TRIUMPH FORSAKEN

Drawing on a wealth of new evidence from all sides, *Triumph Forsaken* overturns most of the historical orthodoxy on the Vietnam War. Through the analysis of international perceptions and power, it shows that South Vietnam was a vital interest of the United States. The book provides many new insights into the overthrow of South Vietnamese President Ngo Dinh Diem in 1963 and demonstrates that the coup negated the South Vietnamese government's tremendous, and hitherto unappreciated, military and political gains between 1954 and 1963. After Diem's assassination, President Lyndon Johnson had at his disposal several aggressive policy options that could have enabled South Vietnam to continue the war without a massive U.S. troop infusion, but he ruled out these options because of faulty assumptions and inadequate intelligence, making such an infusion the only means of saving the country.

Dr. Mark Moyar holds a B.A. summa cum laude in history from Harvard University and a Ph.D. in history from Cambridge University. He is the author of *Phoenix and the Birds of Prey: The CIA's Secret Campaign to Destroy the Viet Cong*. Dr. Moyar has taught at Cambridge University, Ohio State University, and Texas A&M University. At present, he is Associate Professor and Course Director at the U.S. Marine Corps University in Quantico, Virginia.

Triumph Forsaken

THE VIETNAM WAR, 1954–1965

Mark Moyar

U.S. Marine Corps University

 CAMBRIDGE
UNIVERSITY PRESS

CAMBRIDGE UNIVERSITY PRESS
Cambridge, New York, Melbourne, Madrid, Cape Town, Singapore,
São Paulo, Delhi, Dubai, Tokyo, Mexico City

Cambridge University Press
32 Avenue of the Americas, New York, NY 10013-2473, USA

www.cambridge.org
Information on this title: www.cambridge.org/9780521757638

First published 2006
Reprinted 2006 (thrice), 2007 (twice), 2008
First paperback edition 2009
Reprinted 2010

A catalog record for this publication is available from the British Library.

Library of Congress Cataloging in Publication Data

Moyar, Mark, 1971–
Triumph forsaken : the Vietnam war, 1954–1965 / Mark Moyar.
p.   cm.
Includes bibliographical references and index.
ISBN-13: 978-0-521-86911-9 (hardback)
ISBN-10: 0-521-86911-0 (hardback)
1. Vietnamese Conflict, 1961–1975.   2. Vietnam – History – 1945–1975.
I. Title.
DS557.7.M77   2006
959.704'3 – dc22   2006008555

ISBN 978-0-521-86911-9 Hardback
ISBN 978-0-521-75763-8 Paperback

For Kelli, Greta, Trent, Luke, Bert, and Marjorie

Contents

List of Illustrations

1 Parade float in Hanoi depicting Ho Chi Minh shaking hands with Mao
   Zedong. The writing at the bottom of the float reads: "Eternal Friendship."

2 Dwight D. Eisenhower and Ngo Dinh Diem.

3 Strategic hamlet.

4 Army of the Republic of Vietnam soldiers with U.S. Army helicopters.

5 David Halberstam.

6 General Paul Harkins and Major General Ton That Dinh.

7 A Buddhist demonstration in Saigon.

8 Henry Cabot Lodge and John F. Kennedy.

9 Lyndon B. Johnson and Robert S. McNamara.

10 Ho Chi Minh and Sukarno.

Preface

This project began as a single-volume general history of the Vietnam War that would, like most histories spanning such a large conflict, rely primarily on existing books and articles for information, creating a long braid, as it were, by weaving together strands and shorter braids crafted by others. Initial research on the early years of the Vietnam War, however, revealed that many of the existing strands were flawed, and that many other necessary strands were missing altogether. Historical accuracy, therefore, demanded the rebuilding of existing strands and the creation of new strands. The history of the war had to be constructed through the use, whenever possible, of primary sources, rather than another's filtration and interpretation of those sources. This construction process, which involved prolonged exploration of the vast diplomatic, military, and political records of the period, dramatically lengthened the time needed to complete the project, and it increased the number of pages needed to provide the necessary evidence. As a consequence, the history has been divided into two volumes, split at July 28, 1965, the date on which President Lyndon B. Johnson publicly announced the first of many huge increases in the number of U.S. troops in Vietnam. This book is the first of the two volumes.

The inadequacy of the existing historical strands has not been a function of low production volumes. In recent years, new historical books on the Vietnam War have been appearing at an impressive pace, adding considerably to what was already a large body of histories. Like the earlier scholarship, however, the recent historical literature has been concentrated in a relatively small number of areas, and it has been dominated by one major school of thought. Most of the new works are concerned primarily with American policymaking in Washington and Saigon. Most of them come from what is known as the orthodox school, which generally sees America's involvement in the war as wrongheaded and unjust. The revisionist school, which sees the war as a noble but improperly executed enterprise, has published much less, primarily because it has few adherents in the academic world.[1]

Within the last decade, orthodox historians have written a substantial number of prominent books on policymaking during the Eisenhower, Kennedy,
and Johnson presidencies, as well as several noteworthy histories spanning the
entire Vietnam conflict.[2] In addition, some recent specialized books of orthodox persuasion have made significant contributions to the literature on the
period from 1954 to 1965.[3] Other specialized works have challenged some interpretations of the orthodox school while still embracing its overarching tenets.[4]
Still other specialized works do not clearly fit into either the orthodox or the
revisionist camp, largely because most of the fundamental questions dividing
the camps lie beyond their scope. Several such histories have incorporated valuable evidence from Soviet and Chinese archives.[5] The increased accessibility
of Vietnamese and French sources has led to the production of new publications on Vietnamese Communism and Vietnamese anti-Communism, some
of them high in quality.[6] Although most of the recent military histories of the
Vietnam War focus on the period from August 1965 onward, when American
ground forces were fully engaged in the war, a small number examine military
events in the period that ended in July 1965.[7] David Elliott and Eric Bergerud
have produced thorough and informative histories of the conflict in a single
province throughout the course of the war.[8] Recent biographies of American
presidents and other high-ranking figures have also brought new discoveries
on strategic decision making.[9] Studies of other countries and regions have
illuminated international perspectives on the Vietnam War.[10]

The orthodox–revisionist split has yet to become a full-fledged debate,
because many orthodox historians have insisted that the fundamental issues
of the Vietnam War are not open to debate. As Fredrik Logevall has stated
in one of the most widely acclaimed of the recent orthodox histories, most
scholars consider it "axiomatic" that the United States was wrong to go to war
in Vietnam.[11] Some prominent orthodox scholars have gone so far as to claim
that revisionists are not historians at all but merely ideologues, a claim that
is indicative of a larger, very harmful trend at American universities whereby
haughty derision and ostracism are used against those whose work calls into
question the reigning ideological orthodoxy, stifling debate and leading to
defects and gaps in scholarship of the sort found in the historical literature on
the Vietnam War. David L. Anderson, the president of the Society for Historians of American Foreign Relations and an orthodox historian of the Vietnam
War, asserted in his 2005 presidential address that revisionists interpret the
war based on an "uncritical acceptance" of American Cold War policy rather
than analysis of the facts, in contrast to orthodox historians, who strictly use
"reasoned analysis" to reach their conclusions.[12]

Anderson's assertion about revisionists' "uncritical acceptance" of America's
overarching policies can be discredited readily by examining my first book on
the Vietnam War, a revisionist history that was known to Anderson. In that
book, which focused on counterinsurgency during the latter years of the war, I

advanced the revisionist arguments that the Americans and their South Vietnamese allies fought effectively and ethically, and that the South Vietnamese populace generally preferred the South Vietnamese government to the Communists during that period. But I also contended that U.S. politicians were wrong to view the preservation of South Vietnam as a vital U.S. interest.[13] In the course of writing *Triumph Forsaken,* analysis of hitherto unappreciated facts caused me to alter this and other conclusions, an approach diametrically opposed to the ideologically driven approach deplored by Anderson.

During the past ten years, moreover, other revisionist historians have produced some well-researched, well-reasoned works covering the Vietnam conflict between 1954 and 1965, carrying on a relatively small, but strong, tradition of revisionist literature that dates back to the mid-1970s.[14] Drawing on a wide range of new archival sources, Arthur Dommen's history of the two Indochina wars provides a large amount of new information and analysis.[15] *Dereliction of Duty* by H. R. McMaster has shed much new light on U.S. policymaking in 1964 and 1965, particularly with respect to the Joint Chiefs of Staff.[16] Michael Lind has persuasively criticized a variety of orthodox interpretations,[17] and C. Dale Walton has effectively challenged the conventional wisdom on America's strategic options.[18] Several other works have presented new interpretations of the Diem government and the 1963 coup.[19] The strength of the recent revisionist works provides ample evidence that the orthodox school needs to analyze its own interpretations more critically.

There are numerous points of agreement between this volume and the orthodox histories, but there is little agreement on most of the key controversies. This history arrives at some of the same general conclusions as previous revisionist works, as the facts brought it to those points, but differs from them in that it contains many new interpretations and challenges many orthodox interpretations that have hitherto gone unchallenged. It differs from all of the existing literature in its breadth of coverage both inside and outside the two Vietnams and in its use of a more comprehensive collection of source material.

This account first examines the Vietnam War's central characters and countries in the years leading up to 1954. According to the orthodox view, the Vietnamese Communist leader Ho Chi Minh followed in the tradition of numerous Vietnamese nationalists who had defended the country against foreign aggression and who had despised the Chinese and other foreigners. A careful look into Vietnam's past, however, supports no such contentions. Almost all of the conflicts in Vietnamese history before the twentieth century had involved Vietnamese fighting against Vietnamese, not against external enemies. Neither Ho Chi Minh nor Vietnamese of previous generations hated the Chinese, and in fact they both worked amicably with Chinese allies. Ho Chi Minh would serve in the Chinese Communist Army in World War II, he would do whatever his Chinese Communist allies recommended during his war with France, and he would ask the Chinese to send troops to help him in Vietnam on several occasions. Ho generally showed greater deference toward his foreign patrons than did his nationalist rival in South Vietnam, Ngo Dinh Diem, who would ultimately suffer death for refusing to yield to the demands of his American allies. Ho was a fervent believer in the Communism of Marx and Lenin, committed so deeply to Communist internationalism that he would not have sacrificed Communist solidarity for the sake of Vietnam's narrow interests. Thus, contrary to widely accepted interpretations, he never would have turned against his Chinese Communist neighbors, or any other Communist countries, had the United States allowed him to unify Vietnam. Ho Chi Minh would not have let the United States transform his country into an Asian Yugoslavia.

From 1954 to 1965, American leaders correctly perceived that China and North Vietnam were working together to spread Communism across Southeast Asia. They did not view the Communist threat to Vietnam as monolithic in nature, for they were aware of the Sino-Soviet rift that had opened in the 1950s and they knew that the Soviet Union was providing minimal support for Communist expansionism in Southeast Asia. As the war in Vietnam grew in intensity, leading figures in the Johnson administration predicted that the conflict would widen the rift between the Chinese and Soviets, and subsequent history would prove them right.

Whereas the very top leaders of the Vietnamese Communist Party fought the war for ideological reasons, the South Vietnamese peasants who joined the Viet Cong insurgency were attracted primarily by the Viet Cong's leadership capabilities and military strength. They were easily swayed by its charismatic leaders and they wanted to be on the winning side when the fighting ended. Concerned exclusively with local rather than national matters, the peasant masses had little interest in fighting for nationalist causes, and even less interest in Marxist theories or in the collectivization of agriculture that the Communists had in mind. The Viet Cong's temporary land redistribution program did help attract the support of landless peasants, but in the peasants' minds, leadership and strength always outweighed economic policies.

South Vietnamese President Ngo Dinh Diem, who has been incessantly depicted as an obtuse, tyrannical reactionary by orthodox historians, was in reality a very wise and effective leader. In 1954 and 1955, with few resources at his disposal, he brought order to a demoralized, disorganized, and divided South Vietnam. A man deeply dedicated to the welfare of his country, Diem governed in an authoritarian way because he considered Western-style democracy inappropriate for a country that was fractious and dominated by an authoritarian culture. The accuracy of this belief would be borne out by the events that followed his assassination. Diem attempted, with some success, to create a modern Vietnam that preserved Vietnamese traditions, an objective that resonated with his countrymen and with other Asian nationalists to a greater degree than did Western liberalism or Communism. Diem did not stifle religion or kill tens of thousands in the process of redistributing land as Ho Chi Minh did, and he was more tolerant of dissent than his northern counterpart. Most South Vietnamese citizens and officials had a high opinion of Diem, though some disliked his brother and close adviser Ngo Dinh Nhu.

For most of Diem's tenure, the South Vietnamese government held the upper hand in its struggle against the Vietnamese Communists. In the late 1950s, Diem virtually wiped out the secret Communist networks in South Vietnam, thereby precipitating Hanoi's decision to move from political struggle and limited assassinations to a large-scale Maoist insurgency. During 1960 and 1961, the insurgents succeeded in eliminating or reducing the government's power in some areas, and the Diem government was not very effective in employing countermeasures. The problem was not that Diem and his American advisers were interested only in conventional military power, as some would have it. Diem and America's military representatives in South Vietnam fully understood the importance of both conventional forces and counter-guerrilla forces to the defense of South Vietnam. Much of the responsibility for the travails of 1960 and 1961 belonged to U.S. Ambassador Elbridge Durbrow and other American civilians, who chose to provide the South Vietnamese militia and other counter-guerrilla forces with fewer funds and lighter weaponry than they needed. The other key factor was the ability of the Viet Cong to field better leaders on average than the Diem government, the result of political and cultural differences.

During 1960, Diem's forces did score a major success by severing the first Ho Chi Minh Trail, which was located solely within the territory of North and South Vietnam. The North Vietnamese responded by shifting their logistical lines from South Vietnam into Laos, enabling them to intensify the insurgency and mount a very effective, but ultimately inconclusive, offensive in the fall of 1961. President Kennedy, preferring to fight alongside the South Vietnamese rather than the Laotians because of the former's much greater pugnacity, chose not to intervene in Laos and instead tried to solve his Laotian problems through a neutralization agreement. When the North Vietnamese failed to withdraw their forces in the fall of 1962 as stipulated in the agreement, Kennedy refrained from sending American forces into Laos to stop the continuing infiltration. It was a disastrous concession to the enemy, a concession that would haunt South Vietnam and the United States for the remaining fourteen years of the war. Yet despite the heavy influx of Communist personnel and materiel via Laos, the years 1962 and 1963 saw a dramatic turnaround in the war within South Vietnam. Capitalizing on major increases in U.S. military assistance and the coming of age of young leaders whom Diem had begun developing in the 1950s, the South Vietnamese government implemented the strategic hamlet program with great vigor and strengthened its conventional and militia forces. By permanently infusing large numbers of devoted militiamen and officials into the strategic hamlets and by inflicting numerous defeats on the Viet Cong's armed forces, the government reestablished control over most of the territory where the Viet Cong had made inroads in the preceding two years.

Diem's critics were wrong to believe that the Buddhist protest movement of 1963 arose from popular dissatisfaction with a government guilty of religious intolerance. It was, in truth, a power play by a few Buddhist leaders whose duplicity became clear over time as they showed themselves impervious to government attempts at reconciliation and as their charges of religious per-secution were disproved. These leaders had close ties to the Communists or were themselves covert Communists, and other Communist agents participated extensively in the Buddhist movement's protest activities. In Vietnam, where a government lost face if it tolerated sharp public dissent, Diem ultimately had to suppress the Buddhist movement if his government were to remain viable. He suppressed it very effectively on August 21, 1963, by arresting its leaders and clearing the pagodas where it was headquartered. This maneuver was actually the brainchild of Diem's generals, a critical fact lost on those Americans who turned against Diem for his alleged heavy-handedness against the Buddhists. Most remarkably, the anti-Diem Americans would decide that Diem should be replaced with those very generals. While his generals thought that Diem remained the best man for the Presidency, the ensuing renunciations of Diem by the U.S government and press ultimately caused some of them to remove him from power.

In 1963, the American journalists David Halberstam and Neil Sheehan played pivotal roles in turning influential Americans and South Vietnamese against the Diem regime. Their reporting on military events was inaccurate at times, and it regularly overemphasized the South Vietnamese government's short-comings. Colonel John Paul Vann, a U.S. Army adviser and the central fig-ure in Sheehan's book *A Bright Shining Lie*, was more dishonest in dealing with the press than Sheehan ever acknowledged. Vann fed the journalists an extremely misleading version of the Battle of Ap Bac, one that the journalists transformed into the accepted version of the battle. Halberstam and Sheehan presented grossly inaccurate information on the Buddhist protest movement and on South Vietnamese politics, much of which they unwittingly received from secret Communist agents. Ignorant of cultural differences between the United States and Vietnam, they criticized the Diem government for refusing to act like an American government when, in fact, Diem's political methods were far more effective than American methods in treating South Vietnam's prob-lems. South Vietnam's elites, who regularly read Vietnamese translations of American press articles, viewed the *New York Times* and other U.S. newspapers as mouthpieces of the U.S. administration, with the result that negative articles on the Diem government undermined South Vietnamese confidence in Diem and encouraged rebellion. Although the American journalists hoped that their reporting would bring about the installation of a better South Vietnamese government, it actually caused enormous damage to South Vietnam and to

American interests there. Once the coup that they had promoted led to a succession of ineffective governments, exposing them to blame for the crippling of South Vietnam, Halberstam, Sheehan, and fellow journalist Stanley Karnow disparaged Diem with falsehoods so as to claim that South Vietnam was already weak beyond hope before the coup. This turn of events would distort much of the subsequent analysis of the Diem government.

President Kennedy did not consent to the coup that ousted Ngo Dinh Diem on November 1, 1963. Until the very end, Kennedy had serious reservations about the plotting against Diem, in considerable part because many of his senior subordinates opposed Diem's removal, and he unsuccessfully tried to slow the anti-Diem conspiracy. U.S. Ambassador to South Vietnam Henry Cabot Lodge, who was much influenced by Halberstam and Sheehan, instigated the coup without notifying Kennedy and in direct violation of Presidential orders. A few days before the coup began, Kennedy discovered that Lodge was encouraging a group of South Vietnamese generals to rebel and was not informing Washington of his contacts with the conspirators. President Kennedy tried to rein in Lodge and the plotters by sending instructions to the Saigon embassy, but to no avail. He did not take decisive action to stop Lodge, primarily because Lodge was a leading candidate for the Republican Presidential nomination in 1964, and Kennedy did not want campaign accusations that he had kept the Republican ambassador from taking the required actions. Kennedy had appointed Lodge with the intention of hamstringing him and the Republicans by enmeshing them in Vietnam, but it would turn out to be the President who was hamstrung.

Supporting the coup of November 1963 was by far the worst American mistake of the Vietnam War. Contrary to later assertions by the coup's advocates, the South Vietnamese war effort had not entered into a period of decline during the last months of Diem's rule. Proof that the war was proceeding satisfactorily until the coup comes from North Vietnamese as well as American sources – disproving the thesis that American officials were mindlessly optimistic at the time – and also from the 1963 articles of the journalists who would subsequently propagate the myth of a pre-coup collapse. The deterioration did not begin until the period immediately following Diem's overthrow, when the new leaders failed to lead, feuded with each other, and arrested untold numbers of former Diem supporters. Within a few months of the coup, the pacification effort would collapse in most parts of the countryside, and the regular armed forces would be in the first stages of a lengthy period of decline. These changes would help propel Hanoi toward a strategy of seeking a decisive victory through the destruction of South Vietnam's armed forces, which in turn would eventually force the Americans to decide either to introduce U.S. ground troops or to abandon South Vietnam.

Throughout his Presidency, John F. Kennedy was firmly committed to preserving a non-Communist South Vietnam, and he had no plans to abandon his South Vietnamese allies after the 1964 election. Convinced that the defense of South Vietnam was vital to U.S. security, Kennedy vastly expanded the U.S. aid and advisory programs in South Vietnam over the course of his term. Prior to his assassination, Kennedy took no actions that might suggest an intent to abandon Vietnam to the Communists after reelection, and those who knew him best said afterwards that he had never given serious consideration to such a withdrawal. Had Kennedy faced the crisis in Vietnam that Johnson faced in the middle of 1965, he most likely would have come to the same conclusion as Johnson: that saving South Vietnam was so important as to warrant the use of U.S. combat forces.

The effects of the South Vietnamese government's poor performance from Ngo Dinh Diem's death until the middle of 1965 have been understood widely, but its causes have not. According to one standard explanation, the Saigon government failed because its leaders and its American advisers selected the wrong methods for combating the enemy. In truth, however, the problem was not in the concepts but in the execution. An explanation more commonly advanced, closer to the mark but still only partially correct, is that the South Vietnamese government faltered at this time because the country's ruling elite was bereft of strong leaders. Many individuals who occupied positions of power in the post-Diem period, it is true, did lack the necessary leadership attributes, and none was as talented as Diem, but the caliber of the elites as a whole was not a critical problem. The critical problems, rather, were the exclusion of certain elites from the government and the manipulation of governmental leaders by the militant Buddhist movement. From November 1963 onward, the top leadership in Saigon repeatedly removed men of considerable talent, either because of their past loyalty to Diem or because of pressure from the militant Buddhists. And in spite of these purges, the government still had some men, even at the very top at times, who possessed leadership capabilities that would have made them successful leaders had it not been for militant Buddhist conniving. The Buddhist leaders tried to bridle every government that held power after Diem, and in most instances they succeeded, largely because government officials feared resisting the Buddhist activists after watching Diem lose American favor, and his life, for resisting them. As its American advocates had desired, the 1963 coup led to political liberalization, but rather than improving the government as those Americans had predicted, liberalization had the opposite effect, enabling enemies of the government to undermine its prestige and authority, as well as to foment discord and violence between religious groups. Not until June 1965, by which time the United States and most South Vietnamese leaders had come to realize the necessity of suppressing the militant Buddhists and other troublemakers, would political stability return. By then, however, South Vietnam had sustained crippling damage and Hanoi was pushing for total victory.

Lyndon Johnson's lack of forcefulness in Vietnam in late 1964 and early 1965 squandered America's deterrent power and led to a decision in Hanoi to invade South Vietnam with large North Vietnamese Army units. According to the prevailing historical interpretation, the leadership in Hanoi relentlessly pursued a strategy of attacking in the South until it won, with little regard for what its enemies did. In reality, however, North Vietnam's strategy was heavily dependent on American actions. Although Johnson's generals favored striking North Vietnam quickly and powerfully, he chose to follow the prescriptions of his civilian advisers, who advocated an academic approach that used small doses of force to convey America's resolve without provoking the enemy. Because of his chosen strategic philosophy and because of international and U.S. electoral politics, Johnson made only a token attack on North Vietnam following the Tonkin Gulf incidents of 1964 and undertook no military action thereafter. Rather than inducing the North Vietnamese to reciprocate with self-limitations, as the theorists predicted, however, this approach served only to heighten Hanoi's appetite and courage. Johnson's lack of action, as well as his presidential campaign rhetoric, convinced Hanoi that the Americans would not put up a fight for Vietnam in the near future. This change came at a time when the weakened condition of the Saigon government indicated that South Vietnamese resistance to a North Vietnamese invasion would be weak. Consequently, in November 1964, Hanoi began sending large North Vietnamese Army units to South Vietnam, with the intention of winning the war swiftly. The Americans were slow to identify the shift in North Vietnam's strategy and thus lost any remaining chance of deterring Hanoi or otherwise enabling South Vietnam to survive without U.S. combat troops.

Some well-known historians have argued that President Johnson wanted to inject U.S. ground troops into the war whether they were needed or not. Johnson made his decision to intervene, they contend, at the end of 1964 or in early 1965. In actuality, Johnson reached his decision no earlier than the latter part of June 1965, by which time intervention had become the only means of saving South Vietnam. The first U.S. ground troops sent to Vietnam arrived in March 1965, but Johnson deployed them only to protect U.S. air bases, not to engage the main elements of the Communist forces. At the time of the initial ground force deployments, Johnson and his lieutenants did not foresee a major war between American and Communist forces, because they did not know that Hanoi had begun sending entire North Vietnamese Army regiments into South Vietnam. They did not learn of this development until the beginning of April. By the middle of June, abetted by a continuing infusion of North Vietnamese soldiers, the Communist forces had won many large victories and the South Vietnamese Army was losing its ability to challenge large Communist initiatives. The North Vietnamese had entered the third and final stage of Maoist revolutionary warfare, in which the revolutionaries use massed conventional forces to destroy the government's conventional forces. Hanoi's ultimate success, as its leaders repeatedly stated, depended above all on the ability of its conventional forces to destroy the South Vietnamese Army, particularly its mobile strategic reserve units, not South Vietnam's small counter-guerrilla forces. The fighting of 1965 demonstrated that, contrary to the contentions of a multitude of pundits and theoreticians, the Americans and the South Vietnamese had been correct to develop a large conventional South Vietnamese army during the 1950s and early 1960s rather than concentrate exclusively on small-unit warfare.

Lyndon Johnson had always wanted to avoid putting U.S. troops into the ground war if there was any way that South Vietnam could continue the war without them. Like most of his advisers, he doubted that U.S. ground force intervention would result in an easy victory, believing instead that it would result in a long, painful, and politically troublesome struggle against an enemy who might never give up. But in June 1965, Johnson and his military advisers concluded, correctly, that only the use of U.S. ground forces in major combat could stop the Communist conventional forces from finishing off the South Vietnamese Army and government. Even as Johnson became convinced of the need for intervention, he held out hopes of withdrawing U.S. troops from Vietnam relatively soon, regardless of how the fighting was going, in the belief that a brief intervention might achieve as much as a sustained intervention in terms of preserving U.S. credibility and prestige in the world.

Johnson decided that South Vietnam was worth rescuing in 1965 primarily because he dreaded the international consequences of that country's demise. His greatest fear was the so-called domino effect, whereby the fall of Vietnam would cause other countries in Asia to fall to Communism. Historians have frequently argued that Johnson fought for Vietnam primarily to protect himself against accusations from the American Right that he was soft on Communism, which would have harmed his reputation and denied him the political support he needed to carry out his domestic agenda. In actuality, the domestic political ramifications of losing Vietnam had relatively little influence on Johnson's decision on whether to protect South Vietnam. Johnson recognized that the American people were largely apathetic about Vietnam and would be no more likely to turn against him politically and personally if he left than if he stayed and fought. Domestic political considerations did, on the other hand, exert great influence on how Johnson protected South Vietnam, as they discouraged him from bridling Ambassador Henry Cabot Lodge, from taking a tough stance on Vietnam before the 1964 election, and from calling up the U.S. reserves and otherwise putting the United States on a war footing. That there has been great cynicism and confusion about Johnson's motives was partly the responsibility of the President himself, for during this period he repeatedly misrepresented his intentions to the American people and he did not provide decisive leadership that would have clarified his views and inspired the people's confidence.

The domino theory was valid. The fear of falling dominoes in Asia was based not on simple-mindedness or paranoia, but rather on a sound understanding of the toppler countries and the domino countries. As Lyndon Johnson pondered whether to send U.S. troops into battle, the evidence overwhelmingly supported the conclusion that South Vietnam's defeat would lead to either a Communist takeover or the switching of allegiance to China in most of the region's countries. Information available since that time has reinforced this conclusion. Vietnam itself was not intrinsically vital to U.S. interests, but it was vital nevertheless because its fate strongly influenced events in other Asian countries that were intrinsically vital, most notably Indonesia and Japan. In 1965, China and North Vietnam were aggressively and resolutely trying to topple the dominoes, and the dominoes were very vulnerable to toppling. Throughout Asia, among those who paid attention to international affairs, the domino theory enjoyed a wide following. If the United States pulled out of Vietnam, Asia's leaders generally believed, the Americans would lose their credibility in Asia and most of Asia would have to bow before China or face destruction, with enormous global repercussions. Every country in Southeast Asia and the surrounding area, aside from the few that were already on China's side, advocated U.S. intervention in Vietnam, and most of them offered to assist the South Vietnamese war effort. The oft-maligned analogy to the Munich agreement of 1938 actually offered a sound prediction of how the dominoes would likely fall: Communist gains in one area would encourage the Communists to seek further conquests in other places, and after each Communist victory the aggressors would enjoy greater assets and the defenders fewer.

Further evidence of the domino theory's validity can be found by examining the impact of America's Vietnam policy on other developments in the world between 1965 and the fall of South Vietnam in 1975, developments that would remove the danger of a tumbling of Asian dominoes. Among these were the widening of the Sino-Soviet split, the Chinese Cultural Revolution, and the civil war in Cambodia. America's willingness to hold firm in Vietnam did much to foster anti-Communism among the generals of Indonesia, which was the domino of greatest strategic importance in Southeast Asia. Had the Americans abandoned Vietnam in 1965, these generals most likely would not have seized power from the pro-Communist Sukarno and annihilated the Indonesian Communist Party later that year, as they ultimately did. Communism's ultimate failure to knock over the dominoes in Asia was not an inevitable outcome, independent of events in Vietnam, but was instead the result of obstacles that the United States threw in Communism's path by intervening in Vietnam.

It has been said that the Johnson administration, in its first years, could have negotiated a U.S. withdrawal from Vietnam that would have preserved a non-Communist South Vietnam for years to come. Evidence from the Communist side, however, reveals North Vietnam's complete unwillingness to negotiate such a deal. The Communists would not have agreed to a settlement in 1964 or 1965 that could have prevented them from gaining control of South Vietnam quickly. With their list of military victories growing longer and longer, with a clear and promising plan for conquering South Vietnam on the battlefield, the

North Vietnamese had no reason to accept a diplomatic settlement that might rob them of the spoils.

The Americans did miss some strategic opportunities of a different sort, opportunities that would have allowed them to fight from a much more favorable strategic position. In the chaotic period following Diem's overthrow, the Joint Chiefs of Staff and other U.S. military leaders repeatedly advocated an invasion of North Vietnam. Johnson and his civilian advisers rejected this advice, however, on the grounds that an American invasion of the North could lead to a war between the United States and China. Historians have generally concurred in the assessment that Chinese intervention was likely. But the evidence shows that until at least March 1965, the deployment of U.S. ground forces into North Vietnam would not have prompted the Chinese to intercede. Having suffered huge losses in the Korean War, the Chinese had no more appetite for a war between themselves and the Americans than did their American counterparts. Johnson's failure to attack North Vietnam also worked to the enemy's advantage by facilitating a massive Chinese troop deployment into North Vietnam, which in turn freed up many North Vietnamese Army divisions for deployment to South Vietnam and made a subsequent U.S. invasion of North Vietnam much riskier.

Another opportunity not taken – one that never carried a serious risk of war with China – was the cutting of the Ho Chi Minh Trail with American forces. Johnson rejected many recommendations from the Joint Chiefs to put U.S. ground forces into Laos to carry out this task, and on this point, too, historians have backed the President over his generals. The Johnson administration and some historians have argued that the Ho Chi Minh Trail was not essential to the Communist war effort, but new evidence on the trail and on specific battles makes clear the inaccuracy of this contention. The Viet Cong insurgency was always heavily dependent on North Vietnamese infiltration of men and equipment into South Vietnam through Laos, and it could not have brought the Saigon government close to collapse in 1965, or defeated it in 1975, without heavy infiltration of both. Other orthodox historians have argued that an American ground troop presence in Laos would not have stopped most of the infiltration, but much new evidence contradicts this contention as well. The United States, moreover, missed some valuable opportunities to sever Hanoi's maritime supply lines, although it did cut some of the most important sea routes in early 1965.

In sum, South Vietnam was a vital interest of the United States during the period from 1954 to 1965. The aggressive expansionism of North Vietnam and China threatened South Vietnam's existence, and by 1965 only strong American action could keep South Vietnam out of Communist hands. America's policy of defending South Vietnam was therefore sound. U.S. intervention in Vietnam was not an act of strategic buffoonery, nor was it a sinister, warmongering plot that should forever stand as a terrible blemish on America's soul. Neither was it an act of hubris in which the United States pursued objectives far beyond its means. Where the United States erred seriously was in formulating its strategies for protecting South Vietnam. The most terrible mistake was the inciting of the November 1963 coup, for Ngo Dinh Diem's overthrow forfeited the tremendous gains of the preceding nine years and plunged the country into an extended period of instability and weakness. The Johnson administration was handed the thorny tasks of handling the post-coup mess and defending South Vietnam against an increasingly ambitious enemy – and in neither case did the administration achieve good results. President Johnson had available several aggressive policy options that could have enabled South Vietnam to continue the war either without the help of any American ground forces at all or with the employment of U.S. ground forces in advantageous positions outside South Vietnam. But Johnson ruled out these options and therefore, during the summer of 1965, he would have to fight a defensive war within South Vietnam's borders in order to avoid the dreadful international consequences of abandoning the country.

Acknowledgments

This book would not have been possible without the help of many people in many parts of the United States and in other countries. I am forever grateful to Merle Pribbenow, who translated thousands of pages of Vietnamese histories for me on his own time, enabling me to cover the Vietnamese Communist side of the war more comprehensively than it has been covered before. His unflagging efforts have been truly extraordinary. Richard Aldrich, Anthony Badger, John Del Vecchio, Allan Millett, Merle Pribbenow, Tom Schwartz, Bill Stueck, Keith W. Taylor, and James Webb read portions or all of the manuscript and offered many useful comments. I am indebted to my academic mentors – Christopher Andrew, Ernest May, and Akira Iriye – for their ongoing support. B. G. Burkett, John Del Vecchio, Lewis Sorley, Keith W. Taylor, and James Webb have been as steadfast in their support of this project as they were in their service to the United States during the war. Bruce Nichols of the Free Press, the first supporter of this project, originally commissioned the book at an early stage in its development, and he graciously allowed me to transfer to Cambridge University Press when the project turned out to be much larger and more time-consuming than either of us had originally foreseen. Frank Smith of Cambridge University Press energetically saw the book through to its conclusion and served as an outstanding editor. Greg Houle, Melissanne Scheld, and Tamara Braunstein, also of Cambridge University Press, have put a terrific amount of effort into the publicity, sales, and marketing of the book. At Techbooks, Peter Katsirubas made sure that a deluge of modifications and corrections made it into the book in time for publication.

Robert J. Destatte, William Duiker, David Elliott, Chris Goscha, Mike Martin, Edwin Moïse, Merle Pribbenow, Lewis Sorley, and Jay Veith provided or referred me to sources. I was privileged to interview or correspond with William Colby, Roger Donlon, Frederick Flott, Albert Fraleigh, Novarin Gunawan, Hoang Lac, Gayland Lyles, Ted Mataxis, Robert McNamara, John O'Donnell, Andrew P. O'Meara, Nguyen Khanh, Carlton Nysewander, Rufus Phillips, Joseph P. Redick, Carl Schaad, and Fletcher Ware. In addition, I have benefited from interaction with other historians of the Vietnam War – Dale Andrade, Larry

Berman, Anne Blair, John Carland, Olga Dror, Ron Frankum, Chris Goscha, Chen Jian, Bill Leary, Michael Lind, Martin Loicano, Ed Marolda, Matt Masur, Steve Maxner, H. R. McMaster, Ed Miller, David Milne, Stephen J. Morris, Lien-Hang T. Nguyen, Triet Minh Nguyen, Douglas Pike, Jim Reckner, Geoffrey D. T. Shaw, Lewis Sorley, Geoffrey Stewart, Keith W. Taylor, Dave Toczek, Robert F. Turner, Jay Veith, Richard Verrone, and Andrew Wiest.

At National Archives II, I received superlative assistance from Cliff Snyder, Jeannine Swift, and Rich Boylan. Steve Maxner and Richard Verrone went out of their way to help me find documents at Texas Tech University's burgeoning Vietnam Archive, which owes its existence to the tremendous labors of Jim Reckner. Other archivists who assisted me were Frank Shirer of the U.S. Army Center of Military History; Herb Pankratz of the Dwight D. Eisenhower Presidential Library; Tom McNaught of the John F. Kennedy Presidential Library; and Ted Gittinger, Laura Harmon, Linda Seelke, and John Wilson of the Lyndon B. Johnson Presidential Library. I received additional assistance from archivists at the Hoover Institution Archives, the Library of Congress, the Marine Corps Historical Division, the U.S. Army Military History Institute, the National Defense University Library, the University of Virginia Library, and the Public Record Office. I owe much to the interlibrary loan staffs of the Fairview Park Regional Library, the Cambridge University Library, the Texas A&M University Library, and the Library of the Marine Corps, who meticulously tracked down many obscure books for me. I received financial support from Cambridge University, the Lyndon Baines Johnson Library Foundation, the Marine Corps University Foundation, and Texas A&M University.

For the camaraderie and the learning, I would like to thank my teaching partners, Colonel Ritch Rodebaugh, USMC, and Colonel Patrick Redmon, USMC, and the military officers and other students whom I have had the privilege to teach. Thanks also to my other colleagues at the U.S. Marine Corps University, and to Major General Donald R. Gardner, USMC (Ret.); General Thomas Draude, USMC (Ret.); Colonel John A. Toolan, USMC; Dr. Doug McKenna; Dr. Jack Matthews; and Dr. Bill Gordon. My life has been made easier by Carol-Anne Parker, Linda Rohler, Amy Judge, and the rest of Command & Staff College staff. At Texas A&M University, I received help, advice, and knowledge from H. W. Brands; Colonel Joe Cerami, USA (Ret.); Mary Ellen Cole; Kim Isett; Brian Linn; Jim Olson; Jennifer Pestovic; and Nancy Small.

My parents, Bert and Marjorie Moyar, have been extraordinarily supportive, even when it may have been difficult for them. My grandmothers, Lois Moyar and Angeliki Capous, have also been most helpful, and I have been very fortunate that they have been able to see this project reach fruition. My children Greta, Trent, and Luke, all of whom are younger than the book, have been sources of tremendous joy and inspiration, and they have bravely soldiered on through frequent relocations across state and national boundaries. They and I are both immeasurably grateful to my wife Kelli, whose love has not wavered despite the unexpected stress and sacrifices that this project has brought.

TRIUMPH FORSAKEN

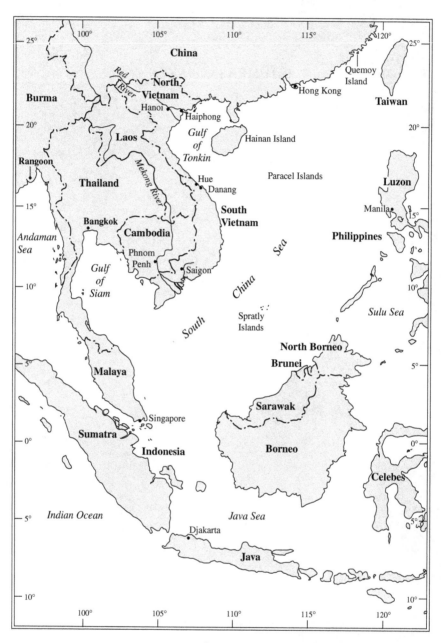

Southeast Asia

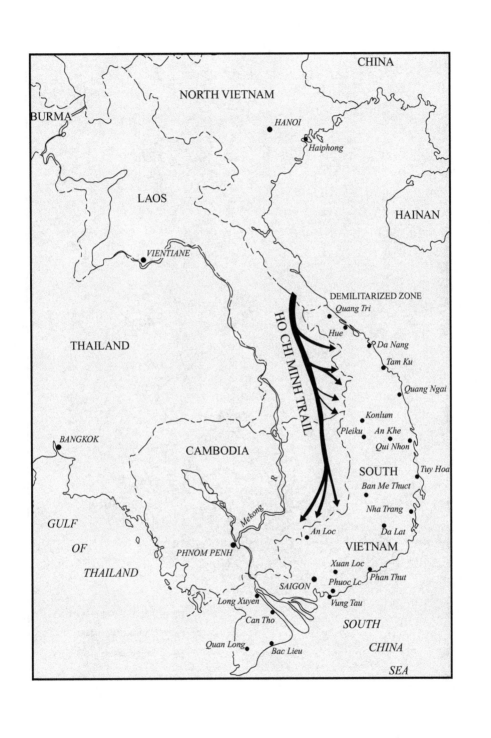

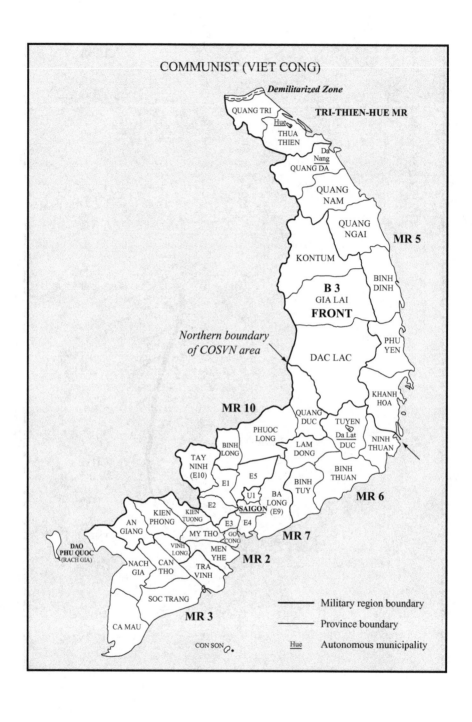

COMMUNIST (VIET CONG)

Demilitarized Zone

QUANG TRI

TRI-THIEN-HUE MR

Hue

THUA THIEN

Da Nang

QUANG DA

QUANG NAM

QUANG NGAI

MR 5

KONTUM

BINH DINH

B 3
GIA LAI
FRONT

Northern boundary
of COSVN area

DAC LAC

PHU YEN

KHANH HOA

MR 10

QUANG DUC

TUYEN DUC

Da Lat

NINH THUAN

PHUOC LONG

LAM DONG

BINH LONG

TAY NINH
(E10)

E5

BINH THUAN

E1

MR 6

U1

BA LONG (E9)

BINH TUY

E2

SAIGON

KIEN PHONG

KIEN TUONG

E3

E4

MR 7

AN GIANG

MY THO

GO CONG

DAO
PHU QUOC
(RACH GIA)

VINH LONG

MEN YHE

MR 2

NACH GIA

CAN THO

TRA VINH

SOC TRANG

MR 3

CA MAU

CON SON

——— Military region boundary

——— Province boundary

<u>Hue</u>   Autonomous municipality

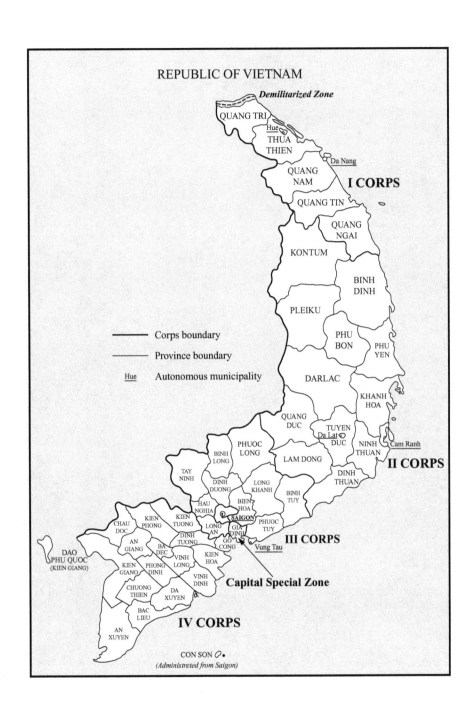

REPUBLIC OF VIETNAM

Demilitarized Zone

QUANG TRI

Hue

THUA THIEN

Da Nang

QUANG NAM

I CORPS

QUANG TIN

QUANG NGAI

KONTUM

BINH DINH

PLEIKU

PHU BON

PHU YEN

DARLAC

KHANH HOA

QUANG DUC

TUYEN DUC

Da Lat

NINH THUAN

Cam Ranh

—— Corps boundary

—— Province boundary

Hue   Autonomous municipality

PHUOC LONG

LAM DONG

II CORPS

BINH LONG

DINH THUAN

TAY NINH

DINH DUONG

LONG KHANH

BINH TUY

HAU NGHIA

BIEN HOA

CHAU DOC

KIEN PHONG

KIEN TUONG

LONG AN

SAIGON

GIA DINH

PHUOC TUY

III CORPS

DAO PHU QUOC (KIEN GIANG)

AN GIANG

BA DEC

DINH TUONG

GO CONG

KIEN HOA

Vung Tau

KIEN GIANO

PHONG DINH

VINH LONG

CHUONG THIEN

DA XUYEN

VINH BINH

Capital Special Zone

BAC LIEU

AN XUYEN

IV CORPS

CON SON

(Administreted from Saigon)

CHAPTER 1

Heritage

FROM ALL DIRECTIONS, FROM HANOI AND FROM THE SURROUNDING countryside, several hundred thousand Vietnamese converged on a large square called the Place Puginier, next to the French Governor's palace. At that square, they had been told, they could hear the man who had suddenly claimed to be the leader of all Vietnam. Ho Chi Minh arrived at the Place Puginier in a black American automobile. He was supposed to speak to the throng at 2:00 P.M., but he arrived several minutes late because the streets of Hanoi were jammed with pedestrians heading toward the square. Having no dress clothes of his own, Ho was wearing a faded khaki suit and a high-collared jacket that he had borrowed from an acquaintance, and atop his head was a pith helmet. Men in suits waved small red flags with gold stars and a band played marches as he headed towards a high wooden platform in the center of the square. Just a few weeks earlier, the Viet Minh had taken over the city from a Japanese occupation force, which had largely stopped functioning after the bombing of Hiroshima and Nagasaki, but Viet Minh leaders still feared that the Japanese might interfere with this momentous event. For that reason, armed Viet Minh guards hovered around the platform and the rest of the square. At Ho's invitation, several American officers from the Office of Strategic Services were standing near the platform, and two American P-38 Lightning fighters happened to fly over the assemblage during the event, both of which created a false impression that the United States government was endorsing Ho Chi Minh.

Ho tailored the beginning of his speech to the American officers standing right in front of him. Quoting from the American Declaration of Independence, Ho pronounced, "All men are created equal. They are endowed by their creator with certain unalienable rights; among these are life, liberty, and the pursuit of happiness." He then read from a proclamation that had inspired a more radical set of men, the French Revolution's Declaration of the Rights of Man and the Citizen: "All men are born free and with equal rights, and must always remain free and have equal rights." Ho proceeded to accuse the French colonialists of violating these American and French principles in all sorts of cruel ways. Asserting that his new government represented "the entire Vietnamese people," he made no mention of his political ideology, and the only political objective he discussed was the formation of an independent Vietnam. "The entire Vietnamese people," he said in conclusion, "are determined to mobilize all their physical and mental strength, to sacrifice their lives and property, in order to safeguard their freedom and independence."[1]

According to many accounts, the Place Puginier speech on September 2, 1945 proved that nationalism, not Marxist-Leninist internationalism, was the locomotive that pulled Ho Chi Minh's revolution. Ho Chi Minh, it is argued, was simply the latest in a long line of Vietnamese nationalists who had resisted foreign aggressors. Had it not been for American determination to support the French colonialists and later to prop up a weak non-Communist South Vietnam, the United States and a unified Vietnam under Ho Chi Minh could have been allies, with Ho's Vietnam turning against Communist China because of nationalist animosity just as Yugoslavia had turned against the Soviet Union. If only the Americans had understood the history of Vietnam, the whole tragedy could have been averted.[2]

The fatal flaw in this line of reasoning is that the history of Vietnam and the history of Ho Chi Minh actually support the very opposite conclusions.[3] Ho Chi Minh was not, in reality, the most recent of many nationalist heroes who had combated foreign aggression. Driving out foreign invaders was not the main chord of Vietnam's national song; infighting was the primary chord, and aggression against the southern neighbors of Champa and Cambodia rivaled the struggle against foreign invasion for second place. For most of the thousand years that are known in the West as the first millennium A.D., Vietnam belonged to what later became China. On a dozen occasions during that period, the residents of Vietnam attempted to expel the ruling officials and soldiers by force of arms, not out of xenophobia – many of the rebels had been born in China or descended from Chinese ancestors – but out of a desire for power or freedom from the central authority. In every case except the last one, the only rebel successes were but brief flourishes that quickly perished along with the perpetrators. The final revolt began in 939, under the leadership of Ngo Quyen, and it ended with Vietnam receiving vassal status from its massive northern neighbor, which entailed the payment of tributes to China in return for Vietnam's autonomy. Vietnam would remain a vassal of China for nearly one thousand years.

From this point onward, in all of the centuries to come, the very extensive fighting within Vietnam consisted almost entirely of one Vietnamese faction fighting another Vietnamese faction. Vanity and cruelty often prevailed in these contests, giving lie to the view of some in the West that it was French colonialism that corrupted Vietnamese politics. The infighting began just five years after Vietnam obtained vassal status from China. Upon Ngo Quyen's death in 944, his brother-in-law Duong Tam Kha and his son Xuong Van went to war over the throne, leading to a succession of usurpations. In 963, while observing his military forces from a boat, King Xuong Van was felled by a crossbowman hidden on the bank. His death plunged Vietnam into a two-year period era of anarchy known as the Period of the Twelve Warlords. Unity returned to the land in 965 when the warlord Dinh Bo Linh put down the other lords. But bloody rebellions would plague his dynasty and all that followed it, becoming more frequent when the king was incompetent or inattentive to subversion. Knowing that deception and treachery were constantly fermenting in the hearts of their countrymen, the kings usually delegated power to their family members, and for this reason revolts normally failed unless they involved members of the royal family audacious enough to despoil the sanctity of kinship. On occasion, however, the entire dynasty was supplanted by feudal lords, in which case there was certain to be considerable brutality, possibly involving wholesale slaughter of the outgoing dynasty.

To support the view that Ho Chi Minh could have become an Asian Tito, numerous commentators have asserted that China and Vietnam had been at war for much of Vietnam's existence and enemies for nearly all of it prior to the mid-twentieth century, ensuring subsequent conflict.[4] The actual history of Vietnam, however, does not bear out this claim. From the end of the tenth century to the middle of the twentieth century, the Chinese and the Vietnamese fought a mere three wars, all of which the Vietnamese initiated. The first of these wars, in 1075, began when the Vietnamese raided China to prevent the Chinese from dominating the buffer zone between Vietnam and China. The Song Chinese sent an army into Vietnam to punish the Vietnamese, and the army withdrew once the Vietnamese apologized for what they had done. In the two subsequent wars, in 1406 and 1789, the Chinese came to Vietnam because one Vietnamese faction invited them in to help fight another Vietnamese faction. The very few uninvited attacks on Vietnam during this thousand-year period were made not by China but by Champa, by the Mongol empire of Kublai Khan, and by France.[5]

In general, amicability characterized relations between China and Vietnam during these thousand years. Having been a Chinese province and a popular destination for Chinese emigrants during the preceding thousand years, Vietnam had thoroughly absorbed the customs, ideas, and religions of China. From the time of its independence through the middle of the twentieth century, Vietnam remained a follower of China in the realms of culture and politics. Although the Vietnamese at times resented Chinese influence and feared excessive Chinese meddling in Vietnam's affairs, as is typical when one nation dominates another, these emotions were not strong enough to either prevent collaboration or create serious hostility. From the middle of the nineteenth century to the middle of the twentieth century, the Vietnamese and Chinese helped each other repeatedly in times of need, much as the Americans during the same period worked together with the British, who had been their colonial masters much more recently. Cooperation was especially close among Vietnamese and Chinese of Communist persuasion.

Ho Chi Minh was one in a long line of Vietnamese leaders who used assistance from abroad to fight their Vietnamese enemies. For most of his career, his successes depended heavily upon large-scale material aid and advice from the Soviet Union and China. His struggles against French colonialism constituted a civil war as well as a war against a foreign power, for more Vietnamese than Frenchmen would take up arms against the Viet Minh, and when Ho's nationalist rival Ngo Dinh Diem came to power in southern Vietnam, the ensuing conflict was purely a contest between two Vietnamese groups that relied heavily on foreign assistance. If one side in that conflict could be said to be less dependent on foreigners than the other, it was not the Communists, as Ho was much more deferential to his foreign advisers than was Ngo Dinh Diem. Ho was to follow the advice of the Chinese with a submissiveness that Diem would never display in his dealings with the Americans. Only Ho Chi Minh would fill towns and villages with propaganda lauding his foreign allies.

Foreign aid to warring Vietnamese factions figured prominently in Vietnamese history from the fourteenth century onward. In 1369, the Vietnamese king perished without leaving an heir, leading to a succession crisis during which royals slaughtered one another in great numbers. Among the victims was Nhat Le, the first man to seize the throne. After Nhat Le's murder, his mother went to the country of Champa to ask for help against the Vietnamese who had taken the kingdom from her son, and, in 1371, the Chams complied. Led by the famed Che Bong Nga, the Chams entered the Red River Valley, tore the Vietnamese army to shreds, and burned the palaces of Hanoi. In 1389, the Chams returned to Vietnam to assist Vietnamese rebels, but just as they were about to defeat the forces of the Vietnamese king, a Cham traitor revealed the location of Che Bong Nga's ship, thereby enabling the Vietnamese to kill the Cham hero and take his head. The Chams, deflated by the death of their mighty leader, returned to their homeland.

In the year 1400, the cunning regent Ho Quy Ly orchestrated the strangling of the young king and massacred huge numbers of his supporters and their male relatives, from babies to old men, in order to take over the throne. Surviving members of the dynastic family appealed to the Chinese for help, and finally, in 1406, Chinese Emperor Yung Lo agreed to do so. He dispatched an army known as the "Force the Barbarians to Submit Army," which, abetted by the ousted dynasty, defeated Ho Quy Ly's forces and drove him from power. Possessed by an enormous appetite for enlarging his domain, Yung Lo did not restore the Vietnamese royal family to power but instead chose to place Vietnam under the rule of his own Ming dynasty. The Ming government in Vietnam, Chinese though it was, enjoyed widespread favor among the people of northern Vietnam. Further south, however, a wealthy Vietnamese landowner named Le Loi formed a powerful group of rebels. A fierce war followed between the Ming and Le Loi's forces, lasting nearly a decade. It ended when Yung Lo's successor decided that Vietnam was not worth the trouble and agreed to let Le Loi have all of Vietnam, returning it to vassal status.

With the start of the early sixteenth century came some of the worst infighting in Vietnamese history, leading to the establishment of two rival regimes, one in the north and one in the south. North Vietnam and South Vietnam were to engage intermittently in inconclusive wars for the next two hundred years. The Nguyen family, which took control of southern Vietnam in the latter part of the sixteenth century, erected two huge walls north of the plains of Quang Tri, running from the sea all the way to the Annamite foothills. Located near the seventeenth parallel, the walls sat very close to the line that would divide North Vietnam from South Vietnam following the Geneva Conference of 1954. After an interval of peace, the North – now led by the Trinh family – attacked the South, beginning a series of wars spanning half a century. Once again Vietnamese leaders sought foreign assistance in order to fight their Vietnamese rivals, with the Nguyen family receiving military equipment and advice from the Portuguese, and the Trinh family obtaining assistance from the Dutch, who were competing with the Portuguese in the scramble for colonies and trading privileges in the Far East. Although the North had a far larger population and army than the South, and although the South expended much of its martial energy in the conquest of lands belonging to Cambodia and Champa, the Trinh were never able to vanquish the Southerners.

In the late eighteenth century, three brothers from the village of Tay Son overthrew both the northern and southern monarchies in an orgy of violence that included ritual cannibalism and every other form of barbarity. The Tay Son brothers cut Vietnam into three sections, North, Center, and South, and ran them as separate states. The deposed royal families called on the Chinese for help in removing the Tay Son brothers, prompting the Chinese emperor to send his troops into Vietnam, the first time Chinese troops had been deployed to Vietnam since 1406. With the assistance of the Chinese, the old dynasties and their supporters drove the Tay Son from the cities and slaughtered many of their collaborators. But the youngest and greatest of the Tay Son brothers, Emperor Quang Trung, built a large army and, in 1789, threw the Chinese back into China while smashing the former dynasties.

Soon thereafter, the former southern king's nephew, Nguyen Anh, stormed into southern Vietnam and seized the commercial center of Saigon and much else in southern Vietnam from the Tay Son. Pigneau de Behaine, a French missionary, persuaded French merchants, missionaries, and naval officers to send Nguyen Anh two ships, a collection of military hardware, and European military advisers so that he could take northern Vietnam as well. From bases in southern Vietnam, Nguyen Anh's forces marched northward into a war that was to last thirteen years. Many of Nguyen Anh's European military advisers grew tired of him during the war and quit. He was overly cautious, they complained, and had no sense of urgency. But in 1802, Nguyen Anh captured Hue and then Hanoi, putting an end to the rule of the Tay Son. He promptly executed the members of the Tay Son family and the families that had supplied the Tay Son with generals. The deposed Tay Son emperor, Nguyen Quang Toan, was forced to watch while Nguyen Anh's men urinated on his parents' disinterred bones, and then he had his limbs tied to four elephants that were driven in four directions until his body was torn into pieces.

Making Hue his capital, Nguyen Anh proclaimed himself the Emperor Gia Long and unified modern Vietnam, to include the Mekong Delta, for the first time. Although both Ho Chi Minh and Ngo Dinh Diem would later claim to be the rightful ruler of all of Vietnam, which they said was a single nation, Vietnam as a unified country had only a very brief and troubled history. Prior to 1954, North Vietnam and South Vietnam would be united for just fifty-eight years, from 1802 to 1859 – a very short period for an area with 2,700 years of history. This unification period would be filled with great tyranny, intrigue, and bloodletting among the Vietnamese, not the sort of unification to merit nostalgia. Nor was it the sort that would help the people develop a strong identification with Vietnam as a nation. For a much longer period, two hundred years in length, the North and South had been divided near the demarcation line established in 1954, and Northerners and Southerners had fought numerous wars against each other during those two centuries. Under the Tay Son and again under the French, Vietnam was divided into North, Center, and South, three regions that developed distinct cultures and identities along with feelings of superiority over the other two thirds. Much of unified Vietnam, moreover, had not been Vietnamese at all for most of Vietnam's history. Until the Vietnamese crushed the Chams in the fifteenth century, ninety percent of what became South Vietnam had belonged to either Champa or Cambodia. Vietnamese settlers did not penetrate the lands at the southern and western extremes of modern South Vietnam until the 1700s, and not until 1757 did the South Vietnamese kingdom reach the southernmost point of the Mekong Delta. While the regions of Vietnam shared the same language and were adjacent grographically, they were not predestined to become unified, any more than were the United States and Canada, or Germany and Austria. Because of its complicated history, Vietnam could legitimately be considered to be one, two, or three countries.

To complicate matters further, much of Vietnam was inhabited by people who were not considered to be Vietnamese by either themselves or by the ethnic Vietnamese who dominated the affairs of prosperous lowland Vietnam. After the annexation of the Mekong Delta, the ethnic Vietnamese were fond of saying that Vietnam was two rice baskets at the ends of a carrying pole, with the Mekong Delta in the south complementing the Red River Delta in the north. This assertion betrayed the contempt of the ethnic Vietnamese for the country's ethnic minorities, for the analogy was apt only if Vietnam were considered to be merely the two deltas and the coastal lowland areas in between them, where virtually all of the ethnic Vietnamese lived. The lowland strip along the central coast was indeed narrow like a pole, but to its west the central highlands extended for hundreds of miles, making them comparable in breadth to the Mekong Delta. Comprising two-thirds of the land mass of southern Vietnam, the highlands were home to tribes from a wide range of ethnic groups. Most of them lived in humble villages on the vast Kontum and Darlac plateaus or in the steep mountains of the Annamite chain, a huge spur of the Himalayan massif running from China's southern frontier down the Southeast Asian peninsula.

By the time Gia Long had established dominion over all of the Vietnamese territories, Vietnam was on a collision course with France. Out of deference to his French benefactors, Gia Long allowed French and Spanish missionaries to convert many Vietnamese to Catholicism – by the 1820s, they had built the Catholic population of Vietnam to 300,000. But Gia Long's successors turned against the missionaries because of their ties to ravenous European governments and their support for opposition groups in a period of great civil strife. During the twenty-year reign of Gia Long's immediate successor, Minh Mang, no less than two hundred different uprisings against the emperor took place, with the opposition particularly strong in southern Vietnam, which remained very resistant to northern authority. At the end of a failed rebellion in 1833, the emperor's forces captured a French missionary with the rebels and, in public, they burned him with red hot pincers, hung him on a cross, and slowly sliced off his chest muscles, buttocks, and other body parts until he died. Emperor Thieu Tri, who came to power in 1840, killed several more missionaries, hundreds of Vietnamese Catholic priests, and thousands of their followers.

The persecution of missionaries and their converts, together with a desire to amass colonies at a time when European countries were racing to expand their empires, caused Emperor Napoleon III to send French forces to Vietnam at the end of 1857, beginning a twenty-five year conflict in which the next Vietnamese emperor, Tu Duc, attempted to fend off French attacks as well as several hundred internal revolts of various kinds. On August 25, 1883, Vietnam surrendered its independence to France. As the Tay Son had done, the French carved Vietnam into three parts – Tonkin in the north, Annam in the center, and Cochinchina in the south. The Chinese, at the urging of the Vietnamese, tried to contest France's colonization of Vietnam by sending their own soldiers to fight the French, but after two years of costly warfare the Chinese relented and agreed to peace on French terms. China officially relinquished its status as protector of Tonkin, bringing to an end the payment of tribute from Vietnam to China. In the next few years, some Vietnamese elites organized further resistance to their new rulers, but most of the prominent and talented Vietnamese decided to cooperate with the French, and a large number of them eagerly absorbed not only the science and technology that gave the French the tools of power but also the ideas that animated them. To maintain their hold on Vietnam, the French colonialists would always rely more heavily on Vietnamese manpower than on their own.

Two strong anti-colonial groups that emerged during the 1920s attempted to throw the French out by force of arms in 1930. The Vietnam Nationalist Party, modeled after China's Kuomintang, incited a mutiny among Vietnamese soldiers in the colonial army, but the French quickly destroyed the mutineers and much of the party. The tattered remnants of the Vietnam Nationalist Party had to hobble into China. The second group was the Vietnamese Communist Party, led by the man who was to become known as Ho Chi Minh.[6] Born in 1890 in the province of Nghe An, Ho was the son of a well-to-do mandarin. During his teenage years, Ho attended the Lycée Quoc Hoc in Hue, the best high school available to Vietnamese boys, a school that would also educate the future Communist Party leaders Vo Nguyen Giap and Pham Van Dong, as well as the two anti-Communists who would ultimately cause Ho Chi Minh the greatest grief, Ngo Dinh Diem and Ngo Dinh Nhu. Ho Chi Minh left Vietnam in 1912 to work aboard a French ocean liner, beginning a long period of life abroad. Following World War I, he settled in Paris and joined the French Socialist Party. Many years later, Ho would explain that he did not understand the party's ideology or platform at the time and he joined simply because they "had shown their sympathy toward me, toward the struggle of the oppressed peoples."[7] French leftists deemed Ho's oratorical skills and appearance unimpressive, but they liked his emotional intensity, which they said could be seen in his dark, flashing eyes.

The French Socialist party would be the stepping stone that took Ho to the Communism of Marx and Lenin. Coming from a country wrapped in authoritarian and communitarian traditions, Ho was not repelled by the lack of democracy and individualism in Soviet Communism, as many of the French Socialists were repelled. Ho later said that he went from being a Socialist to a Communist upon reading Lenin's "Theses on the National and Colonial Questions." He recounted,

> In those Theses, there were political terms that were difficult to understand. But by reading them again and again, finally I was able to grasp the essential part. What emotion, enthusiasm, enlightenment and confidence they communicated to me! I wept for joy. Sitting by myself in my room, I would shout as if I were addressing large crowds: 'Dear martyr compatriots! This is what we need, this is our path to our liberation!' Since then, I had entire confidence in Lenin.[8]

What was in those inspirational Theses? Lenin's Theses laid out a strategy for revolution in colonial and non-European countries, a subject neglected in previous Communist treatises. The struggle against colonialism, Lenin maintained in the Theses, was a key component of Communism's quest to end the enslavement of the world's people by a small number of Western capitalists.

According to Lenin's treatise, the proletariat would first collaborate with the native bourgeoisie to destroy the colonial powers, then the dictatorship of the proletariat would eradicate the bourgeoisie along with "bourgeois prejudices" such as national and racial animosities, and would also destroy the "medieval influences of the clergy, the christian missions, and similar elements" and the "petty bourgeois pacifist confusion of the ideas and the policy of internationalism." Lenin called for "the closest union between all national and colonial liberation movements and Soviet Russia," and demanded "the subordination of the interests of the proletarian struggle in one nation to the interests of that struggle on an international scale."[9]

Ho Chi Minh was a nationalist in the sense that he had a special affection for Vietnam's people and favored Vietnamese unification and independence, but, from his reading of Lenin's Theses onward, he firmly adhered to the Leninist principle that Communist nations should subordinate their interests to those of the international Communist movement. The peoples of the world had to set aside national prejudices, he believed, and they needed to work together as partners to spread the global revolution, themes that he was discussing in his writings as early as 1922.[10] In Ho's opinion, Yugoslavia or an Asian Yugoslavia or any other entity that destroyed Communist unity for the sake of national interests or hatreds was despicable. Like the Soviets, Ho derided those who put nationalism ahead of Communism as "bourgeois nationalists" or "chauvinistic nationalists." When the feud between Yugoslavia and the Soviet Union began in the late 1940s, Ho and his fellow Vietnamese Communists would bitterly denounce Tito for putting national concerns before those of international Communism.[11] They would also praise the Soviets for obliterating the Hungarian Communist regime of Imre Nagy when it tried to leave the Warsaw Pact for nationalistic reasons.[12] In the 1960s, after the conflicts between the Soviets and the Chinese had shattered the unity of the international Communist bloc, Ho Chi Minh would try to gather up the pieces and put it back together.

Throughout his life, Ho Chi Minh greatly admired the leaders of China and the Soviet Union, in whose countries he had lived for many years. He would work for the Comintern – the Soviet organization charged with promoting Marxist-Leninist revolution around the world – and for the Chinese Communist Army. As the leader of the Viet Minh during their war against the French, he would follow Chinese advice as if he had been given orders, and he would invite Chinese soldiers into Vietnam on several occasions.

The only piece of direct evidence employed in arguing that Ho Chi Minh disliked the Chinese and other foreigners was a comment he reportedly made in 1946 while defending his decision to let the French Army into northern Vietnam: "It is better to sniff French shit for a little while than to eat Chinese shit all our lives."[13] This bit of evidence is badly flawed. When Ho allegedly made this comment, China was largely under the control of the Chinese Nationalists, who were fervent anti-Communists and who were actively promoting Vietnamese

Communism's most powerful rival, the Vietnam Nationalist Party. Ho Chi Minh detested the Chinese Nationalists and wanted to be free of their influence, but this hatred did not translate into hatred of the Chinese in general, anymore than Harry Truman's animosity toward the Nazis translated into hatred of the Germans in general. The evidence available overwhelmingly indicates that Ho Chi Minh generally liked the Chinese as a people. Even if Ho had been referring to all Chinese, it easily could have been an attempt to trick his Western adversaries into thinking that there were not strong ties between the Vietnamese and Chinese Communists.

Further evidence of Ho's commitment to Communism came from his single-minded and unswerving dedication to one objective: the imposition of Communist government on Vietnam and the rest of the world. Ho's long career as a practitioner of Marxism-Leninism started in 1920, when he became a founding member of the French Communist Party. Three years later, the Soviets summoned him to Moscow to learn Leninist organizational methods and work for the Comintern. When Lenin died, in January of 1924, Ho waited in line to see the corpse for so long that his fingers and nose became frost-bitten. In a tribute to Lenin, Ho wrote that the Asian peoples "see in Lenin the personification of universal brotherhood. They feel veneration for him which is akin to filial piety."[14] At the end of 1924, the Soviets transported Ho to Canton via the Trans-Siberian Express. Carrying orders to organize Vietnamese émigrés and other Asians into revolutionary groups, Ho was to work under the guidance and financial auspices of the Comintern. In Canton, he started a Communist organization called *Viet Nam Thanh Nien Cach Mang Hoi,* meaning Revolutionary Youth League. In conformity with Lenin's theories, Ho sought temporary alliances with non-Communist Vietnamese. As he wrote in the Revolutionary Youth League's journal, "we must destroy the counterrevolutionary elements," but only "after having kicked the French out of our borders."[15] Ho enrolled some of his most gifted followers in a Chinese military academy, including several who would later become his top generals.

In early 1930, the Comintern sent Ho to Hong Kong, where he welded two factions of Vietnamese Communists into a single new organization called the Vietnamese Communist Party, subordinate to the Far Eastern Bureau of the Comintern in Shanghai. On the day that he founded the Vietnamese Communist Party, Ho made the party's ideological alignment quite clear, asserting that the party belonged to a "revolutionary camp" led by the Soviet Union and supported by "the oppressed colonies and the exploited working class throughout the world." The stated goal of the Vietnamese Communist Party was to "overthrow French imperialism, feudalism, and the reactionary Vietnamese capitalist class," all of which belonged to the "counterrevolutionary camp of international capitalism and imperialism whose general staff is the League of Nations."[16]

The Comintern next sent Ho Chi Minh to Siam, Malaya, and Singapore to preside over the creation of Communist Parties in each of those countries. In Siam, Ho explained to his comrades that "Communists not only should take to heart revolution in their own country, they also should make contributions to the international proletarian revolution."[17] The nascent Communist Parties in Siam, Malaya, and Singapore reported to a new department of the Comintern's Far Eastern Bureau, which was located in a small stone building on Hong Kong island and headed by Ho Chi Minh. Later in the year, Moscow also put Ho in charge of revolutionary activity in Laos and Cambodia, leading to the transformation of the Vietnamese Communist Party into the Indochinese Communist Party.

The year 1930 was one of grand ambitions for Ho Chi Minh and his Soviet patrons. Once he had solidified the party, Ho initiated an insurrection that wrested control of a few northern Vietnamese provinces from the French for several months. During this period, the Vietnamese Communists put their ideas into practice for the first time. They executed large numbers of landlords and Vietnamese colonial officials, then gave their land to tenant farmers, and they burned all tax and land documents. But the revolution was short-lived. The French sent in the Foreign Legion, which killed 2,000 Communists and captured 51,000 more, snuffing out all resistance and crippling the Communist Party.[18] In Hong Kong, the British police incarcerated Ho Chi Minh.

French and Vietnamese moderates, appalled by the violence during the 1930 insurrections of the Vietnamese Communist Party and the Vietnam National-ist Party, looked to the new Vietnamese Emperor to repair relations between French and Vietnamese. The Emperor Bao Dai came to power at the age of eighteen, full of energy and ideas. Believing the mandarins to be outmoded, Bao Dai closed down the high mandarin council and took on its duties him-self. For the position of Minister of the Interior, he chose a thirty-one-year-old mandarin named Ngo Dinh Diem.

The son of the famous mandarin Ngo Dinh Kha, Diem could trace his roots all the way back through Ngo Quyen, the first king of Vietnam.[19] As a youngster, Diem had been a very serious and successful student, awakening before dawn to read by oil lantern. He never missed a day of school; during severe monsoons, when his father told him not to go, he would sneak away from home to go to class. Diem, indeed, often violated his father's will, inviting frequent beatings and whippings. Diem, nevertheless, fully absorbed his father's religious and political beliefs at a young age. Fervently embracing the Catholic faith, Diem took a vow of chastity as a teenager, and he subsequently went to a monastery to become a priest, although he left a short time later. According to one of his brothers, who was to become an archbishop, Diem was too independent to submit to the strict discipline of the church. Diem also absorbed from his father a fierce nationalism and a contempt for the French colonialists. Early in Diem's childhood, his father had quit the imperial court because of his outrage over France's ousting of Emperor Thanh Thai. Moving to the countryside, Ngo Dinh Kha went to work as a farmer, a very unusual job for a prestigious mandarin, and he made his sons join him as he trudged through rice paddies with a water buffalo and plough. These experiences gave Ngo Dinh Diem an appreciation of rural life that most of Vietnam's elites lacked, a fact that would have great influence on the future of Vietnam.

At the Lycée Quoc Hoc, Diem performed so well that the French offered him a scholarship to study in France. He declined the offer, however, and instead studied at the School for Law and Administration in Hanoi. After graduating at the top of his class, Diem received assignment to the position of district chief. Dressed in a mandarin's robe and conical straw hat, Diem rode by horse across his district to mediate disputes among peasants and supervise public construction projects. He helped Vietnamese farmers leave French plantations and settle new lands. Because of his fairness and unwillingness to accept bribes – traits that were greatly revered in a land where public officials often took advantage of their positions for personal gain – Diem acquired an outstanding reputation among both the peasants and the colonial administrators. At the age of just twenty-eight, Diem received a promotion to the post of provincial chief. He asked the French to give the villages in his province better schools and greater control over their affairs, but they rejected the requests. By nature stubborn and averse to compromise, Diem considered quitting, but decided to remain in office on the advice of his elders. "You will lead this country one day," they told him.

Diem lived an austere life. He never had a girlfriend or broke his vow of chastity. Father John Keegan, who worked at a New Jersey seminary where a fifty-year-old Diem stayed a few years before his ascendancy to the South Vietnamese Presidency, remembered: "We didn't know quite exactly what he was all about. He didn't seem to us to be very important. He did dishes with us, and people of importance didn't do that; students did that, or brothers did that, and here was Diem doing dishes at the tables with the rest of the students."[20] At the height of his career, when he was the most powerful man in his country, he would own only two suits – a white sharkskin one for the palace and a khaki one for trips to the villages. Rather than sleep in a luxurious palace bed, he would sleep on an army cot, and he ate a simple peasant's breakfast of bouillon, rice, and pickles. Personal austerity, a vital attribute for a Vietnamese leader, enhanced Diem's aura of impartiality and devotion to the people. Ho Chi Minh projected a similar image of austerity, although in Ho's case the image was based partially on false claims that Ho had never married – he in fact had married a Chinese woman in the 1920s and then, a few years later, a Vietnamese political activist. According to unconfirmed accounts, Ho also wed or had relationships with additional women, including a French Socialist and a Russian.[21] The French scholar and diplomat Paul Mus once remarked, "Only one man could ever hope to challenge Ho Chi Minh for leadership – Ngo

Dinh Diem – because he alone has the same reputation for virtue and austerity as Ho."[22]

Even the Communists, who outwardly denounced Diem as a stooge of the Americans, viewed him as a great nationalist leader. Bui Tin, a Communist who joined Ho's Party in 1945 and thirty years later had the distinction of accepting South Vietnam's surrender at Saigon's Independence Palace, later said, "Although we criticized Ngo Dinh Diem publicly as an American puppet, Ho Chi Minh adopted a more sober appraisal. He realized Diem was a patriot like himself but in a different way. Later many other people came to accept and value Diem as a leader who was imbued with the spirit of nationalism, and who lived an honest and clean life and, like Ho Chi Minh, was unmarried."[23] Bui Tin himself thought that Diem was "an exceptional political figure, with profound patriotism, courage, and integrity, and a simple, unselfish way of life." Because Ho Chi Minh had been involved in a series of romantic relationships and had tried to hide them, and because he had embraced a foreign ideology, Bui Tin decided that a comparison between Ho and Diem "reveals that Ho Chi Minh is far behind and cannot match Ngo Dinh Diem."[24]

A conservative nationalist, Diem wanted to preserve the traditional core of Vietnam's culture while taking advantage of Western science and technology. He embraced the traditional view that the ruler must rule strongly and well and the people must follow. Only through strong leadership, Diem observed, could anyone bring unity to Vietnam, divided as it was into a multitude of squabbling and ineffectual political factions. From early on, Diem recognized that Communists, as well as nationalists, were capable of wielding such strength, and that the Communists sought to unify Vietnam by dictatorial methods in order to destroy the Vietnamese political, social, and religious traditions that he revered. When the Vietnamese Communist Party rebelled in 1930, Diem arrested every Communist he could find in his province, although without the needless excesses that took place in some other provinces.

Diem accepted Bao Dai's invitation to become Minister of the Interior in 1933, and the emperor put him in charge of undertaking reforms, but he would serve only a few months as Minister of the Interior. When it became clear that the French would not delegate real power to Vietnamese officials as they had promised, he resigned. The French reacted by stripping Diem of his academic titles and his decorations for government service. "Take them," Diem shouted. "I don't need them. They are not important."[25] He returned to Hue, where he spent his time reading countless books, attending mass, hunting, and building friendships with other nationalists.

Once Bao Dai had perceived France's determination to deprive him of real authority, he turned to a life of yachting and big-game hunting. Colonial Vietnam coasted along in relative peace until the middle of 1940, when Hitler's panzers overwhelmed France in a period of six weeks. Japan forced the new Vichy French government to allow thirty-five thousand Japanese troops into

Vietnam. The Japanese soldiers left the French colonial government in place since the Vichy French were allies of the Germans, but they appropriated the country's rice, rubber, and minerals.

Ho Chi Minh was serving in China with the Chinese Communist Eighth Route Army when the fall of distant France reverberated across Asia. Following his release from a British prison in 1933, he had gone to Moscow and worked at the Lenin School and the Stalin School until 1938, when the Comintern sent him to China. It was in China that he assumed the name Ho Chi Minh, meaning "Ho the Enlightened One." In early 1941, with the Chinese Communists desirous of hurting the Japanese wherever possible, Ho returned to Vietnam to build up the indigenous Communist movement. Assembling a group of leading Communists shortly after his arrival, Ho convened the Eighth Plenum of the Indochinese Communist Party at a clammy, rat-infested cave near the boundary between Vietnam and China. Towering over the cave was a mountain that Ho dubbed Karl Marx Peak, while 140 feet below the cave flowed a brook that he named Lenin Stream. Perhaps the members of the Party's central committee slaked their thirst at the stream, for the documents they wrote were entirely Leninist in character. The committee members called for a nationalist war in alliance with Vietnamese capitalists, their intention to harness the horses of nationalism until they had defeated the French and Japanese. Once this war had been won, they planned to put those horses to pasture and ride the steeds of Marxist revolution to final victory. During the plenum, the central committee created a new organization called the Viet Nam Doc Lap Dong Minh Hoi, meaning the League for the Independence of Vietnam, or Viet Minh for short. The Party declared it an organization for all Vietnamese that would rely on nationalist, not Communist, propaganda. The Vietnamese Communists would use the Viet Minh as their front organization until the French made peace with them thirteen years later, in 1954.

Numerous Westerners were to believe the claim that the Viet Minh was truly a diverse nationalist movement from top to bottom, deriving its strength from all Vietnamese opposition groups, but from the beginning this conception was inaccurate.[26] While some non-Communists did join the Viet Minh, the Communist Party would always retain control of the Viet Minh's leadership, and few prominent non-Communists ever became members of the Viet Minh throughout its thirteen-year existence.[27] Those Viet Minh leaders who claimed to be non-Communist nationalists were in reality Communist Party members operating at the direction of Ho Chi Minh. The top Viet Minh leaders came predominantly from mandarin families, but they obtained most of their rank-and-file personnel from the uneducated peasantry rather than the independent-minded elites. As a landlord or businessman, one would be permitted to serve in only the lowest ranks of the Viet Minh, and would be monitored and controlled closely. Lasting alliances with other opposition groups did not materialize, for the Viet Minh, determined as they were to maintain complete control over the revolution, either destroyed or alienated those groups willing to put their trust in them. Throughout his career, Ho Chi Minh succeeded not by gaining the friendship of other opposition leaders, but by eliminating them.

Ho Chi Minh went back to China in 1942 to seek support from a variety of Chinese groups and Vietnamese émigré communities. A Chinese Nationalist warlord, wary of Communists, had Ho arrested and chained to the walls of a lice-ridden prison. Chiang Kai-shek, however, released Ho after he promised to work with other Vietnamese to fight the hated Japanese, and he even gave Ho money for this purpose, thereby enabling Ho to build up the Viet Minh's armed forces. After his release, Ho also appealed to the American Office of Strategic Services (oss) for help, changing his name from Nguyen Ai Quoc to Ho Chi Minh in order to hide his Communist past.[28] The OSS began sending arms to the Viet Minh, too, in return for Viet Minh promises to attack the Japanese, hand over intelligence on Japanese forces, and help recover downed American pilots. Although Ho's small army grew steadily, he made little effort to attack the Japanese as he had promised the Chinese Nationalists and the Americans. As the war played out and Viet Minh promises of action mounted, Ho's commanders urged him to unleash the guerrillas against the Japanese, but Ho, mindful that he had only a few chips to play, chose to wait until the odds were clearly in his favor.

In March 1945, fears of an American invasion drove the Japanese occupation force to seize control of Indochina from the French. The Free French leadership in recently liberated Paris appealed to the United States for help in the restoration of French rule. The U.S. government at first did nothing, quickly exciting the wrath of Free French leader Charles de Gaulle, and also that of Winston Churchill, who was working with de Gaulle to preserve both of their empires. On March 13, 1945, de Gaulle informed the Americans, "If the public here comes to realize that you are against us in Indochina, there will be terrific disappointment, and nobody knows to what that will lead. We do not want to become Communist; we do not want to fall into the Russian orbit; but I hope that you do not push us into it."[29]

President Franklin D. Roosevelt opposed colonialism as a general policy, but he had always considered Europe to be more important to American security than Asia, and at this point in time he was already resigning himself to French control over the postwar fate of Indochina. Upon hearing de Gaulle's reaction, therefore, he directed American air units in China to assist French resistance forces in Indochina.[30] His successor, President Harry S. Truman, consented in July to a plan whereby Nationalist Chinese and British forces would move into Vietnam following Japan's surrender to maintain order and facilitate the reestablishment of French rule.

As soon as America's atomic bombs ravaged Hiroshima and Nagasaki, the stunned Japanese dropped the reins of power in Vietnam, leaving them dangling for the first comer. Convinced that the most favorable moment had arrived at last, Ho Chi Minh quickly moved into action. As he had hoped, he preempted the Allied powers as well as the Vietnamese nationalist leaders who possessed armed forces, many of whom were still in China. Vietnamese Communist guerrillas marched unopposed into Hanoi and other cities with the rifles and submachine guns that they had received from their Chinese and American benefactors. Intimidating the inert Japanese-installed regime into submission, they established a new government that had but one stated objective: the end of foreign rule in Vietnam. The Viet Minh avoided any mention of their Communist ideology or their plans to take away the wealth and privileges of the elites. Without delay, the Viet Minh nullified the most hated French policies, including high taxes and the government monopolies on salt, alcohol, and opium. Their anti-colonial rhetoric and their initial actions helped them win over many of the city people, especially in the north, but they owed their success to two other factors as well. Much of their attraction emanated from the personality of Ho Chi Minh. As far as most Vietnamese were concerned, it made little difference whether Ho's ideology was purely nationalist, as he claimed at this time, or whether it was an unoriginal blend of the ideas of Marx, Lenin, Stalin, and Mao, as it was in reality. What counted most were the strength of personality and appearance of austerity that conferred charisma upon him.

Hoang Van Chi, a one-time Viet Minh official who quit the Communist movement because of its excesses, wrote these perceptive words:

> Ho is endowed with an outstanding personality. He has in fact all the qualities necessary in a leader, and his austerity, perseverance, iron determination and whole-hearted devotion to the cause of the Revolution are an inspiration to all who serve under him and to the nation as a whole.... His reputation for honesty and sincerity has contributed greatly to his success, for in Vietnam, as in many underdeveloped countries, the masses put their trust in the personal character and behavior of a leader more than in the political party he represents.[31]

Tran Van Tra, later one of Communist Vietnam's highest generals, sensed Ho's charismatic appeal the instant he met him. Tra remembered his first encounter with Ho: "Just looking at him, I suddenly felt I had endless confidence in him. I respected him and felt intimate with him. His skill could conquer everything. He was the quintessence of talent."[32]

The other key factor in the Viet Minh's rapid rise in prestige during August 1945 was their demonstration of brute strength. From the beginning of their history, the Vietnamese people had always been very inclined to support whichever political faction appeared strongest, in part because theirs was a culture that revered authority, in part because the enemies of a Vietnamese victor so often suffered nasty punishments. At a time when everyone else stood in utter disarray, the Viet Minh could project an image of strength very easily even though they had just five thousand men under arms. Wielding their shiny American weapons, Viet Minh soldiers had the ability to impose their will on most anyone. Further evidence of Viet Minh strength came from the seeming support they enjoyed from the mighty United States, as conveyed by the presence of OSS officers and U.S. aircraft. Many potential rivals were so awestruck by the Viet Minh's prestige that they decided not to resist them at all. Bao Dai himself agreed to step down so that the Viet Minh could form a government for the whole country, although it is not clear whether the Emperor made this decision on his own or under duress.

Unaware that the Americans had already consented to France's return, Ho Chi Minh labored hard to secure the American support that the people thought he already possessed. Ho had manipulated many past adversaries with false offers of friendship, so the idea of hoodwinking the Americans with pretended amicability came readily to him. The citation of the American Declaration of Independence in his Place Puginier speech was only the most prominent of multiple attempts to flatter the Americans into the position of Timon of Athens. To allay concerns over his political affiliation, Ho told the OSS officers in Hanoi that he was not really a Communist, just a patriot seeking national independence. One of those officers, Archimedes Patti, later said that he and others in the OSS admired the Viet Minh and wanted to side with them, only to be thwarted by Washington officials who thought differently.[33] Some of the OSS men were indeed taken in by the Viet Minh's propaganda immediately, but Patti himself at that time recognized that the propaganda was misleading and that the Viet Minh would not be reliable allies. Patti's 1945 OSS reports from Hanoi were not at all of the sort that would suggest to Washington or anyone else that alliance was a viable option. On August 29, 1945, Patti sent Washington a cable stating that "Red elements" were leading the new Viet Minh regime astray, and that the regime's leaders spoke regularly in favor of liberalism and democracy but in fact were preparing to take illiberal and undemocratic actions.[34]

To demonstrate its strength further and enhance its prestige, the Viet Minh government methodically neutralized its opponents. In some instances, the Viet Minh were subtle. They gave respected nationalists positions in the new government and held elections for other positions, then denied the officeholders any real power. Immediately after their march into Hanoi, the Viet Minh quietly took over the printing presses of non-Communist newspapers and ended the publication of material critical of the Viet Minh. More often, though, they acted without subtlety. In the tradition of both the independent Vietnamese emperors and Josef Stalin, Ho had many of his rivals put to death.[35] Without hesitation, the Viet Minh killed the renowned literary and political figure Pham Quynh, who had served under Bao Dai and the Japanese. They apprehended Ngo Dinh Khoi, a prominent and very talented brother of Ngo Dinh Diem, and buried him alive. In Hanoi, the Viet Minh killed Vietnam Nationalist Party leaders Nguyen The Nghiep and Nguyen Ngoc Son, as well as the founder of the moderate Constitutionalist Party, Bui Quang Chieu. Another victim was Ho Van Nga, a conservative nationalist leader in the south. Viet Minh assassins took the lives of Nguyen Van Sam, who had founded the Front of National Union, and Dr. Truong Dinh Tri, a former Viet Minh official who was organizing on behalf of Bao Dai in Tonkin. Others were not killed until 1946, including Truong Tu Anh, head of the influential Dai Viet Party.

Vietnamese Communists who adhered to the Communism of Leon Trotsky, the Soviet luminary who a few years earlier had been murdered with an ice-pick on orders from his archrival Joseph Stalin, were shown no more mercy than the others. For Ho and the other Viet Minh leaders, Stalin was the supreme leader of the world revolution, while Trotsky was a dangerous heretic.[36] The Viet Minh killed some Trotskyites right away, often by tying several people together and throwing them into a river to drown slowly. In 1946, the Viet Minh apprehended Nguyen Ta Thu Thau, the most gifted Trotskyite leader and writer, at the train station in Quang Ngai, then took him to a sandy beach, gave him a mock trial, and put a bullet through his head.

A short time after Ho seized power in Hanoi, Viet Minh guerrillas abducted Ngo Dinh Diem. Diem had spent the years 1942 to 1944 organizing anti-French political subversion in cooperation with exiled Vietnamese nationalists and the Japanese, leading to the formation of a secret political party called the "Association for the Restoration of Great Vietnam." In the summer of 1944, however, the French Sûreté began arresting the party's members and Diem was forced to go into hiding.[37] The guerrillas took Diem to Ho in Hanoi.

"Why did you kill my brother?" Diem asked Ho.

"It was a mistake," Ho claimed. "The country was all confused. It could not be helped."[38] Knowing that Diem possessed rare leadership talents, Ho asked him to become his minister of the interior. Diem said he would accept only if he would be kept fully informed of the Viet Minh's activities and would be privy to all decisions. Ho refused to accept these conditions. "I see it is useless to discuss matters with you while you are so irritable," Ho remarked, "but stay around a little while." Diem still did not budge, though, and after a time Ho released him.[39] That Ho did not kill Ngo Dinh Diem as he killed so many other nationalist leaders was a measure of the respect he had for Diem. It was also the biggest mistake he ever made.

In the northern villages, the Vietnamese Communists implemented a more radical and less discriminate program than in the cities. Stripping the mandarins and the village councils of their powers, they installed revolutionary committees in their place and gave landless peasants the land of landlords who had cooperated with the French. Across the northern countryside, Viet Minh security personnel killed large numbers of village officials and landlords. During August and September, in Vietnam as a whole, the Viet Minh would end the lives of several thousand Vietnamese.[40]

The redistribution of land helped put large numbers of poor peasants on the Communist side, and the Viet Minh gave strong preference to poor peasants when recruiting and promoting within their own ranks. Yet catering to the interests of the peasants was not essential to mobilizing them, whether in 1945 or in centuries past. The essentials were always charismatic leadership and manifest strength, both of which the Viet Minh possessed and used very effectively. Numerous Vietnamese leaders, from Ngo Quyen to Le Loi to Nguyen Anh, had succeeded in mobilizing hundreds of thousands of peasants for war through leadership and strength alone. Consumed by the needs of agricultural work and ingrained with respect for the existing social order, the peasants never led their own rebellions, but they were very willing to follow others.

By eliminating many of Vietnam's finest non-Communist leaders, the Viet Minh hoped to destroy all embryos of resistance before they could grow into mature organisms. That goal, however, was not reached. In the north, stout opposition to the Viet Minh arose under the leadership of the Vietnam Nationalist Party and other exiled nationalists who were on good terms with the Chinese Nationalists. Chinese troops arrived in mid-September to accept the Japanese surrender, and they quickly helped install the Vietnam Nationalist Party in several provinces. In 1946, however, when the Chinese Nationalists withdrew their troops, the Viet Minh started a war with the Vietnam Nationalist Party. Surrounding the provincial and district capitals, the Communist armed forces overwhelmed the nationalist defenders and put the leading elements of the Vietnam Nationalist Party to the sword. Vo Nguyen Giap later wrote that in 1946, "The liquidating of the reactionaries of the Vietnam Nationalist Party was crowned with success and we were able to liberate all the areas which had fallen into their hands."[41] In Vietnamese Communist parlance, the label "reactionary" was applied to anyone who was not a Communist. Many more "reactionaries" would suffer death during the remainder of 1946, bringing the toll of civilians killed by the Communists during the period of Communist rule into the tens of thousands.[42]

While the Viet Minh eventually succeeded in wiping out the organized opposition in the north, they failed in this task in the south. They lacked sufficient strength there in the early moments of the revolution, and were unable to develop it subsequently. Southern political activity was centered in the city of Saigon, which under the French had grown into a modern Asian metropolis, with all the commercial activity, commotion, and vice one might expect. In the autumn of 1945, the native political elite of Saigon jostled for power as frantically as the city's street peddlers sought customers for their fish, rubber, and cinnamon. A bewildering array of political parties, religious sects, and gangsters entered the fray alongside the Viet Minh, resulting in a free-for-all in which countless factions organized demonstrations and processions full of talk and noise but empty of meaning. The people of Saigon had never agreed on anything. They never would.

During September 1945, French soldiers reoccupied Saigon and established control across all of southern Vietnam, which required no great exertion because neither the Viet Minh nor any other Vietnamese group offered armed resistance of any significance. Initially, the French did not try to oust the Communists from the north, owing to the presence of Viet Minh and Chinese troops. Instead, French diplomats attempted to pry concessions from Ho Chi Minh while French clandestine operators developed plans for subverting him. Hoping to avert a war he knew he could not win and to gain time to annihilate the Vietnam Nationalist Party, Ho agreed in March 1946 to let 15,000 French troops plus 10,000 Vietnamese troops under French command into the north for a maximum of six years. The French, for their part, agreed to let the Viet Minh remain in power in the north, and to allow the south to decide by a vote whether it would be united with the north. During the ensuing months, however, further negotiations between the French and the Viet Minh were unproductive and relations deteriorated. Preparing for the worst, Ho doubled the strength of his army, from 30,000 to 60,000.

The showdown between the French and the Viet Minh came at the end of 1946, after a series of small violent incidents. On the night of December 19, Ho's forces in Hanoi knocked out the city's electric power plant and launched an all-out attack against the French. The French Socialist Party, the foreign party to which Ho had first belonged, held power in Paris at this time. As in the past, the French Socialists were generally sympathetic to calls for Vietnamese independence, especially those that came from Vietnamese leftists, but the Viet Minh's recent acts of violence against French civilians and soldiers had convinced the Socialists that the Viet Minh were deceitful and malevolent. The Socialist government, therefore, decided it had to restore order by force before resuming negotiations with the Viet Minh.[43] With their great firepower, the French military easily blasted the Communists out of Hanoi and the provincial capitals, compelling Ho Chi Minh and his associates to flee their offices in the colonial mansions of Hanoi and head into the countryside. The Communists took refuge in jungles and mountain caves from which they would wage war for the next eight years. As their principal redoubt, the Viet Minh chose the Viet Bac, a slice of rugged territory sandwiched between the Red River Delta and the Chinese border. Covered with steep mountains and uncut by roads, the Viet Bac was largely impervious to attack from French aircraft and motorized vehicles. The French were to invade the Viet Bac on a number of occasions, and they did disrupt Viet Minh activities for a time, but they never drove the Viet Minh out altogether.[44]

Ho Chi Minh's army endured numerous setbacks during the first years of the conflict. Lacking sufficient military experience and training, their leaders often reacted to French attacks by holding their ground inflexibly or fleeing in disarray, both of which usually resulted in heavy casualties. They squandered thousands of men in futile assaults. In time, the Viet Minh developed skill in conducting hit-and-run raids, ambushing the long French convoys that traversed Vietnam's narrow roads, and retreating under fire. To inflict losses on well-armed and well-disciplined French forces, his troops still had to take fearsome losses of their own, but Ho accepted these casualties philosophically, believing that his side could stomach the pain of this war longer than the enemy could.

Most of the fighting took place in northern Vietnam, close to the Viet Minh base areas in the Viet Bac. In the south, the Viet Minh were too weak to contest French control in a serious fashion. There, the French used offers of autonomy and riches to enlist the support of the Cao Dai and Hoa Hao religious sects, as well as a Saigon gangster organization called the Binh Xuyen. The Cao Dai sect had been formed in the 1920s, and by the late 1940s it held the allegiance of a million people. At the grand Cao Dai temple in Tay Ninh, one could witness the sect's eclectic character in the collection of effigies honoring favorite saints, whose number included Buddha, Confucius, Jesus, Victor Hugo, and Charlie Chaplin. The Hoa Hao sect was founded in 1939 by a twenty-year-old villager named Huynh Phu So. Said to possess the ability to heal the infirm and other rare spiritual powers, Huynh Phu So began to prophesize events in Vietnam, and each of his prophesies came true. Among the natives of southern Vietnam, word spread that the "living Buddha" had entered their midst, causing hundreds of thousands to flock to the sect. The Viet Minh greatly feared Huynh Phu So because of his ability to mobilize the masses. In 1947, they captured him and bludgeoned him to death, then chopped up his body and scattered the pieces across the country to prevent his remains from inspiring his followers. The grisly murder, however, made the Hoa Hao into the most implacable and fanatical of anti-Communists.

As it became clear that the war would be long and costly, the French attempted to cultivate a strong Vietnamese government that would mobilize the masses against the Communists. They asked Ngo Dinh Diem to join, but he turned them down because their proposals were watered down with special privileges and powers for France. The French found a more receptive man in Bao Dai. In 1949, Bao Dai agreed to form an autonomous and anti-Communist regime within the French Union, and this new government attracted the services of some respected Vietnamese nationalists, who viewed it as a necessary antidote to Communism.

The crucial turning point in the Franco-Viet Minh war came in 1949, when Mao Zedong's Communists won control of the Chinese mainland. To the French and the Americans and the Vietnamese, the enormous implications for Vietnam and the rest of Asia were obvious. Communism now had a massive base in Asia, and Stalin and Mao wanted to use it as a springboard for subverting the other countries of Asia. While French and American politicians agonized, Viet Minh leaders celebrated the "glorious success" of the Chinese Communists and derided the "failure of American imperialism."[45] Ho Chi Minh, in an accurate characterization of both historical relations and his own relations with the Chinese Communists, announced in a published letter, "Brotherly relations have existed between the Vietnamese and Chinese nations during thousands

of years of history. Henceforth these relations will be even closer for the development of the freedom and happiness of our two nations, as well as for the
safeguard of world democracy and lasting peace."[46] In early 1949, Viet Minh
and Chinese Communist units joined together to attack French positions near
the Chinese border, with the Chinese forces briefly holding the Vietnamese
town of Mong Cai before returning to bases on Chinese territory.[47]

Ho hiked to China in January 1950, a journey lasting seventeen days. Just
after he arrived in Nanning, the Chinese announced diplomatic recognition of
Ho's Democratic Republic of Vietnam. The Soviet Union did the same a few
days later. Ho then took a trip to Moscow, where he met with Stalin and Mao
to request weapons and military advisers.

"Toward Vietnam we feel equal concern as we do for China," Stalin told Ho.
"From now on, you can count on our assistance. Especially now after the war
of resistance, our surplus materials are plenty, and we will ship them to you
through China. But because of limits of natural conditions, it will be mainly
China that helps you. What China lacks, we will provide."

"Whatever China has and Vietnam needs, we will provide," Mao intoned.
The Chinese Communist Party "offers all the military assistance Vietnam needs
in its struggle against France."[48] True to his word, Mao gave Ho everything
he requested. During the first nine months of 1950, the Chinese shipped the
Viet Minh 14,000 rifles, 1,700 machine guns and recoilless rifles, 60 artillery
pieces, 300 bazookas, and a variety of other military equipment. The Viet Minh
particularly liked the bazookas and recoilless rifles, which they believed to be
"as powerful as elephants." Two hundred eighty-one Chinese experts came to
advise the Vietnamese Communists from the battalion level on up. At Ho's
request, the list of Chinese experts included Chen Geng, who was one of Mao's
best generals despite the fact that he was so fat that he had to be lifted onto his
horse. The Vietnamese heeded Chen Geng's advice with such readiness that he
became the principal architect of the war effort.[49] As if suddenly grown from a
cub into a bear, the Viet Minh's armed forces for the first time posed a serious
threat to the French military.

For the remainder of the war and for some years afterwards, Ho and his
adherents would follow the Chinese in all things, as an awestruck boy follows
his older brother. Ho acknowledged in 1951, "the Chinese Revolution exerted
a great influence on the Vietnamese revolution, which had to learn and
indeed has learned many experiences from it."[50] A more explicit description
came later from Bui Tin. In the period following Mao's victory over Chiang
Kai-shek, Bui Tin recounted, "We were dazzled by the new light of the Chinese
Revolution, which was acclaimed as our role-model. We accepted everything
impetuously and haphazardly without any thought, let alone criticism. . . . In
truth it has to be said that the thinking of Ho Chi Minh and the rest of the leadership in those days was to regard Mao Tse-tung's thought as the only way to
follow."[51]

The Chinese advisers taught Viet Minh leaders Communist reeducation methods aimed at remaking cadres and soldiers into new men concerned only with Marxism-Leninism. The Vietnamese Communists began a series of radical "land reform" programs under guidance of the Chinese, who had conducted a similar campaign in their own country and had killed over one million people in the process. Viet Minh leaders gave land from landlords to landless peasants and set quotas in each village for the number of landlords who were to receive additional punishments, which would mean death for some. Oftentimes the quotas exceeded the total number of landlords in the village, with the result that other villagers, including some Viet Minh supporters, paid severe penalties for getting caught with a book of French poems or for committing a petty offense against a Party member. Ho Chi Minh himself eventually became aware of these problems, but for a long while he was not willing to contradict Mao's representatives and reform the program.[52] In the name of eradicating feudalism and class distinctions, the Viet Minh killed many thousands of the accused, then buried them inconspicuously to hide the extent of the killing. Many more were permitted to live but were stripped of their possessions and forced to endure the eternal monitoring of the police and the ridicule of the former landless peasants. They became the new lower class.

Prior to the defeat of the Chinese Nationalists in the Chinese Civil War, the United States had remained aloof from the Franco–Viet Minh War. On the one hand, the Americans had no desire to prop up a colonial power, disdaining colonialism as they did. On the other, they did not want to antagonize France by showing support for the Viet Minh, and they distrusted the Viet Minh because of their well-known ties to Moscow. Leading figures in the Truman administration had not considered the Asian mainland to be an area of vital strategic interest for their country before the end of the Chinese Civil War. After World War II, the United States had created a forward line of defense on a chain of Pacific islands lying to the east, southeast, and south of the Asian mainland, which included Guam, the Aleutians, the Ryukyus, Japan, the Philippines, Australia, and New Zealand. From this offshore island chain, as it was called, the United States could launch air, naval, and amphibious attacks against any Pacific foe. It could make sure that key strategic sea lanes and the region's one industrial powerhouse – Japan – stayed out of hostile hands. The Americans had excluded the Asian mainland from their defensive line because it lacked advanced military and industrial capabilities and its defense would require huge numbers of ground forces. The fall of China in 1949, one of America's worst setbacks in the Cold War, compelled the Truman administration to reconsider this policy. Aghast at Communist control of China, besieged with right-wing accusations that he had lost that huge country by cutting U.S. assistance to the Chinese Nationalists, and confronted at the same time with the first Soviet detonation of a nuclear device, President Truman was moving towards the view of some of his principal advisers that the United States now had to defend virtually any country not already under Communist control, not merely nations of high industrial or military value.[53]

Truman had other, more particular reasons to be concerned about Indochina. The fall of Indochina could put at risk America's island defense chain by means of the "domino" effect, a phenomenon widely feared by Truman's diplomats and generals, whereby the loss of Indochina would lead to the fall of other Southeast Asian nations.[54] The loss of Southeast Asia would sever America's island defense chain, and would isolate Japan and India economically and politically, rendering them highly vulnerable to Communist intimidation. Contemporary events readily supported the domino theory. Communism's victory in China had led to a Sino–Viet Minh alliance, to the initiation of Communist insurgencies in Malaya, Burma, and Indonesia, and to the reinvigoration of a Communist insurgency in the Philippines. Recent history also showed the vulnerability of the dominoes to conventional military invasion. During World War II, the Japanese had begun their conquest of Southeast Asia by seizing Indochina and using its ports and airfields to invade Southeast Asia's two greatest prizes, the Malayan peninsula and the Indonesian archipelago. In just a few months, the Soviets and Chinese would in fact back a conventional onslaught by their North Korean allies. Contrary to the caricatures produced by the domino theory's critics,[55] the theory's proponents did not in general believe that the dominoes would necessarily fall immediately or in a uniform manner. Instead, they recognized that intimidation and subversion might be more important than outright conquest and that some governments might ally themselves with the Communists without ceding power to the local Communist Party.

The protection of Indochina also would directly serve American interests that had nothing to do with Asia. By the beginning of 1950, the French were warning the United States that they could not afford to continue the war in Indochina and simultaneously uphold their commitments to the North Atlantic Treaty Organization in Europe. With very large Communist and Socialist parties, France already stood in serious danger of turning away from the United States and the other NATO nations, and continued American indifference towards Indochina, especially if followed by a French defeat there, could push the teetering French into the Communist camp. A cornerstone of the western European alliance, a rampart against a murderous and expansionist Soviet empire that was swallowing up eastern European countries in violation of international agreements, France remained much more important than Southeast Asia as far as U.S. security was concerned, and thus the U.S. government continued to accord it a higher priority.

It was not true, as popular myths had it, that the Truman administration viewed international Communism as an unbreakable monolith and hence dismissed the idea of playing off the Viet Minh against the Chinese Communists.[56] By 1949, leading administration officials clearly understood that Communism was not monolithic and that divisions among Communist countries could and should be exploited. The U.S. government was already supporting Tito in Yugoslavia and seeking other potential Titos elsewhere in Eastern Europe.[57] The Americans viewed the situation in Vietnam on its own merits and concluded, rightly, that Ho Chi Minh could not be made into the Tito of Asia. In any case, supporting the Viet Minh would have antagonized France beyond measure and would have terrified other non-Communist countries that were threatened by Communism. Truman and his advisers similarly decided that they could not split China and the Soviet Union apart at the present time, though they hoped they would be able to realize that end at some future date. This judgment was also correct. From 1949 through 1955, China and the Soviet Union were very close allies. Chinese leaders called Stalin "the sun that shines forever" and the "greatest figure in the world,"[58] while Stalin, although less ebullient, formally committed the Soviet Union to defend China and made Mao his viceroy in East Asia.[59]

When, in the spring of 1950, Chinese and Soviet assistance to the Viet Minh had become obvious to the whole world, Truman made the decision to assist the French in Indochina. Following a formal request for aid from France in May, Truman persuaded the U.S. Congress to fund the French war in Indochina to the tune of $100 million per year. By 1954, the United States would be contributing $1 billion a year, amounting to eighty percent of the French war budget.

For Mao, the investment in the Viet Minh soon began to pay dividends. During the latter part of 1950, with equipment and supplies bestowed by China, Viet Minh forces overran a set of isolated French forts along the Chinese frontier. The French were driven permanently out of northern Tonkin, allowing unobstructed movement of men and materiel between China and the Viet Bac. At the end of 1950, when the specter of despair flew as never before through the spirits of Frenchmen in Indochina, the magnificent General Jean de Lattre de Tassigny took over as the French high commissioner and single-handedly reversed the momentum of the war. General de Lattre revitalized the French forces and made considerable progress in developing a large indigenous army. When, during the first months of 1951, the Vietnamese Communists launched a series of large conventional "human wave" attacks, de Lattre's troops flattened the Viet Minh waves with concentrated firepower and turned the Viet Minh's offensive into a debacle. After stopping the Viet Minh, the French retook key strategic highways in the north that they had lost in 1950. But then chance dealt a momentous blow. Cancer struck the great de Lattre, requiring his evacuation from Vietnam in December 1951, only one year after he had arrived. He died in Paris one month later.

The Vietnamese National Army continued to expand after de Lattre's death, reaching a strength of 205,700 by 1953. Another 100,000 Vietnamese were serving in the French army, and 128,000 more belonged to militia, police, and other armed forces. Over time, the French gave the Bao Dai government control over entire regions. The 150,000 foreign soldiers in Indochina, who were mainly of French, German, or North African origin, focused on destroying Viet Minh troop concentrations in the northern provinces.[60] As war weariness began to mount in France, those who fought for Bao Dai and France did not wither, but continued to fight a nasty war in which the enemy could always flee into the mountains of the Viet Bac or across the Chinese border if too many bullets were launched in their direction. In 1952 and 1953, France's forces consolidated their hold on the Red River Delta and improved their position in central Vietnam. So frustrated was Ho Chi Minh during this period that he asked Mao to send Chinese combat troops to Vietnam, but he was rebuffed.[61] When the Viet Minh invaded Laos in April 1953, French troops swooped into Laos by air at the last moment and thwarted the Viet Minh offensive.

The climactic battle of the war took place in early 1954 at the remote valley of Dien Bien Phu, in the far northwestern corner of Vietnam.[62] The French faced considerable problems at this time, above all dwindling support for the war at home, but the Viet Minh had problems of even greater severity. Janos Radvanyi, a senior Hungarian diplomat, heard General Vo Nguyen Giap tell the story of early 1954 five years later, in front of a papier-mâché model of the Dien Bien Phu battlefield. Radvanyi recounted Giap's lecture: "The battle of Dien Bien Phu, he told us, was the last desperate exertion of the Viet Minh army. Its forces were on the verge of complete exhaustion. The supply of rice was running out. Apathy had spread among the populace to such an extent that it was difficult to draft new fighters. Years of jungle warfare had sent morale in the fighting units plunging to the depths."[63] A variety of Communist sources subsequently revealed that nearly all of the Viet Minh's mobile forces had been sent to Dien Bien Phu, contradicting the dominant belief in the West that the Viet Minh had a vast number of soldiers hidden elsewhere in Vietnam. "Like a gambler, we were staking everything on a single throw and risked losing the entire war," one Communist observed.[64] In short, both sides had the opportunity to win a decisive victory at Dien Bien Phu.

The French high command dispatched 7,000 combat and 3,800 support troops of mixed nationality to hold the valley at Dien Bien Phu. Ho Chi Minh put 50,000 Viet Minh soldiers into the attack. He and his Chinese allies used an equal number of logistical troops, many of them Chinese, and 1,000 Chinese trucks to transport supplies from the Chinese border to Dien Bien Phu. Now relieved of the burden of the Korean War, the Chinese were sending the Viet Minh 4,000 tons of aid per month, ten times what they had sent in 1951. The logistical units were delivering a large supply of heavy weapons, including howitzers and radar-controlled antiaircraft guns, in addition to the small arms and ammunition that Viet Minh forces needed in huge quantities.[65] Some of the most advanced weapons, including a battalion of Soviet-built Katyusha rocket launchers, were operated by Chinese experts.[66] Laying siege to the French position, the Viet Minh dug trenches and tunnels towards the French perimeter outposts.

In mid-March, with the aid of heavy and accurate artillery fire, Viet Minh troops began attacking key posts around the rim of the valley. Concentrated Viet Minh units succeeded in taking some of the objectives, but the defenders inflicted devastating losses on the Viet Minh in these engagements, punching a gaping hole in their morale. At the beginning of April, Ho Chi Minh told the Chinese that the situation had become "hopeless" and he asked his Chinese allies to send its troops into Vietnam to save the day just as they had done in Korea. But the Chinese were not prepared to go that far. Zhou Enlai explained to Khrushchev in secret that the Chinese would not intervene because "we've already lost too many men in Korea – that war cost us dearly." At Khrushchev's suggestion, however, the Chinese gave the Vietnamese Communists the impression that they would eventually come to their rescue if necessary, a Machiavellian ploy designed to bolster the Viet Minh's spirits.[67] This tactic succeeded, for Ho Chi Minh continued the fight at Dien Bien Phu and in the ensuing days the Viet Minh seized some of the strongholds around the valley, enabling them to hurl artillery shells onto the valley floor at will.

The siege of Dien Bien Phu prompted the United States to reappraise the value of Indochina. Occupying the White House now was Dwight David Eisenhower, a man who had already led the U.S. military through the world's largest war before he became President. Eisenhower, whose grandfatherly affability masked an extraordinary grasp of current international affairs, viewed Southeast Asia as an area of high strategic importance where one Communist victory could lead to many others. He was especially concerned about Malaya and Indonesia, believing that the loss of either country would imperil the island defense chain, and he worried that the loss of Southeast Asia could cause Japan to seek alliances with the Communists. On these points, Eisenhower was in agreement with Truman. But Eisenhower was more thrifty and selective than Truman when deploying American aid and military resources, especially in the third world. Eisenhower was less inclined to tangle in peripheral areas where the United States would fight from a disadvantageous position. He also relied less heavily on conventional forces than did Truman, preferring instead to use the threat of "massive retaliation" via nuclear warfare to deter the Communists. That national security posture enabled Eisenhower to attain one of his principal objectives, a reduction in military spending, which he hoped would promote domestic economic development and ultimately lead to victory in the Cold War.[68]

Upon reviewing the situation, Eisenhower decided that Indochina was worth saving if the United States could save it by sending additional military aid or employing more of its air power, but it was not valuable enough to warrant sending American combat troops. Nor did Eisenhower deem Indochina sufficiently precious to threaten China with nuclear devastation and accept the risks involved therein. He was willing to let Indochina fall even though he knew the United States would forfeit strategically valuable territory and antagonize France, which was still in jeopardy of turning its back on the United States. Conditions in the Indochinese states favored America's enemies, Eisenhower had concluded. The President was discouraged by France's inability to develop a strong indigenous army in Vietnam, something he considered essential for victory; like most in the West, Eisenhower did not know that the French and their Vietnamese cohorts were on the verge of crushing the Viet Minh in early 1954. The United States had to hold the line in Southeast Asia, Eisenhower believed, but in Malaya, not Indochina. In contrast to Indochina, Malaya was separated from the Chinese and Vietnamese Communists by one thousand miles of rugged territory, and it had only a small land border to defend. On January 8, 1954, Eisenhower told the National Security Council emphatically, "I cannot imagine the United States putting ground forces anywhere in Southeast Asia except possibly in Malaya, which we have to defend as a bulwark to our offshore island chain." Referring specifically to the use of American troops in Indochina, Eisenhower exclaimed, "I cannot tell you how bitterly opposed I am to such a course of action. This war in Indochina would absorb our troops by divisions!"[69]

After the Viet Minh's initial advances at Dien Bien Phu in late March, Eisenhower began considering a plan put forth by Secretary of State John Foster Dulles called "united action," in which the United States would attempt to convince France, Britain, and several Southeast Asian nations to join a coalition to defend Indochina. If such a coalition were built and France agreed to grant full independence to Indochina, then the Americans would make known their willingness use their bombers to pummel the siege force at Dien Bien Phu. Eisenhower and Dulles viewed united action primarily as a threat rather than as a military measure. Keenly attuned to human nature, Eisenhower and Dulles excelled at employing threatening language and behavior to subdue their adversaries. If America and its allies showed their willingness to act together and strike the Viet Minh, they believed, the Chinese and Viet Minh would back off at Dien Bien Phu and the Americans would not have to bomb at all. In addition, united action would strengthen America's bargaining position in any negotiations on Indochina. Eisenhower and Dulles did not think that dropping bombs on Dien Bien Phu would have much of an effect on total Viet Minh strength, even if it inflicted heavy losses, because of the U.S. military's mistaken assertion that the Viet Minh still had huge numbers of soldiers hidden elsewhere. If the United States wanted to put an end to the Viet Minh, the Joint Chiefs had told them, it should destroy China, because China was giving the Viet Minh forces military hardware and advice as well as sanctuary. In reality, while bombing could not have wiped out all of the Viet Minh forces at Dien Bien Phu, it almost certainly would have thwarted their attack – both by reducing their numbers and cutting their supply lines at key chokepoints – and it would have left them with a sharply reduced capacity for large-unit warfare throughout Indochina.

On April 4, just a few days after Ho had said he was in a hopeless situation and needed a Chinese troop commitment, the French told the United States that they faced a hopeless situation and would suffer defeat unless the Americans immediately bombed the Viet Minh. The heavy fighting had taken its toll on the badly outnumbered garrison at Dien Bien Phu, and the Viet Minh had just captured some critical terrain. French diplomats warned the Americans that if Dien Bien Phu were lost, then France would not be willing to continue the war. After some haggling, the French acceded to America's demand for full independence for Indochina. Dulles took the concept of "united action" to Congressional leaders, and, to his delight, they gave it their consent. In 1954, most Congressmen of both parties favored heavy commitments to anti-Communism abroad. The Congressional leaders were even willing to send American ground forces, but only if other nations contributed large numbers of troops. "We want no more Koreas with the United States furnishing ninety percent of the manpower," was the prevailing view of the Congressional leaders.[70] Eisenhower, though, remained opposed to sending any U.S. ground troops.

The Eisenhower administration then asked America's allies whether they would participate in united action, while Dulles delivered speeches threatening the Communists with the multilateral plan. The governments of Thailand and the Philippines readily expressed a willingness to participate in united action, convinced that the security of their nations would be harmed by a Communist victory in Indochina. Australia and New Zealand were interested in taking part, but they would only act in concert with Britain. Eisenhower himself was not going to act without British participation, so it came down to whether Britain would go along. Unfortunately for the garrison at Dien Bien Phu, the British refused to become involved, on the grounds that the potential danger to Malaya and other British interests was not sufficiently large to justify a possible war. Eisenhower kept his guns in his holsters, and Dien Bien Phu fell on May 7, 1954. The Viet Minh had paid a very steep price for victory – according to Western estimates, they suffered a staggering 22,900 casualties, nearly half their total combat strength – but their victory was to destroy the pro-war consensus in France and give the Viet Minh greater leverage at the ensuing peace negotiations than the overall military situation warranted.

On July 21, 1954, the French and the Viet Minh sealed a peace agreement in Geneva, and the First Indochina War came to an end. Under the provisions of the agreement, Vietnam was to be divided at the 17th Parallel, close to the line where the splendid walls of the Nguyen dynasty had divided Vietnam from the late sixteenth to the late eighteenth centuries. For the moment, Bao Dai would rule South Vietnam's 66,000 square miles and 11 million people, while the Viet Minh would take control of North Vietnam's 61,300 square miles and 14 million

people. Under the terms of the agreement, those people on each side of the
dividing line who wished to live in the other half would be provided transportation. The agreement forbade both Vietnams from introducing additional
arms or foreign troops into their territory and from forming military alliances
with foreign governments prior to unification elections, which were scheduled
for July 1956. To monitor compliance, the negotiators created the International
Control Commission (ICC), composed of observers from Poland, Canada,
and India.

The Vietnamese Communists would later charge that they had expected to
receive all of Vietnam at Geneva but were forced by the Chinese and Soviets
to surrender half of it.[71] The Chinese and Soviets, it is true, worried that
aggressive demands would generate too much friction with the United States
and France, and the Vietnamese Communists were quite deferential towards
China and the Soviet Union at the time. The evidence, however, shows that
the Soviets and Chinese did not pressure their Vietnamese allies into giving up
southern Vietnam against their will. From the start, the Vietnamese Communists concurred in the view espoused by the Soviets and Chinese that partition
was the best possible outcome. Vietnamese Communist leaders confided to the
Chinese and Soviets that because of their heavy losses at Dien Bien Phu and
general military weakness, they sought peace in order to provide a "breathing
space"for rebuilding the army before pursuing further gains. The French and
the anti-Communist Vietnamese, not the Communists, were the ones who
viewed the partition of Vietnam as a great setback.[72]

The Geneva agreement suffered from a congenital defect that would always
obstruct its fulfillment: it lacked the endorsement of the new South Vietnamese
government and the U.S. government, both of which were certain to be leading
actors in the ensuing scenes of Vietnamese history. Bao Dai's representatives,
from whom the Viet Minh and the French deliberately had concealed their
negotiations, refused to sign the agreement. All along they had opposed ceding
the entire northern half of Vietnam to the Viet Minh, because its population
exceeded that of the southern half in size and discipline and because it contained large pockets of staunchly anti-Communist Catholics, who had come to
detest the Viet Minh for persecuting the Church and its adherents during the
war. The Communists obviously intended to establish dictatorial control over
the territory they received, which would ensure that the entire populace within
that territory voted in accordance with the Party's wishes in any all-Vietnam
election, guaranteeing a Communist majority regardless of the outcome in the
less populous South. In protesting against the final agreement, a Bao Dai delegate at the conference declared that "the Government of the State of Vietnam
wishes the conference to take note of the fact that it reserves its full freedom
of action in order to safeguard the sacred right of the Vietnamese people to
territorial unity, national independence, and freedom."[73]

At a meeting of the National Security Council, Dulles explained that the United States would not sanction the Geneva agreement because "we can't get ourselves into the 'Yalta business' of guaranteeing Soviet conquests."[74] But at the same time, the Americans avoided criticizing the settlement, so as not to offend the French, whom the Americans were attempting to entice into the European Defense Community. An American spokesman pledged orally that the United States would "refrain from the threat or the use of force to disturb" the agreement, and "would view any renewal of the aggression in violation of the aforesaid agreements with grave concern and as seriously threatening international peace and security."[75] President Eisenhower announced that he hoped the Geneva agreement would promote peace, but he also asserted: "The United States has not itself been a party to or bound by the decisions taken at the conference."[76]

Unable to resolve the underlying differences between the Vietnamese factions, the Geneva agreement could only postpone the next conflict. The coming conflict, however, would differ from the war that had just ended in that it would clearly be a contest between two groups of independent Vietnamese, like nearly all previous conflicts in Vietnamese history. It would also resemble earlier Vietnamese conflicts in that the two principal parties enjoyed the support of powerful foreign countries. In China, the North Vietnamese Communists had an ally that had been a friend and protector of many previous Vietnamese generations. The Vietnamese Communist leader Ho Chi Minh revered the Chinese Communists, and his Marxist-Leninist internationalism bound him to alliance with China and other Communist countries. In the United States, the new South Vietnamese administration had a friend with immense power, but with little experience in Vietnam. For the moment, the two Vietnams would face very different tasks and obstacles. The non-Communist Vietnamese lacked the depth in experienced and skilled leadership of which the Vietnamese Communists could boast. Powerful non-Communist groups in South Vietnam were not prepared to take orders from the newly formed central government, whereas in the North the central government's potential rivals were relatively weak. The North Vietnamese needed time merely to recuperate and consolidate, while the South Vietnamese needed time to build a cohesive state with materials and tools that were far from ideal. Possessing a massive head start against a staggering opponent, the North Vietnamese had good reason to hope for a quick and easy victory in the looming confrontation with the Vietnamese anti-Communists.

CHAPTER 2

Two Vietnams

JULY 1954–DECEMBER 1955

BY THE TIME THE NEGOTIATORS IN GENEVA WERE UNCORKING THE champagne and nibbling the fondue, Eisenhower and Dulles had already formed a new strategy for Southeast Asia. They intended to create a defensive line running from east to west along the boundary between the two Vietnams up to the Laotian border, then heading northward to encompass all of Laos and Thailand. In order to guard the line, against both conventional invasion and covert subversion, the United States would give aid to allies and participate in a collective defense organization for the region.[1] Eisenhower and Dulles did not want to provide massive sums of military assistance to America's Southeast Asian allies, nor did they want to put large U.S. forces in these countries, for they deemed such measures too costly. If the Communists attacked a Southeast Asian nation in great force, the United States would not try to defend that country at the point of attack, as it could lead to a situation similar to the Korean War. Instead, the United States would threaten China itself with nuclear annihilation and, if threats proved futile, plaster China with nuclear bombs and missiles.

In September, relying on national strength and tough talk to hearten American allies dispirited by Communism's conquest of northern Vietnam, the Americans convinced some of their friends to join a regional defense alliance called the Southeast Asia Treaty Organization (SEATO). Representatives from Australia, France, New Zealand, Pakistan, the Philippines, Thailand, the United Kingdom, and the United States signed the pact in Manila. Cambodia, Laos, and South Vietnam did not sign it because the Geneva settlement forbade them from entering into such alliances, but they were listed as protected nations along with the signatories.[2] In the U.S. Senate, Eisenhower's regional defense strategy received a warm reception from Democrats, who had roundly criticized Eisenhower after Geneva for "losing North Vietnam." The Senate ratified the treaty with just one opposing vote.

Within the countries of Southeast Asia, Dulles and Eisenhower observed, resistance to Communism would depend on indigenous nationalist leaders,

32

for nationalism was rising as European colonialism was falling, and it seemed to be the only power capable of resisting Communism in the region. The United States had to do everything possible to support strong nationalist groups. "The Communists believe they represent the wave of the future," Dulles said in reference to the Far East. "They are fanatic in promoting this idea. We must have people on our side who believe that our way of life is the way of the future. They must also be tough, like the Communists."[3] In order to encourage and assist nationalists in Indochina, the Eisenhower administration intended to cut off French influence gradually while maintaining a façade of cooperation with France.

South Vietnam did indeed have a tough nationalist who could serve as the foundation for a new anti-Communist state, although in the summer of 1954 many Americans were not convinced of it. Ngo Dinh Diem had left Vietnam in 1950, after the Viet Minh pronounced a death sentence against him for developing a new nationalist organization. Arriving in Japan, he met Wesley Fishel, a University of California political science professor who was working for the CIA in Japan at the time. At Fishel's suggestion, Diem went to the United States in 1951 to speak at college campuses and seek the support of government officials. Diem found favor with some Americans of high standing, including Supreme Court Justice William Douglas, Francis Cardinal Spellman, Representative Mike Mansfield of Montana, and Representative John F. Kennedy of Massachusetts. In June 1954, in the middle of the Geneva negotiations, the despairing French at last granted full sovereignty to Bao Dai's government, and Bao Dai asked Diem to become premier. Bao Dai's decision was not motivated by American pressure as some have speculated, but by expressions of support for a Diem government from numerous Vietnamese political leaders. "The county is at risk of being cut in two," Bao Dai said to Diem. "You do not have the right to avoid your responsibilities. The safety of Vietnam requires it." Diem, who had turned down several previous offers of the premiership from Bao Dai, said he would take the job if Bao Dai gave him total control over all civilian and military matters. Bao Dai had never delegated such powers to anyone, but he consented, and Diem became premier.[4]

From the palace office, one man would attempt to repair and reshape a shattered land. The southern half of Vietnam that Diem inherited showed all the symptoms of a country despoiled by prolonged warfare. Many of the bridges had been blown up, and the roads were riddled with deep potholes. Telephone and telegraph lines had been severed. In Saigon and other cities, unemployed peasants who had fled the countryside or emigrated from the north overburdened the country's modest public facilities. French businessmen, consumers, soldiers, and capital were flowing out of the country, tearing the vital organs from the body of the South Vietnamese economy. Gravest of all were the troubles confronting the administrative and military machinery, which were devastated by the departure of the French and the desertion of tens of thousands of Vietnamese. After the ceasefire took effect, American military observers reported, the Vietnamese National Army disintegrated, and army leaders did not try to put it back together. One report explained simply, "The Vietnamese National Army lacks everything which makes a modern army: leadership, morale, training, and combat experience."[5]

One would expect the head of the new central government to assemble the remnants of governmental power and try to restore order, but Diem did not even have authority over those remnants. The French, who scorned Diem as much as he scorned them, retained some of their own officers in the senior command positions of the Vietnamese National Army. The Vietnamese officers in the army had built their careers through subservience to the French, and many remained wedded to French culture, French political authority, and French women. The National Police and the Sûreté were in the hands of the Binh Xuyen, a gang of extortionists and thieves that was paying Bao Dai a monthly stipend of 1.5 million piasters (U.S. $43,000) for the privilege. Although Diem commanded considerable respect among Vietnamese elites for his steady nationalism and his incorruptibility, and although he had built up a network of intensely nationalistic followers and allies over the years, the Saigonese did not think that Diem had a chance of overcoming these massive obstacles. All foreign and domestic observers, in fact, with the possible exceptions of Diem and his brothers, expected the Diem government to sink into oblivion within a matter of weeks.

Upon taking office, Diem adopted some of the traditional practices of the mandarins and the emperors, because of both reverence for the past and confidence that these methods would still work. In keeping with the dignity of his position, Diem assumed a formal and reserved air in public, which untutored Westerners often mistook as a lack of concern for the people. Edward Lansdale, who became one of Diem's closest American confidantes, commented in 1961:

> When someone describes him as an aloof mandarin, I recall how he cried on my shoulder when our close friend, Trinh Minh The, was killed, his anguish over the loss of Phat Diem province in the North to the Communists, and the agony he went through in his final break with Chief of State Bao Dai. He simply doesn't parade his feelings for everyone to see, particularly when things are going wrong.[6]

Like the emperors of centuries past, Diem delegated authority with a miser's hand. He worried that subordinates would use official authority against him, but he also took this approach because the country had relatively few men with strong executive capabilities. Diem insisted that he sign every exit visa for South Vietnamese citizens seeking to travel abroad; he determined where to place the trees at public parks; he chose which government buildings would be equipped with air conditioning. When Diem did mete out authority, it was often to trusted relatives. Receiving the greatest power were his four surviving brothers. Ngo Dinh Can, whose frail heart kept him from walking more than one hundred yards at a stretch, took administrative control of northern South

Vietnam. Ngo Dinh Luyen served in France as a liaison with Bao Dai and Western diplomats, while Bishop Ngo Dinh Thuc played a leading role in the affairs of South Vietnam's Catholic community.

The most influential of the brothers was Ngo Dinh Nhu, who became the president's chief adviser and the head of the secret services. A man of high intelligence, Nhu had studied in France in the 1930s, but had not been won over to Western liberalism as many of his fellow Vietnamese students had been. He possessed a strong grasp of both political realities and abstract political concepts, though his long discourses on the latter were known to befuddle even those close to him. Nhu was, in addition, a gifted leader, which had helped make him one of South Vietnam's most effective political organizers. But because he took a leading role in repressing dissidents and ridding the government of potentially disloyal individuals, Nhu made many enemies among the Vietnamese elites and drew the contempt of Westerners and Vietnamese intellectuals who championed political liberalization. Nhu once told an American journalist:

> Every government has to have the tough guy, the man who does the dirty and unpleasant work. Even Eisenhower had to have a Sherman Adams, in a country as advanced and unified as the United States of America. In Vietnam, where violence and virulence are everywhere, I am the person who takes on the unpleasant jobs. It is I who am vilified, so that others may be spared.[7]

Nhu's wife was born Tran Le Xuan, which means "Tears of Spring." To the world, however, she would always be known as Madame Nhu. Her hair perfectly coiffed and her long nails shining with lacquer, she was energetic and impulsive, and she wielded a sharp tongue. Some in South Vietnam referred to her as the Female Tiger, while the American press nicknamed her the Dragon Lady. Madame Nhu involved herself in the affairs of the state as deeply as Diem and Nhu would permit, working tirelessly on behalf of feminist causes and offering advice on political problems. Her combativeness and desires for sweeping change earned her the disdain of many Saigonese politicians and intellectuals, although these sentiments were partly tamed by her considerable personal charm and beauty. Many Westerners believed that she had tremendous influence over Diem and Nhu, but in reality the President and his brother saw her as a family member who was to be tolerated rather than heeded. As one palace insider observed:

> A proud man like Nhu, a man with an intellect like his, would have a hard time trusting the opinions of such a young wife. In his eyes, she was just a co-ed from a French school who had not even passed her baccalaureate examination. There were a few unusual situations in which Nhu accepted her suggestions, but only as the opinions from someone with the clear eyes of an intelligent, sensitive woman.[8]

Diem and Nhu both favored revolutionary changes but at the same time wanted to preserve central elements of Vietnamese culture. They both denounced Communism as an inhumane and foreign ideology, and criticized Western liberalism for paying inadequate attention to the community and to the poor. For the official national philosophy, they chose the "Personalist" philosophy of the French Catholic Emmanuel Mounier. Personalism sought to balance the competing needs of the individual, society, and state, so as to avoid the excesses of Marxism on the one hand and liberalism on the other. According to Mounier, the people needed to be protected from Communist and Fascist dictatorships, the disintegration of the family, selfish individualism, and unrestrained capitalism. Personalism emphasized the development of one's character through involvement in the family and community organizations. It lauded individual liberty but also warned of the danger that people might abuse that liberty, and it therefore advocated strong governmental control over the people.

Personalism had much in common with Confucianism, which Diem also admired greatly – Diem ordered schools to emphasize Confucianism and he made the anniversary of Confucius a holiday for the first time in the modern era.[9] Personalism and Confucianism both stressed family and community and called for authoritarian rule as part of the divine order of things. But Personalism, as professed by the Ngo brothers, was not a mere rehashing of ancient Confucian precepts or other traditional ideas. Diem and Nhu recognized that a return to pre-colonial ways was not feasible. "The nationalism that would surrender to reaction is doomed," Diem declared, "just as nationalism which allies itself with communism is bound to end up in treason."[10] Vietnamese Personalism, rather, was a synthesis of old and new ideas that would allow Vietnam and its traditions to prosper in the modern environment brought on by French colonialism and other outside influences.

As a cornerstone of their Personalist movement, Diem and Nhu were intent on redistributing land, which they believed would promote the well-being and dignity of every individual, build support for the government, and deny the Viet Minh the opportunity to institute their own land reform. They built schools, hospitals, and places of worship for the masses. Diem and Nhu employed many of the undemocratic political methods used by other authoritarian leaders of the twentieth century, not only because they considered Western democracy incompatible with a Vietnamese culture imbued with authoritarianism and a Vietnamese populace largely ignorant of national politics, but also because democracy inhibited the implementation of drastic change and the suppression of subversion. The futility of democracy in countries such as Vietnam, they liked to point out, was poignantly demonstrated by the antidemocratic coups that had routinely occurred when underdeveloped countries tried democracy.[11] The Diem government's propaganda and its population control methods showed the influence of both Communism and Fascism. Ngo Dinh Nhu and Ngo Dinh Can developed a secret political party called the Can Lao that indoctrinated its members and organized them into cells as Ho's Communist Party did, and, to instill fervor and loyalty more broadly, they created a mass party called the National Revolutionary Movement.

Few people in South Vietnam understood Personalism on more than a superficial level. As a consequence, Western critics would take Diem to task for failing to inspire the masses through ideology.[12] This criticism rested on the premise that gaining the support of the Vietnamese people required such an ideology, a mistaken premise. The Vietnamese masses of the mid-twentieth century were not seeking a leader whose ideas appealed to them, but a strong and charismatic leader who would organize the people, protect them, and treat them justly. If he offered a few catchy slogans such as "save the nation" or "prosperity for all," it was a nice garnish. Diem succeeded in obtaining the cooperation of the masses without the help of a well-understood and inspiring ideology, and the same was true of Ho Chi Minh.

The one major segment of the South Vietnamese citizenry that attached great importance to political ideology was the very small urban elite, which was often termed the "intellectual" class," although it was composed not only of writers and professors but also lawyers, doctors, and technicians. Educated in France or in French schools inside Vietnam, they had been severed philosophically from the rest of Vietnamese society by Western ideas. The tended to advocate Western-style democracy and civil liberties, and for this reason they disliked both Diem and the Communists. In addition, many of them resented Diem for taking away privileges or possessions – especially farmland – that the French had bestowed on them to gain their support. This elite was concentrated in Saigon and had minimal influence over the Vietnamese who lived in the towns and villages, but their power over Western visitors was great, far out of proportion to their numerical size or their inherent worth, because they could speak French or English and they frequented the cafes where Western journalists and officials went for a cup of coffee or tea. No ideology that Diem could have chosen would have both satisfied the intellectuals and permitted his anti-Communist government to survive, for the liberal methods that appealed to the Westernized intelligentsia were the opposite of the authoritarian methods needed to control the masses and shield them from subversives. Diem could afford to alienate the urban elites, because he could run the country by recruiting plenty of other urbanites or well-to-do farmers who did not belong to that small minority, but he could not afford to alienate the masses, because the country's survival depended on mass participation in anti-subversive activities. The unsuitability of liberal governance would be amply demonstrated by subsequent events, during the years 1963 to 1965, when toleration and conciliation of opposition groups led to political disintegration.

A large number of the Americans who came to Vietnam were at first inclined to join with the Saigon intellectuals in denouncing Diem's autocratic ways, because they arrived with the assumption that Vietnam needed to become another Massachusetts, Illinois, or California, with a corresponding respect for political and personal liberties. Like most of its predecessors, this generation of Americans included large numbers from both political parties who believed that foreign political cultures and institutions could and should be swiftly replaced with new political cultures and institutions based on American principles. Some of those who came to Vietnam, particularly those who were not very good at understanding foreigners, continued to subscribe to such ideas throughout their time in the country. Others came to realize that they were looking at a country entirely different from the United States, one that could not be re-sculpted into an Occidental shape. These Americans developed a sound understanding of Vietnamese culture and politics, contradicting the assertions of Robert McNamara and others that the United States suffered from an utter lack of expertise on Vietnam.[13] In general, those who never stopped likening Vietnam to America did not care for Diem, and they wanted either to pressure him to reform the government along American lines or oust him. Those who treated Vietnam on its own terms, by contrast, generally admired and supported Diem. The two groups would remain locked in bitter conflict for the rest of Diem's life.

* * *

"WE'RE SENDING YOU OVER THERE TO INDOCHINA," CIA DIRECTOR Allen Dulles told Edward Geary Lansdale in early 1954.

"To do what?" asked Lansdale, who had recently returned to Washington from the Philippines. "I don't want to help those French."

"No, no, no," Dulles replied. "Just do what you did in the Philippines."[14]

By 1954, Edward Lansdale had already become a legend. A one-time advertising executive, he had joined the OSS during World War II and stayed on afterwards to serve in the Philippines. When the Huks of central Luzon initiated a Communist revolution, the enterprising Lansdale took it upon himself to befriend a Philippine congressman named Ramon Magsaysay, help him advance to the top of the Philippine government, and advise him on combating the insurgency. A very personable man – a colleague once remarked that Lansdale "could make a friend of everybody except Satan"[15] – Lansdale had a special knack for working with Asians. By listening to what they had to say, he earned respect that could not be earned by lecturing them as most of the Americans did. He took their ideas, molded them into practical solutions, and offered them back so subtly that the Asians thought they had come up with the ideas themselves. Relying heavily on Lansdale's counsel, Magsaysay very successfully reformed the Philippine Army and the Constabulary. He went into the field himself, unannounced, to identify and sack incompetent officers. In order to improve relations with the civilian population, Magsaysay trained his troops to become servants of the people instead of parasites and he developed very effective propaganda programs. Ultimately, Magsaysay's counterinsurgency measures transformed the Huk rebellion from a serious threat to a minor nuisance.[16]

Lansdale arrived in Vietnam on June 1, 1954 on board an air-sea rescue airplane. Among the tasks assigned to him by CIA Director Dulles was the creation of a covert CIA team to help the Vietnamese conduct unconventional and psychological warfare. The CIA chief's brother, John Foster Dulles, and President Eisenhower had decided to support Diem soon after Diem took office, despite reservations about his abilities and ideas on the part of some in the State and Defense Departments, because he seemed to be the only Vietnamese politician with the sort of attributes they prized. Diem possessed the nationalist zeal, fervent anti-Communism, and moral purity that might allow him, in the face of tremendous impediments, to break away from the French and mobilize the people against Ho Chi Minh's Communists.

Lansdale's team of twelve, which he called the Saigon Military Mission, and their Vietnamese cohorts began by sending disguised Vietnamese soldiers into Tonkinese marketplaces to spread rumors that a Chinese Communist regiment had laid waste to a northern Vietnamese village and raped its girls. The Americans hired North Vietnamese astrologers to write predictions of doom for the Viet Minh and success for Diem, which were then placed in almanacs and smuggled into Viet Minh territory. Such stunts, however, were much less important than the guidance Lansdale provided to the chief of state. Quickly ingratiating himself with Diem, Lansdale became a regular guest at the palace. While Diem was an expert on Vietnamese politics and culture, he had much to learn about the mechanics of a modernized state and armed forces, and Lansdale made an excellent teacher. For countless hours, from the early morning to the middle of the night, Lansdale and Diem sat together, talking and chain smoking.

Lansdale helped Diem handle one of the greatest challenges facing the government during its first months, the attraction and resettlement of North Vietnamese refugees. Hoping to add determined anti-Communists to the South Vietnamese citizenry and reduce the population discrepancy between North and South, Diem's officials and Lansdale's team launched a campaign of overt and covert propaganda to lure Northerners to the South as the French were preparing to depart. Early in September, they forged Viet Minh leaflets telling the people to prepare for the Viet Minh takeover by making a list of what they owned, so that the new government could decide what to take from them. Northern Catholics were handed leaflets stating that "the Virgin Mary has departed from the North," and "Christ has gone to the South."[17] Trying to get in on the act, the Viet Minh countered that American sailors were going to eat the babies of those who left North Vietnam. But the words of the Diemists found a more receptive audience, thanks primarily to the Viet Minh's long record of brutality, duplicity, and radical social policies. In all, one million people would make their way from the North to the South after the war, the majority of them

Catholics.[18] Viet Minh soldiers prevented the emigration of several hundred thousand additional Vietnamese who wanted to leave the North and go to the South.[19]

With organizational help from Lansdale and other Americans, Diem's government moved the refugees into fertile and under-populated provinces in the western Mekong Delta, with primary emphasis on the Plain of Reeds, long a hideout for bandits and rebels. The government dug irrigation canals, built dikes, and dredged swamplands, enabling thriving new villages of Tonkinese to sprout where no human communities had ever existed before. With funds from the U.S. government and American and French charities, the Diem regime was able to provide all of the refugees with food and shelter for the short term, and farm tools and housing materials to make them self-sufficient in the long term. Roads that once had been prime ambush sites for Communist guerrillas were lined with the homes of industrious and staunchly anti-Communist Northerners. Bernard Fall, one of Diem's fiercest critics, remarked, "To move nearly one million well-trained soldiers in peacetime is a major feat of transportation and logistics. To move that number of disorganized civilian refugees on a 'crash' basis in less than one year surely will remain an accomplishment of note for a long time to come."[20]

Lansdale's exploits in Vietnam would be immortalized in two novels. In *The Ugly American*, by William Lederer and Eugene Burdick, Colonel Edwin Barnum Hillandale was virtually a replica of Lansdale. A swashbuckler with enormous talent for influencing foreigners, Hillandale far outclassed most of the other Americans in the book in combating the Communists. Alden Pyle, a character in Graham Greene's novel *The Quiet American*, was widely seen as a negative portrayal of Lansdale.[21] Pyle's naïve desires to bring liberal government to Vietnam and his zealous pursuit of that objective inadvertently inflicted great harm on the Vietnamese people. Coloring Greene's account was his heavy reliance for information on the French, who had only nasty words for Lansdale because of his blatantly anti-colonial and anti-French attitudes.[22] The real Lansdale, the man who held so much sway during the infancy of the Diem government, was much closer to Hillandale than to Pyle.

There was, nevertheless, an element of truth in Greene's depiction. While Lansdale had a better and more sympathetic understanding of South Vietnam than most Americans, he at times advocated the application of American political concepts in Vietnam without due consideration of the differences between the two countries. Lansdale thought that the Vietnamese people could be won over by offering them democracy and civil liberties, based on the inaccurate presumption that the people thirsted for these things, although he was not dogmatic on the subject or completely blind to South Vietnamese realities as other Americans were. This misperception on the part of Lansdale undoubtedly helped convince Diem and Nhu that the Americans were generally naïve about Vietnamese politics. For most of Diem's time in power, Diem and Nhu would have little regard for American advice on Vietnam's political affairs, except for that from a fairly small number who shrewdly perceived Vietnam's idiosyncrasies, and would try to keep the Americans from gaining too much influence within their country. As Nhu told one confidante, "We have a friend who understands us very well but who likes to poke sticks into the spokes of our wheels – France – and another very valued friend who gives us a great deal of monetary assistance but who understands nothing about Vietnam – the United States."[23]

From the day Diem took office, Saigon was rife with rumors of plots against the President. The leading candidates to mount a coup were either colonial-era officials or commanders of the country's principal armed forces: the National Army, the Hoa Hao and Cao Dai sect armies, and the Binh Xuyen. The top general in the National Army, Gen. Nguyen Van Hinh, was widely respected for his military abilities, but he was also an exceedingly ambitious and vain man, with Francophile tendencies that produced mutual contempt between him and diehard nationalists such as Diem. The Cao Dai and the Hoa Hao wanted complete administrative control over the areas where they had large followings, and they wanted positions in Diem's cabinet. The Binh Xuyen had 2,500 men under arms, much fewer than the army or the religious sects, but they were nevertheless a major threat because their power was concentrated in Saigon, they had a large stockpile of automatic weapons, and they had huge reserves of cash with which to buy off other groups. As a consequence of having joined with the French in fighting the Viet Minh, the Binh Xuyen controlled all of the gambling operations in Cholon, including the massive Grand Monde casino complex, the largest gambling establishment in the Far East. They operated an opium factory, a network of opium dens, a fleet of river boats, and the world's largest brothel, the Hall of Mirrors. Binh Xuyen leader Bay Vien, an illiterate former river pirate, had a moated fortress in the middle of Cholon for his headquarters, with crocodiles in the moat and a caged pet tigress to whom he reportedly fed people who had incurred his wrath.

What made the potential plotters most menacing was the support they began to collect from the French. At an early point in Diem's reign, the French had turned completely against him. Diem had criticized the French for abandoning North Vietnam to the Communists at Geneva and for trying to cozy up to Ho Chi Minh, and he had ignored French advice to include more pro-French individuals in the government. Seeking to protect French interests in South Vietnam and keep the country within the French Union, the government of Radical Socialist Pierre Mendes-France used France's remaining influence to attempt the removal of Diem. That influence was still considerable. In addition to controlling the Vietnamese army and maintaining close ties with the sects, France had 150,000 troops in Vietnam, ostensibly to protect the South against an attack from the North, and French officials exerted more influence than anyone else over several key Vietnamese political figures, including Bao Dai.

Diem had scarcely had time to move his book collection into the palace before the French were stirring up his enemies against him. At first, the greatest threat to Diem came from General Hinh, who was heavily involved in intrigue and was openly telling foreigners that he was going to oust the President.[24]

Lacking military or police forces of his own, Diem would have to rely on his own political skills and the backing of the Americans to neutralize his opponents. Some observers predicted that Diem's honesty and incorruptibility would prevent him from engaging effectively in the intrigue by which Vietnamese leaders traditionally had kept themselves in power, but Diem would soon manifest great skill at manipulation and trickery, as well as at persuasion and placation. These talents would be indispensable to the consolidation of his power. Also indispensable would be the support of the Americans, for by threatening to withhold its all-important aid, the United States could deter every individual who sought to take Diem's place. From July onwards, plotters came to the American embassy almost daily to seek assurances that the Americans would support them after they overthrew Diem. The Americans consistently rejected the overtures, with the result that every plot was aborted. While the United States had not decided to send aid to South Vietnam for the purpose of controlling the country's political life, it had acquired almost unlimited power to preserve or replace the government of South Vietnam as it saw fit, and it had begun to wield that power, even if not by its own choice.

Recognizing the supremacy of American aid, the French spent the first months of Diem's tenure trying to turn the Americans against Diem, employing all manner of calumny. Secretary of State Dulles, however, consistently spurned the French calls for a new government, and chastised the French for their involvement in anti-Diem intrigues. No one had a good chance of bringing South Vietnam under control, said Dulles, but Diem had the best chance of anyone because of his fiery nationalism and his talents, so he ought to be given a chance to prove his mettle. The French found it difficult to counter this contention, for they themselves conceded that the pool of alternative leaders had little to recommend it. In a telling statement, the French Minister for the Associated States said that former prime minister Tran Van Huu was the "best politician available" as a replacement for Diem, but he had "no character and no will."[25]

On August 26, just one month after peace had been made at Geneva, U.S. ambassador to South Vietnam Donald Heath was invited to a cocktail party at the Saigon home of Jacques Raphael-Leygues, a French socialite and intriguer. When Heath arrived, he discovered that it was actually a meeting of high-ranking plotters; the guests included General Hinh, the top sect leaders, and several high French officials. Addressing their remarks to Heath, the conspirators accused Diem of ineptitude and unwillingness to deal with the sects, and they promised that they could do much better. Then, straightforwardly, one of the plotters asked Heath, "Is it all right to go ahead and change the government?"[26]

Ambassador Heath did not consent to a coup, but the sight of so many prominent figures in opposition to Diem made a strong impression on him. Heath was already upset with Diem for refusing to heed American pleas to rely less on loyal friends and relatives and to "broaden" his government by appointing individuals more representative of the population as a whole, which Heath believed would draw the support of various population segments. Heath had been unable to produce a convincing argument as to why diffusion of authority was preferable to concentration in this authoritarian country, or why loyalty ought not be a hiring criterion when the leaders of some population segments disliked Diem and had enough troops to attempt a coup. But such problems did not stop Ambassador Heath from fixing blame on Diem. On the day after the cocktail party, Heath informed Washington that Diem was unable to influence others or act decisively, and that he had lost the support of most of South Vietnam's political groups. Hoping that some better leader was out there who had not yet been seen, Heath concluded, "we must keep our eyes open for another leader."[27]

News of this plotting reached Diem through his informants. On September 10, he fired General Hinh. To allow Hinh to save face, Diem ordered him to undertake a six-month "study mission" in France, a fate that Hinh was perhaps prepared to accept, but Hinh flew into a rage when Diem caused him to lose face in another way, by letting a journalist publicize the dismissal. Hinh declared his outrage and swore that he was going to "take action." To show his defiance, Hinh rode a large motorcycle through Saigon's streets in his shirt sleeves, and on the front of his motorcycle he displayed a Diemist sign that called for Hinh's expulsion. Outside his house, Hinh stationed two armored cars and a collection of guards, saying that he had put them there in order to "protect myself from the President."

The Vietnamese army leadership, Bao Dai, and the French all backed General Hinh, which prevented Diem from expelling him from the country. Bao Dai went so far as to order Diem to resign, but Diem ignored him. Hinh's continued presence began to cause Diem to lose face because in the minds of the Vietnamese, save for those belonging to the tiny intellectual class, the mere presence of unchecked public opposition came across as weakness on the part of the sovereign, as the sovereign was expected to suppress all challenges to his authority. The government that tolerated such insubordination or tried to halt it by a policy of appeasement would suffer a decline in prestige that would encourage its enemies and discourage its friends. On account of this political reality, past Vietnamese leaders had almost invariably done their utmost to stifle political opposition, and those most efficient in wiping out their opponents generally had presided over the periods of greatest public order. Had the Diem government not been besieged by numerous Communists and non-Communists intent on its overthrow, Diem might have been able and willing to try a political experiment as radical as tolerating organized dissent, but the large magnitude of malevolent opposition made such a dramatic break with the past unfeasible. Diem's attentiveness to this reality would guide his behavior towards vocal oppositionists throughout his time in office.

Six days into the crisis, Heath reported to Washington: "With every day Hinh continues stall and appear get away with his defiance, influence and prestige of civil government are diminishing."[28] The American Army attaché reported that South Vietnam was stricken with "almost total political and military paralysis," and that unless the current trends were reversed, which he deemed very unlikely, the Communists would take over South Vietnam "long before 1956 elections."[29] Heath tried to encourage Diem to make peace with Hinh through some sort of compromise, but a compromise with a zealous oppositionist was also likely to convey weakness and reduce Diem's prestige, and it could lead to more demands for concessions. Diem shot back at Heath that if he cut a deal with Hinh, "I would lose all my followers, who would accuse me of being without honor or courage."[30] In Diem's opinion, Hinh would have to be stifled. An exasperated Heath subsequently notified Washington that unless Diem promptly included more army and sect leaders in the government and made the government more efficient, he should be compelled to resign.

News of Diem's difficulties was, in the mean time, making its way to the highest echelons in Washington. Secretary of Defense Charles Wilson was so troubled by the political turmoil in South Vietnam and the rest of Indochina that he recommended total abandonment of the anti-Communist forces in the area. President Eisenhower stood at a junction with many uncertain routes before him. He could give up on the trouble-ridden South Vietnam; he could have Diem replaced; he could pressure Diem to include his rivals in the government; or he could back Diem wholeheartedly. Overruling many of his advisers, Eisenhower decided on the fourth route. He would stand behind Diem and attack Diem's enemies. "Why don't we get rough with the French?" Eisenhower exclaimed in front of the National Security Council. "If we don't do something very quickly, Diem will be down the drain with no replacement in sight. We ought to lay down the law to the French." Eisenhower instructed the State Department to tell the French that they had to "get rid of Hinh."[31]

The policy of roughness worked. France, lacking the economic power of the United States, could not hope to carry on in South Vietnam without American support, and thus they had to yield to American wishes, however resentfully. Hinh left Vietnam for France on November 19, 1954, and did not return. The French, in addition, began turning over control of the army to Diem, and they promised to relinquish all command and staff positions to South Vietnamese officers by July 1, 1955.

Upon making the decision to back Diem completely, Eisenhower ordered the State Department, Department of Defense, and CIA to initiate an emergency program to strengthen South Vietnam's armed forces. In contrast to some of his lieutenants, Eisenhower believed that a strong army was the key prerequisite for a strong government, rather than the other way around. Eisenhower considered this program to hold such importance that he immediately transferred Gen. J. Lawton "Lightning Joe" Collins, the former Army Chief of Staff and U.S. Representative to the NATO Military Committee and Standing Group, to Saigon to take Ambassador Heath's place and oversee all efforts. As Collins was leaving for Saigon, Dulles told him that he put America's chances for success in South Vietnam at one in ten.[32]

Eisenhower and Dulles hoped that Collins would develop a greater respect for Diem than had Heath, the type of respect that would foster a fruitful partnership. Their hopes were soon to run aground. Early in his tour, Collins reported, "Diem is a small, shy, diffident man with almost no personal magnetism. He evidently lacks confidence in himself and appears to have an inherent distaste for decisive action."[33] The remarks about Diem's bearing and personality were the same ones that French leftists had made about Ho Chi Minh after World War I. Like those Frenchmen, Collins mistakenly assumed that the Vietnamese prized tall, outgoing, and self-confident men as Westerners did. Within a few months, Collins would come around to admire Diem's personality, saying that "Diem's integrity, strong nationalism, tenacity, and spiritual qualities render him the best available Prime Minister to lead Vietnam in its struggle against Communism."[34] Collins, nevertheless, would persist in believing that Diem had a poor understanding of politics, and he took it upon himself to "educate" the South Vietnamese President. Like Heath, Collins implored Diem to broaden the government, tolerate dissent, and make various other compromises in order to gain the support of the sects and other elements of questionable loyalty. Diem disregarded this advice for the same reasons he had before.

With Hinh gone, Diem turned his attention to the Binh Xuyen gang, which he had long intended to break. In January 1955, he put the government's hands around the throat of the Binh Xuyen and began to squeeze. He closed the Grand Monde and the Binh Xuyen's other casinos in Cholon, and passed laws restricting the use of opium and prohibiting boys from hiring prostitutes. As a consequence, the Binh Xuyen and Bao Dai both suffered great losses in revenue. Diem hoped to isolate the Binh Xuyen and destroy it completely before moving on to his sect rivals, but this strategy ran into trouble in February when France shut off its subsidies to the Hoa Hao and Cao Dai, which compelled sect leaders to seek funding from the two people with deep pockets, Diem and Binh Xuyen leader Bay Vien. On Diem's behalf, Lansdale met with sect leaders to offer them money and laud Diem's nationalism, and Diem and Nhu themselves dealt directly with sect leaders. Several key sect figures agreed to support the government in return for funds, most significantly the gifted Cao Dai leader Trinh Minh The, who pledged his three thousand troops to Diem's side after Diem flew by helicopter to speak with him.[35] Other sect leaders, however, did not prove so amenable to Diem's entreaties, and they became resentful when they realized that Diem expected them to give up their autonomy. They were particularly worried by Diem's insistence that Hoa Hao General Tran Van Soai hand over control of his administrative region to the Saigon government and by Diem's response to Soai's refusal, which consisted of sending the Vietnamese National Army to the region and cowing General Soai by threatening to level General Soai's headquarters if the Hoa Hao forces resisted. Some sect leaders chose, therefore, to ally with Bay Vien when he offered them money from his huge coffers.

Diem's rivals coalesced at the beginning of March 1955 and sprang an ambush on him. The Cao Dai Pope announced at a press conference that Cao Dai and Hoa Hao leaders were joining the Binh Xuyen in forming a "United Front of Nationalist Forces" to fight the "dictatorship" in Saigon. The Binh Xuyen, emboldened by the rising opposition to Diem, started snatching up strategically located houses in Saigon that could serve as bases for attacks on the Diem government's critical installations. Bao Dai threw his support behind the United Front and told the Americans that Diem was entirely incapable of doing his job. When Diem and the Americans tried to buy Bao Dai's support, he refused, for their offers did not rival the great sums he was receiving from the Binh Xuyen.

Predictably, the members of the United Front tried to obtain American support for dislodging Diem. Much to their chagrin, the Americans gave them a negative reply and a warning that the United States would support Diem if anyone tried to overthrow him.[36] John Foster Dulles had just visited Saigon to meet Diem for the first time and had come away with a heightened admiration for the South Vietnamese President. "I was favorably impressed by Diem who is much more of a personality than I had anticipated," Dulles wrote to Eisenhower.[37]

The United Front proceeded to devise ways of ruining Diem without staging a coup. On March 21, the sects issued a declaration demanding that Diem immediately dissolve his government and create a new one that better served their interests. Collins believed that Diem would be doomed if he caved in to the sects' demands, and that the brazenness of this ultimatum strongly suggested that the sects were going to mount anti-Diem demonstrations in Saigon, which Diem could not afford to tolerate. "Oriental psychology," Collins wrote, "is such that Diem cannot allow demonstrations to be 'successful,' meaning unopposed, and therefore must take action to stop them."[38] He advised Diem to negotiate a compromise with the United Front in order to turn its members into supporters of the government. Initially, Diem agreed to negotiate with the United Front's leaders, but he cast aside any thought of negotiation when they asserted that their demands were not negotiable. To defeat those who challenged his authority, Diem informed Collins, he would use the army. Diem possessed confidence that the National Army would carry out his orders to quash any opposition group, for in recent months he had gained the loyalty of many army officers and had replaced many others whose loyalty he had not gained. But Collins, who underestimated the degree of support for Diem within the army, again told Diem to avoid the use of force and seek a compromise.

Without giving notice to the American ambassador, Diem laid plans to dismiss Lai Van Sang, the chief of the National Police and a leading Binh Xuyen figure, and to seize the Sûreté headquarters from the Binh Xuyen. Both operations were to take place on March 29. Just hours before the scheduled execution time, however, French officials caught wind of the plans and convinced Diem to abort them by promising to evacuate Binh Xuyen commandos from the Sûreté headquarters. That afternoon, Collins paid a visit to Diem to voice indignation at what had nearly transpired. Had Diem acted against the Binh Xuyen, Collins said ominously, it would have been a terrible blunder. It would have caused heavy fighting in the city. The ambassador once more warned most sternly against military action and implored Diem to negotiate a solution with the sects. "If you force the issue now in this manner, you will be making the gravest mistake of your career," Collins intoned, his patience near expiration. "If you continue your present course, we will be under heavy pressure to support a change in the government."[39]

As Ambassador Collins was hurling the gravest threats at Diem, the Binh Xuyen were busy preparing a strike of their own. Suspecting that Diem was going to move against them soon with large elements of the National Army that were now loyal to him, the Binh Xuyen had chosen the desperate option of acting without first seeking America's consent. At midnight, eighty Binh Xuyen troops attacked the Saigon-Cholon prefectural police headquarters, which was under the control of men loyal to Diem. The defenders held off the initial thrust, which provided sufficient time for the National Army to bring in reinforcements in overwhelming numbers. Binh Xuyen troops also attacked a National Army headquarters in Cholon, and met with similarly stiff resistance. On Rue Gallieni, a broad two-mile boulevard dividing Saigon and Cholon, Binh Xuyen troops ambushed several trucks of National Army reinforcements, but the soldiers disembarked with minimal casualties and drove off the Binh Xuyen. All of the Binh Xuyen's attacks came to naught. The Binh Xuyen suffered ten killed and twenty wounded during the night, while the National Army had stopped them at a cost of six dead and thirty-four wounded. The action came to a halt at 3:15 A.M. with the imposition of a ceasefire by French Commissioner-General Paul Ely. To enforce the ceasefire, Ely dispatched 30,000 French soldiers and 400 tanks to key streets and intersections in half of the city. Ely said that he wanted to stop the fighting in order to protect the European residents of the city and their property, but some Vietnamese and Americans suspected that Ely's main aim was to prevent Diem from destroying the Binh Xuyen.

When Collins went to see Diem in the morning, the South Vietnamese head of state told him, "Now that the Binh Xuyen have taken to arms, I see no alternative except to remove control of the National Police and Sûreté from Chief Sang as soon as possible." Collins said that Sang did indeed have to go, since the government would collapse if it tolerated open acts of rebellion, but he added that Diem should do his utmost to prevent further fighting. If Diem should resort to military action, Collins admonished, the National Army probably would not support him. Diem was not persuaded. The sects' armed forces might join with the Binh Xuyen's if he did not act quickly, he said. "The struggle is very hard and there can be no compromise," Diem subsequently remarked. "Every time a compromise is made the problem returns in more acute form. The people do not like this."[40] Collins finally convinced Diem to accept a three-day truce, at the end of which he could relieve Sang, the National Police chief.

The truce was to last much longer than three days because of the French, who extended it repeatedly in order to buy time for new plotting against Diem. Collins, meanwhile, became ever more pessimistic, concluding that if Diem resorted to force the army would turn against him. Even if the Binh Xuyen were driven from Saigon and went underground, Collins said, a civil war would probably ensue, and under such circumstances, the defeat of the Binh Xuyen "would be a vastly difficult task." Collins recommended that the United States seriously consider replacing Diem, though the replacements he suggested were the same unsatisfactory people who had been considered in the past.[41]

In Washington, the reaction to the Binh Xuyen's surprise attack and its aftermath was rather different. Secretary of State Dulles was lunching at the White House with Congressmen from both parties when he heard of the battle. He told them: "This is just the opportunity we have been waiting for to find out whether Diem has the courage and determination to act and whether he has the loyalty of the Army. If these two things are demonstrated, then I think we are over the hump; but if he fails in either respect, then he will have to go. But at least we will have the answer." Eisenhower and Dulles were, therefore, appalled when the French intervened and prevented Diem from continuing the fight with the Binh Xuyen. Collins's talk of replacing Diem took the President and secretary of state very much by surprise, and they notified Collins that they opposed a change in government. Diem, having already shown the will and ability to fight, deserved a chance to destroy the Binh Xuyen, and reports coming to Washington from Lansdale and U.S. military advisers showed that Diem had enough loyal army units to accomplish the task. "We should press the French in the strongest way to permit Diem to assert his authority against the Binh Xuyen," the President declared. "If he fails it will be too bad, but it would be better to find out now rather than later whether the National Army on which we are spending so much money is loyal."[42] Yet Collins kept pressing for Diem's removal. Because he was the man on the spot, as well as a man of high reputation and prestige, Eisenhower and Dulles were very reluctant to disregard his judgment. Finally, Eisenhower asked Collins to return to Washington near the end of April so that they could talk this vital matter over in person.

While the Americans pondered their next moves, the French, the Binh Xuyen, Bao Dai, and large elements of the Cao Dai and Hoa Hao were hurriedly working on new schemes for ousting Diem. Hoa Hao Generals Soai, Ba Cut, and Lam Thanh Nguyen flouted Diem's authority in public. The insubordination of the Binh Xuyen and the Hoa Hao, unchallenged as it was, chipped away at Diem's prestige. The American chargé reported by cable that the Diem government's political position was deteriorating "due largely to apparent inability or unwillingness government take firm action against defiance its authority by Binh Xuyen and Hoa Hao."[43] In Saigon's diplomatic circles, most believed that the Diem government was about to collapse, and French newspapers were predicting Diem's downfall with glee, while the American papers were doing the same but without the glee.

When Collins arrived in Washington, he told President Eisenhower that Diem had to be removed immediately. The President and Secretary of State Dulles protested that French subterfuge was the main cause of South Vietnam's current difficulties, and that replacing Diem would create major problems in Congress and with American public opinion. If a change were to be made, they said, it ought not be made until a strong alternative had been identified. But Collins was adamant. Diem had to go now. Eisenhower decided to honor the decision of the man on the spot, distasteful though it was to him. Dulles penned telegrams to the embassies in Paris and Saigon stating that Collins and Ely would allow Bao Dai and other Vietnamese leaders to select a replacement for Diem. The State Department sent the telegrams on April 27 shortly after six o'clock p.m., Washington time.[44]

Just as it seemed that the Diem regime was headed for the mortuary, Diem seized the initiative and upset all of Collins's plans. Over the critical few hours that followed the sending of the telegrams, Washington received a flurry of messages from Lansdale. Unlike most of the CIA's covert action arms, Lansdale's Saigon Military Mission was totally independent of the local CIA station and embassy, allowing Lansdale to send cables that otherwise might have been edited or thrown in the trash. The timing and nature of these messages suggest that a Diem supporter in Washington had tipped off Lansdale about the decision to forsake Diem, though there is no available proof of such an occurrence. In his first messages, Lansdale asserted that American abandonment of Diem would devastate American prestige in Vietnam, to such an extent that no successor government could survive. Then, shortly before the clock struck midnight in Washington, Lansdale sent word that fighting had broken out in Saigon between the National Army and the Binh Xuyen.

Eisenhower and Dulles, startled by Lansdale's appraisals and the eruption of hostilities, decided that the new circumstances called for the suspension of

Collins's plans. They hurriedly ordered Paris and Saigon to halt the preparations for a change of government and to burn all telegrams on the subject. Preferring a decisive result as before, Eisenhower and Dulles decided that the United States would take no action until the outcome of the battle had been determined.

The battle began in the late morning of April 28, Saigon time, with fighting on Rue Gallieni. Once the shooting started, pedestrians bolted for cover, leaving the boulevard suddenly empty save for armed men and a few ambulances. Accounts of how the fighting started differ sharply, with no single interpretation supported by a preponderant weight of evidence. Some versions hold that the Binh Xuyen decided to attack the army because Diem had just fired police chief Sang. Others state that Diem attacked the Binh Xuyen in order to destroy an old enemy, or to forestall American action against his government. Binh Xuyen mortar rounds began to crash into Independence Palace at 1:15 P.M., wounding two soldiers. During the next thirty minutes, army commanders loyal to Diem ringed the palace with tanks and submachine gun–toting soldiers. On Diem's command, army artillery batteries opened fire on the Binh Xuyen and four paratroop battalions headed toward Binh Xuyen positions. Like potent chemicals mixed in a beaker, the opposing forces came together in a violent frenzy. At Saigon's few hospitals, the beds and hallways and lobbies rapidly filled with injured soldiers and civilians. In the European quarter, which remained under the protection of the French Expeditionary Corps, Americans and Frenchmen viewed the fighting from their balconies. The Americans guzzled beer and rooted for the National Army, while the Frenchmen sipped aperitifs and cheered on the Binh Xuyen.

Contrary to what Collins and many other foreign observers had anticipated, numerous National Army units carried out Diem's orders with a high degree of courage and professionalism. The Binh Xuyen forces, inferior in quantity and quality to the army units, crumpled under the blows of Diem's troops. They soon beat a retreat southward, through buildings and streets, towards their remaining fortified positions. As they went, they set fire to rows of closely packed wooden houses, supplementing fires that had already been ignited by mortar and artillery rounds. Firemen in silver and gold helmets tried to extinguish the blazes, but the flames and choking black smoke continued to fill the sky as thousands of homes burned.

To spare the Binh Xuyen from complete annihilation, Ely asked Diem to halt the fighting. Bao Dai ordered Diem to see him in Cannes, and he announced that he was making his loyal ally General Nguyen Van Vy the supreme commander of the Vietnamese armed forces with a mandate to end all hostilities. Diem refused to pay heed to Ely, Bao Dai, or General Vy, saying, "It's a fight to the finish."[45] After dark, the National Army stormed Binh Xuyen strongholds at the Petrus Ky High School and the Grand Monde. By noon of the next day, Diem's forces had taken most of the Binh Xuyen's posts in Saigon and were pressing on to the banks of the Arroyo Chinois, a narrow river on the city outskirts. When the army reached the river, they were stunned to discover that General Ely had blocked the two main bridges with French troops, ensuring the safety of several Binh Xuyen battalions that stood on the other side. Even more astonishing, French Prime Minister Edgar Faure now became involved directly. Intent on preserving the Binh Xuyen, Faure declared the Diem government unfit at a press conference, and he endorsed Bao Dai's declaration turning the Vietnamese army over to General Vy.[46]

The next day, General Ely went to see Randolph Kidder, who was the acting U.S. ambassador while Collins was in Washington, and called upon the Americans to work together with France to oust Diem. Before he had left for the United States, Collins had told Ely that the United States had decided that Diem had to be removed. Kidder did not actually know the official U.S. government policy on Diem; his bosses had only told him that high authorities in Washington were in the middle of discussing America's future plans in Vietnam. Kidder, the type of man who preferred decision to uncertainty, chose to take matters into his own hands, and out of the hands of Ambassador Collins, Secretary of State Dulles, and President Eisenhower. Kidder had been impressed by Diem's recent successes; he had just notified Washington that the city's population wanted the government to finish off the rebels, and that the "prestige of government has taken upturn which will be maintained only if government presses issue to successful conclusion."[47] Kidder told Ely flatly that the United States would not help remove Diem. Years later, Kidder explained, "I was left no choice but to make up my own mind what our policy was, as I would be damned if I was going to say I didn't know."[48] Had Kidder told the truth, that Washington had not sent the Saigon embassy guidance on U.S. policy toward Diem, the French might have moved more aggressively against Diem than they ultimately did. Had Collins been at this meeting instead of Kidder, he might well have agreed to cooperate with the French in ousting Diem. But that was not what happened.

While Kidder and Ely were arguing with one another, 200 people gathered in the Saigon Town Hall to proclaim themselves the "General Assembly of the Democratic and Revolutionary Forces of the Nation." The assembly's composition and behavior emitted the scent of Lansdale and Diem, though there was no hard evidence that either man was pulling the levers behind the scenes. Those in attendance included representatives of the Cao Dai, Hoa Hao, and eighteen of Saigon's tiny political parties. Leading the assembly were Cao Dai Generals Trinh Minh The and Nguyen Thanh Phuong, and General Ngo of the Hoa Hao. At the start of the meeting, Assembly members tore down a large photograph of Bao Dai, threw it out the window, and stomped on it in the street. Once that mission had been accomplished, they proceeded to denounce the French and their "traitorous henchmen." Then, settling down to business, the Assembly created a list of demands that included Bao Dai's abdication, the withdrawal of all French forces, and the formation of a new government under

Diem. By vote, the Assembly chose a "Revolutionary Committee" of thirty-three members. When the meeting adjourned, the thirty-three committee members immediately went to Diem to deliver the demands, if that was in fact what they were.

Upon arriving at the palace, the Revolutionary Committee was surprised to find General Vy sitting in Diem's office. Vy had come to the palace just a short time earlier and declared that he was taking over the army, as Bao Dai had directed. Brandishing pistols, several members of the Revolutionary Committee forced Vy to cancel his plans. They wanted to kill him, but Diem kept them from doing so. At midnight, a paratroop colonel phoned Diem's office with a threat to shell the palace if General Vy were not released, and therefore Diem let Vy go. The next morning, at a house guarded by paratroopers and howitzer crewmen, General Vy told the press that he was taking control of the army and the government. But no gale could sink Diem's ship now. In the ensuing hours, top National Army officers held deliberations to decide who would lead the nation and it did not take the generals very long to come out in favor of Diem over General Vy and Bao Dai. Once more Diem's personality, his capacity for intrigue, and his good standing with at least some of the Americans had won the day. General Vy fled to Paris at three o'clock that afternoon.

On the other side of the world, in Washington, Collins was still recommending that the United States dump Diem. Diem's attack on the Binh Xuyen, maintained the ambassador, would produce a civil war in which the army would refuse to support Diem. But Eisenhower and Dulles were no longer willing to defer to Collins's judgment. The Darwinian struggle that they had desired was in progress, and it appeared to be progressing in an auspicious direction. The three most influential Americans in South Vietnam at that moment – Kidder, Lansdale, and General O'Daniel – were all supporting Diem's actions. Within the United States, news reports of fighting between an anti-Communist government and a corrupt gang had immediately sparked an upsurge in support for Diem among Congressmen and the public at large. Eisenhower decided to give Diem his full support.

American pressure finally compelled the French to remove their forces from the bridges spanning the Arroyo Chinois. As soon as the French troops had withdrawn, Diem's soldiers galloped across the bridges to attack the remaining Binh Xuyen units on the other side. The young General Trinh Minh of the Cao Dai, one of Diem's most able subordinates, died from a shot to the head while leading his troops over the Tan Thuan bridge. Otherwise, though, the final phase of the offensive against the Binh Xuyen was a smashing success. On May 3, with much of his fighting strength gone and his defenses in disarray, Bay Vien evacuated his remaining forces from Saigon and Cholon. Into the mangrove swamps of the Rung Sat they went, with Diem's battalions in pursuit. The battle for the capital came to an end with 500 combatants and bystanders dead, and another 2,000 wounded. Contrary to the predictions of Western diplomats and newsmen, Diem's crushing of his opponents did not alienate the people but instead achieved the opposite result. Previously uncommitted political leaders and ordinary citizens, seeing Diem's strength, rallied to his side and disavowed his adversaries. The cries "Down with Bao Dai!" and "Off with the head of Ho Chi Minh!" reverberated through the tree-lined boulevards of Saigon.[49]

The failure of the Binh Xuyen, General Vy, and Bao Dai signaled the end of serious French efforts to unseat Diem. One last feeble attempt, though, would be made by French Prime Minister Faure during a series of long meetings with Dulles in mid-May. Repeating the usual litany of criticisms of Diem, Faure charged that the South Vietnamese President had to be replaced. Dulles fired back that the United States "does not agree with the French opinion of Diem. If he had been a non-entity, he would have collapsed, but he did not. He showed so much ability that the U.S. fails to see how he can be got rid of now." Hoping to salvage something of value, Faure dropped his demand that Diem leave, then insisted that Diem and the Americans grant France a number of protections, including the broadening of the government, the cessation of anti-French propaganda, and the safeguarding of French economic and cultural concerns in Vietnam. Dulles replied that the United States could not guarantee France these protections "unless Diem were our puppet. But if he were our puppet, the whole enterprise in Vietnam would fail." Dulles added that the United States would abandon its efforts, largely futile to date, to impose its ideas on South Vietnam's President. "The U.S. cannot undertake to force upon him a government or policies which he does not like," Dulles explained. "He has a mind and will of his own and the fact that he has survived proves he has virtues that are not easily replaced." Dulles dismissed the idea of broadening the government, noting that highly effective Asian leaders such as Syngman Rhee and Ho Chi Minh held power close to their chests rather than sharing it widely.[50]

The days of French influence in Vietnam were over. Accepting the inevitable, and fulfilling the wishes of many in France, Faure slashed the strength of the French expeditionary corps to 50,000. Pushing on a falling tree, Diem was soon asking the French to withdraw all of their forces by the spring of 1956, and the French obliged him, initiating additional troop withdrawals. France would soon be gone from Vietnam.

The disastrous Binh Xuyen guerrilla insurgency predicted by Collins and the French did not materialize. Within a few months, Diem's troops wiped out the remnants of the Binh Xuyen, save for a few small bands that joined forces with the Communists. But another serious challenge to Diem did develop in late May of 1955. Upset that Diem had not granted them enough privileges, Hoa Hao generals Ngo, Ba Cut, Soai, and Lam Thanh Nguyen declared war on the central government. The Hoa Hao leaders knew that they could not survive a direct confrontation with Diem's army, so they burned their bases and sent their troops – a total of 16,000 among the four generals – into the wilderness to operate as guerrillas. The Cao Dai Pope called for a new Cao Dai army to fight the Diem government, though his appeal had less effect because most Cao Dai leaders had rallied to Diem's side after the defeat of the Binh Xuyen.

This time, the Americans did not discourage Diem from fighting back. On June 5, the National Army went on the offensive and bested its enemy again. The army smashed Soai's forces in the middle of June near the Cambodian border, compelling Soai to flee into Cambodia. Disheartened by the ineffectiveness of the rebellion, Generals Ngo and Lam Thanh Nguyen went to Saigon to give themselves up and turn their armies over to the government. Only General Ba Cut continued the guerrilla campaign in South Vietnam. Twenty thousand army troops chased Ba Cut's force of three thousand through the countryside for the remainder of 1955. As for the Cao Dai, Diem left matters to one of their own. General Phuong marched his troops to the Cao Dai headquarters at Tay Ninh, the source of the resistance, where they intimidated the Papal Guard into surrendering their weapons. By declaration, General Phuong deposed the Cao Dai Pope, and thereby put the Cao Dai insubordination to an end.

In order to eliminate what little influence Bao Dai still possessed and to enhance the prestige of the Presidency, Diem held a public referendum on October 23, 1955 in which the people would be asked to select either Diem or Bao Dai as the country's leader. Diem knew all along that he would not lose, for he could make sure that he garnered not only a majority, but an overwhelming majority. In the weeks preceding the referendum, Diem's policemen and soldiers stifled all anti-Diem and pro-Bao Dai propaganda. A committee of pro-Diem parties sent cadres to every single house to tell the occupants why they had to vote for Diem, and it organized village meetings and sent out cars equipped with loudspeakers. Government officials saw to it that the press vilified Bao Dai in exaggerated terms while lauding Diem. Much of the propaganda must have originated with Lansdale, as it very closely resembled other work of his. Through the streets of Saigon, Diem's men paraded a float bearing a dummy of Bao Dai that was grabbing a naked blonde with one hand – most Vietnamese frowned on the mixing of races such as could be seen in Bao Dai's frequent dalliances with European mistresses – and guzzling cognac with the other. A dummy Frenchman could be seen stuffing the emperor's pockets with gold. Diem's propagandists covered building walls and buses with posters displaying slogans that included the following: "Beware of the evil king Bao Dai's preference for gambling, women, wine, milk, and butter. Those who vote for him betray their country." Diem, on the other hand, was described in posters as the "hero of the people" and the "father of all children."[51] When voters arrived at the polls on the twenty-third of October, they were instructed to cast their vote by selecting either a red ballot for Diem – red signified happiness and good luck among the Vietnamese – or a green ballot for Bao Dai – green signified the opposite.

The voting went forward without disruption. Voter turnout exceeded ninety percent except in the few places where the Hoa Hao were still fighting. Ambassador G. Frederick Reinhardt, who had replaced Collins in May, reported that no evidence of fraud or intimidation could be found. According to the final tallies, Diem received 5,721,735 votes, which came to 98.2% of the total vote. This result did not indicate that the entire South Vietnamese people admired Diem; rather, it simply demonstrated the people's lack of interest in democratic procedures and their willingness to follow the dictates of the government, as expressed in its propaganda campaign and selection of ballot colors. These figures did, however, prove useful to Diem's propagandists, who used the enormous margin of victory to show the people that Diem had suppressed his opponents and obtained the cooperation of virtually the entire population, marks of strength in Vietnamese eyes.

With his non-Communist opponents now vanquished, Diem could focus on his last and most dangerous opponents, the Vietnamese Communists. The Viet Minh had begun to establish themselves in the North in October 1954, as soon as French troops had departed in accordance with the Geneva agreement. When the Viet Minh marched into Hanoi, they found the city's streets far less full than they had been in August 1945, for the city's population had plummeted soon after the handover to the Viet Minh had been announced. Under the guidance of the Viet Minh, some Vietnamese shopkeepers and school children massed along streets holding red Viet Minh flags as the troops arrived, but enthusiasm did not pour out spontaneously. Neither Ho nor other Communist leaders delivered stirring speeches or otherwise showed themselves before the people. Explaining his decision not to appear in public, Ho said, "Our mutual love does not depend on appearance."[52] Ho understood what many Western diplomats and journalists did not, that in Vietnam a ruler's effectiveness was neither reliant upon nor demonstrated by the public's visible enthusiasm or the ruler's speeches.

Returning to the methods used in 1945, Ho and his lieutenants promptly compelled all non-Communist political organizations to submit to Communist control, or else disband. They jailed or executed those intellectuals and political leaders suspected of having anti-Communist thoughts. In the North Vietnamese highlands, where tribes rebelled against Communist rule, and in other insubordinate rural areas, Ho used armed force to crush all opposition. Although the Communist government had promised not to censor the press, it in fact seized all media organs and used them to publish only articles that enhanced the government's prestige. In the arts, the Communists prohibited anything that failed to propagate Communist themes, and they forced artists to confess that their prior work was bourgeois nonsense.[53]

The new regime went considerably farther than its Southern counterpart in exerting control over the urban masses. Communist officials compelled Hanoi's residents to meet twice a day for political education meetings, where they were obliged to listen to Party propaganda, partake in self-criticism, and sing revolutionary songs. Party-controlled neighborhood groups convened several times per week for additional political lectures. To indoctrinate and control the educated youth, the North Vietnamese government organized school children over the age of ten into cells and replaced experienced teachers and professors with Party propagandists.[54] The government shut down churches and pagodas or else replaced their leaders with Party men, while at the same time it directly discouraged the people from religious worship.

In a series of extravagant propaganda campaigns, the Vietnamese Communist Party called for solidarity with China's people and leadership. The North Vietnamese imported large numbers of Chinese books, and the majority of North Vietnamese students sent abroad for education went to China.[55] Chinese personnel arrived to replace French commercial and industrial experts, most of whom had already left before the Viet Minh arrived, although a few stayed for a short time – until the Communists began confiscating everything that belonged to French citizens. Chinese engineers built airports and constructed railroads and highways linking northern Vietnam to China. Some of China's best technicians went to work on a modern telecommunications network for North Vietnam. In violation of the Geneva agreement, China transported large quantities of Chinese- and Soviet-made arms into northern Vietnam, most of it crossing the Sino-Vietnamese border at two points that the North Vietnamese prevented the International Control Commission from visiting. Western intelligence services determined that during the seven months after the armistice, the Viet Minh received at least 150 pieces of field and anti-aircraft artillery, 500 mortars, 9,000 automatic weapons, 500 recoilless rifles, and 400 military vehicles.[56]

Ho Chi Minh's Communist patrons also helped him end a famine that reared its head in early 1955, a product of flooding and Communist land reform programs. Responding to desperate North Vietnamese entreaties, the Soviet Union provided Hanoi with 173,000 tons of rice, and the Chinese chipped in another 32,500 tons.[57] In the middle of 1955, Ho went to China and the Soviet Union to seek further aid for economic development. On July 7, the Chinese announced that they would send North Vietnam 800 million yuan (U.S.$200 million) in economic aid and additional technicians, and later that month, the Soviets pledged 400 million rubles (U.S.$100 million) in economic aid.[58] Neither China nor the Soviet Union released figures on military aid to North Vietnam, but military funds and goods continued to flow in at a rapid pace.

The Vietnamese Communists were amassing arms for campaigns in the distant future, not for an imminent strike against the South. For now, they intended to use only low-level subversion in the South and wait to see whether the Southern regime would collapse under political pressure from the Southern Communists or other oppositionists. After Geneva, Ho Chi Minh had withdrawn 120,000 Communist soldiers, supporters, and newly drafted youths from the South for training in the North. The Communists would never divulge how many of their people they left in the South after Geneva, but Hanoi's figures on Southern Communist strength later in the decade suggest that it was in the tens of thousands.[59] The stay-behind personnel received instructions to bury their weapons in burlap and pose as ordinary citizens while secretly engaging in subversive activities. These activities included the infiltration of government organizations, the creation of ostensibly non-Communist political opposition organizations, and the orchestration of public demonstrations lauding the Viet Minh.[60]

Diem was determined to root out the underground Communists, just as he had rooted them out in 1930 and 1931. The first step, he decided, was to expand the government's administrative and military control over rural South Vietnam. In the spring of 1955, he gave top priority to two areas where the Viet Minh had been relatively strong, the Camau Peninsula and the provinces of Quang Ngai and Binh Dinh. In Camau, arriving government troops gave the people pictures of Diem to put in place of Ho's picture, but they did nothing to improve the material condition of the people, and some of them treated the people with disrespect. As a consequence of the Camau operation, Rufus Phillips of the Saigon Military Mission and Col. Le Van Kim created an indoctrination course for two divisions slotted for Quang Ngai and Binh Dinh. For a month, the troops were drilled constantly in courteous behavior. When the divisions went to Quang Ngai and Binh Dinh, they committed no infractions against the civilian populace. They provided medical supplies to the villagers, and they built roads and bridges. In order to improve the government's capabilities for rural administration and development, Lansdale convinced Diem to open centers to train army soldiers and white-collar civil servants in these fields, with some of the training provided by scholars from Michigan State University. Diem's Department of Information and Youth taught its cadres how to how to indoctrinate villagers on Diem's merits and Communism's evils, in preparation for what became the first "Denounce the Communists" campaign. The campaign, unfolding progressively across 1955, saw Diem's security forces and officials fan out into the rural districts and establish permanent control over great numbers of villages while hunting down Communists and preaching Diem's propaganda.

Two weeks after his troops had arrived in Quang Ngai and Binh Dinh, Diem began a series of symbolic appearances in central Vietnamese villages, traveling by jeep. Diem's lieutenants, most likely with the encouragement of Lansdale, organized demonstrations at various points along the tour, which in general was the only way for such events to take place because of rural Vietnam's unfamiliarity with public demonstrations. Hundreds of thousands of rice growers, coolies, and fisherman showed up to greet Diem during his tour. An American who witnessed one of the larger demonstrations remarked, "Fifteen thousand people came charging across the field toward him, screaming, waving straw hats, like the stampede in *King Solomon's Mines.*"[61] Ignoring the threat of Communist assassins, Diem mingled freely and conversed effortlessly with the demonstrators, from farmers to Buddhist monks to lepers. These public events were significant mainly because they were publicized by Westerners who incorrectly took them as proof that the government enjoyed the support of the people.[62] The real proof of the people's support for the government could be found in the establishment of well-led armed forces and administrations in the villages, and in the elimination of organized opposition.

During 1955, Diem's internal security initiatives created far more problems for the stay-behind Communists than Hanoi had anticipated. Most of the Communist political organizations in the cities were quickly exposed and destroyed. The Communist organizations in the villages also sustained heavy damage, though they were not wiped out across the board. On the subject of rural pacification, an official Communist history related, "With an ever-growing network of spies and traitors and an expanding system of guard posts and outposts, Diem and the Americans began to establish puppet governmental machinery at the local level, organizing village and hamlet leaders and interfamily groups. They forced individuals who had participated in the revolution to turn themselves in. . . . Cadre and Party members who were being terrorized by the enemy in the lowlands fled to our old resistance bases."[63]

Having fended off the immediate Communist threat, Diem next had to deal with the proposed 1956 all-Vietnam elections conceived by the French and Viet Minh at Geneva. From the outset, Diem and the Americans had resolved to make sure that the elections did not take place because of their certainty that the North Vietnamese would win the election simply by getting every vote in the more populous North through electoral manipulation.[64] The North Vietnamese, equally confident of their ability to control the outcome of voting in the North, tried to get Diem to engage the South in the elections, but they had little hope that the elections would actually occur because they knew Diem was too smart to allow it. Later, at a plenum of the Vietnamese Communist Party's Central Committee, the Communist leader Le Duan would remark, "Everyone clearly understood that there was no way that general elections would ever be held."[65] Diem, and any other savvy Vietnamese politician, would never willingly let an election decide his fate if he stood a chance of losing. For all but the most Westernized of Vietnamese political figures, elections were a tool for gaining Western approval and supporting domestic propaganda efforts, not a means for conferring power and legitimacy. The leaders of the two Vietnams, for this reason, had little interest in the debates among Westerners over whether the Geneva agreement, the South's rejection of the all-Vietnam elections, or the absence of democracy within both North Vietnam and South Vietnam determined the "legitimacy" of the two governments. They shared the prevailing Vietnamese belief that whoever had actual military and political power was legitimate. Both North Vietnam and South Vietnam were legitimate states by virtue of their effective armed forces and administrators, and they would have to be defeated by overt attack or covert subversion, not by international law or free elections.

As the date scheduled for commencement of electoral discussions neared, the Americans advised Diem to call for elections but insist on stringent protections such as freedom of speech for candidates and an independent supervisory commission. Ho Chi Minh would inevitably reject these conditions, the Americans argued, just as Communist leaders had turned down similar plans in Germany and Korea, and then the Communists would receive the blame for the absence of elections. Diem ignored the counsel of the Americans, because agreeing to such discussions might generate fear among the South Vietnamese populace that the country would be sold out to the Communists. Instead, in the middle of 1955, he rejected the elections outright. "We did not sign the Geneva accords," Diem pronounced over Saigon radio on July 16. "We are not bound in any way by these agreements, signed against the will of the Vietnamese people." No elections for national unification could be held with the Communists, Diem said, "if proof is not given that they put the superior interests of the national community above those of communism; if they do not renounce terrorism and totalitarian methods; if they do not cease violating their obligations as they have done in preventing our countrymen of the North from going south."[66] There would never be any all-Vietnam elections.

As 1955 came to an end, Diem had much cause for satisfaction. He had taken control of a disintegrating country and sewn it together. He had overcome the enmity of the army and the sects, the intrigues of the French, and the contempt of two American ambassadors, and he had fended off the Communists. Steering through the deep water between the shoals of Maoist barbarism on the one side and Western liberalism on the other, Diem had suppressed the opposition without resort to the extensive slaughter employed by the Communists in the North. Many able nationalists, including a significant number of former Viet Minh, had rallied to his side. Expected to last only weeks, Diem's government had now survived for a year and a half, and it was stronger than it had ever been before. As many foreign observers were now saying, Diem had worked miracles.

CHAPTER 3

Peaceful Coexistence

1956–1959

"THERE ARE ONLY TWO WAYS," SAID NIKITA KHRUSHCHEV TO THE delegates, "either peaceful coexistence or the most destructive war in history. There is no third way." Speaking to the Twentieth Congress of the Soviet Communist Party in February 1956, Khrushchev was announcing the new foreign policy line that the Soviet Union would pursue, by and large, until Khrushchev's exit in 1964. The policy of peaceful coexistence, part of a sweeping repudiation of Stalinism, rejected the old notion that defeating capitalism required international confrontation and war. Because nuclear weapons had convinced both sides that a war of the superpowers would mean suicide, Khrushchev, like Eisenhower, had come to the conclusion that the struggle between socialism and capitalism would be resolved by peaceful competition in the economic sphere. "Our certainty of the victory of communism is based on the fact that the socialist mode of production possesses decisive advantages over the capitalist mode of production," Khrushchev explained in his speech. Khrushchev's desire for peace among the major powers did not, however, translate into a desire for peace within countries. Although the working class in some capitalist countries could take power peacefully, through the electoral process, Khrushchev believed that the working class in other countries would have to rise up and destroy the capitalist government by force.[1]

In accordance with the new policy of peaceful coexistence, the Soviets told the North Vietnamese that they should not take up arms against South Vietnam. The people of South Vietnam, maintained the Soviets, would eventually clamor for reunification with the North once they saw the superiority of the Communist economy. The leading Communists in Hanoi grimaced and grumbled, for Diem's crackdowns on the Communists in the South during 1955 had made clear that the North could not defeat the South without an armed struggle. Khrushchev's new ideas so bothered Ho Chi Minh that he began to show less respect for Soviet guidance than before. In April 1956, at the Ninth Plenum in Hanoi, Ho Chi Minh called for peace and proclaimed that the Vietnamese Communists believed "still more strongly in the invincible force of the Soviet Union," but he went on to argue that war against the South might be necessary. "While recognizing the possibility of reunifying Viet Nam by peaceful means," he said, "we should always remember that our people's principal enemies are the American imperialists and their agents who still occupy half our country and are preparing for war. That is why, while holding high the flag of peace, we must be in a position to change the form of the struggle."[2] The North Vietnamese leadership could perhaps reconcile this stand with Khrushchev's policy of peaceful coexistence by arguing that the two Vietnams were really one country and hence a war would not involve international violence. They must have known, however, that the Soviets would find that bit of casuistry less than convincing, for at this same time they stopped informing the Soviets of their plans for conquering the South by force.[3]

Khrushchev's shift at the Twentieth Party Congress occasioned even greater revulsion in China. Mao loathed peaceful coexistence, believing that the transition to socialism was likely to require not only small wars in places like Vietnam but also a monumental war between the Communist and capitalist powers. In fact, the Chinese premier said, he would welcome a nuclear war with the capitalists because it would annihilate their imperialist system without destroying China, as China's people were more dispersed geographically and hence less vulnerable to nuclear blasts. Khrushchev's explicit denunciations of Stalin also infuriated Mao, for Mao regarded Stalin as a "great Marxist-Leninist revolutionary leader" and contended that in rating Stalin, his achievements should count for seventy percent while his mistakes should count for only thirty percent, an opinion shared by Ho Chi Minh.[4] A fissure had opened in the great Sino-Soviet alliance, and during the Cold War crises of the next few years, the issues of peaceful coexistence and Stalin's legacy would drive the Soviets and Chinese further and further apart.

The new Soviet policy reinforced North Vietnam's inclination to rely more heavily on China than on the Soviet Union. In 1956, the Chinese concurred in the North Vietnamese view that defeating Diem was likely to require violent means. Mao, however, told the North Vietnamese not to take any provocative action for the moment, for the Chinese, smarting from the wounds of the Korean War, wanted time to strengthen their economy and military. Ho went along with this suggestion. In March 1956, when Hanoi's representatives in the South proposed a military build up to overcome Diem's increasingly effective security forces, Ho rejected it and ordered the Communist Party's Southern branch to keep concentrating on political organization in the villages.[5]

In the meantime, the massive expansion of the North Vietnamese Army continued. Whereas South Vietnam's armed forces had decreased by 20,000 after the armistice, the Communist army went from seven under-strength divisions to twenty full divisions in the space of less than two years. In addition, thousands of Southerners who had gone North after 1954 began to receive training in insurgency leadership from North Vietnamese officers. To facilitate higher military spending, Ho was pushing ahead with economic development. During 1956, however, Ho had to divert many thousands of men from his grand construction projects in order to combat foes who were trying to demolish the freshly laid bricks. Providing sustenance to the opposition movement was the radical land redistribution program, the fifth phase of which began in January 1956. Many of those killed or otherwise punished during this phase actually owned little or no land. By the summer of 1956, the program had caused such discontent among the masses and the Party membership itself that top Party leaders felt compelled to confess their errors publicly. The Communist Party's Central Committee acknowledged that the land reform program had "dealt indiscriminate blows,"[6] while Ho and Giap personally went to numerous villages to give speeches aimed at soothing the masses and drawing them away from subversive movements. For some of the victims, the government provided funeral services and graves. Nothing was done, however, for the oppositionists and non–Viet Minh landlords who had perished.

In the late summer of 1956, the lack of discrimination in meting out punishments caused the Party's leadership to terminate its land reform initiatives, once and for all. The decision marked the end of the most brutal oppression of Vietnamese non-combatants in recent memory, which, according to a former Communist land reform cadre who is the most well-informed and trustworthy source on the subject, took the lives of 32,000 people over the course of its five phases.[7] The Party's central committee demoted Truong Chinh, who had headed the land reform program, and sacked several other high-ranking land reform officials. The Vietnamese Communists had realized, finally, that the Chinese advisers who had guided the effort were fallible. Ho Chi Minh and the rest of the Vietnamese Communist Party would remain admirers and friends of the Chinese Communists for a long time to come, but they would no longer follow them down every path with the unquestioning zeal of the past.

At this same time, Ho attempted to pacify North Vietnam's urban intellectuals, who were upset about not only the barbarous character of the land reform program but also the general dictatorial character of the regime. In imitation of Mao's "Hundred Flowers" movement, Ho eased the restrictions on political and artistic expression, but, as Mao would also discover, pretty flowers were not the only plants that sprang from the ground. Many intellectuals began criticizing the North Vietnamese regime for denying freedoms and mistreating the people. Discounting the Party's contrition, they loudly denounced the land reform program. Soviet advisers came under fire for behaving imperiously and cruising around Hanoi in large automobiles.

At the end of 1956, after enduring three months of biting criticism, the Party revoked the liberal reforms. The public condemnation posed too great a threat to the regime's prestige in the North, and it was also causing trouble in the South. One Party official, referring to the North Vietnamese intellectual publication Nhan Van, explained: "Nhan Van talked about the 'national unification,' but does it know that the enemy radio station in Saigon has used its slanderous and distorting articles to attack our regime? A number of enemy papers in South Vietnam have used *Nhan Van's* articles to defame North Vietnam, split the people, and create doubts among the people of South Vietnam."[8] The North Vietnamese government shut down all of the independent-minded publications and removed from circulation all issues they could find. Some of the intellectuals who had criticized the Party and Marxism-Leninism disappeared or died under mysterious circumstances. For many others, the end result was incarceration in labor camps along the Bac Hung Hai irrigation canal, where they had to toil in water up to their waists. According to the official North Vietnamese press, the hard work taught these individuals that "culture, literature, and the arts spring from the masses and are destined to serve them."[9] Free of the foreign pressure to coddle intellectuals that inhibited Diem, Ho reestablished his firm grip on the intelligentsia, never to release it again.

The most dangerous opposition to the North Vietnamese regime came to the surface during November 1956, in the Quynh Luu district of Nghe An province. It began when members of the International Control Commission, as part of their supervisory role, rode jeeps into this predominantly Catholic district. Villagers approached the commission's vehicles to complain of oppression, at which point government security troops got in the way and held them back, which then prompted a group of farmers to beat up some soldiers and take their rifles. The resistance movement quickly gained supporters. An article in the North Vietnamese newspaper *Nhan Dan* admitted that "reactionary" leaders "took advantage of our shortcomings in the execution of our agrarian reform policy and our policy on religious freedom committed during the application of the land reform, using the legitimate demands of the masses for correction of these shortcomings to coerce and incite a number of citizens to create disorder and act against the regional authorities."[10]

A few days later, armed with farm tools and simple weapons, several thousand peasants marched on the district capital. They wrote slogans on building walls such as "Down with the country-selling Communists!" and "Let us drive the Chinese Communist troops from North Vietnam!"[11] Communist regulars blocked their path and ordered them to disperse, but the crowd refused. A fight ensued, ending with the deaths of several of the protesters.[12] Hanoi, by now thoroughly alarmed, immediately sent the entire 325th North Vietnamese Army Division to Quynh Luu. For the next three months, the division's troops hunted for the "reactionary ringleaders," and they executed every leader they could find, along with a considerable number of their followers. They deported many thousands of other peasants. The insurrection was annihilated.

In late 1956, under the guidance of Diem, large numbers of saboteurs began entering North Vietnam from Laos.[13] The North Vietnamese suppressed these enemies in 1957, and large-scale armed insurrection would lapse until a series of unsuccessful revolts in 1959, the largest of which saw over one thousand mountain tribesmen seize fifteen villages in Dong Van district before the North Vietnamese Army destroyed them.[14] During 1957, after the stifling of the internal opposition, the North Vietnamese devoted their full attention to economic development, putting primary emphasis on rapid industrialization. Subscribing to the Marxist-Leninist theory that industrial workers made the best revolutionaries, the Party viewed industrialization as a critical task for political as well as economic reasons. To encourage more people to join the proletariat, the Party offered factory workers free housing, water, and electricity. Many of the workers, however, ended up living in bamboo hovels with no water or electricity. Thanks to technical assistance and aid from the Soviet Union and China, the expansion of North Vietnam's industrial base went forward with exceptional rapidity. But while the turbines, high-speed lathes, and conveyer belts were high in quality by Communist bloc standards, the people needed to run the factories were sorely lacking. The Soviets and Chinese were unable to provide enough technicians to compensate for the exodus of French specialists. The textile plants at Nam Dinh, for example, now had twelve thousand employees but not a single engineer, whereas under the French there had been forty-seven French engineers and supervisors. Operating far below their capacity, North Vietnam's industrial facilities were not able to produce substantial volumes for domestic consumption, let alone for exportation.[15]

Near the end of the decade, the Communists completed the takeover of all private businesses. Following the dictates of Marxist-Leninist doctrine, the North Vietnamese reorganized the agricultural economy by forming the peasantry into collectives, taking from the peasants the land given during the war to gain their support. The percentage of peasants belonging to cooperatives rose from less than five percent in 1958 to over eighty-five percent in 1960.[16] To Hanoi's dismay, worker productivity declined, and farmers frequently hid rice from the authorities, which compelled the North Vietnamese government to ration rice and beseech fellow Communist countries for imports of food. The North Vietnamese published grossly inflated rice production statistics in order to hide both their failures and the enormous disparity in agricultural productivity between North Vietnam and South Vietnam.[17] The only people who enjoyed better living conditions under Communist management than before were a select number of industrial workers and the functionaries of the Communist Party.

Diem, like Ho Chi Minh, spent a good portion of 1956 fighting enemies inside his own borders. Hoa Hao rebels continued to harass the government, and the Communists were inserting agents into the rebel forces to increase their numbers and their determination to keep fighting. In addition, the Communists created a few of their own units and disguised them with sect names such as the "Hoa Hao Liberation Company."[18] Near the beginning of the year, the South Vietnamese Army attacked the remaining Hoa Hao rebels in the western Mekong Delta and inflicted crippling losses. General Soai and his 4,600 troops surrendered in February. The last remaining rebel leader was Ba Cut, a man known for his ferocity – his most famous achievement was the invention of a torture procedure whereby a steel nail was driven slowly into the victim's ear. A government patrol apprehended Ba Cut in April, and shortly thereafter the government annihilated his remaining guerrilla units. Convicted in court for a number of murders, Ba Cut was beheaded before the public. In May and June, Communist agents incited 27,000 workers from the metal and shoe industries and from rubber plantations to go on strike. Communist operatives in the cities, working through ostensibly non-Communist organizations, arranged demonstrations demanding "unification."[19] Diem's police, however, went into action against the troublemakers, and by August they had shut down the Communist labor and political organizers.

In the latter part of 1956, the Saigon government organized a new "Denounce the Communists" campaign in the Mekong Delta that reached into even the most isolated of villages. Mobilizing the citizenry, Diem's civic action personnel and several divisions of army troops helped repair roads and bridges and build schools and sports fields. Members of Diem's mass party, the National Revolutionary Movement, plastered photographs of Diem on every building and hut, staged plays in which virtuous farmers shot Communist brigands, and watched for suspicious activity. Most suspected subversives were arrested, and many were thrown in prison. The government itself admitted, in 1956, that it had detained between 15,000 and 20,000 people in "reeducation centers."[20] According to U.S. embassy figures, the number of persons held at the centers would subsequently decline, going down to 10,000 by 1959.[21] Many prisoners spent no more than a few months undergoing indoctrination and were then released, after which they were kept under surveillance by local authorities. Those individuals who were believed to hold leadership positions in subversive organizations, however, might spend much longer in the centers. The director of the reeducation centers was Tran Chanh Thanh, a former Viet Minh who forced upon inmates the same sort of manual labor, strict punishment, and intensive indoctrination that he had employed in his Communist days. Some detainees were tortured during their initial interrogation, but otherwise they generally were not harmed unless they committed an offense.[22] As the result of an ordinance passed shortly before this new Denounce the Communists drive began, captured Communists could be put to death, and sometimes they were. Reports of killing by the Diem government during the Denounce the Communists campaigns, though, were much less plentiful than those on the North Vietnamese side during the same period, despite the West's much greater access to the South and its people. In 1959, the Communists complained that from April 1955 to January 1959, the Denounce the Communists campaigns took 4,971 lives. Even if the Communists were not exaggerating, the number of persons killed was much lower than the number killed by the Communists in 1945 and 1946 and in their later land reform campaigns.[23]

Critics of the Denounce the Communists campaigns would accuse Diem's security forces of catching great numbers of non-Communists in their net.[24]

Facing a threat to its survival, the government was not always willing to put off action until it obtained irrefutable evidence, and so it sometimes convicted suspects on the word of one or two people. Undoubtedly, at least a few witnesses provided false information, as has happened from time to time in most similar situations. No one will ever know how many people were wrongly accused in Diem's Denounce the Communists campaigns, but there is strong reason to believe that the number was small. While the government arrested a considerable number of individuals for participation in opposition groups that were purportedly non-Communist, such opposition was often a good sign of involvement in Communist causes, for the Communists excelled at infiltrating the non-Communist opposition and creating their own "non-Communist" organizations. Independent observers did not find evidence of widespread indiscriminate arrests and killings in the South as had been found in the case of North Vietnam's land reform activities, and Communist histories do not speak of indiscriminate governmental repression in this period. On the contrary, they note that the government reserved punishment for dedicated Communist Party members. The official history of the Vietnamese Communist Party recounted that whereas the South Vietnamese government imprisoned, exiled, or executed those who refused to repudiate Communism, the government released "anyone who agreed to split with the revolution and rip up the [revolutionary] flag."[25] The Denounce the Communists campaigns also differed from Hanoi's land reform campaigns in that they did not produce alienation and unrest on a large scale.[26] It is indisputable, furthermore, that great numbers of people whom the government apprehended or killed most definitely were Communists, for the Communists themselves were to admit as much on numerous occasions.

With the Communist subversive infrastructure gravely weakened, South Vietnam experienced a degree of peace it had not known since war broke out between the French and the Viet Minh in 1946. Only an occasional assassination or Communist propaganda meeting disturbed the tranquility. The subjugation of South Vietnam's enemies translated into additional support for Diem, particularly among the governmental personnel upon whose actions the regime's fate depended.[27] Diem's stature rose in the West as well, and praise abounded. William Henderson of the Council of Foreign Relations wrote in *Foreign Affairs*: "History may yet adjudge Diem as one of the great figures of twentieth century Asia."[28] An advocacy group called the American Friends of Vietnam welcomed into its ranks liberals such as Supreme Court Justice William O. Douglas, Senator Mike Mansfield, and Representative Eugene McCarthy, conservatives such as Senator William Knowland and Massachusetts Governor Christian Herter, the socialist Norman Thomas, and Senator John F. Kennedy.

The only serious threat to the regime during this period was an attempt on Diem's life on February 22, 1957. The Communist Party's Cochinchina committee organized the assassination attempt based on the premise that "if we are able to kill Ngo Dinh Diem, the leader of the current fascist dictatorial puppet government, the situation would develop along lines more favorable to our side." The committee instructed a young Communist commando named Ha Minh Tri to assassinate Diem at an economic fair in the highland town of Ban Me Thuot. Diem had been spending a great deal of his time touring the country with minimal security, to instruct the people on their duties and inspire them with his exemplary comportment. His visits generally left a very favorable impression on the listeners. While Diem was walking through the Ban Me Thuot fair grounds, Ha Minh Tri sneaked up close to the President, then fired a shot from an automatic pistol. The shot missed Diem and instead hit the secretary of agrarian reform, causing serious injury to his left arm. The assassin's pistol jammed, which prevented him from getting off another round, and members of the crowd pounced on him and beat him. Most members of Diem's entourage were visibly upset by the incident, but Diem himself stood still and remained totally calm. The American chargé d'affaires, who witnessed the event, informed Washington that the assassination attempt "has given a striking example to the general public of Diem's strength of character. His calmness and courage also greatly impressed the many members of the diplomatic corps, including the undersigned, who witnessed the incident at close range."[29] In subsequent months, Diem continued to move around the countryside with little armed protection.

During this period, Diem devoted considerable attention to the development of the armed forces. With the departure of the last French troops and advisers in April 1956, the Americans took over complete responsibility for training the Vietnamese army, as Diem had desired. Eisenhower dispatched 350 additional military personnel to South Vietnam in early 1956, on top of the 342 permitted under the Geneva agreement, to help train the South Vietnamese.[30] Leading the advisory effort would be Lt. Gen. Samuel "Hanging Sam" Williams, who had replaced General O'Daniel at the end of 1955. Williams was a man of strong opinions and did not keep his opinions bottled up. In the middle of World War II, Williams was demoted from brigadier general to colonel after screaming about his division commander's "Goddam stupidness" within earshot of said commander. He had acquired his sobriquet while a member of the court martial for an accused murderer. Growing tired of the dull and repetitious cant of the attorneys, Williams at last interrupted by exclaiming, "I've heard enough! Let's hang the sonofabitch!" A strict man with a superb military bearing, Williams was considered one of the Army's best men at training soldiers of all ranks, making him an exceptional candidate for the position of chief military adviser.[31]

Williams was close to Lansdale, and after Lansdale's departure in 1956, Williams established the sort of intimate friendship with Diem that Lansdale had enjoyed. Williams knew how to give the Vietnamese advice and encouragement without seeming condescending or domineering, and for that reason they respected and heeded him. Like all of the Americans who led the military advisory effort during Diem's time, Williams became a strong admirer of Diem. As a military man, Williams appreciated Diem's strength of character, leadership skills, and military savvy, qualities that were never fully appreciated by many American civilians, including in particular Elbridge Durbrow, who would serve as U.S. ambassador to South Vietnam from 1957 to 1961. Williams was regularly appalled by Durbrow's open contempt for the Vietnamese and his efforts to bully them, behavior that helped account for the fact that Williams exerted greater influence on Diem than did Durbrow, much to the latter's displeasure.[32] Williams usually defended Diem when the South Vietnamese President asked for more military aid, or when he emphasized security measures at the expense of social and economic programs, whereas Durbrow would argue that the best vaccines against Communist subversion were programs such as land reform, industrialization, and the development of administrative capabilities. A novice in things military, Durbrow frequently inflamed Williams by involving himself in military matters, leading to numerous shouting matches in front of their subordinates. Williams eventually decided that Durbrow was "better suited to be the senior salesman in a good ladies shoe store than to be representing the U.S. in an Asian country."[33]

In terms of its ability to fight a large-scale invasion force, the South Vietnamese Army that Williams found was only marginally better than the army that Diem had inherited in 1954. Battalions were incapable of operating together as a division. Among the officers, of whom there were too few, experience and training were scarce, and insubordination was rampant in some units. Diem retained much of the military authority at the highest levels, while diffusing the rest across the military commands and the provincial governments, in such a way that several commanders could give orders to the same battalion. In March 1956, the chief of staff of the South Vietnamese Army wrote that he was "certain that many of our units would disappear into the countryside at the very start of the reopening of hostilities."[34]

Williams's objective, handed down from Washington, was to improve the South Vietnamese Army to the point that it could hold off an overt Communist invasion for at least one month. Diem had wanted an army of 300,000 men that could hold its own against the large North Vietnamese Army, but the Eisenhower administration, preferring to limit local spending and rely heavily on nuclear deterrence and nuclear firepower, funded an army of 150,000 men that was simply to hold on long enough for the United States and other SEATO forces to bring overwhelming firepower to bear on the Communists. Williams convinced Diem to reorganize the South Vietnamese army into seven standard infantry divisions. The infantry divisions possessed some trucks and artillery, but they had much less equipment than an American division would have, and they had no helicopter or tank squadrons. Much of the equipment they possessed was inferior and outdated. After the war, the French had quickly shipped out the best U.S. equipment, leaving what they did not want in unprotected dumps or in open fields, where it was corroded by heat and rain until the South Vietnamese army scrounged it up. South Vietnamese divisions were left with old radios that were often in need of repair, and their dilapidated trucks could often be seen on the side of the road with hoods open and smoke wafting out.

American military officers were posted as advisers to South Vietnamese units, and South Vietnamese officers were sent en masse to training courses in the United States, Okinawa, and the Philippines. The American advisers and trainers put the primary emphasis on conventional warfare, as they were most concerned about an invasion of the South by conventional North Vietnamese forces. Williams would often be accused of overemphasizing conventional warfare and underemphasizing the threat of a Communist guerrilla insurgency in South Vietnam,[35] but unfairly. He was far from blind to the possibility of an insurgency. Shortly after his arrival in Vietnam, Williams told Diem: "The Viet Minh will attack only when Moscow tells them to, and that means international war which the Communists do not want. The real danger lies in the local Viet Minh cadres and they must be destroyed like vermin." In a document he handed to Diem at this meeting, Williams deftly laid out the methods that guerrillas historically had used, and the methods, both military and non-military, that had proven effective against them.[36] As chief adviser, Williams recommended that the South Vietnamese units undergo extensive counter-guerrilla training, and he wanted the regulars to have light gear and equipment that would allow them to move quickly on foot. The South Vietnamese army was outfitted with the same type, albeit not the same quality, of equipment as the U.S. Army divisions that had conducted jungle and swamp operations entirely on foot during World War II – the machine guns and some of the crew-served weapons could be carried on foot through any terrain, and others, such as the large 4.2-inch mortars, could be hauled with hand carts. The South Vietnamese conventional forces could march into the mountains and jungles with most of their firepower to ferret out either enemy guerrillas or enemy regulars operating in guerrilla fashion.[37]

At the same time, Williams made sure that the regular army did not concentrate solely on counterinsurgency training and operations, for it would inhibit the army's ability to fight an invasion. Williams liked to point out that the South Korean Army had dispersed to fight guerrillas in southeastern Korea before the outbreak of the Korean War, and as a consequence it was unable to concentrate rapidly near the border to repel the North Korean invasion. Suspecting that the North Vietnamese might likewise initiate guerrilla warfare to spread the South Vietnamese Army thin, Williams advised the South Vietnamese Army leadership to avoid lengthy commitments of the regular army to counter-guerrilla warfare, particularly in the southern parts of the country. The militia forces should take responsibility for most counterinsurgency tasks, Williams said.[38]

Williams and the Diem government did put considerable emphasis on developing mobile and static militia forces. Less heavily armed than conventional units, the militia forces offered an inexpensive and potentially very effective means of countering insurgent guerrillas. They could maintain a constant presence in the villages, and as locals they had excellent access to the information needed in both a guerrilla war and a conventional war.[39] Diem convinced the Americans to provide $12.3 million per year for his static village militia, which he dubbed the "Self-Defense Corps." This money supported a force of twelve militiamen in each village, with a total of 60,000 men nationwide. In 1958, Durbrow tried to cut the funding for the Self-Defense Corps, arguing that only 30,000 men would be needed because of improved security conditions in the countryside. When Diem protested that 60,000 were still needed to protect against a Communist resurgence, Durbrow compromised and agreed to pay for 43,500 men.

The Americans gave greater attention to the 50,000-man Civil Guard, the mobile militia responsible for patrolling entire districts of villages. Responsibility for training the Civil Guard went to a team from Michigan State University, which tried to pattern the Civil Guard after an American state police force, civilian in character. Diem, on the other hand, envisioned the Civil Guard as a paramilitary force that could fight well-armed guerrillas and assist the army in conventional operations. The Civil Guard, in Diem's opinion, ought to have semiautomatic rifles, submachine guns, and mortars, not pistols and nightsticks as the Michigan State group advised. Diem also wanted the South Vietnamese military to have control of the Civil Guard because only the military had adequate manpower to replace the generally poor leaders of the Civil Guard, many of whom were holdovers from the colonial era. Ambassador Durbrow and the United States Operations Mission, however, sided with the Michigan State team over Diem in these disputes, and so the Civil Guard was organized as the professors desired.[40]

Williams's strategic philosophy, with its emphasis on a large conventional army as well as militia forces, was the best available for South Vietnam, even if its implementation would be far from perfect. Large conventional units could be broken down quickly into small detachments to fight guerrillas, but small units created exclusively for fighting guerrillas could not be welded together swiftly into large, cohesive units to fight a conventional opponent. By keeping large numbers of troops in conventional divisions rather than local militia units, South Vietnam made itself marginally more vulnerable to a protracted insurgent war, since local militiamen tended to be more adept at working with the local populace than were regular soldiers. But without large conventional forces, South Vietnam would have been far more vulnerable to conventional North Vietnamese Army attacks, which posed a vastly larger threat to the regime's survival. Communist guerrillas by themselves stood no chance of taking Saigon and the other major centers of governmental power from government regulars, because they lacked the heavy armaments needed for pitched battle, whereas Communist regulars could easily capture those cities if unopposed by large conventional forces. For this very reason, Mao and North

Vietnamese military theorists strenuously maintained that insurgents could win final victory only through large conventional attacks. Even if the North Vietnamese did not launch a massive conventional invasion, such as the one that obliterated the South Vietnamese in 1975, they could still employ substantial conventional units capable of overrunning government centers of power or annihilating counterinsurgent forces dispersed across the countryside for population-control purposes, and indeed they would employ such units from the very beginning of the armed insurgency at the end of the decade. Only conventional counterinsurgent forces possessed the firepower to prevent the insurgent main forces from wreaking such havoc. This reality has largely been ignored by counterinsurgency theorists, who have concentrated on insurgents who operate strictly in small, lightly armed guerrilla units, and that is why such theorists have generally derided the development and use of South Vietnamese and American conventional forces in the Vietnam War.[41]

As part of his effort to strengthen the government's presence in the villages, Diem ended the elections for village governments in some areas. He rescinded this privilege only in villages where the administrative machinery no longer functioned because of the permanent departure of the village elites during the war. Such villages lacked people with experience in village administration, and the absence of an effective local government had enabled Communist subversives to run for office, cast votes, and influence the voting of others. The peasant masses were not especially upset in those villages where the Saigon government appointed local officials in lieu of elections, for they had never actually chosen the village councils. Historically, that task had belonged to the village elites, and the masses had accepted the judgment of the elites without question or complaint. They were willing to tolerate the appointment of village leaders by Diem's district chiefs with similar resignation.

There was, however, a problem with some of the new village councilmen. A large number were former officials of the colonial-era government who were not native to the village, and many of them were not even native to the region, being refugees from northern Vietnam. These outsiders lacked the local knowledge and contacts that were so important for the job, and some were exceedingly lazy, incompetent, or unjust. Whereas Ho had been able to replace the old elites of North Vietnam with a large group of followers built up from the early 1940s to 1954, Diem's secret organization of followers had been limited in size by the arrests of 1944 and his exile in the early 1950s.[42] Diem, therefore, had to put much of the administrative work into the hands of the individuals who had operated the state machinery in the colonial period, as they were the only people available with enough administrative experience to prevent chaos from taking hold. Taxes had to be collected, propaganda had to be distributed, and subversives had to be unmasked without delay.

The same shortage of able administrators could be found at every other level of the government, and it undermined all of the government's programs.

"Generally speaking, the quality of my ministers is very poor," Diem admitted to one American. "Provincial chiefs sometimes do not get out and see all the people in their provinces; district chiefs often do not know what goes on in villages within their districts; and in the ministries in Saigon there are civil servants who never get out in the country to learn about the services which they head within their ministries in Saigon." Explaining why he intervened directly at all levels of the government, Diem said, "I have delegated, and delegated, and delegated, but they have proven unworthy of the delegation of authority and responsibility time and again. This is why I feel constrained to step into the breach which exists and bring order out of the chaos."[43] To improve administrative performance and political organization, Diem began recruiting and training large numbers of young men who had never served in the colonial administration, with the National Institute of Administration serving as the central training venue, but some years would have to pass before these men could supplant the weak bureaucrats who held so many leadership positions.[44]

In terms of social and economic activities, Diem concentrated on those that enhanced national security. He spent more than half of all U.S. economic aid, and a great deal of his personal time, on new settlements and highways in strategically crucial sections of the country. In April 1957, Diem began the large-scale resettlement of ethnic Vietnamese to the vast central highlands, an area that until that time had seen few Vietnamese aside from the emperor, who had used it as his private hunting reserve. Diem wanted to build what he called a "human wall" in the central highlands to block North Vietnamese advances through this area of critical military importance. Using huge American bulldozers, the government cleared forests to create new farmland, and government buses brought the farmers to their new homesteads. Each settler received up to five hectares of land as well as seed, tools, animals, and enough food to last until the first harvest. By the end of 1959, the highlands had 125,000 new residents. The construction of new roads allowed the settlers to trade with the rest of the country, and provided routes for the government to rush reinforcements from the coast to the "human wall" by truck should the need arise.

Among the most significant achievements of Diem's early Presidency was land reform. Diem's land reform efforts focused on the Mekong Delta, where at the time of South Vietnam's creation, forty percent of the rice land was owned by 2,500 people – one quarter of one percent of the rural population. The large majority of the delta's peasants owned little or no land and had to rent rice paddies and draft animals from the large landholders. In the northern sections of South Vietnam, by contrast, less than one quarter of the people owned no land, and a landholder with more than ten hectares could seldom be found.[45] On October 22, 1956, Diem issued a Presidential ordinance that restricted individual land holdings to 100 hectares of rice land. Having resolved to avoid the "methods of piracy and barbaric torture" of the Communist land reform campaigns,[46] Diem instructed his officials to buy the holdings in excess of the limit rather than confiscate them. The government would then sell this excess land in small parcels to landless farmers, who could receive six-year, interest-free loans to make the purchase. The Americans advised Diem to reduce the ownership limit of 100 hectares in order to give ownership to more peasants. Other East Asian land reform programs had set the maximum landholding much lower – in Japan, landholders could keep just four hectares, while in Taiwan they could keep only three. Diem did not heed the warnings. "You don't understand," he replied to the Americans. "I cannot eliminate my middle class."[47] This decision proved to be a costly one, for in much of the Mekong Delta this middle class would be too small to sustain the government's position in the countryside when the landless peasants were given weapons and ordered to attack. Diem's land reform campaign would also suffer from a lack of funds; Diem asked the Americans for $30 million to purchase and finance the land, but the Americans were to provide only $4 million.

Ultimately, Diem's land reform did succeed in breaking up the vast estates in the delta, and it changed the landless peasants in the South from the large majority to a minority. The Communists would later lament that this redistribution of land "seriously interfered" with their subsequent efforts to win over the peasantry through land reform.[48] In the Mekong Delta, however, the landless minority would remain a very large minority. In 1960, forty-four percent of the delta's farming families would still be renting all of their land.[49]

Like his adversary in Hanoi, Diem wanted his country to develop its own wealth but found many obstacles in his way. South Vietnam had few bankers, entrepreneurs, or business managers. "There is only one Vietnamese businessman in the true sense of the word in this country," Nhu explained to Ambassador Durbrow. "This is the man who runs the Lambretta Company. All the rest who have borrowed money to go into business think only of getting themselves a large villa, an air-conditioned office, a Cadillac, and a wife as quickly as possible, and consequently they promptly go bankrupt. Vietnamese only think in terms of quick turnover and quick profits and will not invest money if they have to wait five years to get a return."[50] Foreign capitalists could have provided the impetus for economic development, but Diem and Nhu decided to bar foreign participation in numerous economic sectors, believing that French and Chinese businessmen would enrich themselves at the expense of the country.

Economic development, then, would have to be led and funded by the Saigon government, with U.S. assistance. The Diem government suffered from a lack of experience and training in overseeing economic enterprises, as did most Southeast Asian governments, but the austerity and vigilance of Diem ensured that the government would not suffer from the rampant corruption that plagued most of its Southeast Asian neighbors.[51] In terms of industry, the Diem regime followed American advice to emphasize consumer goods such as textiles, sugar, cement, paper, glass, and plastics. As in North Vietnam, industrial production never reached rates of sufficient magnitude to permit large-scale exportation, and so industrial development did not decrease the government's reliance on foreign aid. Unlike Ho Chi Minh, however, Diem accorded industrial development a much lower priority than agricultural development. Here, too, Diem had taken to heart the counsel of the Americans, who noted that agriculture could create jobs for refugees more quickly and that rapid industrialization required more capital and technicians than were available. In order to provide loans for individual farmers, Diem created the National Agricultural Credit Office, which offered such low interest rates that most of Vietnam's farmers borrowed from it. The agricultural cadres of the South Vietnamese government, with considerable American help, developed new irrigation facilities, introduced better crops, distributed tens of thousands of water buffalo, and ran an agricultural college with 300 students.

South Vietnam's agricultural advancement was one of its finest achievements during the relatively peaceful interval between Diem's accession to power and the end of the decade. Prosperity would return in the southern half of Vietnam in a way it never would in the Communist half. In 1954, South Vietnam's rice production had sunk to 2.6 million tons, barely more than half of what it had been before World War II. By 1959, the country was producing 5 million tons, surpassing the pre–World War II peak. Production of rubber went from 54,917 tons in 1954 to 75,374 in 1959, while the number of cattle, water buffaloes, and pigs rose from 1.3 million to 5.4 million during the same period.[52] The agricultural boom, combined with the opening of hundreds of new primary and secondary schools and new hospitals staffed by American-trained nurses and physicians, raised South Vietnamese living standards at a pace that would have been impressive in any underdeveloped country, not to mention a country that was simultaneously bracing for a massive attack on its homeland.

In the cities of South Vietnam, large segments of the populace supported Diem after the victories of 1955. The intellectuals still disliked him, if not so intensely, but only a few of them were active in dissenting political groups, in no small part because of Diem's intolerance of concerted opposition. Intellectuals could and did deride the government in Saigon's cafes and shops without facing punishment. No other Vietnamese government in history, indeed, had been so liberal in permitting expressions of discontent. Attempts to bring substantial numbers of people into a political organization, on the other hand, were not permitted, whether or not they appeared to have a direct link to the Communists. The government expressly forbade public gatherings of oppositionists and the publication of anti-government material. Douglas Pike recalled, "One of the writer's strongest memories of Vietnam in 1960 was listening to Vietnamese in public places – a sidewalk cafe, the street, a cocktail party – proclaim in loud voices, easily overheard, that 'this is a dictatorship and we have no freedom of speech here,' and then go on to list all the sins of the government.

The unwritten law seemed to be that unorganized hostility was tolerated, organized hostility was not."[53] Group offenders generally were arrested quietly. They might be subjected to torture during interrogation, as was a common practice among Vietnamese of all political stripes.

Diem repeatedly professed a desire for democracy during this period, but he said it could not come right away, and he did not really mean democracy as Westerners or Westernized Vietnamese understood it. He defined it thus: "Democracy is essentially a permanent effort to find the right political means in order to assure to all citizens the right of free development and of maximum initiative, responsibility, and spiritual life."[54] Democracy meant equal protection and care for all, not equal political influence. To assuage the sensibilities of the Americans and the South Vietnamese intellectuals, however, Diem erected a façade of Western democracy, of which the principal component was a legislature called the National Assembly. When Diem held the first National Assembly elections on March 4, 1956, most of the opposition parties boycotted the elections out of fear that they would be rigged – which in fact they were. Diem planned to give the National Assembly no real authority, but he still exerted himself strenuously to assist candidates who supported him unswervingly, for the assembly could become a vehicle for demagogic opponents to gain prominence and challenge his authority. Government campaign committees were charged with screening candidates and they barred anyone whose platform was considered to be anti-Diem or pro-Communist. Candidates were permitted to put up posters and hold meetings in public halls, but the government controlled the printing of campaign materials and radio programming, and gave more support to the preferred candidates. The election yielded the sort of subservient National Assembly that Diem had desired.[55]

The first assembly began by voting unanimously in favor of a constitution that Diem presented to them. Drafted with the help of American legal expert J.A.C. Grant, the constitution assigned considerable power to the legislature and judiciary because the Americans had told Diem that he needed to make provision for the separation of powers, as the U.S. Constitution did. But in practice, both the legislature and the judiciary were firmly in Diem's hands, and therefore Diem retained total control over the entire government. This fact did not cause a major outcry, because except for a few Westernized Saigon gentlemen, the Vietnamese people accepted and expected one-man rule as part of the natural order of the world.

The National Assembly garnered the most attention as a pathway for legislation that Diem wanted to pass with fanfare. In October 1957, Diem let Madame Nhu bring what she called the Family Law before the National Assembly. This law promoted the nuclear family, which was why Diem let her push it, but it also contained feminist reforms more dramatic in nature than anything ever seen in Asia. The Family Law forbade polygamy, concubinage, and adultery – all of the traditional practices by which Vietnamese men had taken multiple women for themselves. The law stipulated that divorce required Presidential approval, and as a Catholic Diem was not at all inclined to give his approval, though he did permit permanent separations. A woman could work in any profession she chose, the law stated, and upon marriage she retained ownership of her property, rather than transferring all of her property to her husband as before. Many men in the National Assembly denounced the legislation, but because of Madame Nhu's influence, the law passed with only one dissenting vote. Much grumbling persisted beneath the surface. The radical reduction in men's privileges and Madame Nhu's uncompromising stance during the process would earn her the lasting enmity of numerous upper-class Vietnamese.

The government held National Assembly elections again in 1959, and again Diem took many steps to control the outcome. In the provinces, Diem's administrators prevented opposition candidates from running, which enabled most of Diem's candidates to receive ninety-nine percent of the votes in their area without any ballot tampering. In the cities, his judges disqualified several independent and anti-Diem candidates for trivial infractions of campaign rules, but some oppositionists were permitted to run because of heavy criticism from the intellectuals. Diem also gave the newspapers wider latitude than before to criticize the government. In Saigon, several pro-Diem candidates lost to opposition figures, of whom the most prominent was Dr. Phan Quang Dan. Ambassador Durbrow asked Diem to let Dr. Dan take his seat, believing that the American people and other Asians would look favorably on the toleration of a "loyal opposition." Diem, however, did not want an opposition of any kind. He was also concerned by Dan's skill at demagoguery. Diem's judges charged Dan with violations of the election laws, such as the promise of free medical care in exchange for votes, and Dan thereby was disqualified from taking his seat.

Although Ambassador Durbrow had opposed Dan's exclusion, he did not object to the shunning of Western liberalism and democracy that it represented. On December 7, 1959, in one of his most insightful moments as ambassador, Durbrow wrote to Washington: "We should be prepared to acknowledge to ourselves that even over the longer term democracy in the Western sense of the term may never come to exist in Vietnam. . . . We should also look with tolerance on the GVN's [Government of Vietnam's] efforts to establish a political system which it considers in conformance with local traditions and needs. We should not attempt to make over Vietnam in our own image. Excellent as the democratic, liberal and parliamentary institutions and methods are for countries like the U.S. and the U.K., recent developments in certain other Afro–Asian countries indicate that they cannot be expected to flower at an early date in such countries."[56]

In May 1957, Diem made a 21-day trip to the United States, the highlights of which were a formal state visit to Washington and a parade in his honor in New York City organized by Mayor Robert F. Wagner. President Eisenhower dispatched his own plane, the *Columbine III*, to bring Diem from Honolulu to Washington. When Diem arrived at Washington National Airport, the American President was there to meet him in person, making Diem the only foreign leader besides King Saud of Saudi Arabia for whom Eisenhower had made such an effort.[57] After Diem spoke to a joint session of the U.S. Congress, members of both parties tried to outdo each other in lauding the South Vietnamese premier. Republican Senator Jacob Javits of New York hailed Diem as "one of the real heroes of the free world."[58] Democratic Senator Mike Mansfield of Montana proclaimed, "The chief credit for holding back the Communist aggression not only in Vietnam, but, because of that, in Southeast Asia as well, lies in the determination, the courage, the incorruptibility, and the integrity of President Diem, who has shown such great ability and has accomplished so much against tremendous odds."[59] The *New York Times* termed Diem "an Asian liberator,"[60] while *Life* dubbed him "the tough miracle man of Vietnam."[61]

On the morning of May 9, Diem went to the White House for a private meeting with President Eisenhower. Diem put his keen analytical powers on display, and even managed to avoid the long monologues that were his habit, knowing that he would have less than an hour with the President. "At the present time, Vietnam is faced with the possibility of a strong Communist offensive from the Viet Minh, who have four hundred thousand men under arms," Diem said to Eisenhower. "My main military requirement is ground forces. I am convinced that because of the poor visibility from low cloud cover prevailing through most of the year, it would be difficult, if not impossible, to give adequate air support to the ground forces. I am afraid, also, that any Viet Minh–Communist attack would probably come down the Mekong River Valley through Laos, which is a scantily populated area where it would not be possible to use tactical atomic weapons since there would be no concentrated targets suitable for A-bomb attacks. While the Laotians are sympathetic to the Vietnamese cause, they do not have a strong army and they hope that the Vietnamese could help defend Laos." Diem said he planned to expand his armed forces from 150,000 to 170,000 without raising costs, by relying more heavily on low-paid conscripts. The expansion would improve South Vietnam's ability to defend against a conventional onslaught as well as an insurgency, though it would only slightly reduce the enormous gap in size between the North Vietnamese and South Vietnamese armed forces.

Then Diem got down to the heart of the matter, the preservation of American aid, which at the moment amounted to two-thirds of South Vietnam's total budget. The United States was in the process of setting its foreign aid budget and, as Diem knew, both Eisenhower and the Congress were interested in reducing spending across the board. The South Vietnamese President implored the American President to maintain the present level of aid. "This aid has permitted Vietnam to build up its armed strength and thus play an important role in Southeast Asia," Diem said. "If this aid should be cut, both the military and economic progress would have to be reduced. This would cause serious repercussions not only in Vietnam but among neighboring countries in Southeast Asia who look on Vietnam as an example of the good U.S. aid can bring."

Offering no reassurance, Eisenhower replied that he had not yet had a chance to review the proposed aid for 1958, and he stressed that the amount of aid would depend on the will of Congress. He then reminded Diem that South Vietnam was protected by SEATO.

"Regarding SEATO," Diem said, "I have studied this question carefully and while SEATO constitutes a good deterrent, there are only two countries which could possibly come immediately to the aid of Vietnam – Thailand and the Philippines. Pakistan is too far away. However, the Filipinos only have about sixty thousand troops and they would be needed to defend the Philippines and could not come to the aid of Vietnam. The Thais only have about one hundred and fifty thousand men under arms and if an attack on Thailand should come by way of Laos, these troops would be needed to defend Thailand itself."

"While the U.S. wants to do all it can to help its friends," Eisenhower intoned, "it must be remembered that we have many international commitments which we must live up to and we have undertaken great obligations from Korea to NATO and the volume of aid we can give is not limitless. For these reasons, we must use our best judgment in allocating the resources we can make available."[62]

Later in Diem's trip, one of his subordinates told an American that the South Vietnamese were troubled by doubts about America's willingness to defend Southeast Asia. Admiral Felix Stump, the commander-in-chief of the U.S. Pacific command, went to see Diem to ease these concerns. Stump said that Eisenhower intended to use nuclear weapons if the Communists attacked any non-Communist country, as the President and Secretary of State Dulles had said several times in public. The United States would not use nuclear weapons against Vietnamese population centers but would use them against targets in China if the protection of South Vietnam demanded it. "If we are unable to stop the Communists in Vietnam or nearby territories in connection with any hostilities, we will not hesitate to use all weapons at our disposal on such areas as the Canton military complex in order to bring about the defeat of the Communists," Stump asserted. "The United States now has military capabilities which can stop and defeat any Communist military thrust."[63]

A few months later, Diem received the news that the United States was cutting aid to his country by twenty percent, the same percentage by which the U.S. Congress had cut the entire foreign aid budget. Ambassador Durbrow, who in most cases thought that Diem requested more American money than he really needed, agreed with Diem that the cut was too large, but Washington ignored Durbrow and Diem and the aid was cut by twenty percent. Over the ensuing two years, Congress cut its total foreign aid budget and the allocation to Vietnam again. South Vietnam still received the highest amount of U.S. aid per capita of any country in the world, but a war was approaching and Diem did not receive all the money he needed for crucial preparations.

* * *

AT THE END OF 1956, THE VIETNAMESE COMMUNIST PARTY TOOK ITS first steps towards the reactivation of the armed struggle in the South. The orders came down from Hanoi to the Party's committee for Nam Bo, a region roughly equivalent to what the French had called Cochinchina, the southern third of Vietnam. At the Second Conference of the Nam Bo committee, the Party authorized its members in the South to kill "traitors," though it also concluded that the time was not yet ripe for a full military struggle. During the ensuing year, the Party undertook isolated assassinations of government leaders, land reform cadres, and spies. Many of the Communists in the South wanted to use force more liberally in order to roll back Diem's spreading security apparatus, and on occasion a guerrilla unit made a small attack without authorization. But the Party did not change its position, and it did not tolerate insubordination. As the year of 1957 neared its end, the Party began using some of the 1,700 Communist troops in the South in armed raids. Many of these troops had come from battered sect units, a fact the Communists exploited by claiming that the attackers were fighting for religious freedom. During the last quarter of 1957, Communist forces initiated 140 terrorist actions and hit-and-run attacks on government posts, mostly in the rugged area along the Cambodian border. On a few occasions, they assembled several hundred men for the attack.

In the summer of 1958, the North Vietnamese notified Beijing that they wanted to commence a full-scale armed insurrection in the South. The Chinese replied that the appropriate time had still not yet arrived, resulting again in North Vietnamese obeisance to China's desire for peace. Hanoi did, however, grant its southern units authority to carry out more assassinations, with special emphasis on eliminating hamlet chiefs.[64] Assassinations rose sharply in 1958 and rose again in 1959. Vo Van An, a former high-ranking Communist official, described the assassination campaign of 1958 and 1959: "The principal purpose of the 'extermination of traitors' movement was to protect the very existence of the Party. Without exterminating the government's hard-core elements, the Party apparatus could not have survived. A second purpose was to aid in the development of the Party by creating fear in the enemy ranks and by creating faith among the masses in the skilled leadership of the revolution. Extermination activities had an enormous psychological impact, because the masses saw that the government hard-core elements were being eliminated." According to An, the Communists publicly proclaimed that they would save the peasants from corrupt or tyrannical officials, and on occasion they would kill such an official, but usually they left them alone. The official they would likely assassinate would be an "honest hamlet chief who has done much for the people" and "is intent on destroying the communist apparatus in his area." The Party also assassinated teachers, An said, "because they were people with a profound understanding about politics, people who were pure nationalists, who might be able to assume anticommunist leadership in their area."[65]

The Communists' acceleration of violence ran headlong into another Denounce the Communists campaign, begun in late 1957 and focused on the Mekong Delta and the provinces encircling Saigon. Adhering to a national campaign plan, Army regulars, militiamen, local officials, and National Revolutionary Movement members organized the villagers and stomped out subversion. The campaign succeeded in strengthening the government's control where it already held power and extended the government's authority into areas that had been neglected previously. In rounding up subversives, the campaign's participants were very aggressive, prompting new charges of improper conduct. Philippe Devillers, one of the foremost French observers of Vietnamese affairs at that time, commented that these crackdowns targeted the regime's non-Communist opponents as well as the Communists, and that many innocent civilians were swept up by mistake. As a result, Devillers wrote, the government hurt itself: "The peasants, disgusted to see Diem's men acting in this way, lent their assistance to the Communists, and even to the sects, going so far as to take up arms at their side."[66]

Subsequent disclosures from the Communist side would prove Devillers wrong. As in 1956, the campaign actually increased peasant support not for Hanoi's representatives, but for Saigon's, and it wrought very heavy damage on the Communists. One Communist account stated that the South Vietnamese government "actively consolidated and strengthened the army, security service, and administrative apparatus from the central to the hamlet level, crudely assassinated people, and truly and efficiently destroyed our Party. By relying on force, the American-Diemist regime was temporarily able to stabilize the situation and increase the prestige of the counter-revolutionaries."[67] Another Communist history described events in the Nam Bo region, where the majority of South Vietnam's population lived: "Early in 1958, the enemy's oppression was intensive. The mass movements ebbed. Many basic structures disintegrated. Many comrades were killed." There were a large number of "shirking and wavering members who denounced others after they had been apprehended and interrogated." Then the Party's problems grew even worse: "In mid-1958 and especially early 1959, with a number of wicked agents already trained, with an espionage system already established in hamlets and some reactionary organizations set up in rural areas, the enemy started a larger scale and more vigorous offensive in the hamlets with the aim of eradicating our movement and our organizations in rural areas. . . . Within just a few months, the enemy succeeded in dismembering 80–90 percent of our organizations in many base areas."[68]

A study supervised by the Vietnamese Communist Politburo acknowledged that the Party lost 90 percent of its members and cadres during the years 1955 to 1958. Cochinchina had 60,000 Communist Party members at the beginning of this period, and only 5,000 at the end.[69]

As Diem lay waste to his enemies and strengthened the government and the economy, his prestige rose ever higher. No one in the armed forces spoke of overthrowing the government anymore, and among the Saigon elite the chatter about coups was as low as it ever would be. From the U.S. press and Congress, there continued a crescendo of praise. On July 7, 1959, the *New York Times* commemorated the five-year anniversary of Diem's accession to national leadership by proclaiming, "A five-year miracle, not a 'plan,' has been carried out. Vietnam is free and is becoming stronger in defense of its freedom and of ours. There is reason, today, to salute President Ngo Dinh Diem."[70]

So bright was the glow of Diem's achievements at the end of the 1950s that it obscured some weaknesses of great future import. By 1959, Diem and his top generals had rid the South Vietnamese army of its worst flaws by removing incompetent leaders, ending insubordination, and teaching the fundamentals of American-style warfare, but many mediocre officers still held important positions because of political considerations and the shortage of experienced officers, and command and control were hampered by multiple chains of command that diffused authority or overlapped. At the end of the decade, the South Vietnamese army remained substantially less competent and much smaller in size than its counterpart in the North.

The militia forces were in even worse shape. The U.S. embassy continued to prevent Diem from putting the Civil Guard under the control of the military or from inserting military officers into leadership positions, so numerous Civil Guard units remained under the command of ineffective men who had served under the French. As a result of the American insistence on making the Civil Guard a police force, the standard Civil Guard unit was armed with .38 caliber revolvers. Diem and Williams had been able to send rifles to some units, but they were French rifles dating back to the turn of the century, and much of the ammunition was unreliable. None of the Civil Guard's weaponry was a match for the submachine guns and rifles Hanoi was beginning to send down the Ho Chi Minh Trail.[71] Professor Ralph Turner, who headed Michigan State's police division in Vietnam, admitted after the war that his division should have adopted Diem's recommendation in the late 1950s to make the Civil Guard a paramilitary force instead of a police force. "In hindsight," Turner said, "obviously the Vietnamese were right."[72] The Self-Defense Corps suffered from the same defects, only to a greater degree. Led mainly by ex-colonial officials, the Self-Defense Corps in many locales became known primarily for stealing chickens, beating peasants, and the other practices traditionally associated with undisciplined Vietnamese soldiers. The ammunition for their antiquated French rifles was so old that only one out of every seven rounds would fire properly, and one third of the men did not have firearms at all.[73] Only in the northern part of the country were the static village militia units very effective, owing to the more enterprising and industrious character of the Annamese people.[74]

Diem's efforts to improve rural officialdom did not yield dramatic results by the end of the 1950s, primarily because the project required more time. Those who had been officials before 1954 still held most leadership positions in all segments of the rural administration. Tran Ngoc Chau, whom Diem had made inspector for the Civil Guard and Self-Defense Corps, toured all of the provinces in late 1959 and found that most positions in the government were held by the same people who had held them in the colonial era. "The French were gone," Chau remarked, "but their policies and their attitudes, particularly toward the rural population, were still in place. As far as the Vietnamese peasant was concerned, it was business as usual. And that meant oppression, duplicity, and corruption."[75] Chau's blanket condemnations of French-era officials and post-1954 governance were somewhat overblown – there were always some honest and dedicated officials – but they contained a good measure of truth.

During 1959, Diem and Nhu attempted to overcome some of the impediments to rural control by moving isolated peasant families into large fortified villages, which they called agrovilles. Each agroville had its own school and market, artificial ponds stocked with fish, horticultural nurseries, and miles of new canals. Every family received farm land and an additional acre of land for a house and vegetable garden, funded by a loan from the government. The Ngo brothers planned to build eighty of these agrovilles, primarily along strategic roads where defense forces could reach them rapidly, with each agroville containing 400 families plus satellite agrovilles of 120 families apiece. For the Diem government, the costs were enormous, and they were especially burdensome because Diem had avoided seeking American financial assistance for the agrovilles in order to avoid American meddling. Agroville residents were required to use the materials from their old houses to build their new houses, and they had to perform work on public agroville projects without pay. Such requirements were nothing new for poor Annamese peasants, as they had for centuries performed work without compensation in lieu of paying taxes. As one Western observer in Annam noted, "Since community responsibility is not internalized by most villagers, they in fact require and expect more policing than an American community would tolerate. ... The average peasant is sorry to be caught in what he regards as a corvée but he also expects the government to organize such projects."[76] In the Mekong Delta, however, where the agrovilles were concentrated, many peasants had not carried such a burden before, and they often resented the Annamese officials who arrived to compel them in the Annamese way, although they would comply if it was necessary. In addition, some peasants became upset because the agroville program obligated them to move considerable distances and leave behind ancestral shrines and fields that they had spent decades improving. The greatest weakness of the agrovilles, however, was that their large size made them extremely difficult to protect against powerful Communist intrusion.

* * *

IN EARLY JANUARY 1959, NORTH VIETNAM'S LEADERS CAME TOGETHER for the Fifteenth Plenum of the Communist Party Central Committee. Because the remnants of the Communist apparatus in the South had suffered intense pounding during the past year, dissatisfaction with the Party's strategy was at an all-time high. Many voices argued that the time had come for a full-blown armed insurrection in the south, involving mobilization of the masses and a level of violence much higher than the Southern Communists were currently employing. Others, however, remained opposed to such a course, warning that the international environment was in the wrong season for such a move. An armed struggle in the South would upset Moscow and China, and it might invite American intervention. Men of both Northern and Southern origin supported each of these positions, though the Southerners in general were more inclined toward armed action.

After hearing all of the arguments, Ho Chi Minh came down in favor of an armed struggle, and his opinion carried the day. The Central Committee then resolved, "[o]ur Party must make active preparations in all fields" for "staging an insurrection to overthrow the U.S.-Diem regime" and "to unify the nation." The war would not just be a local struggle, Ho stressed, but part of a global struggle against the enemies of Communism: "We must include South Vietnam in the over-all revolution of our entire nation and include our nation's revolution in the world revolution. The socialist revolution is gaining in strength and breadth. Imperialism is in decline."[77] Ho shared the concerns about negative international repercussions that had been expressed by the opponents of war, so he insisted that the Communist forces concentrate at first on political organization in the villages and seek only small military victories so as to avoid arousing the Americans and worrying the Soviets and Chinese. In his mind, the initial insurgent campaign should weaken the Diem government and build a base for larger offensives to take place at some time in the future, when the conditions in South Vietnam and around the world were better.

At the beginning of July, Ho traveled to Moscow to see whether the Soviets would support the war for which he was preparing. To Ho's great disappointment, the Soviets told him that he must continue to seek reunification by peaceful means. Could he afford to start a war, however small, without the blessing of the Soviet Union? Perhaps the Soviets would change their minds in a year or two, but then again Ho had entertained similar hopes in 1956 and yet the Soviet minds had not changed. One month after his visit to Moscow, Ho received better news from the Chinese Communists, who expressed approval and promised to send North Vietnam $500 million in arms and supplies for the struggle.[78] After thinking it over, Ho decided that he could wait no longer. He would head into war with the backing of only one of his two big allies.

Over the course of 1959, many of the Southerners who had gone north in 1954 were sent to special North Vietnamese units where they received insurgency training from veterans of the Franco–Viet Minh War and the Chinese Civil War. The instructors inundated them with lectures and readings aimed at teaching them to "hate the United States and Diem."[79] Once trained and equipped, the Southern émigrés of 1954 would become the vanguard of the new armed movement in the South. To get these men and their supplies into the South, the North Vietnamese high command created the 559th Transportation Group and formulated plans to open a route for infiltration into South Vietnam, which would become the first Ho Chi Minh Trail. At the beginning of June 1959, soldiers from the 301st North Vietnamese Army Battalion went to Khe Ho, in the southwestern corner of North Vietnam just north of the demilitarized zone, to determine the location of the route. With the help of the Communist Party committee of Quang Tri province, the northernmost province of South Vietnam, the 301st battalion mapped out a trail that ran southward from Khe Ho along the eastern side of the Annamite mountain range, crossing into South Vietnam at the seventeenth parallel, and ending in Thua Thien province, the province immediately to the south of Quang Tri. It passed through the most difficult of terrain, consisting in some places of sheer cliffs that would necessitate the use of ropes, because the enemy would not closely guard paths that seemed impassable. This trail, unlike later infiltration trails, lay exclusively within the territorial boundaries of North Vietnam and South Vietnam.

Setting off on foot to blaze the trail, the soldiers selected the location of jungle way-stations as they went. The most formidable challenge was crossing Route 9, which, as the principal east-west road near the seventeenth parallel, was heavily guarded by the Saigon government. Communist agents from the local Van Kieu tribe advised the trailblazers to make their crossing between Rao Quan and the junction of the Da Krong River, as this crossing could only be reached by traversing steep slopes and cliffs and therefore did not receive great attention from South Vietnamese soldiers. Reaching Route 9 as the sun was setting, the North Vietnamese troops rolled a nylon sheet over the road, so that they would leave no footprints, and stepped across undetected. Once past Route 9, they crossed through forests of reeds and thick elephant grass, in which many tigers were known to live, until making their final stop at Ta Riep, to the northwest of the A Luoi Airfield in Thua Thien province. At this place, the Communists planned to establish a central depot for the distribution of supplies to combat units.

On July 23, the first porters took possession of guns, ammunition, medicine, and Party documents at the starting point of the Ho Chi Minh Trail. To keep the enemy from discovering that North Vietnam was introducing new weapons and personnel into the South, Hanoi shipped only weaponry that had been manufactured in capitalist countries, and it dressed the infiltrators and logistical troops in the black pajamas and brimmed hats of the Southern Communists – or Viet Cong (VC) as their enemies had begun to call them – rather than North Vietnamese uniforms. Trudging along the difficult trail, the porters took nearly a month to complete the hundred-mile journey. Before August was past, according to Communist sources, porters from the 301st Battalion had transported 60 machine guns, 100 carbines, more than one thousand rifles, 600 submachine guns, 600 pistols, more than 100,000 rounds of ammunition, and 188 kilograms of TNT. By the end of 1959, 31 tons of supplies – including 2,841 infantry weapons – had reached the end of the trail, and several thousand personnel had made the trip or were on their way.[80]

The first act of the new armed rebellion was scheduled to commence at the beginning of 1960. Before the sopranos and tenors sang their arias, however, there would be an overture lasting from September to December 1959, in which the brass section would do most of the playing. From a sanctuary inside Cambodia, a Communist battalion made repeated forays into South Vietnam's Kien Phong province, concentrating its efforts on wiping out the Civil Guard. Elements of South Vietnamese Army companies and a Civil Guard company went into the wooded marshes near the Cambodian border in September, with the intention of tracking down and destroying the Communist battalion. As they came around a bend in their sampans, several hundred Viet Cong ambushed the government soldiers and inflicted thirty-five casualties before departing. On October 10, forty-five South Vietnamese Army troops came under attack in Kien Phong and promptly surrendered. Three weeks later, close to one hundred Viet Cong overran one of the district offices in Kien Phong, killing the district chief, a policeman, six Civil Guardsmen, and four civilians before freeing seventy prisoners and seizing twenty-three rifles. Smaller attacks and ambushes occurred in other provinces during the last months of 1959. According to government figures, which were probably low, assassinations and kidnappings more than doubled starting in October, with an average of thirty-two assassinations and sixty kidnappings per month.[81]

These initiatives did not change the reality that the Communists held almost no power in South Vietnam's villages or the rest of the countryside at the end of 1959. Lacking supporters among the villagers, the Communist guerrillas were spending most of their time trying to avoid detection by government forces. "Our armed forces did not obtain any good results for our movement," stated a Communist history of this period. "On the contrary, when our armed forces appeared the enemy tightly controlled the people and hunted down our forces."[82] For the Communists heading down the Ho Chi Minh Trail to launch the armed insurrection, the chances for success seemed very slim. Whatever the faults of the Saigon government's personnel and the Americans who had come to advise them, Diem's government had turned the villages into fortresses, with most soldiers, officials, and peasants working to strengthen the government and annihilate its enemies. A Communist history of the Nam Bo region described the situation in 1959: "The enemy at this time had completed the establishment of his ruling machinery from top to bottom, being able to build a tight espionage network and to form popular force units in every village. He was able to control each and every family by means of the houseblock system." The government's "oppressive machinery enabled them to control Nam Bo almost entirely, even the remotest areas." The Diem regime "forced everyone to join 'the National Revolutionary Movement,' 'the Republican Youth,' and 'the People's Self-Defense Group.' Nightly, people had to mount guard duty, and when they saw our cadres come to their villages, they would beat on their hollow bamboo stems to ring the alarm. In many villages, which had been in the center of our base areas during the resistance, our cadres, when they appeared, were encircled and hunted by screaming people."[83]

CHAPTER 4

Insurgency

1960

NGUYEN THI DINH WAS SUMMONED TO A MEETING OF SOUTHERN Communist Party leaders at the end of 1959. One of the very few high-ranking women in the Communist movement, Nguyen Thi Dinh hailed from the Mekong Delta province that the Communists called Ben Tre and the Diem government called Kien Hoa. At the meeting, an official named Sau Duong announced that he had important news to share. The Party, he declared, had decided to use military action in conjunction with political action to overthrow the Diem government. The proclamation prompted an immediate and frenzied applause from the audience, who had been convinced by the setbacks of the past few years that armed action was the only possible means of defeating Diem and unifying the country. Returning to Ben Tre, Nguyen Thi Dinh gathered the province's Party leadership in a rice field on the night of January 1, 1960. Although Diem's countermeasures had left the Party with only 162 members in the entire province, the assemblage decided that they had enough experienced people to break the enemy's hold through armed rebellion. The committee therefore resolved to lead an uprising like that in 1945, with a starting date of January 17.

Beating drums and wooden bells, the guerrillas went to several villages and called on the people to revolt. The revolutionaries tore down government flags and burned the plaques on each house that listed the occupants. They chopped down trees and lay them across roads to block enemy movements. Insurgent armed units overran government posts and offices, armed – by their accounts – with weapons captured through chicanery from several government outposts at the beginning of the insurrection, although in all probability they relied partially if not entirely on weapons brought from the North. During the first week of the Ben Tre rebellion, the guerrillas took a total of ten government posts and captured nearly one hundred weapons. Nguyen Thi Dinh recounted the fate of those taken prisoner: "the policemen, tyrants, officials, spies, and landlords with blood debts were led out to be executed in front of the people. Every one of them was guilty of countless crimes and deserved the death sentence. However, in accordance with the lenient policy of the revolution, only the gang leaders – the most cruel and treacherous of them all – were executed." In all, the Communists assassinated forty-three individuals in Ben Tre during the month of January.

Ten days into the uprising, the government sent large regular forces to the area. Fierce fighting ensued. In the village of Phuoc Hiep, Nguyen Thi Dinh recounted, the government stationed "extremely brutal and reactionary" troops who "terrorized the people in an extremely brutal manner." Such terminology, when used by the Communists, usually meant that it was the insurgents, not the civilians, who were brutalized, and Nguyen Thi Dinh's subsequent narrative confirms this case to be no exception. Because of the soldiers at Phuoc Hiep, she wrote, "[t]he villagers' ardor declined noticeably. The comrades in the village pleaded with us to send armed units down to destroy the post. We also wanted to destroy this gang badly and relieve our anger, but our armed forces were still weak." All that the Communists could do was organize thousands of women to surround the district headquarters, defecate on the ground, and demand that the government troops be punished and their victims be compensated. Although the uprising had rejuvenated the Communist movement in the area and put some arms into Communist hands, it failed to achieve its chief objective of establishing a permanent "liberated area." A Communist history acknowledged: "Because the enemy still maintained its governmental apparatus at the district, provincial, and national level, and because his armed forces were still too numerous for us, the enemy was able to gradually reestablish twenty-seven Civil Guard and militia outposts that had previously been forced to withdraw or surrender." After a period of a few months, Saigon withdrew its army forces from the province and returned control to the Civil Guard.[1]

The second major initiative of the Viet Cong's new war took place in Tay Ninh province, to the northwest of Saigon, nine days after the start of the Ben Tre insurrection. During November 1959, upon learning that Hanoi had authorized the use of force, the Nam Bo Party Committee had decided to concentrate its troops for one big strike on the headquarters of the 32nd Regiment of the South Vietnamese Army, or the Army of Republic of Vietnam (ARVN) as it was officially known. An old French fort seven kilometers north of Tay Ninh City, the headquarters was close enough to the Cambodian border that Communist forces in Cambodia could strike it and return to their base areas with little risk of encountering enemy patrols or reaction forces. A Communist history noted that normally the headquarters was "carefully patrolled and guarded day and night," but during the Tet holiday period at the end of January, most of the ARVN regiment went on leave – only 250 men would be present – and security measures were relaxed. The Communists later said they chose to attack during Tet because it was "a time when the enemy was very careless."[2]

The Party assigned the mission to four infantry companies and a sapper company. Early in the morning of January 26, the Communist companies advanced on the South Vietnamese Army base from the north. Aided by agents within the complex, Communist sappers got inside before any shots were fired and placed heavy demolition charges on some key structures. When the firing began, the sappers detonated the charges and destroyed five buildings, including a battalion headquarters, two large barracks, and an officers' billet. A large number of the soldiers in these buildings were asleep in their beds when they were killed. The main Viet Cong strike force swiftly ripped through the sentry posts surrounding the headquarters and stormed the central buildings, killing the acting regimental commander and plundering the regimental arms room. The Viet Cong overran the 1st and 2nd Battalion areas, but were stopped at the 3rd Battalion area. After sixty minutes of fighting, the Viet Cong withdrew, and the South Vietnamese pursued them. The pursuit force reportedly killed thirty of the attackers, and it recaptured two trucks that had been purposefully stalled by Army prisoners forced by the Viet Cong to drive them.

The government unit suffered forty dead and twenty-six wounded, and the Viet Cong absconded with approximately six hundred light firearms, two machine guns, and two mortars.[3] The loss of six hundred firearms was a substantial coup for the enemy, as the Viet Cong were much in need of such weapons, but the worst damage was psychological. Williams called it a "severe blow to the prestige of the Vietnamese Army and [an] indication of the VC ability to stage large-size, well-planned attacks."[4] Appalled and embarrassed, the Vietnamese high command demoted the regimental commander to the rank of captain and forbade him from receiving a promotion for five years. The division commander was fired.

More large clashes followed in March. On several occasions, battalion-sized Communist forces ambushed South Vietnamese Army companies in the Mekong Delta, inflicting from 10 to 100 casualties on the government forces each time. The Communists proved so effective in alternately avoiding and attacking large government units that many suspected the Communists had an agent in the army's upper ranks.

Yet Hanoi, despite some major successes during the first few months, was displeased with the progress of the war. The Southern Communists were undertaking overt action on a larger scale than the North Vietnamese leadership desired and thus were exposing themselves to the enemy's concentrated military power, leading to major setbacks, of which Ben Tre was a prime example. In a March 28 letter to the comrades in the South, the North Vietnamese high command observed that Party leaders in some areas had embarked on "rash adventures" involving the destruction of government of offices, the tearing up of government-issued ID cards, and the digging up of roads, which voided the "legal status of the people." When the people lost their status as legal citizens in the eyes of the government, the Communists could not find shelter by mingling among them, for the government's conventional forces could use their brute force against entire villages without concern for civilian life. "The enemy still have the capacity to concentrate their forces and use their oppressive machinery, and they are still capable of conducting large-scale and fierce attacks," the letter continued. "In this period of contention, we should do our utmost to build up, preserve, and expand our grass root organizations – generally speaking, we should maintain the people's movement under legal cover. We cannot as yet wipe out the enemy government machinery; we can only chip it and damage it." Larger forces needed to be developed before the Viet Cong could take more aggressive actions. Otherwise, they could suffer devastating losses.[5]

Hanoi was also concerned that large-scale revolutionary violence would invite greater U.S. involvement and upset the Soviet Union and China. The Soviets still favored peaceful coexistence and the Chinese still wanted to avoid a conflict on the order of the Korean War. On April 20, at a speech commemorating Lenin's 90th birthday anniversary, Le Duan called for the restriction of violence to South Vietnam and provided reassurance that North Vietnam wanted peace in the rest of the world.[6] Privately, the North Vietnamese leaders continued to view the conflict in Vietnam as part of an aggressive Communist revolution spanning the entire globe, but believed that the international struggle would have to develop slowly. The Party Central Committee noted at the end of April:

> The struggle between the enemy and ourselves throughout the world is now in a tense, back-and-forth situation . . . In Southeast Asia, the U.S. and their imperialist allies have not yet been isolated. They are now working in collusion with one another, and they still have bases of support in Thailand, Malaya, the Philippines, Japan, Laos, etc. For that reason, if we want to further facilitate the revolution in South Vietnam and to gradually create conditions to allow us to progress to the point of seizing the initiative, we need time to let the anti-imperialist movement, and particularly the anti-American movement in Southeast Asia, grow stronger and work with this movement to weaken and isolate the American imperialists and their allies.[7]

Hanoi put a stop to large uprisings and attacks. The war began to take on the shape that was originally intended, that of a rural insurgency that would rely on small guerrilla action initially and rise gradually in intensity. This war would be spearheaded by the infiltrators coming down the Ho Chi Minh Trail, who by the beginning of 1960 numbered 3,500 cadres and soldiers. In accordance with the revolutionary training they had undergone in the North, the infiltrators carried out a systematic program with a high degree of efficiency. After setting up camp at remote bases and taking command of the few Communists who had managed to survive the devastating Denounce the Communists campaigns, the infiltrators used their rifles to kill or drive away village officials, militiamen, and informants. They could obtain relatively few firearms by stealing from the South Vietnamese government or digging up weapons hidden in 1954, so they would have to depend primarily on the arms they carried with them down the trail, and the armed forces they would build would likewise rely primarily on infiltrated weapons.[8]

The assassination and kidnapping rates skyrocketed at the beginning of 1960; during the first five months of the year, the Viet Cong carried out over 150 assassinations and 50 kidnappings per month.[9] In their assassination campaigns, the Communists were very selective in their targeting. Rarely did they use indiscriminate forms of terrorism in villages that they were trying to seize; methods such as the throwing of grenades into markets or the detonating of bombs in restaurants was usually reserved for the cities and those rural areas where the Communists had minimal influence. No form of "punishment" was considered too brutal for the "reactionaries" and "traitors" whom the Viet Cong chose for assassination. Many victims were disemboweled slowly or beheaded in front of their family members. Others had their heads smashed with hammers. Sham trials frequently accompanied the killings, as described by a Communist cadre in his account of the Viet Cong's handling of government representatives: "they seized these men and brought them before a mass gathering and read out their past activities considered as detrimental to the nation and the people's interest. After that they asked the people whether these men were to be released or sentenced. They have their plants among the mass of people. They in turn stood up and gave an opinion and the rest of the crowd had to nod consent. No one dared say anything contrary. Suppose there were six accused. Some were sentenced to death, others were jailed, others discharged." Once the Communists had determined which people were to die, "they beheaded the victims before the crowd."[10]

The Civil Guard and Self-Defense Corps, which Saigon had designated as the primary forces for protecting the rural areas against insurgent violence, proved in a great many villages unable to hold off the Viet Cong, owing to inferior weaponry and leadership. Greatly exacerbating their problems was a decision by the United States to cut off funding to the Self-Defense Corps at the beginning of 1960, the result of a poor judgment by Ambassador Durbrow in late 1959 that Diem did not need these militia forces. When the Viet Cong killed a few government officials or militiamen, the remaining government personnel often moved their residences away from the village and into the district town, which meant that they were no longer in the way of the insurgents, at least during the nighttime. The Diem government's previous domination of the villages began to crack like a clay urn that is struck repeatedly with a mallet.

As the shards of the urn began to fall away, the Viet Cong formed a new vessel to hold the contents. That new vessel was the Viet Cong shadow government. While the Communists ultimately intended to replace the old village governments entirely, they generally refrained from attempting a complete takeover at the outset, in order to avoid exposing themselves to sharp government counterattacks as had occurred at Ben Tre. In villages where the Communists made inroads, the Diem government maintained a certain presence in the villages during the day, and the shadow government conducted its business there at night. The political cadres of the Viet Cong shadow government redistributed the land belonging to landlords, and they collected taxes from all villagers. They created secret informant networks to gather information on the populace, the enemy, and even their own personnel, and organized surveillance teams to watch the fringes of the hamlets for approaching government forces. The shadow government's cadres served as guides for Communist military units and they supervised the transportation of war materials. Most important of all, the Communist cadres acted as recruiting agents. They preferred to recruit peasant boys in their late teens, since they were full of vigor, highly impressionable, childless, and wifeless. They sought out those from families that owned no land, since the Viet Cong's land reform polices held far more appeal for landless families than for landowners. Recruiters also concentrated on boys who already had relatives in the Viet Cong, as they were easier to sway and keep loyal, which helps explain why the Viet Cong were strongest in areas that had sent large numbers of Communists to the North in 1954, such as Quang Ngai, Binh Dinh, Kien Hoa, and the Camau Peninsula.[11] The cadres, in addition, recruited limited numbers of young women, nearly all of whom served as nurses or cooks.

To understand why a large portion of the Vietnamese peasantry was willing to join or support the Viet Cong, it is necessary first to understand the world of the Vietnamese peasant in the middle of the twentieth century. Whereas French colonialism had effected wide-ranging changes on the thinking of urban Vietnamese, the basic outlook of the peasant had changed little since the early centuries of Vietnamese history. As one Saigon newspaper editorialist observed, "Western civilization, which has profoundly influenced the townspeople, has only dug a ditch separating rural areas from cities."[12] The peasant's first loyalty was to his family. He venerated the bones of his ancestors, served his parents dutifully, and hoped that his children would remain to till his land after he was gone. His second loyalty was to his village, with his sense of community considerably stronger if he lived in Annam than in the Mekong Delta, a difference that stemmed from different settlement patterns. Hamlets in central and northern Vietnam were compact clusters, whereas hamlets in the Mekong Delta were frequently strung out along a waterway, resulting in less interaction among residents. To be held in high esteem by one's fellow villagers was the highest honor. To lose face by misbehaving or having one's children misbehave was the worst humiliation.

Although Viet Minh and then Diemist propagandists had swarmed over the countryside in recent years, the villagers remained largely indifferent to political developments beyond their village. Because few peasants had access to newspapers or books or radios, they could not follow external events, and in any case their hard work and their family life left little time for such concerns. Few knew the name of the Saigon government's district chief in their own district, let alone understood the tenets of Personalism or Diem's policies with respect to civil liberties. They knew nothing of Ho Chi Minh's transformation of North Vietnam's schools into indoctrination centers, or of the Cold War. While the Viet Cong insurgency was often described as a nationalist movement, there was actually little nationalism to be found within the peasant communities that provided most of the insurgency's local manpower. "The common people usually pay attention to facts," observed a high-ranking Communist defector. "The Viet Cong promise to give a good future to the people by advocating the liberation of the country, but the people only believe in immediate facts, in something they can enjoy right now. If you give the people what they want right now, that is, tranquility and wealth, you will win in the countryside and, consequently, win the war."[13] Only after young men had joined the movement did the Viet Cong's leaders persuade them to hate the unseen "American imperialists," and even then, the Viet Cong took care to temper nationalism with elements of Communist doctrine, for fear that raw nationalists might ultimately lose interest in the Viet Cong and side with Diem. "It is correct to arouse their national spirit," decreed the central committee of the Viet Cong's front organization, "but it is still a drawback if their class spirit is not evoked."[14]

Marxist-Leninist ideology did not draw the peasants into the Viet Cong any more than nationalism did, and in fact the Viet Cong purposefully deceived the peasants about Communism's tenets because they knew the peasants would recoil at the truth. A high-ranking Communist official explained, "If the Party were to say: in the future you will be a laborer, your land will be collectivized, you will no longer own any farm animals or buildings, but will become a tenant farmer for the Party or the socialist state – if the Party were to say that, the peasants would not heed them.... Indeed, Party cadres are instructed never to mention these things, because, according to the teaching of Lenin, the peasant is the greatest bourgeois of all: he thinks only of himself. Say one word about collectivism, and he already is against you."[15]

Some of the Viet Cong's detractors ascribed the movement's success in mobilizing the villagers to the threatened and actual use of force against peasants. The presence of armed Communists and the occasional execution of uncooperative civilians naturally had some influence on peasant behavior, but it was not the force that the Communists could employ against the citizenry that was most important in gaining the villagers' support. Developing the capability to kill civilians at will did not automatically enable the Viet Cong to obtain the cooperation of the people. What was crucial was the force they employed against the government. Like their ancestors, the villagers of 1960 looked at the power of the opposing forces when deciding which side held the mandate of heaven, and they almost invariably threw their support to the strongest, though they might reserve some support for the other side as a hedge against unforeseen changes. Military power and success and the sustained presence of troops in the village bestowed prestige, while military weakness and defeat and the sustained absence of troops from the village removed it. One report from the southern Communist headquarters explained, "Reality has shown that the stronger the armed activities, the more the political movement of the masses develops."[16] A Communist main force soldier from Tay Ninh province, when asked why young men joined the Viet Cong at the beginning of the insurgency, gave an answer similar to that of hundreds of other witnesses. "The Front was very strong at that time," he replied. "That was the main factor which made many join the Front."[17] Force, then, was crucial for two reasons: it weakened the enemy, and it brought supporters to the movement.

By virtue of the superior quality of its leaders, the Viet Cong possessed that other attribute essential to political success in Vietnam, good leadership. The peasants would follow men who were naturally charismatic, who demonstrated skill and determination, and who served the people fairly and without concern for their own interests. These were the traits of the good mandarin, whom the peasants, unlike the Westernized Saigon intellectuals, still revered. The Communists, employing traditional means to achieve radical ends, trained their personnel to conform to many traditions of the good mandarin, the same traditions that Diem wanted his officials to follow. The best officials on both Hanoi's side and Saigon's side operated as kindly despots, treating the people as their children, not as their brothers or their parents as some outsiders maintained. The peasants expected authoritarianism, and welcomed benevolent authoritarianism. Effective leaders on both sides quashed all opposition and forced people to join political organizations, while at the same time they helped the people with their labors and gave them kind advice. They induced Vietnamese men to trek through hot jungles with little to eat and dangerous insects clawing into their flesh, and to enter battles where only twenty percent of those injured managed to survive.[18]

Good Viet Cong leaders, like good mandarins and good South Vietnamese government officials, excelled at delivering propaganda, an essential task in mobilizing the village masses. Government officials had often maltreated Vietnamese peasants over the course of Vietnam's history, and yet the peasants, docile and fatalistic, had not organized large rebellions to end the abuse. Only an external elite, whether Le Loi or the Tay Son brothers or the Viet Minh or Ngo Dinh Diem's nationalists, could convince them to take up arms. Like the Roman mob of Julius Caesar's day, the Vietnamese peasantry was easily influenced by men with silver tongues, even if the words bore only a slight resemblance to the truth. A Viet Cong instructional directive explained:

> Daily the masses are oppressed and exploited by the imperialists and feudalists and therefore are disposed to hate them and their crimes. But their hatred is not focused; it is diffuse. The masses think their lot is determined by fate. They do

not see that they have been deprived of their rights. They do not understand the purpose and method of the Revolution.... Agitation-propaganda work is necessary to stir up the masses, to make them hate the enemy to a high degree, to make them understand their rights and the purpose and methods of the Revolution, and to develop confidence in our capability.[19]

The Communists spent innumerable hours, day and night, explaining to the peasants that the government was evil and that the liberation movement would provide them a better life. Propaganda could achieve little when the Viet Cong had little else to offer, but it proved highly effective when the Communists could back it with strong evidence that they were superior in leadership or strength. Typical was the case of Le Van Toan, a young man in Kien Hoa province whom the Viet Cong recruited into their ranks even though they had killed his father, a peasant of rather modest means who had worked for the government. Toan said that his decision to join the Viet Cong had much to do with the fact that "the Government side was weak then, and the Viet Cong side was strong." But the Viet Cong's propaganda also played a crucial role. Toan recalled that the Viet Cong "talked very well, even to the point that people who worked for the GVN followed them and accepted their ideas.... They talked to a point where they could convince us that our father did a wrong thing, and I came to hate my father, even though I didn't know what he had done."[20] Lam Ngoc Phu, a Communist Party member and soldier in Phong Dinh province, remembered that the Viet Cong had swayed him and many other villagers with propaganda decrying a poorly led Self-Defense Corps unit, which had been taking poultry and fruit from the people without compensating them. The Communist propagandists, Phu recounted, "spoke very well and very much. I don't remember all they said. Their words scratched just where you were itching. Every time my hamlet had anything which troubled people, the VC took advantage of that and proselytized."[21]

In 1960, the Communists differed from their South Vietnamese opponents not in how they tried to influence the villagers or how the villagers responded to their political ideas, but rather in their capacity for putting large numbers of austere and skilled leaders into the field. Local Viet Cong leaders, in general, were more willing to help the poorer peasants and less likely to harm the citizenry, except for those whom they classified as "reactionaries." A farmer from An Xuyen province, for example, commented that the Communist cadres "are much better than the GVN. They keep strict discipline and never take anything away from the people. When they come to your house, they go to the kitchen and help your wife or to the garden to help you do whatever you do."[22] When asked why villagers supported the Viet Cong, a Viet Cong sympathizer from Binh Dinh province observed, "When they come to your village, you don't have much choice, because they're armed, but you later learn how kind they are and that they don't mistreat you." The Viet Cong did chores for the elderly and showed respect for the people, while the government's forces were not respectful, and "for this reason the villagers will aid the Viet Cong, tell them when ARVN is coming, and help them hide."[23]

Much of the credit for the generally high quality of the Viet Cong's cadres belongs to the leadership skills of Ho Chi Minh and the base of followers he had built up during the 1940s and 1950s. In Vietnam, whether North or South, every organization was a porous pyramid. The leadership that was poured in at the top filtered down into all of the lower sections. If the leadership inserted at the top was of high quality, the whole pyramid would glow with vigor, for good leaders generally picked good subordinates and supervised and motivated them appropriately. If the leadership at the top was poor in quality, the pyramid would rot. Ho and Diem both made their pyramids glow, giving their governments higher levels of integrity and efficiency than most Asian governments of the day. Ho's pyramid, however, glowed more brightly in 1960 because he could fill the echelons of the pyramid with individuals of higher quality than could Diem. Whereas Ho Chi Minh had been able to replace the colonial-era officials of northern Vietnam with experienced Communist followers, Diem still had to rely heavily on ineffective holdovers from the colonial era, whose maximum wattage was rather low. Before he could replace most of the inferior threads in the fabric, Diem would need a couple of more years to train enough young men of strong personality and instill them with mandarin selflessness. Ho Chi Minh, moreover, did not have to contend with the factionalism peculiar to the southern third of Vietnam, sparing him from many difficulties in the areas of leadership selection and command that Diem faced.

The ranks of the Vietnamese Communist leadership also benefited from the use of radical methods to alter the very character of cadres and soldiers. The Communist Party went to great lengths to destroy the primary concerns of the traditional Vietnamese man, namely himself and his family, in order to facilitate devotion to the revolutionary cause and prevent corruption. The Communists termed this preoccupation with the self and the family "individualism," indicating the lack of separation between the self and the family in the minds of the Vietnamese peasants. "The worst and most dangerous vestige of the old society is individualism," Ho Chi Minh once remarked. "It is necessary to build a socialist and a communist man; to have a socialist man and a communist man, it is necessary to shape the socialist ideology and the communist ideology; and to have the socialist and communist ideologies, it is necessary to wipe out individualistic and bourgeois thoughts."[24] Expanding upon the dangers of individualism, a Party study document observed:

> People affected with individualism, when the revolution encounters difficulties, when it meets the increasingly terroristic enemy, when the movement in the villages temporarily withdraws, are very agitated, no longer have confidence, bring up questions of food, are only concerned with their own life, do not think of the people or the Party or the movement. They will abandon the work, even the Party cells; they will abandon the revolution.[25]

To eliminate individualistic thoughts, in the Party's view, it was necessary to sever the man's familial ties. The Southerners who spent the years 1954 to 1960 in the North had already undergone this process. One such Communist said of his time in the North: "Sometimes we were very lonely and wanted to go home to see our families and friends. But we learned after a while not to be lonely, and learned to find strength in our revolutionary struggle. We learned not to think much about our families any more. We learned not to miss our families any more – like Ho Chi Minh."[26] New Viet Cong recruits either were sent to distant provinces, or else were prohibited from living with their families and were inundated with so much work that they had little time to spend with relatives. The Party redirected the natural force of kinship by forming a new "family" composed of the soldiers and cadres. Cells with between three and seven members constituted the "family units," and each cell had a leader who acted as the family head, guiding the others and making sure that they acted properly. With these techniques, the Communists consistently succeeded at replacing "individualism" with a mandarin-like austerity and a zeal for the Party. One Communist commented that among the Viet Cong, the "family bonds seem to break up" over time, and "their new family is their comrades at work." The Viet Cong "have no time to think of religious worship or family burdens, but only the cause of the whole people; it is called by the Party the supreme cause. It becomes a kind of faith everyone has to stick to in order to be saved."[27]

The traditional respect for armed strength and good leadership guided the peasant's political behavior more than anything else. In some places, however, the villagers could not decide whom to follow according to these criteria because neither the Viet Cong nor the government enjoyed clear superiority.[28] Under such conditions, one side might tip the balance by offering material benefits to the villagers. The Saigon government could provide expensive public works projects and agricultural aid. The government paid its employees and let them live with their families either at home or in a guarded compound, whereas the Viet Cong typically lived in jungles or caves, separated from their relatives and short on food and money. The Viet Cong, on the other hand, performed more work for the villagers than did the government. The most compelling benefit that the Viet Cong offered the people, though, was the redistribution of land to landless families, a policy based on exploiting the peasant "individualism" that the Communists secretly despised. Most South Vietnamese peasants remained unaware that the Vietnamese Communists had used land ownership in North Vietnam only as a temporary expedient and had collectivized land after the war, as had the Russian and Chinese Communists before them.

One well-known Communist training document emphasized the critical role of land reform in XB village, a village of 6,000 people in Kien Phong province. At the beginning of 1960, the Party killed some of the village notables and government security agents, but failed to eliminate the government's presence in the village or attract a mass following to the Party. The Communists subsequently distributed propaganda emphasizing that the defeat of the government would give the villagers ownership of their land. As a result, the Communists developed a large following and the village council and many other government supporters fled the village in fear, although a government militia post remained. "The main interest of the farmer of XB village is in land," the study concluded. "In its political and armed struggle, in its administration of the rural area, and in other revolutionary tasks, the Party knew well how to make use of the farmers' interest in land. On it we built a mass movement."[29]

It should be noted that the Saigon government did defend some of its villages very effectively during 1960, thanks to active opposition to Communist intrusion by some government leaders. In areas populated by groups long hostile to the Communists, most notably the Catholics, the Hoa Hao, and the Cao Dai, the government offered particularly stiff resistance. Furthermore, the shock of the Viet Cong's early successes did cause some improvements, top-down in nature, on the government side. Making numerous changes among his officials, Diem replaced bunglers with men of lesser experience or less certain loyalty who would stand up to the Viet Cong. In conjunction with Nhu, Diem began to build the "Republican Youth," a large corps of young men who would undertake political and paramilitary action in the villages.

Huynh Trung Lien, a former Communist Party cadre, remembered that the Communists gained influence in his village at a time when the government's village officials were very selfish and unjust. "Almost every one of them took advantage of their power to oppress the people," Lien recalled. "They worried about their own interests and about the interests of their relatives and of their cliques." Among other things, these individuals stole construction materials earmarked for public projects, thrashed peasants for petty reasons, and carelessly shelled the hamlet when they received reports of Viet Cong activity. The peasants initially held the view that "if a good official is assigned to our village, then tell yourselves you have been lucky. If a bad one comes over to rule us, well, it's only bad luck! We have to accept any fate which befalls us." Lien and other Viet Cong cadres, however, began to gain supporters by holding propaganda sessions in which they denounced the abuses of the government and urged the villagers to join the insurgency. The situation changed when the Saigon government appointed a new district chief, who halted the wanton shelling of hamlets and frequently spoke with the peasants himself to promise better performance on the part of the government. This chief "was very skillful in dealing with the villagers," Lien said. "He became famous in a very short time. At the third month of his incumbency his renown as a good man had spread over the countryside and made the village chapter [of the Communist Party] very uneasy." Lien remarked that "my job of propagandizing for the Front ran into more and more difficulties and the villagers no longer seemed willing to listen to my speeches."[30]

As it became evident that the Civil Guard and Self-Defense Corps could not contain the insurgency in much of the country, Diem began assigning counter-guerrilla tasks to elements of the regular army. By the spring, twelve South Vietnamese Army infantry regiments were dedicated entirely to counter-guerrilla operations.[31] The army fared better than the Civil Guard and Self-Defense Corps, but they could not stop the guerrillas entirely, either. The Viet Cong normally tried to avoid contact with the regular army, knowing that the army usually had more men and weapons than the guerrillas could handle. The regulars seldom could engage the Viet Cong, except when the Viet Cong attacked, for want of intelligence; although the army had much better equipment than the Civil Guard and the Self-Defense Corps, it did not have extensive familial and neighborly contacts among the local populace as the militia did. Some army units had first-rate leaders, but others did not, further stunting their ability to gather intelligence and seek out the enemy. Other agencies were not inclined to give the army information because Diem had deliberately fragmented the intelligence organizations.

The ineffectiveness of the army's early counter-guerrilla operations produced every imaginable accusation and recrimination on both the South Vietnamese and the American sides. Diem and his generals replaced some of the infantry commanders and created several new units. Ambassador Durbrow blamed General Williams for the South Vietnamese Army's inadequate counter-guerrilla training and for its tendency to operate in big units and on the roads, two practices that violated accepted counterinsurgency doctrine. Fiercely resenting Durbrow's latest encroachment into military affairs, Williams denied these charges and assigned blame to the South Vietnamese. Williams pointed out that South Vietnam's generals had ignored his repeated, albeit not insistent, suggestions to conduct counter-guerrilla training, and that when South Vietnamese officers had been handed American training manuals on the subject, they tended to put them on the shelf without reading them.[32] South Vietnam's generals had little time for counter-guerrilla training because Diem required them to employ their troops almost continuously in military operations, guard duty, or construction projects. Diem might have ordered his commanders to devote substantial time to counter-guerrilla training had Williams urged it emphatically, but Diem, and Williams, had intended that the Civil Guard and Self-Defense Corps – which Durbrow had done much to undermine – would take care of most counterinsurgency tasks. Durbrow, moreover, had overemphasized the importance of counter-guerrilla training. While such training was useful, many of the army's officers had learned how to fight guerrillas during the last war, and the rest could learn the basics of guerrilla warfare in the field, as the concepts were fairly simple. Of much greater importance than training were leadership and intelligence.

Durbrow advanced the inaccurate argument that the conventional design of the South Vietnamese army prevented the army from dividing itself into small units and operating on foot. The dissolution of the conventional army, in any case, would have been the greatest folly, for such an army was an absolute necessity given the Communists' ultimate ambition to conduct decisive main force operations, and given the Communists' inability to win without such operations. The one valid criticism that could be made of the South Vietnamese Army's conventional character was that conventional training inclined some Vietnamese officers to conduct large and elaborate military operations in places where the Viet Cong lacked large units. The better option, under these conditions, was to disperse the forces and conduct smaller operations, as dispersed forces could cover more territory and were more difficult for the enemy to detect in advance.

For much of 1960, Durbrow and Williams would tangle over the size and armament of the South Vietnamese armed forces. Diem was pushing for U.S. funding of an additional 20,000 troops in order to carry out a multiplicity of tasks. His government needed soldiers to guard the villages where most of the people lived, the towns that served as the centers of governmental power, the installations that supported the military effort, and the roads that permitted rapid military and commercial movement. Other troops were needed to chase the insurgents around the countryside. Prudence required that still other troops patrol South Vietnam's western border to watch for infiltrators and raiders, and that main force units occupy the highlands and the far north as protection against a North Vietnamese invasion. Diem was, in addition, pleading with the Americans for more equipment. The situation required more helicopters and C-47 transports and L-19 observation planes, Diem believed, as well as amphibious vehicles to fight in the swamps of the Mekong Delta and patrol boats to prevent Communist supply vessels from reaching his shores. Diem also asked for communication equipment, noting that the army had only sixty percent of what it needed.

General Williams favored the addition of 20,000 soldiers and large increases in equipment expenditures, but Ambassador Durbrow argued that such additions were unnecessary. The main problem, Durbrow contended, was not a lack of troops or money, but rather Diem's direction of the government. "There are at present sufficient security forces in the country to meet the problem," Durbrow lectured Diem. "If all the security forces were properly trained, particularly in anti-guerrilla operations, there would be no need for additional forces."[33] It was true, as Durbrow said, that the Diem government was somewhat inefficient in combating the insurgency, but the principal weakness of the armed forces – the quality of its leaders, not its training – could not have been eliminated because too few good replacements were available. If it had been solved partially by eliminating loyalty as a selection criterion, then the stability of the Diem government would have been put at great risk. In light of the Viet Cong's rapid growth, a troop increase and dramatically higher U.S. material assistance were in order. Durbrow's opposition, however, ensured that neither would occur in 1960.

Durbrow did come around to the view that the militia units, which he had done much to emasculate, deserved greater American support. In February, he agreed to the use of U.S. Special Forces personnel in training the Civil Guard, and in the second half of the year he supported the upgrading of the Civil Guard's weaponry, the transfer of the Civil Guard to the South Vietnamese Department of Defense, and the reassignment of Civil Guard training responsibilities to the U.S. military mission. Durbrow, however, did not attempt to resuscitate the Self-Defense Corps after having canceled its funding at the beginning of the year, presumably because the Civil Guard could be improved more quickly and could cover more territory.

The insurgent campaign of 1960 was, on the whole, a remarkable success. The Viet Cong crippled the government's rural apparatus in many places, and large swathes of the countryside came under Viet Cong influence, above all in the areas that had sent men and boys to the North in 1954 for training. The agrovilles, particularly vulnerable because of their large size, were subverted or ransacked. Diem had to scrap the agroville program entirely after completing only twenty-two of the fortified villages. In some parts of the country, the government was left in control of only the district and provincial capitals, which the Communists could not readily capture because they were packed with government troops and policemen. Viet Cong recruitment in the countryside was quite productive, though the Viet Cong's armed forces remained small in comparison with those of the government. By the end of the year, the Viet Cong fielded nearly ten thousand armed troops.[34]

In Hanoi, these achievements did not generate high spirits as might have been anticipated, for the North Vietnamese were confronted with several unsettling developments during this period. In some areas of South Vietnam, effective resistance from the Diem regime was inhibiting the insurgency's development. Little progress had been made in areas of religious fervor, and the entire northern section of South Vietnam – consisting of both the central lowlands and the central highlands – had largely remained free of Communist penetration. The Central Party Committee in Hanoi, bemoaning the lack of success in the highlands, wrote to its subordinate branch in the South in the spring of 1960: "We have seen no mention of the building of a base area in the mountain jungle region in the cables we have received." The Central committee demanded that the Southern committee "devote a great deal of attention to this issue" and emphasized that a base area had to be established before the Communists could station and supply large military units in the highlands.[35] Towards the end of 1960, government forces dealt the Viet Cong a number of defeats in the highlands.[36]

North Vietnam faced continued pressure to restrict the violence from the Chinese and Soviets, who feared the wrath of Eisenhower. The Chinese told the North Vietnamese in May that South Vietnam should be liberated, but through a protracted war involving political as well as military struggle, rather than through a decisive military campaign. "There is no question of winning political power immediately," the Chinese remarked. "Even if Diem is overthrown, unification cannot be achieved right away, for the U.S imperialists would never agree to that."[37] The Soviets advised the North Vietnamese to provide only limited covert support to the Viet Cong because they doubted that "the United States and the bloc of SEATO nations could allow the unification of Vietnam on democratic foundations and thus agree to the loss to the socialist camp of such a first-class strategic position as South Vietnam."[38] For the North Vietnamese, the only consolation was that the Chinese and Soviets satisfied their requests for large loans, over 500 million yuan from the former and 350 million rubles from the latter.[39]

Another cause for unhappiness in Hanoi during 1960 was the widening of the Sino-Soviet split. At a meeting between the Chinese and the Soviets in February, a Chinese delegate insinuated that the Soviets were allowing the United States to drive a wedge between the Communist powers, inciting Khrushchev to declare that Mao was "a pair of worn-out galoshes standing discarded in a corner."[40] In July, the Soviets abruptly withdrew all of their technicians from China and slashed aid to Mao's government. An alarmed Ho Chi Minh implored Khrushchev and Mao to resolve their differences, with a warning that continued disagreements between the Soviet Union and China could be exploited by the "imperialists."[41] When Liu Shaoqi stormed out of an international conference of Communist parties in November 1960 following a row with the Soviets, Khrushchev turned to Ho for help. Ho prevailed upon Liu Shaoqi to leave his hotel, where he had gone to pout, and return to the conference building. Near the end of the conference, it was Ho Chi Minh who had to bring the two sides together. The Chinese and Soviets could not agree on a conference declaration, so Ho asked both parties to compromise, and he succeeded in getting Chinese and Soviet leaders, after much wrangling, to hammer out a solution. The façade of Communist unity was preserved.[42]

The most serious blow to Hanoi's plans occurred at a place far removed from the meeting rooms of statesmen, and from the villages where the insurgents were clashing with Diem's men. In early March, two South Vietnamese Army regiments and some Civil Guard units began sweeping through the area between Cua Viet and Cam Lo, near the demilitarized zone. According to the Communists, these operations were the first to disrupt the traffic on the Ho Chi Minh Trail. During May, the South Vietnamese government used 10,000 troops to sweep through Route 9 in western Quang Tri province, the northernmost province of South Vietnam, and then it sent an Army regiment and two Civil Guard companies into the region between Route 9 and the demilitarized zone. In the words of a Communist historian: "During these difficult days hundreds of revolutionary agents and revolutionary civilians were exposed and murdered, and many of our commo-liaison warriors went to their eternal rest. . . . The trail was exposed and was cut at many points." Unable to hold back the government forces, the North Vietnamese withdrew

the transportation troops of the 301st Battalion into North Vietnamese territory temporarily, hoping to induce the enemy to relax its stranglehold on the
trail.

The Diem government's forces in the area did not let up. After two months,
nevertheless, North Vietnam's leaders decided that they could not afford to
hold infiltration operations in suspense any longer. "The rainy season began,
and the need to support South Vietnam grew more pressing every day, every
hour," stated a Communist source. "Unable to delay any longer, we were forced
to resume the use of the old trail." The passable routes, this source noted, were
now guarded by "a thick network of enemy bases and outposts where the enemy
conducted continuous sweeps" and by new militias that "sprang up in the villages south of Route 9." On many occasions, Communist troops that tried to
move south in significant numbers found their way blocked. The transportation cadres and soldiers soon reached the dire conclusion that "the covert,
secret way is no longer workable. We will have to fight our way through –
either that or seek another route."[43] Unless the Vietnamese Communists could
reopen an infiltration channel, the insurgency would die, deprived of the necessary men and equipment. In order to build main force units, they required
more rifles and machine guns than the insurgents could steal from the enemy,
and while the villagers could be trained to serve in support roles or as local
guerrillas, it was not easy to make them into main force soldiers. The Communist regular forces would not grow much faster than the rate of infiltration
from the North into the South.

As the end of the year came near, the Vietnamese Communists concluded
that victory would be neither quick nor easy. At the Third National Congress
of the Vietnamese Communist Party in September, the Central Committee
acknowledged: "Our patriotic countrymen in the South are still encountering
many difficulties. The U.S. imperialists and the Ngo Dinh Diem clique resort
to all perfidious and inhuman measures to frantically undermine our people's
cause of national liberation. Therefore, the revolutionary struggle of our people
in the South will still be long and arduous." During the congress, the Party
leadership outlined new long-term initiatives that would contribute to the
protracted struggle. As a remedy for unsatisfactory economic performance in
the North, the Party put forth an ambitious five-year economic plan in the style
of Soviet plans, involving further rapid industrial expansion and a reduction
in military expenditures.[44]

It was at the Third Congress that the Central Committee decided to create a front organization in the South on the model of the Viet Minh, for
the purposes of gaining additional adherents and convincing unsuspecting
Vietnamese and foreigners that an independent collection of South Vietnamese
dissidents, not the Vietnamese Communist Party headquartered in Hanoi, was
running the insurgency.[45] To create the front, sixty of the Party's top officials
in the South met on December 20 near the Cambodian border, inside a secret

complex of small buildings that was hidden from view by dense jungle foliage. Adhering to Hanoi's dictates, the assembly officially established the National Liberation Front (NLF) and produced the organization's founding document, which declared the Front an independent organization representing all elements of society that sought to "overthrow the disguised colonial regime of the U.S. imperialists and the dictatorial Ngo Dinh Diem administration, lackey of the Americans." According to the founding document, the Front was fighting for civil and political liberties such as "freedom of opinion, of the press, of assembly, of association, of movement" – none of which could be found in North Vietnam. It also called for liberal, rather than Communist, economic reforms; when land was redistributed, the original landowners would receive fair compensation for the land, aside from those who could be described as "agents" of the "U.S. imperialists."[46]

Communist cadres would hold all of the important leadership positions in the National Liberation Front, and the Front would operate under the direct control of the Southern branch of the Communist Party, which was to be renamed the "People's Revolutionary Party" and portrayed as an independent party. Neither Hanoi's control over the Communists in the South nor any other substantive aspect of the Vietnamese Communist Party was changed. A Communist directive described the underlying rationale for altering the name: "If the Party Chapter for South Vietnam openly kept its old name, identifying it as a Party Chapter of the Labor Party of Vietnam under the leadership of the Party Central Committee in North Vietnam, then our enemies, both domestic and foreign, could utilize that to spread distortions and accusations that North Vietnam was intervening to overthrow South Vietnam, and this would cause problems for North Vietnam in its struggle to gain support for South Vietnam from the standpoint of international legalities."[47]

The Communists had operated for so long in the South that few South Vietnamese were tricked into believing that the National Liberation Front or the People's Revolutionary Party were different from the previous organizations subservient to the Vietnamese Communist Party in Hanoi. The Front's propaganda, however, would take hold in some foreign quarters, particularly in the West. During the remainder of the war, large numbers of Western scholars, journalists, politicians, and students were to claim that the National Liberation Front was led by a coalition with many non-Communist members and that it was not under North Vietnam's control. This development came as a pleasant surprise to the Communists, as they had not predicted that their ploy would fool so many people. Later in the war, the American scholar Jeffrey Race showed two high-ranking Communist defectors some Western articles and books asserting that the southern guerrillas were independent of Hanoi. The defectors, who did not know each other, found these publications "very amusing," Race observed. "They both commented humorously that the

Party had apparently been more successful than was expected in concealing its role."[48]

*   *   *

IN 1960, THE NEWEST AND MOST LUXURIOUS HOTEL IN SAIGON WAS THE Caravelle. Located in the heart of the city across from the Opera House, it stood ten stories high, which made it look like the Empire State Building in comparison with the rest of Saigon. Foreign dignitaries and journalists mingled on the open-air rooftop bar, where they enjoyed an unobstructed view of the city in all directions. Eighteen South Vietnamese oppositionists gathered at the hotel on April 26, 1960 to give the international press a written critique of Diem, an occasion that some observers would interpret as a manifestation of widespread disillusionment. Seven of the eighteen were physicians, and most of the others were men who had served in high positions during the colonial era. All were prototypical Saigon intellectuals, imbued with European ideas and out of touch with the vast majority of their countrymen. The Caravelle Manifesto, as the document became known, called on Diem to remove ineffective officials and eliminate political favoritism in the administration and army, but most of its complaints concerned the absence of democracy and the silencing of oppositionists. "Today the people want freedom," the manifesto stated. "You should, Mr. President, liberalize the regime, promote democracy, guarantee minimum civil rights, recognize the opposition so as to permit the citizens to express themselves without fear, thus removing grievances and resentments, opposition to which now constitutes for the people their sole reason for existence."[49]

Diem and Nhu scoffed at the Caravelle Manifesto and its authors as they did at Saigon intellectuals in general, pointing out that the choice of an air-conditioned luxury hotel as the venue of publication showed how detached the authors were from the masses. The Ngo brothers, and some other observers as well, were suspicious about the similarities between the Caravelle Manifesto and the recommendations that the American embassy was making at this time. Also suggestive of American complicity was the unanimity with which the Saigon intellectuals stated their case, very out of character with their usual internecine strife. No firm evidence emerged at the time, but these suspicions were confirmed years later by Durbrow, who divulged that certain Americans had helped write the manifesto.[50] Durbrow wanted to use the manifesto as evidence of "popular discontent" with the government's "repressions," which would strengthen his argument that Diem had to liberalize in order to obtain "popular support." Durbrow proceeded to hold the Caravelle Manifesto over Diem's head while prodding him to enact liberal reforms.

Just one week after the issuance of the Caravelle Manifesto, Durbrow found yet another reason to criticize Diem. The ambassador received word that the Saigon government, in conjunction with the government of Thailand, had armed one hundred men with French weapons and sent them on a raid into Cambodia. Aside from the Diem government's illiberalism and inefficiency, the issue most galling to Durbrow was Diem's policy of supporting indigenous opponents of the Cambodian government. Prince Norodom Sihanouk, Cambodia's head of state, had enraged Diem by permitting the Vietnamese Communists to use Cambodian territory as a base for operations into South Vietnam, and by laying claim to lands that Diem considered to lie on his side of the border. Durbrow recognized that Diem had legitimate grievances, and, in fact, had asked Sihanouk to kick the Vietnamese Communists out, though without result. Nevertheless, Durbrow wanted Diem to seek better relations with Cambodia, not court opposition elements inside Cambodia.

Rushing to see Diem, Durbrow accused the South Vietnamese President of serious wrongdoing and delivered a very blunt scolding. Diem, appalled that the envoy of his principal ally would utter such words, replied, "I am more concerned with conditions here than in Washington because I see a deterioration between Vietnam and the U.S. based on such false reports." Afterwards, when the Americans were gone, Diem burst into a rage over Durbrow's reprimand. The President was "white with anger," observed Nguyen Dinh Thuan, one of Diem's top executives.[51] Durbrow, meanwhile, wrote to Washington that because "efforts to persuade Diem to see the evils of his ways have been to little or no avail," the United States needed to begin punishing Diem until he changed his ways. Durbrow recommended denial of equipment requests from Diem that were currently under consideration.[52]

Durbrow did not know that Edward Lansdale was following the situation in South Vietnam from his desk at the Pentagon, where he now held a relatively unglamorous Defense Department job. Lansdale was reading the cable traffic between Washington and Saigon and receiving secret letters from General Williams, who was lauding Diem and deploring Durbrow's proposal to deny the equipment requests. Armed with information from Williams, Lansdale told high Defense Department officials that Durbrow's scheme would not cause Diem to do what the ambassador wanted but would instead make him even less cooperative. In one memorandum, Lansdale remarked: "There are few chiefs of state who would sell their nation's honor for a handful of helicopters and swamp boats, and Diem surely is not one of them."[53]

Durbrow's dire message and Lansdale's ripostes brought Vietnam to the attention of the highest authority in the United States. On May 9, at the 444th meeting of the National Security Council, President Eisenhower heard the views of top officials. Robert Amory of the CIA opened hyperbolically with the claim that Diem's government was "crumbling" as the result of dissatisfaction with his "one-man rule." Outside of the government, Armory went on to say, criticism of Diem "is becoming stronger, as indicated by a recent manifesto made public in Saigon by a group of former officials who called for extensive political reforms." Evidently, Amory did not know of the American role in producing the manifesto. Amory also commented, incorrectly, "Diem is not in direct touch with the people since he seldom goes out into the countryside to see the people and talk with provincial leaders."[54] Livingston Merchant of the State Department remarked, "I hope that what happened to Syngman Rhee in Korea will give Diem pause." A few weeks earlier, student revolts had forced Rhee from his position as South Korea's premier.

These dour assessments, however, failed to convince Eisenhower that Diem was a poor leader or that he ought to be bullied. "Diem seems to be calm and quiet and to have an attractive personality unlike Rhee," the President said. "The U.S. ought to do everything possible to prevent the deterioration of the situation in South Vietnam."[55] Heeding the recommendations of Lansdale and Diem's other staunch backers, Eisenhower forbade any efforts to threaten Diem with aid cuts.

For several months thereafter, Durbrow abstained from further calls for punishing or pressuring Diem. At the same time, Diem began to take some of the actions the ambassador was promoting, which delighted Durbrow but failed to persuade him that there existed better ways than pressure to influence Diem. Diem eased tensions with Cambodia, created an improved economic plan, weeded out corrupt officials, and even made public appearances of the sort that an American politician would make. On August 30, in a cable to the State Department, Durbrow lauded Diem for taking these actions and called him the "only dedicated anti-Communist nationalist leader in sight." Yet just a few weeks later Durbrow's insatiable appetite for "reforms" returned to the forefront, with Durbrow warning Washington that if Diem did not undertake dramatic acts of liberalization, the United States might need to consider "alternative courses of action and leaders." Durbrow proposed a long list of demands that included appointing one or two oppositionists to the cabinet, disbanding the secret Can Lao Party, reducing press restrictions, and giving more authority to the legislature. Durbrow also recommended asking Diem to transfer Nhu to a foreign diplomatic post where he would lose all influence. "Rumors about Mr. and Mrs. Nhu are creating growing dissension within country and seriously damage political position of Diem government," Durbrow notified Washington. "Whether rumors true or false, politically important fact is that more and more people believe them to be true."[56]

Diem's advocates pounced on Durbrow's proposed demands. William Colby, who had become the chief of the CIA's Saigon station in June 1960, argued that the reforms ran so contrary to the nature of Vietnamese government and society that they would fail utterly. Colby faulted Durbrow and other Americans for obtaining most of their information on Vietnamese public opinion from English- or French-speaking intellectuals in Saigon's tea shops, who reinforced the tendency of some Americans to equate South Vietnam's politics with those of America.[57] Lansdale derided the proposal to appoint opposition leaders to the cabinet, arguing that no members of the opposition had sufficient popularity or skill, and that Diem needed men of definite fidelity in dangerous times. In reference to the recommended ouster of Nhu, Lansdale wrote, "the proposal is to cut off the President's 'right arm.' What is proposed as a substitute? This is the key second half to any constructive move, and it is missing from the proposal." Running down the list of possible substitutes, Lansdale indicated that none would be as good as Nhu. Lansdale argued that Durbrow's proposals for the Can Lao, the press, and the legislature ignored the need for extensive planning and for U.S. assistance. If the reforms were attempted without such preparation, Diem's support network might collapse, the press would cause serious harm to the government, and an inexperienced legislature would open a Pandora's Box through its public criticism of the chief executive.[58]

Lansdale and Colby, however, proved unable to derail Durbrow and his State Department allies in Washington. On October 7, the State Department authorized the ambassador to take his liberalization proposals to Diem, and Durbrow did so at the palace one week later. Reading to Diem from a typed memorandum, Durbrow expressed serious concern about "what to us seems to be a decline in the popular political support of your Government," and then listed the measures he had presented to Washington. Diem had little to say during the meeting, other than to note that while such changes had merit in theory, they would be difficult to implement in such troublesome times.[59] Diem knew that most of what Durbrow was advocating would harm rather than help South Vietnam, but he also knew that his country was dependent on American support, and so in the following weeks he took some actions to appease the ambassador. He made four changes to his cabinet, three of them involving the key ministries of Defense, Interior, and Information. He allotted more power to the National Assembly, replaced incompetent local officials, and granted more freedom to the press. Durbrow, however, still did not think Diem was doing enough, and he warned Washington that unless Diem reformed the military and centralized his intelligence programs, he would not be able to compete with the Viet Cong.

Very early on the morning of November 11, three battalions from the South Vietnamese Airborne Brigade climbed into armored vehicles and drove off into the dark. The paratroopers at first thought that they were heading to the countryside for an engagement with the Viet Cong. While they were motoring along, however, officers told the paratroopers that they were heading to the palace to rescue the President from a mutiny by the Presidential Guard.[60] The vehicles were indeed destined for the palace, but the Presidential Guard had not mutinied and the only coup attempt that would take place would be spearheaded by these very paratroopers. Among the leaders of the coup were several paratroop colonels who were dissatisfied with Diem because of his inability to stop the Viet Cong insurgency and his favoritism towards staunch loyalists in the officer corps. The ringleader was the thirty-seven-year-old commander of the Airborne Brigade, Col. Nguyen Chanh Thi, characterized by the CIA as "an opportunist and a man lacking strong convictions," and by a U.S. military adviser as "tough, unscrupulous, and fearless, but dumb."[61] The chief civilian conspirator was a wealthy Saigon lawyer named Hoang Co Thuy. It is possible that Ambassador Durbrow or another American who was disenchanted with Diem encouraged the conspirators to revolt – South Vietnamese rebels generally avoided acting without American assurances of support – but no solid evidence of such encouragement has surfaced.[62]

The paratroopers raced down the wide boulevard leading to Independence Palace and arrived in front of the palace at 3:30 A.M. Their objective appeared far more imposing than anything they had faced before, as the palace was surrounded by a high wall, a fence, and a collection of guard posts. Jumping out of the trucks, the paratroopers quickly assembled for an attack on the front gate. Some of the men began charging forward while others provided covering fire, peppering the front of the palace with rifle and machine gun rounds. Most of the palace windows shattered immediately, and the walls began to fill with tiny craters.

Opposing the paratroopers were a mere sixty men from Diem's Presidential Guard, half of them stationed in the building itself and the other half scattered in the posts around the building. But the Presidential Guard had some of South Vietnam's best troops, and they defended their positions with great skill and tenacity against the elite Airborne Brigade. Most of the assaulting paratroopers were gunned down before they made it over the fence, and those who did clear the fence suffered the same fate before getting much farther. The attack stalled. The rebels brought reinforcements to the palace by truck, and the assault resumed at 7:30 A.M. The Presidential Guard again held the attackers at bay with their deadly fire. At 8 A.M., the rebels brought forward five armored vehicles. Circling the palace slowly, they fired blasts at the perimeter posts, while rebel mortars lobbed shells at the defenders, producing terrific, although not especially damaging, explosions on the palace lawn. At 10:30 A.M., the fighting slackened, with the palace still in the hands of the Presidential Guard.

The Diem regime very nearly met its end at the outbreak of the attempted coup. Just seconds after the rebel assault commenced, a .50 caliber machine gun positioned in the nearby Palais de Justice streamed bullets into Diem's bedroom window, one inch above the surface of his bed. Diem had been lying in this bed moments earlier, and he would have been riddled with bullets had he not arisen to get a soda from his refrigerator just before the silence ended. Once Diem heard the bullets tearing apart his bedroom, he located Nhu and Madame Nhu, who went with him into the palace's barricaded wine cellar. They were soon joined by Brigadier General Nguyen Khanh, the thirty-three-year-old army chief of staff, who had been sleeping at his home five blocks from the palace when the battle started. The plotters had tried to arrest Khanh, but they did not know that he had moved to a new house just a few weeks earlier. Awoken by the gunfire, Khanh had driven his car towards the palace, managing to evade the rebel paratroopers despite the fact that the chief of staff flag was fluttering above his hood. Pulling up to the rear entrance of the palace, General Khanh learned that the Presidential Guard was under orders from Nhu to keep the gate shut under all circumstances, so he jumped out of his car, scaled the palace wall, and rushed inside. He was soon coordinating the palace defenses with the help of the Civil Guard's deputy director, Ky Quan Liem, who had reached the palace by bluffing his way past the paratroopers.

Aside from the palace, the rebels had taken all of their main objectives: the headquarters of the Joint General Staff, the central offices of the police, the Presidential Guard barracks, Tan Son Nhut airport, and Radio Saigon. Rebel troops had captured most of the army's top generals, which meant that relief forces would have to be summoned from outside Saigon. Khanh sent an urgent message over the Civil Guard net to Colonel Tran Thien Khiem, the commander of the Fifth Military Region, instructing him to bring his Second Armored Battalion to the center of the capital immediately. The battalion's tank crews warmed up their engines, then sped off from their base, which was located at My Tho, forty miles to the southwest of Saigon. Two of Colonel Khiem's infantry battalions would follow them. Khanh also convinced troops from the 7th Division at Bien Hoa to leave for Saigon, and acting Marine Commandant Le Nguyen Khang agreed to send the 1st and 2nd Marine Battalions to assist the President.

At 2:10 P.M., Assistant Secretary of Defense Nguyen Dinh Thuan phoned Durbrow. He informed the American ambassador that forces from My Tho and Bien Hoa were coming.

"Is the intention to use these troops to try to relieve the Presidential Palace?" Durbrow asked.

"I think so," Thuan said. "Do you consider this a good idea?"

"I hope that the Revolutionary Committee and President Diem can get together and agree to cooperate, as a civil war could only benefit Communists," Durbrow replied. "If one side or the other has to make some concessions in order reach an agreement, I believe that would be desirable in order to ensure unity against the Communists."[63] Durbrow was indeed worried that armed conflict would undermine South Vietnam's national cause, but he also favored compromise for another reason that he did not share with Thuan. At this moment, it was unclear which side would prevail if the fighting escalated, so if Durbrow backed one side over the other and that side ended up the loser, the United States would have a hostile government on its hands.

Unfortunately for Ambassador Durbrow, he ended up alienating Diem anyway with his waffling. Diem now had mutinous soldiers literally in his front yard, yet Durbrow was telling him to give in to the demands of the traitors and let them go unpunished. Governments had always responded with force to armed attacks by traitors, and in few places had they done so done with as much regularity or brutality as in Vietnam. Never again would Diem would have anything but contempt for Durbrow. Later in his life, Durbrow himself decided that he had erred in giving less than full support to Diem, for he began to claim that he had never taken such a position. In 1984, while questioning Durbrow about the coup attempt, a State Department historian asked whether the Embassy had backed Diem completely, adopted a neutral stance, or supported the rebels, to which Durbrow answered that he had been "100 percent in support of Diem."[64]

In the early afternoon, one of the rebel colonels called General Khanh to request a meeting. Khanh agreed to meet in an hour, which bought precious time. Before the hour had passed, the lead vehicles of Khiem's 2nd Armored Battalion, consisting of twelve tanks, two half-tracks, and an armored car, rolled into the center of Saigon. Convincing the paratroopers that the battalion was on the rebel side and had come to relieve them, the task force's commanding officer made his way past the paratroopers and surrounded the palace. The paratroopers collected their gear and began to leave their fighting positions.

Khanh proceeded to the wide boulevard that had been the axis of the initial attack, and there he met with the rebel colonel. Diem must step down, the colonel said, and turn control over to the military. Khanh replied that he would see what he could do. Returning to the palace, Khanh informed Diem, Nhu, and Madame Nhu of these demands. Attaching exaggerated importance to the spectacle of rebel paratroopers and protesters surrounding the palace, Khanh recommended that Diem resign. "It is the will of the population and all the armed forces," Khanh said.

According to Khanh's recollection, Madame Nhu burst out, "No, no, never! You have to kill all of the paratroopers!" Another witness recalled that Madame Nhu paced the floor and told Diem that if he were really the man destined to save the country, he should reject all rebel demands. She wanted him to fight, even it meant that she would die.[65]

Frustrated with Madame Nhu's intransigence, General Khanh got up from the table and snapped, "All right, if you want to take my place, take command. I'm leaving now."

Diem told Khanh to remain, then said to Madame Nhu, "You are tired; we fought too much last night. You'd better get some rest."[66] Madame Nhu withdrew, and Khanh stayed. Expressing agreement with the rebels' basic principles, Diem instructed Khanh to organize a provisional government and mend the troubles between the Airborne and the rest of the army. In addition, Diem had Khanh transmit an offer of negotiation to the plotters. At this same time, the Americans were telling the coup leaders to negotiate a compromise and avoid fighting, for the same reasons they had been pushing this advice on Diem. Confronted with American pressure and unable to take the palace, the rebel leadership accepted the Diem government's offer to conduct negotiations. Both sides consented to a ceasefire.

During the negotiations, Diem informed the rebels that he would create a new government on the condition that he remain the chief of state. Bending little, the rebels said that while they were willing to let him remain in the government, he would have to surrender all real authority. To prevent a halt in the negotiations, Diem slowly offered concessions. If he could buy enough time, friendly troops would flood Saigon, and then at the very least he would not have to accept a settlement under duress. During the night, the Vietnamese Navy was busy ferrying elements of three army divisions, including Colonel Nguyen Van Thieu's 7th Division, across the Saigon River. Rangers from Tay Ninh were on trucks headed for Saigon. If Diem did have any real desire to reach some sort of compromise with the rebels, it began to evaporate because of demonstrations of bad faith by the coup leaders. Over the public radio waves, at 9:00 P.M., the rebels made the false claim that Diem had capitulated, presumably with the intention of winning other military commanders over to the rebel side. In the wee hours of the morning, nevertheless, Diem agreed to create a coalition government in which the generals would have considerable say, and at 6:20 A.M. he announced the arrangement over Radio Saigon.

Just as Diem's message was playing over the radio, rebel troops opened fire on the palace with machine guns and mortars. The intensity of the shooting slackened after ten minutes, but it continued at a lower pace for several hours afterwards, until mid-morning. In radio announcements broadcast throughout the morning, the rebels exhorted the Saigonese to appear at the palace to protest against the Diem regime. Several hundred civilians gathered in front of the palace to shout anti-Diem slogans and wave "Diem must go" banners. A far greater number of civilians gathered in the shady mall next to the palace to watch the confrontation. Colonel Thi addressed the demonstrators. The best way to defeat the Diem government, he explained to them, was to charge the palace. Energized, the mob rushed toward the palace, with high expectations that in some unclear fashion they could change things for the better. Col. Khiem's 2nd Armored Battalion, which still ringed the palace, was determined to protect the palace from all threats. When the unruly mass of protesters came near, tank commanders and soldiers opened fire. Thirteen civilians perished and many more sustained wounds. The rest scattered immediately.

Shaken by this slaughter and by fresh reports of loyalist reinforcements heading towards the palace, Ambassador Durbrow phoned Diem. Durbrow warned that Diem had to put an immediate stop to the shooting, or else "the entire population will rise up against both loyalists and rebels, and the Communists will take over the city. If a bloodbath is not avoided, all of Vietnam will go Communist in a very short time." Durbrow said that he was "extremely perturbed" by the convergence of additional loyalist troops on the palace and their apparent intention to defeat the rebels by violent means.

Diem responded that the rebels had given his troops no choice but to fight, having breached the ceasefire early in the morning and urged Saigon's citizenry to assault the palace. He said he would try to prevent a bloodbath and then said goodbye.[67] At this juncture, Diem had no intention of following the advice of Durbrow, especially since loyal forces now outnumbered the rebels in the city center by a wide margin. The 5th and 21st divisions and other loyalist units received orders to go into battle against the paratroopers. Loyalist troops shot rockets into the central rebel camp, which had been set up in the fifty-acre park behind the palace, and charged. Faced with overwhelming numbers of hostile troops, and now aware that they were part of a coup attempt, the paratroopers offered little resistance. Many of the rebels ripped off their red neckerchiefs, which the coup leaders had issued to the rebel units for identification purposes, and tried to mingle with civilians or loyalist forces. Pro-Diem army units also advanced on the headquarters of the Joint General Staff, the airport, and the police headquarters.

At 2:00 P.M., the leading plotters told their troops to stop fighting and disperse. A dozen of the officers raced to Tan Son Nhut Airport, clambered aboard a C-47, and took off for Cambodia, where they were given asylum by Prince Sihanouk, ecstatic at the opportunity to help Diem's enemies. Crowds of Diem supporters converged on the palace to cheer the President, and civilians quickly filled Saigon's streets, talking cheerfully with the soldiers and thanking them for not looting the city. Contrary to Durbrow's dire predictions, the use of force against the rebels and their civilian allies had not resulted in massive slaughter or harmed Diem's standing with the people or the army. Once again, the Americans had been wrong and Diem had been right, a fact that Diem would remember better than would the Americans.

Diem's success in putting down the insurrection, however, gave him little pleasure. During the days after the coup, in fact, Diem uncharacteristically flew into brief fits of rage in front of his relatives and Vietnamese friends, shouting curses upon his enemies. Much of this anger was directed at Durbrow, because of not only the ambassador's conduct during the putsch but also his renewed lecturing afterwards. Just hours after the defeat of the rebellion, Durbrow arrived to tell Diem that he needed to treat the rebels with lenience, in order to "unify all elements of the country." Diem shot back, "You apparently do not understand that the rebels caused much blood-letting. Many innocent people were killed and many innocent people were duped." The leaders who had misled the paratroopers had to be punished, Diem insisted. Durbrow did concede that "maybe a small number of leaders should not go without some punishment."[68]

Diem subsequently learned that some other notable Vietnamese and American figures had opposed him or refused to support him during the crisis, and unlike Durbrow these individuals could readily be removed from the scene. In the middle of the insurrection, the oppositionist Dr. Phan Quang Dan had declared himself political adviser to the mutineers, spoken in their favor on

Radio Vietnam, and staged a press conference during which a paratrooper grabbed Diem's picture off the wall, ripped it into small pieces, and trampled on the bits. Diem had Dan thrown in jail. General Le Van Kim, whom the rebels had named as premier during the fighting, was put under house arrest for an extended length of time. Saigon's gossip circuit was abuzz with rumors that the plotters had also been in cahoots with General Duong Van Minh, known as "Big Minh" to Westerners because he stood much taller than most of his Vietnamese countrymen. General Minh had failed to come to the besieged President's defense during the fighting and instead had sat idly in his garden, watching his orchids grow. Diem would soon shuffle Minh off to a job where he would no longer wield power.

Diem also found out that two Americans, George Carver and Russ Miller, had spent most of the coup with the plotters, leading him to suspect that Durbrow had sent them there to encourage the conspirators, although in reality the embassy wanted them there simply to facilitate communication between embassy officials and the plotters. Apparently, Diem also learned of Carver's prior friendship with the coup leaders, and he may have been informed that Carver arranged for Hoang Co Thuy's escape from the country when the coup fizzled. Both Diem and Nhu hinted to high-ranking American officials that the situation would be much improved if Carver were deported. "All nations conduct espionage," Nhu told Colby, "and this is not a matter to get upset about. But what no nation can accept, and our government no less, is interference with its political authority and processes."[69] On November 20, Carver opened his mailbox to find a death warrant in his name, purportedly sent by the leaders of the failed coup, which accused him of retracting promises of American support after the coup's prospects soured. When Carver showed the document to Colby, the CIA chief guessed that Nhu was behind it, but he did not worry about its authorship. He thought the ploy was amusing, and that it "looked like a real easy answer." Showing the death warrant to Nhu, Colby said that in order to protect Carver, the United States had decided to remove him and his family from South Vietnam. Nhu looked at the note solemnly, then commended Colby on his wise decision and arranged for armed policemen to escort the Carver family to their departure flight. "Everybody's face was saved," said Colby.[70] Diem was upset, to a lesser extent, with other American officials besides Durbrow and Carver and Miller, and with some American journalists, because these individuals had voiced support for the revolt, which they had interpreted as a popular uprising against an illiberal regime. After talking with high South Vietnamese and American officials in the aftermath of the putsch, a visiting American envoy observed that these expressions of support for the rebels "have been extremely damaging to U.S. interests in Vietnam."[71]

Some Americans, on the other hand, had backed Diem completely, as would be the case in all of Diem's confrontations with rebels. One was Lieutenant General Lionel C. McGarr, who had replaced General Williams as head military adviser a few months earlier and had been in communication with both the rebels and the loyal Army commanders during the insurrection. After the coup, McGarr attributed the defeat of the rebellion to the "courageous action of Diem coupled with loyalty and versatility of commanders bringing troops into Saigon." McGarr believed that "Diem has emerged from this severe test in position of greater strength with visible proof of sincere support behind him both in armed forces and civilian population."[72] In Washington, several important U.S. officials sided openly with Diem and criticized Durbrow for his insistence that Diem compromise with the rebels. "It is most doubtful," Lansdale argued, "that Ambassador Durbrow has any personal stature remaining. Diem must feel that Durbrow sided with the rebels emotionally. Perhaps he even feels that Durbrow's remarks over the months helped incite the revolt. Thus, it would be useful to get Durbrow out of Saigon."[73] General Lyman Lemnitzer, the chairman of the Joint Chiefs of Staff, remarked, "When you have rebellious forces against you, you have to act forcibly and not restrain your friends. The main point is that sometimes bloodshed can't be avoided and that those in power must act decisively."[74]

For the moment, however, it would be Ambassador Durbrow who determined America's policy in South Vietnam. Viewing the coup as proof that Diem was "unpopular," Durbrow exerted maximum pressure on the South Vietnamese President to change his ways.[75] Once again Diem undertook some changes to please Durbrow, beginning with the addition of two posts to his Cabinet and the creation of a new command system for the army. He allowed the creation of an opposition party called the Popular Anti-Communist Front, although it would not accomplish anything of note before the government disbanded it seven months later. Diem incarcerated only a few of the coup leaders, as Durbrow had urged. Ultimately he brought forty-four people to trial, of whom nineteen would be acquitted and twenty-five would receive prison sentences lasting between five and eighteen years. But, as had happened time and again, Diem's actions failed to satisfy Durbrow. The ambassador told Diem that the situation demanded further liberalization, and he cabled Washington that unless Diem's performance improved quickly, "we may well be forced, in not too distant future, to undertake difficult task of identifying and supporting alternate leadership."[76] Now, however, Durbrow had reached the end of his tether, which was beginning to shrink. Assistant Secretary of State for Far Eastern Affairs J. Graham Parsons cabled Durbrow, "Believe for present Embassy has gone as far as feasible in pushing for liberalization and future exhortation likely be counterproductive."[77]

Diem, unaware as he was of the taming of Durbrow, faced a situation at the end of 1960 that would have broken the spirit of many men. His American allies had recently displayed a disturbing dearth of loyalty. The Viet Cong, who had been nearly powerless at the beginning of the year, had by force of arms and personality formed a strong insurgency by year's end. Diem's governing apparatus in the provinces, troubled from the beginning by leadership problems and by weak and ill-conceived U.S. assistance, had suffered bruises and broken bones. And Diem did not know the seriousness of the problems that faced Ho Chi Minh.

As the end of the year approached, the Vietnamese Communist Party developed a plan to restore its lifeline to the South. Because Diem had proven so effective in controlling the South Vietnamese territory abutting the demilitarized zone, the Party's Central Military Committee decided to construct a new Ho Chi Minh trail outside of the two Vietnams, in eastern Laos.[78] By entering Laos from North Vietnam and traveling southwards before hooking back into South Vietnam, North Vietnamese troops and porters could bypass Diem's stout defensive line near the demilitarized zone and territory to the south of the demilitarized zone that was well-suited to defense. Diem's forces might be discouraged from entering Laos by American pressure and by the distance between their bases and the Laotian route, just as they had been discouraged from moving into Cambodia to attack Communist sanctuaries. To reach the new trail, moreover, South Vietnamese forces would have to cross the Annamite mountain chain, which ran from north to south in the Laotian border region and had only a few good passes. Building a trail in Laos was, nevertheless, an option the North Vietnamese would have preferred to avoid. It would require the suppression of Laotian rightist forces, and it carried a substantial risk of provoking the United States. But it was the only way that North Vietnam could get desperately needed personnel and equipment to the southern insurgents.

A landlocked kingdom twice the size of the state of New York, Laos had no railroad and only thirty-five hundred miles of road. With just two million inhabitants, it had a far smaller and weaker population than the powerful, aggressive nations surrounding it. Officials in Washington who knew little about Indochina often suggested that various measures be taken to "seal" South Vietnam's border with Laos in order to prevent the inflow of men and equipment, as one might button up a boat to keep the water out. In reality, however, it was impossible to seal off this border if the infiltrators possessed unfettered access to the full length of Laos, not to mention its southern neighbor of Cambodia, which infiltrators in Laos could readily enter. The long border region between South Vietnam and Laos consisted largely of impenetrable mountains and deep valleys, and it was coated with dense vegetation. Neither South Vietnam nor its allies had enough troops to patrol this area, plus the Cambodian-Vietnamese border region, intensively enough to stop more than a small fraction of the infiltration. The jungle foliage left scarcely a square inch of the ground visible from the air, precluding aerial monitoring. Even in the latter part of the 1960s, when the United States sent half a million troops and the world's best intelligence technology to Vietnam, North Vietnamese men and materiel continued to flow in abundant quantities across South Vietnam's 900 miles of border with Laos and Cambodia. In 1960, the South Vietnamese had to protect only their front door on the north, but if the North Vietnamese entered Laos, the walls on the western side of their house would collapse, leaving them to defend an enormous gap against foes that could appear immediately out of the darkness at almost any point.

The provisions of the 1954 Geneva agreement pertaining to Laos had called for a cessation of hostilities and the removal of foreign military forces from Laotian territory. That fact had not stopped the Pathet Lao – the Laotian Communists – from continuing covert and violent subversion against the government, nor had it caused the Vietnamese Communists to withdraw their advisers who were working with the Pathet Lao. Laotian rightists and neutralists vied with the Communists and with each other for power, and control of the central government bounced back and forth between rightists and neutralists. Eisenhower aided the rightists of General Phoumi Nosovan in the name of containing Communism. The neutralists, led by Souvanna Phouma, received some American support as well, but at times they cooperated with the Pathet Lao, who were led by Souvanna's own half-brother, Prince Souphanouvong. The Laotian Communists received extensive training, support, and guidance from the Chinese as well as the North Vietnamese, both of whom worried that Laos would become an anti-Communist military base and hence a threat to their security and a major obstacle to the conquest of Southeast Asia.[79] In March 1958, large numbers of North Vietnamese Army soldiers and cadres began entering Laos to provide support to the Pathet Lao.[80]

On August 9, 1960, the neutralist paratroop officer Kong Le overthrew a rightist government and put power in the hands of Souvanna Phouma, who then formed a neutralist regime. The United States chose to continue supporting the rightist forces of the ousted General Phoumi, which led Souvanna to accept aid from the Soviets, cooperate with the Pathet Lao, and make goodwill trips to Beijing and Hanoi. The North Vietnamese appear to have played no role in instigating the upheaval in Laos, but once the process began they did their utmost to encourage it along, for it came at the ideal moment from the standpoint of relocating the Ho Chi Minh Trail. Clearing eastern Laos of anti-Communist forces would be much easier for Hanoi with the Laotian government in sympathetic hands.

The neutralists and the Pathet Lao proved unable to drive out the rightist armies on their own. To advance the cause of moving the Ho Chi Mihn Trail, therefore, the North Vietnamese in late 1960 sent large numbers of combat troops into Laos. North Vietnamese units entered into large battles with the rightists for the first time, fundamentally changing the nature of the conflict. With the exception of the fierce mountain tribesmen known as the Hmong, who had a small rightist army underwritten by the United States, the Laotians were not a warlike people; when they fought, it often bore more resemblance to a shoving match between preening teenaged boys than a clash between armies. The rightist forces, aside from the Hmong, showed little appetite for pressing the attack or enduring great hardship. The Laotian Communists and neutralists were similarly weak. When large North Vietnamese units attacked the rightists at the end of 1960, their fierce resolve and their reputation for military prowess usually caused the rightists to panic and run away. Explaining why the military situation suddenly turned against the rightists, the chief North Vietnamese military adviser in Laos reported, "all the victories over the [rightist] armies have been achieved by us. The [neutralist] troops and the Pathet Lao armies have served us but a cover, that is, a mask."[81]

General Phoumi, refusing to be intimidated by North Vietnamese victories over his rightist forces, launched a drive to take the capital city of Vientiane, which was far from North Vietnam and the North Vietnamese troop concentrations. This move induced China and the Soviet Union to unite in support of the neutralist government, revealing that the two big Communist powers were still willing to collaborate on vital tasks in the struggle between communism and its opponents. The Chinese urged the Soviets to send arms to Souvanna for the city's defense, and the Soviets immediately sent howitzers by rail into the Chinese city of Nanning, where they were then loaded aboard black Soviet airplanes and flown to the Vientiane airport for delivery to Souvanna's forces. North Vietnamese troops landed by parachute to stiffen the neutralists and the Pathet Lao. But it was too little and too late. Souvanna's government was forced out of Vientiane, and the Laotian king turned the government back over to the rightists.

Just two days after Souvanna's departure from Vientiane, a North Vietnamese battalion and two Pathet Lao battalions attacked Nong Het, a town in northern Laos near the North Vietnamese border. The Hmong soldiers guarding the town repulsed the first Communist assaults. Hanoi hurriedly brought up reinforcements from the 324th Division and built a 10 kilometer-long road from Muong Xen to Nong Het so that Communist units could tow their artillery up to the edge of the Hmong base camp. The Communists attacked again on December 28, and after three days of fighting they took Nong Het. At this same time, a joint Pathet Lao-North Vietnamese force took Lang Khang in southern Laos.[82] Pathet Lao, North Vietnamese, and neutralist forces began converging in an attempt to cut Laos in two. The Americans considered the situation so serious that they evacuated Vientiane.

On the last day of the year, Eisenhower met with his advisers to discuss the crisis. The United States, he said, should seek British and French support and alert the SEATO Council. Then the United States should warn the Soviets that it was positioning forces to defend the Laotian government and was prepared to fight a major war if necessary. At the end of the meeting, Eisenhower pronounced: "We cannot let Laos fall to the Communists, even if we have to fight – with our allies or without them."[83] Had the Laotian crisis reached this stage at an earlier date, Eisenhower most likely would have set in motion the deployment of U.S. forces into Laos. But with only a few weeks left in his Presidency, he decided to leave the decisions on Laos to the President who would have to see the policy through, a man whose will and ability to wage a war in Laos was a matter of dispute.

CHAPTER 5

Commitment

1961

AS A MEMBER OF THE AMERICAN FRIENDS OF VIETNAM, SENATOR JOHN
F. Kennedy became a great admirer of Ngo Dinh Diem, seeing him as just the type of independent nationalist needed to carry out the struggle in Vietnam. Delivering the keynote address at the organization's 1956 conference, Kennedy lauded "the amazing success of President Diem in meeting firmly and with determination the major political and economic crises which had heretofore continually plagued Vietnam." South Vietnam was an experiment aimed at finding an alternative to Communism in Asia, Kennedy said, and the United States "cannot afford to permit that experiment to fail." Vietnam "represents the cornerstone of the Free World in Southeast Asia, the keystone to the arch, the finger in the dike."[1] Kennedy's views on Diem would change somewhat over time, but he would never lose his respect for Diem or his conviction that the United States had to preserve South Vietnam.

During the Eisenhower years, John F. Kennedy derided the administration's strategy of "Massive Retaliation," believing that it left the United States ill-prepared to fight or support wars of lower intensity, especially wars against Communists in the developing nations of Latin America, Asia, and Africa. It was foolhardy to risk nuclear war over such conflicts, Kennedy argued, and it was pusillanimous to avoid getting involved and letting the Communists prevail. Kennedy preferred "Flexible Response," a strategic approach conceived by General Maxwell Taylor, according to which the United States would broaden its range of military capabilities so that it could meet any enemy challenge without having to bring the country to the brink of nuclear war. Flexible Response dictated a dramatic expansion of America's conventional and unconventional military forces for use in counterinsurgencies and other limited conflicts. Kennedy had a great enthusiasm for counterinsurgency that substantially exceeded his understanding of the topic. In his mind, counterinsurgency involved daring commando raids by soldiers armed with poisonous darts and hand-held rockets, rather than a difficult and laborious undertaking in which success depended heavily on local people and circumstances. Counterinsurgency appeared to acquire additional importance when, a few weeks before Kennedy's inauguration as the nation's thirty-fifth President, Nikita Khrushchev boasted that the Soviet Union would support pro-Communist "wars of national liberation" in current and former colonial areas.

The youngest elected U.S. President, and the second youngest President after Theodore Roosevelt, Kennedy brought youthful energy and charm to an institution normally associated with gray-haired gentlemen in dark suits. He was not, however, a man of ideological fervor. On the ideological plane, anti-Communism exerted the most influence on him, and he took a much greater interest in that subject than in the domestic concerns of his fellow Democrats. Possessing faith in brains and youthful vigor over experience and accumulated knowledge, Kennedy and his followers believed that they could toss out what they termed the "so-called wisdom" of the old and create a new order unencumbered by what had come before. They were, Kennedy said, the men of the New Frontier.[2]

Kennedy's selection for the job of Secretary of Defense, Robert Strange McNamara, was the prototypical New Frontiersman. Blessed with a high level of analytical ability and a terrific memory, McNamara had received an MBA from the Harvard Business School and had also taught as an assistant professor at the school. During World War II, McNamara served as a statistician for the Army Air Corps, and at the end of the war he and a collection of other young Army statisticians went to work for the Ford Motor Company, where they became known as the "Whiz Kids." They brought to Ford a potent combination of cleverness and energy. Henry Ford II took a liking to them because they produced results, enabling Ford to take back market share from General Motors and reap record profits. Several of them were to rise to high positions inside the company. Of all the Whiz Kids, it was said, McNamara whizzed the fastest. He impressed Henry Ford II with his remarkable analytical talents and his ease in recalling any and every statistic in support of his arguments. And McNamara said it all with infinite self-confidence, giving him the appearance of infallibility in the eyes of the unwary. In October 1960, Robert McNamara became the president of the Ford Motor Company at the age of forty-four, the first man to attain that rank without the blood of the Ford family in his veins.

When, two months later, President-elect Kennedy offered McNamara the position of Secretary of Defense, he replied, "I am not qualified." But Kennedy, attaching little importance to the issue of experience, did not relent. "We can learn our jobs together," Kennedy said. "I don't know how to be president, either."[3] McNamara thought it over for a few days, then expressed a willingness to accept the offer under certain conditions. He would have to be given complete control over appointments in the Defense Department, and he would have to be free of obligations to attend Washington social events. McNamara had never cared for cocktail parties and formal dinners, viewing them as impediments to his workaholic schedule. Kennedy agreed to these conditions, and Robert McNamara became America's eighth secretary of defense.

Kennedy appointed McGeorge Bundy as National Security Adviser. A brilliant man and a prodigy, Bundy had become the dean of Harvard's Faculty of Arts and Sciences in 1953, at the age of just thirty-four. He was a systematic thinker who could pull all the extraneous fuzz off an issue and get to the crux of the matter, a quality much prized by Kennedy. If anyone was smarter and more analytically rigorous than McNamara, it was McGeorge Bundy. For the position of Secretary of State, Kennedy chose Dean Rusk, who at various times had been a Rhodes scholar, Army officer, college dean, Assistant Secretary of State for Far Eastern Affairs, and foundation executive. McNamara, Bundy, and Rusk would be the President's most influential advisers on national security affairs for the next six years.

Kennedy and his New Frontiersmen set out to reconstruct the machinery of the government. The Eisenhower administration had been overburdened with cumbersome bureaucracies and stodgy old men, they thought. Kennedy swept away the layers of bureaucracy and instead relied on his own smarts, a few sharp sidekicks, and small task forces composed of New Frontiersmen. Rather than operating on the basis of a grand strategy for handling world affairs as Eisenhower had, Kennedy would employ an ad hoc approach to problems, albeit one based on the general principle of containing communism. McGeorge Bundy was given an office in the White House basement and a staff of intelligent young men to take over many of the roles of Eisenhower's National Security Council staff. McNamara revamped the Defense Department using a cadre of similarly bright young civilians who, like McNamara and his compatriots at Ford, were dubbed the "Whiz Kids." They intended to impose on the Pentagon the same sort of statistical rigor and ruthless economic logic that had worked so well at Ford, whether the slow-moving Pentagon liked it or not. McNamara and the Whiz Kids believed, as well, that they should make important military decisions that the armed services had made heretofore, claiming that their high IQs and their academic theories trumped real-world experience.

Kennedy began his administration by proclaiming from the front of the Capitol, "Let every nation know, whether it wishes us well or ill, that we shall pay any price, bear any burden, meet any hardship, support any friend, oppose any foe to assure the survival and success of liberty."[4] In Saigon, South Vietnamese leaders took heart at these words, and eagerly awaited the translation of the rhetoric into deeds. Kennedy began the translation swiftly, acting on two key reports on South Vietnam that he received as soon as he took office. One had been prepared by the Country Staff Team Committee, an interagency group headquartered in the Saigon embassy. Entitled the Basic Counterinsurgency Plan, the report stated that although Diem was taking more and more steps to improve the counterinsurgency effort, he needed to do much more or else South Vietnam would suffer defeat in the coming months. The document listed a variety of political, military, and economic reforms that Diem needed take, most of them designed to increase the efficiency of existing programs and the government's treatment of the villagers; Washington's rebukes at the end of 1960 had forced Ambassador Durbrow to set liberalization aside. The Country Staff Team also recommended increasing the South Vietnamese armed forces by at least 20,000 men and investing additional money to improve the Civil Guard, at a total cost of forty-one million dollars.[5] Ambassador Durbrow had dropped his previous objection to the expansion of the South Vietnamese military because of the heightened Communist activity in Laos.

The other report came from Edward Lansdale, who at the end of 1960 had finally received permission to visit Vietnam after prolonged efforts by Ambassador Durbrow and the State Department to keep him out.[6] Upon completing his tour of Vietnam in early January, Lansdale reported that South Vietnam was in "critical condition" and required "emergency treatment." Diem remained irreplaceable, Lansdale argued, noting that the opposition lacked constructive ideas. Lansdale observed that the city people were full of gripes about Diem even though they were wealthier than ever before, while the people in the countryside, who had considerably less wealth, were much more supportive of Diem. "Many of the Vietnamese in the countryside who were right up against the Viet Cong terror were full of patriotic spirit," stated Lansdale. "Those who seemed to be in the hardest circumstances, fighting barefoot and with makeshift weapons, had the highest morale. They can still lick the Viet Cong with a little help." Lansdale called for a shift from an adversarial relationship with South Vietnam to an amicable relationship based on mutual respect, which would allow the Americans to regain their influence with Diem. This change, in Lansdale's view, required the immediate removal of Ambassador Durbrow. "The next time we become 'holier than thou,' we might find it sobering to reflect on the Democratic Republic of Vietnam," Lansdale remarked. "Do the Soviets and the Chinese Communists give Ho Chi Minh a similar hard time, or do they aid and abet him?"[7]

Early on the last Saturday morning of January, Lansdale received a call from the White House. "Get down here right away," McNamara told him. President Kennedy, who had previously developed an admiration for Lansdale in the course of reading *The Ugly American*, was impressed by the observations and recommendations in Lansdale's report, and wanted to hear more.[8] Brought before Kennedy and a collection of senior officials, Lansdale reiterated the need for action in Vietnam and for a new ambassador. So taken was Kennedy with Lansdale's criticisms of Durbrow that he promptly decided to remove the ambassador and began considering Lansdale as a possible replacement. Kennedy also asked Lansdale whether the new administration should make a show of its support for Diem. Yes, Lansdale said, it would work wonders.[9]

Lansdale's report and comments helped convince Kennedy to allocate additional resources to Vietnam. Two days after his talk with Lansdale, Kennedy approved the 20,000-man increase in the South Vietnamese Army and the strengthening of the Civil Guard recommended in the Basic Counterinsurgency Plan. Thus did Flexible Response show the first signs of taking hold in Vietnam, reversing Eisenhower's policy of holding down military assistance to the South Vietnamese government.[10] Kennedy also ordered the CIA to send guerrillas into North Vietnam to stir up trouble for the Communists, although these efforts were to be small and largely unproductive.[11] As far as America's own counterinsurgency capabilities were concerned, Kennedy was already pushing for higher spending on elite troops specially trained for counterinsurgency, as well as on conventional forces.

Kennedy's initial moves had little effect on the course of the war in Vietnam. During the first half of 1961, government forces were showing modest improvements in aggressiveness and military competence, and they scored several major victories over Viet Cong forces in the spring, shattering large Communist formations in the delta and the provinces around Saigon. But most of the negative trends of 1960 persisted. The regular army continued to undertake large operations based on insufficient intelligence, and it still suffered from poor organization and coordination. Few government militiamen patrolled at night or defended the villages, preferring instead to button themselves up inside forts or the nearest district or provincial capital. In April, General McGarr estimated that Diem controlled only forty percent of the countryside, and that eighty-five percent of Diem's forces were tied down in static positions, a further indication that government forces lacked the intelligence information or the resolve to undertake more active counter-guerrilla measures.[12] American suggestions aimed at correcting these problems largely went unheeded. The Viet Cong's military forces continued to grow rapidly through recruitment and infiltration, and they conducted more guerrilla attacks than before. Soon they would weaken Diem's hold on the countryside to such an extent that the South Vietnamese government's rice surplus disappeared. During Diem's nine and a half years in office, he fared poorly in the struggle for the villages during only two years: 1960 and 1961.

From Hanoi's viewpoint, on the other hand, the war was not going nearly as well as it might have, either. The Viet Cong, in spite of their accumulating achievements, still remained far from destroying the South Vietnamese regime, which retained a large reservoir of armed strength. "We have been able to carry out our policy of gradually peeling away the enemy's strength and in fact have been able to peel away an initial layer," Le Duan explained in an April letter. "This is only the initial step," for the Diem government's "military forces are still virtually intact." Le Duan noted that the South Vietnamese army continued to carry out orders and was not going to collapse on its own. Communist forces, therefore, would have to destroy the South Vietnamese Army before they could take over South Vietnam. Le Duan instructed the Southern Communists to put greater emphasis on the military struggle.[13]

While Kennedy invested considerable time and money into Vietnam during his first four months in office, the problem that most concerned him at that time was not Vietnam but Laos, where the Communists were continuing to make major advances. At the beginning of 1961, Hanoi sent large elements of the North Vietnamese Army 325th Infantry Division and a number of additional North Vietnamese battalions to fight in Laos, raising the size of the North Vietnamese expeditionary force to 12,000.[14] North Vietnamese, Pathet Lao, and neutralist forces seized several strategic locations from the rightists, including the Plain of Jars, a high plateau in northern Laos containing the highway from North Vietnam to the Laotian cities of Vientiane and Luang Prabang. As the North Vietnamese had hoped, Diem did not send big South Vietnamese units into Laos to interfere with the Communists' activities.

The gravity of the Laotian crisis became clear to Kennedy during a meeting on January 19 between the new President and his Cabinet appointees and Eisenhower and his Cabinet. Secretary of State Christian Herter, who had replaced the dying John Foster Dulles in 1959, explained that the Laotian rightists had proven unwilling to fight, and that although Asian SEATO members favored military action in Laos, the French and British refused to take part, severely undermining the integrity of the alliance. "The Thais, the Philippines, the Pakistanis, who are counting on SEATO for their own self-defense against Communist aggression, are concerned that SEATO is a paper tiger," Herter commented. In Herter's view, the only option for the United States was to undertake military commitments in Laos as mandated by SEATO.

Kennedy asked Eisenhower whether the creation of a coalition government with Laotian Communist participation would be preferable to U.S. intervention alongside SEATO countries. Eisenhower replied, "It would be far better to intervene through SEATO." He pointed to the failed coalition government in China during the Chinese Civil War as evidence that such a government would flop. With the departure of the French from Indochina and the increase in America's presence, Eisenhower now considered Indochina worthy of the sort of U.S. ground commitment he had shunned in 1954. "The loss of Laos would be the loss of the 'cork in the bottle' and the beginning of the loss of most of the Far East," Eisenhower warned. "If Laos were lost to the Communists, it would bring unbelievable pressure to bear on Thailand, Cambodia and South Vietnam. Laos is of such importance that if it reached the stage where we could not persuade others to act with us, then I would be willing, as a last desperate hope, to intervene unilaterally." The odds of intervention leading to a major war were very low, Eisenhower estimated, for the large Communist powers did not want to go to war with the United States over Laos.

"If the situation was so critical, why didn't you decide to do something?" Kennedy demanded.

"I would have," Eisenhower replied, "but I did not feel I could commit troops with a new administration coming to power."

McNamara asked about the U.S. government's capabilities for fighting a "limited war," which in 1961 connoted a war where the United States sought objectives short of complete destruction of the enemy and did not use all of its weapons, such as the Korean War. Eisenhower said that he did not like the term "limited war." It was better, he said, to "go after the head of the snake instead of the tail."[15]

Kennedy decided that he would first attempt to save Laos militarily without the introduction of U.S. ground forces, by bolstering the Laotian rightists and inspiring them to determined military action of the sort that the Eisenhower administration had been unable to elicit. General Phoumi launched a new offensive against the Communists during February, but suffered a string of defeats. In March, the Pathet Lao joined with Laotian neutralist and North Vietnamese forces in a major counterattack, pushing Phoumi's forces back and taking territory of critical strategic importance. Nothing other than a very short amount of time now stood between the Communists and complete control of Laos. Kennedy would have to rush U.S. ground forces into Laos if he wanted to guarantee a non-Communist future for the country.

Eisenhower had been correct when he argued that SEATO or the United States could intervene in Laos without having to fight a big war with the Soviets or Chinese. The Soviets were not particularly concerned with Southeast Asia at this time and did not want a war. China was reeling from the failure of what it called the "Great Leap Forward," an experiment in social engineering that had caused thirty million deaths and cut the nation's birth rate in half.[16] The departure of Soviet experts in 1960 had crippled China's nascent industries, and the Chinese were still haunted by the Korean War and its heavy costs. China, moreover, had no nuclear weapons at this time. The only scenario in which the Chinese might have considered fighting in Indochina involved the massing of U.S. forces near China's border with North Vietnam or Laos. The Americans did not need to get so close to China; the most important part of Laos from the American standpoint, namely the potential infiltration routes from North Vietnam to South Vietnam, lay in southern Laos.

U.S. intervention, however, was fraught with other dangers. The French and the British, two key members of SEATO, remained unwilling to participate in military operations in Laos. With 12,000 North Vietnamese troops already in Laos and further large North Vietnamese troop insertions possible, Kennedy would need to commit multiple divisions of American troops and risk substantial casualties. If the North Vietnamese or Chinese did move large numbers of troops into Laos, the Joint Chiefs warned Kennedy, the United States might need to use nuclear weapons. Kennedy was more averse than Eisenhower and the Joint Chiefs whom he had inherited from Eisenhower to involve the United States in situations that might lead to nuclear warfare. In supporting its ground forces, moreover, the United States would face serious logistical challenges in the untamed mountains and valleys of Laos. But what concerned Kennedy most was the lack of fighting spirit among most of the Laotians who would have to serve as America's principal allies.[17]

Kennedy decided on a show of force, rather than a use of force. He sent the Seventh Fleet into the South China Sea, moved five hundred Marines into Thailand, and put U.S. combat forces in Okinawa on alert. On March 23, the President went on national television. Standing next to three maps of Laos, each six feet by eight feet, he illustrated the advance of the Communist enemy and warned solemnly, "All members of SEATO have undertaken special treaty obligations toward an aggression in Laos. No one should doubt our resolution on this point." The Communist countries could avoid a dangerous conflict, Kennedy explained, by halting their military provocations and joining the United States in establishing a truly neutral Laos.[18]

Kennedy's adversaries, however, refused to back off. Communist forces pushed ahead into key areas during April, putting Vientiane itself into danger. Diem told the Americans at the beginning of May that "Laos must be saved at all costs. Otherwise, the situation in South Vietnam will become untenable. The loss of Laos will open all doors to mass infiltration or invasion of South Vietnam."[19] The Joint Chiefs urged Kennedy to send in U.S. forces, and many of Kennedy's civilian advisers now spoke up in favor of intervention as well, even Under Secretary of State Chester Bowles, the most liberal and usually the most dovish senior official in the Kennedy administration. They advocated such a course in full recognition that it could lead to a major war with China. Bowles himself remarked, "The main question to be faced is the fact that we are going to have to fight the Chinese anyway in two, three, five, or ten years and that it is just a question of where, when and how."[20]

Kennedy was more skeptical about the Joint Chiefs' plans for military action in Laos than he would have been before the 21st of April, one week earlier. That was the day when Fidel Castro's troops had finished crushing an invasion force of fifteen hundred Cuban exiles at the Bay of Pigs. Kennedy had made little effort to consult the Joint Chiefs about the CIA-sponsored operation ahead of time, and he had ignored their calls to provide air support to the struggling invaders, yet he faulted the Joint Chiefs for not voicing their concerns about the operation's success during the planning stages.[21] Kennedy pressed the Joint Chiefs for specifics on intervention in Laos. They told him that American forces would arrive in Laos at two airfields, but upon further questioning the Joint Chiefs admitted that they had not considered the possibility of a large and swift Communist assault force overrunning the airfields before the Americans had landed sufficient defense forces.[22] Kennedy came away with the impression that the Joint Chiefs were unprepared, incompetent, or both.

At this juncture, distraught over the obstacles to U.S. intervention and the ineptitude of the Laotian rightists, Kennedy decided to forswear U.S. military action and seek the neutralization of Laos by purely diplomatic means. He assigned responsibility for negotiating a neutralization agreement to Averell Harriman, an experienced diplomat and former governor of New York who strongly opposed U.S. intervention in Laos. Harriman believed that the Soviets would be willing to join with the United States in guaranteeing Laotian neutrality, as a first step towards a U.S.-Soviet rapprochement that Harriman envisioned. In Harriman's opinion, a neutral Laos should have a coalition government containing members from all of the major political groups, including the Communists, with Souvanna Phouma serving as premier. Harriman dismissed many sage objections to the coalition government concept, objections that would be validated by later events. The most telling of them came from U.S. Ambassador to Laos Winthrop G. Brown, who contended that Souvanna was

> possessed of an infinite capacity for self-deception, convinced (wrongly) that he commands the devout support of 90% of the Lao people, confident that if he could get the Communists in his government he could handle them and keep the country from their clutches, wholly incapable of organizing or running a government, too disposed to compromise, underestimating Communist persistence and ruthlessness, unwilling to believe that his half-brother Souphanouvong, or indeed most of the other Pathet Lao leaders, are really Communists.[23]

Kennedy found neutralization appealing because it allowed him to avoid the dangers of intervention without the appearance of sanctioning the abandonment of Laos. He also liked Harriman's idea of using neutralization to help ease tensions with the Soviets. U.S. Congressional leaders, moreover, were now voicing opposition to the deployment of American troops to Laos, out of concern for the difficult fighting conditions and the Laotians' lack of martial spirit. These leaders expressed a desire to use U.S. troops somewhere else in Southeast Asia, in a country whose people would fight, such as South Vietnam or Thailand.[24]

An opportunity to pursue neutralization arose conveniently on May 3, when the Laotian Communists expressed a willingness to accept a ceasefire and an international conference in Geneva to resolve the conflict. Kennedy immediately directed Harriman to take up the matter of Laotian neutralization with the Communists, hoping that the final settlement would prohibit the Communists from controlling the strategically critical sections of Laos. Unfortunately for Kennedy, many of those areas were already in Communist hands, which meant that he was trying to win by negotiation what had not been obtained on the battlefield, a task seldom achieved. The Communist countries had agreed to negotiate because they had just taken what they most wanted – the long strip of eastern Laos that had been designated as the site of the new Ho Chi Minh trail – and believed that they would retain it at the bargaining table.[25] The 559th Transportation Group had begun shifting infiltration operations from the eastern, Vietnamese side of the Annamite mountain chain, where the blocked trail into

South Vietnam lay, to the western, Laotian side. Hanoi dispatched North Vietnamese engineer battalions to the newly acquired Laotian territory to build bridges and fords so that trucks could use the new infiltration corridor, which consisted of multiple trails although it would always be known as the Ho Chi Minh Trail. During May, to keep the South Vietnamese Army from sending reconnaissance or combat forces to the new trail area, the North Vietnamese Army 270th Regiment crossed into northern South Vietnam and overran a score of small government outposts along Route 9.[26] Supplies were soon flowing down the new infiltration routes, and with far less difficulty than on the old one because, as one Communist account noted, the terrain was easier and the enemy did not get in the way.[27]

At the same time that Kennedy was backing down in Laos, he was preparing to get tougher in Vietnam. Like Eisenhower, Kennedy believed that the United States needed allies on the Southeast Asian mainland and that the Communist conquest of one ally could cause the region's other countries to topple like dominoes. During a discussion with de Gaulle in May, Kennedy likened Vietnam to West Berlin, the loss of which, in the minds of many Western European leaders, would trigger the collapse of anti-Communism across Western Europe.[28] In terms of defending Southeast Asia, Kennedy and Eisenhower differed on where to hold the line, with Eisenhower favoring both Laos and South Vietnam, and Kennedy preferring South Vietnam alone. During a discussion of Laotian neutralization with Rusk, Kennedy said, "If we have to fight in Southeast Asia, let's fight in Vietnam. The Vietnamese, at least, are committed and will fight. There are a million refugees from communism in South Vietnam. Vietnam is the place."[29] South Vietnam's lengthy coast and its terrain, Kennedy believed, would allow the United States to introduce men and supplies and move them around the country much more easily than in Laos. Kennedy could also get the Congressional support for a war in Vietnam that he could not get for Laos.

On April 29, President Kennedy approved a recommendation to increase the number of U.S. military advisers in Vietnam from 685 to 785. The first increase since 1956, it openly defied the rules laid down by the International Control Commission. Kennedy authorized an expansion of South Vietnam's Civil Guard from 32,000 to 68,000 and an intensification of covert action against North Vietnam. A few days later, Kennedy commissioned a study on increasing the South Vietnamese Army from 170,000 to 200,000 men, and he ordered the Defense Department to conduct a "full examination" of "the size and composition of forces which would be desirable in the case of a possible commitment of U.S. forces to Vietnam," though he was not yet ready to send American troops to South Vietnam as the Joint Chiefs were now recommending.[30] These initiatives had been proposed by a newly created Vietnam Task Force, which Kennedy had put under the leadership of Lansdale after strenuous State Department and Defense Department objections had aborted plans to make Lansdale the ambassador to South Vietnam.

The President also heeded a recommendation from Lansdale and the Vietnam Task Force that the newly designated ambassador, Frederick Ernest "Fritz" Nolting, mend relations with Diem by getting on "on the same wavelength" as the South Vietnamese President and by abstaining from demands that Diem satisfy a variety of conditions, since such demands had not worked with the Vietnamese in the past.[31] Lansdale had been particularly emphatic in arguing that Diem should not be pressed to get rid of Nhu, as many in the State Department favored. "The reality is that Diem trusts Nhu for certain activities which he cannot entrust to anyone else, and needs him," Lansdale observed. "We will hardly help Diem be the strong leader we desire by insisting that he get rid of his trusted right-hand man; we would do better to influence that right-hand man more effectively."[32] Soon, Lansdale would be spending little time on Vietnam, and the Vietnam Task Force would be emasculated, but Lansdale had masterminded a new approach for dealing with the South Vietnamese government, one based on persuasion rather than coercion, that the United States would largely follow for more than two years. In time, it would yield excellent results.

Ambassador Nolting arrived in Saigon at the beginning of May. A native of Richmond, Virginia, Nolting held a Ph.D. in philosophy, spoke French, and had a reputation as one of the nation's finest career diplomats. His posting to South Vietnam at the age of forty-nine made him one of America's youngest ambassadors, and it was rare that so young a man would be thrust into a country of such importance and trouble. Personable, intelligent, and attuned to cultural differences, Nolting was adept at handling difficult situations. Walt Rostow, who knew Nolting well, told Kennedy, "You will find him a man of rare strength and character."[33]

During his first months as ambassador, Nolting became fond of Diem, but he also developed serious reservations about the South Vietnamese President's effectiveness. Nolting reported in July that Diem needed to make dramatic progress in the war in order to regain the people's confidence, and if he did not, then the military or the Communists would overthrow him. Nolting noted in this message that he was not expressing these doubts publicly, a tactic that he would employ throughout his tenure to avoid demoralizing the South Vietnamese government and causing it to lose face. "In our attempt to help create a new and winning psychology," he penned, "I have taken a much more optimistic line in conversations with other diplomats and with press here than that reflected above, and I think we should continue to do so, giving benefit of the doubt wherever possible to optimistic assessment."[34] During August, Nolting was to adopt a more positive outlook as the South Vietnamese government improved its performance.

To support the new policy of amicability and assuage fears across Asia that America's Laotian policy might portend abandonment of other countries, Kennedy had Vice-President Lyndon Johnson fly to Saigon and other Asian capitals in May to pledge America's determination to contain Communism. Upon reaching Saigon, Johnson handed Diem a letter from Kennedy that read: "I can now tell you that, for our part, we are ready to join with you in an intensified endeavor to win the struggle against Communism and to further the social and economic advancement of Viet-Nam."[35] Diem was most gratified.[36] While in Vietnam, Johnson also followed through on instructions from Kennedy to make clear America's support for Diem in public. Diem, he proclaimed, was the "Winston Churchill of Asia." As a result of the Vice President's assurances, scheming among Diem's opponents died down, while Diem and his supporters took heart.

Following his visit to Saigon and the other capitals in the region, Johnson notified Kennedy that the impact of America's policy in Laos was even worse than was thought in Washington. Among America's allies in Southeast Asia, it had "drastically weakened the ability to maintain any strongly pro-U.S. orientation." Although his mission had halted the depletion of confidence in the United States, Johnson indicated, America could not restore what had been lost unless it heeded the advice of the region's leaders that "deeds must follow words, and soon." The Vice President cast his vote for strong support of South Vietnam and the other anti-Communist nations of Southeast Asia. Unless the United States maintained allies on the Asian mainland, he contended, its island allies would lose their security and the United States would have to pull its defenses back to San Francisco.[37]

On June 3, President Kennedy headed to Vienna for a two-day summit with Khrushchev. Kennedy wanted to discuss a nuclear test ban and the neutralization of Laos, which he hoped would become the first big steps towards a U.S.-Soviet détente. With his strength of personality and his conversational skills, Kennedy intended to sway Khrushchev in the same way he had swayed so many American politicians and campaign contributors, while at the same time showing Khrushchev that he could not be pushed around. His refusal to send American forces into Laos and Cuba, he knew, had given Khrushchev reason to believe that the new American President had the toughness of a whispering lilac.

The meeting, however, did not at all unfold as Kennedy had desired. It would be Khrushchev who would manipulate his adversary. Kennedy was right about one thing, that from the start Khrushchev considered him weak and susceptible to bullying. After Kennedy's debacle at the Bay of Pigs, two Russian historians revealed in 1996, Khrushchev had scoffed at Kennedy's weakness, chuckling that Eisenhower would not have allowed such an enterprise to fail.[38] Once the Vienna discussions began, Kennedy did little except stagger as he received blow after blow from all directions. Communism was the wave of the future, Khrushchev said, while capitalism was trying to suppress popular aspirations. Through cultural and economic achievements, communism would prove its superiority to capitalism. America was controlled by a handful of wealthy businessmen.

Kennedy scarcely got a word in, and when he did his words resembled the exertions of a youngster pushing against an advancing truck. "He's a little bit out of his depth, isn't he?" remarked Charles Bohlen, a State Department expert on the Soviet Union who was present.[39]

Khrushchev avoided discussing the test ban treaty and most of the other cooperative initiatives proposed by Kennedy, but the two heads of state did talk about Laotian neutralization. Khrushchev said of Laos, "The side supported by the USSR will be more successful because the arms supplied by the United States are directed against the people and the people do not want to take them. . . . If the United States supports old, moribund, reactionary regimes, then a precedent of internal intervention will be set, which might cause a clash between our two countries. The USSR certainly does not desire such a development."

Kennedy said that Laos was "included under the protocol to the SEATO agreement in the Treaty area, and thus we have treaty commitments in that area."

"It would be bad if the United States were to attempt to claim special rights on the grounds that it had vested interests," Khrushchev scolded. "If the President would pardon the blunt expression, such policy stems from megalomania, from delusions of grandeur." After delivering this drubbing, though, Khrushchev said he agreed with Kennedy that Laos should become a neutral and independent nation.[40]

The world's two most powerful men also discussed Berlin at length. A thousand East Germans were fleeing to West Berlin each day, many of them with expertise in fields such as medicine and engineering that could not be replaced for many years. East German leader Walter Ulbricht had complained to Khrushchev that his country was disappearing into West Berlin, and Khrushchev had felt compelled to promise Ulbricht an end to the Berlin problem before the end of 1961. Khrushchev served notice to Kennedy that the Soviet Union would sign a peace treaty with East Germany at the end of the year, which would deprive the United States and its NATO allies of their rights of access to West Berlin. Any American interference in eastern Germany after that time "will be regarded by the USSR as an act of open aggression against a peace loving country, with all the consequences ensuing therefrom."

Kennedy became very defensive about West Berlin. It appeared that he was beginning to believe, as Khrushchev wanted him to believe, that he was a little boy trying to justify himself to a grown man. "The U.S. is committed to that area and it is so regarded by all the world," Kennedy said. "If we accepted your suggestion, the world would lose confidence in the U.S. and would not regard it as a serious country. It is an important strategic matter that the world believe the U.S. is a serious country."[41]

The beating that Khrushchev delivered in Vienna took a heavy toll on Kennedy. "He treated me like a little boy," Kennedy cursed in a fury as he paced his room afterwards. "Like a little boy."[42] British Prime Minister Harold

Macmillan, who met Kennedy in London right after the Vienna talks, recounted his impressions in a letter to the Queen of England: "The President was completely overwhelmed by the ruthlessness and barbarity of the Russian premier. It reminded me in a way of Lord Halifax or Mr. Neville Chamberlain trying to hold a conversation with Herr Hitler." For the first time, Macmillan believed, Kennedy had "met a man who was completely impervious to his charm."[43]

Just after the summit, Kennedy also spoke with James Reston, the Washington bureau chief of the *New York Times* and a personal friend. Reston asked how the meetings with Khrushchev had gone. "Worst thing in my life," Kennedy moaned. "He savaged me." Kennedy slid down on a couch and pulled his hat over his face. "I think I know why he treated me like this. He thinks because of the Bay of Pigs that I'm inexperienced. Probably thinks I'm stupid. Maybe most important, he thinks that I have no guts." After several minutes of distraught rambling, Kennedy calmed down somewhat. "We have to see what we can do," he said, "that will restore a feeling in Moscow that we will defend our national interest. I'll have to increase the defense budget. And we have to confront them. The only place we can do that is in Vietnam. We have to send more people there."[44]

Converging with the need to hearten America's Asian allies and the need to improve the South Vietnamese war effort, Kennedy's desire to confront Khrushchev very quickly drove him to beef up America's assistance to Vietnam and enlarge its conventional forces in Europe. Kennedy was most pleased to receive, on June 14, a South Vietnamese request for an additional $175 million in military aid, which Diem wanted to use to expand South Vietnam's army to 270,000 men, 100,000 men above what Kennedy had already approved. Diem simultaneously requested a "considerable expansion" of the American advisory effort to help train and support the additional forces. Explaining the request in a letter that a South Vietnamese envoy hand-delivered to the White House, Diem asserted that several thousand armed Communists had come to South Vietnam through Laos in the past few months, and that foreign observers believed the Soviet war supplies piling up in North Vietnam were destined primarily for South Vietnam, rather than Laos.[45] Within two months, Kennedy authorized funding for an additional 30,000 regulars, to bring the South Vietnamese Army's strength to 200,000.[46] Kennedy postponed a decision on expanding the army to 270,000 because no decision was needed at present; the Americans projected that it would take Diem until 1963 to build up his regular army to the 200,000 level.[47] Kennedy's military shopping sprees in Vietnam and Europe made an impression on Khrushchev. The Soviet premier did not follow through on his threat to fight over Berlin.

Caution, however, did not take root among the North Vietnamese. During the summer months, despite Khrushchev's promise at Vienna to ensure the neutralization of Laos, the North Vietnamese stepped up the infiltration of men and materiel through Laotian territory and they helped the Pathet Lao attack

Phoumi's forces. During June alone, according to the CIA, 1,500 Communists entered South Vietnam from North Vietnam, and between 500 to 1,000 men came in each of the succeeding months. An official Communist history stated that for the entire year of 1961, the average rate of infiltration exceeded 600 men per month. Viet Cong strength in northern South Vietnam shot up to 8,000 during the summer, as compared with 600 at the beginning of the year, most of the increase coming from infiltration through Laos, as Communist recruiters and trainers in South Vietnam's villages had not yielded enough soldiers to carry out a large-scale offensive. Most of the men who had made the journey to the South in the summer were highly trained soldiers and cadres, and they were inserted into main force units assigned to the Viet Cong's pending offensive. Owing to the beneficence of China and the Soviet Union, the Communist units had more heavy weaponry than before, including a large number of submachine guns, machine guns, automatic rifles, and mortars.[48]

The Viet Cong offensive commenced on the first of September. Its main targets were concentrated in the central highlands, where most of the newly arrived infiltrators were stationed. During the month of September, the Viet Cong launched 450 attacks, thrice the preceding monthly average, and they greatly increased the size of their attacks. On three occasions, the Viet Cong attacked with over one thousand men. Hanoi hoped that its troops would erase the government's presence in key sections of the highlands, establish beachheads in those areas, and from there launch attacks on South Vietnam's cities. If less successful, the offensive could at least cause a loss of confidence in Diem that might precipitate another coup attempt.

The offensive started out well for the Communists. On September 1, over one thousand Communist regulars overran two government outposts thirty miles north of Kontum. The government reported 100 Viet Cong killed in action with only 19 deaths on the government side, but American advisers reported that the government's forces had suffered 92 deaths and 77 missing.[49] On September 17, the Viet Cong's 50th Infantry Battalion and 26th Sapper Reconnaissance Company captured Phuoc Vinh, the first time the Viet Cong had ever overrun a provincial capital. In the main square, the Communists disemboweled provincial chief Nguyen Minh Man, a thirty-three year old major who was considered one of the best provincial chiefs in South Vietnam. They also shot his young wife. To avoid a large government counter-attack, the Communists departed several hours after their arrival, taking with them one hundred rifles and two hundred and seventy Communist prisoners whom they had freed from the town's jail.

"Up until September, I thought we were on upgrade here," Nolting reported to Washington at the beginning of October. "Due to recent infiltrations, which stimulate Viet Cong internal recruitment and aggressiveness, GVN security forces now greatly overextended." Nolting predicted that the government had better than a fifty–fifty chance of winning the war if infiltration were brought under control, but if infiltration continued unobstructed then the government would be defeated. Nolting urged Washington to solve the infiltration problem by abandoning plans for neutralizing Laos and instead seeking a partition of Laos into pro-American and pro-Communist sections.[50] McNamara and the Joint Chiefs wanted to put American infantrymen into Laos. Harriman, however, said that U.S. intervention was too dangerous, and he asserted that the Soviets would prevent the North Vietnamese from infiltrating forces and supplies through Laos.[51] During September, Khrushchev and the Soviet negotiator Georgi Pushkin had given private assurances that the Soviets would keep the North Vietnamese out of Laos and restrain the Pathet Lao. In reality, though, the Soviets had no intention of pressuring the North Vietnamese or the Pathet Lao.

Kennedy heeded Harriman once more. He did, however, agree to send General Maxwell Taylor to Vietnam to analyze two possible options for shoring up South Vietnam – first, the introduction of SEATO or purely U.S. combat troops into South Vietnam, and second, the strengthening of South Vietnamese forces in the absence of such troops.[52] Taylor had become Kennedy's special military adviser after producing an incisive postmortem of the Bay of Pigs debacle. As the author of Flexible Response, Taylor had long commanded Kennedy's admiration. Possessing an unusual blend of charisma, intelligence, glibness, and vigor, he gave advice in the confident and sophisticated way that Kennedy liked.[53] Taylor also shielded the President from the Joint Chiefs of Staff, whose readiness to use U.S. troops and nuclear weapons tended to upset the President. Following Taylor's arrival, the influence of the Joint Chiefs declined sharply until, in the fall of 1962, Kennedy made Taylor the chairman of the Joint Chiefs.

Just a few days before Taylor's departure for Saigon, Diem sent the Americans a request for the deployment of U.S. combat units to South Vietnam. Diem wanted them positioned along the 17th Parallel and in provincial capitals in the highlands, in order to deter the Communists and free up his own forces for mobile operations. Most other Vietnamese leaders had favored introducing U.S. troops before now, but Diem had resisted it, fearing a reduction of national independence. The recent increase in Communist infiltration through Laos had compelled him to change his mind.[54] When General Taylor arrived in Saigon, he told Diem that he agreed on the need for an American combat force in South Vietnam. Taylor viewed the American force as a useful symbol of U.S. strength and as a reserve force in the event of a military crisis, but he suggested dispatching the force with the initial purpose of assisting the victims of recent flooding, so that the move could be portrayed in the press as a humanitarian gesture. Diem then asked for airplanes, helicopters, boats, and trucks. Furthermore, the South Vietnamese President told Taylor, he would like to have Lansdale back in Vietnam on a permanent basis to help him, but this request was doomed to failure because Kennedy wanted Lansdale to work on "Operation Mongoose," the covert program to overthrow Fidel Castro.[55]

Taylor and a team of experts quickly surveyed the situation in South Vietnam, then prepared a long report for Kennedy, which Taylor submitted on November 3. South Vietnam was in deep trouble, Taylor's report concluded, afflicted by self-reinforcing weaknesses. Lacking good intelligence, the South Vietnamese military was compelled to employ between eighty and eighty-five percent of its troops in static guard duty as protection against surprise attacks, which had the effect of conceding the initiative to the enemy. When the Communists launched an attack, the government employed its reserve forces too slowly to stop them. The inability of the armed forces to protect the villages kept the people from supplying the much-needed intelligence. Military ineffectiveness also was responsible for most of Diem's political problems, Taylor concluded: "The record shows that the disintegration of the political situation in South Vietnam since 1959 is primarily due to the government's inability to protect its citizens and to conduct the war effectively."

But the outlook was not entirely bleak. "With all his weaknesses, Diem has extraordinary ability, stubbornness, and guts," wrote Taylor. "Despite their acute frustration, the men of the Armed Forces and the administration respect Diem to a degree which gives their grumbling (and perhaps some plotting) a somewhat half-hearted character; and they are willing – by and large – to work for him, if he gives them a chance to do their jobs." Taylor reasoned that the United States was better off working with Diem and his subordinates than seeking his removal, for South Vietnam had a scarcity of good executives, and a coup could lead to chaos. Taylor also observed that South Vietnam's military performance was going to get better because "within the military and non-military establishment, a new generation of younger men in their thirties is beginning to emerge with a strong will to get on with the job. Some of the new military commanders we met (in divisions, Rangers, Marines) are clearly dedicated, first-class, modern men of whom any nation could be proud. The same is true at the middle level of the bureaucracy." Walt Rostow, who as the Taylor mission's number two man was under orders from Kennedy to gauge popular attitudes towards Communism, reported that the peasants were focused on their own welfare and had little interest in national politics while the urbanites, including Diem's detractors, uniformly despised the North Vietnamese government as the result of its misdeeds from 1954 to 1956.[56]

To save the situation, Kennedy had to act immediately. "From all quarters in Southeast Asia," Taylor warned, "the message on Vietnam is the same: vigorous American action is needed to buy time for Vietnam to mobilize and organize its real assets; but the time for such a turn around has nearly run out. And if Vietnam goes, it will be exceedingly difficult if not impossible to hold Southeast Asia." Taylor recommended sending an American military task force of 8,000 men, with an ostensible mission of providing flood relief, as he and Diem had discussed. This deployment, he asserted, was essential to the survival of South Vietnam. He also called for a large infusion of Americans into South

Vietnam to work on all types of tasks related to the war effort. Expansion of the Army from 170,000 to 200,000 men should proceed if Diem agreed to make the military and political improvements the Americans had long been advocating.[57] In a separate, private report for Kennedy, Taylor noted that the initial troop commitment could conceivably lead to a bigger war requiring additional troop commitments of indefinite duration, but he considered it unlikely because the threat of bombing would likely deter Hanoi, and because the Chinese would face inordinate logistical difficulties and vulnerabilities if they fought in Southeast Asia.[58]

Kennedy liked the Taylor mission's recommendations, with the exception of the American combat force deployment. The champion of Flexible Response, the man who had promised to use American soldiers more readily, still did not want to send those ground troops to Asia. Kennedy, though, did not immediately rule out intervention on the ground. He wanted to see what his advisers and the Congress thought, and he wanted to mull it over in his own mind, both of which required that he buy time. Were it to become known that he was stalling on an urgent troop recommendation from General Taylor, Kennedy would again be accused of giving in to the Communists, especially if the South Vietnamese government began to buckle. To prevent such accusations, Kennedy had his men give the media false stories about the troop issue. The deception worked. The press was soon reporting that Taylor had told Kennedy that no U.S. troops were currently needed in South Vietnam.[59]

Kennedy feared a U.S. combat force deployment for a variety of reasons. Sending American combat forces could lead to a protracted war that would hurt him in the 1964 election. The unwillingness of the French and the British to join the fight in Vietnam would undermine support for an American expedition both at home and abroad. Among his confidantes, several opposed a ground force deployment. Senator Mike Mansfield advised Kennedy to gamble that Diem could get by with only aid and advisers, while Harriman and John Kenneth Galbraith, U.S. Ambassador to India, suggested the neutralization of South Vietnam in the manner of Laos. Galbraith also advised Kennedy that he could avoid a troop commitment by supporting a military coup, as the Army leaders would win the war quickly without Diem. "It is a cliché that there is no alternative to Diem's regime," Galbraith assured the President. "This is an optical illusion arising from the fact that the eye is fixed on the visible figures. It is a better rule that nothing succeeds like successors."[60]

Yet while he dreaded sending American soldiers, Kennedy also dreaded losing Vietnam, which Taylor said would likely happen if he did not send the troops. Kennedy's prestige in the eyes of the American people, the Communist nations, and the rest of the world could suffer irreparable damage. In the United States, public demoralization was likely, as were sharp and effective attacks from the Republicans, who already were criticizing Kennedy in public for his indecision on Vietnam. "There are limits to the number of defeats I can defend in one twelve-month period," Kennedy told Galbraith. "I've had the Bay of Pigs and pulling out of Laos, and I can't accept a third."[61]

For Kennedy, and for most other American officials in late 1961, the prospect of tumbling dominoes in Southeast Asia remained one of the most compelling reasons for holding South Vietnam. "I would like to see the United States out of that area, but would not want its withdrawal to leave control to the North," Kennedy was soon to tell Indian Defense Minister Krishna Menon. "If South Vietnam should fall under the Viet Minh in the next few months, a wave of domination by Communist China could then sweep over Southeast Asia."[62] If the United States abandoned South Vietnam, Kennedy told Walt Rostow, then Southeast Asia would be lost to Communism, the American people would move toward isolationism, and the "loss of confidence in the United States would be worldwide. Under these circumstances, Khrushchev and Mao could not refrain from acting to exploit the apparent shift in the balance of power."[63]

Kennedy and his principal advisers believed, correctly, that China and North Vietnam were working together to knock over the dominoes in Southeast Asia. At this time, the Vietnamese Communist Party sought to remain on good terms with the Soviets as well as the Chinese and it was trying to close the Sino-Soviet rift in the spirit of international revolutionary solidarity, but its primary allegiance remained with the Chinese. Hanoi's views on wars of national liberation, coexistence with the capitalists, and other matters of contention within the Communist world were very close to Beijing's, much closer than they were to Moscow's. From Ho's lips and Ho's pen, there continued to flow words of the highest praise for the Chinese, as in this July 1961 article: "The relationship between the Chinese revolution and the Vietnamese revolution is made up of a thousand ties of gratitude, attachment and love, a glorious friendship that will last forever!"[64]

With respect to South Vietnam, the North Vietnamese solicited advice from the Chinese far more often than from the Soviets.[65] On matters concerning all of Southeast Asia, they deferred to Mao, who was seeking to destroy Southeast Asia's anti-Communist nations through subversion and pressure, avoiding the use of conventional forces so as not to produce another major war with the United States. Inside the other key domino nations, as in South Vietnam, the insurgent movements were coated with the fingerprints of China and North Vietnam. The Communist parties of Indonesia, Thailand, Burma, Laos, and Cambodia all had major training facilities and liaison offices in China at this time, and they were coordinating their activities closely with the Chinese Communists. Offering attractive promises of financial assistance, the Chinese government was pushing these parties to accelerate the Communist revolution across Southeast Asia.[66]

For the United States, the idea of playing off China and the Soviet Union against one another continued to languish in the embryonic stage, its ultimate viability unclear. Despite their squabbles, China and the Soviet Union were still striving towards the common goal of enlarging Communism's domains across the world, and neither one was interfering with the other's work in this direction. Had the Soviets been interested in antagonizing the Chinese in 1961, they would not have chosen Southeast Asia as the place to do it, for they deemed Southeast Asia a region of relatively minor importance. Khrushchev did not get in the way when Beijing and Hanoi expanded their offensive activities in Laos and South Vietnam during 1961, even though he lamented that they could provoke a war with the United States.

Had the United States disengaged from South Vietnam in 1961, it would have removed the only two obstacles to Communist control of South Vietnam – American military aid to the South Vietnamese government and the threat of American retaliation against North Vietnam. The Vietnamese Communists would have quickly taken control of South Vietnam, and Laos and Cambodia then would have had no choice but to submit to complete Communist domination. The domino most likely to fall next would have been Thailand, where the Thai Communist Party had initiated guerrilla warfare against the royal Thai government a few months earlier. The Thai guerrillas were receiving assistance from the Chinese and several other Asian Communist Parties, including the Vietnamese Communist Party, whose leader had eagerly promoted revolutionary activities in Thailand ever since his stint there during the colonial period.

Were Thailand to remain anti-Communist after a Communist takeover of South Vietnam, it would have to fight a difficult counterinsurgency of its own, requiring substantial American aid and advisory support. Once the Communists had free access to the long Thai-Laotian border, they would possess an adjoining sanctuary, something that has been an essential resource for virtually all victorious insurgencies in history.[67] But the United States probably would not even have the opportunity to support such a counterinsurgency effort in Thailand, for Thailand's leaders were warning that if Hanoi took South Vietnam they would be forced to abandon their pro-American position and seek an accommodation with the Communists. For many centuries, the Thais had maintained their independence through a strict policy of aligning with whichever power seemed strongest in the region. In World War II, when Japanese troops tore through Southeast Asia, the Thais had promptly allied themselves with the Japanese and allowed Japanese forces to use Thailand as a base for operations into other parts of Southeast Asia. After seeing the United States surrender South Vietnam and Laos to the Communists, the Thais would have had very little reason to put their trust in American power or in American assurances of support. The domino could thus fall without an insurgency. Kenneth Young, the ambassador to Thailand and a very astute man, predicted in October 1961 that the loss of South Vietnam and Laos would lead swiftly to Communist domination of Thailand, and of the rest of Southeast Asia.[68]

To the south of Thailand lay Malaya and Singapore. Malaya yielded much of the world's natural rubber and tin, materials crucial to the conduct of mechanized warfare. It had a sizeable Communist Party that Ho Chi Minh had organized in 1930, and a third of its populace was Chinese. The Malayan Communists, who for the most part were Chinese in ethnicity, had waged an insurgency against the British that began in 1948 and purportedly ended in 1960, though the insurgency never really stopped entirely and was militarily active, if not very effective, during 1961. Singapore, with a large Communist Party and a population that was eighty percent Chinese, was highly vulnerable to Chinese Communist manipulation. Singapore's Communist Party, which also owed its founding to Ho Chi Minh, was in 1961 supporting a guerrilla campaign against the government. Communist access to Thailand and southern Indochina would expose Malaya and Singapore to attack from abroad, whether by covert infiltration or overt conventional attack – the Japanese had used those two areas to take Malaya and Singapore in 1942. During the Malayan insurgency of 1948 to 1960, the lack of an adjacent base area had stifled Communist attempts to subvert the government. In his memoirs, Malayan Communist Party leader Chin Peng recounted that in 1961 he viewed a Communist Thailand as the key requirement for successful prosecution of the Malayan insurgency. "We desperately needed a common border with a national territory controlled by a fraternal party," he stated.[69]

If Communists in Indochina and Thailand began attacking Malaya and Singapore, the United States might still have a chance of intervening on the ground before the entire mainland was lost. In contrast to South Vietnam, Malaya was relatively far from China and North Vietnam, and the Malayan insurgents were much weaker than the Viet Cong. Unlike Diem's government, however, the Malayan government did not have armed forces that could put up serious resistance to the Vietnamese or Chinese Communists. In addition, the Malayan government might very well have refused to allow American soldiers on its soil at that stage, out of fear that the country would be devastated by a major war or that the United States might back out in the middle, as it had abandoned its South Vietnamese and Thai allies. The Malayans attached great stock to America's actions in South Vietnam during 1961, as shown by their fervent advocacy of American participation in defending South Vietnam. In October, Malayan Prime Minister Tunku Abdul Rahman forcefully called on the United States to protect South Vietnam against the international Communist menace "before it is too late."[70]

The most important of Southeast Asia's dominoes was Indonesia, the giant collection of islands just to the south of Malaya and Singapore, a glittering jewel of sufficient value to justify holding the rougher stones on the mainland from which it could be attacked. Encompassing all of the sea lanes between Southeast Asia and Australia, the Indonesian archipelago occupied a position of tremendous strategic importance. He who held Indonesia could deny his adversaries access to vital trading routes and prevent enemy warships from traveling between the Indian and Pacific Oceans, crucial assets in combating a global naval power such as the United States.

Like Malaya, Indonesia possessed great amounts of rubber and tin, and it also had large petroleum reserves. The Japanese had made the Indonesian archipelago the central objective of their 1941–42 offensive in order to obtain these resources, and the Americans subsequently had cut the sea and air lanes between Japan and Indonesia before attacking the Japanese mainland in order to take away those resources. The sixth most populous country on the planet in 1961, Indonesia had more people than all the countries on the Southeast Asian mainland combined and more Muslims than the entire Middle East. Its Communist Party was the third largest in the world after the Soviet and Chinese Parties. The nation's leader, the eccentric Sukarno, was flirting with the Communists at this time, and in terms of ideology he was much closer to Communism than to democratic capitalism. In 1958, because of Sukarno's coddling of Communists, the Americans had covertly assisted an unsuccessful insurrection against Sukarno, causing Sukarno to gravitate further towards the Communists. By 1961, Moscow had provided Sukarno with a whopping billion dollars worth of aid, far more than the United States had sent and the most the Soviet Union had given to any non-Communist nation except the United Arab Republic. For the moment, Sukarno was trying to maintain good relations with the United States as well as with the Soviets and the Chinese, but if Indonesia's neighbors on the Southeast Asian mainland came under Communist control, Sukarno was almost a certain bet to become a wholehearted ally of the Chinese and Vietnamese Communists. Like most leaders in the region, he preferred siding with the strongest power, and when the Communists amassed naval forces in the ports of Indochina and Malaya he could not have failed to see China as that power.

Momentous events on the mainland also reverberated across the South China Sea to the Philippines, an important segment of America's offshore island defense chain. During May of 1961, Philippine President Carlos Garcia had warned the United States to "put out the fires in Laos and Vietnam now before they get too large." The Philippine Foreign Secretary declared that if the United States did not do more to support anti-Communism in the region, then America's Asian allies would have no choice but to "revise their policies toward the U.S. Government," and the American ambassador in Manila believed that the foreign secretary himself was "beginning to think in terms of a transition toward neutralism of some sort."[71]

Several other countries in the region were somewhat less likely to fall to Communism, thanks largely to geographical separation, culture, or bilateral defense treaties with the United States. Even these nations, though, dreaded Communist aggression and subversion, providing further evidence of the extent of Communism's threat to Asia. One such country was Taiwan, a link in the island defense chain sitting to the north of the Philippines. The Taiwanese were prepared to fight to the death against all odds rather than yield to the Communists, in contrast to some of their opportunistic Southeast Asian neighbors. Taiwan's fiercely anti-Communist leaders urged the Americans to provide greater assistance to anti-Communist Asian nations, especially those in Southeast Asia.[72] The largest link in the island defense chain in terms of land mass, Australia, was similarly adamant in its anti-Communism. During the Communist offensives in Laos, the Australians had lobbied for the use of SEATO ground troops, and they subsequently supported increases in U.S. assistance to South Vietnam and expressed a willingness to fight in South Vietnam if necessary.[73] In the spring of 1962, Australia would send military advisers to South Vietnam and Thailand.

Neutral Burma had been fighting Chinese-controlled Communist rebels for fifteen years. Sharing a border with China, the Burmese would have to yield to the Chinese or suffer destruction if China needed to use their territory for making war. Beyond Burma was Pakistan, which feared that Communist successes in Vietnam and Laos would greatly increase its vulnerability to a Communist attack and for that reason had offered, in the spring of 1961, to send eight thousand of its own troops to fight in Laos.[74] Next door, in India, the threat of war with China loomed in 1961, the result of disputes over border demarcations, China's occupation of Tibet, and India's sheltering of the Dalai Lama's exile government. In 1962, China and India would fight a war in the border region, which would end in a staggering defeat for India.

In geopolitical terms, the most important country in Asia was Japan, as it was the only Asian country that had ever rivaled the nations of Europe and the United States in amassing and employing modern military power. During the 1960s, Japan lacked large military forces, but it possessed great industrial strength that could be turned to military use in a relatively short period of time. Southeast Asia was Japan's largest trading partner aside from the United States; the region's loss to Communism could cause serious economic and hence political problems in Japan. Of greatest concern was the vast and bountiful Indonesian archipelago. The Japanese had a saying that "if Indonesia catches a cold, Japan will catch it, too."[75] Japan, moreover, constituted a critical link in America's island defense chain.

After long days of investigation and contemplation, President Kennedy decided to expand America's commitment to South Vietnam. He held off, however, on committing U.S. ground troops for the time being. Defying Taylor's warning that only an immediate infusion of American troops could save the day, Kennedy was betting that South Vietnam could hold its own in the coming months and that he could send U.S. forces and other SEATO forces at a later date as, in his words, a "last resort."[76] The President approved everything else the Taylor mission had recommended except for sending Lansdale to Vietnam. He authorized much higher amounts of aid for the Civil Guard and Self-Defense Corps, for various other counterinsurgency programs, and for helicopters, planes, and naval craft. A large number of American administrators and advisers would be sent to South Vietnam for insertion into the machinery of the Diem government, and thousands of additional military advisers would be sent to serve with South Vietnamese units.

The State Department instructed Nolting to inform Diem that he had to take a number of actions in return for America's generosity. The list included delegating more authority, broadening his government, and, most intrusively, giving the United States a voice in the decisions of the South Vietnamese government.[77] The imposition of demands was the brain child of William Jorden, a member of the Taylor mission and the State Department's Policy Planning Council who came from the Durbrow school of dealing with the Vietnamese. Sterling Cottrell of the State Department, a Taylor mission member who belonged to the Lansdale school, had lobbied unsuccessfully against such a return to strong-arm tactics, predicting that threats and demands for the use of Western concepts would not work with Diem for reasons of culture. The Americans, he said, had to behave as advisers rather than adversaries.[78]

The wisdom of Cottrell's position became clear as soon as the Americans presented their demands to Diem. "Vietnam does not want to be a protectorate," Diem declared to Nolting. The American demands for concessions "play right into the hands of the Communists," as they would "give a monopoly on nationalism to the Communists."[79] Diem told another listener that the Taylor mission had produced an outcome similar to that of General George Marshall's mission to China during the Chinese Civil War, for in both cases the Americans had decided to force-feed liberal Western concepts that were ill-suited to the local circumstances and culture.[80] Diem also expressed concern that the proposed influx of American personnel would undermine his government's nationalist image and give the Americans more opportunities to impose their views on the South Vietnamese.

In a conversation with Nolting, South Vietnamese Secretary of State Nguyen Dinh Thuan said that "the paucity of people willing to assume responsibility" and "the tendency to analyze and criticize rather than to act" made the proposed reforms unworkable. Diem, he said, would make changes "one by one on a practical basis if the right men could be found, but he would not accept anything that looked to the public as a sweeping reorganization under U.S. pressure." Swayed by these arguments, Nolting told Thuan that the U.S. government might accept such an approach if Diem would assemble a list of improvements he intended to make.[81] To placate the Americans, Diem proceeded to scrape together a list of reforms, which included changes to military planning and organization, delegation of authority to national and provincial councils, and delivery of more Presidential speeches on the radio. Diem also agreed to let select Americans operate inside the government. But he rejected acts of liberalization such as the broadening of the government and the release of imprisoned oppositionists, and he balked at the concept of American participation in his government's decision processes. Grudgingly, Kennedy and the State Department accepted Diem's limited concessions, and dropped their insistence that the United States have partial control of South Vietnamese decision-making.[82] Perhaps Diem's remarks about General George Marshall had reminded Kennedy of his own views at the end of the Chinese Civil War, when the young Congressman had denounced his own party's President, Harry S. Truman, for having slashed aid to Chiang Kai-Shek after Chiang rejected American calls for reform.[83]

Shiploads of American military hardware quickly began arriving in South Vietnam at the end of 1961. Expensive radio interception devices and cameras for aerial reconnaissance were flown in from the United States. Kennedy paid for whatever the military wanted, telling McNamara that "money is no object."[84] Men came, too. By the end of the year, the number of American military personnel in South Vietnam had risen to 2,600, and many thousands more were to follow.

Behind the scenes, Kennedy made some other important moves at year's end. He approved a recommendation from Rusk and McNamara to undertake limited defoliation operations in South Vietnam, starting with the clearance of key routes and then moving on to crop destruction in areas under Viet Cong domination. As part of a shuffling of personnel that became known as the "Thanksgiving Day Massacre," Kennedy installed Averell Harriman as Assistant Secretary of State for Far Eastern Affairs, presumably in the expectation that the ruthless Harriman would overcome resistance to the President's Southeast Asian policies, be it from an enemy, an ally, or an American.

Kennedy also appointed a new U.S. military commander in South Vietnam, a fifty-seven-year-old lieutenant general by the name of Paul Harkins. Harkins had been General George S. Patton's assistant chief of staff during World War II, and he later served as the annotator for Patton's World War II memoirs. Army wags had dubbed Harkins "the Ramrod" because of his effectiveness in making sure that all of Patton's orders were carried out. The nickname was not entirely apt, however, for Harkins was a much more polite and reserved man than Patton. Maxwell Taylor, like Patton, had taken a strong liking to Harkins and had helped push him up through the ranks.

Then there was the matter of the press. As the American commitment had grown, so had press coverage of events in South Vietnam, and journalists in Saigon were uncovering and publishing much hitherto unknown information about American activities in the country. America's new commitment, Kennedy decided, had to be kept secret from these reporters. The State Department, therefore, forbade the Saigon Mission from divulging information on the introduction of U.S. military personnel and equipment. For Kennedy, hiding American involvement had several advantages. It shielded the United States from charges of violating the 1954 Geneva provisions restricting foreign military assistance, a rationale that Kennedy sometimes cited in explaining his policy to subordinates. The Americans believed they were justified in violating the

Geneva Accords because North Vietnam had violated them through its heavy support of the Viet Cong, but public knowledge of American violations could undermine America's claim to the moral high ground. Downplaying the size of America's commitment also satisfied Diem, since his prestige would suffer if his countrymen viewed him as excessively reliant on foreign help. Disclosure of American military support and activities, moreover, might compromise secret military plans.

Secrecy brought other advantages that helped only Kennedy and his political party, not his country or its allies. By hiding and misleading, Kennedy could keep the attention of American voters away from a struggle that was unlikely to provide dramatic gains and had the potential for further deterioration and higher costs. The Republicans would soon be complaining loudly about reports of undisclosed increases in U.S. commitments – the administration continued to claim that it had just 685 men in South Vietnam even after the actual total was many times that figure – and accusing Kennedy of leading the country towards war without its consent.[85] Although Kennedy did not refer to a concern about his electoral popularity on the record, it was probably among the most important of the reasons behind his decision to conceal America's participation. The United States did not suffer much harm when it was cited for violating the Geneva Accords, and in his public and private conversations Kennedy did not mention the issues of Diem's prestige or military security, though these things probably had some influence on him. Like most politicians planning for reelection, Kennedy paid attention to the electoral consequences of all his actions. He also had a documented propensity for hiding the truth to further his political career. During the 1960 campaign, Kennedy had rebuked the Eisenhower administration for allowing the Soviets to create a "missile gap," even after he had been given classified information indicating that Soviet missiles did not outnumber American missiles.[86] In October 1962, on the eve of the Cuban Missile Crisis, Kennedy asked CIA Director John McCone to suppress information on the arrival of Soviet medium bombers in Havana until the completion of the mid-term Congressional elections. If such information became known to the press before that time, Kennedy said, it would become a contentious campaign issue and thus restrict his freedom of action. In addition, Kennedy requested that "all future information be suppressed." The President backed off only after McCone notified him that the intelligence on the bombers had already been disseminated and that a policy of suppressing future information would be "extremely dangerous."[87]

One of the first and most significant attempts to enforce Kennedy's new press policy came in the middle of December, when the USS *Core* traveled to South Vietnam carrying the better part of two helicopter companies. Officers on board the *Core* were under orders to keep secret the number of men and aircraft the ship was transporting. Blowing out billows of black smoke from its single stack, the huge gray aircraft ferry plowed forty-five miles up a tributary of the Mekong River, then followed the Saigon River to the only dock in Saigon suitable for unloading the ship's heavy cargo, which happened to be right in front of the Hotel Majestic and the Café Terrasse, two hangouts of the foreign press.

"Is that an aircraft carrier across the street?" the correspondents asked U.S. officials.

"No comment," came the reply.[88]

Some of the reporters were infuriated by this secretiveness. They quickly typed stories on the Core's arrival and sent them by telegram to their home offices, which promptly published them. The alienation of the American press from the U.S. government had begun.

Just as the Americans were stepping up their assistance to South Vietnam, the North Vietnamese were cutting back on their allocation of resources to the insurgency and reducing the intensity of insurgent military activity. During October, Hanoi decided to scale down its autumn offensive, in spite of its initial successes. To preserve its manpower for later use, Hanoi slashed infiltration from a rate between 500 to 1,000 men per month to a rate between 100 and 200.[89] One reason for these decisions was that Communist leaders had become fearful of American intervention, almost certainly because of Western press reports on the Taylor mission. Another was the stout resistance of some South Vietnamese troops during the offensive. "The enemy still possesses military superiority," the Communist leadership in the South concluded. "The enemy's forces are still strong and his will to fight against our Revolution is still high." The North Vietnamese leadership decided that the Viet Cong would lay low for a while and concentrate on building up their military strength, while watching for a coup against Diem that might allow them to move in for the kill.[90]

In deciding on retrenchment, the North Vietnamese may also have been influenced by pressure from the Chinese to scale down the attacks in the South. The first documented application of pressure, though, did not take place until December, after the Vietnamese Communists had changed their strategic direction. Visiting Hanoi during December, a high-level Chinese delegation told North Vietnam's leaders to avoid attacking Diem's forces in larger than company strength. China's defense minister explained to the North Vietnamese that China was trying to prevent a provocation of the United States, for if the Americans counter-attacked the Vietnamese Communists, the Chinese would feel obliged to enter the war as they had in Korea.[91]

The final months of 1961 marked the beginning of a major turn in the Vietnam War. John F. Kennedy, beleaguered by Hanoi's autumn offensive and by Communist advances elsewhere in the world, became firmly convinced at this time that America needed to build high the dikes at South Vietnam to prevent the surging Communists from flooding the rest of Southeast Asia. He chose South Vietnam as a defensive stronghold not out of utter desperation but out of the conviction that the South Vietnamese could and would fight the

Communists vigorously, more so than the other peoples on the southeast Asian mainland. Kennedy's strategy of providing aid and advisers but not combat troops was based upon confidence in the pugnacity of the South Vietnamese. Diem's armed forces offered encouraging signs by bouncing back from their nadir in September and October 1961, which, together with the massive increase in U.S. assistance to South Vietnam at the end of the year, dashed North Vietnam's hopes for a quick victory. With the falling of the curtain on 1961, the second of Diem's two years of ineffectiveness came to a close.

CHAPTER 6

Rejuvenation

JANUARY–JUNE 1962

THE BEGINNING OF THE NEW YEAR FOUND PRESIDENT KENNEDY AND the top brass in Palm Beach, at the splendid mansion of Kennedy's father, Joseph P. Kennedy. All the top figures of the military establishment were present: Secretary of Defense Robert McNamara, General Maxwell Taylor, the Joint Chiefs, Deputy Secretary of Defense Roswell Gilpatric, and General Paul Harkins. Gilpatric, who was assigned the task of taking notes at the Palm Beach meetings, recorded that the President "emphasized the importance of playing down the number of U.S. military personnel involved in Vietnam." Kennedy also stressed the need to avoid any impression that the U.S. military was participating in combat.[1] The next day, in a memorandum, Gilpatric fleshed out Kennedy's policy on handling reports of U.S. military involvement, assigning the Chairman of the Joint Chiefs of Staff and the Secretary of Defense responsibility for developing "a suitable cover story or stories, a public explanation, a statement of no comment or an appropriate combination thereof."[2]

Kennedy hoped to leave the campaign of concealment to others, but he was forced to become a participant when, at a press conference on January 15, he was asked whether American troops were involved in combat in Vietnam. The President replied that they were not. But in fact they were. Americans were now flying combat missions in World War II-era propeller aircraft, among them A-26 Invaders, AD-6 Skyraiders, and T-28 Trojans, that recently had been brought to South Vietnam and painted with South Vietnamese government markings. On the ground, American advisers were going on combat missions with South Vietnamese forces. While the American high command did not want these advisers to get involved in combat operations, the Americans could not set a good example or keep tabs on the fighting very well if they were not present. Three weeks before Kennedy's statement, James Thomas Davis of Livingston, Tennessee had been killed in the South Vietnamese jungle during a firefight, becoming the first American to die in ground combat.

Robert Kennedy followed his brother's lead during a trip to Saigon the next month. Attempting to downplay American involvement and the extent of the fighting, he announced that it was a struggle, not a war.

"What is the semantics of war and struggle?" a reporter asked him.

"It is a legal difference," he replied. "Perhaps it adds up to the same thing. It is a struggle short of war."[3]

Near the end of February, President Kennedy had the State Department issue a new press directive to his representatives in South Vietnam mandating additional measures to conceal America's involvement from the media. It also called for protection of the South Vietnamese government from the American press's nastier jabs. American personnel were instructed to "emphasize to newsmen fact that success of operation requires high-level GVN-American cooperation and that frivolous, thoughtless criticism of GVN makes cooperation difficult achieve."[4] As a consequence of this directive, the U.S. military command in Vietnam banned journalists from flying aboard helicopters during military missions, and American officials further reduced the amount of information they gave to reporters.

Washington's plan to keep South Vietnam bundled in layers of heavy clothing would prove ineffective against a press corps determined to rip away everything down to the undergarments. Among the Americans in Vietnam, more than a few junior advisers and officials were willing to tell reporters much of what the senior officials refused to divulge. Using such sources, the press corps easily learned the details of American military assistance and combat participation. Much else, like the presence of the USS *Core* or the great collection of U.S. aircraft at Saigon's main airport, could be seen with the naked eye. When the correspondents figured out that American officials in Saigon were being evasive in their answers or spending little time with the press, they often took it as an insult to their profession and to their own talents. Unaware that Washington had ordered these men to keep quiet, the journalists assumed that the orders had come from the top local U.S. officials, Ambassador Nolting and General Harkins in particular, and the press proceeded to attack them.

To shield the war effort and themselves from the newsmen's wrath, high-ranking U.S. officials in Saigon repeatedly asked Washington for greater latitude in speaking with the media, but the requests were usually denied. These officials themselves, though, were reluctant in their own right to speak with entire candor to the press, if not always for the same reasons as Washington. In the main, they worried that foreign press stories on American participation and South Vietnamese weaknesses would undermine the Diem government's prestige among South Vietnam's elites, who regularly read Vietnamese translations of Western newspapers and magazines. Revelations of failure undercut the national morale in any country, but the harmful effects were more pronounced in a county like Vietnam where such revelations caused the leader to lose face, thereby sapping the will of others to follow him. Harsh press attacks, more-over, could reduce the government's willingness to cooperate with American officials. As Ambassador Nolting would come to lament, the American press never appreciated these very important concerns.[5]

In 1962, America's representatives in Saigon could satisfy neither the American press corps nor the Saigon government. The reporters were not getting enough information from U.S. officials to quench their thirst, but they were getting enough information to write damaging articles about Diem's government, thereby undermining Diem's authority. This development was not inevitable, although Kennedy's directives and Diem's desire to keep the press uninformed made it the most likely of outcomes. Nolting and Harkins might have softened the press's attacks had they taken more time to chat and socialize with reporters and use the other methods with which government officials have been known to win the favor of journalists. Both Edward Lansdale and Nolting's eventual successor, Henry Cabot Lodge, achieved excellent results by taking such an approach.[6] Nolting and Harkins were, like Diem, more concerned with being right, working hard, and preserving their dignity than massaging the egos of self-absorbed reporters. "As Ambassador I certainly was not successful with the press," Nolting admitted years later. "Perhaps we did not accommodate the members of the media, socially and otherwise, as much as they expected. My office was always open, and they came in frequently, both singly and in groups, and were occasionally at our home. But we had much to do, and I for one found it difficult to spend hours sitting down, having a drink, and discussing matters with members of the press, some of whom wanted individual interviews to give them a separate story."[7]

The correspondents, for their part, bore some of the responsibility for their lack of contact with senior officials in Saigon. Contrary to common journalistic practice, the resident journalists did not take the initiative in cultivating relationships with these officials. Embassy counselor for public affairs John Mecklin, a former reporter and a good friend of some of the Saigon correspondents, noted that Saigon was the only overseas post he had ever seen where the resident press corps did not interact socially with embassy officials, and he attributed the problem to the fact that reporters never invited these officials for lunch or a drink. "The newsmen," observed Mecklin, "preferred to spend their leisure hours with each other, or their secret sources, talking themselves into a persecution psychology that reached the state of Pavlov's dogs."[8]

Diem wanted to keep information away from the reporters for the same basic reasons as Nolting and Harkins, but his methods for achieving that objective were different. While American officials in Saigon frequently tried to conceal or twist the truth about the war, they rarely engaged in the blatant fabrication of battlefield results that was commonplace among the Vietnamese on both sides of the conflict. The Vietnamese people did not share the foreign press's indignation over the willingness of the Saigon government or the Communists to create a "truth" that served their own interests. In a speech at a South Vietnamese psychological warfare school, Mecklin told a group of South Vietnamese officers that truth was the best propaganda. During World War II, he said, the BBC had been a beacon of hope to the French Resistance because it had broadcast the truth. At present, the Soviet Union blocked radio transmissions because it knew that the truth would destroy it. A smart young Vietnamese lieutenant informed Mecklin that the Vietnamese could not afford to tell the truth all of the time. "What you say may be right in other countries," he said, "but you clearly do not understand the situation here in Vietnam."[9]

When foreign journalists publicized details of government failures and the ever-present Saigon intrigue, the Diem government tried harder to conceal and deceive. Unfamiliar with South Vietnamese psychology, these journalists took offense and proceeded to write more negative stories. As time went on, the American correspondents increasingly viewed Diem as an adversary, which led them to exaggerate the government's weaknesses while understating its strengths. Mecklin was later to write that his main job in Vietnam was to handle the "feud between the newsmen who said 2 + 2 = 3 and the officials who said 2 + 2 = 5."[10] Disdaining both senior U.S. officials and Diem's officials, the resident American press corps received most of its information from South Vietnamese intellectuals and from American personnel who did not work in the embassy or near the top of the military advisory command. The reporters generally overlooked the considerable shortcomings of both groups. Roger Hilsman of the State Department noted aptly in February, "Some United States personnel in all agencies have been in Vietnam too long and carry old grudges and frustrations, or are unduly influenced by the views of various South Vietnamese 'dissidents.' These frustrated old-timers feed defeatist talk to the American press. They also talk to and encourage the 'dissidents' among the French-educated South Vietnamese intellectuals who are concentrated in Saigon."[11]

On the morning of February 27, President Diem awoke early and went to his study, located on the second floor of the yellow stucco Freedom Palace. He was an early riser even by Vietnamese standards, with a work day that typically began at 4 A.M. Diem began to read a biography of George Washington, a man who had long fascinated him, no doubt because the two of them had faced many of the same difficulties and criticisms in their respective struggles for national survival. Diem's reading was interrupted at 7:15 A.M. by the roar of aircraft engines. Hurrying out onto the balcony, the President saw two of his own government's AD-6 fighter-bombers bearing down on the palace. As the planes began bombing the Freedom Palace and strafing it with 20mm guns, South Vietnamese Navy ships in the Saigon River took the renegade pilots under fire with their antiaircraft guns, and the South Vietnamese Air Force sent fighters after them. One AD-6 was shot down and its pilot fell into the Saigon River, to be fished out by the police and taken into custody. The other crash-landed in Phnom Penh, where its pilot was received warmly by the Cambodian government. Damage to the palace was light. Intercepted radio traffic from the conspirators indicated that their sole target was the wing of the palace where the Nhus lived, and this wing was in fact the only part of the palace that was struck by bombs. The only fatality inside the palace was a maid who was struck by a falling beam. When the dead woman was found, she was still clutching the squirmy, but unharmed, infant daughter of the Nhus.

The bombing raid was not part of any larger scheme. No one else moved against Diem or the Nhus or other government leaders during or after the attack. But the foreign press, ignoring this truth as well as the rebel decision to target only the Nhus, argued that the bombing demonstrated the Diem government's "unpopularity."[12] Madame Nhu was correct in noting that American newspaper articles were tinged with an "ill-concealed regret" that the bombing had not destroyed the leaders of the Ngo family.[13] Adding to the bitterness of the South Vietnamese leadership towards the Western press, the captured pilot confessed that he had expected U.S. support for overthrowing the government as the result of reading articles in *Newsweek* and *Time*.[14]

As a result of this affair, the Ngo brothers became increasingly bold in their efforts to stifle reporters who showed contempt for their government. During March, Diem decided to expel Homer Bigart of the *New York Times* and François Sully of *Newsweek* for writing numerous negative articles on the government and its leading family. The Bigart dispatch that raised Diem's temperature over the boiling point asserted that Madame Nhu would soon be taking a trip out of the country, but "reports that she will be absent for several months have been discounted as wishful thinking by Government sources."[15] Amongst Vietnamese, such abuse was generally reserved for sworn enemies. Diem had been embarrassed by some of Madame Nhu's more outrageous public utterances and had tried, with only partial success, to quiet her, but he would still defend her against malicious and ill-informed media attacks. When another American journalist asked Diem about the expulsions, Diem replied, "You belong to a rich and powerful country. You may find that South Vietnam is not quite America. It is your right. But why try to humiliate and defame us while we are fighting a terrible war for our survival and for the defense of a vital border of the free world?"[16]

Ambassador Nolting viewed the reporting of Bigart and Sully as inaccurate and destructive, but he protested the expulsions to Diem on the grounds that they would upset the American people and jeopardize American support for the South Vietnamese government. In response, Diem said that he would not expel Bigart or Sully right away, but he would instead refuse to renew their visas when they expired later in the year.[17] Bigart promptly resumed his criticisms of the government. In an article on Nhu's visit to a village where the Communists had long held sway, Bigart wrote, "The village shows disheartening signs of over-regimentation. Almost everyone who greeted Ngo Dinh Nhu was in uniform.... There was little spontaneous enthusiasm. Security measures were tight and grim soldiers with submachine guns were seen everywhere along the route of inspection." Viewing the East through a Western lens, Bigart had failed to see that security and regimentation were far more important than spontaneous jubilation in South Vietnam. Evidence of that reality could be found elsewhere in Bigart's own article, where he stated, "A year ago this was a very insecure territory. Today one could drive here without a military escort."[18] Bigart was to leave Vietnam in the late summer.

Militarily, the first two months of 1962 were not promising for Saigon. Large and futile operations persisted. Typical was the assault on Binh Hoa, seventeen miles to the west of Saigon, at the end of January. Hoping to catch several hundred Viet Cong who had been spotted at Binh Hoa, four government battalions moved by boat into a nearby staging area, with plans to assault the village the next morning. The Viet Cong, however, detected the large government troop movement and most of them fled Binh Hoa several hours before the assault began. When A-26 Invaders and T-28 Trojans bombed and rocketed the target area right before the attack, the sole victims were five South Vietnamese civilians who were killed and another eleven who were wounded. The government soldiers who swept through the area afterwards killed a total of five Viet Cong and captured a few more.[19]

The Viet Cong, meanwhile, were growing stronger. In February, U.S. intelligence reported, the Viet Cong had increased their strength through recruiting and infiltration to between 20,000 and 25,000, up from 18,000 in December 1961. Admiral Harry D. Felt, Commander in Chief, Pacific, reported to the Joint Chiefs of Staff that the "will, determination, and fighting ability of VC is at least equal to GVN," and "politically VC has support of a significant segment of rural population."[20] Swayed by this and similar reports, President Kennedy was predicting that victory in South Vietnam was ten years away.[21]

The momentum began to shift in the spring. The performance of South Vietnam's armed forces entered into a steady ascent that was to continue for the remainder of Diem's time in office. Government forces started to patrol more aggressively, with greater emphasis on stealthy small-unit operations and night operations. They responded more rapidly and with heightened vigor to distress calls from remote villages and outposts, which themselves were becoming better at fending off Viet Cong attacks. As the government's military successes mounted, the power-minded villagers chose to provide government personnel with more information, which in turn allowed South Vietnamese forces to leave static positions to attack enemy forces.

One of the government's biggest victories in the spring of 1962, on April 6, resulted from a combination of accurate intelligence and military skill. Tipped off in advance that 1,200 Viet Cong would be attacking, several small government garrisons in Tra Bong district positioned heavy weapons outside of their outposts to cover the key approaches. When the insurgents came down off the mountains to attack, they were greeted with a crossfire from machine guns and 155 mm howitzers at close range. Stopped short of the government's perimeter positions, the Viet Cong suffered heavy losses before fleeing back into the hills. The Associated Press reported that the Viet Cong left forty-five dead behind, and presumably they had taken many more with them, while the government reported sixteen of its own dead and thirty-three wounded. The government forces captured two American-made 57 mm recoilless rifles and a collection of French, Chinese, and North Korean machine guns. An American adviser remarked, "A few more wins like this and the back of the Vietcong in the area will be broken."[22]

The foreign press, despite its hostility to Diem and its skepticism about official claims of progress, took note of the military progress. Trustworthy American sources, Bigart reported in April, had concluded that "the erosion of the Government's authority had been slowed if not halted by aggressive action by the Vietnamese Army."[23] *Newsweek,* one of the publications most hostile to Diem, reported later that month that its correspondents had traveled all across South Vietnam to interview American military personnel and had found that these advisers believed South Vietnamese forces were "gradually turning the tide of war against the Communist guerrillas." For instance, one senior American adviser had remarked, "Today we can usually expect a village hit by a surprise attack to fight, where previously the defenders would surrender or flee."[24] By mid-year, the government had staunched the deterioration of the military situation. Kennedy's risky prediction that South Vietnam could survive without U.S. ground forces was being vindicated.

One force driving this rapid improvement was the large-scale introduction of American aircraft, armored vehicles, radios, and other modern equipment. Fixed-wing aircraft could provide firepower in any area where the Viet Cong were present in large numbers. Helicopters allowed government soldiers to reach the enemy's mountain and jungle strongholds in fifteen minutes, whereas in the past the troops had needed to march for three days or more to get there. By accompanying vehicle convoys, helicopters discouraged the Viet Cong from conducting convoy ambushes, the Viet Cong's most effective means of harming the South Vietnamese logistical system. In addition, helicopters could appear and unload troops so quickly that the Viet Cong did not have time to flee in the usual guerrilla manner. One Communist account noted, "It became difficult for our cadre to move around during daylight because the helicopters could see our people walking from a considerable distance away. Just a few helicopters were enough to surround a target and to make a surprise landing of assault troops to capture or kill our cadre and troops in any terrain, and especially in open fields."[25] The M-113 amphibious armored personnel carrier, a ten-ton box of armor plating propelled by tracks and mounted with a powerful .50 caliber machine gun, had the ability to overrun most Viet Cong forces, as the Viet Cong lacked antitank weapons that could penetrate the behemoth's hull.

Radios enabled dispersed government posts to summon help quickly from air, mechanized, or artillery assets.

A second reason behind the change was the massive influx of American military advisers. Growing in number from 2,600 to 11,500 during 1962, American advisers helped transform the South Vietnamese military into an effective modern fighting force, much as Chinese advisers had done for the Vietnamese Communist military in the early 1950s. The U.S. advisers introduced a new degree of sophistication into the planning and execution of military operations. Whereas American political advice to the South Vietnamese was often useless because of cultural ignorance, American military advice contributed mightily to improvements in the conduct of operations. U.S. advisers urged their counterparts to discontinue clumsy and ineffective sweep operations involving thousands of troops and instead run smaller operations and patrols, which were stealthier and allowed coverage of a greater area. They led by example, and their industriousness rubbed off on their counterparts. Trudging into sweltering, leech-ridden jungles with the South Vietnamese, they took the same risks as their counterparts and ate the same meager rations. The advisers could see the South Vietnamese in action and they could count the friendly and enemy corpses on the battlefield afterwards, giving the top U.S. advisers much more information for use in recommending changes to the South Vietnamese. At the highest level, Ambassador Nolting and General Harkins supported Diem unequivocally in accordance with instructions to get along with Diem, and the South Vietnamese President reacted as the authors of this policy had hoped. The South Vietnamese President more often cashiered bad leaders and directed his division commanders and provincial chiefs to take the war to the enemy.

The third factor was the improvement of leadership in the South Vietnamese armed forces and provincial administrations. The year 1962 saw the coming of age of many young South Vietnamese men cultivated by Diem after 1954 in his efforts to replace the colonial-era officials with dedicated nationalists. New division commanders and provincial chiefs took office and filled the leadership slots below them, down to platoon commanders and hamlet chiefs, with officers and administrators who shared their dedication and integrity. Rufus Phillips, a very able protégé of Lansdale, discovered a remarkable improvement in the quality of local officials during an extensive tour of the countryside in mid-1962. "Practically all of the officials I met in six provinces had assumed office within the last year," Phillips observed. "Their conversation and their actions reflected a genuine desire to help the hamlet people and an understanding of their problems. Most of them were working long hours with energy and enthusiasm, inspecting their provinces during the day and going over papers at night."[26]

During the first half of the year, as the government's regular and militia forces gradually improved, a new program came to life that was to revolutionize the war effort. Dubbed the "strategic hamlet" program, it became the core of a new strategy employing military, political, and economic resources in symphony. Most Westerners incorrectly attributed the creation of the strategic hamlet program to Robert Thompson, a Briton who had led the successful counterinsurgency effort in Malaya and who, since September 1961, had headed the British Advisory Mission in Vietnam. The South Vietnamese government itself developed the first strategic hamlets on its own initiative, several months before Thompson's arrival.[27] Much of the confusion over the program's origins resulted from Diem's unwillingness to inform his American patrons about the program in its early stages, a decision made on the assumption that the Americans would interfere in counterproductive ways if they knew about it. Thompson, drawing on his experiences in fortifying Malaya's villages, gave the Vietnamese advice on refining the program, some of which the Vietnamese cast aside. It was Nhu who would lead from the top and bring the program to life as 1962 progressed.

The first step in creating a strategic hamlet was to cut down the vegetation surrounding the hamlet, in order to give hamlet defenders clear sight of approaching enemies and to make room for protective barriers. Next, workers encircled the hamlet with a fence of bamboo and barbed wire. Around the fence they dug a ditch or moat, and for the outermost barrier they used an earthen mound and rows of booby traps and sharp stakes, which protruded out menacingly like the quills of a porcupine. Although these barriers were often flimsy in a material sense, they proved quite useful in encouraging the residents to view the Viet Cong as intruders who were to be resisted.

The principal strength of the strategic hamlet was not its fortifications but its defenders. The representatives of the South Vietnamese government were present in greater numbers than ever before, and they were there twenty-four hours a day, refusing to cede the hamlets to the Viet Cong at night as had been the case in many hamlets since 1960. Defending the hamlet from within were members of the Self-Defense Corps and the Republican Youth, who were generally drawn from the local area and thus had family members upon whom they could rely as informants. In contrast to the Viet Cong, the government tried to harness the power of family bonds rather than destroy them, an approach that did not generally produce the same degree of fanatical devotion to the cause but did produce good results when dedicated leadership was present. The strategic hamlet militia manned observation towers, guard posts, and a central defense post where arms were stored. They were connected to each other with field telephones, and to the district military command with wind-powered radios. At the end of the day, the militiamen rang a bell to signal the imminence of the curfew, and anyone found approaching the hamlet after the onset of the curfew was shot. When they wanted to bring terrible fury onto a Viet Cong attack force after dark, the defenders used torch-lit wooden pointers to guide overhead aircraft, or radioed the enemy's position to the nearest artillery battery.

Civil Guard companies, which were based at the district headquarters, patrolled the areas between strategic hamlets, and they guarded bridges, government bases, and other essential installations. When the Viet Cong attacked a strategic hamlet in force, the Civil Guard were to come to the hamlet's assistance, whether by foot, boat, truck, or helicopter. To meet the strategic hamlet program's demand for militiamen, the Americans funded an increase in the combined strength of the Self-Defense Corps and Civil Guard, from 124,000 to 172,000, over the course of 1962. The central government also issued instructions to eliminate numerous small militia outposts that were scattered across the countryside, many of them distant from the population and highly vulnerable to attack, thereby freeing up additional militiamen.[28] The South Vietnamese Army, which expanded from 168,000 to 196,000 in this time period, attacked Viet Cong forces operating outside the populous areas. Seeking to minimize collateral damage to civilians, the government put major restrictions on the use of air and artillery strikes near the strategic hamlets, although the army was known to disregard the rules at times.

The government cadres who were assigned to the strategic hamlet program carried out the same tasks as the Viet Cong cadres and then some. They recruited and trained villagers, helped tend the fields, and administered medical care. They gave the villagers agricultural loans and wondrous supplies such as fertilizer and rat poison, things that the Viet Cong could never give them. Upon each hut, the cadres nailed a census board listing all of the authorized occupants, and they closely monitored the movements of the peasants and the arrival of strangers. In government-built schools and markets, in rice fields and in thatch-roofed peasant homes, the strategic hamlet cadres preached the virtues of the government and decried the evils of the Viet Cong. They talked of simple things of immediate interest to the peasants, such as government pig-raising programs and the superiority of their rifles to those of the Viet Cong, rather than complicated political theories.

Residents of strategic hamlets were required to participate in hamlet construction projects without pay, with the poorer inhabitants bearing the brunt of the unpaid work because those who were better off could pay others to do their share. Some of the villagers grumbled – especially in the Mekong Delta, which was assigned a lower priority in the program than the country's other regions – but they generally proved willing to cooperate when the government provided adequate leadership. The government's projects and programs were giving the peasants greater wealth than they had ever possessed, and most of the obligatory work took place during the periods of the agricultural cycle when the need to work the family's fields was relatively low. This communal labor pushed villagers, like it or not, towards support of the government side, for the Viet Cong looked down on those who helped the government, and when the Viet Cong came in and destroyed a bridge that the peasants had built with their own hands, the peasants naturally resented it.

The strategic hamlet program differed from the failed agroville program of 1959 to 1960 in that relocation of entire hamlets was unusual, largely because of complaints from peasants during the agroville experience.[29] The strategic hamlets also diverged from the agrovilles and other previous pacification efforts by placing control at the hamlet level instead of the village level. In the past, the village defense forces had typically been located at the village center, with the result that they might be slow in detecting and reacting to enemy initiatives in peripheral hamlets. Now, the Viet Cong would encounter resistance as soon as they attempted to penetrate those peripheral hamlets. This rearrangement also enabled Nhu to bypass the village governments and the Saigon ministries that worked with those governments, both of which still contained large numbers of ineffectual holdovers from the colonial period. Nhu assigned authority in the strategic hamlets to organizations under his direct control, principally the Can Lao Party and the Republican Youth. As part of his design for a Personalist revolution, Nhu was filling these organizations with the new generation of leaders, men who were active and ready to fight. These men were essential. At an early stage in the development of the strategic hamlet program, Theodore Heavner, a Vietnamese-speaking State Department official who examined the strategic hamlets in considerable depth, commented, "One of the brighter aspects of the program at the moment appears to be the remarkable effort to send good cadre into the hamlets to get the program in motion."[30]

When explaining the strategic hamlet program, Diem and Nhu often spoke of its democratic character, but it was a Vietnamese version of democracy rather than a Western version. While the strategic hamlet residents elected hamlet leaders by secret ballot, the elections were not held in the Western way. The government's district chief told the peasants to vote for certain candidates, who were generally members of the traditional village elites despite urgings from Nhu to include less affluent peasants, and invariably those candidates came out on top. The government thus could install people who were competent and loyal and prevent the Viet Cong from influencing the elections. The central government's manipulation of elections did not particularly bother the vil- lagers, any more than the Viet Cong's lack of elections had.[31] What counted in the contest for the support of the peasants was not ideology or democracy, but military power and good leadership that inspired from the top down through the force of personality. Acting with vigor and skill, Diem and Nhu successfully motivated the provincial chiefs, and through them the lower-level officials, to organize the people and carry out the strategic hamlet program.[32]

The Americans were taken aback, and in some cases hurt, when they learned that the Ngo brothers had been developing the strategic hamlet program behind their backs and had sought the advice of a few British experts over that of the sprawling American mission. Ambassador Nolting, however, con- vinced Washington and the U.S. agencies in Vietnam to support the program, and soon it had many enthusiastic advocates on the American side.[33] General

Harkins, who also took a strong interest in the program, helped persuade South Vietnamese army leaders to devote large numbers of soldiers to the protection of the strategic hamlet areas.[34] The Americans, though, did not wholeheartedly endorse the Diem government's methods of implementation, sharing some of the same reservations as the British. The Ngo brothers chose not to follow a British and American plan that would have put much higher emphasis on the strategic hamlets in the southern part of the country than in the northern part. Diem and Nhu favored building strategic hamlets in the highlands, in order to impede the establishment of Communist bases in the mountains, and in the central coastal region, in order to protect the most vulnerable portion of the vital coastal highway. These concepts were, indeed, quite sound. Diem and Nhu also disregarded British and American recommendations to develop the strategic hamlets at a relatively slow tempo with priority given to critical roads, areas of high strategic importance, and areas on the outer edges of human habitation. They planned to convert most of the nation's 16,000 hamlets into strategic hamlets within two years, in the hope that such a rapid pace would generate enthusiasm and confound enemy attempts to damage a large portion of the program.[35] Eventually, Nhu and Diem would find that the rapid tempo of expansion was making it too difficult to develop strategic hamlets of high quality, and so they did reduce the pace of new hamlet construction and set priorities, although rapid expansion would continue in some areas.

Contrary to the government's original plans, the Civil Guard and regular army frequently did not come to the relief of strategic hamlets under attack. When the Viet Cong began attacking strategic hamlets at night, they hid guerrillas along the approaches to the hamlet for the express purpose of ambushing relief forces. Responding to radioed distress calls, the local Civil Guard or army units would walk into a few such ambushes, suffer serious casualties, and then decide that the relief operations were not worth the costs. Out of these experiences evolved new tactics, whereby the hamlets would be made strong enough to resist small attacks on their own, with assistance from air or artillery support. To gain access to the hamlets, the Viet Cong would have to operate in large formations, which made them vulnerable to attack by the Civil Guard and the army.[36] The Civil Guard and army, by inflicting heavy casualties on large Communist units, would discourage or prevent the Communists from operating in sufficient strength to overwhelm a strategic hamlet. If a particularly large Communist unit did manage to reach a strategic hamlet, the defenders were to flee or hide in secret cellars, much as the Viet Cong would do when confronted by large government forces. Some competent government units also developed an ability to predict the Viet Cong's ambush sites during attacks on strategic hamlets and to launch surprise attacks into the rear of the would-be ambushing forces.

During 1962, thanks in part to the Saigon government's achievements in the countryside, the United States did not try to prod Diem into undertaking reforms. Even the State Department, the agency most desirous of reforming and liberalizing South Vietnam, was willing to tolerate Diem's methods at this time, at least as long as they continued to yield good results.[37] Some State officials were even promoting Diem's view that liberalization itself would cause serious damage to South Vietnam. "Diem's strong leadership has been needed to prevent factionalism which is endemic in Vietnamese politics," argued Sterling Cottrell.[38] Theodore Heavner remarked, "Oppositionists in the government or a legal opposition outside the government will not be helpful or possible at this time. Public criticism of the government now would be interpreted by most Vietnamese, many of the Saigon intellectuals included, as a sign of weakness, if not imminent collapse."[39] In the absence of American pressure, Diem enacted a string of American-backed reforms, aimed mainly at promoting efficiency rather than liberalization. He purged officials guilty of abuses, created an organization for investigating complaints, and set up aid programs for disabled veterans and war widows and orphans. Conscription of educated men into the officer corps commenced, while low-ranking soldiers received pay raises.

In June, the Diem government adopted one reform that the Americans did not like in the least, the "Social Purification Law." Conceived and sponsored by Madame Nhu, it put restrictions on divorce, smoking, and alcohol consumption by minors, and outlawed prostitution, dancing, beauty contests, cockfighting, sorcery, and contraceptives. Madame Nhu let it be known that a major target of the law was the vice that the Americans had brought to her country. Like most of the Vietnamese, she objected to intimate relations between American men and Vietnamese women. "Foreigners come here not to dance, but to help Vietnamese fight Communism," she said. "Asians are not used to promiscuity between men and women. If the Americans want to dance, they should go elsewhere."[40] The Diem government went so far as to have General Harkins issue an order prohibiting American servicemen from kissing their Vietnamese girlfriends at the airport. After the Social Purification Law took effect, South Vietnam's cities began looking more like the cities of a country at war and less like Las Vegas. An eerie silence descended on the Rue Catinat, the site of many of Saigon's glitzy night clubs. The swarms of giddy hostesses disappeared, and American servicemen had to turn their attention to less exciting activities, such as games of tic-tac-toe with the barmaids. The changes did not sit well with those city people who had profited from or indulged in these vices, nor did they go over well with the American correspondents, whose entertainment options had been sharply reduced.

In Hanoi, the growth in America's commitment to Vietnam after Taylor's mission and the improvement in Diem's war effort convinced the Communist Party leadership, by mid-1962, that the war was going to be long and difficult. The Vietnamese Communist Party now had no chance of attaining a rapid victory without a massive, overt infusion of North Vietnamese troops, an act sure to invite direct American action on the ground or in the air – the worst possible outcome in the view of the North Vietnamese. Promises to the Viet Cong of a decisive military victory melted away, to be replaced with statements that final victory would require lengthy military and political initiatives. The Vietnamese Communists offered to negotiate with Diem and the Americans, expressing their receptivity to a neutral South Vietnam with a coalition government encompassing all political, social, and religious groups.[41]

Le Duan, among the most militant of the Communist leaders in Hanoi, began advocating a protracted, low-intensity struggle, rather than a swift, high-intensity offensive. In a mid-year letter, Le Duan noted that the Communists would limit their actions to keep the United States from moving from what they called a "special war" – the type of war currently in place, in which the South Vietnamese fought with U.S. support and advisers – to what they termed a "limited war" – a war involving U.S. combat troops. Although previously, in 1961, Le Duan had said that the Communists needed to destroy the enemy army to win, he now said that no such destruction was necessary. As evidence, he cited the recent revolutionary successes in Laos and Algeria. Repeated victories of moderate size over Diem's forces, Le Duan argued, could force the Americans to agree to an ostensibly a neutral coalition government, which would spare the Americans from direct embarrassment but would nonetheless end in Communist control of South Vietnam. Le Duan explained that the Communists would overthrow the coalition government by infiltrating it with South Vietnamese politicians whom the United States deemed non-Communists but who secretly served Hanoi.[42]

The French scholar Bernard Fall, one of the very few Westerners to visit North Vietnam in the early 1960s, heard similar sentiments from North Vietnam's leaders in the middle of the year. Arriving in North Vietnam by air, he was brought from the airport by car into Hanoi, where he caught a glimpse of the changes since 1954. "Not a street seemed to have been paved, nor a house repainted, since the French evacuated the city," Fall observed. No other cars transited the streets, and in once-thriving sections of the town, the shops were boarded up and the buildings were in disrepair. The Frenchman also found striking the rigid regimentation of the people, who were strangely silent and were all dressed in the same black pants and white shirts. He sensed "an atmosphere like that of George Orwell's 1984 – a feeling that Big Brother is everywhere and knows everything." When Fall was taken to North Vietnam's leaders, they revealed that they feared American retaliation, owing to the vulnerability of their nascent industrial base to American military power. Pham Van Dong intoned, "We fully realize that the American imperialists wish to provoke a situation in the course of which they could use the heroic struggle of the South Vietnamese people as a pretext for the destruction of our economic and cultural achievements. We shall offer them no pretext which could give rise to an American military intervention against North Viet-Nam."[43]

Over the course of 1962, the North Vietnamese beseeched the Chinese and the Soviets to provide yet more assistance. Ho Chi Minh, visiting Moscow

himself to seek additional military aid, received an offer of 3,000 firearms
that the Soviets had captured from the Germans during World War II. Ho
growled that the weapons belonged in a museum.[44] Ho made similar pleas
in person to the Chinese leadership, which was now taking a more aggressive approach towards Southeast Asia because Chinese agricultural production
had begun to recover. Proving much more amenable than the Soviets, Mao
decided to ship 90,000 weapons to North Vietnam, enough to equip 230 new
battalions.[45]

* * *

IN WASHINGTON AND ACROSS ASIA, THE DEBATE OVER LAOS BURNED
brighter during 1962. The Joint Chiefs regularly took swipes at Harriman's
plans for neutralization, as did John McCone, the conservative shipbuilding
magnate who had become CIA Director just before the year began. Arguing
that the proposed coalition government would be unable to control the Pathet
Lao or halt North Vietnamese infiltration into South Vietnam, the Joint Chiefs
and McCone called for generous allocations of aid and advisers to Phoumi's
rightist forces. Diem and Nhu relentlessly implored the Americans to clear the
Viet Cong out of Laos, emphasizing that the Greek Communists had not been
defeated until Tito shut off their access to Yugoslavian territory. The Thais,
greatly worried by the prospect of a Communist Laos on their border, pleaded
for an American pledge to defend Thailand unilaterally. The Kennedy administration gave the Thais such a pledge in March.

The chorus of objections failed to move Kennedy off the path towards neutralization or shake his confidence in Harriman as his principal guide. In April,
at Harriman's recommendation, Kennedy cut aid to the royal Laotian government. Within a few weeks, the financial pain induced General Phoumi, the
rightist leader, to agree to a coalition government led by the neutralist Souvanna
Phouma. This turn of events emboldened Hanoi, suggesting as it did that the
United States was giving up on the rightists and was unwilling to send its own
troops to Laos. A few days after Phoumi yielded, Pathet Lao and North Vietnamese troops committed their most flagrant violation to date of the year-old
ceasefire – an attack on the provincial capital of Nam Tha by several of the
best Pathet Lao battalions and six North Vietnamese battalions, supported by
four thousand Chinese logistical troops delivering armaments from China by
truck and mule.[46] The 4,500 royalist soldiers at Nam Tha offered little effective
resistance before fleeing in disarray. After this debacle, the senior American
military adviser in Laos reported that the leadership of the royal Laotian forces
was "gravely deficient," and that the remnants of the royalist army "cannot be
expected to fight with any effectiveness."[47]

At this point, U.S. military leaders and other hawks called on Kennedy to
resume aid to General Phoumi, bomb North Vietnamese railways, and shoot

down Soviet aircraft operating in Laos, so as to convince the Soviets to rein in the North Vietnamese. If such measures failed to move Soviets, they went on to argue, then it would be time to put American troops into Laos. From America's Southeast Asian allies came calls for similar actions. Most troubling of all to Kennedy were the hawkish words that began to emanate from Eisenhower. "If Laos is lost," Eisenhower told McNamara and McCone on May 13, "South Vietnam and Thailand will ultimately go because they would be outflanked. All Southeast Asia will be lost, and Indonesia will follow and the world will be divided. I therefore place the greatest importance on the maintenance of Laos." At the least, Eisenhower said, the United States should seek a partition of Laos into northern and southern sections, with pro-American forces in control of the southern part, which contained the Ho Chi Minh Trail infiltration routes and large Viet Cong sanctuaries. If the United States needed to send troops into Laos, Eisenhower intoned, it should provide "whatever support is necessary to achieve the objectives of their mission, including – if necessary – the use of tactical nuclear weapons."[48]

Dreading a major showdown with the Soviet Union and China, President Kennedy sought other avenues of escape. He moved the Seventh Fleet into the Gulf of Thailand and ordered three thousand American troops already in Thailand to take up positions on the Thai-Laotian border, with the intention of "sending a message" to the Communists, and to the American people, that the President was not as timid as his previous actions might suggest. Continuing to hope that the Soviets would ultimately hold back the North Vietnamese as Harriman claimed they would, Kennedy sent Khrushchev a message decrying the Soviet Union's failure to live up to its promises to support Laotian neutrality. Khrushchev assured Kennedy that Communist forces would not again undertake large-scale military action in Laos, and asserted that the Americans should reciprocate by removing their troops from Thailand. Kennedy began removing the troops from Thailand a few days later. He also had Harriman reach a settlement with Communist negotiators at Geneva on the neutralization of Laos, which involved a coalition government and the withdrawal of all foreign forces.

The neutralization scheme caused great alarm among American hawks and the leaders of Asia's non-Communist nations. When Harriman informed Nolting of the deal, the ambassador replied that he could not, in good conscience, support the plan for a coalition government in Laos.

"You're not working for God," Harriman snapped. "You're working for the Kennedy administration."[49] As he had done on several previous occasions, Harriman lobbied for Ambassador Nolting's removal from South Vietnam, but again without success.

Nolting's opposition, however, was not as problematic for Harriman as was that of Diem, since Diem was the sovereign leader of a critical U.S. ally. Diem flatly refused to sign the final version of the Geneva agreement. Enraged,

Harriman convinced Kennedy to send Diem a letter requesting the South Vietnamese President's signature. In the letter, Kennedy assured Diem that the Soviets would enforce the Geneva agreement, and that the United States had no plans for neutralizing South Vietnam, contrary to many rumors to that effect. "Our policy toward Vietnam must and will continue as it has since my administration took office," promised Kennedy. "We have helped and shall continue to help your country to defend itself."[50] Nolting, having by this time fatalistically accepted the agreement, told Diem that although he himself had little confidence in the agreement, Diem ought to endorse it in order to retain Kennedy's support. Diem had his foreign minister sign the agreement.

The Geneva agreement of 1962 put Laos under the rule of a coalition government containing representatives from Phoumi's rightists, Souvanna's neutralists, and Souphanouvong's Communists. It required the removal of all North Vietnamese troops and American military advisers from Laos by October 7. In addition, Hanoi was forbidden from sending personnel and military goods through Laotian territory, and the Soviets had to discontinue air drops to the Pathet Lao and North Vietnamese troops inside Laos. To monitor compliance with the provisions on foreign military activities, the International Control Commission and the coalition government would carry out inspections, but the main burden of ensuring Communist compliance lay with the Soviets.

The problems in Laos did not overshadow the most important development in the first half of 1962, the strengthening of the South Vietnamese war machine. Abetted by the rise to power of young leaders whom Diem had nurtured and by the influx of American men and equipment, the Diem government effected startling improvements in the armed forces and began to turn the strategic hamlet program into the solid core of pacification. Despite heightened Communist infiltration through Laos, the Diem government succeeded in halting the decline in its fortunes that had begun in 1960. Taking note of these developments, the North Vietnamese abandoned their hopes of defeating Diem through decisive military action and instead turned to a strategy of eroding America's will to support Diem by means of protracted low-intensity warfare.

CHAPTER 7

Attack

JULY–DECEMBER 1962

AT THE AGE OF FIFTY-SEVEN, GENERAL PAUL HARKINS WAS STILL IN excellent physical shape. A former hockey and polo star, he had the energy and enthusiasm needed for the difficult post of senior U.S. military adviser to a country with far flung outposts facing attack. Harkins's enemies in the press corps were to accuse him of spending little time in the field and relying solely on statistical reports for information. The journalist and author Neil Sheehan later claimed that "General Paul D. Harkins and his staff sat in their air-conditioned offices in Saigon and waxed optimistic on the same kind of supposedly impressive statistics the French had comforted themselves with during the First Indochina War."[1] In actuality, as those who worked with him would attest, Harkins spent a great portion of time in the field. "He lived a Spartan military life in Saigon, traveling almost daily around the country in small planes to keep in touch with the war," noted John Mecklin, the embassy counseler for public affairs.[2] At dusty district headquarters and remote mountain militia posts, Harkins sought firsthand information on the war from South Vietnamese and American officers, and then afterwards obtained independent appraisals to make sure the officers in the field knew their stuff and were not sugarcoating anything for the boss.[3]

General Harkins spent much of the year's second half pressing Diem to fix problems in the South Vietnamese armed forces that had not been fixed during the first half. While Harkins was not a brilliant or creative strategist, he was a superb motivational and technical coach, which was what the situation most demanded. The Diem government had a sound strategy, centered around the strategic hamlet program, but it needed further improvement in terms of aggressiveness and tactical proficiency. Advising Diem only behind closed doors, Harkins spoke with enough tact and competence to keep Diem's ear and respect.

"During the preceding week, I visited all the divisions," Harkins said to Diem during a meeting on July 18. "Everywhere, it was reported that there was a serious shortage of company grade officers. In some instances, there were only six officers in a battalion. There were instances of companies commanded by aspirants or sergeants. Leadership is lacking in platoons and companies, the very place where it is needed most – since these are the units which do the fighting." Harkins recommended diverting officers from headquarters or logistical commands to combat units, shortening the training time at the officer school, and bringing more young professional men into the armed forces with abbreviated officer training.

Diem admitted to Harkins, "I am concerned over the number of senior officers who have reached the height of their potential and who lack the education and initiative required in higher grades."

"Such men should be eliminated," said Harkins.

"The situation was inherited from the French, who were too easy and made colonels and lieutenant colonels who had no real capability or training," Diem explained. "One of the difficulties in identifying incompetent officers lies in the fact that my generals do not want to recommend the separation of officers who are old friends." Despite the problems involved, Diem said, "I am considering the thought of elimination."

Harkins brought up the ambush of a South Vietnamese airborne unit a few days earlier. Twenty men had been killed as soon as the Viet Cong opened fire. Two hundred and fifty other paratroopers remained unharmed after the initial volleys and they could have counter-attacked the ambushing force, but instead they hunkered down, allowing the Viet Cong to slip away. "This is an example of the lack of junior leadership," Harkins asserted. Another problem, Harkins said, was the use of large units in counterguerrilla operations, which tended to give the enemy enough advance notice to get away. "Rather than have large, six- or seven-battalion operations, covering eighty square kilometers, which result sometimes in the capture of as little as two VC, better results could be obtained from smaller, battalion-sized operations based on good intelligence and carried out with speed, under the greatest possible secrecy." Harkins emphasized the importance of seizing the initiative by launching attacks relentlessly, asserting, "The only way to win is to attack, attack, attack." Echoing Robert Thompson and other Westerners involved in the strategic hamlet program, Harkins called for a more systematic plan for the development of the strategic hamlets. Contrary to what his detractors would later say, Harkins was concerned not only with conventional military activities but also with pacification.[4]

During a session with Diem on September 7, General Harkins urged him to form a single chain of command in order to eliminate the conflicts among provincial chiefs and division commanders. He emphasized the importance of the strategic hamlets and intelligence collection. Now was the time, Harkins went on to tell Diem, for an all-out effort to crush the Viet Cong. Harkins called it an "explosion" campaign, and he expected that it would curtail the Viet Cong's activities drastically within one year. "Perhaps it would not be possible to kill all the Viet Cong," Harkins said, "but it should at least drive them underground. Even this would not be bad, because it would permit the continuation of the construction of strategic hamlets and the economic development of the country."

"The Viet Cong will not accept a defeat of this kind," Diem responded. "I do not believe the Viet Cong are a worm which can be crushed under one's heel. They have many resources available to them – including Communist North Vietnam." Hanoi might infiltrate large numbers of North Vietnamese troops into South Vietnam through porous Laos if faced with such an offensive, Diem contended. Thus, he said, the Americans and the South Vietnamese ought to consider a period of three years in their planning instead of one. General Harkins, in truth, did not believe that the explosion campaign would eradicate the Viet Cong in one year. Ambassador Nolting subsequently remarked, "There is no thought that this will be a one-time operation: what is involved is moving to a higher intensity of operations which it is recognized may have to be continued indefinitely." The strategic hamlet concept, Nolting also noted, was to remain the centerpiece of the government's strategy during the explosion period.[5] The main concern of General Harkins was getting the Vietnamese to act with greater vigor. He kept telling the team to run a lap in a time he knew they could not achieve, to get them to circle the track faster than they thought they could.

Diem told Harkins that one of the most critical areas of the war remained the Annamite chain of central Vietnam. Particularly crucial were the provinces of Quang Nam and Quang Ngai, where the Viet Cong were still trying to advance from the foothills to the coastal region to obtain supplies. "Recent helicopter operations in this area have helped considerably because they have caused the VC to hesitate in carrying out their plan," Diem said, but "as long as the VC stay in this redoubt, they are safe and even have caves and tunnels in which they can hide."

"The answer is to go in and get them in their tunnels," Harkins replied.

General Harkins recounted to Diem a story he had heard in both Saigon and the delta province of Bac Lieu. A South Vietnamese battalion commander who had encamped his unit along the banks of a river was asked by an observer why he had not moved his troops to the opposite side of the river, where there was a better bivouac. The Viet Cong controlled that side, the battalion commander replied. Then why, the observer inquired, didn't the unit go attack the Viet Cong? The commander responded, "As long as we don't bother them, they won't bother us."

"This commander is a lazy man," Diem said. He recounted telling the commander of I Corps – the northernmost of the four corps areas into which the country was divided for military and administrative purposes – that it was impossible to fight a war without taking casualties, and added that he had admonished the Kien Hoa provincial chief for his passiveness. Despite such efforts on his part, Diem lamented, some commanders were still hesitant to attack.

"This is not right and is certainly no way to win," Harkins protested. "If commanders do not want to fight, they should come to you and tell you so, and you can find others who will."[6]

Diem expressed agreement with most of what Harkins had said that day. For Diem, as for most other South Vietnamese, spoken concurrence often did not reflect actual concurrence; the South Vietnamese were usually too polite for candid expressions of disagreement or disinterest. Diem was, in fact, to ignore some of Harkins's advice. Concerned as always about putting too much power in the hands of any one subordinate, Diem did not unify the chain of command. Diem's actions during the latter part of 1962, nevertheless, indicate that Harkins's advice had considerable influence on him, particularly that pertaining to the selection of commanders and the aggressiveness of South Vietnamese forces.

Diem's government rang in the second half of 1962 with a sensational exhibition of military prowess. On July 20, two days after Harkins had told Diem "the only way to win is to attack, attack, attack," the South Vietnamese 7th Division executed a large night helicopter assault in the Plain of Reeds. Employing thirty U.S. Army and Marine Corps helicopters and one thousand government troops, it was the biggest attack involving helicopters to date, day or night. The heliborne government troops came down almost directly on top of a Viet Cong battalion, but the Viet Cong were unable to gun down the South Vietnamese troops as they disembarked from the helicopters, when they were most vulnerable. Upon realizing the strength of the attack force, the Viet Cong attempted to flee, only to find themselves pursued by South Vietnamese infantry, helicopters, and rocket-firing AD-6 Skyraiders. Many of the retreating Viet Cong were caught in the open, where they had little chance of survival. Before it was over, the government forces had slain 141 Viet Cong, while losing fewer than 30 of their own. A Communist history provided only this description of the results: "This operation inflicted heavy losses on 2nd Company/261st Battalion."[7]

South Vietnam's armed forces were to make even greater progress in the second half of 1962 than in the first. Weak commanders were replaced with aggressive young men from the new generation of leaders. Government units hit the Viet Cong hard in VC-held areas and at night. American advisers in the field elicited better performance from their counterparts by urging them on and by setting an example. Because of American pressure, some South Vietnamese units kept Viet Cong prisoners alive rather than killing them on a whim, thereby allowing interrogators to glean valuable information, and South Vietnamese soldiers were more inclined to treat villagers kindly.[8]

Using American equipment and relying upon American advice, the South Vietnamese made tremendous advances in the conduct of air and armor operations. Enterprising American advisers helped the South Vietnamese develop new concepts for the employment of weaponry and vehicles that had never been tested in combat before, most notably the HU-1A Huey attack helicopters and

M-113 armored personnel carriers that began arriving in large quantities during the second half of 1962. A Communist historical account of 1962 noted, "Our people's war forces were unable to stop the enemy's helicopter-borne and armored personnel carrier assaults, and so our three spearheads [military, political, military proselytizing] became confused and hesitant, and our losses increased. . . . Many units were forced to disperse."[9]

In the latter part of the summer, the number of government victories soared, and the government reasserted its control over many areas that had fallen into Viet Cong hands over the past two and a half years. After repeated maulings of large Viet Cong units, the Communists cut back severely on large-unit operations, making it more difficult for them to overwhelm government units and strategic hamlets. Villagers became much more willing to supply the government with information after seeing government forces kill large numbers of Viet Cong and keep the Viet Cong out of the villages. Optimism surged within the Diem government, invigorating the people responsible for executing the war, and similar changes could be seen in the attitudes of the South Vietnamese populace and American advisers and officials. As the summer came to a close, Ambassador Nolting's deputy William Truehart exclaimed that he was "tremendously encouraged" by progress in the military realm that was "little short of sensational."[10] Even South Vietnamese intellectuals and discontented politicians were impressed, with the result that Saigon witnessed less grumbling and plotting against Diem.

Admiration of the South Vietnamese government was less profuse among the American press corps in Saigon. In August, *Newsweek* published an article by François Sully alongside a photograph of female South Vietnamese militia squads with the caption, "Female militia in Saigon: The enemy has more drive and enthusiasm."[11] Madame Nhu took great offense at the caption, and blamed it on Sully, even though Nolting had explained to her that reporters seldom wrote the photo captions. She also claimed that Sully was working with the Viet Cong to discredit South Vietnamese womanhood and ought to be expelled. Many other observers in South Vietnam and the United States, in fact, including some of Sully's fellow foreign journalists, suspected that Sully was a Communist agent.[12] As usually happened, the Saigon government's criticisms of the foreign press led to further, and more vicious, attacks. Traveling to Hong Kong, Sully wrote that Nhu was "a vicious political in-fighter with an unquenchable thirst for power," while Madame Nhu was "the most detested personality in South Vietnam." Sully predicted that the Diem government would perish "unless the regime gets out of its present slough of apathy and indifference."[13] When *Newsweek* published this extraordinary polemic, the Saigon government publicly condemned the magazine and banned its distribution throughout South Vietnam. In reference to America's insistence on freedom of the press, Madame Nhu told an American correspondent that Vietnam did not need "your crazy freedoms." Even some of Diem's political opponents – the tea-sipping intellectuals of Saigon – agreed that *Newsweek*'s actions represented an inexcusable insult to South Vietnam's national pride.[14]

The foreign press corps protested that the South Vietnamese government had no right to expel Western journalists, because "the United States alone is spending here more than one million dollars a day and has stationed ten thousand of its finest young men in Vietnam to aid in this struggle."[15] In other words, the provision of aid empowered the United States to dictate how South Vietnam should behave. The next month, when Diem expelled Jim Robinson of NBC, the U.S. correspondents in Saigon sent Diem a letter decrying the expulsion as "an unjustifiable infringement of traditional principles of freedom of the press."[16] They evidently were unaware that South Vietnam had no tradition of freedom of the press or of many other freedoms that Americans enjoyed. To many South Vietnamese besides Madame Nhu, these were indeed "crazy freedoms."

After the departures of Sully and Homer Bigart, the resident foreign press corps in Saigon consisted of a handful of relative youngsters. Vietnam in 1962 was not considered a big news story, so the editors of Western publications did not send older, higher-paid correspondents there. A large number of major Western publications did not have full-time correspondents in Vietnam at all, opting instead to rely on reporters who covered several Asian countries and visited Saigon periodically. One of the key resident correspondents in South Vietnam was Malcolm Browne, who headed a team of Associated Press correspondents that included Peter Arnett of New Zealand and the German photographer Horst Faas. An eccentric man in his early thirties, Browne was more objective in his reporting than most of his colleagues in Saigon, that is, more inclined to report on the strengths as well as the weaknesses of the Diem regime. Representing the United Press International was a twenty-five-year-old named Neil Sheehan, who arrived in Saigon in April. Having just entered the profession of journalism, he was the youngest and most inexperienced reporter in a country full of young and inexperienced reporters. Bigart's replacement as the *New York Times'* correspondent was David Halberstam, who like Sheehan hailed from the Northeast and was a recent Harvard graduate. Halberstam was twenty-eight when he came to Vietnam. Before he left, fifteen months later, he would do more harm to the interests of the United States than any other journalist in American history.

The newsmen's animosity towards American and South Vietnamese officials was about to fly to dizzying heights. Sheehan and Halberstam came to Vietnam believing that they were entitled to receive all the information they wanted, and when government officials did not follow their script, the two young men became indignant and vengeful. Their self-righteous insistence on unfettered access to information, and their fury when denied that access, came as a shock to both officialdom and some of the more experienced reporters. Nick Turner, a Reuters correspondent in Saigon, recalled, "I didn't expect everyone to tell me the truth. It was wartime. I didn't carry with me that thought carried by so many American correspondents that I had a God-given right to be informed about everything." Of Sheehan, Turner said, "Neil was a very volatile sort of character, very amusing, sometimes a bit over the top for me, but I liked his company." As for Halberstam, "I could understand Dave being angry and wanting to use his position to change many of the things that were wrong. But it often carried over into personal vendettas and often he saw things in clear-cut ideas that were not always clear-cut."[17] Sheehan himself noted that Halberstam "was a man who saw the world in light and dark colors with little shading in between."[18] Sheehan, for his part, was not immune from the tendency to turn everything into black versus white, either.

When the U.S. military, on one occasion, excluded the press from a large military operation in War Zone D for what it said were reasons of military security, Halberstam penned a letter to Ambassador Nolting declaring that the exclusion "is, of course, stupid, naïve and indeed insulting to the patriotism and intelligence of every American newspaperman and every American newspaper represented here. Let me point out that we, as our predecessors in times of conflict have been, are fully prepared to observe the problems of security, to withhold printing classified information."[19] The U.S. military had been disingenuous in citing military security as the cause for the press exclusion, since the primary reasons were the prestige of the South Vietnamese government and, probably to a lesser extent, Kennedy's political fortunes. Halberstam, however, did not have justification for contending that the journalists deserved access to classified military information because they were responsible patriots. The behavior of some of the journalists suggested that patriotism was not a prerequisite in their profession, and they themselves spurned calls from U.S. government officials to support American policy in South Vietnam, claiming that they were working for independent organs of the news media responsible for monitoring and criticizing the government, not for supporting it. "Too often correspondents seem to be regarded by the American mission as tools of our foreign policy," Homer Bigart had complained dismissively.[20] A journalist who felt no obligation to support the government's policies, and who, in fact, showed disdain for those policies and the individuals who executed them, could not be trusted to protect sensitive information. Even those correspondents who intended to protect the government's secrets would not necessarily do so, for, as military novices with exaggerated opinions of their own knowledge, they sometimes released information that they thought was not sensitive but in fact was. A case in point was a Halberstam article in November 1962 in which he quoted an adviser explaining precisely how the Viet Cong could have attacked government forces much more effectively.[21]

Halberstam, Sheehan, and most of the other American reporters in Vietnam at this time did not set out to compromise the South Vietnamese war effort. Although they regularly denounced American and South Vietnamese leaders and some of their policies, they supported the basic American goal of defeating the Viet Cong in order to preserve a non-Communist South Vietnam and save the Southeast Asian dominoes. The year 1962 was one of the last of an era when almost all Americans, including liberal Democrats such as Halberstam and liberal Republicans like Sheehan, supported an active and forceful anti-Communism in foreign affairs. "We believed totally in the American cause," Sheehan recalled.[22] They also respected the Americans who were serving in Vietnam. Thus, they differed notably from the journalists later in the war, many of whom thought that defending South Vietnam was itself a mistake, that the Viet Cong were more noble than the South Vietnamese government, and that Americans serving in Vietnam were fools or war criminals. They differed as well from their own retrospective self-portraits. In his book *The Best and the Brightest*, published in 1972 after the war had become unpopular among large segments of the American elite, Halberstam claimed that by the fall of 1963 he had concluded that the war "was doomed and that we were on the wrong side of history."[23] Not only was Halberstam not opposed to the war in 1963, he was not even opposed to the war during the much bleaker year of 1965, when he wrote in *The Making of a Quagmire* that Vietnam was "one of only five or six nations in the world that is truly vital to U.S. interests," and, in reference to the Vietnamese and others facing similar challenges, that "we cannot abandon our efforts to help these people."[24]

During the summer and early fall, the new reporters devoted an inordinate amount of time to a single South Vietnamese unit, the Army's 7th Division. One of nine South Vietnamese regular divisions, the 7th Division operated in the northern section of the Mekong Delta. Its headquarters in My Tho occupied a most attractive location for foreign journalists, for it could be reached by a forty-mile drive down one of the country's best paved roads. Although Halberstam and Sheehan and most of the others relied very extensively on Saigon's gossip circuit for information, they did visit the provinces and accompany military operations on a frequent basis at this time, which they and many other reporters would not do in later years.

Another reason for the gravitation of the foreign press towards the ARVN 7th Division was the division's senior American adviser, Colonel John Paul Vann. Shortly after Halberstam's arrival in Vietnam, Vann went out of his way to form a relationship with the young journalist, in the knowledge that winning over the correspondent of the *New York Times* was the surest way to acquire fame and gain the attention of the nation's leaders. Sheehan and Browne, as wire service reporters, reached a larger number of readers each day, but the *New York Times* in 1962 was considered the media's leading authority, the nation's newspaper of record, and Washington's favorite public source of information. Television toddled in infancy at this time, with the television crews often obtaining their information from the *New York Times*' reporter. Not until later in the war could the Saigon correspondents of the *New York*

Times be found glued to a television set furiously scribbling notes. Halberstam and the other journalists were drawn to Colonel Vann as much as he was drawn to them. Vann offered them tools for professional advancement: the ability to go on military operations, access to classified military information, and explanations of military subjects unfamiliar to them. He also provided criticism of the senior American and South Vietnamese officials whom the members of the press disliked, which fanned their animosity and provided material for sensational stories. Sheehan later wrote that of all the people in Vietnam, "Vann taught us the most, and one can truly say that without him our reporting would not have been the same."[25]

John Paul Vann was born in Norfolk, Virginia, to an unwed nineteen-year-old who would spend a good portion of her subsequent life as an alcoholic and a prostitute.[26] His mother used her money on expensive dresses and whiskey while her children lived in a run-down house and never had a Christmas tree or a birthday cake. This miserable rearing did not stifle John Paul's considerable natural talents. As an Army officer, he demonstrated an extraordinary willingness to risk his life for military gain, which would win him much respect. He had charisma, tremendous energy, and a knack for planning military operations. His upbringing, however, undoubtedly contributed to his serious character flaws. One of the most damaging of these flaws was a penchant for lying. Oftentimes Vann would tell awed listeners that he had led the Eighth Army Ranger company in thwarting six Chinese human-wave assaults on a frozen ridge during the Korean War, when in fact the company had been led by Lieutenant Ralph Puckett, Jr., an acquaintance of Vann. In every country where Vann's military career took him, from the United States to Japan to Germany, he relentlessly cheated on his wife, frequently with minors. In 1959, during a stint at Fort Leavenworth, Vann beat a statutory rape conviction by cheating a lie-detector test and convincing his wife to lie on his behalf. In Vietnam, Vann told Halberstam that American prestige was suffering because American men were sleeping with Vietnamese women, but it later came to light that Vann himself had been sleeping with an assortment of Vietnamese women at the time.

Sheehan and Halberstam saw Colonel Vann as a man of great moral courage because Vann had convinced them that he was sacrificing promotion to general by telling the press about the South Vietnamese Army's shortcomings and contradicting the optimistic official line. In reality, Vann knew that in spite of his acquittal, the statutory rape accusation would prevent him from ever attaining the rank of general. Early on in his tenure in Vietnam, when the 7th Division was tearing apart the Viet Cong and he was as happy as could be, Vann wrote a friend that he intended to retire in 1963. He would, indeed, retire during that year. Sheehan, discovering years later that his hero had committed this and other frauds, lamented that Vann had been crusading with "the luxury of believing his career was already lost and he was decorated for conspicuous moral gallantry while deceiving Halberstam and me and all his other admirers."[27] This was the man in whom the young journalists were to place boundless trust during the critical years of 1962 and 1963.

At the beginning of 1962, a few months before Vann became the 7th Division's senior adviser, Vann's predecessor had demanded that the division's commander involve the Americans in operational planning. The division commander refused to do so, but relented when the senior adviser withheld helicopter support. From that point onward, American hands were heavily engaged in the division's operational planning, boosting the unit's effectiveness. Air, armor, and infantry elements were coordinated with greater skill and sophistication, and the number of night-time operations shot up.

The 7th Division was on a roll from the spring to the early fall of 1962, the press corps learned from Vann and the other 7th Division advisers. At one point, it organized six consecutive operations during which one hundred or more Viet Cong were killed. In a typical operation, infantry and armored personnel carriers advanced on covered enemy positions and flushed the Viet Cong troops into the open. As the rebels tried to flee on foot or by shallow-draft sampan across rice paddies, aircraft and the amphibious armored personnel carriers mowed them down with high-power machine guns and rockets. South Vietnamese casualties were remarkably light during these operations, usually fewer than ten in number.

The division hit a bump on October 5, when a South Vietnamese Ranger company that was attached to the 7th Division attempted to flush the Viet Cong from a hamlet. As the Rangers slogged through an open rice paddy toward the hamlet, they came under attack from a VC unit that had dug in along a dike on the hamlet's edge. Unable to find cover or to see the enemy, the Rangers were slaughtered in the flat rice paddy, suffering thirteen dead and thirty-four wounded. At Vann's urging, the 7th Division flew reinforcements into the area, but the Viet Cong raked the helicopters with fire and inflicted additional casualties, then withdrew. In all, twenty of the division's soldiers perished and forty sustained wounds, a much higher total than in previous operations.

According to Colonel Vann, Diem summoned the 7th Division's commander four days after this setback. The commander, Colonel Huynh Van Cao, was one of Diem's most loyal officers, and also one of the most talented.[28] Diem allegedly told Cao that he was paying too much heed to his American advisers and taking too many risks during offensive operations, leading to excessive casualties. Failure to change this behavior could prevent him from getting promoted. Vann's account of Diem chewing out Cao has been neither validated nor discredited by other sources, but it is likely that President Diem did tell more than one of his commanders to avoid taking heavy casualties at about this time.[29] From this point onward, the reliability of Vann's story made a downward descent. Vann told the American journalists that Colonel Cao stopped carrying out meaningful military operations after the meeting with Diem and spent the rest of the year sending his troops on bogus missions in which they stood no chance of running into the Viet Cong. Cao, moreover, was said to have discontinued the involvement of American advisers in operational planning. The American media accepted Vann's account in its entirety and used it as the basis for articles and, later, books. "After the Diem-Cao meeting, the entire momentum of the Seventh Division came to a halt," Halberstam contended in his book *The Making of a Quagmire*.[30] While Halberstam and the other American correspondents did not attribute such behavior to any specific units besides the 7th Division, they went on to contend that the 7th Division's problems were representative of those of the armed forces as a whole.[31]

Colonel Vann, and his journalistic disciples, contended that Diem feared the casualties resulting from aggressive military operations because they would stir up resentment in the armed forces, leading to a coup. This explanation does not hold up under scrutiny. South Vietnamese colonels and generals – the only people capable of pulling off a coup – did not have cause to resent high casualties. They seldom accompanied the infantry during operations, less because of cowardice than because of the small size of operations and the employment of majors as battalion commanders, and therefore aggressive military operations were not likely to endanger their personal safety. Nor was there reason to believe that these officers, hard-bitten as they tended to be, were outraged by casualties in the ranks below them. The events of 1960 and 1961 had shown Diem and other observers that military inaction was likely to increase, not decrease, resentment and plotting within the officer corps.

In another, somewhat more reasonable, explanation for Diem's aversion to casualties, the Vann school contended that Diem was trying to avoid depleting the forces of the regular army upon which he counted for protection against a coup. The 7th Division was considered particularly important because it could reach Saigon quickly by trucking up the forty-mile paved highway connecting My Tho to the capital. In November 1960, it may be remembered, troops from My Tho had taken this highway to Saigon to help rescue Diem. If Diem were worried about losing his counter-coup troops in battle, it would have been a problem peculiar to the 7th Division because of its geographic location, not a problem common to all of South Vietnam's forces as Vann and the newsmen alleged. My Tho was one of the only locations outside the Saigon area from which large numbers of troops could advance rapidly on Saigon; during the coup attempt of November 1963, the 7th Division at My Tho would be the unit outside of III Corps that most worried the plotters, and they would take many actions to keep the 7th Division away from Saigon. But Diem in any case would not have been making operational decisions based on the desire to preserve loyal units, for the 7th Division's losses were far too small to give cause for concern about the division's total strength. No man as savvy as Diem would have believed that the loss of twenty Rangers in a unit of 10,000 men would significantly diminish his capabilities for staving off a coup.[32]

Diem's order to restrict casualties was, in actuality, part of a campaign to keep unfavorable stories out of the international press. The mere loss of a few soldiers, unless accompanied by much larger enemy losses, could be viewed by the South Vietnamese people as a loss of face, and for this reason Diem did everything he could to prevent the South Vietnamese people from hearing of government defeats or high casualties.[33] The Rangers' setback on October 5 was especially troublesome because the Western journalists had not only reported heavy government casualties but also given the impression that it was a victory for the enemy. An article by Browne's Associated Press team, for example, had credited the Viet Cong with delivering "a powerful counterpunch" that "crippl[ed] an entire company of South Vietnamese Rangers."[34] In private, Diem acknowledged the necessity of aggressive military operations that might lead to defeat or heavy casualties. His goal was to strike a balance between undertaking risky military actions and avoiding unfavorable press coverage.

Several days after the loss of the Rangers, Diem instituted new regulations designed to hide information from the press. Americans who wished to interview members of the South Vietnamese military had to submit their questions in writing in advance, and the answers had to be made in writing and officially reviewed before they were handed over. Colonel Cao prohibited American newsmen from traveling by helicopter in the provinces under his authority, and he expelled two reporters from his division's operational area. For the next several months, the 7th Division would continue to implement greater restrictive measures than other units, no doubt because the American reporters had been spending an inordinate amount of time with the conveniently located division and its senior adviser, John Paul Vann. Out of deference to the wishes of the South Vietnamese, U.S. military officers began withholding more information on military activities from the international press, and the American command acquiesced to South Vietnamese decisions to forbid reporters from accompanying several major operations.[35]

These restrictions, condemned by the correspondents as acts of tyranny, were actually quite similar to restrictions imposed by other countries, including the United States, during times of war. Very few have been the countries that impose no constraints on the media in wartime. The parallels with America's own war between the North and the South are particularly striking. During the Civil War, Union officers denied Northern newspapermen access to certain areas and often censored their writings. General William Tecumseh Sherman prohibited all members of the press from accompanying his army, and he threatened to hang several reporters. In discussing the press in an 1863 letter to his brother, Sherman remarked: "the day must come when the army will make short work with this class of enemies. Now they succeed in intimidating some officers by their vindictive power, encourage discord by their false praises and abuses, and do more to prevent unity, concord and discipline than any other possible cause."[36] President Lincoln went so far as to suppress several newspapers that were not supportive of the government, such as the *New York World* and the *Philadelphia Evening Journal*.[37]

The allegations concerning Diem's aversion to casualties were discredited most powerfully by subsequent military events in South Vietnam. The frequency and quality of military operations did not plummet after the setback of October 5, not even in the 7th Division's area of operations. Clearly, Diem had only told his commanders to be a bit more careful in how they conducted business, not to close up shop, and they acted accordingly. South Vietnamese leaders continued to launch aggressive military operations in areas dominated by the Viet Cong after October 5, including some operations that penetrated areas of the central highlands where government troops had not ventured since 1960. South Vietnamese soldiers were still out in the rice paddies and jungles tracking down the enemy and disrupting their activities with the same determination, and they were still running into ambushes and dying quietly in suffocating heat. Following the loss of the Rangers, weekly South Vietnamese casualty and weapon losses actually increased, a development the American embassy attributed to the "increasing aggressiveness of [government] units in small actions."[38] At just this time, government forces started capturing more weapons from the enemy than they lost – during October and November 1962, Diem's troops captured 860 Viet Cong weapons while losing 736 of their own.[39] These figures were a sure indicator that government forces were fighting not only aggressively but also effectively – of all the war's statistical indicators, weapon losses were among the most reliable, since the South Vietnamese could not misrepresent them to the Americans as they could other statistics.

It just so happened that an important outsider was about to arrive in South Vietnam. At the age of twenty-six, Richard Tregaskis had been the lone war correspondent to land on the beach at Guadalcanal with the U.S. Marines. Accompanying the Marines as they drove the Japanese back, he recorded what he saw and published it as a book entitled *Guadalcanal Diary*, which became one of the most highly acclaimed books of World War II. The book and its young author gained the adoration of American boys who grew up in the 1940s and 1950s, including some of the young correspondents who were now living in Saigon. Tregaskis came to Vietnam in 1962 to write another chronicle, this one entitled *Vietnam Diary*. Traveling to all of the major areas of fighting, Tregaskis spoke with a great many American advisers. From his first entry, on October 9, 1962, to the last entry, on January 11, 1963, Tregaskis described a war that was very different from the one that Halberstam and Sheehan later depicted in their enormously influential books. The American advisers Tregaskis met during those three months gave no indication of frustration with the level of aggressiveness among South Vietnamese leaders; to the contrary, they generally thought that the South Vietnamese were prosecuting the war effectively. "Patrols are going on constantly," said Major Lloyd Picou, the American operations officer for II Corps. "We want to get into new areas, so that there will be

no area where the VC can say, 'This is a safe area.'" Pointing to a map of Vietnam, Picou showed Tregaskis a province where the government had gone from
controlling very little two-and-one-half months earlier to controlling three
quarters of the rice land.[40] The main gripes of the U.S. advisers in Vietnam,
Tregaskis discovered, concerned the U.S. government's unwillingness to intervene in Laos, a prohibition against shooting from helicopters before being fired
upon, and the unfairly negative coverage of the war in the press. Lieutenant
Richard C. Hamil of Rome, Georgia told Tregaskis that he had read pessimistic
press stories about the war in Vietnam before arriving, but "what you read in
the papers and what you hear over here are two different things."[41]

Tregaskis's narration of individual operations was also very telling. On
November 14, he encountered, of all people, Colonel Vann and Colonel Cao,
both of whom were busy preparing for an operation. Vann had definitely not
been left out of operational planning as he would subsequently maintain, and
Cao was clearly not directing the sort of worthless operation, in an area devoid
of Viet Cong, that Vann later described to Halberstam and Sheehan. Pointing
to a map with an overlay showing the troop positions, Vann explained the
day's operation to Tregaskis. "Our only concern now is that the enemy is in
there," Vann began. The plan involved encircling the Viet Cong with airlifted
troops at the tip of a river delta where government forces had not operated
previously. Commented Vann, "This area has always been safe to them, but by
moving troops in by a river force and helicopters, we have the opportunity to
cut them off." Tregaskis took off in a helicopter loaded with South Vietnamese
troops at the start of the operation, and he observed the ferrying of numerous
South Vietnamese soldiers for the better part of the afternoon. Returning to
the 7th Division's command post at the end of the day, Tregaskis learned that it
had been a reasonably successful day. According to Vann's count, government
forces had killed nine Viet Cong, captured fifteen, and taken another sixty Viet
Cong suspects into custody.[42]

Tregaskis's diary entry for December 8 described an operation involving fifty
South Vietnamese troops in the enemy-infested Camau peninsula. Tregaskis
accompanied these troops as they advanced into a partially dry rice field toward
a village where they suspected the Viet Cong were located. When gunfire erupted
from the village, the South Vietnamese soldiers ran in the direction of the firing.
At a canal at the far end of the rice field, they regrouped in preparation for an
assault into the village. Huey helicopters, meanwhile, began to fire into the area
where Tregaskis and the South Vietnamese troops had landed fifteen minutes
earlier. An American adviser, Captain Richard A. Jones of Berkeley, California,
recommended that they go back to the landing zone, but his South Vietnamese
counterpart, Lieutenant Van, insisted on pressing ahead into the village. Van
spoke rapidly in Vietnamese and motioned towards the small arms fire coming
from the village. Conveying Lieutenant Van's thoughts, an interpreter told
Jones, "Say VC in village." The government soldiers crossed the canal on a

bamboo bridge that led to a row of gray thatch houses. "Our troopers were moving into town now, and I admired the way they worked," Tregaskis wrote in his diary. "They kept a security screen out on both sides of the river, with well-spread riflemen scanning the fields for any further VC."

When the government unit entered the village, the guerrillas stopped firing and attempted to hide. The soldiers did, however, apprehend several suspicious men of military age. Once the search was finished, Jones and Lieutenant Van entered into a heated dispute concerning when and where the helicopters should pick them up. Jones eventually won with the argument that the helicopters could not wait as long as Van wanted before retrieving them. Once the helicopters had taken them back to Soc Trang, Captain Jones told Tregaskis that he was not bitter towards Lieutenant Van over the quarrel. "At least he's eager, he wants to fight," Jones said of the South Vietnamese lieutenant. "You have to give him that."[43]

Other American journalists who visited Vietnam in late 1962 came away with the same general impressions as Tregaskis. Touring Vietnam for *Newsweek* after Sully's removal, Kenneth Crawford wrote, "In the opinion of Diem's responsible American advisers, his strategy is right and he has made a promising start." Crawford also noted, "Missionaries scattered through the country report that the Communists are in fact complaining about lack of support."[44] Writing in *The Saturday Evening Post* in late November, Harold Martin concluded that the huge American investment of men and materiel had begun paying dividends in recent months.[45] *Time* commented that the war in South Vietnam "looks far more hopeful than it did a year ago," and "U.S. advisers are confident that the Viet Cong now have virtually no hope of achieving their goal of setting up a separate Communist-ruled puppet state in South Viet Nam."[46]

Most remarkably, the reporting from the Saigon correspondents themselves in late 1962 confirmed that the South Vietnamese government had not cut back on aggressive military operations and that the South Vietnamese armed forces were fighting well. On October 20, according to a dispatch from Browne's Associated Press team, seven hundred troops from the South Vietnamese Army's 21st Division engaged in fierce clashes with the Viet Cong along the Gulf of Siam, killing sixty-six Viet Cong and capturing seventeen others while sustaining seventeen casualties themselves.[47] On October 31, Browne reported, a battalion from the 21st Division came to the assistance of an outpost in Vinh Long province that was under heavy Viet Cong attack, leading to several days of fighting. Browne reported that government troops killed 100 Viet Cong in a single day. The government forces had not shied away from taking casualties; Browne noted that "South Vietnamese losses also were big." Summing up the operation, Browne wrote that "the South Vietnamese Government scored one of its biggest successes in months against the Communist guerrillas."[48]

From mid-October until the end of the year, Halberstam and Sheehan spent little time covering the 7th Division. In their articles, they continued to bemoan the Diem government's political practices and the lack of support for the government among some South Vietnamese, but they did not mention South Vietnamese efforts to avoid the enemy. Their allegations about the government's concern with minimizing casualties would not appear until this period had passed, after their main source, Colonel John Paul Vann, had become embittered for other reasons. They were generally upbeat on the war. "The Government is showing much more military initiative than it did a year ago," Halberstam reported on October 20. "The war is going better than it went a year ago."[49] On November 14, Halberstam reported on the fighting in one section of the highlands, where he found a regiment of South Vietnamese soldiers and its American advisers marching straight up and down the mountains under a scorching sun. Small unit patrols during the past month, Halberstam informed his readers, had resulted in the killing of twenty Viet Cong and the capture of twenty-three weapons.[50]

Twelve days later, he penned an article on a Viet Cong attack on the Phuoc Chia outpost. The government had established this outpost and garrisoned it with one hundred men only two months earlier in an area that, in Halberstam's words, "has been a Communist stronghold for years." In the early hours of November 25, soldiers from the 4th and 70th Viet Cong Battalions and local guerrilla units attacked the outpost with at least a few hundred and perhaps as many as one thousand men. Directing two nearby howitzers with great skill, the garrison smashed some of the Viet Cong troop clusters at the outset. Some attackers reached the barbed-wire perimeter and tried to storm it in the face of heavy machine gun and automatic rifle fire, but never made it past the barbed wire. Once the attack began to peter out, government forces counter-attacked, pushing their way into the battered enemy ranks. The Viet Cong retreated from the battlefield after three hours, having suffered at least 124 dead, including two battalion commanders. Halberstam reported that the figure of 124 dead came from American advisers, who had counted the bodies for themselves. The Viet Cong also left behind several 57mm recoilless rifles and a collection of machine guns. The government defenders suffered ten wounded and no dead. Halberstam remarked that American advisers were especially pleased by the outcome because it was "entirely a Vietnamese victory. The Vietnamese fought as they had been trained to fight and they won not because they had helicopters or fighter planes, but because they were well prepared and fought well."[51] In December, Halberstam reported on effective government operations in the Camau Peninsula. "Government troops have been striking hard against the villages of the Vietcong," he wrote, "in an attempt to divert guerrilla attacks from the armada of boats bringing desperately needed charcoal from this essentially enemy area to homes in Saigon."[52]

During the last three months of 1962, Neil Sheehan reported on a series of aggressive military operations in the operational area of the 7th Division, most of them involving militia forces rather than the 7th Division's regulars. They corroborated a U.S. Army appraisal that stated that military activity did not fall off in the 7th Division's area without indicating whether the division's regulars or the militia forces were carrying out most of the operations.[53] The negative publicity surrounding the October 5 mission may have caused the South Vietnamese to rely more heavily on militia units in the 7th Division's operational area, a logical approach since the journalists had not usually reported on militia activities. The activities of the 7th Division itself between October 5 and the end of 1962 remain shrouded in mystery, for the division began conducting some of its operations without the participation of its American advisers, the source of most documentation on the division still in existence.[54] The dispatches of Sheehan and Tregaskis as well as Communist sources, though, do indicate that the division continued to mount some productive operations.

On October 19, observed Sheehan, government forces in the eastern Mekong Delta killed seventeen Viet Cong and recovered their bodies while suffering sixteen killed, three wounded, and one missing.[55] During a night battle in the Plain of Reeds a few weeks later, according to Sheehan, two battalions of government troops swooped in on helicopters and killed sixty-four Communist guerrillas. U.S. military sources show that the government battalions belonged to the 7th Division.[56] Another night battle occurred on November 25, this time in Vinh Binh province, when a Civil Guard company bumped into an estimated Viet Cong battalion. The government sent another Civil Guard company and an infantry battalion into the fray, while a C-47 transport plane fired flares so that the government troops could press the attack. By the time the battle had ended, Sheehan reported, the government had sustained eight killed and thirty-two wounded, while Viet Cong casualties were unknown.[57] At the end of November, Sheehan filed another report stating, "Intense fighting raged in the northern Mekong Delta and the Communists were reported suffering heavy losses."[58]

Much other evidence shows that Diem's war effort did not falter between October and December 1962. In some areas, especially those distant from Saigon, American military advisers witnessed successful operations during this period that entirely escaped the attention of the press corps. Among the most noteworthy was a series of joint air-ground assaults in III Corps near the Cambodian border. U.S. advisers praised the South Vietnamese for their use of tactical air support during this endeavor, and reported that as many as one thousand Viet Cong were killed during a single assault.[59] Theodore Heavner, following a visit to Vietnam from October 18 to November 26, noted that American advisers "say that the GVN forces are doing more and better night work," with the result that "the night no longer belongs only to the VC." The South Vietnamese armed forces were performing much better on the whole, he noted, adding that many South Vietnamese officials now expected that the war would be won within one to two years.[60]

Most compelling of all, the Communists themselves acknowledged that the Diem government was attacking the Viet Cong energetically and adeptly during the last months of 1962. Meeting on December 6, the North Vietnamese Politburo remarked, "The enemy is using his military superiority to expand the war in a determined effort to annihilate our forces." It conceded that "our armed forces are still weak," and that if the Communists continued the armed struggle at the present level, they would be unable to maintain the movement in the South.[61] One official Communist history noted that South Vietnamese government leaders "obstinately continued to strengthen their forces and wage an increasingly fierce 'special war' against our people in the South" through the end of 1962.[62] A Communist document concerning the upper delta – the 7th Division's own area of operations – in late 1962 acknowledged that "the enemy succeeded in mopping up our weak areas, repressing the people's political movement, expelling our forces, and activating strategic hamlets. The enemy then employed concentrated Civil Guard, Self-Defense Corps, and Ranger units to attack liberated areas."[63] Similar descriptions appeared in a Communist history of Military Region 6, which encompassed six coastal and highland provinces in central South Vietnam.[64] According to these Communist histories, South Vietnam's regulars as well as its irregulars caused great harm to the Viet Cong in this period, a strong indication that the South Vietnamese Army was becoming more proficient in counterinsurgency operations.[65]

The latter part of 1962 also witnessed major advances in the implementation of the strategic hamlet program.[66] A good illustration of the progress came from a Communist report on two villages where the government had built strategic hamlets during the fall. In conjunction with the establishment of the strategic hamlets, the author noted, the government had succeeded in recruiting many of the local males into the Republican Youth and the militia. Day and night, the militia patrolled inside and outside the hamlet fences. Once these strategic hamlets began functioning, according to the report, the Viet Cong movement "declined very rapidly." Because so many local families had members in the militia and the Republican Youth, the villagers "very often make contact with and give information to the men of the [militia] stations, and consequently our cadres are usually pursued when they come to the village." The strategic hamlet program thwarted all of the Viet Cong's political and military activities, for when cadres and soldiers tried to operate in the hamlets the government forces attacked them and drove them away.[67]

A considerable number of very effective strategic hamlets dotted the South Vietnamese countryside at the end of 1962, though they were less numerous than Nhu or Diem had wanted by that point in time. Taylor concluded in November that of the 3,353 strategic hamlets reportedly complete, only 600 had all of the necessary equipment, fortifications, security forces, and cadres. Many others had been partially completed. The outlook for the future was nonetheless bright, Taylor asserted, for the six hundred fully functioning strategic hamlets were proving significantly more capable of resisting Communist intrusion than other hamlets. With roughly three hundred additional hamlets now reaching true completion each month, the program was on pace to cover every hamlet by 1966.[68]

Some of the most successful strategic hamlets at the close of 1962 could be found in the critical highlands region, home to the many tribes known collectively as the Uplanders or Montagnards. Over the course of 1962, half of the country's one million Uplanders had left their mountain villages and headed toward areas under the control of a government they had long distrusted, in order to escape the escalating war in the highlands and Communist rapacity. As the war had intensified, Viet Cong demands for rice and livestock had risen. Highland villages that failed to hand over what the Viet Cong wanted were now greeted with a company of Viet Cong troops who, lacking the respect for the populace that they generally showed in ethnic Vietnamese areas, would torture, massacre, and burn. Entire villages disappeared, like plants ripped up from the soil, roots and all. The South Vietnamese government, by contrast, actively courted the highland tribes, on orders from Diem, who had greater sympathy for the tribal minorities and understood them better than most Vietnamese. The tribesmen were also impressed when they saw an army coming to battle in loud metal birds that shot arrows of fire into the Viet Cong. The Uplanders proved quite receptive to resettlement in strategic hamlets, and the Diem government went to remarkable lengths to resettle them. The CIA recruited the tribesmen into paramilitary units called "Civilian Irregular Defense Groups," replacing their spears and crossbows with Swedish submachine guns and American rifles. By the end of the year, the CIA had brought 38,000 Uplanders into the paramilitary units, many of which were as capable in combat as ethnic Vietnamese units.[69]

Communist sources show that the strategic hamlet program, despite the relatively limited number of hamlets completed, was already having a substantial effect on the war in much of South Vietnam before the year ended. One of Hanoi's postwar histories credited the Diem government with reducing the Viet Cong's "liberated areas" in Cochinchina, the southern third of Vietnam, by the end of 1962 through the creation of 2,000 strategic hamlets.[70] As the hamlets sprouted up across the country, Hanoi ordered the Viet Cong to set the destruction of the strategic hamlets as their top priority. The Viet Cong, however, were not capable of annihilating the new hamlets, not even in the Mekong Delta, where the program was making the least headway and was most vulnerable. The Communist history of the upper Mekong Delta noted that when the Viet Cong tore down the strategic hamlet fences and guard posts, "the enemy would just force the people to rebuild them, this time even stronger, and would tighten his defensive alert procedures, tighten his controls on the population, and aggressively hunt down our guerrilla organization inside the hamlet to suppress it, making it more difficult for us to conduct our operations.... When we destroyed a strategic hamlet they usually rebuilt it and then built even more."[71] The official Communist history of the southern Mekong Delta region stated,

"We expended tremendous efforts in the program to destroy strategic hamlets but in fact accomplished very little."[72]

* * *

AFTER THE CONSUMMATION OF THE GENEVA AGREEMENT ON LAOS, THE United States promptly began pulling its advisers out of Laos and the Soviets stopped parachuting supplies over Laotian territory.[73] The North Vietnamese were soon proclaiming that they had withdrawn all of their troops from Laos, but in actuality they withdrew only a small fraction of the 9,000 who had been in Laos when the agreement was signed. At the International Control Commission's checkpoints, where all foreign personnel were supposed to exit Laos, the commission's observers counted a paltry forty North Vietnamese soldiers departing.[74] The Pathet Lao's armed forces refused to join the new government's army, and they prevented the neutralists and the International Control Commission from entering areas under their control, which included the entire Ho Chi Minh trail area. Without interruption, North Vietnamese men and armaments continued to move along the Laotian infiltration routes, leading the critics of Laotian neutralization to give the Ho Chi Minh Trail a new nickname – the Averell Harriman Memorial Highway. By the end of the year, the annual total of Communist infiltrators would come close to 10,000.[75] The first movements of large artillery pieces, mortars, and machine guns over the Ho Chi Minh trail also began in 1962.[76] The Communist armed forces in South Vietnam were, by this time, so reliant on the Chinese and Soviet aid that was funneled through North Vietnam and Laos as to render absurd the oft-repeated argument that South Vietnam was not a viable country because of its reliance on the United States.[77] No small nation could long survive the assaults of an enemy lavishly supported by two great powers unless it received substantial assistance from another great power.

Near the end of the year, Kennedy received reports of post-Geneva infiltration and recommendations for counter-measures, but he did not change course. Some of the force had by now gone out of the arguments of the hawks, for evidence had accumulated that Kennedy could guarantee the safety of the Southeast Asian mainland without sending American combat forces. Although the loss of eastern Laos had removed one pillar from Kennedy's defense structure in the region, the South Vietnamese pillar had gained enough strength to keep the structure up, under current international conditions. Kennedy's tacit surrender of eastern Laos would not have fatal consequences unless North Vietnamese Army units poured down the Ho Chi Minh Trail *en masse* or the South Vietnamese government came apart, events that by no means were certain to happen. At the end of 1962, the North Vietnamese government had no intention of undertaking the former, and the South Vietnamese government was showing no signs of succumbing to the latter. All observers in South

Vietnam at the time, even the American journalists who would later claim that the war effort was deteriorating at this time, reported that the Diem government dramatically improved its position in the countryside relative to that of the Viet Cong during the second half of 1962. It did so in the face of extensive North Vietnamese infiltration of men and materiel that continuously replenished the Viet Cong's forces. The Australian Wilfred Burchett, a pro-Communist journalist who lived with the Viet Cong during this time and spoke with many of their leaders, accurately summed up the year. "In terms of territory and population, Diem made a considerable comeback in 1962," Burchett observed. Government armed forces "registered a number of successes and held the strategic and tactical initiative." In the final analysis, stated Burchett, 1962 was "Diem's year."[78]

CHAPTER 8

The Battle of Ap Bac

JANUARY 1963

JUST BEFORE THE NEW YEAR BEGAN, A SPECIALLY-EQUIPPED AMERICAN airplane traced Viet Cong radio signals to the hamlet of Tan Thoi in Dinh Tuong province, the province where the ARVN 7th Division was headquartered. Tan Thoi stood next to the hamlet of Bac, which would later be called Ap Bac after U.S. journalists covering the battle added the prefix *ap* (hamlet). Jutting abruptly upwards from flat rice paddies, the two hamlets stood out like small islands in a calm green sea. The Americans relayed the location of the Viet Cong radio transmitter to the South Vietnamese high command, which then ordered the 7th Division to take Tan Thoi at the beginning of January. Intelligence reports indicated that the Viet Cong forces guarding the radio transmitter consisted of a reinforced company of 120 men. Thus, the South Vietnamese leadership was aware that the infantry attack was likely to involve significant South Vietnamese casualties.[1]

The Viet Cong actually had a total of between three and four hundred men at Bac and Tan Thoi, most of them belonging to the 261st and 514th Battalions. The 261st Battalion was among the best Viet Cong units in the country, a fact attributable to its fine leadership. Afterwards, American advisers were to say that the Viet Cong soldiers at Bac and Tan Thoi were the most determined Communist fighters they had encountered in more than one year.[2] Equipped with an array of powerful weapons that the North Vietnamese had smuggled to South Vietnam by boat, including machine guns, 60mm mortars, and rifle grenades,[3] the Viet Cong troops were deployed along canals to the north, east, and south of Bac, with the northernmost forces in Tan Thoi. Closely packed fruit trees and dense undergrowth cloaked them well and provided remarkably good protection from heavy weaponry. On thick zigzagged dikes, studded with trees and built up like levees, the Viet Cong dug foxholes so deep that a man could stand inside. Only a direct hit from an artillery shell or bomb could kill the occupant. They dug all of the holes from the rear so that no trace of excavation could be seen from the fighting side. From these foxholes, the Communists could very easily fire down on anything that moved across the surrounding area, so open and flat were the paddies. An American who inspected the Viet Cong positions after the battle remarked that it was akin to firing across a high school football field from the third or fourth row of bleachers.[4] Behind the foxhole line, invisible from the air, ran an irrigation ditch that allowed the Viet Cong to communicate and move men and supplies swiftly along their defensive line, either by sampan or on foot. The Communists' defensive position at Ap Bac, with its fortified dikes overlooking open rice paddies, bore a striking resemblance to the position from which they had mauled the Ranger company in October 1962.

The Viet Cong, in short, would enjoy tremendous advantages over any foe that tried to attack them. The Communists, indeed, most probably were trying to lure the government forces into attacking by sending out radio signals that understated their strength. In an after-action report, the Communists confided that they had viewed Ap Bac as a much-needed opportunity to demonstrate strength to the peasants and to their own followers, for government victories during the previous year had gravely undermined the prestige of the Communist movement in this part of the delta.[5]

An American adviser, Captain Richard Ziegler, worked with members of the 7th Division's staff to draft the South Vietnamese battle plan. Certain that the Viet Cong had no more than 120 soldiers guarding the transmitter, the planners created an operational scheme suited for attacking a much weaker enemy than actually existed. According to their plan, an infantry battalion from the 7th Division would fly by helicopter to the north of Tan Thoi and attack southwards. From the south, a Civil Guard regiment under the command of the Dinh Tuong provincial chief would attack northwards. An infantry company riding with a mechanized company of thirteen M-113 armored personnel carriers, also under the provincial chief's command, would launch an assault from the west. The attack force had a total of twelve hundred troops, with an additional three companies in reserve. No forces would attack from the east. On the basis of the Viet Cong's past performance, the South Vietnamese officers and their American advisers expected the Viet Cong to flee eastwards when attacked from the other directions. Never had the Viet Cong stood their ground against a large government force outfitted with armored personnel carriers. American aircraft and South Vietnamese artillery would pummel the exposed Viet Cong as they attempted to move east across the rice paddies.

The provincial chief's units moved forward from the south on January 2 at 6:35 A.M. One hour later, while crossing the flat rice paddies, the Civil Guard came under heavy fire from Viet Cong troops hidden in a tree line. Their forward movement was halted. The Civil Guardsmen attempted to assault the enemy positions twice in the ensuing two hours, but were thrown back each time with high casualties, which included the task force commander, who was shot in the leg, and the lead company's commander, who was killed. Deprived of its best leaders and facing terrain that heavily favored the enemy, the task force lost all forward momentum. Provincial Chief Lam Quang Tho held the Civil Guard units in place for the rest of the morning and awaited the attack of the 7th Division. The Civil Guard would initiate further offensive action in the afternoon, but without success.

The battalion from the 7th Division that had been scheduled to land by helicopter and assault Tan Thoi from the north was several hours late in attacking, on account of fog that interrupted the helicopter flights. As a result, the guerrillas were able to concentrate troops in the south to fend off the Civil Guard, then concentrate troops to the north to defend against the enemy regulars without fear of simultaneous attacks. The South Vietnamese battalion approached Tan Thoi along three separate axes. Well-concealed Communist troops waited until the government soldiers were twenty yards away, then opened fire. Immediately the attackers were pinned down. In the course of the next five hours, this battalion attempted three assaults against the Viet Cong defenses, all of which failed to break the Viet Cong line.[6]

With the attacks in the north and the south bogged down, the 7th Division's brand new commander, Colonel Bui Dinh Dam, attempted to stretch out the defenders or find a soft spot by organizing an attack from the east or the west. He asked Colonel John Paul Vann to investigate two possible landing zones for the reserve troops, one to the east of Bac, the other to the west. Flying above the hamlet in an L-19 reconnaissance plane, Vann decided that the western zone offered a better location. Vann said that he did not see any enemy forces near the landing area. One of the 7th Division's reserve companies clambered aboard a fleet of H-21 helicopters, ungainly old two-rotor machines nicknamed "Flying Bananas" because their eighty-six foot long bodies were shaped like the fruit. The Flying Bananas hauled the infantrymen to a landing site one hundred and eighty meters west of the tree line. Later, in his after-action report, Vann claimed that he had ordered the choppers to drop off the men at a distance of three hundred meters from the tree line – the minimum distance at which .30 caliber small-arms fire was considered ineffective – but the lead pilot had ignored him and taken the helicopters in closer.[7] The responsibility for this fateful decision would become clear later.

During his reconnaissance flight, Vann had failed to see that the Viet Cong had several strong points on the western side of the tree line. The reserve company landed directly in front of these points. As soon as the Flying Bananas touched the ground, they began taking fire. A group of Hueys, escorting the Flying Bananas to provide fire support, closed on the tree line while strafing the guerrillas with their twin .50 caliber machine guns and shooting 2.75-inch rockets in their direction, but their fire failed to suppress the Viet Cong. At one hundred and eighty meters, the Viet Cong could hit the exposed Flying Bananas with considerable accuracy and effect. One of the ten Bananas sustained enough damage that it could not take off after depositing its troops. A second, which had just left the ground, set down again to assist the disabled chopper and was then knocked out of action. A third had to land two kilometers away as the result of hits suffered while unloading troops. One of the Hueys, more heavily armored than the Flying Bananas, came to the aid of the two Bananas that were stuck in the landing zone, but enemy fire ruined the Huey's tail rotor, causing the helicopter to turn on its side and crash.

The landing zone became a slaughter yard. Droves of South Vietnamese soldiers were shot as they disembarked from the helicopters, their bodies and equipment slumping into the mud. "When those poor Vietnamese came out of the choppers," one U.S. officer noted afterwards, "it was like shooting ducks for the Viet Cong."[8] More than half of the company's 102 men were killed or wounded in the early stages of the fighting. Facing an expertly entrenched opponent and needing to cross one hundred and eighty meters of open and mushy paddy to reach the tree line, the remnants of the company stood no chance of mounting an attack that had any hope of success. One of the first men to appreciate this truth was a helicopter pilot stranded in the paddy, Chief Warrant Officer Carlton Nysewander of Pasadena, California, who had seen combat in Korea as an infantryman. When standing in the paddy, Nysewander noted, a soldier's feet sank eighteen inches below the surface into dark mud, preventing him from travelling faster than a slow trot. To slosh through open rice paddy at such a pace was to ensure death at the hands of Viet Cong machine gunners. Even a large and able American infantry unit could not have taken the Viet Cong position on its own, Nysewander believed, an assessment that would be validated when American combat units came to Vietnam later on. Defeating the enemy in this setting would require either the utter devastation of the hamlet with large bombs and napalm or the employment of armored vehicles that could shield advancing infantry from the zipping Viet Cong machine gun bullets and pour fire into the Viet Cong defenses. "If you didn't have something to shield you until you got to the tree line, then you'd be cannon fodder," observed Nysewander. "Charlie had dug in real well. They had done a wonderful job."[9]

Vann, who could see the wrecked helicopters from the L-19 and knew that two of the American crewmen were seriously wounded, asked Colonel Dam to send the mechanized company and all other available forces to the landing zone. From a military perspective, Vann's plan was a poor one, as the landing zone was the most difficult place from which to attack the enemy, but Vann was determined to rescue the American helicopter crewmen, knowing that he bore considerable responsibility for their predicament. It took an hour for Colonel Dam to order the mechanized company to the landing zone, purport-edly because of communication difficulties. The company commander, Captain Ly Tong Ba, was slow in moving the company, which was two kilometers west of Bac when he received the order. His reluctance came as a surprise to Captain James Scanlon and Captain Robert Mays, the American advisers assigned to the mechanized company, because Ba was considered one of the most aggressive of the South Vietnamese officers. With Vann screaming over the radio at Scanlon and Mays for Ba to make haste, the two advisers had to badger the South Vietnamese captain to move the company forward. The Americans were not certain what was in Ba's head. Later, very plausibly, Scanlon speculated, "Perhaps Ba was thinking that because the helos were down and the crews were in danger, the Americans were very excited and emotions were causing them to exaggerate the situation."[10] It is also possible that one of Ba's commanders had warned him that the exposed landing zone was a death trap.

While Ba's carriers were heading east, artillery and air strikes showered down on the Viet Cong positions. To direct the strikes, Vann repeatedly flew a spotter plane over the Viet Cong at a low altitude, a feat of such daring that he was subsequently awarded the Distinguished Flying Cross. The artillery and air assets, however, inflicted little damage on the enemy. The Viet Cong's superlative camouflage made it exceedingly difficult for Vann and others to pinpoint the fighting positions, and the heavy vegetation and the Viet Cong fortifications kept the blasts from wreaking large-scale destruction. "We got a fix on one machine-gun position and made fifteen aerial runs on it," one U.S. adviser noted. "Every time we thought we had him, and every time that damned gunner came right back up, firing."[11] Vann also summoned two Flying Bananas and three Hueys to rescue the men marooned in the rice paddies, but one of the Flying Bananas was brought down by enemy fire, becoming the fifth and final helicopter casualty of the battle. Vann then aborted the helicopter rescue operation.

At one-thirty in the afternoon, the armored personnel carriers reached the site of the disastrous helicopter landing, their metallic skin repelling the Viet Cong's bullets. The vehicles stopped to pick up some survivors and unload infantrymen, then readied themselves for a frontal assault on the tree line. Mays boarded the carrier of Lieutenant Cho, the most aggressive of the platoon leaders. Like the other Americans, Mays believed that the Communists would fire a few shots at the armored personnel carriers and then run for their lives, as they had in the past. The numerous and spectacular successes of the M-113s had made the vehicle one of the most dreaded enemies of the Viet Cong, who called them the "green dragons." Although they had fought very well thus far, the Viet Cong had little desire to face the dragons on this day. They had, in fact, planned for this battle with the intention of avoiding the M-113s, for they had predicted that no M-113s would be able to reach the battlefield before the fighting was over. If the guerrillas stood up to the dragons to fight, they could be swallowed up, yet if they retreated, they would have to flee across open paddy, exposing themselves to merciless pursuit by the fire-breathing dragons as well as helicopters. Colonel Hai Hoang, an outstanding officer who was in command of all the Viet Cong forces at Bac and Tan Thoi, concluded that a retreat through the muddy rice fields meant certain death and therefore they would stay put and throw everything possible at the enemy. "Do not let your men leave their fighting positions," Hoang told his company commanders. "If they abandon their foxholes, if we leave our positions, we will lose."[12]

Shortly before two o'clock, the M-113s steamed towards the tree line. Dismounted South Vietnamese infantrymen, accompanied by Scanlon, fanned out and ran forward while firing their rifles. It was exactly what the Americans had trained the South Vietnamese to do. When the foremost two vehicles came within fifty yards of the tree line, a VC machine gunner took them under fire, and other Viet Cong quickly joined in. Because the government's attacks had already stalled to the north and south, the Viet Cong were able to concentrate their troops on the segment on their western edge where the South Vietnamese were now attacking. Lacking cover and unable to see any enemy targets, the dismounted government troops began dropping. After witnessing the volume of enemy fire, Scanlon concluded that the infantrymen would be wiped out if they continued to charge ahead.[13] He and the infantry unit retreated behind the downed helicopters, to wait until the armored personnel carriers had knocked out the enemy's strong points.

Advancing on the tree line, the company of M-113s sprayed the fortified enemy positions with their powerful .50 caliber machine guns. The gunners, however, did not know where to shoot because they could not see the enemy. So dense was the vegetation that they could not even locate the Viet Cong's muzzle flashes. The main victims of the M-113 machine guns turned out to be the trees. The Communist fire, on the other hand, struck the M-113 crewmembers with deadly precision. In order to operate the .50 caliber machine guns, the M-113 gunners had to stand up in the command hatch, leaving themselves unprotected from the waist upwards. In the past, this arrangement had not been a problem, since the Viet Cong had not offered serious resistance. It was a major defect in the design of the American vehicles, one that would be corrected later by adding armor for the gunner's upper body. Fourteen South Vietnamese soldiers were killed that day while manning the machine guns on the thirteen M-113s. Eventually, after the first assault had come to naught, the vehicles retreated to a safe distance and then began to attack in groups of two or three, except for one occasion when the carriers moved in unison. The Americans had taught the M-113 commanders to attack in small formations, rather than as a whole group, and this approach had worked when the Viet Cong had fled in fear of the machines.[14] Now that the Viet Cong were holding their ground, however, this method permitted the revolutionaries to concentrate their firepower on a small number of exposed gunners.

Captain Ba's vehicles engaged in repeated duels with the Viet Cong machine gun on the right side of the enemy line, which had inflicted horrific casualties on the attackers. If this gun were eliminated, then the government forces could outflank the defenders with ease. Ba's men shot the head off of one of the weapon's gunners, but could not silence the weapon because of the efforts of one very brave man who kept on firing. The armored company tried some other solutions, too. An M-113 with a flamethrower drove within effective range of the tree line and attempted to fire, only to have its flamethrower malfunction. Ba's carrier and two other carriers moved forward to a position fifteen yards from the irrigation dike, and from there the carrier crewmen lobbed grenades at the critical Viet Cong machine gun. The Viet Cong, however, responded with a storm of grenades, which compelled the carriers to retreat. Vann wanted the Vietnamese to drive the carriers straight into the Viet Cong position and jump out there, but they did not, for American armor officers had taught them that enemy soldiers would pounce on the vehicles and throw grenades in as soon as a hatch opened. Finally, after two M-113s were put out of action, the entire mechanized company pulled back to a safe distance.

Colonel Vann and a few of the Vietnamese field commanders wanted all of the government ground forces to renew the attack, based on the belief that the Viet Cong would not have enough troops to defend on the north, west, and south sides simultaneously. This plan, however, was tossed out by the newly promoted corps commander, General Huynh Van Cao, who had come to the 7th Division's command post to direct the battle. Cao preferred to use heavy weapons against the Viet Cong and request reinforcements. Upon his instructions, artillery and AD-6, T-28, and B-26 aircraft pounded Bac again. Some would later cite this decision, and earlier decisions at the northern and southern ends of the battlefield to use heavy firepower and await reinforcements, as evidence of South Vietnamese aversion to casualties. While some South Vietnamese officers squandered opportunities during the battle because of excessive caution, as a whole the conduct of the South Vietnamese at Bac and Tan Thoi did not demonstrate a strong propensity for avoiding losses. In each of the instances in question, the troops had already suffered heavy losses during repeated assaults on extraordinarily well-defended positions. Under such circumstances, it made sense for a commander to change his method of attack. Most armies with heavy firepower at their disposal, moreover, prefer to use it liberally against well-defended positions, rather than simply launch repeated infantry assaults, in order to save soldiers' lives. Commenting on the South Vietnamese decision to halt the ground attacks and call in the air and artillery during this battle, Lt. Gen. Dave R. Palmer wrote: "those cautious tactics were, in spite of the very sincere exhortations of the U.S. advisors, precisely the same that any American commander would have used after U.S. troops were committed in 1965. Moreover, the American's fate for accepting human losses in lieu of calling for firepower to do the job would have been the same as that of the South Vietnamese commander – removal from command."[15]

The South Vietnamese Joint General Staff decided to send one of its strategic reserve units, the 8th Airborne Battalion, to the battle. Vann asked Cao to have this battalion land to the east of Bac, so that it could stop the Viet Cong if they tried to withdraw to the east, which at present remained the only direction in which there were no government forces. This move would also enable the South Vietnamese units to attack the Viet Cong from all directions. Cao, however, chose to drop the airborne battalion to the west of Bac. Vann, and hence his press protégés, would claim that Cao had sent the paratroopers to the west with the intention of holding them in place rather than attacking, because Cao had wanted to let the enemy escape so as to avoid further South Vietnamese casualties.[16] In reality, Cao wanted to use the elite airborne battalion, in concert with the M-113s and air support, to flush the Viet Cong eastward before nightfall and hammer them with heavy firepower once they were in the open, as envisioned in the original battle plan drawn up by the Americans and the South Vietnamese. The paratroopers received clear orders to attack the Viet Cong position as soon as they landed.[17] Cao's approach was consistent with a Sun Tzu maxim that he and other South Vietnamese officers held dear: "To a surrounded enemy you must leave a way of escape."[18] A surrounded and entrenched enemy would fight more fiercely and from a much more advantageous defensive position than a retreating enemy.[19] Another likely factor in Cao's decision on the airborne battalion was a loss of confidence in Vann's judgment. The abrasive adviser had already made many mistakes, berated his counterparts in front of others, and put the South Vietnamese forces in an unfavorable position in order to rescue a handful of stranded Americans.[20]

In the late afternoon, the three hundred paratroopers of the 8th Airborne Battalion flew towards Bac in C-123 Providers. As the whale-shaped Providers approached, the Viet Cong peppered them with machine gun fire, prompting the pilots changed course. Either the jumpmaster or the lead pilot did not adequately compensate for the change and therefore when the paratroopers jumped, they came down much closer to the enemy than planned, with some of the paratroopers floating down directly over Viet Cong positions. The Viet Cong shot many paratroopers while they were still in the air or caught in tree branches. Once on the ground, the surviving paratroopers had little cover from close-range enemy fire and they could not move with any speed because the water in the rice paddies came up to their knees. Some tried to break through the Viet Cong's perimeter, but, despite their bravery and their excellent military skills, they could not advance very far under such conditions. "They kept trying to move ahead," said Fletcher Ware, an American captain who parachuted in with the 8th Airborne Battalion, but "they couldn't move very fast and were just getting picked off."[21] The battalion quickly sustained fifty-two casualties, including Ware and Russell Kopti, the other American adviser present. Sporadic fighting continued until sundown.

Colonel Hai Hoang knew that the government forces around him were growing stronger, and that the government had troops to his north, west, and south but not to his east. Many of his guerrillas had been killed or wounded, and the others were low on ammunition and energy. After the sky turned black, he ordered all of his forces to assemble at Tan Thoi. From there, sheltered by darkness, they headed eastwards with most of their dead and wounded. No bullet or bomb disturbed their escape.

All told, eighty South Vietnamese government troops were killed and one hundred and nine wounded during the battle of Ap Bac. Casualties among the American advisers totaled three dead and six wounded. Based on the number of Viet Cong bodies recovered and reports from civilian witnesses inside the hamlets, Colonel Vann estimated that the battle had claimed the lives of more than one hundred Viet Cong.[22] This estimate may have exceeded the actual total, as some of the men whom Vann counted as dead may have been wounded soldiers who had been evacuated by stretcher or other ancillary means.[23] On the other hand, Communist sources, which are inconsistent with one another, almost certainly understated the Viet Cong's losses by a large margin, presumably in order to brighten their achievements, a practice as common on the Communist side as on the government side. Hai Hoang reported that only eighteen of his men had been killed, while Communist military region commander Le Quoc San said that just twelve Viet Cong had perished and thirteen had been wounded. Actual Communist casualties must have exceeded one hundred, and may have been substantially larger. Supporting this conclusion are the civilian reports, evidence that large numbers of Viet Cong forces were subjected to heavy weapons fire, and a statement by Le Quoc San that Hai Hoang had wanted to attack the Airborne troops during the night but had decided against it because of substantial Viet Cong losses sustained that day.[24]

The government's attack on Ap Bac constituted a tactical failure, for government forces did not annihilate the Viet Cong and they suffered heavy losses despite having many more troops and far better weaponry. On the other hand, Ap Bac was a defeat for the Viet Cong in a strategic sense. At the beginning of 1963, the government's regular forces outnumbered the Viet Cong's regulars by approximately ten to one, yet the ratio of government to Viet Cong casualties at Ap Bac was no higher than two to one, so the Viet Cong lost a much higher portion of their total armed strength. The government's casualties at Ap Bac amounted to only a few hundredths of one percent of total strength.

Soon after the battle ended, Colonel Vann gave Sheehan, Halberstam, and other reporters a highly distorted version of the events, in which all of the day's failures were the fault of the South Vietnamese. "It was a miserable damn performance," Vann told the reporters, "just like it always is. These people won't listen. They make the same goddamn mistakes over and over again in the same way."[25] Vann sought to expose South Vietnamese flaws as a means of pressuring the South Vietnamese into accepting the changes he favored. He was also trying to escape responsibility for the day's unpleasant results by putting all of the blame on his South Vietnamese counterparts, whom he especially resented for failing to overcome the difficulties created by his mistakes. The journalists gobbled it up. Sheehan, for example, wrote that American advisers faulted the South Vietnamese commanders for a "lack of aggressiveness," and the Americans were "disappointed – and angered – that the South Vietnamese troops should fail one of their biggest tests after more than a year of training."[26] The South Vietnamese inaction at Ap Bac, Vann went on to tell the reporters, was the result of serious defects in the Diem government. "The advisers feel that there is still too much political interference in the Vietnamese army and that promotion too often depends on political loyalty rather than military ability," wrote Halberstam in the *New York Times*. "Some commanders are said to feel that they will not be promoted and may lose command if they suffer too many casualties."[27]

Vann neglected to tell the young journalists the many details of the battle that reflected positively on South Vietnamese forces or reflected negatively on him and other Americans. The newsmen's stories did not state that the American advisers had expected the enemy to field a much smaller force, or that they had assumed the enemy would flee once attacked as in the past. Nowhere was it written that the Americans had landed the 7th Division's reserve company much too close to the tree line based on Vann's faulty assessments, or that Vann had concentrated the government's forces at a landing zone that was a most inauspicious point for launching attacks, or that design defects had consigned the machine gunners on the M-113s to death. The correspondents largely overlooked the Communists' enormous defensive advantages and the numerous and costly government attacks that did take place. They did not write that the Vietnamese armored unit had been following procedures learned from the Americans when it attacked piecemeal and when it refused to drive into the middle of the enemy position, and in fact they wrote the opposite. Nor did they mention that a reputedly hard-charging American adviser, Scanlon, had called off an infantry attack across the rice paddies because he considered it to be suicidal, or that the 8th Airborne Battalion had been ordered to spearhead a concerted attack before nightfall but had been prevented from accomplishing this mission because one person's inability to adjust the drop location properly had landed them in the wrong place.

Initially, the journalists emphasized the downing of the five helicopters, in support of their argument that the government had suffered a major setback. The damage to the helicopters, however, was one negative aspect that Vann wanted to play down. He succeeded in getting the correspondents to deemphasize it by deliberately misleading them about the disastrous landing zone selection that had led to the loss of all five helicopters. In the after-action report that Vann wrote for his superiors, as has been mentioned, Vann blamed an American helicopter pilot for the proximity of the landing site to the enemy-infested tree line. With the reporters, he spun a different tale. Based on Vann's claims, Halberstam was to write the following on the loss of the helicopters: "Many Americans view this as virtually inevitable. The helicopters went into an area protected by deeply entrenched, well-armed, well-trained Communist troops."[28] Thus, according to this account, the helicopters could not possibly have landed the necessary three hundred meters from the enemy because the enemy was everywhere. Whereas Vann had blamed all of the other setbacks on South Vietnamese weakness rather than Viet Cong strength, in this one instance the Viet Cong were all-powerful. Halberstam toured the battle site, yet apparently did not notice that the area to the west of the tree line was wide open rice paddy that could not possibly have harbored swarms of guerrillas with guns at the ready. The helicopters could have landed safely in an open area three hundred meters away from the tree line or much further. The reason Vann lied about the helicopter fiasco was that he himself bore full responsibility. Although Vann adroitly conned the younger newsmen, he admitted to Richard Tregaskis a few days after the battle that he had made the decision to put the helicopters so close to the tree line, the most costly mistake anyone made during the battle.[29]

A variety of observers immediately recognized that Colonel Vann and his journalistic disciples had greatly exaggerated both the South Vietnamese mistakes at Ap Bac and the significance of the battle. This group included many of the other American military advisers present at the battle and officials who spoke with these advisers. Colonel Daniel Boone Porter, who had observed the battle as Vann's boss, recalled later that most of the advisers were pleased that the South Vietnamese had engaged the large Viet Cong force at Bac and Tan Thoi, and believed that South Vietnamese officers had done their best in the difficult task of integrating infantry, armor, artillery, helicopters, fixed-wing aircraft, airborne, and militia units – something that they had never attempted before.[30] Roger Hilsman, an OSS veteran with degrees from West Point and Yale who had never been a great admirer of the Diem government, was in Vietnam at the time of the battle and had access to the Americans who witnessed it. Ap Bac "contained some mistakes, but it was not nearly the botched up disaster that the press made it appear to be," asserted Hilsman. "The American press representatives are bitter and will seize on anything that goes wrong and blow it up as much as possible."[31] Richard Tregaskis remarked that the press, and Sheehan in particular, had misunderstood the ultimate importance of the battle and had held naïve expectations of perfection from the South Vietnamese, something that Tregaskis knew from experience was never achieved in battle.[32] Captain Andrew P. O'Meara, whose unit arrived at Ap Bac on the morning after the fight, concluded that Vann had disparaged the Vietnamese unfairly and had himself contributed mightily to the failure.[33]

Later in 1963, during the fall, Halberstam himself would reveal one of the critical points that Vann had omitted from his account of the battle – the enormous difficulty of attacking across wet rice paddies on foot against an entrenched enemy. Vann and other American advisers had not been aware of this problem before Ap Bac, which helps account for Vann's decision to land South Vietnamese forces in the middle of the paddies. In an October article, Halberstam related the story of an adviser who had toured the mushy paddies surrounding Bac on the morning after the battle. This American told Halberstam that the day of the Ap Bac battle was "the day the Americans began to learn just how tough these Indochinese rice paddies can be." Halberstam added: "A rice paddy deals an awesome advantage to a well-armed defender."[34] After 1963, however, Halberstam's accounts of Ap Bac made no mention of the tremendous problems involved in attacking across rice paddies. Sheehan, years later, would make mention of the difficulties that the paddies created for U.S. combat forces once they arrived, though he ignored this point in his lengthy rendition of the battle of Ap Bac. The American combat units that later went to Vietnam, Sheehan noted, avoided assaulting hamlets on foot when it entailed crossing open paddy, preferring instead to blast such hamlets with overwhelming firepower. Referring to costly U.S. combat operations in the rice paddies of the Bong Son Plain during early 1966, Sheehan wrote, "To have taken these hamlets chiefly by infantry assault across the flooded paddies would have meant massive casualties. The punishment of the first couple of days . . . had a sobering effect. The commanders began to settle for pummeling a hamlet with shellfire and air strikes until the enemy abandoned it."[35]

The claim that Ap Bac exemplified general South Vietnamese ineptitude was also erroneous. The government had been waging war effectively in late 1962, and it would do so again in the months after Ap Bac. It was true, as critics often pointed out, that Diem still appointed some officers of mediocre ability because they were likely to oppose rather than support efforts to oust him, but the naysayers failed to understand that Diem had sound reasons for engaging in this practice. In a country so prone to factionalism, appointing an officer of uncertain loyalty might well lead to a coup regardless of who the premier was. Diem believed that none of the potential rebels could lead the nation as well as he could, and that if given power such individuals would be at least as likely as he to choose subordinates on the basis of fealty. Later events would fully vindicate Diem's analysis. Despite the politicization, moreover, Diem still succeeded in employing able men in many key positions, within both the armed forces and the provincial administrations.[36]

Knowing little about their own country's history, Vann and his journalist allies did not comprehend that U.S. leaders – and the leaders of every other country in history, for that matter – often had appointed senior officers for their loyalty or for other political reasons, rather than for their military abilities. During America's Civil War, President Abraham Lincoln repeatedly appointed militarily inexperienced or inept men to the rank of general in order to raise troops and otherwise gain support for his government and the war. To win over Democrats, he commissioned a large number of well-known Democrats as generals, men such John A. Logan, John A. McClernand, and Daniel E. Sickles. To satisfy the foreign-born population, Lincoln bestowed generalships on prominent ethnic figures, including Carl Schurz, Franz Sigel, and Thomas Meagher. In addition, he made generals out of some prominent leaders, such as Benjamin F. Butler, as a means of keeping them out of the 1864 Presidential race. Although some of the appointees became able generals, many others failed badly and their mistakes cost many lives. Soon the label "political general" acquired great currency and a connotation of military incompetence. "It seems little better than murder to give important commands to such men as Banks, Butler, McClernand, Sigel, and Lew Wallace," lamented Union Chief of Staff General Henry W. Halleck, a West Point professional, "yet it seems impossible to prevent it."[37] On the Confederate side, Stonewall Jackson criticized President Jefferson Davis for giving generalships to unqualified politicians such as William Taliaferro and John Echols. "The great interests of the country are being sacrificed by appointing incompetent officers," Jackson exclaimed in the spring of 1862. "I wish that if such appointments are continued, that the President would come in the field and command them, and not throw the responsibility upon me of defending the district when he throws such obstacles in my way."[38]

The appointment of political loyalists to all types of high offices was commonplace in the United States for most of the nineteenth century. The passage of the controversial Pendleton Civil Service Act in 1883 reduced the number of such appointments, but the practice was never eliminated completely. In the summer of 1963, in fact, political concerns would lead President Kennedy to choose the blundering Henry Cabot Lodge for ambassador to South Vietnam. Adding absurdity to chicanery, Ambassador Lodge was to become the most important critic of Diem's loyalty-based appointments. Shortly after Ap Bac, a perceptive American adviser took note of America's hypocrisy in its expectation that South Vietnam would be free of such scheming. "I find it curious that we, as a nation of maturity, wealth and skills, demand levels of political virtue and competence in a relatively new and lacking nation like Vietnam that we do not always apply in our own country," he observed. "I have sometimes noticed in myself that I tend to project upon Vietnam my own desire for perfectionism, something I would know better than to do in any state or municipal government in the United States."[39]

In comparison with other new countries, South Vietnam did not look bad at all. Of the numerous countries that had gained their independence from colonial rule after World War II, very few had developed strong military capabilities in their first decade. When Nguyen Anh attempted to create a unified Vietnam for the first time in the late eighteenth century, it may be recalled, he needed thirteen years to develop strength in southern Vietnam and drive the Tay Son out of northern Vietnam. Nguyen Anh's success owed much to external aid, and to foreign military advisers who sharply criticized him for passivity and excessive caution. When, during this same period in history, thirteen North American colonies formed a new and independent nation, they suffered from many of the same deficiencies as Diem's South Vietnam. The armed forces of both countries lacked adequate leadership and discipline at times, and the leaders of both countries sought assistance from foreign military men out of military necessity.

The foreign helpers in the American case, of whom the most distinguished were Baron Friedrich von Steuben, Marquis Gilbert de Lafayette, and Baron Jean de Kalb, sometimes commanded units in addition to providing advice. These men often faulted America's leaders for the inability of the Continental Army to live up to the standards of more seasoned armies, just as the Americans of the 1960s would fault Diem and his subordinate leaders. Scathing attacks poured forth, for example, after the Continental Army suffered a calamitous defeat at the Brandywine River on September 11, 1777, two and a half years into the war. General George Washington rarely used the Continental Army against large enemy forces as he did at Brandywine, and the results of the battle showed why – by the end of the engagement the Americans had suffered over twelve hundred casualties and had lost eleven cannons. After the fiasco, de Kalb complained that Washington "is too slow, too indolent and far too weak. ... In my opinion, whatever success he may have will be owing to good luck and the blunders of his adversaries, rather than to his abilities."[40] When von Steuben, on another occasion, went to a Virginia courthouse to lead five hundred American volunteers into battle and only five Americans showed up, the Prussian fumed, "I shall always regret that circumstances induced me to undertake the defense of a country where Caesar and Hannibal would have lost their reputation, and where every farmer is a general, but where nobody wishes to be a soldier."[41] The Americans' abundant problems did not drag them down to defeat in their war for independence, but they needed time and much outside help to improve their performance. Seven years of war were to pass and Washington's troops were to suffer many humiliating defeats before they won the climactic battle at Yorktown, a victory that itself would require the contributions of 7,800 French soldiers and a French war fleet.

In a new country short on professional military men, the best one could expect was sustained incremental improvement. During 1962 and 1963, the South Vietnamese government was making such progress. Shortly after the battle of Ap Bac, *Time* magazine reported that "U.S. advisers are pleased with the progress made by government troops over the past year." It quoted one adviser as saying: "The Viet Cong are improving their arsenal and techniques. We're doing the same – and on balance we're still way out ahead of them."[42] Colonel Daniel Boone Porter, the senior American adviser in the Mekong Delta, where the government's armed forces were at their weakest, reported in February 1963 that "tremendous progress has been made in virtually all areas of training, operations, logistics, civic action programs and in the fields of leadership and command since 1 January 1962."[43] None other than Vann himself was to say, in his final report before leaving the country in April, "There is not the slightest doubt that significant improvements have occurred in practically every facet of the counterinsurgency effort in this tactical zone during the past year."[44] Steady improvement was to continue for the rest of Diem's tenure, and Diem's government would never again suffer another setback on the scale of Ap Bac.

A central contention of Vann and the journalists, and hence of the numerous histories based on their assertions, was that the most strategically important area in South Vietnam was the Mekong Delta, where the government was experiencing its greatest difficulties in 1963 by all accounts.[45] In actuality, however, the Mekong Delta was the war's least important area. The delta was useful to the Viet Cong because it provided them opportunities to undertake low-scale guerrilla activities. Bursting with green flora and vibrant villages, the delta supplied more foodstuffs and recruits to the Viet Cong than any other part of the country during the early 1960s. The Mekong Delta, however, was a lousy place for Hanoi to try to win the war. The Communists would never take enough of the delta's resources to cause a major shift in the relative strengths of government and Viet Cong forces, and the terrain was not at all conducive to large insurgent attacks. Against an enemy equipped with attack helicopters and fixed-wing aircraft, insurgent units would be pulverized if they traversed the delta's flat, open rice paddies in large numbers. The Vietnamese Communists had learned that such territory was ill-suited to large operations when the French mauled them repeatedly in the Red River Delta, and consequently they had then sought decisive victories against the French elsewhere, on territory covered with steamy jungles and high peaks and valleys. The provinces of the Mekong Delta, moreover, were the furthest from North Vietnam, making it exceptionally tedious and difficult to bring men, heavy equipment, and vehicles overland from the North.

In the Mekong Delta, Hanoi was never to build the powerful main force units that it constructed in the other three corps areas. All of North Vietnam's attempts to gain a decisive victory by force of arms – in 1961, 1965, 1968, 1972, and 1975 – involved major thrusts in areas other than the Mekong Delta, and only minor offensive activity in the delta. Nor was the delta vital as a source of food or recruits for the main forces fighting elsewhere. The Communists staged their largest offensives, in 1972 and 1975, despite having little access to the delta's food and manpower.

Diem understood that the delta was flimsy as an attack platform for the Viet Cong. The real threat to South Vietnam, he knew, lay not in the present type of war, a guerrilla war with extensive activity in the delta provinces, but rather a big-unit war with Communist main forces concentrated in areas outside of the delta. Later in the year of 1963, in reference to his Vietnamese Communist adversaries, Diem confided to U.S. embassy chief-of-staff John Michael Dunn, "There'll be a time when they'll come at us with tanks in division strength when they're ready, and I don't know where the other forces will come from, whether from your country or France or from nowhere; we may have to fight and die alone. But this business that it will forever and a day be a guerrilla war is nonsense. We can handle the guerrillas. What we can't handle is the main force units which are going to be built up and built up and built up until an invasion takes place." Diem pointed out the places where he expected the enemy forces would invade, none of them in the Mekong Delta, and they turned out to be precisely the places where the enemy main forces came during their subsequent main force offensives.[46]

In the view of both South Vietnamese leaders and North Vietnamese leaders, the area of greatest military importance in South Vietnam was the central highlands, the vast interior space covered by the Annamite mountains, steep-sided valleys, forested plains, and marshy basins. Diem and Giap were both reported to have said, "He who controls the highlands controls the country."[47] Le Duan called the central highlands "the strategic backbone" of South Vietnam, and said that the Communists had to maintain the highlands as a base area "at all costs."[48] Sparsely populated and rugged, the highlands had fewer roads than the rest of the country, despite Diem's road-building programs, and the western edge of the highlands abutted Laos and Cambodia, with the Ho Chi Minh Trail feeding into many highland areas. As a consequence, the central highlands offered Hanoi the best places to infiltrate, forge, hide, and use armies against the mobile South Vietnamese armed forces. Much as the Viet Minh had used their mountain bases in the Viet Bac as the launching pad for most of their operations against the French in northern Vietnam, the Communists sought to use the central highlands as their principal base of operations against Diem. The eastern edge of the highlands lay so close to the coast of northern South Vietnam that forces based in the highlands could reach the narrow lowland plain with very little marching. Invading the central lowlands from the highlands was considerably easier than relying on local lowland forces, as the Communists had found it difficult to build and maintain large military forces amid the government-dominated villages of the lowlands. The southern end of the highlands extended into the provinces immediately north of Saigon, close enough to make it a staging ground for attacks on the capital.

A high-level Communist cadre, in a notebook written during early 1963 and captured by Allied forces during Operation Crimp in 1966, explained that in the central highlands, "we are able to endure a prolonged struggle against the enemy even under the most difficult of circumstances and at the same time have the capability of every day engaging in activities in the delta areas, particularly those in the Fifth Region, and, when the opportunity presents itself, to advance into the heartland of the enemy including Saigon." By delta areas, the author meant all lowland areas, not just the Mekong Delta; the Communists' fifth region to which he referred comprised six of South Vietnam's central and northern coastal provinces, from Khanh Hoa in the south to Quang Nam in the north. The cadre noted that the Communists were not faring well in the struggle for the highlands in early 1963, because "the enemy is also aware of this vital area and therefore has and will use every scheme to compete with us in this area."[49]

As the cadre's remarks about the fifth region indicated, the lowland areas that most interested the Communists in 1963 lay in the northern part of South Vietnam. If the Communists dominated the lowlands of military region five, they could send new recruits and rice to the mountain bases, while at the same time providing intelligence and logistical resources to main forces sent from the highlands to the lowlands. A North Vietnamese Politburo directive explained: "The destruction of the enemy's apparatus of oppression in the lowlands of Region 5 is a matter of great importance, not only in order to expand our control of the rural areas in order to gain manpower and resources, but also because it will have a very important effect in building and expanding our bases in the Central Highlands."[50] Conquering the lowlands in some of the northern provinces would allow the Communists to split the country in two, which is what the Communists tried to do repeatedly during large offensives later in the war, and succeeded in doing during their final offensive. The lowlands in III Corps, between the highlands and the Mekong Delta, were important because the Communists would have to move through this area to assault Saigon, the ultimate prize as far as Hanoi was concerned.

Correctly perceiving the relative importance of each region of the country, Diem put the greatest emphasis on fighting the Viet Cong in the provinces outside the delta, both before Ap Bac and afterwards. When allocating resources for military activities and strategic hamlets, Diem made the Mekong Delta the area of lowest priority.[51] Only two of the regular army's nine divisions operated in the delta, even though one half of all Viet Cong guerrillas were there, and the delta's armed forces received poorer commanders and less equipment than those in the other regions. In addition, the government faced greater natural difficulties in the delta than in the other, more important areas. Militia units in the delta had improved dramatically since the end of 1961, but they were still not as able as those further north in 1963 owing to the easygoing nature of the delta's residents and to the improvements in the rest of the country since 1961. Implementing the strategic hamlet program was inherently more difficult in the delta than elsewhere because the delta's hamlets were more dispersed and hence more difficult to defend, with many hamlets consisting of a set of houses strung along several miles of canal, like strands of spaghetti, whereas in other parts of the country the dwellings were clustered together like meatballs. In the second half of 1962 and for much of 1963, the war in the delta was close to a stalemate, except in a few provinces where the government was definitely winning. With the government clearly outperforming the enemy outside of the delta and fighting with a slight overall advantage in the delta, the government most definitely held the upper hand in the war at the time of Ap Bac.

One more subject on which wisdom and historical perspective were wanting was the U.S. military's relationship with the press. The Saigon correspondents became outraged when, at a news conference shortly after Ap Bac, Admiral Felt scolded them for being so critical and told them to "get on the team." Believing that they were not obliged to support American policy, the young reporters viewed Felt's comments as naïve at best, and manipulative at worst. At this same press conference, Felt and General Harkins proclaimed Ap Bac a success. "I consider it a victory," said Harkins. "We took the objective." The reporters, who knew that the primary goal of the operation was not to capture Bac and Tan Thoi but to destroy the enemy forces, were appalled that Harkins had tried to put a good face on the battle. Some suspected that Harkins was consciously distorting the truth to avoid embarrassing the South Vietnamese, while others concluded that Harkins had deluded himself into believing it was a victory by disregarding unpleasant facts.[52]

What was transpiring in the heads of the U.S. military leadership was rather different from what the newsmen imagined. Harkins and Felt believed that the war was generally going well – as indeed it was – but they did not ignore the faults of the South Vietnamese at the time of Ap Bac or, as has been seen already, at other times. Contrary to his public statements, Admiral Felt privately expressed considerable dissatisfaction with the South Vietnamese performance in the battle.[53] So did General Harkins. Reporting through military channels on the performance of the South Vietnamese, Harkins wrote, "In some cases they could have done better, and I think they should have."[54] Harkins asked the South Vietnamese leadership to relieve two commanders for their failures during the Ap Bac battle,[55] and in the ensuing weeks and months he would continue to press Diem to make improvements in the South Vietnamese armed forces.[56] The top South Vietnamese leadership, for its part, also demonstrated in private a clear understanding of the mistakes at Ap Bac.[57]

General Harkins exuded optimism and downplayed the negative in his remarks to the press and to others with very clear purposes in mind. He sought to stave off the despair that the ravages of war are wont to breed in the hearts of men, and to maintain the prestige of the South Vietnamese government in a culture where face was easily lost. As Harkins had told Ambassador Nolting a short time before Ap Bac, it was necessary to "whistle while we work," in order to sustain "our own and everyone else's morale here."[58] Harkins was simply following the example set by many great men before him. As Supreme Commander of the Allied Forces during World War II, General Dwight Eisenhower had written that by the end of 1942 he had reached the conclusion that "without confidence, enthusiasm, and optimism in the command, victory is scarcely obtainable.... Optimism and pessimism are infectious and they spread more rapidly from the head downward than in any other direction." As a result of this realization, Eisenhower recorded, "I firmly determined that my mannerisms and speech in public would always reflect the cheerful certainty of victory – that any pessimism and discouragement I might ever feel would be reserved for my pillow." General Eisenhower consistently gave upbeat press conferences, and he was given to putting pretty clothing on the ugliest of goblins.[59] The press assisted Eisenhower by giving little attention to negative developments and maintaining a generally upbeat attitude in their articles, in furtherance of the cause. Harkins and Felt assumed, mistakenly, that the Saigon correspondents would act in a similar manner.

When journalists were not around, Eisenhower acted vigorously to correct the major weaknesses of the war effort. Harkins did so as well, and he achieved excellent results by exerting influence over Diem. Among military officers of both eras, an unwritten code dictated that an officer should fix problems behind the scenes and not enlist the press in his cause. It was Vann's violation of this code, plus his insensitivity to the inticracies of South Vietnamese prestige, not his criticism of the South Vietnamese, that was to elicit the wrath of American and South Vietnamese leaders.

Some of the most important evidence on General Harkins surfaced in a private letter that Colonel Daniel Boone Porter wrote to graduate student Thomas J. Lewis in 1971 and in a 1982 oral history interview with Porter that the Lyndon Johnson Library released in 2004. As the senior adviser in IV Corps and the link in the chain of command between Harkins and Vann in 1962 and 1963, Porter had been in an ideal position to see whether Harkins was ignoring criticisms of the South Vietnamese from Colonel Vann and others. Vann's admirers in the press corps, it should be noted, were to praise Porter for supporting Vann right after the battle and for presenting Vann's complaints to Harkins. In his 1971 letter, Porter directly attacked the claim of Halberstam and others that General Harkins had not comprehended the shortcomings of South Vietnam's forces: "I cannot agree with their findings of 'loss of objectivity' and 'unrealistic optimism.' In my discussions with Admiral Felt and General Harkins I found that they clearly recognized from the start that under the political restraints which were in effect, and with the GVN military establishment just beginning to show evidence of having the will and strength to fight, that the struggle was going to be long and hard."

At the same time, Porter commented, when Felt and Harkins wrote private reports lauding the South Vietnamese, they exhibited a strong appreciation of the facts rather than self-delusion. "I believe that Admiral Felt and General Harkins had ample justification for submitting reports reflecting substantial progress," Porter asserted. In the oral history interview, Porter noted that Harkins acted on negative reports but kept quiet to avoid causing political problems for the South Vietnamese. Explaining why Harkins always displayed optimism, Porter remarked, "Those of us that knew him well think that General Harkins was thinking of himself pretty much the same as Vince Lombardi or Knute Rockne or one of the great football players. That it would be highly improper for him, in the presence of his subordinate commanders and his staff, to say that we had suffered a defeat over something that was as trivial as Ap Bac was." Porter testified that "I have always been very, very much disturbed" by the press attacks on General Harkins, for "I think he was a very great man."[60]

Paul Harkins was, indeed, one of the most poorly understood and most underestimated men of his era. The primary cause of the misunderstanding was the foreign press in Saigon. Harkins himself, though, bore a degree of responsibility because he did not combat the negative press reports. His distrust of reporters and his adherence to an Army culture that shunned media exposure kept him from gaining favor among the correspondents and from using the press to defend himself. During General Harkins's tour in Vietnam, Brig. Gen. Michael Greene told him to let the truth be known in order to clear his name, but Harkins did not follow this advice, and so the journalists went on harboring the illusion that Harkins was the fool and they were the wise men. Following Harkins's retirement, Greene kept pressing Harkins to reveal his side of the story. Harkins, however, would only tell Greene, "I don't think I want to do that, Mike."[61]

The Battle of Ap Bac was, like its most famous participant, not what it first appeared to the outside world. Far from being the "golden opportunity" for the South Vietnamese forces that Halberstam was to call it in *The Making of a Quagmire*,[62] the battle was a golden opportunity for the Viet Cong, as they entered the battle with tremendous advantages, thanks to the terrain. The South Vietnamese forces did not perform well at Ap Bac, but neither did they display gross ineptitude or cowardice. Most of their troubles could be traced to the terrain, to the prowess of crack Viet Cong troops, or to Clausewitzian friction – the inevitable mishaps that make easy tasks difficult in war. Colonel John Paul Vann committed the most grievous error of the battle by landing the reserve company too close to the western edge of the Viet Cong's defensive positions, which he mistakenly believed to be free of enemy forces. Vann succeeded in misleading the American press corps, and hence the world, about the events at Ap Bac by exaggerating the faults of the South Vietnamese and hiding his own. The mischaracterization of Ap Bac as the epitome of the Diem government's incompetence would not take root so quickly, since contrary evidence abounded at the time. The rise of that misinterpretation, like that of many other denigrations of the Diem regime, would have to await the overthrow of the Diem government.

CHAPTER 9

Diem on Trial

FEBRUARY–JULY 1963

AS 1963 PROGRESSED INTO THE SPRING AND SUMMER, THE SOUTH Vietnamese government continued to improve its counterinsurgency capabilities and its position in the countryside.[1] Increasing in size and quality at the same time, the Civil Guard reached a strength of 75,000 men, the Self-Defense Corps 100,000, the Civilian Irregular Defense Groups 40,000, and the regular armed services 215,000.[2] At Diem's command, the South Vietnamese continued to eliminate small and isolated outposts in the countryside and transfer their personnel to more productive duties. The government's forces aggressively sought battle with the Viet Cong and inflicted many defeats during this time. Colonel Bryce F. Denno, upon completing an eleven-month tour as the I Corps senior adviser in July 1963, reported that in his region, "the Self-Defense Corps units are defending their villages against enemy attacks with much greater confidence and success than in the past. The ARVN is reaching out into the deep jungle to attack Viet Cong 'secure' areas." The population, moreover, was giving more information on the enemy to government forces in his corps area.[3] In a mid-year assessment, III Corps senior adviser Colonel Wilbur Wilson remarked that pacification had experienced substantial gains in every province of the corps area.[4]

Major General Victor H. Krulak, the special assistant for counterinsurgency for the Joint Chiefs of Staff, traveled to all four corps areas in late June and observed that "offensive operations against the Viet Cong are widespread and varied, and are growing steadily in intensity." In Khanh Hoa province, Krulak found that the 23rd ARVN Division had been broken down into small units and was ably patrolling the mountains in the western parts of the province. In Quang Ngai province, a province that long had been a hotbed of Communist activity, the 25th Division had pushed the Viet Cong from the coastal plain into the Annamite mountains. The strategic hamlet militia and the 25th Division, aided by information from numerous villagers, had repulsed large Viet Cong attacks on the strategic hamlets in April, dealing the Viet Cong several hundred casualties.[5] In the country as a whole, the Communists initiated only seven battalion-size attacks during the first half of 1963, whereas they had managed thirty-five in the first six months of 1962.[6]

Western observers noted that the strategic hamlet program continued to make great strides. Phase I of the National Campaign, which involved implementation of two-thirds of the strategic hamlet program, was completed by mid-1963, ahead of schedule, in every part of the country except for the Mekong Delta.[7] A large number of hamlets were functioning effectively, even though some of them were still only partially complete. U.S. officers who visited each of South Vietnam's provinces in the first half of 1963 remarked that local governments had undergone dramatic improvements and had greatly extended their reach, while the hamlet militia were repelling the Viet Cong with determination and skill. They also noted that the rural population and local officials now had much greater confidence in the government and their morale was up.[8] Colonel Ted Serong, a guerrilla warfare expert who headed the Australian training mission in South Vietnam, told top Washington officials in May 1963 that "the big success story in Viet-Nam is the strategic hamlet program and this story has not yet been fully told."[9] Sir Robert Thompson, who like many other observers had shifted to an optimistic view of the war effort after holding a distinctly pessimistic view in the bleak days of 1961 and early 1962, observed that in the strategic hamlet program, "the energy displayed has been remarkable by any standards."[10] In Thompson's opinion, the government was now winning the war and it might be able to shut off the Viet Cong's access to the people by the middle of 1964, even in the Mekong Delta.[11]

The beginning of May saw the production of a noteworthy report on the strategic hamlets by Rufus Phillips, the chief U.S. adviser to the strategic hamlet program. In the report, Phillips observed that some South Vietnamese officials were still creating strategic hamlets too rapidly, thus sacrificing quality for quantity. Phillips pointed out that the program faced the worst problems in the Mekong Delta, where "except in a few provinces, the apparent progress is largely illusory." Despite these problems, Phillips noted, "the strategic hamlet program has so well proven itself in those areas where it has been well executed that there is every reason for optimism and confidence."

Later it would be alleged with great regularity that the optimism surrounding the strategic hamlet program was the result of uncritical acceptance of inflated South Vietnamese statistics. In reality, Phillips and most other advisers did not rely solely on statistics or other reports from the South Vietnamese. In every province, American civilian and military advisers personally inspected numerous hamlets and talked with villagers and government employees, then sent reports to Phillips's staff and other U.S. organizations. The Americans also received pertinent information from captured documents and Viet Cong defectors.[12] Phillips's report made very clear that the optimism about the program was not based upon official statistics. Stated Phillips, "In general, highly significant progress has been made in the Strategic Hamlet-Provincial

Rehabilitation program in many provinces. Progress is measured in terms of the establishment, in steadily increasing number, of viable hamlets with inhabitants who have the will and the means to resist the Vietcong. There is a sharp difference between the number of such hamlets, and the total number of strategic hamlets officially listed as complete by the Vietnamese Government."[13] On a variety of other occasions, U.S. military advisers and South Vietnamese leaders – including Diem and Nhu – acknowledged that the official total of strategic hamlets completed greatly exceeded the actual total.[14]

During the middle of 1963, those watching the war also noticed major advances in the aggressiveness and effectiveness of South Vietnamese forces in the problematic Mekong Delta. Once again, the careful entreaties of General Harkins and Ambassador Nolting exerted a positive effect on Diem. "The Viet Cong have taken it on the chin these past few weeks," observed Paul Smith, a helicopter pilot from Nebraska who was flying South Vietnamese troops into combat across the delta, in a May letter to his brother. "The government troops are growing increasingly aggressive, and their leaders are assuming a more positive attitude about winning battles."[15] In late July, the ARVN 7th Division dispatched a large task force to attack two heavily-entrenched companies of the 514th Viet Cong Battalion, one of the two battalions that had fought the 7th Division at Ap Bac. Employing aircraft and armored personnel carriers as well as infantry, the task force assaulted two Viet Cong strong points that, like the fighting positions at Ap Bac, were defended by heavy machine guns and surrounded by open rice paddies. After two hours of bitter fighting, the 7th Division overran the two Viet Cong positions, compelling the remaining soldiers of the 514th Battalion to flee through escape tunnels. Government troops recovered fifty-eight Communist bodies, and the fleeing Viet Cong were believed to have taken many more with them. For the 7th Division, casualties totaled eighteen dead and forty-five wounded. David Halberstam reported, "American advisers were pleased not only with the planning of the operation, but also with the way the plans were carried out under difficult conditions."[16] In reference to the 7th Division, an American adviser told the press, "Everything they did wrong at Ap Bac they did right Saturday."[17]

Once again, North Vietnamese documents and histories corroborate the American and other foreign reports on the Diem government's effectiveness. One North Vietnamese account stated that in the first six months of 1963, the South Vietnamese government conducted between 1,500 and 2,000 infantry operations per month, and it noted: "Protracted and large-scale operations launched unremittingly against any given region were more numerous and fiercer than in the previous year."[18] A top-level Communist report on this period asserted that the government strengthened the rural militias and it still possessed much stronger military forces than the Viet Cong. "Due to the results attained in the recent sweeps and due to his grinding efforts to gather in the people and establish strategic hamlets," the report acknowledged, "the enemy seized a large number of people and constricted our liberated areas, causing us many manpower and materiel difficulties." It also stated that government forces had launched successful operations deep into Communist base areas, destroying Communist forces and disrupting Communist lines of communication that ran from North Vietnam and Laos into South Vietnam.[19]

The history of the Communists' critical Region 5 noted that during 1963, "the enemy recaptured practically everything we had captured." The Diem government expanded the strategic hamlet program to cover most of the hamlets in the region, causing "enormous problems" for the Viet Cong. Communist forces that tried to impede the program's progress were driven from the lowlands.[20] Another account explained, "With a network of outposts and strong points and a web of roads, airfields, and 'strategic hamlets,' the enemy was able to establish fairly tight control over Region 5. In the rural lowlands, our self-defense guerrillas and local force troops were few and weak."[21] Concerning Cochinchina, meaning the Mekong Delta and the provinces surrounding Saigon, a Communist account stated that the Viet Cong had few full-time soldiers at this time, and noted that the Viet Cong troops were dispersed into small groups, which prevented them from defeating government forces engaged in either mobile operations or the construction of strategic hamlets.[22] Le Quoc San, the Communist commander in the upper Mekong Delta for most of the war, remembered that the Viet Cong were hurting badly in Ben Tre province, which had been one of the most troublesome provinces for the government since the Ben Tre insurrection in January 1960. By the middle of 1963, the government had established 195 strategic hamlets across Ben Tre. "Our Party members and guerrillas who had previously lived with and been close to the people," explained Le Quoc San "were now driven out and forced to return to conducting secret operations or to living in the fields in bushes and on riverbanks. District and provincial local force troops could no longer rely on the people. Without this support, they were forced to disperse to conduct low-level operations, evading the enemy's constant sweep operations and patrols."[23]

These developments reinforced the pessimism that had taken hold during the middle of 1962 in Hanoi. In a prominent Party journal, a senior North Vietnamese official named Minh Tranh wrote that the Americans and the South Vietnamese government "resort to all shrewd and cruel measures" and therefore "the South Vietnamese revolution must go along a long, arduous and complicated path." The fighting capabilities of Diem's forces, he predicted gloomily, "will not diminish during 1963 but can grow even fiercer."[24] In line with the strategy, established in mid-1962, of seeking a coalition government rather than decisive military, Hanoi let it be known that it would support the creation and preservation of a neutral South Vietnam led by a coalition government, but did not find any takers on the opposing side.

After 1963 had come and gone, Halberstam, Sheehan, and other reporters would claim that South Vietnam's counterinsurgency efforts crumbled over the course of 1963, up until the end of October, and that they had been aware of the crumbling at the time.[25] It was a myth crafted afterwards to justify their support of the disastrous November coup. During this period, some members of the Saigon press corps – particularly Halberstam and Sheehan – did report fewer government successes and were more critical of the Diem government in general than American officials, because they so despised the regime. Albert Fraleigh, one of the top U.S. advisers to the strategic hamlet program, received frequent visits from Halberstam, Sheehan, and other correspondents. On many occasions, Fraleigh discussed with them the achievements of the strategic hamlet program, but they showed no interest in such topics because they quite obviously were not seeking positive information about the Diem government. "Halberstam and Sheehan were always looking for glaring errors on the South Vietnamese side," Fraleigh explained.[26] Major General Edward Rowny recalled from firsthand experience that some journalists, especially Halberstam, "were more interested in pursuing their own political agendas than they were in reporting on the military situation." After Halberstam and Rowny accompanied one operation that resulted in combat with the Viet Cong, Halberstam wrote an article stating that the government troops had performed poorly and blaming their ineffectiveness on the unpopularity of Madame Nhu. Rowny told Halberstam, "You know, Dave, that the operation was rather successful. And whether it was or not had nothing to do with Madame Nhu. The soldiers don't even know who she is." Halberstam replied, "Ed, the readers don't want to read anything about these military skirmishes. What they are interested in is the Dragon Lady."[27]

The correspondents' general appraisals of the war, nevertheless, differed little from the private views of senior American officials for most of 1963. Both the reporters and the officials recognized that in spite of some significant shortcomings, Diem's military was outperforming the Viet Cong except in the delta, where the war was close to a standoff. The two groups differed mainly on secondary issues, with the journalists contending inaccurately that the delta was the key battleground and criticizing Diem's military for failing to attain a level of competence that had eluded the armies of Washington and Lincoln. Exemplifying the journalists' coverage of the war during the middle of 1963 was a Halberstam article dated July 28, 1963. The young *New York Times* correspondent repeated some of the criticisms he had made at the time of Ap Bac, which in some cases were similar in character, if not in tone, to the criticisms that Harkins and other American advisers were delivering to the South Vietnamese in private at this same time. Government forces were inhibited by fear of heavy casualties, and the strategic hamlet program in the delta faced some problems. The war in the delta, Halberstam stated, "is now considered stalemated at best." Outside of the delta, though, the war was going well for Diem. "In some large areas north of Saigon," Halberstam wrote, "there has been substantial progress. This includes the central coastal region, where the

Government is pushing hard on the strategic-hamlet program.... Progress is also substantial in the central highlands, where Montagnard tribesmen, trained by the United States Special Forces, are being used to cut off Vietcong infiltration routes."[28]

The military issue that most worried American experts in the first part of 1963 was not the performance of Diem's forces, but rather the infiltration of North Vietnamese personnel and war materials.[29] Despite the impressive successes registered by the CIA-trained Uplanders and other South Vietnamese forces in the border regions, Communist soldiers and porters continued to stream across in large numbers.[30] American analysis indicated that 500 men from the North were arriving in the South each month, similar to the estimated rate in the months preceding the Geneva Agreement on Laos.[31] The American estimates actually were far too low; according to Communist figures, the monthly infiltration average during 1963 was close to 1,500 men per month. Chinese heavy weapons, including recoilless rifles and .50 caliber machine guns, were popping up throughout the country. Some had been carried overland through Laos, while others had been moved by sea either directly to South Vietnam or through Cambodia. Hanoi later acknowledged that during the years 1961 to 1963 it transported 165,600 weapons by bicycle, elephant, and human porter into South Vietnam, and had shipped large quantities of heavy weapons, munitions, and other equipment to the South by sea.[32]

For a Viet Cong regular army with roughly 23,000 men, a monthly influx of 1,500 men or even 500 constituted an addition of great magnitude. Heavy Viet Cong losses, in fact, would have resulted in a substantial decline in Viet Cong strength starting in mid-1962 had it not been for the infiltration. As it was, the infiltration only sufficed to offset Viet Cong combat losses, desertions, and defections,[33] leaving total troop strength unchanged. The infiltrators were much superior to peasants recruited in the South since they were already trained, they were firmly devoted to the cause, and they often did not have access to relatives on the government side who could lead them astray. Many of them were assigned to important leadership positions. It was thus not surprising that a high-ranking Communist leader observed in early 1963 that southern Laos was "vital to all of South Vietnam and all of Indochina."[34]

Laos began to come apart entirely in April, when ten thousand Pathet Lao and North Vietnamese troops seized part of the Plain of Jars from neutralist forces. Aghast at the duplicity of the Communists, Souvanna beseeched the Soviets and British to intercede. Kennedy, yet again, rejected recommendations from his advisers to deploy ground forces into Laos, though he did authorize limited air strikes. He sent Harriman to Moscow with instructions to tell Khrushchev to take the steam out of the Pathet Lao. In conversation with Harriman, the Soviet premier pledged his allegiance to the Geneva agreement, but he also repudiated his previous claims of influence in Laos, the claims upon which Kennedy had built his Laotian policy. "The Soviet Union has no one in

Laos except its Ambassador," Khrushchev explained. But no such influence was needed, Khrushchev assured Harriman, for the Pathet Lao were acting in good faith, and Laos in any case was unimportant.[35] Returning to the United States, Harriman once more expressed hope that the Soviets would help enforce Laotian neutrality, though by now even he must have been stricken with serious doubts about the likelihood of Soviet assistance. As it turned out, Khrushchev did not lift a stubby finger to slow the Pathet Lao. Souvanna's control faded in patches, like grass wilting in a summer drought, and ever more men from North Vietnam marched through Laos en route to South Vietnam bearing machine guns and ammunition belts.

During May, an even more dangerous crisis began to brew in the city of Hue, the Ngo family's own hometown. Like the vapors from the city's famed fish soup, it started at the hands of a few chefs, then wafted through the city streets, drawing others towards it. What ostensibly prompted the chefs to fill their kettles was an attempt by the police to keep Buddhists from flying religious flags on May 7, a Buddhist holiday. Just a few days earlier, during religious celebrations in Hue and Da Nang, government officials had permitted Catholics to fly the Vatican's gold and white flags. After the Catholic celebrations, however, Diem decided that the government ought to begin enforcing a longstanding but hitherto unobserved ordinance that prohibited outdoor flag flying by all religious groups, Catholics included.[36] Diem most probably made the decision in order to preserve the government's prestige – in the eyes of most Vietnamese, regardless of political affiliation, the flying of flags was an assertion of power that had the potential to undermine the prestige of the political authorities. For this reason, the Viet Cong regularly prohibited the people in areas under their control from flying Buddhist flags and other religious flags.

Although the ordinance applied to all religious groups and its enforcement came in response to Catholic activities, certain Buddhist activists asserted that it was an act of discrimination against Buddhists because the government had recently tolerated Catholic flag-waving. At the urging of activist leaders, thousands of Buddhist flags popped up in Hue on May 7, and on the next morning five hundred Buddhist protesters gathered at Tu Dam pagoda in Hue with banners protesting the flag prohibition. The monk Tri Quang, who was the head chef, told the crowd that the government favored Catholics and persecuted Buddhists. "Now is the time to fight!" he proclaimed.[37] Later in the day, the protesters took their demonstration to Hue's radio station, whereupon they demanded that the government give air time to Tri Quang. In the past, government leaders had permitted Buddhist monks to go on the air, but the radio station's director refused because Tri Quang wanted to broadcast a tape recording critical of the government. Next, the provincial chief arrived on the scene and attempted to convince the demonstrators to go home. They refused. At some point, probably because of rock throwing by the crowd, the provincial chief decided that the time for a firmer hand had come. Using fire hoses, government security personnel sent thick jets of water into the throng, but some of the protesters still did not leave. Soldiers arrived, and a disorderly melee of uncertain origin ensued. In the hope of dispersing the crowd, the soldiers fired artillery blanks and shot their rifles up into the air.

What happened next has never been determined with certainty. According to the Buddhist activists, government troops unjustifiably opened fire on the Buddhists and threw grenades at them. The South Vietnamese government contended that a Communist or some other agitator detonated plastic explosives in the midst of the crowd with the intention of sowing dissension.[38] It is most likely that some people were shot by troops and others were struck by the blast from one or more explosives set off by an agitator, in a sequence that cannot be inferred from the existing evidence. What is certain is that nine civilians died and fourteen were wounded, most of them Buddhist protesters.

Two days later, five thousand Buddhists assembled at Tu Dam pagoda. Boisterous and defiant, the demonstrators waved banners emblazoned with anti-government slogans. Tri Quang urged the people to adhere to the policies of Ghandi; they were to carry no weapons, but should be prepared to die. Another Buddhist leader, however, arose to declare that the Diem government was a good one. The provincial chief also spoke before the gathering, expressing sorrow for those killed on May 8 and promising that the government would provide compensation to their families, which prompted the crowd to erupt into applause. Observing these developments, the American consul in Hue concluded, "Believe crisis nearing end."[39]

Tri Quang and certain other leaders, however, refused to be conciliated. They organized new demonstrations and issued a set of demands, which included punishment of the officials involved in the May 8 incident, removal of all restrictions on the display of flags, and, most fantastically, a prohibition against the arrest of Buddhists. Diem started a dialogue with the Buddhist leaders, but did not yield to most of their demands. Making further concessions would, in Diem's view, suggest that his government was guilty of the killings and convey an impression of weakness. A potpourri of other factions and minorities might inundate the government with new demands that the government could not afford to meet. And fulfilling the Buddhists' demands would severely reduce Diem's ability to protect himself from Communists and other subversives – if the police could not arrest demonstrators who claimed to be Buddhists, the government could not possibly prevent rioting and the accompanying erosion of national morale. In the coming months, though, Diem would not systematically round up Tri Quang and other militant Buddhist leaders, even as the venom began to issue forth from their lips in large doses. The costs of this decision would be enormous, for it allowed the protesters time to gain the sympathies of the foreign press. Had Ho Chi Minh been assailed by protesters such as Tri Quang, he would have arrested them when they first criticized the government, and possibly he would have tortured or killed them. Ho, in fact, already had used brutal methods to stamp out all independent impulses amongst North Vietnam's Buddhists. Two factors account for this difference in behavior. The first is that Diem, despite his own strong aversion to political opposition, was more willing to grant freedom to religious leaders than was the anti-religious Ho. The second is that Ho's Chinese and Soviet patrons wanted him to eliminate dissidents by whatever means necessary, whereas the American government put considerable pressure on Diem to tolerate the Buddhist protesters and other dissidents.

The American press corps in Saigon seized on the Buddhist protests as evidence that the Diem government lacked public support and was hopelessly repressive and therefore deserved to be overthrown.[40] It soon became their principal means for attacking Diem, as they were finding it harder and harder to deplore the South Vietnamese war effort. The reporters developed friendships with the militant Buddhist leadership, thanks largely to their common contempt for Diem's government. The activists gave the newsmen tips and other information in English, carried protest signs and banners written in English, and made the young men feel important, as indeed they were. In return, the correspondents penned favorable stories about the Buddhist protesters. The militant Buddhists, in fact, were so much more skillful at pandering to the Western media than almost any other Vietnamese group, then or since, that one could sensibly deduce that they were receiving guidance from their American press allies. The American correspondents, because of their hatred of the Diem government and their unfamiliarity with the Vietnamese political environment, uncritically accepted their Buddhist friends' claims about the political situation, many of which were fallacious. The journalists were similarly credulous in their dealings with South Vietnamese intellectuals and other English-speaking schemers who regaled them with ominous stories of dissatisfaction with Diem and plots against him, oftentimes unaware of these individuals' own political agendas and political myopia. Halberstam later acknowledged that the individuals upon whom he and the other reporters depended for political information "were regrettably limited in their larger vision."[41]

Two of the sources upon whom the journalists relied most heavily, Pham Ngoc Thao and Pham Xuan An, were actually Communist agents. Pham Ngoc Thao, a colonel in the South Vietnamese Army, was touted by the American media as a brilliant Young Turk who could help turn South Vietnam around.[42] Thao regularly gave the correspondents information on dissension and intrigue against the government, which they in turn eagerly passed on to their readers. Pham Xuan An was a member of the international press itself, for he worked as a stringer for Reuters. Muoi Huong, the Communist who recruited both Pham Ngoc Thao and Pham Xuan An, later said that he had told An to become a journalist for the very purpose of influencing foreign reporters. Muoi Huong explained that he wanted An to become a journalist because "in 1945, when our people had just seized political power, a number of foreign journalists sought to speak ill of our young government. Uncle Ho always reminded our leaders to be careful in dealing with these journalists because they were the 'fourth power' whose voice was of great influence."[43] In fulfillment of Muoi Huong's vision, Pham Xuan An brilliantly manipulated and misled the foreign press. After the war, journalist Stanley Karnow would acknowledge his heavy reliance on Pham Xuan An during the war: "We would huddle together in the Brodard or the Givral, his favorite cafes, as he chain-smoked and patiently deciphered the puzzles of Vietnam for me."[44] Halberstam and Sheehan relied heavily on information from Pham Xuan An; Halberstam considered An to be their best source on the South Vietnamese officer corps because of his supposed contacts among the officers.[45] The newsmen's reliance on Pham Xuan An goes a long way toward explaining why the press kept reporting dissatisfaction among the officers in 1963 that did not actually exist.

Armed by deficient informants and driven by passionate hatred, the reporters wrote highly inaccurate and biased stories on the Buddhist protest movement. The flaws in their argument began with the claim that seventy or eighty percent of the South Vietnamese population was Buddhist, which implied that to alienate "the Buddhists" was to alienate the nation's majority. While a large proportion of the South Vietnamese populace had some loose affiliation with Buddhism, those who considered Buddhism to be their religion, and who therefore may have felt an affinity for the Buddhist political movement in 1963, constituted a much smaller fraction. In a country of fifteen million, there were between three and four million Buddhists, and of these perhaps only fifty percent could be considered practicing Buddhists. In other words, the number of Buddhists in the country was between ten and twenty-seven percent of the populace, depending upon whether non-practicing Buddhists were counted. Most of South Vietnam's Buddhists lived in the countryside and knew nothing of political disturbances in Saigon and Hue, so that only a very small minority of Buddhists were potential members or supporters of the Buddhist opposition movement. Confucians, for whom ancestor worship remained the principal spiritual activity, also numbered four million. One and a half million, about ten percent, of the nation's citizens were Roman Catholics. The Cao Dai and Hoa Hao sects, with a total of between two and a half and three million members between them, were close in total size to the Buddhists. That fact was particularly significant in light of the claims made in 1963 that Diem could not afford to take on such a large segment of the population as the Buddhists – Diem had successfully resisted and then destroyed the Cao Dai and Hoa Hao opposition in 1955 even though these sects had their own armies. Most other South Vietnamese citizens were animists, Taoists, Protestant Christians, Hindus, or Muslims.[46]

The American press accepted and advanced the spurious claim of the militants that the deaths of Buddhists on May 8 were the result of a governmental policy of persecuting Buddhists. Diem, in stark contrast to Ho Chi Minh, had done much to help Vietnam's Buddhists. From the beginning, Diem had given the Buddhists permission to carry out many activities that the French had prohibited.[47] Of South Vietnam's 4,766 pagodas, 1,275 were built under Diem's rule, many with funds from the government. The Diem government also provided large amounts of money for Buddhist schools, ceremonies, and other activities.[48] Diem's accusers said that he blatantly discriminated in his selection of officials, with the result that most officials were Catholics, but they were mistaken.[49] In some parts of the government, Catholics did hold a disproportionately high number of positions, and at certain times and places Catholics received limited preferential treatment in hiring and promotion, which South Vietnamese leaders might justify by pointing to the fact that Catholics, and especially Northern Catholic refugees, had repeatedly shown themselves to be more dedicated in their anti-Communism than the average non-Catholic. The primary cause of Catholic over-representation, though, was not discrimination but the higher proportion of educated persons in the Vietnamese Catholic population, a legacy of the colonial era. But what is most significant is that Catholics did not come close to dominating the Diem government, not even at the highest levels. Among Diem's eighteen cabinet ministers were five Catholics, five Confucians, and eight Buddhists, including a Buddhist vice-president and a Buddhist foreign minister. Of the provincial chiefs, twelve were Catholics and twenty-six were Buddhists or Confucians. Only three of the top nineteen military officers were Catholics.[50]

Like many U.S. officials, the journalists assumed that the Diem government's repeated attempts to prevent or break up Buddhist demonstrations in the spring and summer of 1963 appalled the South Vietnamese populace, in the same way that crackdowns on religious demonstrations in the United States might offend American sensibilities. The Vietnamese people, however, did not see it that way.[51] As had already been made clear in 1955, the Vietnamese tended to look favorably on a government that suppressed public demonstrations, so long as they themselves were not among the demonstrators and the crackdowns were carried out effectively. No successful leader in Vietnamese history had tolerated the sort of vicious and organized public attacks that the Buddhist militants began to make on Diem in May 1963. In the rural areas, moreover, where the war was being fought, no one cared about the Buddhist crisis. Even among the educated elite, a large number understood and supported Diem's actions during the Buddhist disturbances.[52]

The journalists rejected the claim of Diem and many other South Vietnamese officials that some militant Buddhist leaders were secret agents of Hanoi, capable of influencing the movement's behavior as well as duping their press contacts. The Buddhists, they swore, were only concerned with ending religious persecution or discrimination.[53] Most American officials did not give credence to accusations of Communist complicity, either, at least in part because of their own confidence in the professions of the Buddhists and the press. It is undeniable that a large number of the Buddhists who demonstrated from May 8 onwards were protesting solely to end what they had been told was religious oppression, not to support the North Vietnamese politburo. It is equally undeniable that significant numbers of the protesters were Communist agents, including some of the monks. The Vietnamese Communists had a long history of posing as monks and infiltrating Buddhist organizations, a very easy task as any Vietnamese man could become a Buddhist monk at any time simply by shaving his head, donning a monk's robe, and acting with humility.[54] None other than Ho Chi Minh had concealed his Marxist-Leninist intentions by masquerading as a Buddhist monk during the late 1920s.

A few captured Communist documents, available at the time to both the Americans and the South Vietnamese, revealed Communist participation in the Buddhist protest movement. One Communist document, dated July 27, 1963 and captured a few weeks thereafter, stated that in some areas Communist personnel "have pushed the political struggle movement by initiating the demonstrations against the terrorization of Buddhism at the province and districts."[55] For many years, Hanoi kept silent about the very sensitive subject of its involvement in the Buddhist movement, but in the early 1990s it began publishing detailed accounts of its early and intimate complicity. One Communist history divulged that immediately following the May 8 incident, "Revolutionary agents among the Buddhists and students, laborers, and *petit bourgeoisie* from the Dong Ba Market called on the people to struggle to demand justice for those who had been killed." In the ensuing period, "our Party provincial and city committees stayed close to and directed the movement from the inside through the use of our agents in the mass organizations and in the Buddhist Church."[56] Another Party history asserted that "the NLF Central Committee quickly directed the people of all classes of the population to cooperate actively with the Buddhist monks and nuns in a resolute struggle until the goals were achieved." This account credited the National Liberation Front with organizing a variety of demonstrations in provincial capitals during the subsequent months, in which the demonstrators denounced the United States and Diem for the "repression of Buddhism" and demanded "freedom of religion" and "democracy."[57] Communist sources also state that Party agents successfully infiltrated the leadership of the Buddhist movement in the capital city of Saigon and incited the Saigonese to protest against the government while making far-reaching demands in the name of Buddhism.[58]

While Hanoi had plenty of its own operatives working in the lower and middle echelons of the Buddhist opposition, Hanoi's influence at the top level is less certain. Tri Quang, the foremost leader of the militant Buddhist protesters, was often accused of being a Communist. The Vietnamese Communist government never acknowledged that he was an agent, as it would with some of its other prominent agents after the war, but considerable evidence points in this direction. In a nation where Buddhist monks rarely participated in political activities, Tri Quang's ardent political activism immediately gave cause for suspicion. A Northerner by birth, Tri Quang had served with the Viet Minh in their struggles against both the Japanese and the French, and he may have spent time in Hanoi after 1954. When the Buddhist uproar began in the South, Tri Quang's brother was a senior official in Hanoi's Ministry of the Interior and was responsible for organizing subversion in South Vietnam.[59] During his sermons, Tri Quang argued that Buddhism and communism were compatible. His political methods, particularly with respect to the spreading of propaganda and the manipulation of crowds, were strikingly similar to those of the Vietnamese Communists, and were very different from those of traditional Vietnamese Buddhists, which accounts in part for his ability to mobilize the masses far more effectively than traditional Buddhists. Over and over again, Tri Quang would refuse to accept generous concessions from the government, both in 1963 and later. During the summer of 1963, he openly stated that he would not stop protesting until the Diem government fell,[60] and on an at least one occasion he went so far as to advocate collaboration with the Communists.[61]

Beginning in 1964, other Buddhist leaders would begin accusing Tri Quang of working for the Viet Cong. Several of those accusers had previously been among his most prominent followers.[62] In 1965, Tri Quang was to oppose, without success, a resolution by other Buddhists denouncing Communist terrorism against civilians and Communist efforts to control the Buddhist masses. Tri Quang, with few pauses, would attempt to undermine the South Vietnamese government from mid-1963 all the way until June 1966, when Premier Nguyen Cao Ky banished him to a mountain retreat. He returned to a life of protest when the Republic of Vietnam neared its end and, on March 31, 1975, as the Saigon government was reeling from the blows of North Vietnamese divisions, he took part in a public demonstration demanding the resignation of President Nguyen Van Thieu.[63]

The sum of the evidence strongly suggests that Tri Quang was a Communist operative. If the Communists did in fact control him, it was one of the most ingenious and effective uses of covert action in history. Tri Quang caused enormous harm to every South Vietnamese regime that held power from 1963 to 1966, despite those regimes' often extraordinary efforts to appease him, and he would have destroyed the South Vietnamese government entirely had some of its leaders not decided in the end to stop him. If Tri Quang was not a dedicated Communist, then he must have been operating under the assumption that he could hold off or control the Communists himself once the South Vietnamese government collapsed, a delusion that would grip other Vietnamese politicians near the end of the war.

As the Buddhist disturbances unfolded, Harriman, Hilsman, and other State Department officials in Washington came to the conclusion that President Diem was not doing enough to placate the militant Buddhists. Belonging to the school of thought that equated South Vietnamese politics with American politics, they were particularly concerned that the South Vietnamese President was not undertaking a large public relations campaign aimed at gaining the Buddhists' sympathies. Harriman and Hilsman also sought to use the Buddhist disturbances to browbeat Diem into adopting liberal reforms, an approach the two men had begun resurrecting several months earlier. Harriman was naturally heavy-handed and close-minded, and these traits were exacerbated whenever he dealt with Diem and the other pro-American strong men of East Asia, a fact that probably had much to do with Harriman's own autocratic tendencies and his liberal political views.[64] Harriman had averred, not long before the crisis began, that "we must start calling some of the tunes and Diem must take our advice,"[65] and he would do his utmost to achieve that end in the coming months. Soon after the May 8 incident, Harriman and Hilsman compelled Ambassador Nolting to tell Diem to take additional conciliatory actions, make a public statement, and appoint a commission to review the incident thoroughly. Diem slowly began to act on these measures.

Ambassador Nolting had been scheduled to leave Vietnam with his wife and daughters for vacation on May 9, but he postponed the trip when the demonstrators died in Hue. Two weeks later, though, it seemed that Diem and his local officials had defused the crisis and so Nolting decided to depart. He was to be gone for a month and a half, with a vacation in the Aegean followed by consultations in Washington. Before Nolting left, he received a promise from Truehart, who would be acting ambassador in his absence, to notify him of any emergencies or dramatic changes in America's Vietnam policy. Truehart was to send any such notification to the CIA station chief in Athens.

Soon after Nolting's departure, the Buddhist opposition flared, with protesters filling city streets to denounce the government, fueled by false rumors that the government had killed Tri Quang and other militant Buddhists. Some demonstrations ran their course without incident, but in other cases the demonstrators became unruly and refused to leave when instructed to do so by government officials, prompting government security forces to disperse them with tear gas. Acting Ambassador Truehart discerned at the end of May that the charges of religious oppression were "being used as label and façade behind which other groups seek to express opposition to Diem government and exploit situation for various aims," which, he said, forced the South Vietnamese government to deal with the protesters as political opponents. While Diem had started to carry out acts of conciliation that the Americans had insisted he carry out, Truehart noted, these gestures were not working. A South Vietnamese government communiqué issued on May 29 that reaffirmed constitutional protections of religious freedom and firmly forswore discrimination "appears to have had no effect on militants."[66] When the South Vietnamese government replaced its top officials in Hue in early June to please the Buddhists, Truehart noted a few days later, it "apparently had no effect unless it was to stimulate further agitation."[67] Yet the State Department kept instructing Truehart to demand further concessions from Diem.

On June 5, Diem and Nhu reached a tentative agreement with many of the Buddhist leaders to resolve the impasse. Under the terms of the deal, the Buddhists would cease all demonstrations and agitation. They would fly the national flag at all times outside pagodas and would fly religious flags outdoors on holidays, while they could fly religious flags indoors whenever they wanted. In return, the government would remove all uniformed personnel from the pagodas and punish officials who interfered with Buddhist religious activities or made arbitrary arrests. In addition, the National Assembly would pass a new law officially giving Buddhists equal status with Catholics.

A few days later, before the agreement had been made final, Madame Nhu endangered the reconciliation with a public statement attacking the Buddhist activists. Madame Nhu, a born Buddhist who had converted to Catholicism upon marrying Ngo Dinh Nhu, began with words of respect for Buddha and Buddhist philosophy. She then insinuated that Communists and neutralists were controlling the demonstrators, and implored the government to "cease allowing itself to be deafened by the idle clamor of political inspiration and immediately expel all foreign agitators whether they wear monks' robes or not; that it keep vigilance on all others, particularly those inclined to take Viet Nam for a satellite of a foreign power or organization; that it treat, as deserved, those who seek to disrupt public order."[68] Madame Nhu's words contained considerable truth, but her biting tone and her timing disconcerted certain Vietnamese and Americans. Afraid that Madame Nhu's assault would wreck the tentative deal with the Buddhists, Truehart asked Diem to repudiate her statement. Diem himself was well aware that his sister-in-law was a political mischief-maker, and on a variety of occasions he had lost his temper with her over these sorts of matters, but he allowed her some leeway because she was Nhu's wife. Publicly, Diem did not say anything about Madame Nhu's latest outburst, but he did order Vietnamese newspapers and radio stations to avoid mentioning her resolution.

Madame Nhu was not the only person whose actions threatened to wreck the agreement. Tri Quang, for whom the tentative agreement was far more wor-risome than for Madame Nhu, was preparing a spectacle that would leave a far greater impression on the Americans than anything the Ngo family had done. At Tri Quang's behest, Buddhist activists notified several American newsmen that something big was going to happen at Xa Loi pagoda on June 11. Of the reporters, only Malcolm Browne made his way across Saigon's streets to the pagoda that morning. At ten o'clock, a seventy-three-year-old monk named Quang Duc and two younger monks pulled up in an Austin sedan. Browne watched the two younger monks help Quang Duc out of the car and seat him on a square cushion. According to some witnesses, the elderly monk appeared to be drugged. Surrounded by several hundred bonzes and nuns, the saffron-robed Quang Duc assumed the lotus position, then ran his fingers across his prayer beads while his associates doused him with gasoline from a plastic five-gallon container. Calmly, Quang Duc struck a match and set himself on fire. The crowd fell silent. Pulling out his camera, Browne snapped pictures of the burning monk, much to the satisfaction of the militant Buddhists. With loud-speakers in hand, activist monks proclaimed in English and Vietnamese that Quang Duc was dying in protest of the government's refusal to meet their demands, feigning ignorance of the settlement between the government and Buddhist leaders on these demands. A few policemen tried to reach the burning monk in order to extinguish the fire, but a large group of bonzes blocked them until Quang Duc's blackened corpse fell onto the melted asphalt.

One of Browne's photographs of the burning Quang Duc soon circulated throughout the international media. In the United States, this photo did much to transform Vietnam from a Cold War sideshow into a major foreign policy issue. Americans unfamiliar with recent events in Vietnam were inclined to believe that such a self-sacrifice could have occurred only if the government had engaged in severe religious persecution. A group of American ministers took out full-page advertisements in the *New York Times* and *Washington Post* to protest the alleged injustices, with Browne's picture of Quang Duc placed over a caption that read, "This Buddhist priest, the Reverend Quang Duc, has just set himself on fire. He dies to protest South Vietnam's religious persecution of Buddhists (70% of population)."[69] Of greatest significance was the reaction of certain senior American officials who jumped to the same conclusions. With the permission and support of Harriman and Hilsman, Acting Ambassador Truehart notified Diem that he had to meet all of the Buddhists' demands immediately or else the U.S. government might publicly denounce his handling of the Buddhists since May 8.

Demonstrating a knack for subterfuge that would come into play again later, the State Department did not inform the President that it had delivered this grave ultimatum to Diem. Kennedy did not learn about it until it appeared on his intelligence checklist two days later, on the same day that it appeared in a *New York Times* story that did much to damage Diem's prestige. Furious that he had not been notified of the ultimatum, Kennedy promptly halted the State Department's scheming. The White House issued a memorandum stating that the President "wants to be absolutely sure that no further threats are made and no formal statement is made without his own personal approval."[70]

In spite of this admonition, State Department officials continued to scheme in the days that followed, albeit with more subtlety. While Kennedy received messages on some of their activities, they did not report everything, and the President did not give them the attention that was warranted after the unau-thorized ultimatum. At first, Kennedy was preoccupied with civil rights prob-lems in the South, and then, a week later, he embarked on a ten-day tour of

Europe. During this period of Presidential distraction, Harriman and Hilsman instructed Truehart to tell Vice-President Tho that if political problems
rendered Diem incapable of ruling, the United States would back Tho as his
successor. They also advised Truehart to build up covert and overt contacts with
oppositionists.[71] Truehart, however, did not act on these instructions, for just
after he received them, on June 16, the government and the Buddhists issued
a communiqué affirming the agreement formulated on June 5. Because of this
positive development, Truehart decided, Tho should not be approached for the
time being, though such an approach should be considered in the future if Diem
misbehaved. But Truehart went on to propose that the United States "press
Diem directly and indirectly to accept Buddhist crisis as blessing in disguise
and to use agreement reached as stepping stone to concessions to other groups
(before they demand them)." Truehart conceded, "This scheme will doubtless
be regarded as naïve by anyone who knows this country (and it certainly is the
longest of shots)."[72] Naïve it was indeed, in addition to counter-productive.

Just a few hours after Buddhist leaders and Diem announced the accord,
two hundred and fifty young men attacked policemen who had been positioned at Xa Loi pagoda to deter large demonstrations. Pelting the police with
rocks, bricks, and bicycle chains, they inflicted a considerable number of major
injuries. Finally, the police force became fed up and broke up the crowd with
fire hoses and tear gas. Thirty policemen had to be hospitalized as a result of
the attack, whereas none of the protesters sustained injuries requiring hospitalization. Truehart notified Washington, "Embassy officers present throughout
this riot and report no doubt whatsoever it provoked by crowd, not police."[73]
Occurring immediately after the announcement of the settlement, the violent
demonstration almost certainly had been orchestrated by Tri Quang's militant Buddhists, by Communist agents posing as ordinary civilians, or by both.
Neither the militant Buddhists nor the Communists wanted a reconciliation to
occur – for both groups, the chief objective was not religious freedom but political upheaval. Upon learning of the June 16 communiqué, an English-speaking
militant Buddhist leader informed Halberstam that he was greatly troubled
by President Diem's success in appeasing large numbers of Buddhist leaders.
Halberstam, it would later be revealed, now had his first inkling that the more
militant of the Buddhists wanted to topple the Diem government regardless
of its religious policies.[74] Halberstam, however, would not fully appreciate this
reality until it was too late. For the remainder of Diem's term of office, Halberstam and the other correspondents failed to report that the militant Buddhists
had no intention of making peace with the government or that Diem had made
numerous concessions in vain, preferring instead to portray the militants as
sincere individuals with legitimate grievances and Diem as an inflexible despot
who was unresponsive to those grievances.

Harriman and Hilsman permitted Truehart to proceed with his ill-conceived
plan to pry ever more concessions from Diem. The acting ambassador told

Diem to make new gestures of good faith towards the Buddhists, such as the release of all the people arrested after the rock-throwing riot. In reply, Diem said that his people were processing the detainees as fast as they could, but some of those arrested had turned out to be members of Communist youth organizations and would not be released. Diem also made clear that he was reluctant to release people who had thrown rocks at policemen. Both were good reasons not to release all of the detainees, but Truehart did not appear to find them persuasive. At the end of their meeting, Diem said, "The Buddhist affair has been blown up all out of proportion. What people should be worried about is the situation in Laos." Truehart responded, "This might be the right judgment strategically but, as you know, politics do not always follow strategy."[75]

One week later, as rumors began to swirl that the Buddhists were planning another suicide by fire, Truehart told Thuan that "Diem must accept that he cannot afford to have more demonstrations and bonze burnings, virtually no matter what concessions he has to make."[76] Truehart was advocating a political program that was certain to destroy Diem, for concessions would only undermine the government's prestige and authority and beget demands for more concessions from Tri Quang and others who did not want to stop until Diem had conceded away so much power that he no longer could govern. One CIA report, addressing Buddhist charges of religious oppression, stated that militant Buddhist spokesmen "convey the unmistakable impression that even if the government can satisfactorily refute these charges, the Buddhists will raise new charges and the militant wing indicate they intend to keep up the pressure until the Diem regime is overthrown."[77]

Compounding the tensions between South Vietnam and the United States at this moment was the announcement that Henry Cabot Lodge would be arriving in August to replace Ambassador Nolting, who two months earlier had requested a permanent transfer to the United States for family reasons. The descendant of two of the nation's most prominent families, Henry Cabot Lodge had been an important figure in the Republican Party since his election to the United States Senate in 1936 at the age of just thirty-four. During World War II, Lodge had become the first person since the Civil War to resign from the Senate to join the regular Army. After the war, Lodge won reelection to the U.S. Senate, but lost his seat in 1952 to John F. Kennedy, then lost to him again in 1960 as the Vice President on the Nixon ticket.

Lodge possessed only one qualification that set him apart from the other candidates for the ambassadorship: he was a famous Republican with a strong chance of gaining his party's Presidential nomination in 1964. By enmeshing a prominent Republican in a controversial cause, Kennedy could insulate himself from Republican charges of botching Vietnam and also jeopardize Lodge's own political fortunes. Arthur Schlesinger, Jr. said of Kennedy, "the thought of implicating a leading Republican in the Vietnam mess appealed to his instinct for politics."[78] Lodge, on the other hand, believed that the high-profile appointment could provide him a springboard to the Presidency. It was rumored that Lodge accurately perceived Kennedy's partisan motives and that if the posting to Saigon did not bring him fame and glory, Lodge would thwart Kennedy's designs by resigning and accusing Washington of bungling the whole affair. Lodge's ability to make such charges stick would depend on the degree of control the Kennedy administration tried to exert over him, a fact that was to loom large in the coming months. Lodge had three other key attributes that would come into play during his tenure as ambassador. First, he was by nature a man who preferred to act independently, with little or no guidance from anyone. Second, he possessed no knowledge of Asia's people or its ways. Third, he was, as one of the most liberal members of the Republican Party, inclined to favor remaking Vietnam in America's image, in the tradition of Durbrow rather than that of Nolting.

Although Diem knew scarcely more about Lodge than Lodge knew about him, the appointment of the new ambassador at such a difficult juncture led the South Vietnamese President to fear that it signified a new determination to shove American prescriptions down his throat. Diem told Thuan, "They can send ten Lodges, but I will not permit myself or my country to be humiliated, not if they train their artillery on this palace!" When Thuan related Diem's concerns to Truehart, the acting ambassador asserted that he did not know what Lodge's instructions would be. The Saigon government, Truehart chided, should concern itself with carrying out the agreement with the Buddhists and otherwise conciliating them. He confided that the "burden of proof is rigidly and wrongly on the government, and Diem simply cannot afford to have a revival of demonstrations or bonzes burning in the street." Articulating the principle underlying all of his thinking on the Buddhist problem, as well as the thinking of senior State Department officials in Washington and the American press, Truehart pronounced that Diem ought to "start acting like an American politician."[79]

With reluctance, Diem did some more of the things that the Americans demanded. Under his auspices, Nhu publicly told the Republican Youth to comply with the June 16 agreement, and Tho sent conciliatory messages to the Buddhists. After the Buddhists roughed up a South Vietnamese Ranger who was distributing pro-government propaganda, Diem prevented the Rangers from staging an anti-Buddhist demonstration. The government-controlled *Times of Vietnam*, however, continued to publish sharp criticisms of the Buddhist activists, in order to preserve the government's prestige. The Americans received reports of government noncompliance with the June 16 agreement, but little of this information had been verified and, as Truehart noted, much of it came from Tri Quang, a person with a motive and a penchant for fabricating information.[80] Diem's acts of conciliation failed to sway Truehart, Harriman, or Hilsman. On July 1, while Kennedy was in Rome, the State Department advised Truehart to threaten Diem with dissociation if he did not do more to remedy the Buddhist problem, which Truehart then did.

South Vietnam's problems with the American press took a turn for the worse a few days later, on July 7, when government policemen decided to halt a Buddhist procession in Saigon, presumably because they did not want it to turn into a political demonstration or a riot. Foreign journalists began snapping pictures and, according to the police, they objected vehemently to the stopping of the procession. Either a correspondent or a policeman – it is not clear who acted first – resorted to fisticuffs and touched off a scuffle between the correspondents and plainclothes police officers. The policemen knocked Peter Arnett to the ground, kicking him repeatedly. Malcolm Browne could have come to Arnett's assistance, but instead shinnied up a telephone pole and photographed the beating. Several of the journalists had their cameras broken or confiscated before it was all over.

With the greatest of indignation, the correspondents descended on the American embassy to demand action for what they termed an unprovoked assault on the press. Truehart, however, refused to take action, commenting that he had been pressuring Diem enough in recent weeks and that he could do nothing more before the imminent return of Ambassador Nolting. Truehart did not reveal his main reason for rejecting the correspondents' demands, namely that he did not believe their version of what had happened. Referring to South Vietnamese police claims that the foreign journalists had protested the halting of the procession and that one of the reporters had struck the first blow, Truehart informed Washington, "Given extreme emotional involvement of correspondents these days – amounting regrettably to intense hatred of all things GVN, in certain cases – I would not feel sure about refuting police."[81] Dismayed by the embassy's inaction, Halberstam, Sheehan, Browne, and CBS's Peter Kalischer wrote a sharply-worded letter to President Kennedy demanding that he "protest against this attack and obtain assurances that it will not be repeated."[82] With President Kennedy's permission, Press Secretary Salinger notified the newsmen that the U.S. government had lodged a protest with the South Vietnamese government and that Assistant Secretary of State for Public Affairs Robert Manning, a former *Time* correspondent, would soon be coming to Saigon to evaluate the situation. The tempers of the journalists subsided slightly as they awaited Manning's visit.

Arriving in Saigon in mid-July, Manning spent most of his time learning about the press situation from American officials and correspondents and trying to improve relations between the two groups. He also met with Diem and Nhu, at which time he assured them of continued American support but also warned them to leave American reporters alone. At the end of month, Manning returned to Washington, whereupon he delivered to the President a most astute report on the press situation. Manning remarked that the correspondents who worked exclusively in Vietnam, most notably Halberstam, Sheehan, and Browne, "seem for the most part to be given to quick-rising emotionalism, and they unquestionably are severely afflicted with 'localitis,' the disease which causes newsmen long assigned to the confines of one given situation to distort perspective by over-concentration on their own irritations, adventures, and opinions." Manning also attributed some of the media's animosity to "wounded ego on the part of the correspondents who have a highly developed sense of importance." More balanced reporting, he said, was coming from correspondents who were reporting from Vietnam but were not residing there, of whom the leading figures were Keyes Beech, Pepper Martin of *U.S. News and World Report*, and NBC's Jim Robinson. Manning concluded that there was no way to close the rift between the South Vietnamese government and the American press corps, given their incompatible interests, but U.S. officials could improve their relations with the press by speaking frankly to the reporters and treating them "as politically important individuals, rather than as a group of socially objectionable and professionally incompetent young cubs." Manning recommended that officials "give them an 'in' feeling, and invite them more often not only to ritualistic type functions but specifically to, say, small dinners given by the Ambassador for Vietnamese officials and leading personalities."[83]

In the meantime, the American reporters pressed on with their assault on the Diem government. A central theme of their writings in July was that the government's mistreatment of the Buddhists was likely to spark a coup, provided that American officials expressed approval as the journalists were arguing that they should. "Some Vietnamese military officers," Halberstam wrote, "are reported ready to act but they give the impression that they would like the Americans to make a public statement calling for a change." In what was probably an attempt to push U.S. officials in this direction and encourage would-be plotters, Halberstam added that "the Americans" wanted a new government.[84] In actuality, the top three Americans in Vietnam – Ambassador Nolting, General Harkins, and CIA Saigon station chief John H. Richardson – preferred the existing government, as did a large number of other civilians and military officers. South Vietnam's elites, aware that Diem could not survive without the cooperation of the Americans and his own military leaders, took such articles as evidence that Diem might soon be gone, which led the more opportunistic among them to tilt towards the opposition. Presuming that the American press was similar in nature to the South Vietnamese press, they viewed the purported facts and opinions in American articles as those of the U.S. government. Halberstam was the most influential American journalist among the South Vietnamese, for of all media outlets they considered the *New York Times* to be the leading barometer of U.S. government attitudes toward Diem. Shortly after Diem's ultimate undoing, one of the coup leaders would say that during the Buddhist crisis he had believed that the *New York Times* "represented the true U.S. position."[85]

One day after Halberstam announced that "the Americans" wanted a change in government, a coterie of senior Vietnamese generals invited Lou Conein of the CIA to meet them at a loud Saigon bistro. The date of the meeting, the importance that the plotters subsequently ascribed to the *New York Times*, and the similarity between the content of the article and the content of the meeting all suggest that Halberstam's article spurred the generals into action, though no hard evidence on the cause of the meeting has survived. The most prominent of the generals at the bistro were Big Minh, who remained bitter about his relegation to a meaningless job in 1960, and General Don, now the acting chief of staff. Don, who had had known Conein since 1945, had no doubt invited Conein because of the CIA's prior involvement in coups elsewhere and because of Conein's known dislike for Diem and Nhu. During their meeting at the bistro, Don told Conein that the South Vietnamese generals were unhappy with the Ngo brothers, especially Nhu, because of their handling of the Buddhist troubles, and he asked how the United States would view a military coup. Most of the generals, asserted Don, would support him in overthrowing the regime.[86]

Conein took this message back to his superiors. CIA analysts who reviewed the matter pointed out that Don did not have the backing of most of the generals as he had claimed. The generals were not in agreement, they observed, and Nhu was actively maneuvering among them to forestall or redirect the plotting.[87] The Americans did not pursue the matter further with General Don, for the time being.

During his tour of the Greek isles, Ambassador Frederick Nolting repeatedly phoned the CIA station chief in Athens to check for messages from Truehart. Nolting made one of these calls after picking up a small Greek newspaper on Mykonos that contained Malcolm Browne's photo of the burning monk, Quang Duc. On this occasion and the others, there was no message in Athens for Nolting. The vacationing ambassador did not learn about the new problems with the Buddhists until his arrival on July 1 in New York, where he found a letter waiting for him from Thuan that read, "President Diem asks you to return as soon as possible." During Nolting's vacation, in fact, Thuan twice had asked the embassy to notify Nolting that Diem wanted him to return to mediate the crisis. Truehart had promised to send the message, but did not follow through on either occasion. Truehart's conniving earned him an official rebuke from Nolting and tarnished a long personal friendship between the two men.[88] Had Nolting been contacted during his Aegean trip, he no doubt would have returned to Vietnam at once and relieved some of the tension between the South Vietnamese government and the Americans. Whether he could have done enough to save Diem, however, is questionable, for it would not have changed the fact that Lodge would soon become the new ambassador to South Vietnam.

When Nolting returned to Vietnam, he found Diem carrying out many of the tasks that the State Department had wanted him to carry out. On July 18, Diem broadcast a message in which he again called on all his personnel to implement the joint communiqué of June 16. He allowed the bonzes to return to pagodas that had been barricaded, and he punished a lieutenant colonel who had organized a protest against the Buddhists. After government units beat up a group of unruly protesters, Diem ordered that force no longer be used against any Buddhist demonstrators, and he was obeyed.[89] Madame Nhu, at the insistence of her husband and brother-in-law, was refraining from verbal assaults on the Buddhist activists. These measures, although quite substantive, failed to placate the militant Buddhists or the high State Department officials in Washington.

During his last days as ambassador, Nolting did his best to convince Washington that the Buddhist troubles were subsiding and that the United States should vocally support Diem, whom he still considered irreplaceable. Hilsman, disregarding Diem's numerous concessions and gestures of good faith, responded that Diem had to be pressured because the South Vietnamese government had not yet tried very hard to conciliate the Buddhists. A coup was likely to occur in the next few months, if not weeks, cabled Hilsman, and therefore the expression of support "runs obvious risk of putting us in position of having backed loser, and even of prolonging crisis and increasing violence, with all bad effects on war effort that would flow from such error."[90]

As the period of decision approached, as South Vietnam teetered near the brink, the communication of information between Saigon and Washington was increasingly polluted with misunderstanding, falsehood, and deceit. Fanatical Buddhists and covert Communists had made great headway in misleading both the American press and elements of the U.S. government into believing that the Saigon government was committing religious oppression. As Truehart and Hilsman and Halberstam and other Americans besieged Diem with ill-begotten demands for conciliation, they turned their eyes away from two critical truths: that the South Vietnamese war effort continued to make major strides forward, and that South Vietnam's real main problem was the rising infiltration through Laos.

1. Parade float in Hanoi depicting Ho Chi Minh shaking hands with Mao Zedong. The writing at the bottom of the float reads: "Eternal Friendship." *Source:* Department of Defense.

2. Dwight D. Eisenhower and Ngo Dinh Diem. *Source:* National Archives.

3. Strategic hamlet. *Source:* National Archives.

4. Army of the Republic of Vietnam soldiers with U.S. Army helicopters. *Source:* National Archives.

5. David Halberstam. *Source:* AP/Wide World.

6. General Paul Harkins and Major General Ton That Dinh. *Source:* National Archives.

7. A Buddhist demonstration in Saigon. *Source:* The Vietnam Archive, Texas Tech University.

8. Henry Cabot Lodge and John F. Kennedy. *Source:* National Archives.

9. Lyndon B. Johnson and Robert S. McNamara. *Source:* Lyndon Baines Johnson Library.

10. Ho Chi Minh and Sukarno. *Source:* AP/Wide World.

CHAPTER 10

Betrayal

AUGUST 1963

"I CANNOT SEEM TO CONVINCE THE EMBASSY THAT THIS IS VIETNAM – not the United States of America," said Diem at the beginning of August 1963. His conversation partner was a reporter from the *New York Herald Tribune* named Marguerite Higgins. The first female war correspondent to win the Pulitzer Prize, Higgins had become a celebrity through her daring reporting during the Inchon landing. Many of the other reporters covering Vietnam did not care for Higgins, as they resented her reluctance to collaborate with them, her willingness to criticize them, and her continued admiration for Diem. Higgins was to talk with South Vietnam's leader for five hours in the oppressive afternoon heat. Diem, clad in his white sharkskin suit, sat baking in a deep chair the entire time. Occasionally he toyed with a tiny cup of green tea. Otherwise, the President remained remarkably still and calm, like a mountain unmoved by the fury of tempests and floods. The strains of recent months had taken their toll on Diem nonetheless, as evidenced by a plump and pinkish appearance. Higgins later remarked, "It was hard to imagine him as the revolutionary who had exhorted his people upon assuming power in 1954: 'If I advance, follow me! If I retreat, kill me! If I die, avenge me!'" Diem's superb intellect, however, had not been dulled. Diem had invited Higgins to the Presidential palace for the purpose of issuing a conciliatory statement to the Buddhists, and he fulfilled this task, but he also took the discussion far off into other realms. The interview turned out to be one of Diem's last and best articulations of his principles and policies.

Diem told Higgins he was proud to call himself a modern mandarin. "We are not going to go back to a sterile copy of the mandarin past," he vowed, but instead, "we are going to adapt the best of our heritage to the modern situation." Diem pointedly criticized the Americans for telling him how to run his country based on the experiences of the United States. "Procedures applicable to one culture cannot be transplanted wholly to another culture," the South Vietnamese President pronounced. "It is impossible – a delusion – to think that a solution for Asia consists in blindly copying Western methods." No Asian or African nation, Diem emphasized, had successfully adopted the sort of political liberalization that the United States was trying to force upon South Vietnam. He noted that although Vietnam had long possessed a certain degree of democracy in the villages, democracy of the Western sort could not be extended to the national level, at least not during a war.

Without using authoritarian methods, Diem explained, he could not prevent his countrymen's inherent factionalism and the Communists' scheming from tearing the country apart. "Your press and radio mock the idea of discipline and respect for authority and glorify so-called civil liberties and the right to criticize and the need for political opposition," Diem said, "but this country is in a life-and-death struggle," and "even Western democracies suspend civil liberties during war emergencies." The Buddhist movement, Diem asserted, was a political movement bent on overthrowing his regime, and some of its members were Communists. If he let the agitators do whatever they pleased or gave them everything they wanted, he would appear feeble in Vietnamese eyes and the agitation would accelerate. Exasperated by American calls for tolerance and appeasement of the Buddhist protesters, Diem exclaimed, "The Americans are breaking Vietnamese psychology and they don't even know what they are doing." The South Vietnamese President voiced great displeasure with American threats of aid reduction, and with reports that certain Americans were courting oppositionists. "Am I merely a puppet on Washington's string? Or – as I had hoped – are we partners in a common cause?" Diem demanded. "If you order Vietnam around like a puppet on a string, how will you be different – except in degree – from the French?"[1]

During the first part of August 1963, the Buddhist crisis largely proceeded along the path it had followed before. Hard-liners within the Buddhist protest movement continued to interfere with the reconciliation efforts. Buddhist activists refused to cooperate with a governmental committee established to resolve the crisis under the leadership of Vice-President Tho, who was a Buddhist. A monk set himself ablaze in Phan Thiet, although the monks in the province could think of no government impositions on them other than an order to fly the national flag on Buddha's birthday,[2] and three more committed suicide during the next eleven days. Large public demonstrations erupted again, featuring Buddhist orators who accused the government of tyrannizing the people and trying to eradicate Buddhism. On the other side, Madame Nhu let her sharp tongue fly again. The monks were guilty of deception and treachery, she charged, and Diem was being too soft on them. During a CBS news interview that aired on August 1, Madame Nhu declared, "What have these so-called 'Buddhist leaders' done? They have neither program nor man to propose in place of program. All they have done is barbecue a bonze, and that not even with self-sufficient means, since they had to use imported gasoline." The remarks gave new ammunition to Diem's detractors within the American government, and they added to the perception among South Vietnamese elites that Madame Nhu was a reckless menace.

On August 18, a few days after Ambassador Nolting's departure, twenty thousand protesters massed around Xa Loi pagoda in Saigon. Brash monks called for the overthrow of the government, to cheers and thunderous applause from the sea of protesters. The massive crowd appeared to be composed of ordinary Buddhist clergy and laymen, but that was not entirely the case. The Vietnamese Communists would later credit their agents with bringing large numbers of protesters to this demonstration and instructing them to vilify the government while acting as if they were simply devout Buddhists.[3] In accordance with the political psychology of the land, the vicious and unchallenged protest rally at Xa Loi caused the government's leadership to lose face.

There was considerable truth to the claim of Diem's detractors that some government officials were growing dissatisfied with his handling of the Buddhist protesters. The critics were wrong, however, in believing that the dissatisfaction stemmed from repressive actions by Diem, for the dissatisfied South Vietnamese officials tended to believe that Diem was being too soft, not too tough. Vice-President Nguyen Ngoc Tho, a Buddhist whom Diem's American and Vietnamese foes later installed in power to end Diem's alleged persecution of the Buddhists, had told a group of foreign diplomats just a few days earlier that the regime ought to crush the Buddhist movement "without pity."[4] On the evening of August 18, ten of the South Vietnamese Army's senior generals met to discuss the mounting crisis. The majority of them were Buddhists, and among the group were most of the generals who later would lead a coup against Diem, including Duong Van Minh, Tran Van Don, Ton That Dinh, Tran Thien Khiem, Nguyen Khanh, and Le Van Kim. Neither Diem nor Nhu attended the meeting. The ten generals concluded that Diem had let the protests go on for too long. The militant Buddhists now could endanger the war effort, for the Viet Cong had seeped into the Buddhist protest movement and the Buddhist leaders did not intend to relent until Diem had been swept from power. Of particular concern to the generals was Thich Duc Nghiep, an English-speaking bonze who had ingratiated himself with David Halberstam and other American journalists and officials. The consensus among the generals was that the government needed to put an end to the protest movement once and for all by removing the monks from the pagodas and sending them back to the areas from which they had come. Some amount of force would have to be used, since the Buddhist agitators had made clear that they would not go home willingly.[5]

The generals went to Diem and urged him to authorize the forced evacuation of the pagodas and the imposition of martial law. "Continued disorders cannot be tolerated," General Don argued. "These disorders deeply undermine the people's faith in the power of the government to keep the situation under control. The ring leaders of the disorders have to be rounded up. . . . The pagodas cannot be privileged sanctuaries for subversion." Don asserted that "the 8 May affair in Hue could have been settled" were it not for the fact that "the VC had penetrated the Buddhists in Xa Loi pagoda." The generals also pointed out to Diem that forceful action against the sects in 1955 had ended a similar crisis. After hearing the generals' arguments, Diem consented to the clearance of the pagodas and to martial law, but insisted that none of the bonzes be harmed.[6]

Just after midnight on August 21, a collection of South Vietnamese police, Republican Guard, and Special Forces personnel surrounded the Xa Loi pagoda, while Army regulars occupied many key locations elsewhere in the Saigon area to protect against subversion and assist the police in strictly controlling the movement of civilians. To keep the Americans in the dark, South Vietnamese technicians severed the telephone lines running to and from the U.S. embassy and the residences of U.S. officials. South Vietnamese officials shut down the building from which reporters sent stories to the United States. These actions were conceived and largely run by South Vietnam's generals, although some of the activities in Saigon were put in the hands of Nhu and Special Forces commander Col. Le Quang Tung, one of Diem's most loyal officers. General Dinh, who was a Buddhist and the son of a Buddhist nun, was in command at the tactical level in Saigon,[7] while General Don, another Buddhist, had overall supervision of the operation. Don went on Radio Saigon himself to announce the implementation of martial law.

In defiance, the monks at Xa Loi locked the doors and threw bottles and ceramic pots at government troops from the upper floors of the pagoda. But it was to no avail. The government forces moved in swiftly, arresting hundreds of monks, nuns, and other Buddhists. Many resisted arrest strenuously, which resulted in the hospitalization of nine bonzes and bonzesses, and twenty police-men. Similar fracases took place in the other major cities where government forces evicted the militants from the pagodas. In the northern part of the coun-try, Army troops cleared out the pagodas without assistance from the police and Special Forces, and in its own radio program the Army announced that it had orchestrated the evacuation of the pagodas in Hue. In all, government forces seized thirty of the nation's nearly five thousand pagodas and arrested a couple of thousand people, most of whom were returned promptly to the areas from which they had come, although some of the top leaders were to remain in jail for an extended period of time. In an after-action report prepared for Diem, General Dinh noted that government forces had discovered weapons and Viet Cong documents in several of Saigon's pagodas, which he said proved that the Buddhists had been colluding with the Communists.[8]

Militant Buddhist activity fell off dramatically after the clearance of the pago-das on August 21, and during Diem's lifetime it did not regain its force. The government's use of force and the silencing of the militant Buddhists strongly impressed the populace, eliminating much of the griping about the government and bringing eminent monks over to the government's side. As in 1954 and 1955,

Diem had ended harmful internal strife by suppressing his opponents, not by accommodating them as so many of his critics had demanded. Even among Western observers, a large number concluded that Diem had nimbly handled a serious threat to his government. Gordon Cox, the Canadian representative on the International Control Commission, told U.S. officials that the Diem regime's actions on August 21 were "justified in light of the warlike preparations in the pagodas and the clear intent of the Buddhist leadership to go on with political agitation until the government was overthrown." The raids had increased the government's prestige, he observed.[9] British ambassador to South Vietnam Gordon Etherington-Smith commented, "From the 18th of July onwards the bonzes in the Xa Loi pagoda increasingly defied and even mocked authority, to the point at which the majority of observers became convinced that the Government must act or fall." Etherington-Smith added, "Given the passive nature of the majority of Cochinchinese and the very loose hold of Buddhism in South Vietnam, it seems improbable that there will be a further open explosion of resentment for a long while."[10]

Success would prove to be short-lived, for the regime's opponents were about to mount an incredibly effective campaign to distort the pagoda raids and the events preceding them. Noticing that the American press was condemning the pagoda raids as horrid acts of repression, these individuals decided to attribute the whole affair to Nhu, an easy target since many Americans and Vietnamese already disliked Nhu and his wife. Some of the Ngo family's enemies took their claims straight to the foreign press, where like-minded journalists were ready to publish unsubstantiated gossip that supported their views. Halberstam wrote a string of fallacious front-page articles on the pagoda raids that would shape the views of many Americans on the event and help him win a Pulitzer Prize. "Hundreds of Buddhist priests were arrested and many were beaten in the military and police action," Halberstam stated in an initial report, written on August 21. "The police charged the pagoda gate with fixed bayonets, smashing through. They were heavily armed. The Buddhists had barricaded themselves upstairs. Some monks trying to flee were fired on. Others were hurled down stairs. Witnesses said they saw priests bayoneted and clubbed." At Hue, the action was "particularly bloody," wrote Halberstam. "Army troops attacked the pagoda there about 3:00 A.M. There was much shooting, then a loud explosion." Halberstam did not at first blame Nhu, but instead reported that the military had taken the leading role in the operation.[11]

On the twenty-second of August, Halberstam reversed his position on the military's complicity in planning the evacuations, reporting, "Highly reliable sources here said today that the decision to attack Buddhist pagodas and declare martial law in South Vietnam was planned and executed by Ngo Dinh Nhu, the President's brother, without the knowledge of the army." General Don, Halberstam claimed, had not been informed of events in Saigon until the pagodas had been emptied. From this point onwards, Halberstam and the other

American reporters in Saigon would contend that Nhu alone had master-minded the pagoda raids, a claim that the journalists would use first to promote a coup and then afterwards to justify their promotion of the coup. Opposition to the government, Halberstam maintained in his dispatch, "is acknowledged to be extremely widespread." In addition, Halberstam claimed to have received reliable reports of mass defections among troops of the Vietnamese Army's Second Corps because of the "attacks" on the Buddhists. All of the forego-ing information from Halberstam's August 22 reporting came from unnamed sources in Saigon whom Halberstam had been too eager to trust, and all of it was false.[12]

A day later, Halberstam reported that at least thirty people had been killed and at least seventy wounded during the evacuation of Tu Dam pagoda in Hue.[13] He repeated this claim a couple of years thereafter in *The Making of a Quagmire,* though not in his subsequent and more famous book, *The Best and the Brightest.*[14] Halberstam's reporting on Hue, together with his account of the bayoneting and shooting of Buddhist monks at Xa Loi pagoda, created an international stir that eventually caused the United Nations to send an investigative commission to South Vietnam. The commission did not reach Saigon until October 24, by which time the alleged total of Bud-dhist dead during the pagoda evacuations had shriveled to four, two of them in Hue and two in Saigon. Upon investigation, commission members actu-ally met and interviewed all four of these monks.[15] One other false mas-sacre story emerged from Halberstam's typewriter on August 24, never to be retracted: "According to unconfirmed reports, Catholic and Buddhist troops fought each other at Seventh Division headquarters in Mytho, 35 miles south-west of Saigon, Thursday. The reports said 60 men were killed and 120 were wounded."[16]

During the remaining days of August, in other news articles, Halberstam grossly exaggerated the opposition to Diem amongst the South Vietnamese and the Americans. South Vietnam "is ruled by a strikingly unpopular gov-ernment," and "key Vietnamese have long waited for Washington to give an indication that it has had enough of the Ngo family." In reality, the "key Vietnamese" – the government's top military and civilian officials outside of the ruling family – had not held such views in the past. Nor did any of them share Halberstam's confidence that the government could be overthrown with ease, for they knew that Diem loyalists held the top command positions in both III Corps and IV Corps, the two areas most crucial for any coup undertaken in Saigon. Halberstam asserted that "Americans" believed that Diem and his government "have lost all popularity," and that Diem "is no longer a serious political figure." Halberstam advertised General Duong Van Minh as an excel-lent replacement for Diem, claiming that Minh "is considered to be as close to an authentic hero as South Vietnam has."[17] Minh would later show himself to be utterly incompetent as a national leader.

To South Vietnamese politicians and generals, who always had trouble understanding that the U.S. government did not necessarily hold the views espoused by the *New York Times* and other U.S. press organs, Halberstam's unmistakable contempt for the Diem government and his admiration for Duong Van Minh indicated that the Kennedy administration wanted Diem replaced for treating the Buddhists roughly. Halberstam's reports on American and South Vietnamese opposition to Diem reduced Diem's prestige and raised fears among South Vietnam's military leaders that they would come under attack for their complicity in cracking down on the militant Buddhists. To avoid the wrath of the Americans, some of the generals began backing the claim that the army leadership had not been involved in the pagoda raids. Among this group were some of the generals who had proposed the raids to Diem in the first place.

A few days after the pagoda raids, American representatives had crucial conversations with several South Vietnamese officials who had made or heard this false claim about the paternity of the pagoda raids. The first was General Kim, one of the generals who on August 20 had urged Diem to clear out the pagodas. In a meeting with Rufus Phillips, Kim claimed that Nhu had tricked the army into enforcing martial law and had orchestrated the emptying of the pagodas, while the Army "knew nothing of plans to raid Xa Loi and other pagodas." Nhu, having already been blamed for the raids by Halberstam and others in the press, was the obvious choice of a scapegoat. General Kim spoke in favor of keeping Diem, but he wanted the Americans to demonstrate their opposition to the Nhus, in which case he promised that the Army would remove Nhu and his wife.[18] Vo Van Hai, chief of Diem's private staff, said much the same to State Department official Paul Kattenburg. Hai had particularly strong reasons for attributing unpopular actions to Nhu, for, as Hai himself admitted, he resented that Nhu had taken away the influence he had once enjoyed with Diem.[19] The animosity was quite personal. "Hai truly hated Nhu and his wife," one senior South Vietnamese official recalled.[20]

Secretary of State Nguyen Dinh Thuan, speaking with Rufus Phillips, blamed Nhu for the raid on Xa Loi pagoda and said that the generals had known nothing of it beforehand. Thuan said he saw "no alternative to the President as a leader for Vietnam. No one else is as widely respected, or would be generally acceptable within Vietnam." But the Nhus needed to be removed. "Under no circumstances," Thuan pronounced, "should the United States acquiesce in what the Nhus have done." The United States government, he advised, ought to make clear that it would not continue supporting the regime so long as Nhu held a position of authority. Then the generals would force Nhu's removal.[21] Whether Thuan absolved the generals of complicity in the raids because he had received incorrect gossip, or because he wanted to feed the Americans information he knew to be false, is unknown. He certainly bore a personal animus towards Nhu; like Vo Van Hai, Thuan had suffered a loss of influence with the President that he blamed on Nhu.[22] Thuan's recounting of events carried great weight with the Americans, for he was the South Vietnamese official who enjoyed the greatest respect within the U.S. State Department.

In the fourth key conversation, General Don talked with Lou Conein of the CIA. Don admitted to Conein that he and other generals – and not Nhu – had convinced Diem to evict the militant Buddhists from the pagodas and to impose martial law. Like the other three, Don argued that Diem was the best man for the Presidency. No civilian exile would be a suitable replacement, Don said, and "within the military there is no one who could replace Diem." He did not think Nhu could be removed and he instead hoped for unspecified changes among Diem's top ministers. Confused, wondering why the Americans denounced the pagoda raids publicly but refused to force changes on Diem, Don urged the United States to make clear where it really stood.[23]

On the twenty-fourth of August, upon receiving reports on these four conversations, three men in Washington feverishly set to work on a memorandum to Ambassador Henry Cabot Lodge. The group consisted of the two State Department figures most active – and most arrogant – in the conduct of American affairs in Vietnam, Averell Harriman and Roger Hilsman, and the third was Michael Forrestal, Harriman's adopted son. The Buddhist crisis, these three had decided, was jeopardizing the whole war effort. They concluded that it was Nhu's idea to empty the pagodas based on the statements of Kim, Hai, and Thuan, disregarding contrary statements from Don and the South Vietnamese minister of the interior and other reliable informants. In arriving at this conclusion, they may have put stock in the international journalists in Saigon, whom they were watching closely and who by this time had told the world that Nhu was the sole instigator. This mistaken attribution of the pagoda raids to Nhu instead of the generals would become the single most important factor in America's falling out with the Ngo regime. It would cause those Americans who were disgusted with the pagoda raids to offer power to the very generals who had advocated and carried out the raids.

Harriman, Hilsman, and Forrestal described the events of August 21 in the same manner as the American press, asserting that the government had chosen to "smash the pagodas." They showed no appreciation of the provocation and treasonous intent that had led to the removal of the militants from the pagodas, and, unfamiliar with South Vietnamese culture, they failed to understand that toleration of protests such as that at Xa Loi caused a Vietnamese leader to lose face. In the minds of these three Americans, the pagoda clearings were merely an attempt by Nhu to persecute Buddhists and deny the populace the right to free speech, and as such they must have turned the public against the Ngo family.[24]

Hilsman would say that he was much impressed by Thuan's statement that "under no circumstances should the United States acquiesce in what the Nhus had done." He and Harriman had long hoped to see Nhu gone, and now a terrific opportunity seemed to have presented itself. In their memorandum, the drafters wrote, "U.S. Government cannot tolerate situation in which power lies in Nhu's hands." They authorized the Voice of America and other U.S. government information channels to announce that Nhu, and not the South Vietnamese military, was at fault. Moving well beyond what the four Vietnamese sources had advised, they asserted that Diem ought to be given a chance to get rid of Nhu, but if he failed to do so, "then we must face the possibility that Diem himself cannot be preserved." The message's authors instructed Ambassador Lodge to tell the generals that if Diem did not remove Nhu and make major concessions to the Buddhists, the Americans would stop supporting Diem and would be willing to support an alternative leader. At great peril, Harriman, Hilsman, and Forrestal had disregarded the statements from General Kim, Vo Van Hai, Nguyen Dinh Thuan, and General Don during the past two days that Diem was the nation's best leader and had to be kept in power.[25]

On that Saturday afternoon, Harriman and Hilsman took the cable to the ninth tee of the Chevy Chase Country Club, where Under Secretary of State George Ball was playing golf. Ball liked the tough approach. He had been disgusted by Diem's crackdowns on the Buddhists, as reported by the U.S. journalists, to whom he had paid great heed. On one occasion, Ball would tell Kennedy that "you get more by talking to the correspondents" who were working in Vietnam than by talking to U.S. government officials.[26] Ball recommended asking President Kennedy's permission to send the message to Saigon.

The cable's authors and Ball phoned the President, who was spending the weekend at his estate in Cape Cod, and urged him to give the cable his approval. Kennedy had started to lean towards the view that the Nhus needed to go and Diem needed to be pressured, in considerable measure because of the uproar in the press over the pagoda raids. Kennedy, though, most likely did not recognize the harm that the message portended for Diem. He still held Diem in high regard, and later, when the message's full implications had become clear to him, he would deplore it. From his chair in Cape Cod, Kennedy told the State Department officials that he approved of the cable on the condition that they obtain the agreement of their boss, Dean Rusk, and of Roswell Gilpatric, who was filling in for Secretary of Defense McNamara while he was mountain climbing in Wyoming. The President was particularly concerned about the views of the Defense Department because of its steadfast support for Diem.

Reached by phone at Yankee Stadium, Secretary of State Rusk was told that Kennedy had already approved of the message, not that Kennedy's approval was conditional on his concurrence and on that of Gilpatric. Rusk expressed approval of the message. Forrestal contacted Gilpatric and asked him to sign off, emphasizing that Kennedy and Rusk already had given their consent. Forrestal likewise neglected to mention the conditional nature of Kennedy's approval, leaving Gilpatric, too, with the impression that his consent was being sought merely as a rubber stamp for a policy that the President had already selected.

Gilpatric expressed concurrence. To prevent the CIA from feeling left out, Harriman contacted CIA deputy director for plans Richard Helms, rather than attempting to get in touch with CIA Director John McCone, who was strongly pro-Diem. Harriman informed Helms that the President had chosen a new course of action for South Vietnam but did not ask Helms for his opinion or that of the CIA before saying goodbye. The cable's authors did not seek the consent of JCS Chairman General Maxwell Taylor, another powerful Diem supporter. Had McNamara, McCone, or Taylor been contacted, or had the cable's authors properly communicated the President's stipulations to Rusk or Gilpatric, there is little doubt that the cable never would have left Washington, given the respect McNamara, McCone, and Taylor had for Diem and the fury with which they subsequently reacted to this trickery. The cable was sent to Ambassador Lodge that evening.

The telegram's recipient had only just arrived in Vietnam. Landing at Tan Son Nhut airport on the night of August 22, Lodge had blown past General Paul Harkins and the other American officials awaiting him on the runway and headed straight for a group of U.S. newsmen. The new ambassador and former reporter spent his first five minutes in the country talking with those journalists, telling them that they were a vital component of American democracy. The character of his relationships with his subordinates and the press was set. A short time later, in adherence to Robert Manning's advice, Lodge arranged lengthy private dinners with the three most influential journalists in Saigon: David Halberstam, Neil Sheehan, and Malcolm Browne. In contrast to Nolting and Harkins, Ambassador Lodge welcomed the reporters' ideas, treated them as equals, and avoided debating with them. Lodge leaked information in almost colander-like fashion to the resident American correspondents, satisfying their thirst for headline-worthy information and serving his own needs at the same time. Lodge's coddling of the journalists and his contempt for the Diem regime transformed these young men into self-perceived insiders and adoring supporters of the American ambassador.

The three journalists also supplied Lodge with information and advice on the South Vietnamese government. Their words resonated agreeably in Lodge's ears, since he shared their tendency to treat Vietnam as if it were fundamentally the same as the United States. Unlike Nolting and Harkins, who traveled all over the countryside to see what was going on, Lodge chose to stay in Saigon and get all of his information from journalists and two trusted subordinates, Major General John Michael "Mike" Dunn and Frederick Flott. Dunn, who served as Lodge's chief of staff, recalled that American journalists "used to come into my office at the embassy and tell me what was going on. They weren't sitting out there as neutral observers. They were players. I think it's fair to say that Ambassador Lodge depended upon them very heavily as sources of information, not from just what they were sending home in their dispatches, but from what they told him in private."[27]

Shortly after Lodge's arrival, some of the more experienced journalists who visited Vietnam periodically, most notably Marguerite Higgins, Keyes Beech, and Joseph Alsop, defended Diem and attacked his media opponents. In a profession where public criticism of one's colleagues was rare, they resorted to open warfare out of a conviction that the resident American journalists in Saigon had stepped far outside the bounds of responsible conduct and had jeopardized their country's interests. Higgins, during a trip to Vietnam in August, produced devastating critiques of Halberstam and his cohorts, bringing to light glaring factual and analytical errors in their coverage of the Buddhist crisis and the military situation.[28] Higgins's August articles in the *New York Herald Tribune* deeply impressed government officials and newspaper editors in the United States. One editor at the *New York Times* went so far as to send Halberstam a letter by special pouch stating: "Some of what she has been writing would tend to balance the material we have been getting from Saigon recently.... I am sure that you will take care of this aspect of the Vietnamese story as soon as you can."[29] Diem's advocates in the U.S. media, however, would not be able to influence Lodge to nearly the same extent as Diem's detractors, largely because they were not in Vietnam permanently and did not write articles continuously on Vietnam.

The anti-Diem sentiments building in Lodge through his exposure to the press and through his projection of the American way of thinking onto the Vietnamese did not initially cause him to push for a change in government. Just hours before he received the critical August 24 cable, he had advised against encouraging the generals to remove Nhu or Diem, stressing that the key generals still supported Diem and that some of the generals had favored the emptying of the pagodas.[30] But upon receipt of that cable, Lodge quickly embraced most of its recommendations, and from then on, Lodge was to share Halberstam's, Hilsman's, and Harriman's fierce contempt for the Diem regime. He jumped into the anti-Diem camp with such passion that he recommended taking the cable's proposed course of action one step further. Based on what he had been told in his first few days, he had decided that Diem would never remove Nhu, which pushed Lodge to one option – have the generals remove Nhu immediately and decide for themselves whether to retain Diem, rather than insist that the generals first ask Diem to remove Nhu. On the twenty-fifth of August, Lodge proposed this option to Washington, and Ball sent Lodge authorization the same day to move forward with this plan.[31]

On the following morning, Lodge directed the CIA station in Saigon to transmit the message to the generals. The Voice of America, apparently acting on orders from Hilsman, announced that the regular South Vietnamese Army had not played any part in the pagoda raids, and that "Washington officials say the raids were made by police under the control of President Diem's brother, Ngo Dinh Nhu. They say America may cut its aid to Vietnam if President Diem does not get rid of the police officials responsible."[32] This announcement caused

Diem to lose face, and the labeling of Nhu as the chief culprit undermined Nhu's prestige to an even greater degree. A few hours later, at 12:45 P.M. Saigon time, Lou Conein of the CIA conveyed Lodge's message to General Khiem. As the South Vietnamese Army chief of staff and a man who had Diem's trust, Khiem was probably the most powerful of all the generals. Up until this moment, the generals had wanted Diem to remain in power, even though some were trying to distance themselves from the pagoda raids as a result of American condemnations. Khiem himself, shortly after the pagoda raids, had spoken favorably of the raids and had remarked that over the years he had "come to respect and admire the leadership and wisdom of Diem."[33] But Lodge's message and the Voice of America's warning of an aid cut-off promptly transformed many of the generals into conspirators. Convinced that Diem and Nhu were inseparable, Khiem and the other generals believed that they had to oust both brothers if they were to satisfy Lodge's demand for Nhu's removal, a demand that they had to satisfy because their country could not survive the loss of U.S. aid. Khiem would later state that the military leadership decided to overthrow Diem in order to "please the United States. We thought that was what the Kennedy administration wanted." Khiem explained, "If the United States was so angry with Diem that it would cut off aid, it was even possible that the United States would pull out of the war," which "would have been the end of everything."[34]

A few hours after Conein delivered the message to Khiem, the Monday work day began in Washington. Kennedy, alerted early in the morning to mounting outrage among some of his lieutenants, called a noontime meeting to discuss the weekend's events. McNamara, McCone, and Taylor, who by now knew that they had been circumvented by the drafters of the August 24 cable, were boiling with anger. One aide said that Taylor's fury was "blood-curdling to behold."[35] Kennedy himself was furious, a fact that McGeorge Bundy, the National Security Adviser, believed was exacerbated by the President's realization that he himself bore some of the responsibility for the fiasco.[36] Later on, in a solitary dictation, Kennedy would say, "That wire was badly drafted. It should never have been sent on a Saturday. I should not have given my consent to it without a roundtable conference at which McNamara and Taylor could have presented their views."[37] The State Department, moreover, had defied the President's authority by approving Lodge's change to the plan and by directing the Voice of America to broadcast the dreadful threat.

At noon, with the administration's top figures assembled in the White House, Kennedy lashed out at the men who had pushed through the momentous cable. Rarely did the President speak with such ferocity to anyone. When the President's tirade ended, Forrestal offered to resign. Forrestal had never been as enthusiastic about ousting Diem as his adoptive father or Hilsman – earlier in the year, upon meeting Diem for the first time, Forrestal had concluded that Diem was the strongest figure he had ever encountered.[38]

"You're not worth firing," the President growled at Forrestal. "You owe me something, so you stick around."[39]

Kennedy suggested to the attendees that the August 24 cable had been inspired by none other than the press, and by one reporter in particular. The President had been following David Halberstam's reporting in recent days, and had ordered special inquiries that had revealed some of the journalist's errors. "Halberstam of the *New York Times* is actually running a political campaign," exclaimed Kennedy before the group. "He is wholly unobjective, reminiscent of [Herbert] Matthews in the Castro days. It is essential that we not permit Halberstam unduly to influence our actions." The President remarked, "Diem and his brother, however repugnant in some respects, have done a great deal along the lines that we desire and, when we move to eliminate this government, it should not be a result of *New York Times* pressure."[40] In the course of the meeting, Kennedy asked McNamara, McCone, and Taylor if they wanted to issue orders canceling the new policy. They all said no. Such a quick turnabout in U.S. policy, they believed, would undermine America's credibility, and it might have little effect in any case because by this time Lodge had already entered the forest. McNamara and Taylor did recommend one more approach to Diem for the purpose of requesting Nhu's removal, but this proposal was turned down.

Twelve hours later, in Saigon, General Khiem gave the generals' reply to Conein. Some of the generals would stage a coup within one week, Khiem said, with General Minh and Vice-President Tho playing leading roles. Khiem observed that several key individuals stood in the plotters' way: General Cao, commander of IV Corps, whose troops in My Tho could reach Saigon swiftly by paved highway; General Dinh, military governor of Saigon and III corps commander; and Colonel Tung, commander of the Special Forces.

Kennedy sent cables to Lodge and Harkins on the evening of August 27 asking for their opinions on the coup's prospects. Above all else, the President wanted to make sure that if a coup were attempted it would succeed, for a failed coup could poison relations with Diem irrevocably and give Kennedy an embarrassment on the order of the Bay of Pigs. Lodge reported back that the coup committee's generals "are the best group that could be assembled in terms of ability and orientation. Certain of them (Big Minh, Khanh, and Kim) are considered to have personal force of character." The plotters, Lodge asserted, controlled more forces than the loyalist commanders, though it was uncertain whether they could attain victory quickly in Saigon.[41] In a quite different reply, General Harkins contended that the composition of the pro- and anti-Diem factions remained unclear, and therefore the United States did not have cause to give the plot its blessing right away.[42]

On the next day, August 28, Kennedy brought together a large group at the White House to discuss the impending coup. Kennedy was especially interested in hearing former Ambassador Nolting's arguments on the inadvisability of overthrowing Diem. The previous day, Harriman had barked at Nolting in front of the President, "You've been wrong from the beginning. No one cares what you think."[43] Kennedy, beset by serious doubts on the wisdom of dumping Diem, had interrupted Harriman to say that he liked Nolting and wanted to hear his views.

"I have grave reservations about proceeding against Diem," Nolting told the group. "Only Diem can hold this fragmented country together." Nolting also said, "I think President Diem could be persuaded to remove Madame Nhu from the scene and at least to make brother Nhu less conspicuous."

Hilsman countered, "The generals could put the Vice President of Vietnam in power and govern the country the way the generals have in Korea." He admitted, however, that "we have little information on how the generals plan to run the country if they are successful."

Harriman, who continued to maintain that the generals had not been a party to the pagoda raids, contended, "We had been winning the war with Diem because the generals were with him. The generals are defecting now because of the recent actions which Diem has taken against the Buddhists."

Ball said, "We can't win the war against the Communists with Diem in control. The U.S. position in the eyes of the world is being badly damaged." It was too late, Ball maintained, to renege on support for the conspirators. "We are already beyond the point of no return," he avowed.

"I do not believe we should take the position that we have to go ahead because we have gone so far already," Kennedy responded. "If a coup is not in the cards, we could unload." Kennedy was particularly troubled by the generals' lack of enthusiasm and by a report that pro-Diem forces within the Saigon area outnumbered anti-Diem forces by a two-to-one margin. "At present, it does not look as if the coup forces could defeat Diem."[44] The White House transmitted the President's reservations to Lodge and asked him for more information.

On this same day, in Saigon, Diem unfurled a warning that he was not going to cave in to American demands or surrender to any rebels. To Paul Kattenburg, the South Vietnamese President swore, "I'm ready to die, at once, if the sweat and blood of the last nine years now are to be sacrificed to a small group of agitators in Buddhist disguise, whom the population in any case despises."[45]

But neither Washington's doubts nor Diem's ominous message stopped Lodge. At 6:00 P.M. Saigon time on August 29, the ambassador informed Washington, "We are launched on a course from which there is no respectable turning back: the overthrow of the Diem government. There is no turning back in part because U.S. prestige is already publicly committed to this end in large measure and will become more so as the facts leak out. In a more fundamental sense, there is no turning back because there is no possibility, in my view, that the war can be won under a Diem administration." Aware that the coup committee remained hesitant, Lodge wanted to prod them into acting quickly. No one would act, he noted, unless assured of continued U.S. support. As a means of demonstrating America's sincerity, Lodge recommended that General Harkins give the plotters a collection of CIA messages previously sent by Conein. If this gesture failed to sway the generals, the United States should suspend its aid to the regime and announce the suspension publicly, on the condition that the generals set their plan in motion.[46] President Kennedy authorized Lodge to pursue this course of action, in spite of his own very strong reservations about a coup. Lodge was the man on the scene, and a leading contender for the Republican Presidential nomination.

The imminent revolt, however, would fail to come to life. Nhu, having learned of the plot from his informants, told a gathering of the top South Vietnamese generals that he knew of a plot to overthrow the regime, and he put the Special Forces on full alert. The conspiring generals, at the same time, concluded that they lacked adequate forces to defeat the loyalist units. At 2:39 A.M. on the thirty-first of August, just a day and a half after Lodge's foreboding message about the impossibility of turning back, Richardson, the chief of the CIA's Saigon station, informed Washington that the United States had no choice but to turn back. "This particular coup is finished," he reported.[47] The White House ordered U.S. officials in Saigon to destroy all copies of every cable sent or received during the past week, starting with the cable of August 24.

Because the plotting of late August was aborted, Hilsman would later say of the August 24 cable, "nothing happened as a result of that cable."[48] By that time, in 1977, the war had been lost, and Hilsman was attempting to distance himself from the catastrophe that followed the 1963 coup, as many others would attempt in their own ways. But his claim was not correct. The cable helped persuade Ambassador Lodge that Nhu and perhaps Diem should be removed and that Kennedy would sanction a coup, considerations that would guide Lodge after August. The message of August 24 also caused the Americans to forge enduring clandestine ties with the generals who, two months hence, would work with the United States to overthrow Diem, and it let those generals know that the United States had an interest in changing the government. These generals, who had strenuously promoted and executed the pagoda raids that had created so much contempt for Diem and Nhu among far away State Department observers, had not favored replacing Diem until they were advised to do it as a result of the August 24 cable. What this message had started, however, would be finished not by Harriman, Hilsman, Ball, or anyone else in Washington, but by the ambassador in Saigon.

CHAPTER 11

Self-Destruction

SEPTEMBER–NOVEMBER 2, 1963

AFTER THE INSURRECTION FAILED TO BLOSSOM, OPINION IN THE highest ranks of the U.S. government remained divided along lines similar to those before. Harriman, Hilsman, Ball, and Forrestal continued to attack Diem. Relying to a considerable degree on press reports, they argued that mid-level South Vietnamese officers and soldiers were growing weary of the regime's repression of the Buddhist activists. They acknowledged that the counterinsurgency effort had not yet been harmed seriously by morale problems, but predicted that it was going to come apart soon. In their minds, a successful South Vietnamese regime needed to tolerate public protests, conduct fair elections, broaden the government, give numerous public speeches and press conferences, and otherwise conduct itself like an American government. They believed that there existed individuals within South Vietnam who could lead the war against the Communists as well as or better than Diem, though they seldom specified exactly whom they meant. A State Department cable exemplifying this type of thinking read: "Seems clear from our studies that Vietnam has no lack of qualified leadership or executive talent if available personnel resources are put to effective use."[1]

The list of Washington officials who opposed Diem's removal remained filled with men of greater clout, including Secretary of Defense Robert McNamara, Chairman of the Joint Chiefs of Staff General Maxwell Taylor, Attorney General Robert Kennedy, and CIA Director John McCone, as well as others of past and future significance such as former Ambassador Nolting, CIA Far East Division Director William Colby, and Vice-President Lyndon Johnson. The pro-Diem Americans maintained that dissatisfaction with the government's handling of the Buddhists existed almost exclusively in the cities, and was primarily the result of Buddhist demagoguery, inaccurate American press articles, and the government's initial indecisiveness in silencing the opposition – not of outrage over serious injustices. The government's popularity in the cities had not slipped to the extent that it had weakened the nation's ability to fight in the countryside or maintain order in the towns. Diem's proponents observed that continued government military successes were bolstering Diem's popularity in the villages, where the fighting was taking place and where the Viet Cong tried to obtain most of their recruits.

On the subject of Americanizing the government, Diem's American friends argued that during a period of civil war, Diem could not be expected to grant the civil liberties enjoyed by Americans in peacetime. Taylor, for instance, contended, "We need a strong man running this country. We need a dictator in time of war and we have got one. I seem to recall that in our civil war we also had a dictatorial government. We also suspended the writ of habeas corpus."[2] Some of Diem's defenders stressed that Western democratic political methods were particularly difficult to employ in Asia, where force was respected more than liberality. Robert Thompson, whose British Advisory Mission unanimously supported Diem, remarked shrewdly in October, "Western thought is overly influenced by phrases such as 'lack of public support' which have little relevance in the Asian, still less in the Vietnamese, context. In my view all this is wasteful and wishful thinking."[3] In humanitarian terms, Thompson argued, Diem compared favorably with the leaders of similar countries. "Why withhold support from Diem now? Is he as bad as all that? In any list of Afro-Asian leaders (not to mention Governor Wallace) he would be far from the bottom. . . . In so far as emergency measures are concerned, he has certainly not been as ruthless as we were in Malaya under both Labour and Conservative Governments."[4] The pro-Diem faction steadfastly maintained that there was no suitable replacement for the President.

Kennedy was ambivalent. The arguments of Diem's proponents, which were far better than those of Diem's opponents, made an impression on him, particularly because the pro-Diem group contained his most trusted advisers while the State Department group led by Harriman and Hilsman had lost considerable influence with President Kennedy as a result of their deviousness in promoting a coup.[5] Kennedy, however, did not side unequivocally with Diem's advocates. For one, the media's gross misrepresentation of the Buddhist crisis had caused public approval of Kennedy's Vietnam policy to fall to twenty-eight percent, with fifty-six percent opposed.[6] Thanks also to the media in considerable part, Kennedy had some worries about support for Diem within South Vietnam. The President, therefore, took a middle course that had been suggested by Secretary of State Dean Rusk, who had not sided firmly with the pro-Diem or anti-Diem groups, in which Kennedy would apply pressure but not seek Diem's overthrow. Late on the same day that Richardson pronounced the coup dead, the State Department told Lodge to talk tough with Diem. Two days later, from his backyard at Hyannis Port, Kennedy gave Diem a stern warning in a nationally televised interview with Walter Cronkite. "We are prepared to continue to assist them," the President said, "but I don't think the war can be won unless the people support the effort, and in my opinion, in the last two months, the government has gotten out of touch with the people.

The repressions against the Buddhists, we felt, were very unwise." Cronkite asked whether Kennedy thought the Diem government could win back the people's approval. "I do," Kennedy answered. "With changes in policy and perhaps with personnel, I think it can. If it doesn't make those changes, I would think that the chances of winning it would not be very good."[7] In Saigon, friends and foes of the Diem regime immediately took heed of these ominous words.

President Kennedy, his confidence in Lodge and other Saigon officials shaken by the collapse of the plot, sent a task force to Vietnam in early September composed of U.S. Marine Corps General Victor Krulak – whom McNamara had selected – and Joseph Mendenhall of the State Department – whom Harriman and Hilsman had picked. Krulak traveled to ten locations spread throughout all four corps areas and talked with eighty-seven American advisers who had marched through the heat and rain with the South Vietnamese, plus twenty-two South Vietnamese officers. Some of the advisers put their opinions down in writing, and Krulak attached their remarks to his report, which was the most thorough survey of the military situation that had been conducted by an American outsider. Based upon the remarks of these 109 individuals, Krulak concluded that the war was going well, and that no serious desire existed among South Vietnamese officers to take up arms against Diem. With respect to the thirty-five advisers with whom he spoke in the troublesome Mekong Delta, Krulak observed, "All thirty-five were enthusiastic about the progress of the war and were emphatic that their counterparts were laboring at the war and not at politics."[8]

Contemporaneous reports from other observers in Vietnam confirmed the validity of Krulak's conclusions. Writing in the *Chicago Daily News*, Keyes Beech reported, "Contrary to the Saigon rumor mill, the war in the countryside has not 'ground to a halt.' Just the opposite is true." Government forces in the delta had intensified their efforts to destroy the Viet Cong, Beech asserted, and "on more than one occasion Vietnamese soldiers have in the last few days fought and fought well."[9] Captain Donald Koelper, a thirty-two-year old adviser to South Vietnam's 4th Marine Battalion, wrote home in September, "We have been in action against the Viet Cong almost every day and we hurt them a little more each time."[10] At the beginning of September, four large government task forces attacked Viet Cong camps in Quang Tin province, killing forty-seven Viet Cong and capturing twelve, at a cost of five dead and sixteen wounded.[11] In the jungles of Kontum province, near a suspected infiltration route, the South Vietnamese 42nd Regiment decimated a Viet Cong company.[12] On September 9, the Viet Cong 261st and 514th battalions – the two Viet Cong battalions that had fought at Ap Bac – were pummeled by the ARVN 7th Division, which had suffered heavy losses at Ap Bac and then had beaten up the 514th battalion in July. After the engagement ended, American advisers counted eighty-three dead Viet Cong bodies at the scene – more than the total number of government troops killed at Ap Bac – and they estimated that the retreating Viet Cong had taken at least one hundred additional casualties with them. A Communist account of this battle conceded that the "261st battalion suffered heavily." On the government side, losses totaled twenty-two dead and twenty-eight wounded. An Associated Press piece concluded with these words: "American advisers regarded it as a most significant victory against the guerrillas."[13]

In the late summer, the Viet Cong were intensifying their attacks against the strategic hamlets in the Mekong Delta, the area that habitation patterns and Diem's geographic priorities had made the most vulnerable to enemy initiatives. The guerrillas concentrated their offensive in four delta provinces: Long An, Dinh Tuong, Vinh Binh, and Kien Hoa. These provinces were auspicious for the Viet Cong because their proximity to Saigon made them easily accessible to Western journalists and because they lay within the operational zone of the ARVN 7th Division, the unit that the American newspapers had derided so much in the past. During this period, these four provinces experienced more Viet Cong attacks than South Vietnam's other thirty-seven provinces combined. In the country as a whole, however, the scope and scale of Viet Cong attacks did not change appreciably, as their initiatives elsewhere declined.[14] Although the government's forces in the delta were patrolling the countryside and defending the strategic hamlets with increasing vigor, they were not always able to prevent large Viet Cong forces from overwhelming the hamlets in portions of the delta. The delta's lengthy coastline and its labyrinthine network of rivers allowed the Viet Cong, with relative ease, to introduce troops and weapons from Cambodia or North Vietnam into the delta and move them from one delta province to another. Exploiting the favorable terrain, Communist units succeeded in overrunning a significant number of the strategic hamlets in two of the target provinces, Long An and Dinh Tuong. Typically, they tore down the hamlet fence, delivered propaganda lectures, and, if possible, took weapons from an inadequately organized hamlet militia. While the nationwide rate of Viet Cong weapon losses remained at approximately the same levels as in the period preceding the four-province offensive, the rate of government weapon losses experienced a moderate increase because of increased Viet Cong weapon seizures from the delta's strategic hamlets.[15]

The strategic hamlets in most parts of the delta, nevertheless, were not atrophying but building muscle. At the beginning of September, reporting on a just-completed tour of all the delta provinces, Thompson's British advisory mission concluded: "Generally, steady progress has been made in these provinces over the last six months in the strategic hamlet program and in the restoration of roads and bridges, with the result that Government authority is being gradually restored over large areas of the country and an increasing degree of security is being provided for greater numbers of the population."[16] That report was issued at the same time as a status report from Rufus Phillips and the other American advisers to the strategic hamlet program, which stated that the strategic hamlets were gaining steadily in effectiveness across the three corps areas to the north of the Mekong Delta as well as in the delta provinces of Vinh Binh and Kien Hoa – two of the four provinces targeted by the Viet Cong's offensive – plus Kien Phong, An Giang, and Kien Giang. Progress was unsatisfactory only in the sparsely populated delta provinces of An Xuyen, Chuong Thien, Ba Xuyen, and Kien Tuong – the government had yet to make a serious effort in these provinces – and in the other two provinces under heavy attack, Long An and Dinh Tuong.[17] As shall be seen, Communist sources would later reveal that even in Long An and Dinh Tuong the strategic hamlets had not been hurt as badly as the Americans thought. Corroborating this depiction of a flourishing strategic hamlet program was a simultaneous assessment from the central Communist leadership organ in South Vietnam, which credited the Saigon government with creating 5,000 strategic hamlets nationwide thus far. "The enemy has been able to grab control of population and land from us, and he has drawn away for his own use our sources of resources and manpower," the Communist appraisal stated. "We have not yet been able to stop them. On the contrary, from an overall perspective, the enemy is still pushing his program forward into our areas."[18]

These developments attracted little attention from Joseph Mendenhall, the State Department official who had gone to Vietnam at the same time as General Krulak. A longtime advocate of replacing Diem, Mendenhall had spent his visit in three South Vietnamese cities, where he spoke primarily with South Vietnamese officials, city dwellers, and U.S. officials. In the presentation he prepared for Kennedy and the National Security Council, Mendenhall warned that if Nhu remained in power, the Diem government was certain to fall victim either to the Viet Cong or to a religious civil war. Mendenhall omitted from his presentation two important conclusions that were contained in his written trip reports: that the military leadership and the provincial and district chiefs had not turned against Diem, and that discipline in the lower ranks of the military had not declined.[19]

Krulak and Mendenhall presented their conclusions to President Kennedy and the National Security Council on September 10. After listening to the recitations of Krulak and Mendenhall, the President quipped, "The two of you did visit the same country, didn't you?" Rufus Phillips, who also happened to be in attendance, advised Kennedy to seek Nhu's removal while keeping Diem, for most Vietnamese wanted Diem to stay but wanted Nhu to go. "The war is going well in the first, second and third corps," commented Phillips, "but it is emphatically not going well in the fourth corps." In the delta, he remarked, the Viet Cong were overrunning the strategic hamlets, as they had recently destroyed fifty of them. Phillips was painting a darker picture of the strategic hamlet program in the delta than he had in his September 1 report, almost certainly to reinforce his claim that Nhu had to go. He later wrote that the fifty strategic hamlets he mentioned to Kennedy were all in one province, Long

An,[20] one of just two provinces in the entire country that had suffered major setbacks in the strategic hamlet program during the Viet Cong's summer offensive. Phillips also muddled the issue at hand by equating the war in the delta with the strategic hamlet program in the delta; the government's mobile armed forces in most parts of the delta were fighting with skill and aggressiveness. The comments of Mendenhall and Phillips provoked a strong reaction from John McCone, whose CIA station in Saigon had collected much more information than either Mendenhall or Phillips. "The current view of the intelligence community is not as ominous as that expressed by the civilian reporters today," McCone asserted at the end of the meeting. "The Vietnamese military officers will work with Nhu."[21]

After the abortive coup, Ambassador Lodge initially concurred with the administration's new middle-of-the-road approach, advocating an effort to limit Nhu's role and to bring in Thuan as prime minister. At the beginning of September, Nhu informed the Americans that he would remove himself from the government entirely, provided that the United States withdrew its agents who were dealing with potential traitors. "Everybody knows who they are," Nhu said of these agents. Nhu promised that Buddhist prisoners would be freed as Lodge advocated, and that Madame Nhu would go abroad on an extended trip.[22] Several days later, Madame Nhu left the country, although she continued to denounce the Buddhists and certain Americans from abroad, and the brash Archbishop Thuc also departed.

Rather than taking these promising initiatives as a cue to work amicably with Diem and Nhu to resolve the remaining problems, as Lansdale or Nolting would have done with success, Lodge chose to threaten Diem. Visiting Gia Long Palace a few days later, Lodge warned Diem of strong opposition to the South Vietnamese regime in the United States. "It is my personal view," Lodge said, "that without some change of policy the suspension of aid will become a very real possibility." For the first time, Lodge told Diem of his desire to take away Nhu's powers. "Mr. Nhu should go away, not returning at least until the end of December – after the appropriations have been voted."

"Why, it would be out of the question for him to go away when he could do so much for the strategic hamlets," replied Diem. "He has been very unjustly accused. He was not the one who organized the raids of August 20. He was always the influence in favor of a flexible solution of the problem." Lodge's threat and the sharp criticisms of Nhu emanating from American spokesmen and journalists made Nhu's removal into an issue of face for Diem. Nhu had said he would leave the government, and Diem, at one point, had expressed a willingness to consider removing his brother, but now Diem decided against it. According to an official who was close to the South Vietnamese President, Diem refused to let go of Nhu because "the Vietnamese people would think that the Americans had made him do it. He did not want to be perceived as a puppet or lackey of the Americans."[23]

The problem was not with Nhu, Diem told Lodge, but with the Americans. "If American opinion is in the state you describe, then it is up to you, Ambassador Lodge, to disintoxicate American opinion." In his account of the conversation, Lodge noted that Diem became evasive when confronted with American suggestions for change, though at the end he promised Lodge that he would give serious consideration to all that Lodge had said.[24]

Walking away from this meeting in frustration, Lodge again began advocating a coup. On September 11, he cabled the State Department that "the time has arrived for the United States to use what effective sanctions it has to bring about the fall of the existing government and the installation of another." The only such sanction, contended Lodge, was the suspension of U.S. aid. He had yet to determine who would replace Diem, as evidenced by this statement: "Renewed effort should be made to activate by whatever positive inducements we can offer the man who would take over the government – Big Minh or whoever we would suggest."[25]

Washington was not ready for another coup attempt, and it told Lodge to wait and keep talking with Diem. But Lodge was in no mood for patience. Without telling his superiors, Lodge proceeded to explore the possibility of igniting a coup on his own. On this occasion, however, Washington snatched the match from his hand before he could light the tinder. On September 13, based on a report from a CIA officer who had just made an inspection trip to Vietnam, McCone revealed to President Kennedy that Lodge was considering fomenting a coup in cooperation with General Don.[26] Shortly thereafter, the State Department notified Lodge, "I am sure you share our understanding that whatever course we may decide on in the next few days, no effort should be made to stimulate coup plotting pending final decisions which are still being formulated here."[27] The South Vietnamese generals, in any case, were showing considerably less enthusiasm than Lodge for a putsch at this time. In the middle of the month, the generals asked Diem for some important cabinet posts, to which Diem replied that they would have to wait until after the national elections on September 27. The generals agreed to wait until that time for the prized positions.

From September onwards, Lodge relied very heavily on U.S. newspaper correspondents for information. The assessments that he telegraphed to Washington much more closely resembled the assessments of the press than they did the assessments of the American military and the CIA, the only U.S. organizations that had large numbers of officers and informants in the field. Lodge did not dispute that the military situation was improving at present, but he predicted a dim future, in which the hostility of the urban elite would cause "the soldiers to get less aggressive."[28] The media was invoking the same arguments, and was devoting little attention to the positive military developments across the country. On September 14, Neil Sheehan wrote favorably of American civilian officials who believed that "the Diem government's war against the Viet Cong rebels cannot be won unless the Diem regime is replaced with a more liberal group that can win the support of the whole population."[29] Stanley Karnow, who made a trip to Vietnam in September, wrote the following in the *Saturday Evening Post:* "No matter how much the United States supports the unpopular regime of Ngo Dinh Diem, this regime's chances of victory over the Communists are just about nil."[30]

General Harkins, by contrast, continued to emphasize the robust character and achievements of the South Vietnamese war effort. South Vietnamese officers all agreed on the necessity of suppressing the Buddhist disturbances, he reported, and they remained willing to support the Diem regime.[31] CIA station chief Richardson emphasized to Washington that Tri Quang and other Buddhist agitators had, from the beginning, sought political change rather than just religious privileges, and that the generals had conceived of the pagoda raids and had been deeply involved in executing them. The generals were willing to work with Diem, despite the recent conspiratorial debacle. While the Ngo family had alienated the urban classes to some extent, Richardson observed, "there are few points of no return in Asia," and he himself was "inclined to believe we should be able to resume successful prosecution of [the war] in military and civil sectors."[32]

Richardson's praise for Diem and his private conversations with Nhu, which the generals took as an indication of American support for Nhu, grated on Lodge. On September 13, in a message to Secretary of State Dean Rusk that he typed himself to maintain the highest level of secrecy, Lodge requested the removal of Richardson.[33] Lodge wanted Lansdale to take Richardson's place, having been told by Rufus Phillips that Lansdale would serve as a good "coup manager." Phillips had not told Lodge that Lansdale remained sympathetic to Diem, or that Phillips sought Lansdale's presence as a means of saving Diem while ousting Nhu.[34] McCone, however, refused to remove his Saigon station chief. In a letter to Rusk later that month, Lodge lamented, "It is a real pity. Had my request been granted, I believe the coup might have been pulled off."[35]

Lodge's press allies would help him deal with the Richardson problem by means of articles contending that the CIA station chief in Saigon was out of touch with the situation. In a September 15 piece, David Halberstam contended that whereas the station chief advocated supporting Diem, nearly everyone else in the CIA was appalled by the regime's expulsion of the Buddhist activists from the pagodas.[36] In actuality, some CIA officers in Saigon opposed Diem, but a large number of others favored Diem and understood that the generals had instigated the pagoda raids.[37] At the beginning of October, Richard Starnes wrote in an article for Scripps-Howard that "the story of the Central Intelligence Agency's role in South Viet Nam is a dismal chronicle of bureaucratic arrogance, obstinate disregard of orders, and unrestrained thirst for power. Twice the CIA flatly refused to carry out instructions from Ambassador Henry Cabot Lodge."

Starnes made Richardson's name public for the first time, blowing his cover.[38] Starnes's information apparently originated with Lodge or Harriman. James Reston of the *New York Times* told McCone that the media attacks on the CIA had been "obviously planted ... probably a good deal of it from Harriman."[39] Two days later, Halberstam gave the matter wider circulation with an article in the *New York Times.* Although he noted, correctly, that Richardson had not disobeyed the ambassador, Halberstam reported in approving tones that Lodge was dissatisfied with Richardson.[40]

The disclosure of Richardson's identity by Starnes and Halberstam may explain why the CIA abruptly yanked Richardson out of the country at that point in time. CIA policy required relocating officials such as Richardson when they were identified in public. The available evidence, however, is not entirely clear on this point, and the main reason may have been Lodge's demands for Richardson's removal. The end result, in any case, satisfied the desires of Lodge and Harriman. No longer would a senior CIA official in Saigon stand in their way.

The Richardson fiasco came at a time when Kennedy's disgust with Halberstam was climbing high into the mountains. Halberstam and his Saigon colleagues had just come under attack again by another prominent journalist, Joseph Alsop, the most influential media figure of the day and one of President Kennedy's favorite journalists. In one report from Vietnam, Alsop described a visit to the delta province of Kien Hoa, one of the four provinces bearing the brunt of the Viet Cong's attacks. "In the five months I've been here," Major John S. Ames told Alsop, "no night has passed without an attack on at least one of the strategic hamlets. We have more than two hundred and fifty of them by now. In all that time, not one of them has failed to resist. In the great majority of cases, the VC has been beaten off, quite often with heavy losses. And although some hamlet forts have been lost, no actual hamlet has ever been overrun." Alsop observed, "There is something oddly inconsistent here with the widely propagated picture of Vietnamese masses with no will to resist and a positive tendency to regard the Communists as the preferable alternative."[41] In a September 23 article, Alsop noted that he had recently met a group of U.S. advisers who expressed indignation at the press for reporting, completely contrary to the truth, that they viewed the Vietnamese soldiers in their province as ineffective. Alsop also likened the Saigon correspondents to the American journalists of the 1940s who had denigrated Chiang Kai-Shek and praised Mao Tse-Tung as a "great man and above all a humane man," as well as to Herbert Matthews, the reporter who had idealized Fidel Castro during the Cuban revolution.[42] On the morning that this article appeared, Kennedy told a group of top officials in the White House that there was "a great deal of truth" in Alsop's assessment of the Saigon press corps.[43]

Distraught, Kennedy proceeded to ask the CIA for a detailed analysis of David Halberstam's reporting. In the resultant assessment, the CIA cast great doubt on Halberstam's objectivity, noting, "Other observers writing from South Vietnam indicate that large segments of the American military community have been and still remain optimistic about the course of the war. Such optimistic sources are almost never quoted by Mr. Halberstam." A great amount of evidence, the CIA assessment stated, contradicted Halberstam's assertion that the Buddhist crisis was turning the rural populace and the army against the ruling family. Halberstam was slanting the news, the CIA decided, to support his contention that South Vietnam would lose the war if Diem remained in power.[44]

A few weeks later, Kennedy invited New York Times publisher Arthur Sulzberger to lunch at the White House. After complaining at length about the newspaper's coverage of Vietnam, the President suggested that the Times remove David Halberstam from Vietnam. Unbeknownst to Kennedy, the top men at the Times had recently decided that they would bring Halberstam out of Vietnam soon for at least a temporary period. Kennedy's request, however, caused the Times' leadership to cancel the plans for withdrawing Halberstam, because the newspaper did not want to give the appearance of succumbing to pressure from the U.S. government – any more than Diem did.

Kennedy continued to harbor similar suspicions about biased analysis from Lodge and the State Department officials in Washington who opposed Diem. In late September, for the purpose of assessing the situation, Kennedy sent a team to Vietnam led by McNamara and Taylor, Diem's most powerful defenders in Washington and two of Kennedy's top three advisers on matters of national security. The third of the three top advisers, Dean Rusk, had begun to lose the confidence of Kennedy because of his fence straddling.[45] Ambassador Lodge, who no doubt perceived Kennedy's distrust, argued in vain against a visit by McNamara and Taylor, claiming that it would yield no new insights and would necessitate a meeting with Diem that would suggest an end to American displeasure with the regime.

McNamara and Taylor arrived on September 24 for a ten day visit. Working from six-thirty in the morning until eleven at night, they spoke with many people of varying perspectives and opinions. U.S. military officers expressed optimism on the military situation based on their personal observations, while embassy officials warned that the regime was in deep political trouble, despite the apparent calm. Early on in the trip, Taylor met General Big Minh at the Saigon Officers' Club for a game of tennis, with McNamara looking on. Taylor and McNamara had heard that General Minh wanted to speak with them about an important matter in private, which they presumed would be the generals' views on a coup. A scorching heat covered the court, with the result that the running and swinging of rackets quickly became laborious. During a break in the match, McNamara and a very sweaty Taylor gave less-than-subtle hints to Minh to persuade him to open up. But Minh chose to avoid any mention of maneuvering against Diem. A few days later, in a second meeting with Taylor, General Minh complained about the organization of the military and the preferences given to Catholics over Buddhists, but he did not offer any suggestions for improving the situation, and he asserted that there was no good alternative to the current government. "It would be tragic to retard the military campaign by a cutback in aid," Minh said. "I see no opposition to the present government which might rally domestic and foreign support."[46]

Ambassador Lodge escorted McNamara and Taylor to the palace on September 29 for a three-hour meeting and dinner with Diem. The ambassador had not spoken with Diem in three weeks, believing that an aloof posture would compel Diem to yield to his wishes, although in fact Diem and most of his other countrymen were best persuaded by those who cultivated a close and amicable personal relationship. Quite at ease, puffing away at cigarettes and pointing at maps, Diem spoke almost continuously for the first two hours about the progress in the war.

Finally, McNamara spoke up. Relaying President Kennedy's worries about support for Diem in the United States and South Vietnam, McNamara asserted, "Public opinion in the United States seriously questions the wisdom or necessity of the United States government's aiding a government that is so unpopular at home and that seems increasingly unlikely to forge the kind of national unity or purpose that could bring the war to an early and victorious conclusion."

In reference to the negative perceptions of his government, Diem said, "I ascribe all this to inexperience and demagoguery within Vietnam and to misunderstanding in the United States of the real position in Vietnam because of the vicious attacks of the American press on my government, my family, and me." Diem defended his actions and made no promises to do any of the things that the Americans had requested.

"This is not satisfactory," McNamara retorted. "The problems of which I spoke are real and serious and will have to be solved before the war can be won or before Vietnam can be sure of the continued American support that I sincerely hope it will merit and receive."[47]

Upon returning to the United States on October 2, McNamara and Taylor delivered their report to the President. The war was proceeding very well, they reported, so well that the United States could withdraw one thousand military advisers by the end of the year.[48] McNamara and Taylor predicted that the political difficulties would not harm the war effort in the near term, but if the trouble persisted, they could not be certain that the military realm would remain impervious. McNamara argued, and Taylor reluctantly concurred, that the United States should cut aid enough to compel Diem to undertake various reforms but not enough to disrupt the war effort seriously. Diem should be given two to four months to comply with America's wishes, and if he failed to perform, the United States should consider supporting a coup to remove him. The report stated that a change at the very top would have a 50–50 chance of improving the South Vietnamese government, which was a very optimistic estimate, particularly given Big Minh's negative views on the alternatives to

Diem. Whether the proposal to cut aid resulted from a change in McNamara's own views or a change in Kennedy's views is uncertain.[49]

Kennedy immediately transformed the McNamara-Taylor recommendations into America's policy. He ordered a cut in aid and directed Ambassador Lodge to avoid giving "active covert encouragement to a coup," but he also called for "urgent covert efforts with closest security under broad guidance of ambassador to identify and build contacts with possible alternative leadership as and when it appears."[50] The aid cut was to have portentous consequences that Kennedy had neither intended nor desired. When word of President Kennedy's action spread in Saigon, it did much to reduce the Diem government's prestige in the eyes of its potential opponents and allies, and to persuade the senior South Vietnamese military leadership that South Vietnam would lose American support and hence the war if Diem remained in power.[51] And rather than gaining Diem's cooperation as Kennedy had envisioned, the cutting of aid made him even less cooperative. While the Ngos released some additional Buddhist prisoners, they continued to reject the far-ranging political reforms demanded by the Americans. Articles in the government-controlled press attacked the United States for reducing aid in the name of senseless reform.[52] In conversations with an Italian journalist and an Australian novelist, Nhu said that South Vietnam had no need for American military advisers. In fact, commented Nhu, the Americans reduced the government's ability to make appropriate social changes and conduct military operations. Nhu recommended that the Americans adopt the same policy toward South Vietnam that they practiced with Yugoslavia – send helicopters and money, not men.[53] The Ngo brothers, moreover, undertook a series of austerity measures and bureaucratic realignments that would enable the country to continue with less American aid than before. In combination with the aid cut, the austerity measures created economic difficulties that upset many South Vietnamese officials and officers, which in turn further eroded confidence in the government.[54]

On October 5, with the aid cut in effect and Diem stalling on the appointment of the generals to the cabinet positions they had requested, General Minh told CIA operative Conein he wanted assurances from the U.S. government that it would not attempt to thwart a coup that he was planning with Don, Kim, and Khiem, and that it would continue to provide aid at current levels after their coup.[55] Ambassador Lodge now saw an opportunity to push matters ahead much more quickly than the two-to-four month time frame that Kennedy had adopted based on the advice of McNamara and Taylor. Firing off a cable to the President straightaway, Lodge requested authorization to assure General Minh that the United States would not try to stop him, and that it would maintain aid to a government it considered capable of obtaining popular support and defeating the Communists.

In his reply, dated October 9, Kennedy instructed Lodge to obey the earlier command to avoid giving "active covert encouragement to a coup" but at the

same time to "identify and build contacts with possible alternative leadership."
Kennedy's telegram contained two additional key points. The first: "While we
do not wish to stimulate coup, we also do not wish to leave impression that U.S.
would thwart a change of government or deny economic and military assistance
to a new regime if it appeared capable of increasing effectiveness of military
effort, ensuring popular support to win war, and improving working relations
with U.S." The second point: "With reference to specific problem of General
Minh you should seriously consider having contact take position that in present
state his knowledge he is unable present Minh's case to responsible policy
officials with any degree of seriousness. In order to get responsible officials even
to consider Minh's problem, contact would have to have detailed information
clearly indicating that Minh's plans offer a high prospect of success. At present,
contact sees no such prospect in the information so far provided."[56]

Lodge decided to heed only a small portion of Kennedy's directive. Determined to give Minh the assurances he had requested, Ambassador Lodge seized
on the section within the first point concerning America's desire to avoid leaving the impression it would thwart a change in government. He ignored the
second point, which advised him to hold off on revealing the American policy
contained in the first point, and he also disregarded Kennedy's order against
providing "active covert encouragement" to potential coup leaders. Quite aware
that he was violating Kennedy's orders, Lodge would not inform the White
House of his subsequent actions.

On the next day, October 10, Lodge had Conein tell the generals that the
United States would not "thwart a change of government or deny economic
or military assistance to a new regime if it appears capable of increasing the
effectiveness of the military effort, assuring popular support to win the war,
and improving working relations with the United States."[57] With promises of
non-interference and continued aid from the Americans, the conspirators now
had the promises coveted by all those who had plotted against Diem from
1954 onward. These promises, combined with the aid cut and other recent
U.S. demonstrations of dissatisfaction with the Diem government, induced the
generals to commit themselves to a coup. General Minh said later, "The final
consideration that encouraged all of us to go ahead was the knowledge of the
disenchantment of the United States with Diem's government and that the revolutionary government would probably be quickly recognized and supported."[58]

The intrigue in Saigon and the conflict between Diem and the Americans
did not prevent the South Vietnamese armed forces from plowing forward
through October at the same speed as before. In the books Halberstam wrote
after leaving Vietnam, he maintained that the South Vietnamese military was
in shambles at this point in time.[59] As a journalist in October 1963, Halberstam
failed to report on numerous government successes, but even so his writings
from that month gave a far more positive view than what Halberstam the
author was later to claim. In one dispatch, Halberstam reported on an attack

by the ARVN 21st Division against Bai Ai village in Chuong Thien province, in which South Vietnamese infantrymen slogged through open rice paddies toward a village defended by heavy machine guns. The terrain and the Communist defenses resembled those at Ap Bac, but this time, Halberstam appreciated the enormous difficulties confronting the assault force. He penned, "Military sources described the situation as almost impossible for the attacking infantrymen, who advanced through water and mud up to their hips." Supported by napalm and bombs from fix-winged aircraft, the 21st Division's forces repeatedly attempted to take Bai Ai by maneuvering across the open paddies that surrounded the village on all sides, but the Viet Cong's interlocking automatic weapons fire stopped them. In the late afternoon, the South Vietnamese attempted to surround Bai Ai with blocking forces. As they prepared to put the final blocking unit in place, however, the weather suddenly turned foul and the helicopter flights had to be cancelled. After dark, the surviving Viet Cong were able to slip away through the gap left open by nature's whims. The South Vietnamese Army suffered forty-one dead and eighty-three wounded at Bai Ai, and they found eighty-two Viet Cong corpses. In contrast to Ap Bac, where the friction of war similarly had prevented the South Vietnamese from moving forces to the proper location late in the day, neither the American advisers nor Halberstam alleged that the failure to contain the enemy forces constituted a horrid mistake. In summing up the performance of the South Vietnamese troops, the correspondent of the *New York Times* wrote, "American advisers said the Vietnamese regulars had reacted well under heavy fire."[60]

Other U.S. press and advisory reports from October confirmed that the war effort had not lost its locomotion. In the week after Bai Ai, *Newsweek* noted, government forces in the delta scored two major victories, in which they killed 159 guerrillas at low cost to themselves.[61] Further north, in Binh Dinh province, elements of the Viet Cong 32nd Main Force Battalion attacked the An Tuong village office on October 7 and laid ambushes for government relief forces, but the wily South Vietnamese sector commander anticipated the ambush locations and attacked the would-be ambushers from the rear, killing a confirmed sixty-four Viet Cong, including the commander of the 32nd Main Force Battalion.[62] Several government main force battalions, supported by two howitzer batteries and two militia companies, went in search of the 60th and 70th Viet Cong battalions during the last week of October and found them near the junction of the Khanh and Tranh rivers in Quang Tin province. Several days of intermittent clashes resulted in the killing of a confirmed thirty-two Viet Cong, the capture of an additional seventeen, and the seizure of seven tons of rice.[63]

Halberstam later asserted that the strategic hamlet program in the delta was hopeless by October 1963, citing Rufus Phillips, the chief U.S. adviser to the program, and Lieutenant Colonel Elzie Hickerson, the leader of an interdepartmental investigation of the delta's strategic hamlets, as key sources.[64] Phillips's views at this time, as has been related, were not nearly as pessimistic as Halberstam subsequently alleged. Nor were those of Hickerson. Near the end of October, Halberstam himself wrote an article about Hickerson's recently completed investigation in which he described Hickerson's final report as "hardly one of despair."[65] The text of Hickerson's report stated that there continued to be a "virtual stand-off in the Delta," as "both the GVN and the VC have made improvements in their positions and capabilities. . . . The performance of [government] troops in combat has been good. This is especially true of the Civil Guard and Self-Defense Corps." The Viet Cong had overrun some strategic hamlets either because the government armed forces had been stretched too thin or because the Communists had employed heavy weapons smuggled in from Cambodia.[66] Other knowledgeable Americans believed that Hickerson's report was actually too pessimistic because it gave the impression that problems encountered in certain parts of the delta existed throughout the delta when in fact many provinces were much better off.[67] Even Ambassador Lodge, who was never inclined to report the Diem government's positive achievements, confirmed at the end of October that the strategic hamlet program in general was in good shape across the country.[68] Furthermore, a multitude of Communist sources depicted the strategic hamlet program in the delta as generally effective all the way up until November 1, 1963, a subject that shall be detailed further.

On the evening of October 22, many of the principal protagonists and antagonists attended a party at the British embassy. While mingling among the guests, General Harkins tracked down General Don and gave him a shock. Two nights earlier, Harkins said, a Vietnamese colonel had asked an American officer whether the United States would support a coup involving General Minh and several other generals. Harkins warned Don that he opposed a coup, pointing out that the war was going well. General Don pretended to know nothing of such a plot.

Don hurried away from the party. The generals had already scheduled the coup for October 26, Armed Forces Day, when the holiday's martial festivities would allow the conspirators to place their forces in Saigon without raising undue suspicions. But the warning from Harkins, along with reports that Diem had learned a rebellion was brewing, convinced Don and his fellows to postpone the putsch. Desperate for a clarification of the American position vis-à-vis a coup, General Don arranged a meeting with his CIA contact, Lou Conein, at a Saigon dentist's office the next morning. While their teeth were being examined, Don explained the generals' deep concern over General Harkins's remarks. Don asked whether the coup leaders could still count on the blessing of the United States. Conein assured Don that the views of General Harkins did not represent official American policy, and that they actually ran contrary to orders sent by President Kennedy. Adhering to a script prepared by Lodge, Conein reiterated that the American government would not get in the generals' way and would not cut off aid to a new regime.[69] General Don went to confer with his fellow plotters and then returned to the dentist's office the next day, at which time he notified Conein that the coup would take place before November 2.

General Harkins's interference, in addition to scaring the plotters, brought the conspiracy to Washington's attention sooner than Lodge had desired. Believing that Harkins would communicate his encounter with General Don directly to Taylor, Lodge was forced to start informing Kennedy of the plotting. The White House was stunned by the imminence of rebellion. Even more troubling for Kennedy was the surfacing of evidence that Lodge had been conspiring with the South Vietnamese generals behind his back. On the twenty-third of October, presumably at Kennedy's command, the CIA prepared a chronology of contacts with the plotters, and on that document was listed an abortive plan for a meeting between Lodge and the generals on October 18, which Lodge had not reported to Kennedy.[70] On the same date, Washington also received reports of another encounter between Don and Harkins and a subsequent conversation between Don and Conein, which together suggested further that Lodge was making unauthorized commitments to the generals. According to a CIA telegram, General Don told Conein that Harkins had said, "My previous comments to you yesterday concerning the non-desirability of a change of government were actually contrary to a presidential directive." Don said, in addition, that Harkins had arranged for him to meet with Ambassador Lodge. Yet Harkins soon notified Washington that he had not made the alleged statement to Don, and the CIA telegram stated that no one on the American side had scheduled a meeting between Lodge and General Don.[71]

By now, Kennedy was convinced that he had erred gravely in selecting Lodge as ambassador. On October 25, in front of a small group of high-ranking officials, he and McNamara held forth at length on the terrible problems that Lodge had created. With respect to the intrigue involving Lodge and the generals, McNamara said, "We ought to take our association with it out of the very amateurish hands that have been controlling it so far. Those hands are, particularly, the ambassador and Conein. . . . We're dealing through a press-minded ambassador and an unstable Frenchman." In a voice of exasperation, McNamara denounced Lodge for collaborating with the generals without obtaining permission from above and without notifying Washington of his interaction with the plotters. Lodge "has never said a word about these Conein contacts," McNamara piped. "That's no way to run anything. . . . It's the damnedest arrangement I've ever seen." Kennedy told McNamara that they should consider removing Conein or other anti-Diem officials in the embassy such as Truehart and Mecklin. Kennedy agreed with McNamara's assessment of Lodge, but he was not prepared to remove Lodge, for the same reason he had not been willing to do so earlier – Lodge's ability to use a dismissal for partisan purposes in the 1964 election. The President lamented, "Everybody on this issue has more or less the same reservations about Lodge's conduct, but he's there, and because he's there we can't fire him. So we're going to have to give him direction. We ought to make sure we give as much thought as we can to how we're going to handle Lodge and try to get him to do it in the way we want him to do it, when he comes back.... We've got to end up where we want him to go, not end up where he wants us to go."[72]

To keep the ambassador from determining their destination, the President sent Lodge a stern message via National Security Adviser McGeorge Bundy. "Certain aspects of the Don-Conein contacts give us considerable concern," the message stated, especially "Don's reference to a Presidential directive and to a scheduled meeting with Ambassador Lodge, for which there was no basis." The message emphasized that evidence on whether a coup would succeed was lacking, and it instructed Lodge and Harkins to obey the directive of October 9, which forbade the stimulation of a coup as well as the conveyance of the impression that the United States would thwart a coup.[73]

In his reply, Ambassador Lodge brushed aside the President's concerns about Conein, the mention of a Presidential directive, and the likelihood of success. He argued that the United States should not obstruct those who wished to topple the regime, for two reasons. First, "it seems at least an even bet that the next government would not bungle and stumble as much as the present one has." Second, "whenever we thwart attempts at a coup, as we have done in the past, we are incurring very long lasting resentments, we are assuming an undue responsibility for keeping the incumbents in office, and in general are setting ourselves in judgment over the affairs of Vietnam."[74] Lodge gave no explanation as to why his encouragement of the plotters did not amount to "setting ourselves in judgment over the affairs of Vietnam."

On October 27, at Diem's invitation, Lodge and his wife flew to the distant mountain resort town of Dalat for a brief stay at one of the presidential villas. After an exquisite dinner, Diem brought up the recent cutbacks in aid. Lodge asked whether Diem would reopen certain schools and appease the Buddhists if the aid were restored. In response, Diem said that he was making progress in those areas. Diem then went on to accuse John Mecklin and the CIA of assisting the government's opponents.

"Give me proof of any improper action by any employee of the United States government," Lodge declared, "and I will see that he leaves Vietnam."

Once again assuming the blunt negotiating posture that never worked with Diem, Ambassador Lodge repeated America's concerns and its demands for reform. "We do not wish to be put in the extremely embarrassing position of condoning totalitarian acts which are against our traditions and ideals," Lodge warned.

Diem replied, "*Je ne vais pas servir.*" The literal translation from the French was "I am not going to serve." Lodge informed Washington that Diem's response "makes no sense," and surmised that Diem must have really meant to say something else. Perhaps nothing better exemplified Lodge's inability to understand Vietnam in 1963 than his failure to comprehend Diem's unwillingness to be a servant of the United States.

Near the end of their conversation, Lodge said, "Mr. President, every single specific suggestion which I have made, you have rejected. Isn't there some one thing you may think of that is within your capabilities to do and that would favorably impress U.S. opinion?" Demonstrating the usual Vietnamese aversion to direct confrontation, Diem did not answer the question and began speaking on a different topic.[75]

The next day, Ambassador Lodge told South Vietnamese Secretary of State Thuan about his seemingly unproductive talk with Diem. But Thuan, who had played a critical role in turning U.S. opinion against Nhu and thus inadvertently against Diem, suggested that the meeting signaled the start of better relations between Diem and the United States, for it had convinced Diem that he had to grant some of the Americans' wishes. Diem, Thuan revealed, had said that the regime could not survive without U.S. aid. Thuan asked Lodge what Diem ought to do to appease the United States, noting that he intended to communicate the answer to Diem. Lodge mentioned the usual political reforms. The Americans should be hearing from Diem again, Thuan indicated.

Lodge, watching this late opportunity for rapprochement surface and float toward him, let it pass by. That evening, Conein met once more at the dentist's office with General Don to discuss the conspiracy. "My group and I have no political ambitions," Don avowed. "Our only desire is to win the war against the VC and re-establish the prestige of Vietnam and the Army." Don divulged some of the military units that would participate in the coup. When questioned by Conein about timing, Don refused to reveal the date, and said that the Americans would be informed of the plans and the timing only four hours before the coup commenced, not two days before as was promised earlier, though he did vouch that the coup would begin no earlier than October 30 and no later than November 2. The problem of General Dinh had been solved, Don explained. Because they remained unsure of Dinh's loyalties, the plotters were leaving Dinh out of the coup planning and surrounding him with men committed to the conspiracy who "have been given orders to eliminate Dinh if he shows any signs of compromising the coup."[76]

Ambassador Lodge reported to Washington on the following day that a coup was "imminent." Although he conceded that he had some doubts about its chances for success, he asserted that the United States could stop it only at an inordinately high cost, warning, "No positive action by the U.S. Government can prevent a coup attempt short of informing Diem and Nhu with all the opprobrium that such an action would entail." Furthermore, the generals' decision to reveal the kickoff time only four hours in advance "rules out my checking with you between time I learn of coup and time that it starts. It means U.S. will not be able significantly to influence course of events."[77]

Just as he had done two months earlier, Lodge was making a false claim that the coup could not be stopped in order to prevent a reluctant Kennedy and others in Washington from interfering with his enterprise. Even at this late date, however, the generals were willing to step back if they doubted whether American support would be forthcoming, as they had after Don's encounter with General Harkins at the British embassy. Diem had not dismembered the military leadership after the August conspiracy and most likely would not do so if this plot fizzled. At this time, moreover, the plotters still had a few more logs to tie down before they set off on their raft. They still intended to ask Diem for concessions before taking action against him, and they had yet to finish checking the allegiance of key generals, some of whom they still suspected of supporting Diem.

Diem's American defenders were not prepared to stand back and let Lodge steamroll the South Vietnamese President unopposed. General Victor Krulak distributed the findings of an eight-member Congressional delegation that had just returned from Vietnam, where it had met with many of the key anti-Diem Americans, including Lodge and Mecklin, as well as with Harkins and others more sympathetic towards Diem. According to Clement J. Zablocki, a Wisconsin Democrat who headed the delegation, all members had come to agree on the following:

> a. Diem, with all his faults, his autocracy, his tolerance of venality and brutality, is durable, and has been winning.
> b. There is no visible substitute for Diem – at least none which guarantees improvement; thus, actions by U.S. representatives to join with coup plotters, as was apparently true in August, is harmful.
> c. The conduct of the resident U.S. press is a grave reflection upon their entire profession. They are arrogant, emotional, unobjective and ill-informed. The case against them is best expressed by their having been repudiated by much of the responsible U.S. press.[78]

The conservative writer and political activist Clare Booth Luce took out a full page ad in the *New York Times* to defend the Diem government. Echoing Alsop's earlier accusation, she wrote: "Is the history of the liberal press in Chungking and Havana going to repeat itself? The evidence is that it is." With respect to the Buddhist issue, Luce asserted, "In America, if a Catholic priest were to burn himself to death in protest of the government's failure to provide free bus rides for parochial school children, or if a Protestant minister were to make himself a living torch to express his opposition to the Supreme Court decision against prayer in public schools, we would consider them religious maniacs. And our government would take stringent measures to prevent any emulation of such acts. This is precisely the view Madame Nhu has taken of the self-immolating bonzes."[79]

Kennedy brought together his senior advisers at 4:20 P.M. on the twenty-ninth of October. William Colby, director of the CIA's Far East Division, began the meeting by presenting a map marked with the Vietnamese military units in and around Saigon. By Colby's count, the pro-palace and pro-coup forces in the area each numbered 9,800, and the remaining 18,000 troops were considered to be neutral. Colby remarked that the critical factor was not the opinion of the average soldier in Saigon, but rather the conduct of the most powerful and best-positioned units. As the key units, he listed the Presidential Guard, the Special Forces, the Airborne, the Marines, the Air Force, and an armored unit. Half of these forces were pro-palace and half were anti-palace, said Colby.

Harriman and Rusk argued that the Diem government had to be removed. "I think that we're gradually going to find that there will be less and less enthusiasm for this regime," said Harriman. "We're gradually going downhill, and at the end of the year we'll have found ourselves in increasing difficulties unless something else has happened in the meantime."

"I just don't see that this makes any sense on the face of it," Robert Kennedy said of the projected coup. "What we're doing, really, is putting the whole future of the country and southeast Asia in the hands of somebody that we don't know very well." Diem "is a fighter. He's not somebody like [Dominican Republic President Juan] Bosch who's just going to get out of there. He's a determined figure who's going to stick around and I should think go down fighting. He's going to have some troops there that are going to fight, too. . . . If it's a failure, I would think Diem's going to tell us to get the hell out of the country." The younger Kennedy finished by warning, "We're just going down the road to disaster."

Taylor and McCone concurred with the younger Kennedy. "I found absolutely no suggestions that the military didn't have their heart thoroughly in the war," Taylor said, in reference to his earlier trip to Vietnam. "I would be willing to step further and say even a successful coup would be a detriment to the conduct of the war. First, because you'll have a completely inexperienced government, and second, because the provincial chiefs, who are so essential to the conduct of the war, will all be changed." Laying out the CIA's position, McCone said, "I think our opinion is somewhat the same as General Taylor expressed. We think that an unsuccessful coup would be disastrous. A successful coup, in our opinion, would create a period of political confusion that would seriously affect [the situation] for a period of time which is not possible to estimate. It might be disastrous."

"What are Lodge's existing instructions?" the President inquired.

Rusk read from the message of October 9 containing the order to avoid "stimulating a coup," which Lodge had long since violated. McNamara said of Lodge, "We have, rightly or wrongly, led him to believe that we would support a coup, or at least we would keep hands off." McGeorge Bundy interjected, "I don't think we've said that to him, but I think it's clear that that's what he thinks." Kennedy's inner circle had now figured out just how Lodge had twisted and exploited the October 9 instructions.[80]

As the meeting wound down, President Kennedy said that if pro-Diem and anti-Diem forces were equal in number, as Colby had reported, then a coup would be unwise. Unless Lodge could produce information showing that the rebel leadership would control the larger part of the armed forces in Saigon, then the United States should discourage the conspirators from launching a coup.[81]

Once the assemblage adjourned, Bundy wrote to Lodge on the President's behalf. Rejecting Lodge's spurious contention that the coup could not be stopped, the message stated, "We believe that what we say to coup group can produce delay of coup and that betrayal of coup plans to Diem is not our only way of stopping coup." Lodge was instructed to notify the generals immediately that the United States did not believe the coup plans were sufficiently promising. Lodge, Harkins, and the CIA were to assess the probability of success, and then a decision would be made on whether ultimately to encourage the coup, discourage the coup, or maintain a hands-off policy.[82]

Lodge received Bundy's cable on the morning of October 30, but did not reply until that evening, at which time he argued against telling the generals that the coup might not succeed. Lodge, in fact, never would order Conein to convey the message to the plotters that the President had ordered him to convey. The United States could not delay or avert the coup, Lodge maintained, short of informing Diem and Nhu of the plot, which would cause Diem and Nhu to remove a substantial segment of the leadership needed to fight the war and would "make traitors out of us." Further down in his response, Lodge undermined his own assertion that stopping the coup would be catastrophic, writing, "If we were convinced that the coup was going to fail, we would of course do everything we could to stop it." Lodge did not provide any new information about military units loyal to the coup leaders. Concerning Washington's skepticism about the plot's viability, Lodge wrote, "I do not know what more proof can be offered than the fact these men are obviously prepared to risk their lives and that they want nothing for themselves. If I am any judge of human nature, Don's face expressed sincerity and determination on the morning that I spoke to him."[83] Kennedy hardly could have been reassured to learn that Lodge's confidence in the coup was based on his interpretation of a treacherous general's facial expressions.[84] With respect to a White House suggestion that Harkins assume control of the U.S. mission in Lodge's absence, Lodge argued, "It does not seem sensible to have the military in charge of a matter which is so profoundly political as a change of government," apparently having forgotten who was in charge of the coup on the South Vietnamese side.

That same day, General Harkins sent three cables to Washington, each of which promptly landed on Kennedy's desk. Harkins objected that the ambassador's active encouragement of a coup violated official American policy, as did Lodge's failure to keep the head military adviser apprised of the plotting.

Whether the coup would succeed was unclear. The generals remained willing to cooperate with Diem, Harkins observed, although many disliked the Nhus. Harkins, who unlike Lodge had first-hand knowledge of the South Vietnamese generals' capabilities, warned that South Vietnam had no adequate replacement for Diem. "In my contacts here I have seen no one with the strength of character of Diem, at least in fighting Communists," he asserted. "Certainly there are no generals qualified to take over in my opinion."[85]

These cables added substantially to Kennedy's already considerable reservations about the overthrow of the South Vietnamese government.[86] Late that night, the President sent Lodge another cable expressing serious doubts about the coup and Lodge's views on how to handle the situation. "We do not accept as a basis for U.S. policy that we have no power to delay or discourage a coup," the message stated bluntly. As evidence, it cited Lodge's contradictory statement that he would try to forestall an unpromising coup. The embassy should discourage the coup leaders not only if their undertaking was likely to fail, the message read, but also if the chances for success were less than high. If the ambassador in Saigon had been someone other than a potential Republican Presidential nominee, Kennedy more likely than not would have gone further and ordered him to halt the plotting altogether, but the President authorized Lodge to make the final decision on support for a coup based on his own assessment of its viability.[87]

On the thirty-first, one day before the coup was set to begin, Nhu ordered General Dinh to the Presidential Palace. The Dinh Tuong provincial chief had informed the palace that General Dinh's deputy, Colonel Nguyen Huu Co, had asked him to join in a coup. Confronted with this information, Dinh told Nhu that he knew nothing of it, which in all likelihood was true given the conspirators' distrust of him, and he exclaimed, "We must arrest Co and chop off his head!"[88] Diem and Nhu, however, decided that they would keep Co alive in order to get more information about the plot.

General Don also paid a visit to the palace on this day, to inquire about the request that he and General Dinh had made in September for cabinet posts and new policies. Diem and Nhu informed Don that the improvement in the situation rendered such changes unnecessary. An unspoken but very important rationale was that the Ngo brothers, based on years of interaction, believed that the generals were poorly qualified for work outside the military sphere, an assessment that events would soon validate. Had Diem granted the cabinet posts even at this very late date, the generals might have aborted their insurrection; Don later said that the rejection of this appeal led the generals to make the definitive decision to rebel.[89]

On the morning of November 1, the kickoff date, Lodge and Admiral Felt met with Diem. "I know there is going to be a coup attempt, but I don't know who is going to do it," Diem told the two Americans.

"I don't think that there is anything to worry about," said Lodge.[90]

Diem asked Lodge to meet with Colby and Nolting when he visited Washington so that they could discuss Nhu, upon whom Diem so greatly depended. The South Vietnamese President then implored the ambassador, "Please tell President Kennedy that I am a good and frank ally, that I would rather be frank and settle questions now than talk about them after we have lost everything. Tell President Kennedy that I take all his suggestions very seriously and wish to carry them out but it is a question of timing."

This conversation, Lodge admitted in reporting the proceedings to Washington, suggested that the United States could achieve a reconciliation with Diem.[91] But Lodge sent this report back to Washington as a cable of the lowest possible priority, and it would not arrive until several hours after Washington had begun receiving high-priority cables on a coup in the South Vietnamese capital.

That morning, just a few hours before their mutiny was scheduled to start, the plotters remained unsure of themselves. A teary-eyed General Khiem approached General Dinh and asked that he tell no one what he was about to say. When Dinh promised to keep quiet, Khiem said that he wanted to cancel the coup. "Dinh, I think we still have time to talk to the old man," Khiem sobbed. "I don't want to hurt him. Have pity on him!" Taken aback by this display, Dinh weighed the situation. Finally he said that he still wanted to go ahead with the coup. Perhaps Dinh thought that he was being tested; the plotters were obviously wary of him, as they still had not given him the details of their planning, nor had they invited him to join them at their command post. At this point in time, the opportunistic Dinh most probably intended to avoid a firm commitment to either side until one showed a clear preponderance of strength. Whether Khiem himself was actually entertaining doubts and whether he would have opposed a coup had Dinh chosen to do so are uncertain. Khiem later told Don that he had sprayed Chinese medicinal oil into his eyes to give the appearance that he had been crying, and had then approached Dinh to test his loyalty. This claim, however, may have been simply an attempt to dissolve suspicions about his own loyalty.[92]

Shortly before the rebellion commenced in Saigon, Colonel Co arrived at My Tho, home of the Seventh Division. With a show of automatic weapons, soldiers accompanying Co forced the division's officers into submission, and Co took command of the unit. In addition to neutralizing this critical division, Co was able to use the division's forces to transfer all ferries in the area to the north bank of the Mekong river, thereby preventing other regulars in the delta from going to Saigon to rescue Diem, a maneuver of great import.

Another of Diem's loyal commanders, the chief of naval operations, was alarmed by mysterious troop movements near Saigon that morning, and he determined to notify Diem. Before he could make contact, however, some of his fellow officers convinced him to join them for lunch, as it was his thirty-sixth birthday. On the way to the restaurant, his deputy killed him.

The coup leaders summoned many other generals and colonels who knew nothing of the coup to the Joint General Staff headquarters, and upon arrival arrested those whose loyalties remained suspect. Among the officers taken prisoner were the commanders of the Airborne Brigade, the Marine Brigade, the Special Forces, the Air Force, the police, and the Civil Guard, which were arrests of great value because these men commanded all of the key units within Saigon that could support Diem except for the Navy and the Presidential Guard, and they were men of considerable talent. Perhaps the most gifted of them all was Colonel Cao Van Vien, who commanded South Vietnam's finest fighting force, the Airborne Brigade, and who from 1967 to 1975 would serve as the chairman of the South Vietnamese Joint General Staff. One observer testified that Vien "broke down completely" upon learning of the coup and handed his insignia to General Minh in resignation.[93]

Also at the headquarters of the Joint General Staff was Conein. Earlier that morning, General Don had contacted him and asked him to bring all the money he could. Conein arrived at the South Vietnamese headquarters with three million piasters – the equivalent of forty-two thousand American dollars – and a radio that enabled him to maintain direct contact with the CIA's Saigon station. The plotters told Conein that if the coup failed, he would have to come with them as they attempted to fight their way to Cambodia in nine armored cars, which had been loaded with extra gasoline and set aside for this purpose.

At one forty-five in the afternoon, the coup began in Saigon. Troops under rebel command attacked the headquarters of pro-Diem military and police units, although it was rather difficult to tell who was on whose side. As in 1960, most of the troops participating in the revolt had been kept in the dark about the planned operations until the last minute, and then were told that they were going on a mission to rescue Diem from mutinous units.[94] Capturing the governmental radio station, the coup forces broadcast reports of their success, until the Presidential Guard retook the radio station. Several government headquarters succumbed quickly to attacks by overwhelming numbers of rebel troops.

Many loyalist forces in the Saigon area did not come to Diem's aid because their leaders had been arrested at the coup headquarters. Only a few units offered serious resistance: the Special Forces, the Presidential Guard, and the Navy. Diem also benefited from the loyalty of Colonel Lam Son, commandant of the Infantry School, who foiled an attempt by the conspirators to gain the assistance of two cadet battalions. The Special Forces provided substantially less punch than Diem would have hoped, for the plotters had removed several Special Forces companies from Saigon by assigning them to distant operations just before the coup. This relocation was made possible by the U.S. embassy, which one week before the coup had used the threat of aid suspension to compel the Diem government to put Tung and the Special Forces entirely under the authority of the Joint General Staff.[95] In addition, a large contingent of the Special Forces in Saigon capitulated after coup leaders put a pistol to the head of Special Forces Commander Colonel Le Quang Tung, held a phone to his mouth, and compelled him to order his men to surrender. The conspirators executed Tung afterwards. That the coup forces had gained the upper hand soon became evident to General Dinh, and so he committed himself to the insurrection.

Diem and Nhu monitored events from the basement of the Presidential Palace, which the insurgents were attempting to surround. At three-thirty, Diem reached General Don by telephone.

"We request that you resign with no conditions or strings attached," Don asserted. "We will then send you and your family out of the country." Don said that the generals had launched a coup because of Diem's refusal to reorganize the government.

Diem protested that he had intended to announce a reorganization this very day.

"Why didn't you tell me that yesterday?" Don demanded. "Now it's too late."

Nhu got on the phone with Don. "Why did you have to attack us?" Nhu asked. "If there is something that you do not like, we can talk about it. Why have you shown this ingratitude toward us?" Nhu invited the generals to the palace to negotiate.

Don conferred with the other generals standing around him. Afraid that Diem was merely trying to buy time for loyal troops to arrive as he had during the 1960 coup, the generals rejected the offer.[96] They then warned the Ngo brothers that unless they surrendered in the next five minutes, rebel forces would strike the palace from the air and on the ground. Diem refused to yield, holding out hope that loyalist troops from inside or outside Saigon would foil the rebellion. He hung up the phone. The threatened attack did not materialize.

Later in the afternoon, the rebels again asked Diem to surrender. If he did not, Minh vowed, the palace would be "blasted off the face of the earth."[97] Diem again refused. Now the generals' troops began to attack the 1,500 crack Presidential Guard troops who were defending the palace.

Just as the rebel troops commenced their assault, with the possibility of limiting the violence evaporating, a Special Forces brigade commander proposed to Diem an audacious plan involving a strike on the rebel headquarters by loyalist armor and infantry. Success was certain, the commander explained, because only inexperienced military trainees were guarding the generals, which was true enough. With the leading conspirators in custody, Diem's foes would be thrown into complete disarray. But Diem decided against the armored strike. "The brigade should conserve its forces to fight the Communists and avoid bloodshed," Diem intoned. "In the meantime, it should protect Gia Long Palace, the Post Office, and the Treasury."[98] One person who was with Diem at the time elaborated that the President chose not to attack the Joint General

Staff Headquarters because it "represented the authority of the armed forces," and because he "did not want to cause more harm, more death, more suffering for the soldiers. The President was confident that his forbearance would make the coup forces realize that he was a President who always stood on the side of the masses of the population."[99]

At four-thirty, Diem telephoned Ambassador Lodge. The official report filed by Lodge rendered the dialogue as follows:

> **Diem:** Some units have made a rebellion and I want to know what is the attitude of the United States.
> **Lodge:** I do not feel well enough informed to be able to tell you. I have heard the shooting, but am not acquainted with all the facts. Also it is 4:30 A.M. in Washington and the U.S. Government cannot possibly have a view.
> **Diem:** But you must have some general ideas. After all, I am a Chief of State. I have tried to do my duty. I want to do now what duty and good sense require. I believe in duty above all.
> **Lodge:** You have certainly done your duty. As I told you only this morning, I admire your courage and your great contributions to your country. No one can take away from you the credit for all you have done. Now I am worried about your physical safety. I have a report that those in charge of the current activity offer you and your brother safe conduct out of the country if you resign. Had you heard this?
> **Diem:** No. (And then after a pause) You have my telephone number.
> **Lodge:** Yes. If I can do anything for your physical safety, please call me.
> **Diem:** I am trying to reestablish order.[100]

Other witnesses to this conversation remembered its content differently. They testified that Lodge urged Diem to stop resisting the coup and flee the country, and to facilitate the latter he offered Diem transportation to the Philippines aboard a U.S. jet aircraft that had been brought in recently for the ambassador's own use. Frederick Flott, who was standing next to Lodge as he spoke, recalled that the American ambassador told Diem, "You're a great man. You've done great things for your country. I think the prudent thing for you to do would be to get out of here and not fight it further. I would be prepared to send my car and one of my officers whom you know to meet you. We can appeal to reason on both sides to let you be taken to the airport, and I just happen to have this plane here." Flott was to pick up Diem in a limousine flying American flags and take him to the airport, where he would board Lodge's plane. According to Flott, Diem replied to Lodge, "No, no, you're panicking. You're exaggerating the danger." Flott remarked that Diem "didn't even thank Lodge graciously for the offer."[101]

Diem's reply was not merely lacking in grace, according to one of Diem's bodyguards, whose account of the conversation is similar in many other respects to Flott's. The bodyguard recalled that Diem shouted the following at Lodge:

"Mr. Ambassador, do you realize who you are talking to? I would like you to know that you are talking to a president of an independent and sovereign nation. I will only leave this country if it is the wish of my people. I will never leave according to the request of a group of rebellious generals or of an American ambassador. The U.S. government must take full responsibility before the world in this miserable matter."[102]

For several more hours, Diem and Nhu tried to summon friendly units to Saigon, but with little success. Although a large number of provincial chiefs openly supported Diem, they could not come to his assistance because the plotters had severed their communication lines or blocked the roads or waterways leading from their provinces to the capital. As many as half of the division commanders remained loyal to Diem after the coup began, according to a rebel tally, but the loyal division commanders similarly could not reach Saigon because of rebel obstruction or lack of transportation.[103] General Huynh Van Cao, the IV Corps commander, ordered the 9th Division to Saigon to save Diem, and division commander Colonel Bui Dzinh eagerly ordered the unit into action, only to discover that the division's troops could not cross the Mekong River because Colonel Co had repositioned the ferries. The commanders of I and II Corps – General Do Cao Tri and General Nguyen Khanh – and several division commanders located far from Saigon neither supported nor opposed the rebellion at the outset. They had been encouraged to join the plot by the words of fellow officers and by the actions of the U.S. government and press, but they still preferred Diem as the nation's leader. General Khanh, in fact, reportedly had prepared a force for assisting Diem in the event that the coup seemed headed for defeat.[104] Eventually, however, these individuals decided that the coup forces in Saigon were too strong and they belatedly declared their support for the revolt.

At eight o'clock P.M., Diem and Nhu climbed down a secret set of palace stairs, which brought them to a deep underground tunnel. Hurrying through the dark passageway, they came to another long set of stairs and climbed it until reaching a street in the middle of Saigon, far enough from the palace that rebel troops did not see them. Nhu wanted them to split up. One of them could go to the Mekong Delta to join with General Cao's units, and the other could do the same in the central highlands with the formidable II Corps forces led by General Khanh. The plotters would not dare kill one of them if the other were still alive, Nhu argued. Diem rejected the suggestion. According to one account, Diem told Nhu, "You cannot leave alone. They hate you too much; they will kill you. Stay with me and I will protect you." Another version had Diem saying, "We have always been together during these last years. How could we separate in this critical hour?"[105] The two brothers took refuge in the house of a prominent Chinese citizen in Cholon.

Sixty minutes later, rebel artillery and tanks began an intense attack on the palace. The three Presidential Guard battalions defending the palace, who were as unaware as the attackers that Diem and Nhu had fled, fought back ferociously. Magnesium parachute flares and a spectacular volume of gun flashes made the night almost as bright as day. At 10:00 P.M., four hundred infantrymen and seventeen tanks of the Presidential Guard moved out from the palace and counter-attacked one thousand rebel troops. Loyalist and rebel tanks, scarcely able to maneuver in the streets and alleys surrounding the palace, pumped shells into each other at point blank range. Crouching on nearby rooftops, American and South Vietnamese civilians watched the action, fascinated. There was much courage and letting of blood to be seen.

Leading the rebel assault on the palace was Colonel Nguyen Van Thieu of the 5th Infantry Division. In August, the CIA had concluded that Thieu was loyal to both Diem and Nhu, and was a "strong supporter of Nhu."[106] During the November 1960 putsch, Thieu had brought the 7th Division to Saigon and helped defeat the mutineers. Thieu did not immediately commit himself to the coup of November 1963, and he seemed willing to side with Diem if the coup was failing or the United States sided firmly with Diem. Many of the plotters, indeed, distrusted Thieu and made plans to eliminate him should he come down on Diem's side.[107] Thieu later said that he had agreed to participate in the coup only after coup leaders had convinced him that the United States and other countries supported the coup and that Diem would not be killed.[108]

The Presidential Guard held their ground through the night, but they were surrounded and the rebels had prevented loyalist relief forces from entering Saigon. At 6:45 A.M. the next morning, Diem decided that continued defense of the palace would only cause needless bloodshed, and so he ordered the Presidential Guard to surrender. Upon entering the palace, rebel commanders were dismayed to discover that Diem and Nhu were not there, and so were the Americans. According to General Don, Conein kept saying, "Where have the two of them gone? They must be arrested, no matter what. This is very important. You don't make an omelet without breaking the eggs."[109] If Diem slipped away, all of them knew, he might meet up with loyal troops elsewhere in the country or flee into exile to scheme from abroad against the new government.

After telling the Presidential Guard troops to lay down their weapons, Diem and Nhu left the Cholon safe house and went to a church. As they departed, Diem told the man who drove them, "I don't know whether I will live or die and I don't care, but I want you to tell Nguyen Khanh that the President loves him and he should avenge me."[110] At the church, Diem phoned the American ambassador. Lodge would never inform Washington of this conversation, but two different sources affirmed its existence, including Lodge's senior aide Mike Dunn, who was present as Lodge spoke. Lodge told Diem that he would provide asylum and do whatever else he could, but he would not arrange any transportation for the deposed President, contrary to his offer the previous day to fly Diem to the Philippines. Dunn told Lodge that he was willing to go pick up Diem and Nhu himself, to protect them from the conspirators, but Lodge forbade it. "I was really astonished that we didn't do more for them," Dunn recalled.[111]

The embassy also received a call early that morning from Conein. What had prompted the call was a conversation between Conein and the conspirators in which the latter had asked whether the Americans could get a plane to fly Diem out of the country, although it was not clear how serious the plotters were about carrying through with such an operation. The previous afternoon, it may be recalled, Lodge had offered Diem the use of a jet aircraft that was ready for immediate use, yet when Conein relayed the rebels' question to the embassy officer who answered the phone, the officer replied that obtaining a suitable plane would take twenty-four hours. The embassy officer explained that Diem would have to be flown to a country that had already offered him asylum, with no intermediate stops in closer locations where Diem might disembark and form a government-in-exile, and such countries could only be reached by a long-range aircraft that would have to be flown in from Guam.[112] And yet Lodge could have flown Diem to Clark Air Force Base in the Philippines, which was sovereign U.S. territory and presumably was the place Lodge had in mind when he had offered to transport Diem to the Philippines the previous day. The most likely explanation for the embassy's about-face is that when Lodge had offered the jet the day before, he had done it to induce Diem to give up at a time when the outcome of the insurrection was very much in doubt. Now that the coup clearly had succeeded, Lodge no longer needed to offer such an incentive to Diem. Lodge's primary concern at this point was ensuring the continued success of the coup leaders, something that Diem and Nhu could jeopardize if they agitated against the new government from a foreign country. Lodge, in fact, later expressed relief that the Ngo brothers did not get away. "What would we have done with them if they had lived?" Lodge said to Halberstam. "Every Colonel Blimp in the world would have made use of them."[113] Rebel efforts to send Diem out of the country ended with Conein's phone call to the embassy.

Diem, discouraged by his conversation with Lodge, called the generals. General Don got on the phone. He and Diem came to an agreement that the generals would give Diem and Nhu safe passage to the airport, and then the brothers would depart the country by plane. The generals readied an armored personnel carrier and two jeeps for the task of retrieving Diem and Nhu from the church. After consulting with only a few of his colleagues, General Minh took it upon himself to determine the ultimate fate of Diem and Nhu. At 7:30 A.M., as the task force was about to speed off, Minh gave them a prearranged hand signal that meant they should kill the Ngo brothers.

When the three vehicles arrived at the church, they found a large crowd gathered around the building. Diem and Nhu were taken aboard the armored personnel carrier, and the convoy drove towards Saigon until it reached a railroad crossing, where the carrier driver pulled over. Two soldiers, one armed with a Thompson submachine gun and the other with a Colt .45 pistol, fired numerous rounds into Diem and Nhu from behind. Then the soldiers pulled out knives and punctured the flesh of the deceased men over and over again. The generals proceeded to notify the Americans that the Ngo brothers had committed "accidental suicide."

Minh and the other rebel leaders who favored these killings had several reasons for wanting Diem and Nhu dead, which were similar to Lodge's. Perhaps the most important was that offered by Tran Van Huong, a future prime minister who, having spent several months in prison for opposing the Diem government, was no great friend of Diem. "The top generals who decided to murder President Diem and his brother were scared to death," Huong explained to a British diplomat. "The generals knew very well that having no talent, nor moral virtues, and no popular support whatsoever, they could not prevent a spectacular comeback of the President and Mr. Nhu if they were alive."[114] General Minh gave this rationale for destroying Diem: "Diem could not be allowed to live, because he was too much respected among simple, gullible people in the countryside, especially the Catholics and the refugees." As for the President's brother, Minh said, "We had to kill Nhu because he was so widely feared – and he had created organizations that were arms of his personal power."[115]

While South Vietnam's President was ousted and killed by certain of his countrymen, ultimate responsibility for his fate belonged to Henry Cabot Lodge, to the President who appointed and refused to fire Lodge, and to the individuals who were giving Lodge information and advice on the political situation – a few State Department officials in Saigon and Washington and a handful of resident journalists. Lodge had overridden a much larger and better informed group of Americans who had opposed a coup, including most of Kennedy's top advisers, the top CIA and military officials in Vietnam, and veteran American journalists, and he had disregarded orders against encouraging a coup from President Kennedy, who himself was torn by serious doubts about removing Diem. Hiding his actions from Washington, Lodge pushed South Vietnamese generals into launching a coup that they had not wanted to undertake in the first place and were hesitant to undertake until the very end. He did it to remove the South Vietnamese President for rejecting culturally ignorant political advice from the Americans and for implementing internal security policies that these very generals had eagerly helped create and implement. Although Kennedy eventually discovered his ambassador's conniving, Lodge's potential role in the 1964 election dissuaded the President from firing him and led the President instead to try, in vain, to steer Lodge and the plotters away from a coup.

When the coup came, the South Vietnamese armed forces were not nearly so united in opposition to Diem as would often be portrayed. By arresting or killing many key leaders, blocking roads and waterways, cutting communication wires, and sending elements of the Special Forces out of Saigon, the conspirators kept a large number of powerful loyalist units from assisting Diem. Even so,

Diem probably could have overrun the rebel command post with loyalist forces had he given the order. At the very end, Lodge still had the power to save Diem from death, but he refused to exercise that power. At the time of Diem's demise, despite the political turmoil of September and October, the South Vietnamese armed forces and the strategic hamlet program were still thriving, building on the great gains that had been registered since early 1962. Events were soon to prove, however, that the proper functioning of the counterinsurgency machinery depended heavily on the skills of the chief mechanics, skills that were most difficult to find.

CHAPTER 12

The Return of the Twelve Warlords

NOVEMBER 3–DECEMBER 1963

TO THE OBSERVER WHO LEARNED ABOUT THE COUP BY READING THE foreign press, nothing suggested that one of the worst debacles in the history of American foreign relations had just transpired, or that the war against the Viet Cong would soon unravel. Praise for the plotters surged forth from journalists in Saigon and Washington. The editorial page of the *New York Times*, enlisting many of David Halberstam's arguments, pronounced, "The coup in Saigon was inevitable, and, given the stubborn refusal of President Diem to institute political reforms that had long been urged upon him, it was by this time highly desirable."[1] The *Washington Post* published an editorial entitled "HOPE IN SOUTH VIET-NAM" immediately after the coup. "It long has seemed almost impossible to continue with the Diem government any effective resistance to the Communist conquest of this part of Southeast Asia," the *Post* asserted. "Nothing was more certain than the ultimate collapse of such a monument to vanity and cupidity."[2] The foreign media gave wide coverage to anti-Diem demonstrations in the streets of Saigon, to the burning of the offices of the state-run *Times of Vietnam*, and to the toppling of a statue of the famed Trung sisters that bore resemblance to Madame Nhu. American onlookers unfamiliar with Asia were inclined to view these events as proof that "the people" despised the Diem regime, particularly since the media did not report that the rebels had staged many, if not all, of these demonstrations.[3] In the bars of Saigon, now free of Madame Nhu's social purification law, American reporters danced gleefully with young South Vietnamese women. Unmentioned in the American press were the anguish and weeping of many Vietnamese military personnel over the death of President Diem and the complete absence of joy and celebration out in the provinces, where the fighting was actually taking place.[4]

Unsurprisingly, Ambassador Lodge was relieved and elated that the coup had succeeded. A couple of days after the event, he informed Washington, "We should not overlook what the coup can mean in the way of shortening the war and enabling Americans to come home."[5] Equal jubilation could be found among Lodge's allies in the State Department. John Kenneth Galbraith wrote to Harriman right after Diem's death: "Dear Averell, The South Viet Nam coup is another great feather in your cap. Do get me a list of all the people who told us there was no alternative to Diem."[6]

In the White House, however, the death of Diem occasioned only sorrow. Having admired Diem, having tried to halt the rush of events without paying the political cost of throttling his rival Lodge, Kennedy watched in horror as Lodge engineered Diem's removal and – even more galling – allowed the generals to put Diem to death. When Kennedy learned of the killing of Diem and Nhu, Maxwell Taylor recalled, the President "leaped to his feet and rushed from the room with a look of shock and dismay on his face which I had never seen before."[7] Michael Forrestal described Kennedy's reaction to the assassinations thus: "It shook him personally . . . bothered him as a moral and religious matter. It shook his confidence, I think, in the kind of advice he was getting about South Vietnam."[8] When a friend tried to console Kennedy by saying that Diem and Nhu had been tyrants, Kennedy snapped back, "No. They were in a difficult position. They did the best they could for their country."[9]

The White House ordered Ambassador Lodge to do his utmost to protect Diem's brother Ngo Dinh Can, who had turned himself in to the Americans. The man best suited for leading the country after Diem and Nhu, Can was the most likely rallying point for Diem supporters and others who opposed the new regime. The generals who had led the coup asked Lodge for custody of Can, promising that they would guarantee Can's safety and treat him in accordance with the law. Lodge, who himself must have feared the possibility of Can returning to power, handed him over to the rebels. In light of the generals' assurances of good treatment, Lodge remarked, "It seems to me that our reason for giving him asylum therefore no longer exists. I also consider that we would be subject to justified criticism if we attempted to obstruct the course of justice here, particularly as Can is undoubtedly a reprehensible figure who deserves all the loathing which he now receives."[10]

On November 5, the generals announced the composition of the new government. Occupying the most powerful position was General Minh, who received the titles of President and Chief of the Military Committee. Minh headed a committee of generals, and beneath these generals – not above them, as had been promised – was a civilian cabinet led by Nguyen Ngoc Tho, formerly the vice president and now the prime minister. The members of Tho's cabinet included no public political figures and few individuals with any political experience, almost assuredly because the generals assumed that such persons would be too difficult to control and might attempt to put themselves in charge. General Don became the Minister of Defense, and General Dinh the Minister of Security. All of the generals who played central roles in the coup were appointed to key positions of power, calling into question Lodge's claim on October 30 that the plotters "want nothing for themselves."

The new regime promptly freed those student and Buddhist leaders who were still in prison. Upon the advice of their American advocates, the generals promised to implement many of the Western political reforms long championed by the Americans, including freedom of the press, toleration of non-Communist political opposition, and meritocracy in government appointments. The junta vowed to make more public speeches and appearances in order to bolster popular support. Military operations would be intensified and the strategic hamlets would be strengthened by implementing the modifications that the Americans advocated, such as a slower pace of expansion and reduced reliance on forced labor.

On November 22, at 12:30 P.M. central standard time, President Kennedy was shot on his way to the Dallas Trade Mart. Rushed to Parkland Hospital, he was pronounced dead at 1:00 P.M. An hour and a half later, aboard Air Force One, Vice-President Johnson was sworn in. The implications of Kennedy's assassination for the Vietnam War have been debated ever since. Several of Kennedy's admirers would later allege that Kennedy had said, near the end of his life, that he viewed Vietnam as a futile endeavor and intended to withdraw from Vietnam after the 1964 election. That such a plan implied a willingness to squander lives and money for reelection purposes seems not to have occurred to these individuals. A considerable sum of evidence, however, supports the opposite conclusion, that Kennedy viewed Vietnam as crucial to American interests and had no plans for withdrawing so long as U.S. assistance was needed. It is possible that Kennedy told certain people of a desire to withdraw, but if so he was merely telling them what they wanted to hear. Those individuals were not the closest people to the President; Kennedy never mentioned disengagement plans to Taylor, Rusk, or McGeorge Bundy, nor to his closest confidante, Robert Kennedy. Time and again, President Kennedy voiced a determination to prevent South Vietnam from falling as Laos had fallen. In 1964, Robert Kennedy asserted unequivocally that President Kennedy "felt that he had a strong, overwhelming reason for being in Vietnam and that we should win the war in Vietnam." When asked what the overwhelming reason was, he responded, "The loss of Southeast Asia if you lost Vietnam. I think everybody was quite clear that the rest of Southeast Asia would fall. It would just have profound effects on our position throughout the world and our position in a rather vital part of the world. It would affect what happened in India, of course, which in turn has an effect on the Middle East. It would have, everybody felt, a very adverse effect. It would have an effect on Indonesia, with a hundred million people." When his interviewer inquired whether there was ever "any consideration given to pulling out," he flatly replied, "No."[11]

During the last weeks of his life, in public and in private, Kennedy repeatedly vowed to persist in the fight against the Vietnamese Communists, with such vehemence that he would have suffered great embarrassment were he

to abandon South Vietnam later. In the nationally televised interview with
Cronkite on September 2, for example, Kennedy said, "I don't agree with those
who say we should withdraw. That would be a great mistake."[12] Kennedy also
remained firmly opposed to the neutralization of South Vietnam, the only
means by which he could have withdrawn from South Vietnam. It would not
work, he had indicated to top administration officials, because it was not working in Laos.[13] From the first month of his administration onwards, Kennedy was
engaged in building up the U.S. advisory presence and aid to South Vietnam.
Near the end of 1961, he opened wide his nation's wallet to give South Vietnam
far more advisers, money, and military hardware than ever before, knowing
full well that a commitment this large would make a subsequent withdrawal
much more damaging to American prestige. He ordered the Defense Department and Maxwell Taylor to examine the use of U.S. forces in Vietnam and
expressed a willingness to send U.S. combat troops there as "a last resort."[14]
Had Kennedy intended to get out of Vietnam in 1963, he could have used the
negative publicity surrounding the Buddhist crackdowns and Madame Nhu's
anti-American outbursts as pretexts for backing out. Or he could have refused
to continue funding South Vietnam after the November 1 coup, something he
never seriously considered.[15]

After becoming the thirty-sixth President of the United States, Lyndon Baines
Johnson resolved to continue America's commitment to South Vietnam. He
had long approved of Kennedy's policy of supporting South Vietnam and,
having just inherited the Presidency from a widely admired martyr, Johnson
in any case had no choice but to maintain this policy if he wished to avoid
accusations of betrayal from Robert Kennedy and other Democrats, as well
as from Republicans. Johnson kept most of Kennedy's top officials, for while
he viewed many of them as too Eastern, too Ivy League, and too snobbish, he
was impressed by their talents and their skill in dealing with the media and
the intellectuals of the eastern establishment. Getting rid of them, moreover,
could have pushed them deep into the camp of Robert F. Kennedy, a group that
Johnson quickly came to view as a threat to his power.

Johnson, though, was going to make some changes to America's approach to
Vietnam. During a visit to Washington in late November, Ambassador Lodge
listened to the new President lay out some strong reservations about America's
involvement. "A great many people throughout the country question our course
of action in supporting the overthrow of the Diem regime," Johnson said.
"Strong voices in the Congress feel we should get out of Vietnam. I am not at
all sure we took the right course in upsetting the Diem regime, but this was
a decision that I did not have to make as it was a *fait accompli*. Now that it is
done, we have to see that our objectives are accomplished." Johnson bluntly
informed Lodge that attempts to transplant American political methods to
Vietnam were no longer welcome. Americans did not need to remake every

Asian in their own image, nor did they need to press the Vietnamese so hard for social reforms.[16]

The ousting of Diem and its miserable consequences had appalled Johnson to a greater degree than he revealed to Lodge during this conversation, and would bother him more over time as South Vietnam continued to slide.[17] Lodge's instigation of the coup and his refusal to work with others so irritated Johnson that he wanted to remove Lodge from Saigon, but the new President did not withdraw Lodge for the same reason as Kennedy: the fear that Lodge would use the dismissal as a weapon against the Democratic President during the Presidential race. Others, however, did not enjoy the same protections as Ambassador Lodge. Shortly after taking office, Johnson fired Hilsman for his role in precipitating Diem's overthrow. Administration discussions and decisions on Vietnam would no longer involve Harriman, who himself confessed during an interview several months later, "As you look back on it, Diem was better than the chaotic condition which followed him."[18]

Unfortunately for Johnson, and for many others, changes that would have done much to fortify the South Vietnamese government a few months earlier could not stop the decay of the government that Lodge, Hilsman, and Harriman had set in motion. Diem had served as the immune system of South Vietnam, keeping factionalism at bay as antibodies ward off infection. When the Diem government ceased functioning, nothing was left to prevent South Vietnam from contracting debilitating diseases. Just as Vietnam had descended into the chaotic Period of the Twelve Warlords after the assassination of King Xuong Van in 963, so did South Vietnam splinter after Diem's assassination, exactly one thousand years later. On November 4, the CIA issued a report from a source close to General Tran Van Minh indicating that "the generals are quarreling among themselves" and that if the differences were not resolved in the next day, some units would stage another coup.[19] One major point of contention was the execution of Diem. Conein observed that the slaying had undermined the cohesion of the successor government because most of the leading coup participants had not desired Diem's death and consequently "many of those conspirators who joined the coup d'état now feel a tendency to disassociate themselves from the coup."[20] Among the most upset was General Khanh, whose only stipulation for going along with the plotters had been that Diem would not be killed. Other matters of dispute amongst the generals included the prevalence of looting and the rapid promotion of certain individuals after the takeover. This crisis would subsequently be defused, but the resentments lingered, soon to resurface.

To their chagrin, Ambassador Lodge and other American officials found that the new South Vietnamese government, despite its amenable rhetoric, did not go very far in adopting American political practices. The generals' initial experiments in political liberalization led to a reduction in the new government's prestige and disruption of the war effort, prompting the swift abandonment of such measures. President Minh and Prime Minister Tho had not been in power long before they drew words of contempt from quarrelsome factions of the liberalized Vietnamese press, and therefore the new regime took action to stifle its media critics. On November 30, a CIA officer reported that the Minister of Information had issued the South Vietnamese press a long list of topics that they were not permitted to cover.[21] A few weeks later, Prime Minister Tho berated a group of one hundred journalists in his palace office for inaccuracy, irresponsibility, and disloyalty. Shouting and banging his fist on his desk, he declared that the journalists were lying when they claimed that his civilian government was merely a front for Minh's military junta. One of his press accusers was a Communist, the prime minister insisted, and another was an opium smoker. If the press did not shape up, the government would "take steps to meet the situation." The next day, Tho's Ministry of Information shut down three newspapers for disloyalty to the government.[22]

The honeymoon with the international press also had a very short lifespan. Although most of the American correspondents had favored the coup, and some had lavished praise on the Minh government, a number of them did not refrain from reporting on certain aspects of the new regime that the regime did not want people to see. Two of the most significant articles appeared in mid-December, one in *Time* and the other in *Newsweek*. The *Time* piece stated that President Minh and his committee of generals were so ineffectual that South Vietnam had "a power vacuum at the top."[23] *Newsweek*, which had long been a proponent of replacing Diem, took note of the new government's crackdowns on the Vietnamese press and commented that the new government "is all too plainly divided and indecisive."[24] A few days after these articles appeared, a group of senior South Vietnamese generals said, in a meeting with McNamara, McCone, and Lodge, that the United States "could do them a big favor if they could dissuade *Time* and *Newsweek* from publishing untrue articles about division among the generals." Tho explained that such articles caused them extraordinary trouble because American press articles were translated into Vietnamese and given wide circulation in the Vietnamese press. It was at this meeting that one of the coup leaders said that he had equated the opinions of the *New York Times* with those of the U.S. government during the Buddhist crisis. Ambassador Lodge said he was surprised to learn that English-language publications had such power, something he indeed would have benefited from knowing months before.

At this same meeting, the Americans advised the generals to deliver rousing speeches to the people, just as Lyndon Johnson had done after the death of President Kennedy. It was the same advice that the Americans had given Diem for years, with little to show for it. Lodge recorded the response: "The generals were quick to point out that things were different in Vietnam from what they are in a democracy and stressed the fact that Vietnamese people are 'extremely difficult.' If many speeches were made, they would be considered to be dictators; whereas if they accomplished things and solved problems province-by-province and did not talk, they would come to be appreciated for their works."[25] They sounded just like Diem.

The Buddhist problem, the root cause of Diem's downfall, did not disappear. Although the generals had released all jailed Buddhists following the coup, three Buddhist suicides occurred during the regime's first month in office, and in the four months succeeding Diem's death, more Buddhists would kill themselves with fire than during all the years of Diem's rule combined. As *Time* noted, though, these deaths did not receive the intense publicity that the Western press had accorded the Buddhist suicides in the Diem period.[26] Such occurrences blatantly contradicted the prediction of the American resident correspondents that a new, less heavyhanded government would solve the Buddhist problem.

Arrests of suspected oppositionists, particularly those who had served the Diem regime loyally, were commonplace from the regime's inception. Preferring to have loyal friends in positions of power, the junta arrested many government employees who had served in Diem's Can Lao party or otherwise shown strong support for Diem, and it dismissed many others. The junta replaced nearly all of the district and provincial chiefs – the men charged with running the strategic hamlet program, the various militias, the police, and the economic and political programs in the villages – and dissolved the vibrant organizations most responsible for making the strategic hamlet program a success – the Republican Youth, Ngo Dinh Can's Popular Forces, and the strategic hamlet coordinating committee. Many of the ousted district and provincial chiefs were strong executives and diehard anti-Communists whom Diem had cultivated for many years,[27] while their replacements tended to be individuals of modest experience and questionable ability. During November and December, the generals disarmed large numbers of strategic hamlet militia units because of doubts about their loyalty to the new regime, and they gutted the leadership of the Civil Guard and the Self-Defense Corps.[28] The military leaders, moreover, fought more against one another than against the Viet Cong; within a few weeks of the coup, nine of the twenty-two top military commanders had been replaced.[29] Maxwell Taylor had predicted such an outcome, but had not been heeded, partly because the generals had promised to avoid large-scale purges and eliminate politics from the appointment process. A report filed by a State Department official at the end of December concluded that the imprisonment of Diem supporters had reached epidemic proportions. "This raking over the coals of the past has become a national pastime," the report observed, "and it has helped to freeze most of the machinery of government."[30]

After the coup, the Viet Cong launched a new wave of attacks in the countryside, intended to test the new government and capitalize on the movement of government troops from the countryside to Saigon during the coup. The new government quickly demonstrated that it lacked its predecessor's ability to wage war. In a country where all activity required instruction and exhortation from the top, Big Minh and his cohorts provided neither. "We soon began to notice an aimless drift developing on the Vietnamese side in Saigon, and a growing erosion of popular confidence," recalled Albert Fraleigh, a senior pacification adviser. "There seemed to be no new initiatives or programs, and no one seemed to be leading."[31] Lodge himself conceded in December, "I am disconcerted by an apparent lack of drive in conducting the war. The members of the junta give me splendid clear-cut answers and say all of the right things, yet nothing much seems to happen."[32] The new provincial chiefs, inexperienced and bereft of guidance from above, did little to halt the Viet Cong, and their inactivity caused inertia to take hold at the district, village, and hamlet levels.[33] Deprived of good leadership and support from mobile reaction forces, the hamlet militiamen in a multitude of areas turned in their weapons and stopped fighting. Aggressive South Vietnamese army patrols, which in the past had done much to weaken the Viet Cong and keep them from massing, came to a halt. When the Communists realized that they now could move through the countryside and launch attacks without incurring substantial casualties, they intensified their rampage, devouring government outposts and strategic hamlets as cats gobble up beached fish. In many villages, the government lost all capacity for reconstituting its influence.

On December 6, in a private conversation with Ambassador Lodge, the Australian counterinsurgency expert Ted Serong asserted that the new government's leadership was so weak that the patient was quickly nearing death, and could only be saved through radical emergency surgery. Said Serong, "In its five weeks of existence, the GVN has shown itself incapable – the job is far too big for these little men. They are still groping blindly around the edges of it. Meanwhile the war and the nation are disintegrating." Unless the United States assumed direct control of the South Vietnamese government, Serong declared, "this war will be over in 1964 – via Geneva."[34] Lodge, who by this time recognized that South Vietnam was in a very dire predicament, knew that Serong's advice had considerable merit, but he was not prepared to resort to such drastic measures for an illness that he himself had caused.

In contrast to the upbeat stories about Saigon's war effort that Halberstam, Sheehan, and others wrote after the coup, the American government that the reporters had earlier derided as incurably optimistic could be heard making quite pessimistic observations. The Department of Defense warned at the beginning of December that government weapon losses had shot up since the coup, and that there was not a corresponding increase in Viet Cong weapon losses.[35] A short time later, General Krulak reported that the government's operations had plummeted after the coup and that the government's position in the Mekong Delta was far worse than it had been in October.[36] The CIA, at this same time, noted that the Viet Cong had made dramatic gains in some parts of the country since the coup, with the strategic hamlet program suffering much of the damage.[37] On December 21, upon returning from a visit to Vietnam, Secretary of Defense Robert McNamara reported, "The situation is very disturbing. Current trends, unless reversed in the next two to three months, will lead to neutralization at best and more likely to a Communist-controlled state. The new government is the greatest source of concern. It is indecisive and drifting."[38] CIA Director John McCone, who went on the same trip, stated, "There is no organized government in South Vietnam at this time."[39]

In their trip reports, McNamara and McCone commented that during the Diem era some Americans had made use of South Vietnamese government statistics on the war that exaggerated the government's successes. Supporters of the coup would later cite these remarks as evidence that the strategic hamlet program and other elements of the South Vietnamese war effort were crumbling during Diem's last months.[40] This contention was erroneous. As mentioned earlier, top U.S. government officials had long distrusted South Vietnamese statistics and had based their views of the war on what they had learned from American advisers in the field and other reliable sources. Up until the time of Diem's death, they had believed, correctly, that the war in general was proceeding well, and after the coup they perceived, with equal accuracy, a spectacular decline in performance.

Coup proponents were also to misuse a statement in McCone's report that statistical indicators of South Vietnamese performance in the war had begun a downward turn in July. They argued that these statistical trends showed that the Viet Cong had held the upper hand in the war from July onward, but in truth these statistical trends resulted from the increase in Viet Cong attacks on fledgling strategic hamlets in a few delta provinces, which, it has been seen, in no way demonstrated that the war had begun to turn against the government. These provinces had little strategic value, and Diem had been faring well in the rest of the country. At the time of the December report, McCone himself and the rest of the CIA knew that until the coup the problems had been confined to a few provinces, and that the sharp downturn did not begin until November.[41] In February 1964, moreover, after all of the claims of statistical error had been analyzed, an independent CIA team of experts pinpointed November 1, 1963 as the date at which the strategic hamlet program and the militia entered into a steep decline.[42]

Communist sources were to confirm that the government had held the upper hand until the coup, and quickly lost it after the coup. In April 1964, reporting on the general situation, their southern command would state that the Viet Cong had struggled during 1962 and the first ten months of 1963, but after November 1 they began to re-establish themselves in areas where they had been weakened.[43] A Communist assessment prepared in March 1965, by which time the Saigon government stood very close to total defeat, was to describe the government's collapse in the sixteen months since Diem's killing in the following manner:

> The balance of forces between the South Vietnamese revolution and the enemy has changed very rapidly in our favor.... The bulk of the enemy's armed forces and paramilitary forces at the village and hamlet level have disintegrated, and what is left continues to disintegrate.... Eighty percent of the strategic hamlets, which are viewed by the Americans as the 'backbone of the special war,' have been destroyed, and most of the people and land in the rural countryside are in our liberated zones.[44]

Consonant with U.S. sources, Communist accounts indicate that the Viet Cong took longer to capitalize on the coup in some areas than in others. In the crucial lowlands of Communist Military Region 5, according to Hanoi's official history of the region, the destruction of strategic hamlets built under Diem did not begin until the middle of 1964, for the Communist forces needed the intervening period to recover from the losses sustained during Diem's final years. Between the middle of 1964 and the middle of 1965, the history stated, the Communists destroyed 2,100 of the 2,800 strategic hamlets that had been built in the region before the coup of November 1963.[45] A similar situation prevailed in Communist Military Region 6. The official Party history of that region stated that between Diem's assassination and the middle of 1964, Communist forces accomplished little in the way of destroying strategic hamlets and retaking control of the population. The reason, again, was Communist weakness, not governmental strength; the history noted that the Minh government's rapid disbandment of Diemist organizations and prosecution of Diemist officials had quickly caused the collapse of the government's ruling apparatus in the villages, while the major advances did not begin until mid-1964. From that point until mid-1965, the number of civilians under Communist control in Military Region 6 jumped from 25,000 to 203,345.[46]

In the central highlands, the strategic hamlet program sustained very little damage prior to November 1963. It came under attack in the months immediately following the coup, suffering substantial injury well before the programs in Communist Military Regions 5 and 6. The Communist history of the central highlands front observed that the ousting of Diem and the resultant disorganization of the South Vietnamese militia forces enabled the Viet Cong to cause the strategic hamlet program serious harm for the first time; within a few months, they destroyed forty percent of the region's strategic hamlets. The strategic hamlet program in the highlands continued to suffer losses throughout 1964 and the first half of 1965. Many of the most geographically important hamlets in the highlands did not fall under Communist domination until the Communists' summer offensive of 1965.[47]

The southern command's April 1964 report acknowledged that before Diem's demise, the campaign against the strategic hamlets had attained significant momentum only in the Mekong Delta, and that even there, the Viet Cong's achievements had been rather modest up until November 1963, at which point they began to grow rapidly.[48] Even in Long An and Dinh Tuong, the two provinces where the Viet Cong had inflicted substantial pain on the strategic hamlets prior to the coup, the strategic hamlet program suffered much greater damage after the coup than before. The official Communist history of Long An province stated that September 1963 was the "period when the province faced its greatest difficulties. Enemy strategic hamlets and military outposts practically covered the entire rural area of the province. Most of the civilians had been moved into the hamlets." The Viet Cong's mobile company in the province had been so weakened in recent battles with the enemy that neither it nor the district and village forces could destroy any strategic hamlets completely. Whenever Viet Cong forces injured a strategic hamlet, the history asserted, the government came back the next day to repair the damage.[49] Of the 273 strategic hamlets established in the province under Diem, the history recounted, only 20 had been put out of order before the coup. In the six months after the coup, "virtually all the strategic hamlets throughout Long An province were destroyed."[50] In Dinh Tuong, the other province where the Viet Cong had made the most headway against the strategic hamlets before November 1963, the bulk of the destruction likewise took place after Diem's assassination. The Communists did not publish statistics concerning the pre-coup period in Dinh Tuong, but they did state that soon after the coup, they destroyed 33 government posts and over 100 of the province's 184 strategic hamlets. Concerning the post-coup period, one Communist veteran from Dinh Tuong recalled, "At no other time were members of the Front so enthusiastic."[51]

The last point worth mentioning in connection with the claims of a major decline preceding the November coup is that almost all of the supporting evidence originated with Diem's successors, who, even if they had always respected Diem and had turned against him primarily to appease the Americans, had a desperate need after the putsch to save face with the Americans and with their own people. Like Halberstam and Hilsman and the other American proponents of the coup, South Vietnam's new rulers inaccurately claimed that the abysmal situation at the end of 1963 differed little from the situation preceding November so as to show that the coup they had instigated had created no new problems. An American assessment of the strategic hamlet program at the beginning of 1964 noted that because of "political or personal considerations," the Minh government had replaced the original statistics on the pre-coup period with new, less positive statistics in order to support the "denigration of the old regime" and establish "a favorable data base for the new incumbent."[52] The deceitful misrepresentation of the pre-coup situation by coup supporters, American and Vietnamese, would color analysis of the Diem regime for many years to come.[53]

Because of Diem's accomplishments in 1962 and 1963, the Viet Cong lacked
the ability to defeat the government at the time of Diem's death, and for a
considerable period thereafter. Had Diem lived, the Viet Cong could have
kept the war going as long as they continued to receive new manpower from
North Vietnam and maintained sanctuaries in Cambodia and Laos, but it is
highly doubtful that the war would have reached the point where the United
States needed to introduce several hundred thousand of its own troops to avert
defeat, as it would under Diem's successors. Quite possibly, indeed, South
Vietnam could have survived under Diem without the help of any U.S. ground
forces. Those who led South Vietnam from November 1963 to the time of the
American intervention prosecuted the war far less effectively than Diem had,
and this weak performance helped overcome Hanoi's great reluctance to send
the North Vietnamese Army into South Vietnam. If the North Vietnamese
Army had invaded the South at some later date while Diem still ruled, South
Vietnam might very well have withstood the onslaught with the help of U.S.
air power but without U.S. ground troops, as it would in 1972.

The Communists, unlike most of the Americans, were very quick to grasp
the profound significance of the November 1963 coup. Upon hearing of Diem's
assassination, Ho Chi Minh remarked, "I can scarcely believe that the Americans would be so stupid."[54] Demonstrating astonishing foresight, the North
Vietnamese Politburo predicted:

> The consequences of the 1 November coup d'état will be contrary to the cal-
> culations of the U.S. imperialists.... Diem was one of the strongest individuals
> resisting the people and Communism. Everything that could be done in an attempt
> to crush the revolution was carried out by Diem. Diem was one of the most com-
> petent lackeys of the U.S. imperialists.... Among the anti-Communists in South
> Vietnam or exiled in other countries, no one has sufficient political assets and
> abilities to cause the others to obey. Therefore, the lackey administration cannot
> be stabilized. The coup d'état on 1 November 1963 will not be the last.[55]

The pro-Communist Australian Wilfred Burchett, who spent time with Vietnamese Communist leaders shortly after the coup, told an American journalist
in late 1964, "We never believed the Americans would let Diem go, much less aid
and abet his departure. Diem was a national leader, and you will never be able
to replace him – never. You haven't had an effective government in Saigon since
and you won't have one." Burchett said that Vietnamese Communist leaders,
amazed by their good fortune, called the coup a "gift," and exclaimed that
"the Americans have done something that we haven't been able to do for nine
years and that was get rid of Diem."[56]

Hanoi soon adjusted its grand strategy to capitalize on the infighting, disor-
ganization, and listlessness resulting from the overthrow of Ngo Dinh Diem.
In December 1963, at its ninth conference, the Vietnamese Communist Party's
Central Committee began by observing that the leaders of the new South

Vietnamese government were squabbling amongst themselves, resulting in the weakening or destruction of South Vietnam's principal sources of power. Since Diem's demise, the committee noted, "the confusion among the puppet army and administration and the disintegration of Diem's oppressive agencies (such as the Labor and Personalist Party, the Republican Youth Group, the espionage networks, the reactionary Catholic factions, etc.) have created many favorable conditions for us to step up the destruction of strategic hamlets." So greatly had the Saigon government debilitated itself, the conference resolution explained, that the enemy had lost its capacity to fend off large-scale military attacks. The North Vietnamese wanted to take full advantage of these changes, but to do so they first would need to increase their military capabilities in the South dramatically. In December, following the post-coup spike, Viet Cong attacks subsided because the Viet Cong were not yet ready to sustain a high level of offensive activity for more than a few weeks.[57] The central committee, therefore, called for a huge expansion of Communist military forces in the South and an intensification of offensive military actions. The Party leaders predicted that they would need two to three years to build up sufficient strength and fight the final battles.[58]

Twice in Vietnam the Americans would forsake the successes that they had attained at a heavy cost in men and dollars. The first took place on November 1, 1963.

CHAPTER 13

Self-Imposed Restrictions

JANUARY–JULY 1964

LYNDON BAINES JOHNSON GREW UP IN THE HILL COUNTRY OF SOUTH Texas, at a time when it was one of the poorest regions in the United States. Later in his life, Johnson liked to assume the airs of a rough-and-tumble Texan, but like much else about the man, the appearance veered from the reality. Although he was always tall for his age, young Lyndon Johnson shied away from the fist-fighting that kept most boys in the hill country occupied. As a college student, he received an F in physical education, and when one of his underhanded deeds put a fellow student into a fighting mood, Johnson did not stand and trade punches, but instead hopped onto his bed, lay on his back, and kicked frantically with his long legs to keep the would-be adversary away.[1]

Elected to Congress in 1937 at the age of twenty-eight, Johnson took a leave of absence after Pearl Harbor and became an officer in the Navy. He quickly become impatient with having to take orders from superior officers; his closest adviser, Alvin J. Wirtz, tried unsuccessfully to get President Roosevelt to give Johnson an instant promotion to the rank of admiral. Johnson's sole encounter with the enemy came on June 9, 1942, during an inspection trip in the Pacific, when he rode as a passenger on a B-26 that was scheduled to bomb New Guinea. During the mission, one of the plane's engines failed, and just as it was turning back it came under attack from Japanese Zeros. Swerving and firing its guns at the Zeros, the bomber took a large number of hits from enemy machine guns and cannon, but the pilot managed to bring her home safely. Johnson headed back to the United States the next day. For the remainder of his life, Johnson would tell journalists and visitors that he had spent months braving enemy fire in numerous bombing missions against the Japanese, and that the 22nd Bomb Group had nicknamed him "Raider" Johnson. He would also wear a Silver Star that he had undeservedly received for his single passenger flight – the only medal given to anyone who had been on the aircraft that day.

Johnson won a Senate race in 1948 by eighty-seven votes, thanks only to the arrival of several hundred fraudulent votes six days after the election. In 1951, he became the Democratic whip, and two years later he became the Senate minority leader. Perfecting the art of influencing other Senators, he proved extremely adept at moving legislation forward. Johnson acquired a reputation as a firm Cold Warrior during his years in Congress, enthusiastically supporting the tough policies of the Truman and Eisenhower administrations. Johnson was one of the Congressional leaders who, during the Indochina crisis of 1954, had endorsed John Foster Dulles's plan for united action on the condition that other nations contribute substantial numbers of troops.[2] The collapse of that plan and the subsequent French failure at Dien Bien Phu led Johnson to declare, "American foreign policy has never in all its history suffered such a stunning reversal."[3] International affairs, however, had been of relatively little interest to Johnson during his Congressional years, with the result that he came into the Presidency with a rather limited understanding of this vast subject.

Under the Johnson administration, the most important deliberations on Vietnam took place in small groups or as a tête-à-tête, with participation restricted to a few of Johnson's most trusted lieutenants. This setup minimized unauthorized leakage of information to the press, something Johnson despised obsessively, especially when it concerned dissension within the government. Johnson was open to contrary views and often encouraged people to express them, but, for reasons of partisan politics and national morale, he did not want the public or the government's rank and file to know of internal objections to his policies. The three men who would most greatly influence the President's decisions on Vietnam in the first years of the war were McGeorge Bundy, Dean Rusk, and Robert McNamara. With Johnson less sure of himself in foreign affairs than Kennedy, Secretary of State Rusk more often took a firm position on issues instead of merely laying out the various alternatives as in the past. Rusk was now an opinionated waiter rather than a bus boy stocking the buffet. The adviser who played the largest role in helping Johnson on Vietnam, though, was McNamara, whose confident manner and quick mind captivated Johnson. Alexander Haig, one of McNamara's assistants at the time, recalled that in the early days of the Johnson Presidency, "Men who had been listening to testimony all their lives listened to McNamara's briefings with the rapt faces of religious converts. Standing behind McNamara as I placed the charts on the easel, I saw that Lyndon Johnson was one of them."[4] In a 1965 interview, Johnson said of McNamara: "He's like a jackhammer. He drills though granite rock till he's there.... No human can take what he takes. He drives too hard. He is too perfect."[5] To McNamara, Johnson assigned primary responsibility for managing the war in Vietnam. Neither Johnson nor McNamara paid much attention to the Joint Chiefs of Staff. This fact did not escape the Joint Chiefs, nor did the fact that the administration's leading civilians thought they were more adept at solving military problems than the men in uniform.[6]

Johnson's views on the geopolitical value of Vietnam were quite similar to those of his predecessor. Many historians were to contend, wrongly, that the Johnson administration deemed the defense of South Vietnam strategically important primarily because it would preserve the credibility of American security guarantees throughout the world.[7] Much of the confusion stemmed from a document written by Assistant Secretary of Defense for International Security Affairs John McNaughton in March 1965 and reproduced in the *Pentagon Papers*. In the document, McNaughton stated that U.S. aims in Vietnam were:

> 70% – To avoid a humiliating defeat (to our reputation as a guarantor).
> 20% – To keep SVN (and then adjacent) territory from Chinese hands.
> 10% – To permit the people of SVN to enjoy a better, freer way of life.[8]

McNaughton did not have access to the information needed to pass such judgment for, as an Assistant Secretary of Defense, he was not present at most of the top-level deliberations on Vietnam. He had significant access to only one member of the President's inner circle, McNamara, and McNamara himself later said that McNaughton did not know enough about policymakers' views to ascertain the relative importance of their motives.[9] William Bundy, the brother of McGeorge Bundy and the Assistant Secretary of State for Far Eastern Affairs beginning in February 1964, was to decry the importance ascribed to McNaughton's memorandum. "It isn't serious evidence," he remarked. The only thing that it proved, Bundy asserted, was that bureaucrats "could write a memorandum at the end of the day to themselves."[10]

It was true that protecting the global credibility of the United States did make the administration more inclined to stay in Vietnam. Johnson and his principal advisers had some concerns that America's security treaties and guarantees would lose their force around the world if Vietnam fell, thereby discouraging non-Communist nations from resisting Communism. Global credibility, however, was for them a much less important reason to protect Vietnam than the distribution of power within Southeast Asia.[11] Subscribing to the domino theory, they believed that the fall of South Vietnam would lead to Chinese domination of all Southeast Asia, whether by diplomacy, covert action, or war. Chinese control of Southeast Asia, in their view, would severely degrade America's power in the Pacific, even if the Sino-Soviet rift continued to widen.[12]

For the Johnson administration, as for previous administrations, the most important domino in Southeast Asia was Indonesia. "More is involved in Indonesia, with its 100 million people," said Rusk in January 1964, "than is at stake in Vietnam."[13] During the months leading up to Johnson's presidency, a precarious conflict between Indonesia and Malaysia had begun. In response to Malaya's suppression of a rebellion in Brunei, Sukarno had vowed to "crush" the new Malaysian federation and take some of its territory. He made political and economic moves to isolate Malaysia, and sent Indonesian infiltrators to clash with Malaysian forces. Britain, Australia, and other Commonwealth countries dispatched tens of thousands of troops in 1963 and 1964 to defend Malaysia, which had a far smaller population than Indonesia.[14] Indonesia's belligerency also alarmed other non-Communist countries nearby. In the summer of 1964, Philippine President Diosdado Macapagal told the Americans that Indonesia had to be prevented from sliding completely into the Communist camp, for if Indonesia were lost to Communism, then "we are lost – we are sunk." Macapagal was willing to go to war to prevent that outcome, and he promised, "If the U.S. and Indonesia got into a fight, the Philippines would fight with the U.S. against Indonesia."[15]

As 1964 moved along, Sukarno looked with increasing favor on China and strengthened his ties with the Indonesian Communist Party, which was closely aligned with Beijing and, with three million members, was the strongest party in Indonesia and the largest Communist party outside of the Communist bloc. Having moved steadily leftward himself, Sukarno now held political views very close to those of the Indonesian and Chinese Communist Parties. Sukarno was working to reduce the influence of anti-Communist officers within the Indonesian military, the only entity in the country with enough power to resist the Communist Party.[16] During 1964, Sukarno's relations with the United States fell apart as he intensified his attacks against Malaysia and the Americans vainly tried to stop him with the threat of aid cuts. "When any nation offers us aid with political strings attached, then I will tell them, 'Go to hell with your aid!'" Sukarno declared in March.[17] In the summer, with Indonesian military initiatives accelerating, Johnson granted requests from Malaysian Prime Minister Tunku Abdul Rahman for American military trainers and the sale of ships and aircraft.[18] A short time thereafter, Sukarno officially recognized North Vietnam, broke off diplomatic relations with the South Vietnamese government, and prayed in front of the Presidential Palace that Vietnam would be "reunited in freedom" by the Viet Cong.[19]

Lyndon Johnson's critics, contemporary and subsequent, would fault him for rejecting the concept of neutralizing Vietnam in 1964.[20] Johnson allegedly forfeited a chance to reach a peace settlement without harming American interests when, on several occasions, he dismissed Communist expressions of interest in neutralization involving a withdrawal of U.S. forces coupled with promises by Hanoi to refrain from further military action. Some of Johnson's critics, taking the North Vietnamese at their word, argued that North Vietnam would not have seized control of a neutralized South Vietnam, or at least not for several years. But the arguments against neutralization, most of which the Johnson administration advanced at the time, were far more compelling. The mere pursuit of negotiations by the Americans in 1964 most probably would have caused a sharp drop in the cohesion of the South Vietnamese government and society, suggesting as it would American abandonment, and might have caused the South Vietnamese to go directly to the North Vietnamese to end the war. Were a neutral government established in South Vietnam, its non-Communists members would either capitulate to the Communists as soon as the Americans disengaged, or else fall victim to Communist subversion. It would be obvious that non-Communist politicians could not survive without American protection – South Vietnam's non-Communist leaders were struggling and demoralized in fighting the North Vietnamese at this time even with massive aid from the world's most powerful country. North Vietnam's flagrant violation of the neutralization agreement on Laos, moreover, provided ample reason to believe that it would not remain faithful to a neutralization agreement on South Vietnam.[21]

Subsequent revelations from the Communist side were to confirm that the North Vietnamese never had any interest in creating a truly neutral South Vietnam. The "neutral" government envisioned by Hanoi was composed of members of the National Liberation Front and intellectuals who were ostensibly neutral but were actually working for the Communists.[22] The North Vietnamese were determined to prevent the Saigon government's present leaders from serving in a neutral coalition government, because, in Bui Tin's words, the Communist Party leadership "considered all these people to be irrecoverable; such persons could be overthrown or assassinated, but one could never shake hands with them."[23]

Neither was it possible, as some critics would maintain, that the Viet Cong would make neutralization work by turning against the North Vietnamese and protecting the neutral government from Northern interference. Rebellious Southern Communists could not have survived against the ruthless central leadership in Hanoi, particularly since many of the Viet Cong's leaders and soldiers were now Northerners who had infiltrated down the Ho Chi Minh Trail. In any case, the Southerners had no inclination to break with Hanoi – for the past few years, they had dutifully risked their lives for the very purpose of unifying Vietnam.

For Lyndon Johnson, the potential domestic consequences of losing Vietnam were much less worrisome than its international consequences. Johnson was not pulled into Vietnam by fear of the public's reaction to withdrawal, as has often been depicted,[24] but instead he was trying to pull the public along with him into Vietnam in order to prevent the dominoes from tumbling. The claim that Johnson decided to hold on in Vietnam to appease the American Right would not be made until after he left office, and it was advanced by Johnson himself and other Democrats in an effort to shift blame from Johnson to conservative America. The records from 1964 and 1965 show that President Johnson did not believe that abandoning Vietnam would generate widespread domestic opposition. Discussing the possibility of U.S. intervention in Vietnam in May with his old friend Senator Richard Russell, Johnson said, "I don't think the people of this country know much about Vietnam, and I think that they care a hell of a lot less."[25] Poll data supported this view.[26] Johnson attempted to obtain favorable press coverage of the war in order to increase public support for preserving Vietnam, as well as support for himself, though his efforts to steer the press generally led only to increased press hostility, as they had for Kennedy.[27] Johnson, moreover, recognized that fighting in Vietnam could cripple his domestic power just as easily as withdrawal could. He told Russell that the deployment of U.S. troops would lead to many American deaths, which in turn would undermine public support and spawn Republican claims that the President ought to act more forcefully than Johnson was willing to act.[28] As Johnson told Senator George Smathers, the Republicans would attack him whether he intervened or not.[29]

While domestic politics did not cause Johnson to defend South Vietnam, they did influence the President's thought process at other forks in the road. In the first half of 1964, Johnson tolerated many unsound actions by Ambassador Lodge, who by this time, according to polls, was the frontrunner for the Republican Presidential nomination. When Washington sent Saigon a highly regarded diplomat to manage the expansive activities of the embassy, which Lodge had been ineffectual at managing, Lodge denied this man the authority needed to accomplish his mission. When they sent a new man to head the public affairs section, Lodge forbade him from having any interaction with the press. Relations between Lodge and General Harkins remained so poor that Washington officials were saying that one of them had to go.[30] This suggestion never came to fruition because Johnson would not replace Lodge, and Taylor and the other Joint Chiefs, appalled by Lodge's previous behavior, blocked Harkins's removal. "He ain't worth a damn," Johnson said of Lodge in May. "He can't work with anybody. He won't let anybody else work." Questioned as to why he did not remove Lodge, Johnson replied, "He'd be home campaigning against us on this issue every day."[31] As a further precaution against giving Lodge election-year ammunition, Johnson resolved to approve whatever Lodge recommended, without regard to its merits, a policy that would last until Lodge gave up the ambassadorship in late June to help other liberal Republicans fight against the nomination of Barry Goldwater for the Presidency.[32]

To avoid losing votes prior to the November election, Johnson sought to prevent Vietnam from attracting great public attention, an objective he candidly divulged to subordinates on several occasions.[33] Johnson, therefore, shunned more forceful measures in Vietnam. At the same time, though, he had to prevent the sickly South Vietnamese government from perishing prior to November. Seeking to achieve the latter without resort to the former, he sent more American advisers and aid to Vietnam in as inconspicuous manner as possible. "We must not let any arbitrary limits on budget, or manpower, or procedures stand in our way," Johnson directed.[34] During May, Johnson convinced Congress to increase Vietnam appropriations by $125 million, and he sent another 1,500 military advisers.

* * *

AT THE BEGINNING OF 1964, SIXTY-TWO POLITICAL PARTIES VIED FOR power in Saigon. Avoiding any form of constructive action, they busied themselves with denouncing the government and each other. Their unbridled attacks caused the government to lose face, potentially fatal for a government as weak as Big Minh's. Diem's predictions about the harmful effects of political liberalism in an authoritarian-minded and factious South Vietnam were coming true. The *Saigon News* commented: "Are we to think that, to our political parties and our politicians, democracy means only the right to criticize and not the obligation of accepting responsibilities and incurring criticism? If that is so, then Nhu and Diem were right, because they held that Vietnam was not ripe for democracy."[35]

Hindered by weak leadership at the top and by ongoing purges, the South Vietnamese war effort remained in disarray at the beginning of 1964. Ambassador Lodge informed Australian adviser Francis Serong in January that the pacification effort was "at bottom."[36] Soon, the incompetence of the junta became unbearable to Americans and Vietnamese alike, most importantly the thirty-seven-year-old General Nguyen Khanh. In explaining later why he decided to take action, Khanh said: "After the November coup, there was much relaxation, wining and dining, and little serious prosecution of the war effort. The intelligence organization which I had helped President Diem build up over six years was completely destroyed and many of the hard-core Viet Cong whom we had collected so painstakingly over the years were released."[37] Khanh was also upset that the leading generals had murdered Diem, in violation of promises made to Khanh and others, and that they had neglected to give Khanh a top position in the post-coup government. In proposing his coup to the Americans, though, Khanh emphasized that he had a more immediate cause for concern. Some pro-French generals were themselves about to stage a coup, he told the senior U.S. adviser in I Corps, Colonel Jasper Wilson, and once in power they intended to neutralize South Vietnam. Khanh claimed that their putsch would have a high chance of success, unless he were to arrest the conspirators and seize control of the government himself. Whether such a plot existed and whether Khanh believed it existed remain uncertain. Khanh then asked Colonel Wilson whether General Harkins would mind if he mounted a pre-emptive coup.

When the question was relayed to Harkins, his response to Khanh was, "No, I think you are a very fine general." Asked later why he had not informed the Minh junta that Khanh was plotting against them, Harkins explained that the generals "weren't getting along anyway, so maybe it was a change for the better. I thought it was." Harkins believed that, in general, a single ruler could act more quickly and decisively than a committee, and that, in particular, Khanh was a better leader than any member of the disordered junta. News of Wilson's dealings with Khanh was also passed along to Lodge, and the ambassador likewise chose not to interfere with Khanh's plans.[38]

Gaining the cooperation of the key military commanders in the Saigon area, who shared his low opinion of the current government, Khanh launched his coup at 4:00 A.M. on January 30. General Khiem sent paratroopers, tanks, and armored cars to surround the homes of top military and civilian leaders and take them into custody. The arrests took place without incident, and the regime was entirely overthrown without any violence. After incarcerating Minh and his closest associates, Khanh made himself prime minister.

A natural leader, Khanh had risen faster than any other officer in the Vietnamese National Army during the Franco-Viet Minh War. In 1950, at the startling age of just twenty-three, he became the first commander of the Vietnamese National Army's elite airborne battalion. Enthusiastically supporting the Diem regime from its inception, Khanh became the first man to command the South Vietnamese Air Force, and by the time he was thirty he had reached the rank of general. In terms of providing national leadership, Khanh would prove to be more decisive and capable than the Minh junta. But Khanh also displayed some of the inattentiveness and administrative weakness that had plagued the preceding regime. Khanh, furthermore, suffered from a critical lack of political experience, which caused him to turn primarily to Ambassador Lodge for advice on political matters.[39]

Upon taking office, Khanh asked Lodge whom he should appoint to a new cabinet, to which Lodge responded, "One good rule of politics in any country is to include rather than to exclude, and to give all elements in the community a sense of participation." With Lodge's help, Khanh appointed officials from every significant religious, political, and regional group. This approach, however, failed to yield the positive results anticipated by Lodge. Many of the appointees lacked experience or skill, and, because of their diverse backgrounds, they did not work well together but instead took to squabbling and scrambling after their own group's interests. On Lodge's advice, Khanh made American-style public appearances. During February, *Time* reported approvingly, "From the way he buttonholed passers-by on Saigon sidewalks, the pint-sized Vietnamese officer in green fatigues could have been Nelson Rockefeller campaigning in the New Hampshire primary. He shook hands, introduced himself, asked, 'Have you any suggestions about how we can do a better job for Vietnam?'" In the same article, *Time* unwittingly provided evidence that activities of this type would bear no fruit in South Vietnam: "For all his efforts, Khanh has as yet made no great impression on the mass of the population."[40]

Like the leading figures in the Minh junta, Khanh had a rather limited appetite for liberalization. Harking back to the Diem era, he prohibited the people from dancing the twist. South Vietnam could begin to build the institutions of a democratic state, Khanh remarked, but "we cannot achieve full democracy for some time, perhaps for another generation or two."[41] Lodge had instigated Diem's removal because he had suppressed dissenters and because other leading Vietnamese did not like him, and he could have convicted Khanh on exactly these same charges, but he was starting to gain some understanding of Vietnamese politics and therefore did not hold such matters against

Khanh. When Khanh asked for Lodge's opinion on the possibility of a South Vietnamese declaration of war, which would involve austerity measures, the suspension of many civil rights, and "getting rid of the so-called politicians," Lodge replied that, "given the state of the country, winning the war must come first. After the war is won, there will be plenty of time to go ahead with democratic forms."[42] At a conference of American officials in early June, Lodge said that the only way to protect South Vietnamese pacification programs from the Viet Cong was to make "a police state out of South Vietnam similar to the Ho Chi Minh regime."[43]

Like Big Minh, Khanh had promised the Americans before his coup that he would not reshuffle the national leadership following the coup, and then broke the promise as soon as he came into office. Khanh promptly replaced numerous provincial and district chiefs, in some instances with able officials whom the Minh junta had fired for their loyalty to Diem. The re-installation of Diem's former officials precipitated outlandish charges from Tri Quang and other militant Buddhists that Khanh's government, which was predominantly Buddhist, was reverting to Diemist persecution of Buddhists. Khanh, fearful of the militant Buddhists, then switched over to sacking and incarcerating officials who had served Diem loyally.[44] To protect himself against the coup plotting that would be the constant scourge of his government, Khanh filled some key positions on the basis of loyalty rather than merit, and he did not delegate authority as generously as the Americans wanted.

Although Khanh had succumbed to the Buddhist pressure on the issue of appointments, he would have no greater critic during his first months in office than Tri Quang, who, in contrast to many other Buddhist leaders, relentlessly accused him of denying religious freedom to Buddhists. As in the case of Diem, concessions from Khanh only caused Tri Quang to demand more, but unlike Diem, Khanh continued to satisfy Tri Quang's never-ending stream of demands. Part of the explanation for Khanh's behavior lay in his belief that resisting the Buddhists would completely turn the Americans against him, a logical conclusion to be drawn from Diem's overthrow. The other part was that the politically naïve Khanh was intimidated by the demagogic skills of the militant Buddhists, especially Tri Quang.

In order to appease Tri Quang, Khanh had the Army remove all of its Catholic chaplains. Pressure from Tri Quang induced Khanh to give a life sentence of hard labor to Dang Sy, a Catholic officer who had been involved in the mysterious and bloody confrontation with Buddhist protesters on May 8, 1963. Unlike most prominent Buddhists, Tri Quang demanded that the government try Diem's brother Ngo Dinh Can and sentence him to death in order to thwart "Diemism." Lodge, who had turned Can over to the generals in November 1963 with the comment that "Can is undoubtedly a reprehensible figure who deserves all the loathing which he now receives," now beseeched Khanh not to execute him, protesting that the South Vietnamese government had "made no case at all" against Diem's brother.[45] By this time, Lodge also had begun to sour on Tri Quang and his incessant condemnations of the government, as had many other members of the diplomatic community and the press corps who had supported the militant Buddhists in 1963.[46] Following the advice of Tri Quang, not that of Lodge, Khanh ordered the execution of Diem's ailing brother. Khanh's men tied Ngo Dinh Can to a post and a firing squad ended his life in front of three hundred spectators.

During the first months of the year 1964, North Vietnam was also undergoing a leadership transition, but in a way that was smoother, slower, and far less damaging. Ho Chi Minh, his health deteriorating, was becoming less and less involved in governmental decisions. Responsibility for the country's detailed business no longer belonged to Ho at all but to Le Duan, and on large strategic issues Le Duan was becoming the dominant figure. No longer a devout follower of Ho Chi Minh – "I am better than Uncle Ho," he later explained to one associate[47] – Le Duan intended to take the country in a new direction, involving closer relations with China and adherence to Chinese Communist ideology, with correspondingly less regard for the Soviets. As the Sino-North Vietnamese alliance tightened at the beginning of 1964, Hanoi sharply rebuked the Soviets for signing the nuclear test ban treaty with the United States and for pursuing the policy of "peaceful coexistence," which the North Vietnamese derided as "ridiculous pacifism." Le Duan and other militants in Hanoi undertook a campaign to discredit so-called revisionists within the Vietnamese Communist Party, most notably Giap and Truong Chinh, who supported the Soviet position on peaceful coexistence and other major issues. Dozens of military officers suspected of harboring revisionist thoughts were arrested, hustled away in cars with dark windows, and thrown into detention centers. Ho Chi Minh lectured Giap, Truong Chinh, and several other top leaders in order to correct their thinking, and although Giap kept the title of minister of defense, the anti-revisionist General Nguyen Chi Thanh was put in charge of the war in the South.[48]

The triumph of the anti-revisionists resolved a dispute between revisionists and anti-revisionists over military strategy. Giap had opposed rapid intensification of the struggle, worried by the prospect of large-scale U.S. retaliation and alienation of the Soviets, who alone could provide the equipment and training that North Vietnam would need to defeat South Vietnamese forces equipped with American aircraft, armor, and artillery. Le Duan and Nguyen Chi Thanh, on the other hand, had wanted to fight large battles soon in order to annihilate the South Vietnamese Army and capture Saigon, contending that U.S. and Soviet weaponry were of secondary importance while "man and spirit are decisive factors."[49] Meeting in early 1964, the Central Military Party Committee and the Ministry of Defense officially ruled in favor of the anti-revisionist position of Le Duan and Nguyen Chi Thanh. To make ready for large battles, the Viet Cong main forces would be expanded through heightened recruitment in the South and more rapid infiltration of native Northern draftees – by early 1964, most infiltrators from the North were native Northerners, for the supply of Southerners who had gone north in 1954 had by this time dried up.[50] North Vietnam's decision makers did, however, pay some heed to Giap's warning that sharp intensification of the war would invite American reprisals, for they chose not to send complete North Vietnamese units to the South, opting instead to assign all of the infiltrating Northern soldiers to Viet Cong units, and they put limits on the pace of the Viet Cong's expansion. The enlargement of the main forces would be gradual and the climax would not be rushed.

Hanoi's new strategy had the effect of pushing the North Vietnamese still further from the Soviets and closer to the Chinese. When Le Duan went to Moscow in February, Khrushchev told him that Hanoi had to abandon its militant strategy to avoid undermining the world Communist movement and harming relations between North Vietnam and the Soviet Union. Hanoi's refusal to change course in subsequent months caused Moscow to scale back its aid to North Vietnam.[51] Mao, on the other hand, encouraged Hanoi to insert more troops into South Vietnam and Laos to fight a larger war. "Ineffective and indecisive skirmishes will not solve problems," Mao told North Vietnamese envoys. "Only large and decisive battles can solve problems." If the Viet Minh had not destroyed France's conventional forces in major combat ten years earlier, Mao noted, France would not have given in.[52] On the question of American retaliation, Chinese Premier Zhou Enlai asserted that the risks of American intervention were low, based on their reading of American public opinion. "Many people of American monopolistic capital are not in favor of the adventurist policy of Goldwater, because that might possibly bring about American failures," Zhou contended. "The American people in a broad extent also oppose this war because they are of the opinion that while no country in the world is invading their country, why should they launch a major war and a nuclear war?"[53] During the spring and early summer of 1964, Mao promised the North Vietnamese that if the United States invaded their country, China would send its soldiers to North Vietnam.[54]

As part of their new strategy, the North Vietnamese transformed the Ho Chi Minh Trail into a thoroughfare for trucks and other motorized vehicles. North Vietnamese laborers widened the main route to twenty feet, enlarged and strengthened the bridges, and set up refueling and repair stations. Once these improvements were completed, trucks could travel all the way from North Vietnam to the eastern Laotian town of Tchepone, from which point porters could carry the cargo into South Vietnam on mountain footpaths. The hauling power of the trucks would enable Hanoi to send four times as many tons of supplies to South Vietnam in 1964 as in 1963.[55] To solidify their hold over the Laotian infiltration routes, North Vietnamese and Pathet Lao forces made new advances into non-Communist territory at the beginning of 1964, culminating in the ejection of neutralist and rightist forces from the Na Kay Plateau.

These developments coincided with intelligence reports from CIA-supported Laotian ground forces and U-2 surveillance aircraft of large enemy troop concentrations, new supply bases, and new roads suitable for trucks in southeastern Laos. The Joint Chiefs and other hardliners in the United States consequently demanded stronger military measures in Laos. American Ambassador to Laos Leonard Unger, however, objected to such measures, arguing that continued U.S. adherence to the Geneva framework would put international pressure on the Communists and limit the Communists' options, although recent events gave little support to this contention. In addition, Unger said, Laotian Prime Minister Souvanna Phouma opposed such actions, as they would subject his country to a destructive East-West confrontation. "When buffaloes fight, it is the grass that gets hurt," was how a Laotian proverb put it.[56] The State Department came down on Unger's side, and therefore the United States did not move to counteract the Communist territorial gains. Nor did it undertake large intelligence gathering missions in Laos that the military recommended. Whereas the Joint Chiefs advocated South Vietnamese ground reconnaissance operations into Laos in at least battalion strength, with U.S. advisers accompanying the troops, Unger and the State Department convinced Johnson to limit the operations to 100 men and prohibit American participation, so as to avoid upsetting the Geneva agreement. The Joint Chiefs had predicted that reconnaissance operations on that scale would be a debacle, and they were. Then, in May, the Pathet Lao and North Vietnamese began a new offensive across the Plain of Jars, causing Souvanna to abandon his hopes for a reconciliation with the Pathet Lao and North Vietnamese, and to approve the use of American T-28 bombers in his country. The Johnson administration, however, sharply limited the air strikes based on the hope that Soviet intercession would wrest eastern Laos from the Communists, a most desperate hope in light of the Soviets' continuing assertions that they would do nothing of the kind.[57]

Another major type of Communist infiltration, by the sea, received considerably less attention from the Americans during this period. In 1964, the North Vietnamese Navy started moving materiel with steel-hulled ships that were capable of carrying 100 tons to the southern tip of South Vietnam in a week. Sending the same load over the Ho Chi Minh Trail, by comparison, would require the employment of an entire division as porters for up to one year.[58] Heavy weaponry and equipment, essential to Hanoi's plans for large battles of annihilation, could be moved far more easily by ship. At this time, moreover, the Ho Chi Minh Trail extended only to the northern border of Cambodia, so overland shipment to provinces further south required exceptional toil and risks. Once they were loaded to the brim with supplies, the steel ships traveled to secret docks on the South Vietnamese coast, or else to Cambodia, where the cargo would be moved into South Vietnam by inland waterway with the cooperation of the Cambodian government.[59] In June, Hanoi ordered the deployment of several Viet Cong regiments to South Vietnam's coastal regions to facilitate the delivery of supplies.[60]

South Vietnam's attempts to detect and stop the sea infiltrators were most feeble in the year of 1964. Diem's ouster had prompted numerous changes in the South Vietnamese naval command, most of them for the worse. In the opinion of the head U.S. naval adviser, the Diem coup had completely undone major improvements to the Navy made in the preceding two years. Diem's chief of naval operations, assassinated during the coup, was replaced by Captain Chung Tan Cang, described by the head U.S. adviser as "a very poor officer" who was "certainly not the kind of person you would want for a senior job in the Vietnamese Navy." So many commanders were replaced with less qualified men that half of all the Navy's commanding officers were deemed insufficiently experienced for their jobs. Because of the leadership deficiencies, the South Vietnamese Navy tended to stay in port rather than go out and interfere with the Viet Cong's activities. Interception of Communist shipping in 1964 was minimal.[61]

The North Vietnamese Navy was to deliver 3,600 tons of weapons to the Viet Cong during 1964, nearly three times the amount sent by sea in 1962 and 1963 combined.[62] More supplies were to transit the sea route in 1964 than had moved down the overland Ho Chi Minh Trail during the entire war to date, producing fundamental changes to the strategic situation in the South.[63] "These supplies had a tremendous impact," one Communist history noted, "especially with regards to the armament of our troops."[64] Many Viet Cong units were now outfitted with AK-47 assault rifles and other modern light weapons, and they had much more heavy weaponry than before, to include flamethrowers, 7.62mm machine guns, RPG-2 rocket launchers, 90mm bazookas, 57mm and 75mm recoilless rifles, and heavy mortars, almost all of them of recent Chinese, Soviet, or Eastern European manufacture.

Without the importation of such equipment, whether by sea or overland, the Communists would have had no chance of destroying the South Vietnamese Army. Contrary to popular mythology, the Communists obtained less than ten percent of all the weapons they needed in the period from 1960 to early 1965 by capturing weapons from South Vietnamese forces and installations.[65] Communist forces in the South were also heavily dependent on externally supplied ammunition, especially for the heavy weapons that they were to use extensively in the large battles that were to come. Le Quoc San, the commander of Communist Military Region 8 from 1961 to 1975, said after the war that infiltration from the North to his region "was our most important source of weapons and ammunition and was of decisive importance for the entire course of the war." Hanoi provided the heavy weapons essential to success, he noted, particularly artillery, mortars, anti-aircraft guns, and anti-tank weapons, which gave Communist forces "sufficient firepower to eliminate enemy troops and destroy enemy heavy weapons and equipment."[66] Only heavily armed conventional units could destroy South Vietnam's conventional forces and win the war, a reality at the forefront of Hanoi's thinking when it decided to seek decisive victory by force of arms. At its ninth conference, the Central Committee of the Vietnamese Communist Party noted that Saigon's regular army divisions were South Vietnam's critical forces, of much greater significance than the militia units. "As long as these regular force divisions are not disintegrated and destroyed," the committee observed, the militia forces "will have enough support to conduct their activities."[67] As General Samuel Williams had recognized when he organized the South Vietnamese Army into conventional divisions in the mid-1950s, the greatest obstacle to Hanoi's ambitions would always be the regular forces.

During the spring of 1964, as the result of a directive from the top, the Communist military forces in the South increased both the size and frequency of their attacks.[68] Fierce clashes followed, with each side scoring some major victories. The South Vietnamese Army had not suffered as much damage from personnel changes as had the provincial administrations, so some units still had able leaders and continued to perform effectively, especially the Airborne and Marine battalions that comprised the South Vietnamese general reserve. On several occasions, South Vietnamese forces killed more than one hundred Viet Cong in a single engagement. The Viet Cong's successes, however, were more numerous. During one week in April, the Viet Cong overran a district capital and a government training center in the Mekong Delta and inflicted over 1,000 casualties, the highest weekly total the government had ever suffered, while Viet Cong losses for the same week were estimated at 710. In July, the Viet Cong launched more large attacks than it had launched in any previous month, with twelve of battalion strength and seven of company strength. Hampered by poor leadership during these engagements, government forces lost far more personnel and weapons than the enemy.

A dramatic clash at the Nam Dong Special Forces camp in Thua Thien province, on July 6, underscored the leadership problems on the South Vietnamese side, as well as the value of American advisory and air support.[69] Led by Captain Roger Donlon of Saugerties, New York, the U.S. Special Forces detachment at Nam Dong of two officers and ten NCOs was advising a 300-man South Vietnamese Strike Force. Also present at the camp were 60 Nung guards, one Australian NCO, and an American anthropologist. At two-thirty that morning, white phosphorous mortar shells began exploding inside the camp, followed by grenades and small arms fire. Acting on detailed information obtained through espionage, the Viet Cong targeted the camp's most vulnerable and important points, and their weapons rapidly hit the command post, supply facility, and dispensary, engulfing each in fire. With 800 men in the attack, the Viet Cong soon breached portions of the camp's innermost wire fence and opened gaping holes in the perimeter of the South Vietnamese Strike Force. Before much time had elapsed, the Viet Cong had completely overrun the Strike Force's section of the camp. One hundred members of the Strike Force were killed or wounded, while the others fled the camp to protect their family members, who were living in a shanty town one kilometer away.

The Viet Cong who had seized the Strike Force's area joined with the rest of the assault force in attacking the other section of the camp, held by the American advisers and Nungs with less than one quarter of the numerical strength of the Strike Force and less than one tenth the strength of the attackers. The Americans and Nungs, however, proved to be very formidable opponents, refusing to let the Viet Cong penetrate their perimeter despite the absence, at first, of air support. With the inner perimeter fence still intact in this section of the camp, the defenders gunned down many Viet Cong as they ran toward or tried to cross the fence, in some cases at point blank range with shotguns and rifles. In his book *A Bright Shining Lie,* Neil Sheehan was to call the Vietnam War a "war without heroes,"[70] but that contention does not do justice to those who fought at this battle, or at many others. Sergeant Terrance D. Terrin, a medic from St. Johns, Arizona, lost the use of an arm early in the battle but continued firing an AR-15 from the hip, earning him one of the five Silver Stars awarded for the Battle of Nam Dong. Captain Donlon, after salvaging what he could from the command post as flaming pieces of roofing fell around him, directed the defensive effort. While the two sides blasted each other, Donlon ran around the perimeter from one position to another barking out orders, shouting encouragement, and directing fire. Donlon killed several Viet Cong himself, and on multiple occasions he was seen throwing back hand grenades that the Viet Cong had tossed at him. Without assistance, Donlon dragged a wounded sergeant, a 60mm mortar, a 57mm recoilless rifle, and several boxes of ammunition to the rear, all the while braving what witness Gerald Hickey, the American anthropologist, called the "extreme danger" of "intense Viet Cong fire from small arms, automatic weapons and mortars." Donlon continued to function after receiving four successive wounds, including a shrapnel wound in his stomach the size of a quarter. For his efforts, Donlan would receive the Congressional Medal of Honor, making him the first American to win the nation's highest combat award in Vietnam.

When daylight came, the Americans and Nungs still clung to their positions, and they now had the ability to cast massive air strikes on the exposed Viet Cong. The Viet Cong commander, recognizing his predicament, ordered a retreat. Departing in haste, the Viet Cong left behind fifty-four dead and hauled away an uncertain but probably large number of additional casualties. In total, Nam Dong's multinational garrison suffered 55 dead during the battle, including two Americans and an Australian, and 65 wounded. The two American dead were forty-five-year-old Team Sergeant Gabriel Alamo of Newark, New Jersey, and twenty-two-year-old Sergeant John Lucius Houston of Fort Knox, Kentucky, both of whom received the Distinguished Service Cross for their valor at Nam Dong. The story of Houston's family epitomized the fortitude of a great many

American families of the 1960s, an attribute that helped make America's armed forces a stalwart adversary, even if their nation's leaders and press were not always so stalwart. As soon as Houston's wife received the news of her husband's death, she prematurely delivered twins, only one of whom survived. At the ceremony in which Mrs. John Houston accepted her husband's Distinguished Service Cross, Captain Donlon asked her what she would do if her son wanted to join the Army when he grew up. "I would say to him the same as I said to his father," she replied. "My son would have to make the decision himself. If he wants to go into the military, I would be as proud of him as I was of his father."

In the struggle for control of the villages during the spring and summer of 1964, the successes were almost entirely on the Viet Cong's side. In Washington, many blamed the Saigon government's pacification woes on its inattention to political and economic matters, which they attributed to overemphasis on the military side.[71] The proponents of this interpretation failed to appreciate the primacy of security – the government could not obtain popular support and carry out political and economic programs in the villages without first using force to ward off the Viet Cong. They also did not understand that the foremost obstacle to good governance was not strategic or tactical thinking but deficient South Vietnamese leadership from top to bottom.[72] Good leadership was not attainable now because most of the experienced and dynamic leaders had been replaced with a rotating slate of generally inexperienced and nonthreatening individuals. By the spring, many of the entities that had controlled and employed the rural populace had been razed by the Saigon government or the Viet Cong, and in the limited number of provinces where the governmental apparatus still functioned in some capacity it was deteriorating. "The political structure in the hamlets and villages has almost disappeared," observed McNamara in April. "Frequent changes of hamlet leaders and village chieftains have produced a vacuum into which the Viet Cong have moved."[73] With the disintegration of the government's village presence, monthly recruitment tumbled to less than half of what was needed, causing the South Vietnamese armed forces to slide far below authorized strength.[74]

Efforts to fill the void in the villages by inserting the South Vietnamese Army usually met with little success. General William Westmoreland, who would often be accused of failing to understand pacification, noted quite perceptively in June 1964 that the army's renewed emphasis on large sweep operations – an outgrowth of leadership problems and growing enemy strength – was undermining its efforts to establish the lasting security upon which all other aspects of pacification depended.[75] The only national pacification program that showed much promise in 1964, the Counter-Terror Team program, was initiated not by the Saigon government but by the CIA. Armed with folding-stock carbines that could be concealed beneath their clothing, Counter-terror Teams of three to six men attempted to hunt down Viet Cong leaders in areas where other government forces were loathe to go. This program, however, was too small to have a significant impact on the war as a whole.

In Washington, the Saigon government's inability to stop the Viet Cong also was raising the level of interest in actions beyond South Vietnam. President Johnson himself, soon after taking office, had initiated planning for the intensification of covert operations against North Vietnam.[76] The men who drafted the initial plans favored a greatly expanded effort that included psychological warfare, intelligence collection, sabotage, and the organization of indigenous resistance groups that could tie down large numbers of North Vietnamese forces, as the Viet Cong were tying down South Vietnamese forces. The success of all these efforts, emphasized the authors of the covert operations plans, required the formation of indigenous resistance, which they believed could be done very effectively through recruiting from the tribal minorities and Catholics in North Vietnam,[77] two groups that had a proven capacity for organized and fierce anti-Communism. But Johnson and his advisers, early in 1964, nixed the resistance movement and other major operations, on the grounds that they might provoke a severe reaction from North Vietnam or China.[78] Johnson approved a much more limited covert plan, entitled OPLAN 34-A, and entrusted its implementation to McNamara, who was much more sanguine about its prospects than the military planners, the Joint Chiefs, and the CIA, despite his comparative lack of experience in such ventures.

The covert action program was to turn into a major fiasco. The South Vietnamese personnel assigned to the program suffered from poor morale, because ineffectual leaders had been installed at the top and they were not well received by the personnel below them, who for the most part had been loyal to Diem and Colonel Le Quang Tung, the Special Forces commander who had been executed on November 1, 1963. North Vietnam's own internal security services noticed that after Diem's overthrow, the South Vietnamese forces responsible for covert missions in North Vietnam declined in leadership and morale and were "no longer capable of implementing their plans."[79] Because of the prohibition against forming a resistance movement, the covert teams did not have a network of sympathizers to shelter and guide them once they arrived in North Vietnam. North Vietnamese security forces quickly captured all of the teams sent to the North.[80] Naval commando raids carried out under OPLAN 34-A fared slightly better, resulting in the destruction of a few North Vietnamese bridges and installations at a heavy cost in South Vietnamese commandos.[81] By mid-March, McNamara was admitting that the covert action program as a whole was "so limited that it is unlikely to have any significant effect."[82]

Certain senior Americans, disappointed by the limited character of OPLAN 34-A, called for much more forceful actions from early 1964 onward. The Joint Chiefs of Staff told Secretary of Defense McNamara that "the United States must be prepared to put aside many of the self-imposed restrictions which now limit our efforts, and to undertake bolder actions which may embody greater risks." In addition to forfeiting opportunities to harm the enemy, they noted, these restrictions "may well now be conveying signals of irresolution to our enemies – encouraging them to higher levels of vigor and greater risks."[83] General Harold K. Johnson went so far as to argue that if the United States were unwilling to "go all the way" in Vietnam, then it should not go at all.[84] Contending that North Vietnamese support was vital to the insurgency, the Joint Chiefs recommended using South Vietnamese ground troops and U.S. air strikes to disrupt the Laotian infiltration routes, and U.S. ground troops and air strikes to attack North Vietnam. They proposed, furthermore, putting an American general in command of the South Vietnamese armed forces. Addressing the possibility of Chinese intervention, the Joint Chiefs argued that economic troubles would discourage the Chinese from entering a major war in Southeast Asia. During the first half of 1964, the Joint Chiefs were to repeat these recommendations over and over again.[85] CIA Director John McCone put forward similar recommendations.[86]

Johnson and his principal advisers rejected all of these measures. One major factor in the rejections was the President's desire to keep Vietnam in the background until the November election. In explaining this consideration to subordinates, Johnson said that dramatic U.S. actions in Vietnam prior to the election could harm the Democrats at the ballot box, and that the public would be more amenable to forceful measures once he had been elected President in his own right.[87] The election was not, however, the only factor. The civilians whom Lyndon Johnson had inherited from John F. Kennedy believed that the Viet Cong insurgency was largely self-sustaining, and hence actions in Laos or North Vietnam would not have dramatic effects on the war in South Vietnam.[88] Like everyone else in the upper echelons of the U.S. government, these individuals had access to the numerous intelligence reports showing rising infiltration of equipment and personnel from North Vietnam, but whereas the senior military and CIA officers knew the importance of logistics and leadership from years of military or paramilitary service, many of New Frontiersmen had no such experience. Thus, they paid more attention to counterinsurgency theories that emphasized the importance of local rather than external support, and of popular opinion rather than charisma and organizational skill.

Johnson and other top civilians contended that sending U.S. combat troops to Vietnam would smack of colonialism and decrease the drive of the South Vietnamese, and that handing control of South Vietnamese units to American officers would alienate the South Vietnamese leadership. Powerful U.S. initiatives in Laos or North Vietnam would provoke major North Vietnamese and Chinese retaliation, they believed, leading to a major war in which the U.S. government would face tremendous pressure to use nuclear weapons, and Johnson and his advisers were no more interested in nuclear brinksmanship than Kennedy had been.[89] Fighting the Chinese without nuclear weapons would, in the minds of Johnson and his civilian advisers, mean a bloody and inconclusive war similar to the Korean War. Haunted by the specter of another Korea, Johnson feared that China, with four times as many people as the United States, could endlessly pump bodies into battle until American losses became intolerable.[90] Johnson's fear of repeating the Korean War experience, it should be noted, was based not on real evidence of China's current intentions and capabilities, but rather on a general fear of history repeating itself and the recognition that an enemy – especially a fanatical one such as Communist China that had killed tens of millions of its own people – can react in unpredictable ways. In 1950, as Johnson well remembered, the Chinese had intervened in Korea despite confident predictions from MacArthur that they would stay out.

For some of Johnson's closest civilian advisers, although not for Johnson himself, placing major restrictions on U.S. action was also attractive for what they considered to be more sophisticated reasons, derived from the "limited war" theories advanced by social scientists in the 1950s and early 1960s, which were much in vogue with civilian government leaders in the Kennedy and Johnson administrations.[91] In what was perhaps the most influential work produced by the limited war theorists, the 1960 book *Strategy of Conflict*, Harvard professor Thomas Schelling contended that the opponents in a conflict acted rationally and therefore could be restrained through limited actions that made heightened conflict seem contrary to their interests. A limited war was acceptable because it could be kept from turning into a nuclear war, Schelling and his advocates believed. Here they stood in stark contrast to America's military leaders and former President Eisenhower, who believed that one ought to go after the head of the snake rather than fight a limited war, and that limited war theories and simulations were "academic and useless exercises played by a bunch of eggheads."[92]

By taking a limited action initially, Schelling theorized, one side could communicate to the other side its commitment to its cause, thereby inducing the adversary to back down. When one side accepted limits on its behavior, rationality would induce the other side to limit its own behavior. Relying on logical analysis of what perfectly rational beings would do, Schelling failed to consider the history of actual human behavior, which has shown time and again that men often act irrationally, that they often misinterpret their enemies, and that a man can deter his foes better by brandishing a broadsword and howling a battle cry than by holding a dagger delicately and promising to avoid serious bloodshed.[93] For McNamara and other leading civilians, the Cuban missile crisis seemed to have validated the limited war theories because a limited demonstration of force, in the form of an American naval blockade, had seemingly cowed the Soviets by signaling strength and determination. In reality, as would become clear to Americans only after the Cold War, the Soviets had relented not because of the blockade but out of fear that the Americans would invade Cuba or attack it with nuclear weapons.[94] That the Soviets were very different from the Communists of Asia, or that the Soviets prized Cuban missiles less dearly than North Vietnam and China prized South Vietnam, were also not factored into the administration's calculations.

During March, Prime Minister Khanh began advocating the same aggressive actions as the Joint Chiefs, out of the same frustrations. Khanh called for attacks on North Vietnam and the Laotian infiltration trails, with a warning that if America and South Vietnam did not try for a clear victory in this manner, it would be senseless to continue the carnage of the war, for the South could not win the war by fighting strictly within its own borders. But Johnson and his advisers were not swayed. To reduce public pressure on President Johnson for taking action against the North, in fact, anonymous administration officials leaked word to the press that Khanh was opposed to attacks on the North.[95] Khanh made arrangements with the Laotian rightist General Phoumi Nosovan for South Vietnamese air strikes and regimental-sized ground operations in eastern Laos, but the U.S. government compelled Khanh to cancel these activities before they got started. The Johnson administration also rejected a proposal by Khanh for more direct U.S. involvement in his government's war effort.[96]

Khanh would have been more encouraged had he known that Johnson was, at this same time, moving towards the view that the United States would have to strike the North at some point to avert defeat. At a White House dinner on May 24, 1964, Johnson told his advisers that if diplomacy failed to solve the Vietnam problem, then the United States would hit North Vietnamese targets. Not surprisingly, however, the attacks on North Vietnam would not commence until after the election in November.[97] A few days thereafter, Johnson arranged for delivery of a threat to the North Vietnamese via Canadian diplomat J. Blair Seaborn, a man whose exceptional height was expected to intimidate the diminutive North Vietnamese. Arriving in Hanoi on June 18, Seaborn notified Pham Van Dong that the United States was determined to keep North Vietnam from expanding beyond its present boundaries, and that if the conflict escalated, North Vietnam would suffer "the greatest devastation." The Americans did not want to overthrow North Vietnam, Seaborn said, they only wanted peace, and he stressed that North Vietnam could secure financial favors from the United States in return for an end to the hostilities. Pham Van Dong, making no effort to conceal North Vietnam's control over the Viet Cong, replied that the North Vietnamese were intent on continuing the struggle – which he said had turned very much in their favor since Diem's assassination – and swore that "we shall win."[98]

In the meantime, America's opposition to tough measures so frustrated Khanh that he made contacts of his own with the Communists, to find a way out of the long and gruesome war he foresaw. One of his ministers approached the Viet Cong during June to discuss peace negotiations, but the overture appears to have been futile.[99] In July, Khanh was back to clamoring for attacks on North Vietnam, highlighted by a massive public ceremony on July 19. In front of a crowd of 100,000 in Saigon, Khanh took earth from two small containers, representing North and South Vietnam, and mixed them in one large container to signify the unification of Vietnam under an anti-Communist regime. "We have often heard that the people have called for the war to be carried to the North," Khanh declared. "The government cannot remain indifferent before the firm determination of all the people who are considering the push northward as an appropriate means to fulfill our national history." Khanh led the crowd in chanting, "To the North!"[100]

By July, Lodge was no longer around to keep Khanh in line. Less than two weeks before Khanh's ceremony, Maxwell Taylor had arrived in Saigon to succeed Lodge as America's ambassador to South Vietnam. Johnson had chosen Taylor because, as he put it, the American people "are gonna look at him as a reasonable, fair, good man who has the respect of everybody." Taylor, the President said, "can give us the cover that we need with the country and with the Republicans and with the Congress." Johnson noted, furthermore, that Taylor was the American most capable of bolstering Khanh and building Khanh's confidence in the United States, a most ironic statement in light of what was to come.[101] It thus fell upon Taylor to inform Khanh that the United States had no desire to be pressured by Khanh's public statements into attacking the North or supporting South Vietnamese attacks on the North. When Taylor delivered this message to Khanh, the South Vietnamese premier replied innocently that his "to the North" campaign was not intended to pressure the United States – it was just that his people were weary of fighting and the war had to be ended quickly. Khanh brought up the rapidly expanding presence of Northern regulars among the enemy forces, which American and South Vietnamese intelligence had confirmed through prisoner interrogations. This development, he said, signified that the war had entered a new phase, one in which new countermeasures were needed. Khanh refused to retract his call for conquering the North.[102]

Coincident with Taylor's arrival was the accession of General William Childs Westmoreland to the command of the U.S. military advisory mission. A native of South Carolina, Westmoreland had been recognized for his exceptional leadership talents since joining the Boy Scouts at age twelve.[103] As a cadet at West Point, Westmoreland had become a master of the drill field and barracks, standing perfectly straight, bellowing out commands with supreme confidence, and remaining calm under the most unnerving of conditions. At graduation, Westmoreland received the Pershing Award, given to the cadet who had demonstrated the highest degree of military proficiency. Following Pearl Harbor, young Westmoreland received command of the 34th Field Artillery Battalion and arrived in North Africa just as Rommel was demolishing the U.S. II Corps at the Kasserine Pass. Rushing through Tunisia with the rest of the 9th U.S. Infantry Division, the battalion helped bring Rommel's advance to a halt, earning the unit a Presidential Unit Citation. Westmoreland also participated in the invasion of Sicily in July 1943 and the invasion of France in June 1944, in both cases gaining renown for the performance of his troops. During the Korean War, he commanded the 187th Regimental Combat Team, and in 1956 he attained the rank of brigadier general. Westmoreland then took command of the 101st Airborne Division, firmly ensconcing himself with Taylor and the other officers of the "Airborne mafia," a group that dominated the highest ranks of the U.S. military for many years.

When Westmoreland had first shown up in Vietnam, he had been taken aback by the optimism displayed by General Harkins. But once he had spent some time in Vietnam and had gained an appreciation of the situation, Westmoreland too became an eager promoter of optimism. In one order, he insisted on "the maintenance of an optimistic outlook on the part of all advisors."[104] Westmoreland's own private appraisals of the situation, like those of Harkins, were sober and fair, ignoring none of the weaknesses of America's South Vietnamese allies.

As this period drew to a close, the critical question was whether the American armed forces would step in before the Communists could conquer South Vietnam. Convinced that South Vietnam had to be protected in order to save the other Southeast Asian dominoes, President Johnson sensed that tougher measures were required, and he was under pressure from Khanh and his own generals to adopt them. He did not, however, want to act prior to the election, because he feared that dramatic initiatives would upset his electoral lead and because he had less confidence than his generals that such actions would save the day, based on two erroneous beliefs – that the Viet Cong were not heavily dependent on North Vietnamese assistance and that attacks on North Vietnam would incite North Vietnam and China to aggressive actions that they would not otherwise take. Khanh, after taking power at the end of January, slowed the downward slide of the South Vietnamese war effort that began in November 1963, but the slide was continuing, thanks in considerable measure to Tri Quang's meddling in the appointment process. Consequently, Johnson could not be certain that the Saigon government would stave off collapse until the U.S. election in November, and so he felt compelled to do everything possible to assist South Vietnam short of deploying U.S. combat forces and sending an effective ambassador to Saigon. The Vietnamese Communists were building their forces in the South through heavy infiltration of North Vietnamese soldiers and materiel, with long-range plans for large conventional battles that they hoped would vanquish the South Vietnamese without drawing in the Americans. The Communists found themselves in a quandary, too. If their offensive were too small or too slow, it would give the United States enough time to accumulate the resources in South Vietnam to foil their designs. If, on the other hand, it were too big or too fast, it could quickly arouse the American giant and cause it to swing its fists.

CHAPTER 14

Signals

AUGUST–OCTOBER 1964

THE BEGINNING OF AUGUST FOUND THE AMERICAN DESTROYER USS *Maddox* engaged in a "De Soto patrol" in the Gulf of Tonkin, off the North Vietnamese coast. The highly classified De Soto patrols had been conducted sporadically since 1962 for the purposes of gathering information on North Vietnamese radar and decrypting North Vietnamese communications. When, on the morning of July 31, the *Maddox* had crossed the 17th Parallel on its way northward, it had come within four miles of six South Vietnamese commando boats that were speeding southward after bombarding North Vietnamese island installations as part of OPLAN 34-A. Later, it was widely believed that the North Vietnamese attacked the *Maddox* because they mistakenly concluded that it had just participated in these raids. Communist histories, however, make clear that no such confusion existed. North Vietnamese radar had begun tracking the *Maddox* long before it entered the area of the 34-A attack, and tracked it for another two days before the attack order was issued in Hanoi.[1]

The North Vietnamese were, nevertheless, more troubled by hostile naval operations than the U.S. government thought. As they monitored the northward movement of the *Maddox,* the North Vietnamese feared that the American destroyer would attack the coast or the islands as previous vessels had done. It had not occurred to the Americans that the North Vietnamese would take this view of the *Maddox,* which was larger and was moving much slower than the commando boats, but that is what happened. With the *Maddox* lurking off the North Vietnamese coast under the watchful eye of North Vietnamese radar, the Politburo met in Hanoi to decide what to do. "We need to make good preparations to deal with this situation, but we will not strike first," Ho Chi Minh said. "If they strike first then we will retaliate immediately." Noting that the *Maddox* had not crossed into North Vietnam's territorial waters, General Giap concurred.[2] The increasingly powerful Le Duan, however, in no mood to let the country's aging founders restrain him, issued an attack order through military channels on the afternoon of August 2. Later in the day, this order was countermanded by another message, presumably at the behest of a displeased

Ho Chi Minh, but the countermanding order arrived too late to stop the North Vietnamese Navy, which by that time had already sent three P-4 torpedo boats to attack the *Maddox*.[3]

From intercepted North Vietnamese communications, the *Maddox* learned of the impending attack in advance, prompting the destroyer's captain to increase speed to 25 knots and head away from the North Vietnamese coast. The spry, Soviet-built torpedo boats, however, were swifter than any destroyer, capable of reaching speeds as high as 52 knots. They came within ten miles of the *Maddox*, at which point they began a high-speed run, but of very poor conception. The torpedo boats attacked one at a time, which allowed the *Maddox* to concentrate all of her 5-inch guns on each boat as it moved forward, and they launched their torpedoes at extreme ranges from which a hit was nearly impossible. Responding to calls from the *Maddox*, four F-8E Crusaders took off from the aircraft carrier *Ticonderoga* and raced to the scene of the confrontation. The aircraft hit two of the boats with nine-foot long Zuni rockets and 20mm gunfire, while the guns of the *Maddox* tore holes in the third torpedo boat.[4] At 4:30 P.M., the North Vietnamese boats chose to withdraw, having inflicted no harm on the *Maddox* or the American aircraft.[5]

Prime Minister Khanh publicly urged the Americans to retaliate against the North Vietnamese in order to save face and avoid looking like a "paper tiger."[6] Ambassador Taylor notified Washington that if the Americans did not strike back, it "would immediately be construed in Saigon as indication that U.S. flinches from direct confrontation with North Vietnamese."[7] President Johnson, however, refused to strike back, for he and his top officials had concluded, incorrectly, that a local North Vietnamese shore commander or shore station had initiated the attack against the wishes of the North Vietnamese high command.[8] Johnson told the Navy to continue the patrol with an additional destroyer – which would be the USS *Turner Joy* – and air cover.

On the evening of August 4, the *Maddox* decrypted enemy messages suggesting that unspecified North Vietnamese vessels would soon attack it and the *Turner Joy*, and one hour later, radar operators on board the *Maddox* spotted what appeared to be surface vessels advancing toward the two destroyers at speeds of 35 to 40 knots. Aircraft soared off the deck of the *Ticonderoga* to defend the ships. When the fast-moving radar blips had closed within 7,000 yards of the *Turner Joy* and the *Maddox*, both destroyers began firing salvos. Their fire control radar indicated that they were hitting the targets. The *Turner Joy* and *Maddox* split up, and the remainder of the perceived enemy action involved only the *Turner Joy*. Over the next four hours, radar contacts kept appearing and disappearing on the *Turner Joy*'s radar, and as the ship's guns fired, the radar indicated that hits were being scored and vessels sunk.[9] Multiple crewmen on the *Turner Joy* reported seeing enemy boats, enemy gunfire, and torpedo wakes at various times during the incident, and the *Turner Joy*'s signal bridge personnel testified that they had seen an enemy searchlight aimed at their ship. The most compelling evidence that enemy vessels had attacked, the Americans believed after the incident had ended, came from signals intelligence, which included not only what appeared to be an attack order but also messages stating that the North Vietnamese had shot down two U.S. aircraft and that two North Vietnamese boats had been "sacrificed." The sum of the evidence convinced the destroyer commanders, and then Pacific Commander-in-Chief Admiral Ulysses S. Grant Sharp and the Joint Chiefs of Staff, that an attack had occurred.[10] Not until much later, long after the Johnson administration had acted in response, would considerable evidence become available suggesting that an attack had not taken place. Most important among this evidence was the conclusion by many National Security Agency and Central Intelligence Agency officials that the intercepted North Vietnamese messages that seemingly mentioned an August 4 attack actually referred to the August 2 battle or to ensuing salvage operations.[11] No one has found a "smoking gun" showing irrefutably the absence of an attack on August 4, but most of the information now available supports the view that an attack did not occur.[12]

Upon receiving the military's verdict that the North Vietnamese had attacked for the second time in three days, Johnson and his triumvirate of Bundy, Rusk, and McNamara decided that the time for retaliation had arrived. Rusk, drawing on the limited war theories of Thomas Schelling and like-minded academics, explained, "We have been trying to get a signal to Hanoi and Peking. Our response to this attack may be that signal." Rusk called for a "limited" response that would "limit the escalation" by showing "that we are not going to run out of Southeast Asia, but that we have no national ambitions either in a war to the north."[13] Persuaded by this act of deduction, Johnson ordered a surgical bombing strike on the North Vietnamese naval bases that housed the torpedo boats.

Johnson called Congressional leaders to his office on the evening of August 4 to sell them on the need for retaliation and for a Congressional resolution giving him a free hand to use force in Southeast Asia. Johnson's commanders in the Pacific had already received orders to execute the retaliatory attack by the time this meeting began,[14] but he acted as if no such orders had been given, tossing around what seemed to be proposed reactions. When the Congressmen eventually expressed support for both retaliation and the resolution, Johnson said, "I had that feeling but I wanted the advice of each of you and wanted to consult with you. We felt we should move with the action recommended by the Joint Chiefs, but I wanted to get the Congressional concurrence." Johnson read the legislators a statement he intended to deliver to the nation. Several Congressmen, most notably Republican Senator Leverett Saltonstall of Massachusetts, objected to the repeated use of the word "limited" in the text. Senator Saltonstall remarked, "Three times in that little statement you use the word 'limited.' Why not use the word 'determined' and let the limitations speak for themselves? If you use the word 'limited,' maybe we won't go any further."

Dwight D. Eisenhower and John Foster Dulles never would have used the word "limited" in such an announcement, knowing that it was antithetical to instilling fear in the enemy. Johnson responded, "We want them to know we are not going to take it lying down, but we are not going to destroy their cities."[15] The President kept the word "limited" in the statement. "Our response, for the present, will be limited and fitting," Johnson said in announcing the retaliatory strikes to a national television and radio audience later that night. "We Americans know, although others appear to forget, the risks of spreading conflict. We still seek no wider war."[16]

In Operation Pierce Arrow, U.S. carrier aircraft bombed the North Vietnamese torpedo boat bases. At Vinh, the oil tanks caught fire and exploded, spitting out a column of smoke that extended 14,000 feet into the air. Over the skies of North Vietnam, antiaircraft guns shot down two U.S. planes, resulting in the death of one pilot, Lieutenant Junior Grade Richard C. Sather, and the capture of the other pilot, Lieutenant Everett Alvarez. After ejecting from his damaged plane, Alvarez landed on North Vietnamese territory, breaking his back in the process, and he was thrown in a Hanoi prison where he would spend the next eight and a half years. In the cities of South Vietnam, the retaliatory strikes received near-universal approval, with Khanh, the Saigon press, and many other South Vietnamese urging the Americans to continue attacking the North.[17] America's Southeast Asian friends applauded, too. "I sleep very well now," declared Thai Air Chief Marshal Dawee. "Before, I got up in the middle of the night thinking of what my American friends would do if the Communists attacked us."[18] For Malaysian Prime Minster Tunku Abdul Rahman, the retaliation was "not only justified but also necessary if peace is to be restored and respected in Southeast Asia."[19]

Wasting no time, Johnson sent the Congress a proposed resolution that gave him authority to "take all necessary measures to repel any armed attack against the forces of the United States and to prevent further aggression" in Southeast Asia.[20] Johnson believed that he already possessed the authority to use U.S. forces abroad without Congressional approval; administration officials considered a declaration of war necessary only if the United States undertook a massive military enterprise such as it had in the two world wars. The purpose of this resolution, the Tonkin Gulf Resolution as it became known, was merely to get the Congress on record in support of tougher action, which would give the impression that the whole country supported the resolution and would discourage Congressional opposition in the future. On August 6, to build support for the resolution, Johnson had McNamara address a joint session of the Senate Foreign Relations and Armed Services Committees. McNamara testified that the *Maddox* had been "carrying out a routine patrol of the type we carry out all over the world at all times." He did not mention the ship's involvement in intelligence collection. Despite his own conviction and that of the President that the 34-A raids had provoked the enemy into attacking, the Secretary of

Defense asserted that the North Vietnamese attacks were "unprovoked and deliberate."[21]

During the Senate's deliberations, only two Senators – Democrats Wayne Morse of Oregon and Ernest Gruening of Alaska – spoke against the resolution. Morse's suspicions had been aroused when someone in the Pentagon informed him of the 34-A raids and the *Maddox's* intelligence activities. Morse denounced the proposed resolution as a "predated declaration of war," and alleged that the United States could not win a war in Vietnam even if it scored numerous military victories, for "eventually the white man will be engulfed in that Asiatic flood and drowned." Instead of fighting, Morse said, the United States should negotiate a settlement with the assistance of the United Nations. Gruening said that he opposed American involvement in Vietnam because South Vietnam had no strategic value and the struggle in any case would be futile. Ignorant of the realities of Southeast Asia in 1964, Gruening contended that the problem could be solved with a ceasefire supervised by a United Nations police force. What Gruening did not tell his Senate colleagues was that he also was worried that military escalation would lead to a Republican victory in the 1964 Presidential election.[22]

Morse and Gruening were not men of substantial influence in the Senate, and their colleagues paid them little heed. Numerous Senators from both parties stood up to endorse the resolution. Most emphasized the need to show American firmness in resisting what appeared to be unprovoked Communist aggression on the seas, and some mentioned the importance of preventing further Chinese gains in Asia. A sizeable minority of Senators in both parties said that they had been dissatisfied with Johnson's Vietnam policy up to this point in time, either because the administration was showing too much or too little restraint, but now their patriotic duty obliged them to support the administration. Democrats, moreover, were very reluctant to oppose Johnson on any matter at the beginning of August 1964 because the party's national convention was just a few weeks away. "When U.S. forces have been attacked repeatedly upon the high seas," pronounced Democrat Albert Gore of Tennessee, "whatever doubts one may have entertained are water over the dam. Freedom of the seas must be preserved. Aggression against our forces must be repulsed." Frank Church, Democrat of Idaho, proclaimed, "There is a time to question the route of the flag, and there is a time to rally around it, lest it be routed. This is the time for the latter course, and in our pursuit of it, a time for all of us to unify."[23] Congress's sentiments were in line with the views of the bulk of their constituents. Before the incident, the American people had disapproved of the Johnson administration's handling of Vietnam by a 58–42 margin, and had been opposed by a 37–31 margin to military action against North Vietnam. Now they approved the Johnson administration's handling by a 72–28 margin and favored military action against the North by a margin of 50–25.[24]

A few keen Senators asked for clarification of certain points, some of which President Johnson had hoped would remain unclear to the Congress. Democrat Daniel B. Brewster of Maryland inquired if the resolution would permit the landing of large American forces in Vietnam or China. Senate Foreign Relations Committee Chairman J. William Fulbright of Arkansas, a Democrat who was promoting the resolution on Johnson's behalf, responded, "There is nothing in the resolution, as I read it, that contemplates it," although "the language of the resolution would not prevent it." Fulbright assured Brewster that "I have no doubt that the President will consult with Congress in case a major change in present policy becomes necessary."[25] The Tonkin Gulf Resolution passed in the Senate by a 98–2 vote.

The resolution was considered for just forty minutes in the House of Representatives, where Democratic leaders were more explicit, and more misleading, than their Senate counterparts in describing the resolution's limits. "This is definitely not an advance declaration of war," averred Thomas E. Morgan of Pennsylvania, the Democratic chairman of the House Foreign Affairs Committee. "The committee has been assured by the Secretary of State that the constitutional prerogative of the Congress in this respect will continue to be scrupulously observed."[26] The resolution passed 416–0 in the House, with two abstentions.

American hawks, as well as large segments of South Vietnam's urban populace, hoped that the Tonkin Gulf incidents and the Congressional resolution would cause Johnson to undertake additional aggressive actions. Taylor, Sharp, and the Joint Chiefs recommended another destroyer patrol in the Gulf of Tonkin, for the purposes of asserting strong American resolve and determining whether the North Vietnamese intended to attack again, and they called for additional air strikes in North Vietnam and along the Ho Chi Minh Trail.[27] Sharp and Westmoreland went so far as to recommend sending U.S. military personnel to protect American airbases from major North Vietnamese ground attacks. Johnson's top advisers, however, convinced him to do just the opposite. Johnson suspended the De Soto patrols and halted the covert 34-A attacks on the North. He refused to authorize further air strikes or U.S. troop deployments. For at least the next few weeks, the administration was determined to avoid anything that could be viewed as provocative and that would, in the words of William Bundy, "in any way take the onus off the Communist side for escalation."[28] The onus for escalation would, ultimately, rest on the Communist side, but the damage incurred by the United States through its restraint was far more harmful than any onus.

Prime Minister Khanh, like President Johnson, believed that this moment of high international tension presented an excellent opportunity to strengthen his political hand, and so, on August 7, he declared a "state of urgency." By decree, Khanh authorized government personnel to ban demonstrations, imprison dangerous persons, search private homes at any time of day, and execute

terrorists and speculators. The government would impose censorship and prevent "the circulation of all publications, documents, and leaflets considered
as harmful to public order."[29] Khanh also drafted a new constitution, which
increased his own powers.

Instead of elevating Khanh to new heights of authority, however, as Johnson's
Tonkin Gulf Resolution had done for him, these moves sparked a devastating
political crisis that would knock Khanh off the ladder. At large demonstrations in the cities, Buddhist and student groups demanded that Khanh revoke
the new constitution and end the "state of urgency." They falsely charged that
Diemists in the government, particularly Can Lao Party veterans, Catholics,
and Dai Viets, were conspiring to oppress Buddhists.[30] Grossly exaggerating
the strength of Catholic governmental officials, Buddhist leader Tri Quang
told U.S. embassy officials that "the Buddhists could not accept government
by·Christians" and would abandon the anti-Communist struggle unless the
Americans dispossessed the Diemist groups of their remaining influence in
the government.[31] Under the inspiration of Tri Quang and other militants, a
mixture of riotous Buddhists, students, and other troublemakers set Catholic
houses and churches afire and ransacked a Catholic school, the offices of a
Catholic newspaper, and Catholic shops. One Catholic youth was hauled by
Buddhists to Saigon's central market, stabbed, and killed with clubs. Mobs
demolished the government's Information Ministry offices as well as a government radio station.[32] In Da Nang, three days of clashes between anti-Catholics
and Catholics claimed the lives of twelve people, including four hospital patients
who were dragged from their beds and beaten to death, and a mob of 2,000
shouted anti-American slogans as it stoned an American army billet.[33]

Government soldiers and policemen did not intervene to halt the violence,
even when rioting and murder were occurring right in front of them.[34] From
Diem's downfall, Khanh had learned that suppressing demonstrations, especially those involving Buddhists, would invite angry accusations of illiberalism from the Americans, and he was also intimidated by the large crowds of
protesters, just as he had been during the failed putsch on November 11, 1960.
To calm the oppositionists, Khanh resorted instead to the granting of their
demands. In Vietnam, where the strongman was venerated, such softness in
the face of virulent opposition caused the sort of dramatic drop in prestige that
Diem had so strenuously sought to avoid during his confrontations with the
Buddhists. "The emergency, and indeed any other laws, are being mocked," the
British embassy commented. "The grave element in all this is the failure of the
Khanh regime to assert themselves even in the face of small demonstrations.
In their desire to avoid appearing dictatorial they are showing themselves to be
ineffective."[35]

Most observers, including those in the American press, now believed that
Tri Quang and other Buddhist militants were wielding great influence over the
students who were responsible for much of the mayhem, and that Communist

agents were playing a significant role in both the Buddhist and student movements. Some of the protesters were moving in military formations guided by whistles and drums, and they established elaborate defenses against government forces that were well beyond the capacities of ordinary civilians.[36] A postwar Communist history divulged that the Communists made considerable headway in infiltrating student groups and faculties in the Saigon area in the aftermath of the coup of November 1, 1963.[37] The South Vietnamese police had been able to hold down Communist activity in the cities until Diem's overthrow, but the police were rendered largely ineffective after Diem's assassination by the purging of its leaders and the infiltration of the organization by Viet Cong agents.[38]

More and more people, including some high-ranking U.S. officials, were coming to the conclusion that Tri Quang himself was a Communist. One reason was that the targets of his false accusations were the most dedicated anti-Communists in the government. Another was his closeness with the People's Revolutionary Committees that had just been formed in the coastal towns of Annam, particularly the one in Hue, which was headed by one of his lieutenants, Dr. Le Khac Quyen. The committees' avowed aims bore striking similarities to those of the Communists, and in the handful of towns where they temporarily gained power, they sabotaged the government apparatus. U.S. intelligence strongly suspected that the Viet Cong had significant influence over the committees' leadership.[39]

On the night of August 24, Prime Minister Khanh asked Tri Quang, Tam Chau, and Thien Minh to come talk with him at Vung Tau. The three monks refused, prompting Khanh to rush to Saigon for the same purpose, to the obvious detriment of his negotiating position. When Khanh got there, the monks presented him with a written list of demands. First on the list was the nullification of the August 16 charter. Next, the leading generals who comprised the Military Revolutionary Council had to elect a president, after which the council would be disbanded, thereby removing the army from politics. Khanh also had to dismiss all former members of Diem's Can Lao Party who were still serving in the government, which would include some of the ablest and most important military officers. Lastly, in case Khanh still had any prestige remaining after those concessions, Khanh had to announce publicly that he was meeting the Buddhists' demands. If Khanh refused to carry out these actions, warned the monks, the Buddhist leadership would organize a massive resistance campaign.

After this meeting, Khanh asked Ambassador Taylor to come to his home. Taylor hustled over, arriving at one o'clock in the morning. As he listened to Khanh describe the monks' demands, Taylor received the impression that Khanh was inclined to meet them. The South Vietnamese premier suggested that concessions to the Buddhists would stop the fighting between Buddhist and Catholic civilians and prevent it from spreading into the armed forces. Religious fighting within the armed forces, Khanh believed, would make victory in the war impossible. He then asked Taylor what he thought ought to be done. Taylor answered, "I think it is a mistake to give in to pressure from a minority group on an issue of this importance, particularly to an ultimatum with a short deadline. To do so may only create further demands."[40] Taylor had identified this danger from observing the last months of the Diem regime. Khanh, however, had not learned this lesson, and therefore he did not take heed of Taylor's counsel.

Within a few hours of his meeting with Taylor, Khanh released a communiqué in which he promised to revise the constitution, cut back press restrictions, permit public demonstrations, and correct past abuses with special "field courts." As Taylor had predicted, these concessions only led to more demands and protests from the Buddhists and students. Khanh then drew up a new plan that satisfied the other demands made by the Buddhist leaders the previous night.[41] Astute observers in Saigon recognized that Khanh's capitulation meant that power had effectively been transferred from those desiring order and military success to Buddhist agitators intent on promoting their own interests, and perhaps those of the Communists as well. So outraged were some of the generals that they formed a cabal to seek the replacement of Khanh with Big Minh. Their conspiring was halted, however, when the Americans turned down their request for permission for a coup on the grounds that another change in leadership would throw the government into further disarray.

On August 26 and 27, at meetings of the Military Revolutionary Council, the dissension within the military burst into the open, culminating in a verbal joust between Khanh and Khiem. Khanh attributed the government's troubles to members of the Dai Viet Party in the government, who he said were spending more time plotting for power than fighting the war. Khiem, deploring the insecurity in the countryside and the rioting in the cities, put the blame on Khanh. Several of Khiem's supporters, including Generals Thieu and Nguyen Huu Co, called for Khanh's removal and the installation of Big Minh. But Minh himself then said that he was unwilling to take power and that everyone should support Khanh, because Khanh was the only person the Americans were willing to support. Khiem, his anger still burning, cried, "Obviously, Khanh is a puppet of the U.S. government, and we are tired of being told by the Americans how we should run our internal affairs." Shuddering beneath the weight of these blows, Khanh said in turn that he did not want to stay on because he did not have overwhelming support.[42] By the end of these deliberations, nothing had been resolved, except that Minh, Khanh, and Khiem were to meet afterwards to continue discussing what to do.

The three generals eventually agreed to form a triumvirate that would govern for two months, until a new government could be created. In Saigon, they restored order by using paratroopers with fixed bayonets to round up the rioters and herd them into trucks. Khanh was able to gain the dominant position in the interim government, but he continued to cede his decision-making power to the

Buddhists and the People's Revolutionary Committees. He dismissed numerous able civilian and military officials opposed by these two groups, prompting General Westmoreland to declare that "actions best calculated to destroy the morale, the unity, the pride and confidence of the Armed Forces have transpired in a manner which leads me to believe that a relative free hand has been given to those who aim to destroy the Armed Forces."[43] Buddhist demands, in addition, caused Khanh to order the release of all the people arrested during the rioting, of whom at least eleven were known Viet Cong leaders.[44]

The weakening of Khanh and the government intensified the calls on the American side for direct U.S. military action to stave off defeat. General Westmoreland advocated air strikes on the Ho Chi Minh Trail, while Ambassador Taylor and some of the Joint Chiefs favored bombing North Vietnam itself. The U.S. Air Force should bomb the North Vietnamese "back into the Stone Age," said Air Force Chief of Staff General Curtis E. LeMay, which in his opinion would cause the North Vietnamese to end the war and dissuade China from intervening.[45] Most pronounced was the rise in bellicosity among civilians. Assistant Secretary of State for Far Eastern Affairs William Bundy suggested using 34-A raids and a De Soto patrol to provoke the North Vietnamese into military action, in order to give the United States an excuse to bomb North Vietnam.[46] John McNaughton and Daniel Ellsberg, two of McNamara's Whiz Kids, favored air strikes in Laos and North Vietnam, though "if worst comes and South Vietnam disintegrates or their behavior becomes abominable," then the United States should "disown" South Vietnam and attempt to portray it as "a patient who died despite the extraordinary efforts of a good doctor."[47] National Security Adviser McGeorge Bundy wanted to employ American troops within South Vietnam, while U.S. Army Chief of Staff General Harold K. Johnson advocated the insertion of four U.S. divisions into Laos to sever the infiltration routes and destroy the Communist supply network.[48] The advocates of ground force intervention deemed air power incapable of stopping Hanoi, a conclusion that in many minds was supported by the recent SIGMA war games, although close scrutiny of these simulations shows that they supported no such conclusion.[49] The CIA, the U.S. agency that studied North Vietnamese intentions in the greatest depth, was predicting that air and naval action against Laos and North Vietnam would cause Hanoi to scale back its aggressive activities and seek a temporary truce.[50]

The various recommendations for direct U.S. military action deeply worried Johnson, for they could leak to Congress and the public and thereby put pressure on him to act before the election. Such pressure would become especially intense were it known that all of the country's top military leaders favored a more aggressive strategy. Presumably it was at Johnson's direction that a Pentagon spokesman told the press, on September 4, that the Joint Chiefs had not recommended the forceful measures that they were in fact recommending.[51] In the second week of September, Johnson did approve the resumption of 34-A

operations and De Soto patrols, as well as limited South Vietnamese ground
and air operations into the Ho Chi Minh Trail area. During the next De Soto
patrol, on September 18, two U.S. destroyers in the Gulf of Tonkin detected
several seemingly hostile objects on their radar and fired on them until they
disappeared, but the evidence of an attack was much thinner than it had been on
August 4, and therefore Johnson chose not to retaliate.[52] Over the objections of
his generals, Johnson discontinued the De Soto patrols for the remainder of the
year. Johnson had confidence that he could afford to put off stronger action,
based on reassurances from two of his most trusted subordinates, Maxwell
Taylor and Robert McNamara. At a September 9 meeting, Taylor had said
that the South Vietnamese government and armed forces would be able to
survive as long as they believed the Americans were on their side. McNamara,
at the same meeting, had assured the President that the risks of waiting a few
months before striking the North were minimal and that a period of waiting
would give South Vietnam valuable time to bolster its defenses against a North
Vietnamese counteraction.[53] They were both wrong, because they had both
mistakenly assumed that the enemy was not considering the launch of a large
conventional offensive in the near future.

North Vietnam's decision to shift its strategy had begun in the aftermath
of the Tonkin Gulf incidents. The one-time U.S. bombing raid on August 5
convinced the North Vietnamese that the United States was escalating the war,
jeopardizing Hanoi's chances for victory. Further endangering their prospects
was China's feeble reaction to the raid. On a variety of occasions during the past
year, two of them less than one month before the Tonkin Gulf incidents, the
Chinese had promised to fight the Americans with their own sea, air, or land
forces if the United States attacked North Vietnam.[54] Yet when the Americans
bombed the North Vietnamese torpedo boat bases, no Chinese planes or ships
attempted to defend North Vietnam or attack the American aircraft carriers.
Nor did the Chinese even produce a strong verbal response, stating only that
the Vietnamese would fight and defeat the Americans if they expanded the war
but making no mention of a Chinese intention to participate in the fracas.[55]
Chinese leaders tried to ease the disappointment of the North Vietnamese by
offering them one billion yuan, though with a condition that Hanoi reject
all offers of aid from the Soviet Union. The Soviets were looking increasingly
attractive as allies to the North Vietnamese not only because of China's failure
to resist the United States, but also because of the Soviets' sophisticated military
equipment.[56] The North Vietnamese chose not to reject all Soviet aid at this
time but, as a sop to the Chinese, they did not seek an increase in Soviet support
either. It was the first of what would become many instances where American
firmness in Vietnam exacerbated the Sino-Soviet schism and increased tensions
between North Vietnam and the two Communist giants.

China's fear of the United States during and after the Tonkin Gulf incidents
was, in fact, even greater than the North Vietnamese suspected, of such magnitude as to make the Chinese put self-preservation ahead of international

hegemony, solidarity with other Communist states, and all other concerns. The Chinese military leadership issued orders to prepare against an American invasion of mainland China, and Mao initiated an enormous program of industrial development in western and southwestern China so that his government and armed forces could retain some industrial assets if an American invasion compelled them to retreat inland.[57] Mao was also alarmed by the possibility of getting dragged into a smaller war in Vietnam because, like President Johnson and many of his advisers, he had no desire to fight another war like the Korean War and mistakenly believed that his former adversary would not hesitate to fight such a war again.[58] In the Korean War, the Chinese had learned that American forces, with their devastating air and artillery, were vastly superior to their own forces in conventional combat. Chinese forces would need enormous numerical superiority over American forces to have any chance of success, and in 1964 Mao could not come close to attaining such superiority. The Chinese and North Vietnamese could undertake a conventional offensive in Southeast Asia with a maximum combined strength of roughly twenty divisions, most of them equipped lightly and with outdated weapons, according to American intelligence estimates. U.S. military planners believed that even without resort to nuclear weapons, the United States would need only five to eight of its divisions, a total of 300,000 men, to stop a joint Chinese-North Vietnamese advance in Southeast Asia. The American military could assemble such a force in a short period of time, and it had the ability to deploy as many as eighteen out of its twenty-eight powerfully armed divisions to Southeast Asia, giving it more than enough muscle to counter-attack and drive into China.[59]

After the Tonkin Gulf reprisals, in violation of previous promises, the Chinese made clear to Hanoi that if American forces invaded North Vietnam, China would not send its troops to fight the Americans. They also told Hanoi that North Vietnamese forces should not try to defend North Vietnam's installations and population centers against invading Americans, but should instead withdraw into the mountains and fight from mountain bases as they had done against the French.[60] The North Vietnamese did not like the thought of yielding their cities and national infrastructure to the Americans, but they knew from their war with France, as well as from the experience of the North Koreans in 1950, the terrible costs of defending fixed positions against an aggressive enemy with overwhelming firepower. Concurring with the Chinese, the North Vietnamese made plans to retreat into the mountains in the event of an American invasion.

This revelation of Chinese and North Vietnamese contingency plans for an American invasion of North Vietnam permits, for the first time, a well-grounded analysis of the prospects of such an invasion in late 1964, a subject that has been fiercely debated ever since it was first proposed. An American invasion followed by a North Vietnamese retreat into the mountains and a Chinese abstention from fighting was, for the United States, a far better strategic scenario than the one the Americans ultimately accepted by not invading. While a ground war fought in both Vietnams would not have been easy for the United States, considering the ability of the North Vietnamese to hide in the mountainous areas, it had many advantages over the war that ended up taking place. The Communists would have lost the supply system that began in the North and reached into the South via the Ho Chi Minh Trail, and they would have been denied the importation of foreign war supplies by sea into Haiphong, the North's primary port, compelling them to rely on the vulnerable roads and railways from China for logistical support. The frightened Mao, moreover, might not have been willing to send massive military assistance into a war-stricken northern Vietnam as he had done during the Franco-Viet Minh War. The American invasion would have sharply reduced the Communists' access to North Vietnamese manpower, an essential resource for the Communists in a protracted ground war against the Americans and their Vietnamese allies.[61] The French, faced with similar conditions and tremendous Chinese logistical assistance to the Viet Minh, had come close to vanquishing the Communists in 1954 with only 150,000 of their own troops, a far cry from the 550,000 troops whom the Americans eventually sent to South Vietnam.

After the war, General Giap was to say that during 1964 and 1965 he had lived in great fear of an invasion of the North by American and South Vietnamese forces. Had the Americans invaded the North, Giap asserted, "the war would not have evolved in our favor as it did." Giap believed that the United States could have invaded the North successfully using three ground divisions plus naval and air units, far fewer forces than the Americans were to deploy to South Vietnam in the second half of the decade. Even a limited American invasion that did not capture all of the populous areas, said Giap, would have wrecked the Ho Chi Minh Trail and prevented Hanoi from sending large numbers of North Vietnamese troops to the South.[62]

President Johnson had sound reasons for refusing to invade North Vietnam prior to March 1965, the month in which China returned to expressing a willingness to fight in North Vietnam. He and most other Americans still hoped that South Vietnam could hang on without substantial U.S. participation in the ground war, which was a reasonable hope based on what they knew at the time – prior to April 1965, the Americans were unaware of the North Vietnamese strategic shift that would ultimately necessitate U.S. intervention. But Johnson and his civilian advisers also rejected a promising strategic option that did not carry large risks either in 1964 or in succeeding years, the use of U.S. ground forces to cut the Ho Chi Minh Trail.[63] The United States would not have found it inordinately difficult to sever the North Vietnamese supply lines in Laos by placing ground troops along the 175 mile-long Route 9, which ran from Dong Ha on the South Chinese Sea to Savannakhet on the Lao-Thai border. During the colonial era, the French had built up the road bed and filled it with culverts so that it could accommodate vehicles even under rainy conditions, making it a far easier line to patrol than the mountainous, roadless, and far longer Lao–South Vietnamese border. In 1960, at which time the North Vietnamese infiltration had involved no motorized traffic, a South Vietnamese force roughly the size of one division had severed the first Ho Chi Minh Trail by controlling the South Vietnamese section of Route 9, which comprised one-fourth of the road's entire length. In 1964, with the infiltration effort heavily reliant on trucks because of the high demand for large equipment and supplies, the United States could have detected and stopped most infiltration of materiel much more easily because the Laotian segment of Route 9, winding as it did through rugged territory, had only a few intersections where trucks could cross. If North Vietnamese forces managed to cross Route 9 on foot once American and South Vietnamese forces had occupied it, they would then find themselves in an area where they had no local allies or North Vietnamese comrades to provide supplies and hiding places. By moving troops rapidly via helicopter, the Americans could contain or encircle the slow-moving North Vietnamese intruders. American troops were to show a remarkable ability to attack, defend, and keep their supplies flowing in remote regions of Vietnam, and they certainly would have done the same in Laos.[64] The Americans, furthermore, could employ their heavy firepower without restraint in this area, for the region lacked the civilian settlements that hindered the use of force in much of South Vietnam.

Were the Americans to cut the Laotian infiltration routes, the North Vietnamese would find it extraordinarily difficult to move the Ho Chi Minh Trail into Thailand.[65] They would need to transport the materiel 100 miles westward to Thailand and another 100 miles eastward back to South Vietnam through very unaccommodating terrain, which would slash the trail's capacity. In addition, the North Vietnamese would have to cross the Mekong River once to get into Thailand and once to get out, forcing them to float across open water where they would be exposed to American air and naval power. U.S. forces could move into Thailand to interdict the new routes, and they would enjoy the assistance of the 125,000–man Thai armed forces.[66] The North Vietnamese might respond by invading Thailand in force; North Vietnamese and Chinese leaders were already considering such an invasion. This type of initiative, though, would have broken with the longstanding policy of Hanoi and Beijing of avoiding large attacks that could not be disguised as purely indigenous rebellions, a policy based on a well-justified fear that overt warfare would provoke the United States and other countries into a massive counter-attack. Hanoi's other possible alternative would be to increase the shipment of materiel and men by sea to the South Vietnamese coast and to Cambodia. The former route, however, would soon be closed, while the latter route could have been closed in 1964 by a blockade or an invasion of Cambodia, though the Americans would not actually close the Cambodian route until 1970.

General Dong Sy Nguyen, the Communist commander in charge of the Ho Chi Minh Trail for much of the war, told a comrade on one occasion that his

great fear was an American ground force intervention across the Ho Chi Minh
Trail. "They can bomb it, no sweat!" he said of the trail. American bombers
rarely caused major damage, the general noted, even when, later in the war, the
Americans began bombing the infiltration routes with mighty B-52s. "What
worries me most is that they will send in troops or use choppers to land some
commandos or drop paratroopers, who would then occupy a chunk of the trail.
This would throw the entire complicated system out of whack." Senior officers
of the North Vietnamese Joint General Staff told Bui Tin, "All they have to do
is to use two or three divisions, both Americans and Saigon troops, to occupy a
chunk of the Ho Chi Minh Trail; then we would be in trouble! The higher-ups
have just this one huge worry!"[67]

Despite these vulnerabilities and despite the cowering of Hanoi's Chinese
allies following the Tonkin Gulf incidents, the North Vietnamese did not lose
heart in the ensuing weeks, for events led them to believe that the United States
had lost the will to inflict serious damage on their country. Although the United
States was increasing its military activities in Indochina, they observed, it was
doing so only at a slow pace, a reality that they attributed to a lack of resolve. After
August 5, they pointed out, the Americans did not take further military action
against North Vietnam or deploy combat troops to South Vietnam.[68] President
Johnson suspended the De Soto patrols for six weeks and then suspended them
again after the September 18 patrol, giving the impression that, as Mao put it
to North Vietnamese Prime Minister Pham Van Dong, the U.S. Navy had been
"scared away" from the Tonkin Gulf.[69]

From reading American newspapers, the North Vietnamese knew that some
leading Americans openly opposed U.S. involvement in Vietnam, which the
North Vietnamese took to mean that internal dissension was shackling Johnson.
Johnson himself, in his speech preceding the August 5 air raid, had unwisely
stressed the "limited" nature of American action, and a few days thereafter
the Americans had notified Hanoi through the Canadian intermediary J. Blair
Seaborn that they did not intend to overthrow the North Vietnamese government, which suggested to North Vietnam's leaders that they could send more
troops to South Vietnam and take other provocative actions without endangering their existence.[70] A Communist history described the Party leadership's
perceptions in September: "Neither the international situation nor the domestic situation in the United States would permit the warmongers of the ruling
class to immediately and all at once commit the full force of U.S. military
might to the Vietnam War."[71] For a decade, the North Vietnamese had been
held at bay by the fear that the United States would attack North Vietnam or
send ground troops to South Vietnam. Johnson had squandered that deterrent
power with a couple of months of timorous behavior.[72]

On the campaign trail, as the fall of 1964 unfolded, Johnson provided further
supporting evidence for Hanoi's interpretation of the United States by por-
traying himself as the candidate of peace and denouncing Republican nominee

Goldwater as the candidate of war, part of his strategy of painting Goldwater as an irresponsible fanatic. Johnson announced that while he did not intend to abandon South Vietnam, he would not send U.S. ground troops to Vietnam – the only surefire way of preventing defeat – or otherwise expand the conflict. On September 25, at Eufaula, Oklahoma, Johnson declared, "We don't want our American boys to do the fighting for Asian boys. We don't want to get involved in a nation with 700 million people and get tied down in a land war in Asia."[73] Some of Johnson's lieutenants, worried about the potential inconsistency between the "peace candidate" rhetoric and the administration's future actions, advised him to tone down the talk of peace and restraint and speak more of the defense of South Vietnam. McGeorge Bundy warned Johnson, "It is a better than even chance that we will be undertaking some air and land action in the Laotian corridor and even in North Vietnam within the next two months, and we do not want the record to suggest even remotely that we campaigned on peace in order to start a war in November."[74] Johnson had not changed his mind on post-election attacks on the North since he began planning them in May, but he refused to rewrite his campaign playbook. After receiving Bundy's admonition, on October 21, he told an audience at the University of Akron, "we are not about to send American boys nine or ten thousand miles away from home to do what Asian boys ought to be doing for themselves."[75]

Unlike the hypothetical adversaries in Schelling's academic games, the North Vietnamese did not impose limits on themselves when the enemy limited itself, but instead became more aggressive to exploit the enemy's self-imposed restrictions. America's intellectuals and their civilian admirers in the administration were proving inept at predicting enemy behavior, while the hardheaded military leaders, to whom Lyndon Johnson was paying little attention, were becoming America's Cassandras. In late September, the apparent unwillingness of the United States to employ its full power in the near future, combined with the continuing deterioration of the South Vietnamese governmental structure, led the North Vietnamese to accelerate their plans for intensifying the war in the South. The Communists resolved to destroy the South Vietnamese government within one to two years, convinced that the Americans would not build enough strength in South Vietnam within that time to stop them. At a meeting that lasted from September 25 to 29, just after Johnson had told the crowd of Oklahomans of his desire to keep America's boys out of Asia, the North Vietnamese Politburo expressed a determination to "move quickly to seize this opportunity and strive to completely defeat the puppet army before the U.S. armed forces have time to intervene."[76] The Communists decided that the Viet Cong were not strong enough to win this victory on their own, despite the accelerating inflow of native Northerners, so they decided to send whole North Vietnamese Army main force regiments to the South to help fight the large battles that would have to be fought if South Vietnam's conventional units were to be crippled.[77]

At this time, the North Vietnamese also suggested to the Chinese that if a larger war began, the international Communist movement should expand the armed struggle across all of Southeast Asia. Every Communist party in Southeast Asia, the North Vietnamese stressed, had built networks at the local level. Mao, however, chastened by the Tonkin Gulf events, wanted to take matters more slowly. The revolution could succeed right now in South Vietnam and Laos, Mao told Le Duan, but Thailand and Burma might not yet be ready for major revolutionary warfare. It could take five to ten years to launch a full-scale armed insurrection in Thailand, Mao divined. He agreed with Le Duan, nevertheless, that North Vietnam should work hard to assist the Thai Communist Party in building its military forces. Even a small insurgency could help convince the Thai government to switch allegiance from Washington to Beijing and Hanoi. Thailand was critical to the struggle for power in Southeast Asia, Mao intoned, and the United States would be hard pressed to fight in the region if deprived of its alliance with Thailand.[78]

At the end of September, the North Vietnamese Politburo for the first time sent one of its own members, General Nguyen Chi Thanh, to the South, where he was to command all of the Communist forces.[79] The Communist headquarters in South Vietnam began preparations for taking Saigon with main forces, supplemented by an urban uprising.[80] The dispatch of North Vietnamese units to South Vietnam, however, which was the action most likely to attract international attention, did not take place in October, most probably because Hanoi wanted to watch for further indications of American intentions. Abeyance would, above all, allow them to see first whether Johnson, the candidate of peace, would defeat Goldwater, the alleged warmonger, in the U.S. election.

The Johnson administration had no inkling that the strategic landscape in Hanoi was changing. Believing the Saigon regime to have less strength relative to North Vietnam than the North Vietnamese themselves believed, U.S. intelligence analysts concluded that Hanoi was sure to prevail if it kept increasing the insurgency gradually and therefore it would not need to accelerate its military efforts precipitously. They contended that the fear of provoking the United States into attacking North Vietnam's industrial bases and the concentrated North Vietnamese military forces required for a large conventional offensive would keep Hanoi from pursuing such a strategy. It was an egregious underestimation of the degree to which recent American timidity had reduced North Vietnam's fear of U.S. retaliation.[81] Such conclusions served to reinforce Johnson's belief that his restraint, procrastination, and campaign rhetoric could not make possible the death of South Vietnam, regardless of that country's internal ailments and the stones cast at it.

The newest ailment afflicted South Vietnam on September 13, in the predawn hours. Ten rebellious battalions spearheaded an insurrection in Saigon, under the leadership of General Lam Van Phat, who until recently had been the Minister of the Interior, and General Duong Van Duc, who had been working as a waiter in Paris before Prime Minister Khanh appointed him the commander of IV Corps. Dissatisfied with Khanh's weak leadership and his subservience to Buddhist demands, the two generals had been among those whom Khanh had just agreed to remove in response to Buddhist pressure. With their ten battalions, the coup leaders took the city center without firing a shot. They were unable, however, to locate Khanh. Broadcasting from the national radio station, General Phat announced the overthrow of the government, and he vowed to rely on the philosophy and prestige of Ngo Dinh Diem in building a new government. Most of the army's senior commanders, similarly fed up with Khanh, either abetted the conspirators or sat back and did nothing.

Khanh had escaped Saigon when the trouble began and taken refuge in the mountain city of Dalat. On orders from the American embassy, William Sullivan of the State Department and Major General Richard Stilwell flew to Dalat to urge him to return to Saigon. Khanh had to take charge immediately, they told him, before the situation worsened. Khanh replied that he would go back to Saigon if the United States broadcast a statement supporting him and his government. After questioning Khanh about his plans, Sullivan and Stilwell concluded that he had none, which they duly relayed to the State Department, along with Khanh's request for an expression of support.[82] Fortunately for Khanh, the Americans who were on the phone with General Phat concluded that the coup leaders themselves lacked plans for a new government. For this reason, the U.S. embassy urged the head conspirators to end the revolt, and it announced that the United States still supported Khanh's government, which together, in a short time, dissuaded other officers from joining the rebellion and convinced Phat and Duc to give up. Returning to Saigon following the American declaration of support, Khanh put the coup leaders in prison for sixty days and replaced an extraordinary number of top commanders – three of the four corps commanders and six of the nine division commanders – for failing to assist him during the abortive putsch.[83]

Shortly after this event, out of enormous frustration with the persistent instability in Saigon, the Americans warned prominent South Vietnamese figures that continued internal feuding could cause the United States to write off South Vietnam. These warnings, however, failed to halt the centrifugal motion. From observing Khanh's concessions to the Buddhists and his indecisiveness, other groups decided that now was the time to demand concessions for themselves. On September 19 and 20, Upland tribal soldiers seized four paramilitary camps in Darlac province, killing seventy South Vietnamese soldiers and taking a number of U.S. and South Vietnamese personnel hostage before adroit American military advisers convinced them to desist. On the twentieth, the 300,000-member Vietnamese Confederation of Labor staged a forty-eight-hour general strike which, among other things, deprived Saigon and other cities of electricity.[84] To defuse the unrest, Khanh made lavish concessions to both the Uplanders and the Confederation of Labor. Khanh's concessions to every group that had pressured him, Ambassador Taylor reported to Washington, had whittled away the government's authority close to the point at which it would cease to be a government at all.[85]

Other disorders continued in the cities after the September 13 coup attempt and the general strike, with Viet Cong participation in the unrest growing still further. In Qui Nhon, where rioting temporarily shut down the government, and in other cities in the northern part of the country, government commanders did nothing to stop the agitators. Many government ministries stopped functioning altogether, even in Saigon.[86] Under pressure from some of the other generals, Khanh put his rival Big Minh in charge of appointing a seventeen-member High National Council that would oversee the creation of a new government. Minh's handpicked council quickly came out in favor of giving overwhelming authority to a new chief of state, a position that the council members expected would be filled by Minh. Khanh, however, discerned their scheme and sabotaged it, with the help of the Americans, who had lost all confidence in Minh after the implosion of the Minh junta. The Americans convinced the council to dilute the chief of state's authority to such a large degree that Minh would find the office unattractive, which caused Minh to turn down the position and go abroad on a "goodwill tour" financed by the United States. Ultimately, in late October, the High National Council chose the aging Pham Khac Suu as chief of state, and Suu selected Tran Van Huong, the mayor of Saigon, as prime minister. Khanh officially left politics to become the commander-in-chief of the armed forces.

In the few months preceding the tumult of the late summer and early fall, the Americans had noticed some improvement in pacification and in the manpower growth and combat effectiveness of the South Vietnamese Army.[87] The political turmoil resulted in a sharp disruption of the remaining pacification efforts, with the most pronounced declines in the northernmost provinces of South Vietnam, where pacification previously had not suffered as much damage as in most parts of the country. Having gained control over much of the piedmont in those areas since Diem's demise, Communist forces were now launching operations into the coastal plain. Large numbers of Northern-born soldiers were entering the northern provinces, bringing the number of Communist soldiers in Communist Military Region 5 to 11,000, the most of any region in the country. Viet Cong prisoners from this region stated that their units contained 30 to 40 percent Northerners.[88] Nationwide, the administrative disorder and the Communists' advances produced an ominous drop in the number of men entering into the government's armed forces, with monthly conscription plunging from 4,400 in August to 1,600 in September, far below the government target of 10,440, and voluntary enlistments plummeting from 4,000 to 1,700.[89] The numerical strength of the regular army began to fall at an alarming rate.

The momentous changes of the late summer and early fall all grew out of the Johnson administration's attempt, on August 5, to send a signal with a small and solitary air attack.[90] Rather than convincing Hanoi to "limit the escalation" by indicating that the United States meant business, as was the intent, the August 5 strike encouraged Hanoi to escalate precipitously by suggesting that the United States had lost the will to defend South Vietnam with its full might, the one thing that had held Hanoi in check for the previous ten years. The dramatic deterioration of the South Vietnamese government that had begun on November 1, 1963 progressed rapidly between August and October because of Khanh's capitulation to the demands of Buddhist leader Tri Quang and other dissidents, providing ample grounds for Hanoi to believe that South Vietnam was ripe for the taking. After the air raid of August 5, American certitude that Hanoi would not dare escalate led Johnson to refrain from hitting North Vietnam again and to talk of peace in his campaign speeches, each of which supplied additional evidence to North Vietnam that the United States would not thwart a great Communist offensive. Whereas America's civilian leadership thought that strong action against the North would cause the North Vietnamese to attack the South, it was the absence of strong action that prompted them to attack.

CHAPTER 15

Invasion

NOVEMBER–DECEMBER 1964

ON NOVEMBER 1, JUST AFTER MIDNIGHT, A VIET CONG MORTAR company rode sampans down a river that led to the Bien Hoa air base, home to some of the most sophisticated U.S. aircraft in South Vietnam. On orders from General William Westmoreland, a South Vietnamese Airborne battalion was guarding the base, but the mortar company managed to evade the paratroopers' patrols. One and a half miles from the airfield, the guerrillas brought the sampans ashore and set up their 81mm mortars in a meadow of shoulder-high brush. Over the next thirty-nine minutes, they lobbed 100 rounds at the airfield and hit an important target with almost every round, a sure indication that Viet Cong spies had infiltrated the base beforehand and paced off the range to the targets. The shells shattered the airfield's control tower and an American barracks, killing four Americans and wounding thirty. Aircraft casualties totaled twenty-seven, including eleven B-57 bombers worth 1.25 million dollars apiece.

Ambassador Taylor, General Westmoreland, and Admiral Sharp demanded immediate retaliation, to show the enemy that such attacks would not be tolerated and to inspire the South Vietnamese government. The Joint Chiefs of Staff called for both heavy air strikes in North Vietnam and Laos and the introduction of Marine units into South Vietnam to protect American installations. So important did the Joint Chiefs consider the matter that they warned the President, through Secretary of Defense McNamara, that if he refused to respond militarily, then the United States should get out of Vietnam.[1] Johnson, keenly attuned to the political atmosphere in the United States with the election only a few days away, was most concerned with the domestic ramifications of his reaction. Voters might view retaliation as an election ploy and turn against him. On the other hand, the Tonkin Gulf incidents had shown the American people to be enthusiastic supporters of retaliation, and they might want it in this case. Just a few hours after the savaging of the air base, at Johnson's behest, Special Assistant to the President Bill Moyers phoned Louis Harris of the Harris Poll. Moyers told Harris, "The President would like to know if a failure to respond to this attack immediately will be taken by the voters as a sign of weakness by the administration." Harris assured Moyers that the majority of people would approve if Johnson did not act immediately.[2] Soon thereafter, Johnson decided against retaliation. He and his civilian advisers offered Ambassador Taylor and the generals most every possible excuse for inaction, some of which had not been considered significant issues before. The most important reason, though, was contained in a separate message sent solely to Taylor and labeled "Literally eyes only Ambassador." In the message, Secretary of State Rusk informed Taylor, "In this one case we are inevitably affected by election timing. Quick retaliation could easily be attacked as election device here."[3]

Visiting the Joint Chiefs the following day, McNamara assured the distraught generals that he and Johnson wanted to undertake major military action in Vietnam and also in China, just not right away. He characterized the President's intentions as the legacy of a Texas cowboy youth, although Johnson's true intentions were much closer to the legacy of his actual youth, when he lay on his bed and fearfully kicked at his adversary, afraid of using force and ignorant of its ways. "The President, being born in Texas, is inclined to take some action," said McNamara. The President wanted to hit all the high-priority targets in North Vietnam and, McNamara commented, "I don't believe that he will be able to stop there. I would recommend that when that point is reached, we should strike against the Communist nuclear facilities. This nuclear capability of the Chinese Communists is a greater threat over a long period of time."[4] The sole purpose of these words was to prevent the generals from denouncing the President's Vietnam policy right before the election, for Johnson and McNamara had no intention of smiting China. Three days later, after the election was over, McNamara would tell the President, "I don't think there's any strong sentiment for trying to go in and clobber China at the moment, other than [from] a strictly military organization. I'm sure we can sit on top of that."[5]

Critics would later say that the Joint Chiefs should have resigned in protest of Johnson's mishandling of Vietnam and his inattention to the recommendations of the military.[6] This charge, however, was neither realistic nor fair. The resignation of one of the Joint Chiefs likely would have been followed by a public commotion that faded after a few days or weeks and by the installation of someone more willing to go along with the President. In the end, American policy would remain unchanged, the Joint Chiefs would have one less man willing to question policy in the future, and a general's career would be over. The resignation of all the chiefs at once would have provoked a crisis between military and political authorities even more serious than the showdown between Truman and MacArthur during the Korean War, as it would call into question the subordination of the military to the civilian government. The outcome would have been either the subordination of civilian authority to the military on matters of national security or else the installation of yes-men into all the slots in the Joint Chiefs of Staff. By trying to sway Johnson while staying within the system, the Joint Chiefs chose the best of the inferior options available.[7]

As Taylor and America's military leadership had feared, the absence of American air strikes and ground force deployments following the Bien Hoa attack reinforced Hanoi's perception that the Americans lacked resolve. The North Vietnamese received the most encouraging news two days after the attack, when Western newspapers announced that Johnson had defeated Goldwater in the Presidential election. The U.S. President for the next four years, it seemed, would be a man whose pronouncements and actions had shown him unwilling to get tough over Vietnam.

At this very same time, the North Vietnamese also became convinced that tensions between the United States and France were about to shift the global distribution of power in the favor of America's enemies. At the beginning of November, the Western press was filled with indications of an imminent French withdrawal from NATO on account of intractable disagreements with the Americans over NATO's organization and a proposed mixed-nation nuclear fleet. The *New York Times,* which North Vietnamese government officials read as ravenously as their South Vietnamese and American counterparts, commented that NATO "today faces the most serious crisis in its history." Simultaneously, the French were agreeing to give $356 million in trade credits to the Soviets and applauding a Chinese proposal for an international disarmament conference.[8] The Soviet Union, which had just experienced the ouster of Nikita Khrushchev and the installation of Leonid Brezhnev and Alexei Kosygin, appeared to be moving away from the policy of peaceful coexistence towards a militantly anti-American policy; the Soviets informed Prime Minister Pham Van Dong during the second week of November that they intended to repair relations with North Vietnam and provide it with much greater military assistance.[9]

In the middle of November, the Political Bureau of the Communist Party Central Committee convened in Hanoi for final deliberations on strategy. The United States, the assemblage concluded, would not attack North Vietnam or send its troops to South Vietnam, because of both internal and external problems. In their analysis, the Political Bureau also noted that the infighting in South Vietnam was progressively weakening the South Vietnamese government and armed forces, to the degree that Communist subversives in the cities could overthrow it once Communist main forces had thrashed the South Vietnamese Army. Citing the successes of the Russian Revolution in Petrograd and Moscow in 1917, the bureau asserted, "It is presently possible to expand the movement in the cities very rapidly. . . . The rule of one day being equivalent to 20 years, as Lenin said, can apply to the cities of South Vietnam."[10]

As soon as the Political Bureau adjourned, the exuberant North Vietnamese leadership set the invasion of South Vietnam in motion. The 325th North Vietnamese Army Division received orders to send its three regiments to northern

South Vietnam at once via the Ho Chi Minh Trail. While Hanoi had sent thousands of North Vietnamese soldiers to serve in Viet Cong units, it had rarely sent complete North Vietnamese units to the South heretofore, and it had never sent anything larger than a single battalion.[11] The first of the 325th Division's regiments left its base on November 20, with the intention of commencing offensive operations in the South no later than March 1965. Hanoi also ordered the 320th Infantry Regiment, the 545th Viet Bac Battalion, and several other North Vietnamese battalions to proceed to the South.[12] North Vietnam's leaders refrained from committing numerous other units at their disposal, because they still had some fear that the United States or other countries would react strongly if they detected a massive invasion, and detection would be more likely the larger the North Vietnamese forces were. Fear of detection also caused the North Vietnamese to disguise the invading units by outfitting them in the black pajamas and rubber sandals of the Viet Cong, giving them Viet Cong unit designations, and chiseling the markings off weapons that had been produced in China or Eastern Europe.

At this same point in time, Communist ambitions were also surging on another front of the Asian Cold War. Chinese Premier Zhou Enlai told Sukarno in November that he should arm Indonesian farmers and workers in order to defeat anti-Communist elements within the Indonesian military, and he offered to provide firearms for this purpose. Zhou, in addition, promised Sukarno economic aid and assistance in both the conventional military and nuclear fields. Visiting Djakarta in November, Chinese Foreign Minister Chen Yi urged Sukarno to participate in a joint Sino-Indonesian offensive against Malaysia, with China supporting a guerrilla war in northern Malaya.[13] Indonesian Foreign Minister Subandrio told his country's diplomats the following month that Indonesia, China, and North Vietnam would work together to drive the Americans and British from South Vietnam, Malaysia, and the rest of Southeast Asia, with South Vietnam serving as a base for attacking Malaysia across the Gulf of Siam, as it had served the Japanese in World War II.[14]

In Saigon, November was the month when Tran Van Huong assumed power. Huong was, like Ngo Dinh Diem, a stubborn and conservative nationalist who had opposed both sides during the Franco–Viet Minh War. In 1954, Huong agreed to work for Diem and was appointed mayor of Saigon, but resigned from that position in the late 1950s because of political differences with the President. A man of integrity and determination, Huong was one of the ablest civilian executives in South Vietnam in 1964, and, had it not been for insidious Buddhists and other unusual problems, he most likely would have been a successful national leader.

Huong was intent on restoring law and order in Saigon, sharing as he did the view of Diem and most other knowledgeable Vietnamese that unrestrained opposition was anathema to effective governance. "There must be respect for public order, and there must be national discipline," Huong declared upon taking office.[15] Like Diem and unlike Khanh, Huong viewed Tri Quang as an implacable menace and an accomplice of the Communists.[16] Quickly recognizing Huong's intolerance of political chaos and rabid opposition, Tri Quang and other militant Buddhists hurried to organize demonstrations denouncing the new government. Buddhist leaders issued a communiqué calling Huong "stupid, a traitor, a fat, stubborn man without any policy,"[17] and they charged that the governmental leadership contained extensive "vestiges of the Diem regime," which was a major exaggeration.[18] Buddhist spokesmen fiercely condemned Huong's plans to curb public protests, with some even calling for a reduction in the government's military activities,[19] undisturbed by the reality that continued disorder and the disintegration of the Huong government would abet the Viet Cong. "It is better to have a political vacuum than have Huong in power," one Buddhist leader snarled.[20]

Huong broke up the Buddhist demonstrations with troops wielding nightsticks, fire hoses, and tear gas. The government's enemies claimed that government security forces caused numerous fatalities and injuries in the first few days of Huong's rule, but no one actually died and the number of injuries was far lower than was alleged.[21] Huong also imposed censorship and shut down ten newspapers suspected of colluding with the Communists. At the end of November, frustrated by Huong's initial resistance to pressure, the Buddhists turned to more violent methods. Assembling a large number of anti-government demonstrators in Saigon, they pelted policemen with rocks and hit them with clubs. When members of a Buddhist mob threw concussion grenades of the sort used by the Viet Cong, a paratroop officer fired his pistol in their direction and killed a fifteen-year-old boy. The militant Buddhists then issued an ultimatum demanding that the army and police not touch any demonstrators and that Huong be removed from office. Huong rejected the demands, opting instead to declare a state of siege, which involved a prohibition of public gatherings and the closing of schools. On the radio, Huong announced that the disorders were the fault of "irresponsible people who have either innocently or deliberately fallen in with the Communist plan."[22] Huong's firm actions quelled the unrest in Saigon for the moment.

Inheriting a government that had already been devastated by purges and infighting, Huong found that many cabinet members and military leaders did not like each other and did not like him. Khanh and other generals were secretly conspiring with Tri Quang against Huong, while at the same time a different group of officers was making plans to install General Nguyen Van Thieu in place of General Khanh. The debilitation of the government under his predecessors and the rampant factionalism denied Huong the opportunity to bring the provincial administrations up from their disarray. Huong did, on the other hand, have some success in repairing the government organs in the towns and cities and in bolstering the regular army. During the first two months of Huong's rule, military recruitment rebounded to such a degree that the South

Vietnamese Army began to increase in size.[23] The growth, however, did not keep pace with that of the Viet Cong.

By the end of 1964, Viet Cong strength would rise to 51,300 main and local force troops in sixty-nine main and local force battalions, thanks to heavy recruitment in the South and to accelerated infiltration that brought the total number of North Vietnamese infiltrators to 17,000[24] for the year 1964. Toward the end of the year, moreover, Hanoi increased the shipment of war supplies to South Vietnam by sea in order to meet a greater demand for weapons.[25] Using weapons newly arrived from the sea, Communist forces in the coastal provinces of Communist Military Region 5 intensified the war during November and December. In Military Region 5 and the highlands, the Communists initiated a substantial number of large-scale military attacks, most of them successful. Taylor noted, "The northern provinces of South Viet-Nam, which a year ago were considered almost free of Viet-Cong, are now in deep trouble."[26] Across the country, the Viet Cong armed forces generally fared well in the last two months of the year. The number of provinces where U.S. advisers reported adequate government control of the rural population fell from seventeen provinces out of forty-five in November to ten out of forty-five in December.[27]

Some of the fiercest fighting in late 1964 took place in Binh Dinh province, located in the middle of Communist Military Region 5. In accordance with standard counterinsurgency doctrine, Westmoreland had advised the South Vietnamese Army commanders in Binh Dinh to break down their forces into small units and spread them out to provide security for a large number of villages. The South Vietnamese had followed this advice, and it had brought them some early rewards. Their initial successes, however, led the Communists to introduce large main force units – the 2nd Regiment and the 409th Sapper Battalion – into Binh Dinh. Attacking the small government detachments one by one, the Communists were able to bring overwhelming strength to bear on each occasion. One government unit after another was mauled by the Communist battalions. Lacking large and capable reserve forces, the government could not halt the rampage or attack the Communists in their base areas.

From the Binh Dinh campaign, Westmoreland came away with a most important lesson, one that was to guide all of his subsequent thinking on how to fight the war. "Ignore the big units and you courted disaster," was how Westmoreland put it. "Failure to go after them in at least comparable strength invited defeat."[28] Because of their main force capabilities, the Viet Cong could and would respond to a dispersion of government forces by concentrating their own forces, just as they often responded to a concentration of government forces by dispersing their forces. While some dispersion of the counterinsurgent forces was necessary in order to exert control over the villages and their resources, a substantial number of counterinsurgent forces would have to operate in large mobile units to battle with the large insurgent units and keep them away from the small, dispersed counterinsurgent units. The revolutionary mobility afforded by the helicopter dramatically increased the efficiency and effectiveness of such mobile reserve units, but they were still needed in large numbers against an enemy with as many conventional troops and as many potential targets as the Vietnamese Communists had in South Vietnam. These reserve forces had to seek out the enemy's big units away from the uninhabited areas as well as react to enemy initiatives. If they merely reacted to the enemy, they would always have to face one of two unappealing scenarios: fighting at the time and place of the enemy's choosing, or arriving after the enemy had overrun its target and departed. A purely reactive approach would also require government forces to do most of their fighting in populated areas, where they would face restrictions on the use of firepower and where combat might drive away pro-government civilians. If left unmolested by large government operations in unpopulated areas, moreover, the Viet Cong could concentrate in great numbers at will. The inability to appreciate these realities would lead to the production of a library's worth of articles and books wrongly condemning the Americans and South Vietnamese for using large conventional forces to search for and engage the Communists.[29]

The largest and most fruitful Communist attack of the year came at Binh Gia, a hamlet in Phuoc Tuy province, just forty miles to the east of Saigon.[30] Binh Gia, which means "people of peace," had been considered an exemplary strategic hamlet during the Diem era, and in late 1964 it was one of the few hamlets that still had an effective militia force, owing to the fervent anti-Communism of the 6,000 North Vietnamese Catholic refugees who comprised its population.[31] The hamlet had provided the South Vietnamese government with many fine soldiers, so Saigon could be expected to rush substantial relief forces there if the Viet Cong seized control. Located in a lowland forest, Binh Gia afforded the Viet Cong ideal conditions for engaging relief units. The approaches to the hamlets and the surrounding fields lay within striking distance of tree-covered areas where the Communists could mass troops and heavy weapons unseen.

The newly arrived North Vietnamese commander-in-chief, General Nguyen Chi Thanh, chose to commit to this battle two of his three main force regiments in Cochinchina, the 1st and 2nd Viet Cong Regiments. He also deployed several smaller Viet Cong units and, for fire support purposes, the 80th Artillery Group, which was led by North Vietnamese officers. In all, the Viet Cong fielded a force that was equal in size to a full division, larger than anything the Viet Cong had ever put onto a field of battle. These forces were extraordinarily well equipped because of the exertions of the North Vietnamese Navy, which had secretly delivered an astounding 500 tons of weapons to the attack force shortly before the battle. The infantry carried AK-47s and an array of high quality machine guns, while the four battalions of the 80th Artillery Group possessed an abundance of the heavy armaments needed in a large conventional battle – 81mm mortars, 75mm recoilless rifles, 70mm pack howitzers, and 12.7mm heavy antiaircraft machine guns. General Thanh intended to take and hold Binh Gia with a portion of his men, then use the full weight of his forces to pounce on government relief troops from a variety of directions.

The engagement began on the morning of December 28, with the Viet Cong's 1st Regiment and 445th Company sweeping into Binh Gia with overwhelming force. They drove the hamlet militiamen to flight, much as large South Vietnamese units had driven off Viet Cong guerrillas so many times before. In the center of the hamlet, the 1st Regiment erected its command post, and along the hamlet's edges the Viet Cong prepared defenses in expectation of a government counter-attack. At this point in time, the top leaders of the South Vietnamese Army were preoccupied with the newest national political crisis, and they would spend most of the Binh Gia battle in Vung Tau trying to resolve political problems behind closed doors, which left the battle in the hands of less capable subordinates. Upon learning that a Communist force of uncertain size had taken Binh Gia, the acting commander sent two South Vietnamese Ranger companies to land to the west of Binh Gia and advance on the hamlet with the assistance of Skyraider attack bombers and UH-1 B Huey helicopters. These forces, however, were much too small to breach the densely defended Communist defensive line, and so the South Vietnamese corps command then used the entire 30th Ranger Battalion to attack from the west. But still they lacked the strength to penetrate the Viet Cong's defensive line.

The South Vietnamese command next decided to attack Binh Gia from multiple directions simultaneously to compel the enemy to spread his forces out around the hamlet rim. Two companies of the 33rd Ranger Battalion flew by helicopter to the northeast of Binh Gia and marched forward to assault the hamlet. The first company made it intact to the edge of Binh Gia, but was unable to break through the Communist defenses. The commander of the other company attempted to outflank the Viet Cong by moving through a coffee plantation to the southeast of Binh Gia, but was outwitted by the Viet Cong regimental commander, who was carefully tracking this company's movement. The Viet Cong commander ordered his battalions to push into the coffee plantation from the north, south, and west in order to drive the Ranger company to the east, to what might seem to the Rangers a safe area because of the absence of Viet Cong soldiers but was in reality an ideal killing zone because it was flat, open, and within close range of the Viet Cong's concealed heavy weapons. When the Viet Cong's 1st Battalion stormed into the coffee plantation at 3:00 P.M., some of the Rangers fled eastward and were quickly slaughtered by heavy weapons fire. The remaining Rangers attempted to fight their way to the northwest, into the center of the hamlet, but they could not get past a Viet Cong blocking force. Surrounded and outmanned, they were quickly obliterated. Of all the Rangers sent into the melee by the 33rd Ranger Battalion that day, approximately seventy percent became casualties.

To the west of Binh Gia, the afternoon's events progressed more favorably for the government. Several companies of the 30th Ranger Battalion broke through the Viet Cong's defenses, which had been thinned out to deal with the 33rd Rangers in the east. The hamlet's residents helped the advancing Rangers by cutting Viet Cong telephone wires, hauling wounded Rangers into their homes for protection, and retrieving weapons and ammunition from the dead to give to the living. Attacking into the afternoon sunlight, the Rangers battled their way forward to the center of the hamlet. By evening, the commander of the 1st Viet Cong Regiment became convinced that the Viet Cong could not maintain a foothold in the hamlet much longer. Under cover of darkness, he withdrew all Viet Cong units from the hamlet to positions in the forest where, along with the other Viet Cong elements, they could strike the government's relief forces.

Little fighting took place on the next day, December 30, but that evening, a Huey helicopter that was pursuing Viet Cong troops was shot down by a 12.7mm antiaircraft machine gun, another instance where the newly infiltrated weapons from the North inflicted grievous damage. With flames pouring from its wounds, the helicopter crashed through the rubber trees of the Quang Giao rubber plantation before hitting the earth. The III Corps command ordered the 4th South Vietnamese Marine Battalion to the crash site to retrieve the Americans, be they dead or alive. Early the next morning, two of the Marine battalion's companies moved eastwards along a gravel road from Binh Gia and into the rubber plantation, reaching the helicopter wreck at noon. The South Vietnamese Marines found that the Viet Cong had buried the four American crewmen, who had been killed when the helicopter hit the ground and exploded.

The Marines had just begun digging up the corpses when the Viet Cong, who had been watching them since the beginning of their approach to the rubber plantation, hit them with an avalanche of artillery shells and an infantry charge. The rubber trees, so large that a man could not get his arms all the way around them, made it most difficult to determine the enemy's location and strength. The Communists described this stage of the battle as follows: "Under powerful attack from the south, the enemy force closed ranks and put up ferocious resistance." The two Marine companies desperately repulsed several Viet Cong assaults, but it appeared doubtful that they could continue to hold the large enemy forces at bay for very long. Guided by an L-19 reconaissance plane that was dropping smoke markers, American aircraft hammered the Communist positions, which forced the Viet Cong to pull back and allowed the two Marine companies to escape from the rubber plantation. A Viet Cong force attempted to pursue them once they were in the open, but was halted by rocket-firing helicopters that had just arrived on the scene.

On their way back to Binh Gia, the two South Vietnamese Marine companies linked up with the remainder of their battalion, which had headed for the rubber plantation on hearing the din of battle. With all of its companies together now, albeit two of them reduced by combat losses, the 4th Battalion returned in the direction of the helicopter crash site. Keeping their eyes on the Marines, the Viet Cong readied three battalions to attack them in the rubber plantation. Encountering no opposition initially, the Marines arrived at the crash site at 2:00 P.M. and loaded the dead Americans onto a helicopter that had flown to a landing zone nearby. Before the South Vietnamese Marine battalion could get away, the three Communist battalions attacked it from three directions. The Marine battalion commander and battalion surgeon were shot dead in the opening moments of the fighting, and the battalion executive officer suffered a mortal wound. The Marines called for air strikes, only to be told that no air assets were currently available. Two of the Marine companies fought their way northward out of the plantation and, despite heavy Viet Cong infantry and artillery attacks along the gravel road, made it back to Binh Gia in an orderly manner. Of the two Marine companies that remained in the rubber plantation, one was eventually overrun and decimated, with all but a dozen or so of its men perishing. The other clung desperately to a hilltop inside the plantation, its ranks depleted but not broken by numerous Viet Cong artillery barrages and large infantry assaults. At sundown, the company moved off the hilltop and daringly slipped through the Viet Cong lines to safety. By the end of the day, the Marine battalion of 426 men had endured total losses of 122 dead and 46 wounded.

The last major clash at Binh Gia occurred two days later, when a task force of Rangers and armor went in search of the Viet Cong several kilometers to the southwest of the hamlet and ran into the Viet Cong's 2nd Regiment. South Vietnamese tanks and armored personnel carriers, enjoying one of their very few opportunities to engage a large enemy force in a conventional battle, exchanged fire with Viet Cong recoilless rifles and .50 caliber machine guns. The government task force suffered nearly one hundred casualties, and Viet Cong recoilless rifle fire destroyed two of its M-113s and a tank. The Viet Cong's losses were not known. After this encounter, the Viet Cong main forces withdrew entirely from the Binh Gia area.

The South Vietnamese armed forces sustained serious damage during the Battle of Binh Gia, taking casualties of 445, most of them elite Rangers or Marines. The Communists never revealed the extent of their total losses in the battle, but they must have been quite high, for had their strength not fallen substantially they would have had little reason to flee the battlefield at this time. The Viet Cong's prebattle numerical strength far exceeded the numerical strength of the South Vietnamese units deployed around Binh Gia at the end of the battle, despite the arrival near the end of several Airborne battalions, and in the absence of heavy losses they would have been in very high spirits and eager to continue inflicting heavy losses on the government forces. The Communists withdrew from Binh Gia, Le Duan recounted afterwards, because they lacked sufficient strategic reserve forces to defeat the South Vietnamese units assembled at Binh Gia. For the moment, the Saigon government's vital strategic reserve forces remained stronger than those of the Viet Cong. Hanoi's conventional forces had not, by the end of 1964, reached the point where they could fight the series of large and decisive battles that Le Duan and General Nguyen Chi Thanh had envisioned at the year's beginning. General Hoang Van Thai, one of Hanoi's top generals, explained later, "the puppet army was still large and was monitored and directed by tens of thousands of American advisors. Meanwhile, our armed forces were still small and we lacked the 'main force fists' needed to take action one step ahead of the general uprising."[32] The Viet Cong had, however, shown an aptitude for massing troops and employing imported heavy weapons on such a large scale that they could wipe out entire companies of the South Vietnamese strategic reserve. And the "main force fists" were on their way.

*   *   *

FOLLOWING HIS VICTORY IN THE ELECTION, WITH HIS ACTIONS NO longer so heavily dependent upon electoral concerns, President Johnson ordered an interdepartmental working group to analyze two options for attacking North Vietnam. One of the options involved major U.S. military action against the North that would intensify rapidly until the Communist leadership relented. The other involved a lower level of violence at first and a much slower rate of intensification, with the United States deciding as it went along whether to increase, maintain, decrease, or terminate the attacks.[33] These options were known to their proponents, respectively, as the "sharp blow" and the "gradual escalation" options.

The leaders of the working group – William Bundy, John McNaughton, and Michael Forrestal – favored gradual escalation from the outset, as did the administration's top civilians, and the group's output portrayed gradual escalation as the option with the greater chance of success, although they admitted that they could not predict the outcome of either option. The great damage to North Vietnamese capabilities resulting from the sharp blow was unimportant, the working group put forth, for America's principal target ought not be Hanoi's capabilities but rather its will, since Hanoi's capabilities could not be completely destroyed but its will could.[34] Coming into play, again, were the civilians' misperceptions about the importance of North Vietnamese support to the war in the South. The lower level of destruction might even be an advantage for gradual escalation, asserted the working group, because "the prospect of more to come" was "at least as important psychologically as present damage,"[35] a contention derived mainly from abstract academic theorizing rather than analysis of history. In theory, gradual escalation was less risky than the sharp blow, because the United States could de-escalate the attacks as soon as the Communist powers began reaching for their weapons, and because gradual escalation would allow South Vietnam more time to strengthen itself in advance of enemy counter-escalation. In addition, the working group noted, U.S. experts on China believed that dramatic U.S. action against North Vietnam would strengthen the alliance between China and North Vietnam. In actuality, major U.S. actions against the North Vietnamese had been undermining North Vietnamese-Chinese solidarity since August 1964, and they would continue to have this effect in the future.

Ambassador Taylor favored gradual escalation, but with the proviso that escalation continue unconditionally; if the United States was willing to see the Saigon government go down to defeat, said Taylor, North Vietnam should at least be left in "smoldering ruins."[36] The Joint Chiefs of Staff voiced very strong and powerful objections to gradual escalation. Most objectionable to them was the working group's claim that "the prospect of more to come" was "at least as important psychologically as present damage." Rather than deterring the Chinese and North Vietnamese, the chiefs asserted, gradual escalation would likely cause them to underestimate U.S. resolve and, consequently, to accelerate their military activities. Neither the chiefs nor any other Americans, of course, knew that this very process had already occurred, in the aftermath of the Tonkin Gulf incidents. The Joint Chiefs much preferred the sharp blow, and they favored unconditional continuation. "A sharp blow, because of the boldness and resoluteness of its delivery, will discourage rather than encourage the enemy to escalate," they argued to Secretary of Defense McNamara. The chiefs also stressed that a lack of intensive attacks up front would give the Communists time to enhance their defensive capabilities and infiltrate more men and war goods.[37]

President Johnson showed his usual disregard for the Joint Chiefs. The working group and the highest civilian advisers succeeded in persuading him that North Vietnamese assistance to the insurgents was of minimal military importance,[38] and that gradual escalation offered an important advantage in allowing more time for improving the South Vietnamese government before the North Vietnamese attacked the South in great strength. On November 29, he made the working group's gradual escalation option the new official U.S. policy. Explaining the decision to his top officials, Johnson remarked, "I do not want to send a widow woman to slap Jack Dempsey. . . . If need be, we should create a new Diem, so that when we tell Wheeler to slap, we can take a slap back."

In reply to this assertion, Taylor said, "I doubt that Hanoi will slap back." U.S. intelligence estimates stated that neither Hanoi nor Beijing would respond to tough U.S. actions with major attacks.

"Didn't MacArthur say the same thing?" Johnson countered, referring to General Douglas MacArthur's mistaken prediction early in the Korean War that China would not enter North Korea to fight U.S. forces.[39] No amount of expert assurance or diplomatic information could break the President's fear of repeating the Korean War. William Bundy would later assert that fear of

Chinese intervention was the main reason why Johnson and other top officials chose gradual escalation over the sharp blow.[40]

Toward the end of this discussion, President Johnson told JCS chairman General Earle G. Wheeler that he liked the Joint Chiefs' proposals to attack the North, but first he would give Ambassador Taylor one more chance to turn things around in the South. The President assured Wheeler that if the situation in South Vietnam did not improve, "then I'll be talking to you, General."[41]

Subsequent to this meeting, Johnson approved a detailed two-phase plan for the implementation of gradual escalation. Phase one, to begin on or near December 15, would consist of intensified covert raids on the North Vietnamese coast and two small air attacks per week on the Ho Chi Minh Trail. If, after a minimum of thirty days, the South Vietnamese government "improves its effectiveness to an acceptable degree," then the United States would commence phase two, consisting primarily of a bombing program that would "give the U.S. the option at any time (subject to enemy reaction) to proceed or not, to escalate or not, and to quicken the pace or not." The second phase might also include sending American forces in division strength to South Vietnam to discourage the North Vietnamese from invading.[42]

Some prominent historians have recently contended that President Johnson made up his mind to bomb North Vietnam and use American ground forces to save South Vietnam at this point in time.[43] The most significant evidence cited is Johnson's promise to Wheeler that "I'll be talking to you, General" if the military situation did not get better. But the evidence fails to sustain the interpretation. Johnson's comment to Wheeler was sufficiently ambiguous that Johnson could easily disregard it in the future or take only small initiatives. Johnson had a history of treating vague promises on Vietnam in such a manner – for many months, he had been making unfulfilled promises to the Joint Chiefs that he would get tougher over Vietnam, and just one month earlier, Johnson had sent McNamara to feed the Joint Chiefs false talk of striking China. Johnson, moreover, did not anticipate a major ground war, believing still that Hanoi would not invade the South with great numbers of North Vietnamese soldiers. Most important of all, the language of the new policy itself made clear that Johnson was not firmly committed to war in December 1964, that he was still considering backing out. Intensification would take place only "if the GVN improves its effectiveness to an acceptable degree," a criterion sufficiently imprecise as to permit withdrawal under any circumstances. The plan explicitly left the President with the flexibility to choose whether "to proceed or not." It was this very conditionality to which Taylor and the Joint Chiefs had objected during the deliberations.

In accordance with the new strategy, U.S. Ambassador to Laos William Sullivan asked Prime Minister Souvanna Phouma to consent to the bombing of the Ho Chi Minh Trail. Souvanna quickly and eagerly gave his consent, telling the Americans that if they "see anything moving on the road, either day or night, attack it."[44] On December 14, U.S. air attacks commenced in Laos under the code name Barrel Roll, with four American jets attacking Communist infiltration routes and installations twice per week. Both Souvanna and the Joint Chiefs beseeched Johnson and his civilian advisers to run a greater number of sorties, but they refused, saying that the primary purpose of the air campaign was not to inflict damage but to "send a signal" of American determination to the other side.[45] CIA analysts soon discerned the impact of Barrel Roll, concluding that because of the program's small scale, it was neither causing significant physical harm nor conveying the desired signal to the North Vietnamese.[46] The same could be said of the secret raids on the North Vietnamese coast.

Upon Ambassador Taylor's return to Saigon in early December, he undertook new efforts to reduce opposition to the South Vietnamese government from the Buddhists and other groups. One approach that appeared to hold promise was the isolation of Tri Quang and Tam Chau from the rest of the Buddhists. By now, many other Buddhist leaders had become disenchanted with Tri Quang because of his fanatical and underhanded opposition to successive governments that had demonstrated no religious intolerance and had made numerous concessions to the Buddhists. In December, at its seventh conference, the World Federation of Buddhists warned that the "martial zeal" displayed by the Vietnamese monks would "most tragically diminish Buddhism's high spiritual value" and was "quite as disturbing to Buddhists as to non-Buddhists."[47] Tam Chau himself was drifting apart from Tri Quang because of the latter's extreme views and methods. Taylor's initiatives apparently had an effect, for at the end of the year the Cochinchinese Buddhists, led by Mai Tho Truyen, broke with Tri Quang and his close supporters. Rampant factionalism, however, prevented the various Buddhist groups from working in unison against Tri Quang. Taylor also attempted to turn down Tri Quang's volume by telling him, along with other Vietnamese leaders, that the United States would stop supporting South Vietnam unless everyone got behind the Huong government, a counter-productive threat since Tri Quang would have been happy to see the Americans abandon South Vietnam. Simultaneously, the CIA was approaching Tri Quang's lieutenants covertly and urging them to help moderate his behavior. None of the American actions had a softening effect on Tri Quang.

A new political crisis sprouted in the middle of December, sparked by Khanh's decision to join forces with a group of generals known, fittingly, as the Young Turks. Khanh and the Young Turks tried to convince the High National Council to retire all military officers who had served for more than twenty-five years. Having come of age under Diem, both Khanh and the Young Turks had been inspired by Diem's intense nationalism, and they viewed the older officers as decaying relics of the colonial era with excessive sympathies for the militant Buddhists. The High National Council, however, did not hold the older generation of officers in such low regard, at least in part because many council members were themselves older men – humorous Saigonese referred to the council as the High National Museum. The council rejected the retirement proposal. Outraged, Khanh and the Young Turks dissolved the High National Council and sent troops to arrest eight of its members.

Khanh and the Young Turks did not give Taylor advance notice of the arrests or the dissolution of the council, as they were sure that he would not approve. Several days earlier, over a steak dinner at General Westmoreland's house, Taylor had told the generals that he wanted unity and that there should be no more changes in government. The generals had assured him that he had nothing to worry about, a fact that contributed to Taylor's rage when he learned what had occurred after the fact. Most upsetting to Taylor, though, were what he believed would be the disastrous political consequences stemming from this maneuver. Without the High National Council, Taylor reasoned, the government could not create a legitimate national assembly, an entity Taylor considered essential for the long-term viability of the government and the war effort. Taylor's strong attachment to the concept of a national assembly came as a surprise to the Young Turks, and it made little sense, for no part of Vietnam had ever had an effective legislature and yet the Vietnamese had repeatedly fought wars with great tenacity. Taylor also suspected that Khanh planned to use the termination of the High National Council as a vehicle for gaining personal control over the government, something that Taylor adamantly opposed on account of Khanh's previous failures. Taylor had misperceived the motives animating the key players, for the Young Turks had supported the dissolution of the High National Council to give more power to Huong, not to Khanh, and they had attained this result.

As soon as Taylor learned that the generals had dismantled the High National Council, he asked Khanh to see him at the U.S. embassy. Khanh refused to go and instead sent four of his top military officers – General Nguyen Van Thieu, General Nguyen Cao Ky, General Nguyen Chanh Thi, and Admiral Chung Tan Cang. When the four men had sat down in Taylor's office, the ambassador snapped at them, "I told you all clearly at General Westmoreland's dinner we Americans were tired of coups. Apparently I wasted my words." The four South Vietnamese officers were astonished by Taylor's tone, which they took as an affront to both their personal and their national pride. Ky later complained that Taylor "talked to us as errant schoolboys who had been caught stealing apples from an orchard."[48] Taylor lectured them that he had made clear that military success required governmental stability. The disbandment of the High National Council was "totally illegal," he said, and was tantamount to a military coup. "Now you have made a real mess," he steamed on. "We cannot carry you forever if you do things like this."

The four officers, indisposed to direct confrontation like most Vietnamese, did not rise to Taylor's level of vehemence and bluntness, but instead defended their actions calmly and circuitously. General Ky explained to Taylor that "the political situation is worse than it ever was under Diem," and some changes had to be made. "We know you want stability, but you cannot have stability until you have unity," said Ky. The High National Council had been undermining national unity by spreading coup rumors and sowing doubts about the armed forces. Ky promised that the generals would explain their actions at a press conference, then would return to their military units and stay out of politics.

"I do not see how our action has hurt the Huong government," added General Thieu. "Huong now has the full support of the Army and has no worries from the High National Council, which we have eliminated."

Taylor said sternly that the arrests took power away from Huong and Suu and ran contrary to their wishes. The Vietnamese officers replied that they had promised full support to Huong and that Huong had consented to the generals' action, the first of which was true, while the second may not have been true. Their words did nothing to placate Taylor. "I don't know whether we will continue to support you after this," Taylor said, fuming, at the end of the meeting. "You people have broken a lot of dishes and now we have to see how we can straighten out this mess."[49]

Taylor next went to see Huong. The prime minister said that although the generals had not consulted him before making the arrests, he and Suu had agreed to take over the duties of the High National Council. Taylor, nevertheless, advised Huong to reject as illegal the military decree dissolving the High National Council and to demand that the military release the prisoners. If Huong accepted what the generals had done, warned Taylor, the military would dominate the government, and such an arrangement might cause the United States to terminate its support to South Vietnam.[50] These arguments failed to win over Huong. The Vietnamese people, Huong commented a short time later, "take a more sentimental than legalistic approach," and thus the role of the High National Council was far less important than the "moral prestige of the leaders."[51]

The next morning, the ambassador proceeded to Khanh's office to condemn the disbandment of the High National Council. The generals' action, Taylor lectured, was inconsistent with the stability and loyalty that the Americans wanted from the South Vietnamese government. Khanh shot back that loyalty was a two-way street, and he recalled that Diem once had said that the United States had not been loyal to him. Vietnam was not a vassal of the United States, Khanh bristled. Taylor then declared that he had lost confidence in General Khanh.

"You should keep to your place as Ambassador," Khanh warned, "and, as Ambassador, it is really not appropriate for you to be dealing in this way with the commander-in-chief of the armed forces on a political matter, nor was it appropriate for you to have summoned some of my generals to the Embassy yesterday." Later in the conversation, however, Khanh expressed a willingness to step down from his position, and he asked Taylor whether his resignation would help the situation. "Yes, it would," Taylor replied. Khanh told Taylor that he would get back to him once he had decided what to do.[52]

At midnight, Khanh called Taylor to say he was ready to resign, and he requested funds for him and several other generals to travel abroad. Taylor responded that if Khanh would give him a list of the generals, he would look into it. Khanh proceeded to ask Ambassador Taylor to repeat back the proposal to send several generals abroad, which Taylor did, unaware that Khanh was secretly taping the conversation. After they hung up, Khanh played back a few carefully selected snippets to his fellow generals as proof that Taylor had insisted on their departure from the country.[53] Reneging on his offer to Taylor to leave the country, Khanh embarked on a new voyage of political intrigue. He opened a public offensive against the Americans by announcing over Radio Vietnam that "We make sacrifices for the country's independence and the Vietnamese people's liberty, but not to carry out the policy of any foreign country." It was "better to live poor but proud as free citizens of an independent country rather than in ease and shame as slaves of the foreigners and Communists."[54] In an interview published by the New York Herald Tribune, Khanh asserted that Taylor's attitude and activities "have been beyond imagination as far as an ambassador is concerned," and that in order to succeed in Vietnam, the Americans would have to be "more practical and not have a dream of having Vietnam be an image of the United States, because the way of life and the people are entirely different."[55]

Through his defiance of Ambassador Taylor, who in the minds of most Vietnamese leaders had insulted the entire South Vietnamese armed forces, and through the suppression of the High National Council, Khanh regained a degree of prestige among some of South Vietnam's generals. American personnel in contact with the senior South Vietnamese military leadership were reporting that the generals viewed the army as the highest authority in Vietnam and considered it unimportant that the abolition of the High National Council had violated any laws. The American concerns about legal niceties were, in their minds, unwarranted and harmful.[56]

On the evening of December 23, Khanh persuaded the other generals to join him in urging Huong to declare Ambassador Taylor persona non grata and demand his removal from the country. Confident that Huong could not but side with them, considering that the alternative was to side with a foreign ambassador against his own military, the generals planned to see Huong the next day to state their case. But one of the attendees quickly related the contents of the generals' meeting to the CIA,[57] which gave the Americans precious time to work on the generals individually before they took their proposals to Huong. Under American pressure, the generals abandoned the idea of declaring Taylor persona non grata and demanding his removal. Instead, in their recommendations to Huong the next morning, they merely denounced Taylor's conduct at the meetings on December 20 and 21 and called on Huong to "take appropriate measures to preserve the honor of all the Vietnamese armed forces and to keep national prestige intact."[58]

Taylor and the State Department were coming to realize that both Huong and the generals were unwilling to yield to the United States on key points, and that further attempts to shove political solutions on them would only alienate the country's leading anti-Communists. On Christmas day, Taylor sent Lieutenant General John Throckmorton to smooth things over with the four general officers whom he had berated. Explaining to the generals that they had misinterpreted some of Taylor's remarks, General Throckmorton assured them that Taylor had not asked Khanh to resign. Khanh seemed to respond favorably. On December 30, Khanh announced that he was not as anti-American as the press was saying, and he expressed a desire for Admiral Cang and General Thieu to get together with the Americans to resolve any remaining differences. At this same time, however, Khanh was secretly making contact with Huynh Tan Phat, Vice President of the Central Committee of the National Liberation Front. Phat would tell Khanh that they should work together to save their homeland, but they would not delve into substantive discussions before Khanh's involvement in South Vietnamese politics came to an end two months later.[59]

During the final days of this brouhaha, the anti-Communist cause suffered one more wound, in the form of another strong enemy provocation. On Christmas Eve, two Viet Cong agents clothed in South Vietnamese Army uniforms drove into central Saigon with a 200-pound explosive charge in their trunk. They stopped at the Brink Hotel, a six-story, 193-room monstrosity that was now serving as an American bachelor officers' quarters. The two Communist agents convinced one of the South Vietnamese sentries that they were awaiting an American officer who, according to Communist intelligence, would not be at the hotel at that hour. This officer was not, in fact, in the hotel at the moment, so the sentry allowed the two agents to park the car in the hotel's garage. Leaving the car in the garage, the two went to a nearby café, from where they would eventually make a safe getaway.[60] At 5:45 P.M., the timer on the explosives went off, blowing away the entire ground floor of the hotel, save for the steel girders, and blasting gaping holes in the three floors above it. The gas tanks of trucks parked in the garage exploded in sequence, which shot flames and debris through the first three stories of the building, as in an extended fireworks display. At the time of the detonation, a large number of U.S. field grade officers were in their rooms getting ready for a party at the rooftop officers club, and two of them were killed, while 38 others were injured. Another 25 civilians suffered injuries, including several Vietnamese children. With this act of terrorism, the Viet Cong had been trying to kill comedian Bob Hope, who had just flown in to perform a Christmas show for the troops and was planning to stay at the Brink Hotel, but Hope had not yet reached the hotel because he had been delayed by the unloading of his cue cards at the airport.[61]

The Brink Hotel attack came on the heels of renewed pleading from Ambassador Taylor to unleash American air power on North Vietnam, and it seemed to offer the perfect justification for doing so. The Joint Chiefs joined Taylor in recommending retaliation, as did Admiral Sharp, who commented that force "is the language the VC understand."[62] To discuss these recommendations, President Johnson summoned his advisers away from their Christmas celebrations to his Texas ranch. Rusk and McNamara both advised the President to reject Taylor's request and, once more, Johnson took their advice. As in the case of the Bien Hoa attack, the President sent Taylor a response containing almost every conceivable objection, some of them bordering on the absurd. The most important reason for refraining from action, Johnson stated, was the political turbulence in Saigon. He expressed doubts about the Viet Cong's culpability, despite the availability of compelling evidence that included National Liberation Front broadcasts claiming credit for the act. In an effort to shift some of the onus for inaction onto Taylor, Westmoreland, and other hawks in the military, Johnson sniped, "I also have real doubts about ordering reprisals in cases in which our own security seems, at first glance, to have been very weak. . . . I do not want to be drawn into a large-scale military action against North Vietnam simply because our own people are careless or imprudent." Taylor was told, in addition, that the war could not be won from the air and that Johnson would look more favorably on a request for U.S. ground forces than a request for air strikes – although Johnson and other civilians were not actually convinced at this time that air power alone was incapable of deterring Hanoi.[63] The most important reason may have been one not contained in Johnson's message, as had been the case with the message after Bien Hoa. One day later, General Wheeler informed General Westmoreland that administration officials believed that too much time had elapsed since the actual attack. The embassy had needed four days to determine that the Viet Cong had perpetrated the act, and Johnson and other civilian policymakers believed that reprisals had to take place within thirty-six hours of the depredation – otherwise, according to their theories, the reprisals would constitute unprovoked escalation by the United States.[64]

When Johnson refused to retaliate for the Brink Hotel attack, he missed what was probably his last opportunity to prevent the North Vietnamese from undertaking an offensive that the Saigon government, gravely weakened as it was by disunity and Buddhist conniving, would be unable to stop. Massive U.S. air or ground attacks in North Vietnam or Laos at a subsequent date might still have caused Hanoi to abort its offensive, but Johnson had no inclination to go that far, as he had unwisely made apparent to the enemy on multiple occasions. North Vietnam's remaining worries about U.S. intervention melted away after the bombing of the Brink Hotel.[65]

A few months later, when the Communists were assembling their forces for what they expected to be the decisive offensive, Johnson would figure out that his inaction and his public statements in the last months of 1964 had emboldened the enemy. He would rue the days when he had rejected the military's proposals for hard action in Laos and North Vietnam, when he had sided with smart civilians who had embraced specious academic theories, misinterpreted enemy intentions, and undervalued the men and arms infiltrated from the North into the South. At a news conference on April 27, 1965, Johnson lamented, "When our destroyers were attacked in the Gulf of Tonkin, as you will remember last summer, we replied promptly with a single raid. The punishment then was limited to the deed. For the next six months we took no action against North Vietnam. We warned of danger, we hoped for caution in others. Their answer was attack, and explosions, and indiscriminate murder. So it soon became clear that our restraint was viewed as weakness; our desire to limit conflict was viewed as prelude to our surrender."[66]

CHAPTER 16

The Prize for Victory

JANUARY–MAY 1965

THE POLITICAL DISPUTE IN SAIGON WAS OSTENSIBLY SOLVED ON January 6 of the new year. The army officially ceded political control to a provisional civilian government led by Tran Van Huong, and this government was instructed to organize the election of a civilian legislature in the near future. Some of the generals, however, soon engaged in intrigue with Tri Quang aimed at subverting the new government.[1] Buddhist and student leaders organized new demonstrations, issued fresh denunciations of Huong, and rejected pleas from an interfaith committee to discuss their alleged grievances with Huong's representatives. Tri Quang implored Taylor to force Huong's resignation, but the ambassador refused, and in fact Taylor secretly encouraged Huong – who had impressed the Americans with his limited successes in suppressing Buddhist agitators – to stand firm against efforts by Khanh and Tri Quang to usurp his power. Tri Quang then told the Americans that the new government had perpetrated acts of religious persecution, including the killing of four Buddhists who were walking to a pagoda for prayer. The Americans investigated the charges and found them to be false.[2] After one of his meetings with Tri Quang later in the month, Taylor complained, "All we got was another repetitious airing of grievances which ring true only in the ears of the leaders of the Buddhist Institute,"[3] and Khanh himself conceded that the militant Buddhists' accusations were baseless.[4]

On January 18, in a break with his usual hard-line stance, Prime Minister Huong tried to placate the militant Buddhists by dismissing two ministers whom they disliked. But concessions served Huong no better than they had served Diem or Khanh. At a press conference two days later, Tri Quang and several of his followers announced that they were starting a hunger strike, to last until Huong stepped down. Thien Minh, Tri Quang's closest comrade in the Buddhist movement, added that if Huong were not removed, then the Buddhists would "call for peace" with the Communists, a complaint that coincided with new evidence of collaboration between the Communists and

Buddhist leaders who were close associates of Tri Quang, most notably Secretary General of the Buddhist Institute Thich Huyen Quang and his deputy Tran Dinh.[5]

Buddhist leaders promised that there would be no demonstrations during the hunger strike,[6] but broke their promises almost immediately. On January 23, Tri Quang and Tam Chau opened a rabidly anti-American protest campaign with major participation from Communist operatives, and little participation from the Buddhist masses, who by and large were repulsed by the militants' politicking.[7] Swirling outside the U.S. embassy and the U.S. Information Service's Abraham Lincoln Library in Saigon, hordes of demonstrators shouted that Huong was Taylor's "lackey" and demanded that the U.S. ambassador leave the country. Among the most outrageous of charges came from Thich Huyen Quang, who released a communiqué stating, "The policy of the United States Ambassador and Huong, lackey of the United States Ambassador, is to let leaders of Vietnamese Buddhism die and to exterminate Vietnamese Buddhism." The demonstrations in Saigon eventually turned violent, with the mobs breaking windows and casting stones at riot policemen. Buddhist ruffians lit a Catholic man on fire. In the end, the government had to send paratroopers to disperse the mobs with tear gas and clubs. In Hue, a crowd of 5,000 sacked the two-story U.S. Information Service Library, then burned 8,000 books, and in the cities of Da Nang, Quang Tri, and Nha Trang, militant Buddhists organized strikes in which Vietnamese businesses either refused to serve Americans or else shut down completely. General Khanh and his co-conspirator, General Nguyen Chanh Thi, took no action in the northern provinces to rein in the mobs, nor did they protect American and South Vietnamese property, for they hoped that the chaos would lead to Huong's ruin.[8]

As the windows were shattering and the books were burning, Khanh struck a deal with the leaders of the militant Buddhists that would secure the removal of Huong. Khanh vouched that the armed forces would get rid of Huong, take control of the government, allow the Buddhist militants to do as they pleased, and purge any supposed Diemists who remained in office after the countless purges occasioned by previous Buddhist demands. In return, the Buddhists would support the new government for at least two years, and would send Tri Quang, Tam Chau, and a third Buddhist leader out of the country. At 10:00 on the morning of January 27, assisted by General Thi and Air Marshal Nguyen Cao Ky, Khanh led a bloodless coup. Because of assurances from Khanh that he would leave politics once a twenty-man advisory group appointed a civilian chief of state, the Armed Forces Council agreed to dismiss Huong and put Khanh in charge. Some of the generals, however, were far from enthusiastic about the transition. A large number strongly opposed collaboration with the militant Buddhist leadership, and among them the coup increased sentiment for a complete and permanent suppression of the militants. One general said that many of his colleagues had voted in Khanh's favor "in the conviction that they were giving Khanh sufficient rope to hang himself."[9]

On the very day of the coup, the tireless Tri Quang was already talking of ousting his fellow conspirator Khanh, and the next afternoon he began efforts in that direction. First, Tri Quang notified the generals that the Buddhists would no longer honor the promises they had just made – to stay out of politics, support the government, and send the three leaders abroad. The promises were null and void, according to the Buddhists, because the military had promised to oust the government on January 25 or 26 but had not done so until January 27. This explanation was as dishonest as it was preposterous, for Tri Quang had known all along that the coup would not take place until January 27.[10] The Buddhists' duplicity infuriated some of the generals; one of their rank notified the Americans that if Khanh failed to resist the Buddhist Institute now, then Khanh's "life would be in danger."[11] Khanh did not stand up to the Buddhists but instead yielded to their demands once again, like a man confronted by wolves who lacks the nerve to shoot and instead runs away while dropping his food in the hope of satiating the beasts. On January 31, Khanh pushed the Armed Forces Council into transferring General Pham Van Dong, who had upset the Buddhists through his effective suppression of Buddhist demonstrations in Saigon, from command of the capital military district to command of II Corps. The transfer moved him from the center of power to an area where he would have minimal influence over Saigon and its politics.

Khanh's machinations led to agonized discussions and a change of policy in Washington. Throughout the month of January, President Johnson had been receiving pleas from Ambassador Taylor, the Joint Chiefs, and some leading civilians to move beyond the Phase I actions in striking North Vietnam. The most stirring appeal had sprung from the pen of Taylor, who argued that if the United States continued to wait for a good government in Saigon before acting, South Vietnam would soon cease to exist. "Until the fall of Diem and the experience gained from the events of the following months," Taylor wrote to the President, "I doubt that anyone appreciated the magnitude of the centrifugal political forces which had been kept under control by his iron rule." Taylor lamented that "there is no adequate replacement for Diem in sight."[12] Johnson staved off the requests for firmer action until January 27, the day on which Khanh removed Huong from power. It was on that date that McGeorge Bundy and McNamara arrived at the same conclusion as Taylor, whereupon McNamara used his great influence to convince the President that the United States could not afford to wait any longer. "Stable government or no stable government," Johnson resolved on the twenty-seventh, "we'll do what we ought to do. We will move strongly."[13] The President dispatched McGeorge Bundy to Vietnam, where he was to ask the embassy what sort of damage ought to be visited upon the enemy.

Arriving in Saigon with his entourage on February 4, the national security adviser spent a good portion of his first few days with Taylor developing a plan for the sustained bombing of North Vietnam. Bundy's trip was punctuated early on the morning of February 7 by two Viet Cong surprise attacks in Pleiku province, the main strike coming at Camp Holloway, where Viet Cong saboteurs detonated satchel charges in the aircraft parking areas while Viet Cong soldiers unloaded mortars and bazookas into the troop billets. The Viet Cong killed seven Americans, wounded more than one hundred, and damaged or destroyed twenty-five aircraft.[14] Making contact with Washington by phone, Bundy reported that the country team unanimously recommended retaliatory air strikes. This phone call triggered a meeting of the National Security Council in Washington. Everyone present at the meeting favored reprisals except for Senator Mike Mansfield, who argued that reprisal strikes could touch off a major war with China and close the Sino-Soviet rift.

President Johnson's fuse had reached its end. "I have kept the shotgun over the mantel and the bullets in the basement for a long time now," Johnson exclaimed, "but the enemy is killing my personnel and I cannot expect them to continue their work if I do not authorize them to take steps to defend themselves." The President averred that "cowardice has gotten us into more wars than response has," and remarked that the United States could have avoided getting into World War I and World War II had it been more courageous early on.[15] Johnson approved the lightest of three air strike plans presented by his generals, consisting of attacks on four North Vietnamese barracks. On the afternoon of February 7, in an operation dubbed Flaming Dart, 49 U.S. Navy A-4 Skyhawks and F-8 Crusaders took off from the USS *Coral Sea* and USS *Hancock*, bolted into North Vietnamese airspace, and then descended through the monsoon clouds to bomb the North Vietnamese barracks at Dong Hoi. Because of poor weather, most of the sorties against the other three barracks were cancelled.

McGeorge Bundy's team left Saigon later that day. During the flight home, Bundy completed his recommendation for a long-term bombing campaign over North Vietnam, which he delivered to Johnson upon his arrival in Washington. Bundy's campaign consisted of sustained strikes that would be justified publicly as reprisals for Viet Cong depredations in the South. To encourage Hanoi to scale back its efforts, the United States would increase or decrease the intensity of the bombing raids based on the intensity of Viet Cong attacks. If the Viet Cong failed to cut down on their offensive actions, the reprisals would increase gradually, never reaching America's full bombing capacity so that there would always be "a prospect of worse to come." Eroding Hanoi's will, though, was only a secondary and long-term objective, Bundy explained. The principal and immediate purpose was to demoralize the Viet Cong and shore up support for the Saigon government among the South Vietnamese, who had made clear that the dearth of U.S. action thus far had undermined confidence in the United States and the Saigon regime. Bundy estimated that the program had a chance of between 25 and 75 percent of altering the course of the war.[16]

Johnson's other advisers agreed with Bundy on the need for sustained bombing of North Vietnam, although CIA Director John McCone favored a much faster pace than Bundy had recommended, for McCone believed that the bombing could, in fact, erode Hanoi's will and capabilities. After his advisers had laid out their arguments, Johnson decided upon a sustained bombing campaign with a slow, escalating pace as specified in Bundy's plan. He preferred the slow initial tempo because he shared Bundy's view that air power could not do serious harm to the North Vietnamese government's will or ability to continue, and because it seemed to carry a lower risk of war with China.[17]

The bombing campaign, named "Rolling Thunder," began on March 2 at a rate of one strike per week, with the frequency and size scheduled to rise slowly over time. In conceiving Rolling Thunder, the central figures of the Johnson administration badly underestimated the importance of the physical damage wrought. Not until April would the United States learn that the 325th Division had arrived and that Hanoi had shifted its strategy[18] – had the Americans known of these developments earlier, they would have been encouraged to intensify the bombing sharply and target the vulnerable logistical elements required for a conventional offensive, such as trucks, ammunition depots, bridges, and oil storage tanks. When Johnson did receive this information in April, though, he would not exploit it.

In the first months of 1965, the continued inadequacy of U.S. intelligence on North Vietnam's plans also affected U.S. decisions on sending ground forces to Vietnam, for the Americans persisted in the belief that the enemy would continue relying primarily on small attacks that the South Vietnamese ground forces could handle.[19] If President Johnson had been aware that the gears of the major offensive had begun turning months earlier, and if in fact Hanoi by this time was not already immune to deterrence, Johnson might have cooled Hanoi's passion with a large and rapid US troop deployment. The attack on Camp Holloway on February 7 did cause the Joint Chiefs and General Westmoreland to argue strenuously that the United States needed its own ground forces in Vietnam, but not for the purpose of deterring Hanoi with overwhelming numbers or smacking the Viet Cong – any desire they had for such actions was muted by the previous unreceptivity of the civilian leadership. Instead, the generals proposed using the troops to protect American assets, most importantly the air base at Da Nang, which was believed to be within striking range of twelve Viet Cong battalions. The destruction of such a base, it was clear, would constitute a gigantic military and moral victory for the Communists.[20]

In the second half of February, some of Johnson's civilian advisers came around to the view that the situation demanded a U.S. troop deployment, and on the evening of February 26, Johnson consented to the dispatch of two U.S.

Marine battalions to Da Nang, with a scheduled arrival date of March 8. The President did not envision the deployment of troops to Da Nang as the first step in enmeshing U.S. forces in the war, but instead viewed it as what the military labeled it – a stopgap measure to protect the Da Nang air base. On the day he agreed to send the troops, Johnson revealed his thoughts to McNamara: "I'm scared to death of putting ground forces in, but I'm more frightened about losing a bunch of planes from lack of security."[21] The Marines could conceivably end up getting entangled in the ground war, Johnson acknowledged, but the odds were against it.[22] In terms of the possible consequences of inserting U.S. troops, President Johnson was less worried about a ground war with the Vietnamese Communists than about provoking the Chinese or the Soviets or pushing the American Congress and public into a divisive debate that would undermine support for the war and Johnson's domestic agenda. Conservatives would accuse him of employing too little force and liberals of employing too much. While most liberal Democrats were expressing support for war in Vietnam at this time – even George McGovern, the antiwar Presidential candidate of 1972, was saying that the United States should fight in Vietnam rather than "surrender the area to communism"[23] – a significant minority was already criticizing him for excessive use of force, and Johnson also suspected, correctly as it would turn out, that pro-war liberals would turn against the war when the going got tough.

The President decided that the best way to avoid these frightening consequences would be to minimize the visibility of the ground troop deployments. He suggested to Secretary of Defense McNamara that they refer to the first contingent of Marines as "security battalions," rather than Marine battalions. McNamara dissuaded him with the remark that the press would know the difference and accuse the administration of falsification. The Secretary of Defense, however, came up with another way to reduce the attention given to the Da Nang troop deployments: he deliberately announced them late on a Saturday night so that the story would miss the morning newspapers on Sunday, the only day when there were no afternoon editions.[24] Johnson's efforts to mask the deployments would work for a short time, but they would prove a disastrous error in the long run, for the people ultimately were to recognize his deceitfulness and his failure to inspire the people for war. At first glance, it seems inexplicable that such a savvy politician would have believed that the American people and Congress would not aggressively seek the truth about the troop deployments. It was not unrealistic, however, if one expected, as Johnson did, that the troops would not engage in major combat.

When the Marines landed at Da Nang ten days later, they were assigned responsibility for defending the airfield and other U.S. installations. Their instructions, handcrafted in Washington, stated that they would "not engage in day to day actions against the Viet Cong."[25] During an appearance on the CBS television program "Face the Nation," Dean Rusk explained, "The purpose of those Marines is to provide local close-in security for the Marines who are already at Da Nang with the Hawk missiles and other American personnel there in connection with aircraft. It is not their mission to engage in pacification operations."[26]

* * *

THE NORTH VIETNAMESE UNITS THAT HAD BEEN SENT TO THE SOUTH in late 1964 found the journey even more grueling than they had expected. Traipsing up and down steep mountains, the soldiers swore that they could feel the weight of each fly that landed on their backpacks. Before the trip, the logistical command had informed the 325th Division's commander that the warehouses on the Ho Chi Minh Trail contained enough rice to a feed a division. The rice had been in storage for some time and was infested with worms, the division commander was told, but it was still edible. This report proved to be overly optimistic. The further down the Ho Chi Minh Trail the soldiers went, the more worms and mildew the rice contained, and the more foul stenches it emitted. Toward the end of the journey, when the soldiers attempted to scrub off the worms and mildew, the rice turned to powder. In these cases the regimental cooks mixed unscrubbed rice, with all the mildew and worms, together with wild jungle vegetables to make a smelly, mushy green soup. Only when the North Vietnamese soldiers reached South Vietnam did the food situation improve.[27]

The 325th Division and two other North Vietnamese Army units, the 320th Regiment and the 545th Viet Bac Battalion, arrived in the highlands of South Vietnam during the first months of 1965.[28] They established base areas, then joined with the Viet Cong in a winter-spring offensive, which was to feature numerous operations in battalion strength on the part of both the North Vietnamese Army and the Viet Cong main forces. In some of the substantial clashes that ensued, the South Vietnamese army fared better than Hanoi had hoped. In January, government forces inflicted more losses on Communist forces than in any previous month.[29] The Communists, on the other hand, enjoyed their share of major successes as well, especially as the number of North Vietnamese Army troops in the highlands mounted. The Communists performed considerably better in February than in January, inflicting 4,114 casualties on the government, a tremendous increase from the 1,593 inflicted in the same month the previous year, while suffering 1,873 killed. The Saigon government lost 2,376 weapons in February and captured only 1,384 weapons from the Communists.[30] Communist forces in I Corps strengthened their grip on the piedmont and encroached further into the lowlands, isolating district and provincial capitals from one another. In Binh Dinh province, the Communists gained complete control over four districts, which compelled the South Vietnamese government to commit precious reserve forces to these districts. Communist units blocked the coastal highway from Phu Yen to Quang Ngai, and they cut Route 19, which connected the strategically crucial highland capitals of Pleiku and Kontum to the coast. A South Vietnamese Airborne task force, however, fought its way up Route 19 at the end of February and destroyed or scattered the Communist forces that had been strangling it.

Hanoi's principal military setback in early 1965, however, did not involve the clashing of thousands of men on South Vietnam's roads and fields. Since the end of 1964, North Vietnam's Group 125 had been transporting war supplies by ship to Communist Military Region 5, along the central and northern coast of South Vietnam, arriving at night and unloading their cargo rapidly in order to escape before daylight. The influx of heavy weapons accelerated at the beginning of 1965, with 75 mm pack howitzers appearing in the cargo lists for the first time. In January 1965 alone, Group 125's ships delivered over four hundred tons of materiel to secret South Vietnamese docks.[31] A North Vietnamese history noted that the shipments to Military Region 5 in late 1964 and early 1965 made possible the considerable Communist victories in that region during the winter-spring offensive.[32] As a result of the maritime infiltration, supplemented by smaller shipments of equipment via the Ho Chi Minh Trail, many Viet Cong main force units were re-armed at this time with new AK-47 assault rifles and other new Communist bloc 7.62 mm automatic and semiautomatic weapons.[33]

On February 15, sailing under the flag of a commercial vessel as a disguise, Ship 143 of the North Vietnamese Navy was on its way to Cochinchina to deliver armaments when the crew received reports of trouble at the intended unloading area. The ship altered its course for Vung Ro Bay in northern South Vietnam, a deep and almost perfectly circular bay that was ringed by enormous cliffs and rocks. Arriving at Vung Ro at 3:00 A.M., the crew frantically unloaded crates of weapons and ammunition at a dock hidden among the rocks, but as the morning approached they came to the realization that they would not finish before sunrise. Choosing to remain for the day and finish unloading the next night, the ship's skipper had his men camouflage the vessel with tree branches, which they were able to accomplish before dawn. A few hours after daybreak, a keen-eyed U.S. helicopter pilot spotted the camouflaged ship and radioed for air strikes, which were soon forthcoming. South Vietnamese aircraft pelted the ship, eventually causing it to roll over on its side. The Communist military region headquarters sent an engineering squad with a one-ton charge to incinerate the ship, so as to destroy the evidence of its covert activities. The engineers detonated the charge successfully, but to their dismay the ship merely broke in two. Several companies of government troops subsequently arrived, some of them making amphibious landings onto one of the bay's beaches, others descending from the high ground around the bay, and they entered into a lengthy battle with the ship's crew and local guerrilla platoons. Ultimately, the numerical superiority of the government forces overwhelmed the Communists, driving them away and putting the wreck into the possession of the Saigon government.

The search at Vung Ro turned up 100 tons of weapons and supplies, including 2,500 rifles, 1,000 submachine guns, seventeen machine guns, 1,500 grenades, one 57mm recoilless rifle, and one million rounds of small arms ammunition. Almost all of this materiel had been manufactured in China or Eastern Europe.[34] While the Americans and South Vietnamese had received many unconfirmed reports of major sea infiltration, the Vung Ro incident provided the first solid evidence, so it served as a rallying cry for those favoring more stringent measures to block infiltration from the North. To anyone who had witnessed the debilitation of the South Vietnamese Navy after November 1963, it was obvious that the Saigon government lacked the capability to stop this type of infiltration, and therefore General Westmoreland and the Joint Chiefs called for the use of the U.S. Seventh Fleet, the greatest symbol of American military power in the Far East. President Johnson promptly approved the recommendation. In what was to become known as "Market Time," the Seventh Fleet's destroyers, minesweepers, SP-2H Neptune reconnaissance aircraft, and carrier-based A-1H Skyraiders began sweeping the South Vietnamese coast for enemy vessels.

Market Time swiftly brought Hanoi's maritime infiltration operations to ruin, as if the stopper had been pulled and all of South Vietnam's coastal waters had gone down the drain. One Vietnamese Communist account explained, "On many voyages our ships were blocked by enemy warships and forced to turn back. A number of ships managed to penetrate the enemy's outer patrol perimeter, but they ran into enemy naval vessels close to shore." From February 1962 to February 1965, North Vietnamese vessels had embarked on eighty-nine voyages to the South, and the ships had reached their destination on eighty-six occasions, delivering approximately 5,000 tons of equipment and supplies. From March 1965 all the way to the end of the war in April 1975, the North Vietnamese Navy would attempt only eighty voyages to the South, and of these only fourteen would reach their destination, resulting in total delivered cargo of less than 800 tons.[35]

The Joint Chiefs, General Westmoreland, and Ambassador Taylor also wanted to mine or blockade North Vietnamese harbors. Eighty percent of North Vietnam's foreign trade was transported by sea, including almost all of its oil imports,[36] and if the harbors were blocked, most of the imports would have to come from China by roads or rail lines, which could be cut by destroying bridges. Mining or blockading would also put a halt to North Vietnamese ships that were moving cargo from Haiphong to ports in southern North Vietnam, which became crucial when, in mid-1965, bombing severed the rail line between Hanoi and Vinh. Some American generals also recommended a blockade of Cambodia, for U.S. and South Vietnamese officers were reporting large amounts of war goods entering South Vietnam from Cambodia. President Johnson, however, refused to approve mining or blockading in the cases of both North Vietnam and Cambodia, having been convinced by his advisers that the Communist armed forces in South Vietnam were still not heavily dependent on external support and that a dangerous crisis could arise if any damage should come to the many Soviet ships frequenting Haiphong.[37]

The full effects of Market Time would not be felt on the battlefield until much later, for the North Vietnamese had already stockpiled large quantities of weapons and ammunition in the South by February 1965. Market Time, therefore, did not dissuade Hanoi from launching the great summer offensive. During February and March, the Communist leaders solidified the details of their strategy. "Has the opportunity to defeat the United States in the 'special war' arrived?" Le Duan wrote to General Nguyen Chi Thanh. "Can we defeat the Americans before they have time to change their strategy? I believe our opportunity has arrived and I believe there is still a possibility we can restrict the enemy enough to defeat them in the 'special war.'" By "special war," it may be recalled, the Communists meant a war in which the Americans served only as advisers to the South Vietnamese, as was currently the case, which they considered far preferable to a "limited war," in which large numbers of U.S. combat troops participated, as in the Korean War. "The puppet government is in a serious political crisis, but it is still able to rely on a rather strong army," Le Duan explained. "We must cause the complete and utter disintegration of the puppet army before the U.S. has a chance to react." To achieve this goal, Le Duan believed, they had to destroy three or four of Saigon's nine regular divisions in a series of large battles. They also had to pound down the eleven elite battalions of the South Vietnamese strategic reserve, which could be done by drawing them into battle repeatedly with numerous, geographically dispersed attacks. Once the South Vietnamese Army had been spread out and mauled, according to the strategic plan, the conventional Communist units would conquer Saigon in conjunction with an urban uprising. A supposedly neutralist front composed of secret Communist agents would then create a supposedly neutralist regime and demand an American withdrawal.[38]

At the end of March, during its 11th Plenum, the Party Central Committee in Hanoi resolved to accelerate the decisive campaign, with the objective of winning the war by means of a summer-fall offensive. Rapidity of victory now had become even more critical because earlier in the month the Americans had commenced Rolling Thunder and deployed the first U.S. ground forces to South Vietnam.[39] Steeling his countrymen for the climactic battles, Ho Chi Minh invoked the principle of international Communism that had guided him throughout his political career: "Our country has the great honor of being an outpost of the socialist camp and of the world's people who are struggling against imperialism, colonialism, and neocolonialism.... Let all of us single-mindedly unite as one man and be determined to defeat the U.S. aggressors!"[40]

On the international front, Hanoi was reaping the benefits of the recent shift in Soviet policy. Soviet SA-2 surface-to-air missiles, IL-28 jet light bombers, and MiG-15 and MiG-17 fighters arrived in North Vietnam during the spring, along with large quantities of food and ammunition. Soviet military aid to North Vietnam for the year 1965 would exceed the previous year's total by tenfold.[41] Near the end of March, in response to a public National Liberation Front appeal for fellow socialist troops, Brezhnev announced that many Soviet citizens were volunteering to fight on the side of the Vietnamese Communists, adding that "if the American aggressors hope that their actions in Vietnam will be forgotten in the course of time, that time will wash off the disgrace of the crimes, they are profoundly mistaken."[42] The Soviet display of support went beyond what the North Vietnamese actually were seeking from the Soviets; Hanoi responded by informing Moscow privately that the National Liberation Front had issued its call to drum up international support and sympathy, and did not yet need actual volunteers.[43]

The Soviets, however, were not the loyal socialist allies that they appeared to the rest of the world. At this same time, they were conniving to deny the North Vietnamese a decisive victory, for two reasons. First, the destruction of South Vietnam would substantially enhance China's prestige and power within Asia and the Communist world, undermining the Soviet Union's position. Second, the imminence of a North Vietnamese victory or a victory itself could provoke a sharp U.S. reaction that might harm Soviet relations with the United States or lead to a war between the United States and China in which the Soviets, because of their 1950 treaty with China and their concern about Soviet prestige in the Communist world, would feel obligated to assist the Chinese in some way. Describing Soviet views of the North Vietnamese, Anatoly Dobrynin said that Soviet leaders "cursed them behind their backs" because the Soviets "did not want to aggravate Soviet-American relations."[44] At the beginning of the summer, the Soviets would take the extraordinary measure of revealing to the Americans the unseen soft spot in North Vietnam's armor. Anatoliy Aleksandrovich Danilov, a Soviet official in London, confided to an American that the United States "should increase its force by five divisions in Vietnam, seal off the 17th Parallel, cut off the Viet Cong from their northern logistics, then ignore the North and wait for Viet Cong to come to terms because they are 'starved' by lack of Northern support."[45] The number of U.S. divisions suggested by the Soviet official was the same number put forward by U.S. military planners who had assessed the task of severing the Ho Chi Minh Trail, and was slightly higher than what the North Vietnamese believed the United States would need for the job. The Johnson administration, however, failed to heed this precious counsel.

In contrast to the Soviets, the Chinese remained in a cautious, defensive mode during the first months of the year, their intent to pacify the Americans. On January 9, Mao told American journalist Edgar Snow, "China's armies will not go beyond her borders to fight. That is clear enough. Only if the United States attacked China would we fight." More specifically, Mao said that "the Vietnamese can cope with their situation," which should have eliminated any doubt that he was foreswearing an attack on U.S. forces in any part of Vietnam.[46] Fortune was on Hanoi's side again, for Johnson did not capitalize on the opportunity here presented to march into North Vietnam without risking Chinese intervention.

The Chinese reacted to Flaming Dart and Rolling Thunder in much the same way that they had reacted to the Tonkin Gulf reprisals, by issuing verbal warnings that committed them to no firm action and by taking steps to protect themselves from American attack.[47] China's tepid responses to the U.S. air strikes alarmed North Vietnam's leadership, which had begun to regain some fear of American intervention after Mao's comments to Snow. Much did the North Vietnamese now fear that the United States would perceive China's unwillingness to fight in Vietnam, plainly stated as it was, and loose the full fury of its weapons on North Vietnamese territory.[48] But once again, in spite of their professed expertise in the business of "signals," Johnson and his advisers missed the signal.

China's fears of the United States were not so intense as to cause the Chinese to reduce their support to Communist causes across Southeast Asia, or to seek an end to the war in Vietnam. Zhou Enlai told a Vietnamese military delegation on January 22 that they should "continuously eliminate the main forces of the enemy when they come out to conduct mopping-up operations," and said that victory could come "even sooner than our original expectation."[49] The Chinese objected most strenuously to peace negotiations during this period; when Yugoslavia and fifteen other non-aligned nations called for negotiations on Vietnam without preconditions in March, the Chinese took it upon themselves to declare that the Vietnamese people would never negotiate without preconditions, and they denounced Tito and other leaders involved in the non-aligned nations' proposal as "monsters and freaks."[50] Beijing was worried that the peace proposals were part of a sinister U.S.-Soviet plot to halt the expansion of pro-Chinese Communism, and that the North Vietnamese, distraught by China's failure to protect them from the United States, might seek favor with the Soviets by agreeing to a peace settlement that undermined China's prestige.[51] In reality, Beijing had no need to worry about Hanoi reaching a peace agreement, for the North Vietnamese at this time were intent on resolving the conflict not with pen and paper but with heavily armed main force units.[52]

During late February and March, China's stance on Vietnam shifted, because the risks associated with greater involvement were decreasing while the risks associated with less involvement were increasing. American behavior eased Chinese fears that assisting North Vietnam would result in an American attack on China or a clash between U.S. and Chinese forces in North Vietnam. Rolling Thunder was progressing at a slow pace and it remained far from Chinese territory. The American ground troops were staying within South Vietnam. Repeating a most unfortunate mistake, the Johnson administration kept announcing that it did not intend to conquer North Vietnam or attack China.[53] The intensification of China's rivalry with the Soviet Union, meanwhile, compelled the two large Communist powers to lavish support on North Vietnam so as to lay claim to the foremost position in the Communist camp.[54] While American doves were arguing that heightened U.S. involvement in Vietnam was engendering Communist solidarity, it was actually exacerbating the tension between China and the Soviet Union. It fostered mistrust, moreover, between these two countries and North Vietnam.[55] At the end of February, in response to an urgent North Vietnamese request for surface-to-air missiles, the Soviets sought permission to fly missiles over Chinese territory to North Vietnam, but the Chinese refused, prompting new recriminations from both the Soviets and the Chinese and arousing suspicions about the Chinese in the minds of the North Vietnamese.[56] Zhou Enlai went to Hanoi in March and asked Ho Chi Minh to reject all Soviet offers of military assistance, warning that Soviet military instructors who came to North Vietnam might engage in subversion. If the Chinese and North Vietnamese were not careful, cautioned Zhou, "the relations between our two countries may turn from good to bad, thus affecting cooperation between our two countries."[57] Ho politely rejected Zhou's request.

Brezhnev's public offer to send Soviet volunteers to Vietnam, together with Johnson's spoken and manifest unwillingness to move U.S. troops into North Vietnam or strike China, led the Chinese to abandon the caution that had characterized their policy towards Vietnam since August 1964. On March 25, two days after Brezhnev extended the Soviet offer, the Chinese countered with a more specific pledge: "We are ready to send our men, whenever the South Vietnamese people want them, to fight together with the South Vietnamese people to annihilate the American aggressors."[58] In contrast to the Soviet offer of troops, the Chinese offer found immediate favor in Hanoi. Le Duan informed Chinese Chairman Liu Shaoqi on April 8: "We want some volunteer pilots, volunteer soldiers . . . and other volunteers, including road and bridge engineering units." Liu Shaoqi responded, "It is our policy that we will do our best to support you. We will offer whatever you are in need of and we are in a position to offer."[59] Before Le Duan took leave of his Chinese hosts, the Chinese would sign an agreement to send troops to North Vietnam.[60] China found, much to its relief, that it remained North Vietnam's preferred ally, and a very trusted one at that. Only a highly trusted ally would be invited to bring massive numbers of soldiers into a country that was unlikely to experience ground combat on its own soil and that was preparing to send much of its own army out of the country.

Ho Chi Minh and Mao met subsequently to flesh out the details of the Chinese force deployment. "We need China to help us build six roads from the border areas," Ho said, referring to the border between North Vietnam and China. "These roads run south through our rear. And in the future they will be connected to the front. At present, we have thirty thousand people building these roads. If China helps us, those people will be sent to the South. At the same time, we have to help Lao comrades to build roads from Samneua to Xiengkhoang and then from Xiengkhoang to Lower Laos, and to the South of Vietnam."

Mao agreed to provide seven divisions of Chinese troops for road construction and other projects, and he offered to provide any additional support that the North Vietnamese needed. Demonstrating his ambitions for lands beyond Indochina, Mao added, "Because we will fight large-scale battles in the future, it will be good if we also build roads to Thailand."[61]

Chinese armament deliveries to North Vietnam would rise sharply over the course of 1965. China sent 221,000 firearms to Vietnam, versus 80,000 in 1964; they sent 4,439 mortars and artillery pieces, versus 1,205 in 1964; they sent 114 million bullets, versus 25 million in 1964.[62]

* * *

FOLLOWING TRAN VAN HUONG'S OVERTHROW, THE MOST INFLUENTIAL force in creating the new South Vietnamese government proved to be the Buddhists, not their accomplice Khanh. The top position went to Dr. Phan Huy Quat, a man whom Tri Quang had long been promoting for the premiership. Some observers, in fact, suspected that Quat was entirely under the control of Tri Quang. Formerly the minister of education and minister of defense under Bao Dai, Quat had often been mentioned as a possible replacement for Diem during the early days of the Diem regime, and he had gone to prison in 1960 for signing the Caravelle Manifesto. Most other members of the new Quat government also were Tri Quang allies known for their strong opposition to "Diemism."

On February 19, just three days after the new government officially took power, another coup rocked the South Vietnamese capital. The rebel leadership consisted largely of men who had orchestrated the coup of September 13, 1964, with General Lam Van Phat and Colonel Pham Ngoc Thao the top figures. Tanks and infantry under Colonel Thao's control captured the Saigon post office and radio station, and they surrounded Khanh's house and Gia Long palace. General Phat led Marine, Airborne, and Special Forces troops to Tan Son Nhut, where they captured the airport and began parking tanks across the runways to prevent planes from taking off or landing. On the airfield, Khanh was preparing an escape in his personal airplane when he saw Phat's tanks beginning to park on the tarmac. With great haste, his pilot took the plane down an open runway and lifted it into the air before the tanks could block it in. Khanh flew to Vung Tau, and from there he ordered the commanders of III and IV Corps to send troops to Saigon to put down the insurrection. But these commanders refused to obey Khanh's order because they, like most of the other generals, had been appalled by Khanh's submissiveness toward the

Buddhists. Most other units in the vicinity of Saigon chose not to take sides in the dispute, either.

On Saigon Radio, the rebels announced that they were creating a new government. They praised Ngo Dinh Diem and denounced former Ambassador Henry Cabot Lodge for inciting his overthrow.[63] They intended to get rid of Khanh, the plotters said, but would retain other members of the government. Then, however, in secret negotiations, Generals Phat and Thao struck a bargain with Air Marshal Nguyen Cao Ky to leave the current government in place in exchange for Khanh's removal. At the command of Phat and Thao, the rebel forces dispersed quickly and without incident. Returning to his coup headquarters, General Phat took off his uniform, beneath which was a set of civilian clothing. He shook the hand of an American military observer, muttered, "I go now," and sped away in a civilian car.

The next morning, in a meeting at Bien Hoa, the Armed Forces Council gave Khanh a vote of no confidence in absentia and ordered him to leave the country immediately. Khanh, however, refused to give up. He spent most of the day flying from province to province in his personal airplane to rally supporters, only to find that very few people still supported him. Late that night, his plane ran out of gas in Dalat, and Dalat had no place to refuel at that hour. While Khanh sat ingloriously on the runway, he listened as Colonel Jasper Wilson, whom Westmoreland had sent because of his close relationship with Khanh, urged him to resign in order to end the crisis. Seeing now that the game was lost, Khanh sighed that he was willing to leave office if he could do so in a dignified manner. The generals promptly arranged an elaborate departure ceremony for Khanh, complete with several bands and an honor guard. After attending the ceremony, Khanh was officially sent to the United States to "report to the United Nations," serve as "ambassador-at-large," and perform other meaningless tasks.

Many of Khanh's adversaries had hoped that his removal would slow, if not halt, the government's flood of concessions to the militant Buddhists. They were quickly disappointed. Once the Quat government settled in, it adopted a host of measures that Tri Quang had championed. It set free everyone whom government forces had detained during anti-Huong demonstrations. Quat and his top military supporters – General Thi above all – carried out yet another round of purges within the military to satisfy Tri Quang and keep opposition to the new regime from congealing. Among the casualties of these purges were Pham Van Dong, Tran Thanh Ben, Tran Van Minh, and Dang Van Quang – able officers whom Tri Quang opposed because they had suppressed Buddhist protests or otherwise obstructed his endeavors. Some vigorously anti-Communist military officers who survived these purges subsequently criticized Quat for failing to incarcerate suspected Communists and neutralists, and they soon found themselves staring out prison windows as well. So extensive were the purges and the changes to the command structure that the chain of command turned into a heap of broken links.[64] The inevitable result was a serious weakening of the officer corps and the armed forces. During no other period in its twenty-one-year history would the Republic of Vietnam perform so poorly against the Communists as during Quat's rule. The miserable performance of the Quat regime verified what some had long believed, that a government dominated by Tri Quang and his Buddhist followers would not prosecute the war against the Communists with skill or vigor.

During Quat's first month in office, the Communist main forces concentrated their attacks in the provinces east of Saigon, the northern coastal provinces, and the central highlands, bent on destroying the government's best main force battalions and gaining experience in large main force attacks.[65] At the beginning of March, a South Vietnamese Army battalion in Kontum province was decimated by several heavily armed Communist battalions that, unbeknownst to the South Vietnamese, belonged to the 325th North Vietnamese Army division. As a result of this defeat, the South Vietnamese command in Kontum initiated contingency planning for abandoning the entire province. In other sections of I Corps and II Corps, multibattalion Communist attacks in the first weeks of March compelled South Vietnamese commanders to avoid operating in less than battalion strength. Because small units no longer could operate safely, the government had to cut back severely on the number of mobile operations, giving the Viet Cong free reign over most of the countryside. In response to the enemy's advances in I and II Corps, the South Vietnamese high command sent most of its general reserve battalions there to engage the enemy, removing the strongest element of the Hop Tac pacification program in the areas around Saigon.

In the bulk of the rural areas, the Communists could recruit at will, a trend that would continue for most of 1965. In their sixth military region, for example, the Communists would recruit 2,689 youths into their armed forces during 1965, the most for any year of the war and nearly half of the region's total of 6,000 recruits for the entire war.[66] Hai Chua, the head of the Party chapter in one Cochinchinese village, recounted that during this period the Viet Cong could obtain every villager's cooperation without threatening or killing anyone "because the people were nearly certain that the future lay with the Communists." Even villagers with relatives in the government, Hai Chua said, avoided reporting the Viet Cong's activities to the government.[67]

The Communists reduced their offensive military activities in mid-March, and for the next two months they rarely committed battalion-size units to combat, relying instead on small attacks of the hit-and-run variety. Several additional North Vietnamese battalions arrived in the South during this period and they, like the other Communist battalions in the South, undertook preparations for large battles scheduled for May and June. Because the Saigon government's presence in the villages had shrunk to almost nothing, South Vietnamese forces lacked intelligence and thus they seldom could locate Communist units and force them into battle. In early April, the South Vietnamese armed forces did score a few substantial victories, in large measure due to timely air support and the competence of the elite general reserve battalions, but the deterioration of the war effort continued. Most observers on both sides viewed April 1965 as a new low point for the South Vietnamese government. Looking back on the period from the Diem coup in November 1963 to the end of April 1965, Westmoreland commented, "Government effectiveness steadily declined throughout this entire period. South Vietnamese civil servants became dispirited and inactive in the face of the continued political instability. Institutions of government formed during the regime of President Diem progressively deteriorated and in some instances, particularly elements of the intelligence and police forces, disappeared altogether." Because of the weak leadership of the armed forces, he observed, "the overall effectiveness of these forces decreased markedly."[68]

Although Tri Quang and his subordinate leaders at the Buddhist Institute expressed approval of the new Quat government and abstained from creating disturbances, they did not resist the temptation to engage in other forms of mischief. The Yale-educated monk Quang Lien and several additional Buddhist Institute figures openly espoused a peace plan that entailed the withdrawal of all foreign forces from Vietnam. Other high officials of the Buddhist Institute, Tri Quang among them, told the Americans that they disagreed with Quang Lien, but in front of different audiences these individuals endorsed the peace plan. In an interview with the *Hong Kong Standard*, Tri Quang said that Hanoi and Washington should "start immediate talks" to negotiate a peace.[69] With negotiations widely expected to produce nothing better than a frail neutralist regime that enjoyed no U.S. protection, the Americans became very nervous upon hearing such talk, and therefore they asked Tri Quang about the interview. Tri Quang then claimed that he did not really mean the United States should negotiate immediately.[70] In May, Tri Quang displayed anti-American and anti-Catholic sentiments so virulent and unreal in nature that they could only have come from the mind of either a maniac or a subversive or both. In one letter to the Americans, he warned that they would lose the war unless they stopped favoring Vietnamese Catholics over Vietnamese Buddhists because the Vietnamese people thought that the United States was "using Catholics to exterminate Buddhists."[71] While Quat was proving surprisingly fierce in suppressing new groups that were demanding peace and neutralism, he did not crack down on anyone in the Buddhist Institute for making such demands.[72]

The frailty of the Quat government and the progressive corrosion of the military situation generated new sentiment among certain Americans for intensifying Rolling Thunder. On March 8, Ambassador Taylor urged Washington to move the strikes northward more quickly than was planned in order to make a greater impression on the North Vietnamese.[73] The Joint Chiefs favored immediate and sharp increases in the pace and scope of the bombing, with high priority given to the railroads and highways between North Vietnam and China and to the Soviet surface-to-air missiles and aircraft that were arriving in North Vietnam.[74] Most emphatically, CIA Director McCone told the President, "We must hit them harder, more frequently, and inflict greater damage. Instead of avoiding the MiGs, we must go in and take them out. A bridge here and there will not do the job. We must strike their airfields, their petroleum resources, their power stations, and their military compounds." By avoiding such targets, McCone argued, "we signal to the Communists that our determination to win is significantly modified by our fear of widening the war." In the absence of intensified bombing, North Vietnamese infiltration would continue at a high rate, with the result that "we can expect requirements for an ever-increasing commitment of U.S. personnel," and "we will find ourselves mired down in combat in the jungle in a military effort that we cannot win, and from which we will have extreme difficulty in extracting ourselves."[75]

President Johnson himself, in scant time, became frustrated with the failure of Rolling Thunder to alter the situation in South Vietnam. The bombing program had been his most serious hope of averting defeat without American intervention in the ground war, although he had never had great confidence in it and had viewed it primarily as a means of quickening the gallop of the South Vietnamese government. Johnson rejected all of the recommendations to bomb the North more heavily because of his belief that air power could inflict little real damage and his civilian advisers' warnings that heavy bombing could lead to war with China or the Soviet Union. He was out of good options, he believed, and time was running out. Discussing Vietnam at the dinner table one evening, he thundered, "I can't get out. I can't finish it with what I have got. And I don't know what the hell to do!"[76]

Turning to hope of the most desperate variety, Johnson frantically rummaged around for new devices that would achieve a miraculous turnaround without U.S. ground forces and without action outside of South Vietnam. "We played the first half of the game, and the score is now twenty-one to zero against us," he told the Joint Chiefs on one occasion. "Now I want you to tell me how to win." Looking at General Wheeler, the President huffed, "You're graduates of the Military Academy and you should be able to give me an answer. I want you to ... tell me how we are going to kill more Viet Cong."[77] In a telephone conversation with Secretary of Defense McNamara, exposing the full extent of his ignorance of military affairs, Johnson said, "I don't guess there's any way, Bob, that through your small planes or helicopters ... you could spot these people and then radio back and let the planes come in and bomb the hell out of them." McNamara did not inform the President that the Americans and South Vietnamese had been using such methods for years, but instead replied, "This is what we are trying to do, but it's very difficult when they're under the trees."[78]

To come up with new ways to kill more Viet Cong, the President ordered Army Chief of Staff General Harold K. Johnson to visit Vietnam in the middle of March. On the morning before the general's scheduled departure, the President issued him instructions as they rode the White House elevator. President Johnson shoved his finger in the general's chest and barked, "Get things bubbling, General." General Johnson, who had not been treated so shabbily when he was a second lieutenant, recalled, "His finger was boring literally in my chest."[79]

General Johnson made a quick trip to Vietnam, and returned to the White House on March 15 to deliver his report. The much-weakened South Vietnamese armed forces, he told the President, were incapable of handling the Viet Cong, and the United States therefore needed to introduce its own troops into the war. The general advocated sending a division of U.S. combat forces to defend several provinces in the central highlands, and asserted that the United States might need to deploy an anti-infiltration force of four American divisions along the 17th Parallel, from the South China Sea across Vietnam and Laos to the Thai-Laotian border, to cut the Ho Chi Minh Trail. What shocked the President most was General Johnson's warning that victory could require five years and 500,000 U.S. troops, well beyond what the President and the rest of the civilians had expected.[80] President Johnson approved a series of smaller actions put forward by the Army Chief of Staff, but he did not act on the recommendations to insert U.S. ground troops directly into the fighting in Vietnam and Laos.

A debate over the deployment of major U.S. ground forces ensued, pitting General Westmoreland and the Joint Chiefs, who favored such a deployment, against Ambassador Taylor, who opposed it. Taylor admonished that the arrival of U.S. forces could cause the South Vietnamese to sit back and let the Americans take over the fighting, and that it would lend credence to Communist propaganda that French imperialism had been replaced by American imperialism.[81] South Vietnamese leaders themselves raised objections to an infusion of American combat troops, arguing that it would cause South Vietnamese civilians to demand an end to the war. General Thieu expressed confidence that accelerated military mobilization efforts would yield enough South Vietnamese troops to render the use of foreign ground forces unnecessary.[82] Westmoreland, however, who was following the mobilization efforts closely, believed that the South Vietnamese could not add enough men to the armed forces in time. In late March, Westmoreland estimated that the preservation of South Vietnam would require the insertion of 33,000 American troops, consisting of the third and fourth Marine battalions, a full U.S. Army division, and a separate Army Airborne brigade. Westmoreland also evaluated a plan that involved deploying three more U.S. divisions and two divisions from Southeast Asian allies across the 17th Parallel to block the Laotian infiltration routes. Such a move would have major military advantages, Westmoreland believed, but it might come too late. For logistical reasons, the five divisions probably could not be deployed for another nine months, by which time there was a strong chance, in Westmoreland's view, that Rolling Thunder would have compelled Hanoi to call off the insurgency.[83] Thus did Westmoreland decide, fatefully, against putting troops in Laos at this time.

A short while later, the gloomy news on government troop shortages and Communist strength convinced McNamara and his statisticians that the United States did need to send more ground troops immediately to guarantee the safety of U.S. facilities. As the President's most influential adviser on Vietnam, McNamara promptly persuaded Johnson to pursue this course, and so on April 1, Johnson ordered the deployment of two additional Marine battalions and 20,000 additional support troops. Johnson, furthermore, approved a request from the Joint Chiefs to authorize U.S. forces in Vietnam to participate in "counterinsurgency operations." The President, though, was not ready to plunge the United States into the middle of the ground war and introduce several hundred thousand American troops as some in the military wanted, but instead was still concerned primarily with protecting U.S. bases. He did not approve the recommendations of the Joint Chiefs and Westmoreland to send U.S. Army units to Vietnam, and he authorized the Marines to undertake counterinsurgency operations only from a defensive posture and on an experimental basis.[84] U.S. forces were to remain in enclaves around the key installations. President Johnson was still unaware that the North Vietnamese Army was streaming across the Annamite mountains, which would soon render the enclave strategy untenable. At the beginning of April, Johnson had not ruled out a withdrawal of U.S. forces in the event that the experiment failed or the whole enterprise seemed doomed, although he was loathe to pull out before American prestige in the region had been adequately bolstered. As with the first Marine deployment, President Johnson made every effort to conceal the new deployment and the authorization of counterinsurgency operations. On his instructions, National Security Adviser McGeorge Bundy sent out word that U.S. troops should carry out their new mission "in ways that minimize any appearance of sudden changes in policy."[85]

In an effort to mute criticism from the liberal American intelligentsia, from left-wing European political parties, and from certain foreign leaders who were calling for peace, Johnson gave a speech at Johns Hopkins University on April 7 in which he offered to participate in "unconditional discussions" on Vietnam, a reversal of his previous stance on negotiations. The speech immediately reduced criticism of America's Vietnam policy among the groups Johnson was hoping to placate, while it reduced confidence in Johnson among staunchly anti-Communist allies. The Communists did not respond at all favorably. Hanoi dubbed Johnson's proposal a "deception" full of "all the tricks of the most wicked sorcerers." North Vietnamese Premier Pham Van Dong insisted that any peace negotiations had to be conditional, with the United States

consenting beforehand to the withdrawal of the U.S. military from South Vietnam, to the settlement of South Vietnam's internal affairs "in accordance with
the program of the South Vietnam National Front for Liberation," and to the
reunification of Vietnam. In an internal memorandum, Le Duan explained that
these conditions really were "intended to pave the way for a U.S. withdrawal
with a lesser loss of face."[86] When Johnson subsequently attempted to mollify
his most demanding critics by accompanying an offer of unconditional negotiations with a suspension of Rolling Thunder, the North Vietnamese merely
denounced the bombing pause as "a deceitful maneuver designed to pave the
way for new U.S. acts of war."[87]

Not long after the Johns Hopkins speech, the American view of the war
underwent a drastic change. The origins of this transformation can be traced
to March 23, when a discontented soldier from the 101st North Vietnamese
Army Regiment crept away from his comrades and turned himself in to a
South Vietnamese Army unit. The defector divulged that his entire regiment,
one of the 325th Division's three regiments, was operating in Kontum province.
Next, he guided the South Vietnamese 21st Ranger Battalion to a valley northwest of Kontum City where the 101st Regiment was hiding, sparking a fierce
and inconclusive clash between the Rangers and the heavily equipped North
Vietnamese unit. The CIA and U.S. military intelligence then concluded that
elements of the 325th North Vietnamese Army Division were in South Vietnam,
four months after the first regiment had left North Vietnam and nearly two
months after its arrival in the South.[88] This discovery quickly led American
intelligence analysts to alter their views on Hanoi's intentions, for they knew
that the North Vietnamese would not undertake so provocative an action as
sending a North Vietnamese Army regiment unless it was seeking the greatest
of prizes. On April 15, the CIA distributed a prediction that the Vietnamese
Communists were preparing for a very large and ambitious offensive, and two
weeks later, interagency intelligence bodies in Saigon and Washington accurately forecast both the timing and the location of the coming offensive.[89]

The identification of the 101st Regiment and the revised assessments of North
Vietnamese intentions inspired America's military leaders to advocate additional ground force deployments. In the middle of April, General Wheeler recommended sending three entire U.S. divisions to South Vietnam, while General
Westmoreland argued that the situation demanded at least an American brigade
in the vicinity of Bien Hoa and Vung Tau. Wheeler's proposal failed to take root
with President Johnson, who said that such a large increase could provoke a
sharp reaction from North Vietnam and China and would not find favor with
Congress, but the President did grant Westmoreland's wishes, agreeing to send
the 173rd Airborne Brigade to the Bien Hoa-Vung Tau area. Johnson, in addition, sent another 5,000 Marines to participate in combined counterinsurgency
operations with the Vietnamese Marines. At this same time, Johnson told the
Saigon embassy to undertake a large collection of new initiatives concocted by

his Washington advisers, to include experimental integration of U.S. personnel into South Vietnamese Army units and the provincial administrations, a
new recruiting campaign guided by American experts, and new programs for
dispensing food and medical care.

Ambassador Taylor had not been consulted before President Johnson made
these decisions, and he was not at all pleased when learned of them after the fact.
Still skeptical of the value of American troops in Vietnam, Taylor recommended
postponing deployment of the 173rd Airborne Brigade until the results were in
from the Marine experimentation. Taylor characterized the other new plans as
"crash projects of doubtful value," and remarked that the Americans in Vietnam
had already tested many of the concepts and either implemented or discarded
them. The South Vietnamese government was currently overwhelmed with
the ninety initiatives he had been given during his last visit to Washington.
The critical problem for the Saigon government, Taylor knew, was not a lack
of concepts but a lack of action. "We are going to stall the machinery of the
government if we do not declare a moratorium on new programs for at least
six months," he protested.[90]

McNamara promptly invited Taylor, Westmoreland, and the Joint Chiefs to
Honolulu for the purpose of gaining their acquiescence in the new recommendations. At Honolulu, events largely proceeded to McNamara's satisfaction.
The argument that convinced Ambassador Taylor to yield on most points was
that the enemy, newly reinforced by the 325th Division, would likely launch a
major offensive that could inflict a catastrophic defeat at one of the major U.S.
bases.[91] Taylor consented to the deployment of two U.S. Army brigades, three
more Marine battalions, and 18,000 additional support troops, which would
boost U.S. troop strength from 33,000 to 82,000. McNamara agreed to back
away from some of the administration's other proposals because of Taylor's
protestations, most notably the integration of American troops into South
Vietnamese Army units. After the Honolulu conference, McNamara would
inform President Johnson that the conferees were perfectly content with the
tempo and geographical restrictions of Rolling Thunder, although in fact some
of the Joint Chiefs had recommended a major expansion of the program during
the conference.[92]

Ambassador Taylor presented McNamara's deployment plans to Premier
Quat. The South Vietnamese leader initially showed little enthusiasm and
expressed doubt that his country needed more U.S. troops at the moment.
South Vietnam's generals and most of the country's civilian leaders, on the
other hand, welcomed the proposed augmentations, and after a few days of
deliberation, Quat yielded on the issue of the troop deployments. The South
Vietnamese leadership proved to be much more resistant, however, on the issue
of a joint U.S.–South Vietnamese command, which the U.S. government was
also advocating. Air Marshal Ky and General Thieu said publicly that South
Vietnam had neither the desire nor the need for a joint command, while the

Saigon press objected that it would mean a loss of Vietnamese sovereignty. The Americans shelved the idea.

The new U.S. units arrived in early May, just in time to see the war enter its next phase. Commencing in the second week of the month, the Viet Cong and the newly arrived North Vietnamese Army units attacked the South Vietnamese in many areas to compel the Saigon government to disperse its forces and send them into the mountains and jungles, making them vulnerable for annihilation by massed Communist forces. The offensive that began in the second week of May greatly exceeded all previous Communist offensives in strength and ambition. The North Vietnamese leadership sought to kill South Vietnamese regulars at such a pace that the South Vietnamese Army's total combat losses for the year would reach a level of between 30,000 and 40,000, which they predicted would be high enough to allow Communist forces to capture Saigon and the other cities before the Americans could stop them.[93] While Western pundits were still calling the war a guerrilla war, and some Western historians would later describe the first seven months of 1965 as a period of guerrilla warfare,[94] the war was now much closer to a conventional war. Generously equipped with heavy conventional armaments such as pack howitzers, flamethrowers, and 12.7mm machine guns, the Viet Cong and North Vietnamese main forces had entered the third and final stage of Mao's revolutionary war, in which the highest priority was no longer on political organization and hit-and-run strikes but on massed attacks on the enemy's conventional forces and its bases and cities.[95]

The first punch was thrown at Song Be, the capital of Phuoc Long province, on the night of May 11. Powered by the 840th Viet Cong Battalion, the 1st Battalion of the 1st Viet Cong Regiment, and a startling eight heavy weapons companies, the attack was the largest on a provincial capital since the assault on Phuoc Vinh in September 1961. The remainder of the 1st Viet Cong Regiment and the entire 2nd and 3rd Viet Cong Regiments conducted supporting operations and established ambush positions in areas around Song Be where the Communist commander expected South Vietnamese reinforcements to arrive by land and by air. The Communists thus had the strength of a full division on the field of battle. Soon after the Communist heavy weapons lit up the sky above Song Be, the assault battalions overwhelmed Song Be's outnumbered defenders at many points and captured most of the town. They failed, however, to seize the South Vietnamese provincial headquarters and the U.S. advisory compound, both of which had stout fortifications and vigorous defenders. Witnesses credited the survival of the advisory compound to the bravery and ferocity of six Americans who held their positions for four hours under continuous howitzer, mortar, recoilless rifle, and machine gun fire that consumed a large fraction of the Viet Cong's total ammunition supply. Compelled by circumstance to carry their weapons and supplies through mountains and across fast-flowing rivers without motorized transport, the Viet Cong units had arrived at Song

Be with relatively small supplies of the bulky ammunition required for their big weapons. At the end of four hours, their supplies near exhaustion, the Viet Cong had to curtail their heavy fire sharply.

In the morning, helicopters carried a South Vietnamese Army regiment to a site near Song Be. Aided by air strikes that tore apart the landscape around the regiment's landing zone, the South Vietnamese troops organized themselves on the ground and advanced on the capital before the enemy regiments could attack them. Intent on holding their ground, the two Viet Cong battalions in Song Be braced for the attack, but the South Vietnamese regiment, through a series of fierce assaults accompanied by devastating aerial bombardments, drove the Viet Cong out during the afternoon. It was a poignant demonstration of the importance of conventional military assets – mobility, mass, and firepower – for both the Communist main forces engaged in third-stage warfare and for the South Vietnamese forces trying to stop them. All told, the battle claimed the lives of least several hundred Viet Cong, against thirty-seven South Vietnamese and five American dead.[96]

While the Saigon government had won the first round, the next rounds would go to the Communists. In the remainder of the offensive's opening week, the Communist main forces made five attacks in battalion strength or greater, and for the rest of May the intensity of large-scale attacks remained high in all regions of South Vietnam except the Mekong Delta. By the end of the month, the Communists had mounted a total of eighteen large attacks, including eleven in at least battalion strength. Although government troops performed reasonably well in some of these engagements, the Communists usually outfought them, and on several occasions they shattered the cohesion of government units, sending their men running away in panic. The government would lose nearly twice as many weapons as it captured from the enemy in May.[97]

The most successful Communist attack of May opened in Quang Ngai province on the 29th. The Communists brought the equivalent of two regiments into what became the battle of Ba Gia – the 1st Viet Cong Regiment, several local force battalions, and the 45th Battalion, a unit of the North Vietnamese Army that had been sent to South Vietnam in the spring of 1963. With a heavy weapons battalion plus two batteries of 75mm pack howitzers and an anti-aircraft battery equipped with 12.7mm machine guns, the Communist forces held organic firepower superiority over the South Vietnamese forces they were to face. The 1st Viet Cong Regiment opened the battle near Ba Gia district headquarters by ambushing a company of the 1st Battalion of the South Vietnamese Army's 51st Infantry Regiment. The Communists expected that other units from the 51st Regiment would come to assist the company, followed by larger South Vietnamese Army relief forces, and they were ready to ambush these units in turn. In accordance with their hopes, the commander of 1/51 Battalion sent a second company to help the first. It too met stiff resistance. Then the South Vietnamese battalion commander left Ba Gia by truck with two platoons from his remaining company in order to take command. The Communists allowed the government troops to reinforce with little interference, to give the impression that they had only a small force in the area. Once the South Vietnamese battalion had completed its movements, the Communist regulars slammed into it from two directions and overran the entire unit. Only a few South Vietnamese soldiers and U.S. advisers escaped with their lives.

The next day, in further fulfillment of Communist expectations, the commander of the South Vietnamese Army's 2nd Division sent larger forces to Ba Gia, three battalions in all. Departing from Quang Ngai City at 9:00 A.M. the 2nd Battalion of the 51st Regiment, the 39th Ranger Battalion, and the 3rd Marine Battalion proceeded by truck and armored personnel carrier to the Lam Loc intersection and from there advanced on foot to the area where the 1/51 Battalion had been crushed. They took up positions on three widely dispersed areas of high ground, a very unwise course of action. The battalions were too far apart to support each other, and the terrain objectives were too large to be held by single battalions.

As on the previous day, the Communists had forces nearby but let the government troops move to their positions unopposed, then struck quickly before the government troops had time to solidify their defenses. From 2:00 P.M. through the afternoon and into the evening, the Communists bit into the perimeter at all three locations. American and South Vietnamese fixed wing aircraft hit the attackers hard, flying more sorties in this battle than in any previous engagement. Communist sources indicate that the air strikes seriously impeded their attacks. The government, moreover, had artillery batteries within range of the assailants, and the artillery killed some Viet Cong and North Vietnamese Army soldiers, too. The air support and artillery, however, were considerably less effective than they might have been, for communication was lost with the Ranger and Marine battalions, and the forward observer of the 2nd Battalion, 51st Regiment was killed.

During the night, the Marine battalion fared the best of the three government battalions. Having taken refuge in a moat, it held off three large Viet Cong charges. The 2/51 Battalion sustained the loss of an entire company in the middle of the night. The other companies, depleted but intact, fought their way out with the assistance of M-113 armored personnel carriers and a devastating napalm strike. Suffering the worst fate was the 39th Ranger Battalion. The 45th North Vietnamese Army Battalion and a company from the 1st Viet Cong Regiment cut the Ranger battalion into three pieces and wiped out two of them, annihilating an entire Ranger company and the battalion headquarters. Only 115 of the 265 Rangers survived. A subsequent inspection of the battlefield revealed that the Communists had killed wounded Rangers and cut open some of their stomachs. Shortly before dawn, the Communists broke off their attacks at all three places and withdrew.

The two days of fighting at Ba Gia left the South Vietnamese Army with 107 dead, 123 wounded, and 367 missing. The Communists completely destroyed one battalion and rendered two more combat-ineffective. Confirmed Communist dead totaled 84, though the American command estimated total Communist casualties to be 800, based on the observations of forward air controllers who saw large Viet Cong forces subjected to powerful and accurate air strikes in open terrain. In post-battle appraisals, American advisers stressed that senior South Vietnamese officers had committed glaring tactical errors and demonstrated cowardice during the engagement, making it one of the worst performances in the history of the South Vietnamese Army. Most of the blame for these troubles belonged to General Thi, who recently had replaced key commanders in this part of the country.[98]

For proponents of South Vietnamese anti-Communism who began the year despondent about the war, the outlook had, in some ways, become much worse by the end of May. The fall of Huong had removed from the scene one of the few men capable of throttling the militant Buddhists. The removal of additional capable officers under Khanh and then Quat brought South Vietnam's military strength down to a precariously low level, just as the Communists were beginning a great offensive. The Chinese, emboldened by the unwillingness of the Americans to send ground troops into North Vietnam, agreed to deploy seven Chinese divisions to assist the North Vietnamese. The anti-Communists, however, had one critical new asset on their side of the balance sheet, the armed forces of the United States, and that asset was growing rapidly. American aircraft were now dropping bombs over both Vietnams, American ships were keeping the South Vietnamese coast clear of Communist vessels, and American ground forces were guarding bases on South Vietnam's soil. President Johnson, though, was clinging to a hope that the first deployments of American forces would not entangle the United States in the ground war, and he had yet to decide whether the U.S. forces would continue to grow or whether they would even remain on the balance sheet.

* * *

AS 1965 PROGRESSED, FEAR OF THE DOMINO EFFECT ROSE IN SEVERITY at the top levels of the Johnson administration. An observer in the White House would have seen increasingly grim looks on the faces of President Johnson and his principal lieutenants as they fretted that the fall of South Vietnam would topple the Southeast Asian dominoes and shatter the American position in the Far East. In the event of a precipitate American withdrawal from Vietnam, Johnson told his advisers on one occasion, the Southeast Asian nations would label the United States a "paper tiger," and the United States would see its credibility plummet in the region. It would be "an irreparable blow."[99] At the same time, the top Americans were showing less concern than before about the issue of global credibility. No less than Secretary of State Dean Rusk, who heretofore had been the most concerned about harmful consequences beyond the Asian continent, was now worried mainly by the domino effect within Asia. Rusk informed the President on one occasion that if South Vietnam fell, the United States would lose its alliances with Laos, Thailand, Malaysia, South Korea, Taiwan, and Japan, and in addition the Chinese would dominate India, while America's European alliances would remain intact.[100] Johnson and his advisers continued to believe that China posed the main threat to the dominoes, and that a loss in Vietnam would encourage Hanoi and Beijing to seek further gains in Thailand and beyond,[101] conclusions that were shared by the U.S. intelligence community at the time[102] and were well supported by contemporary and postwar evidence.

In connection with the domino theory, President Johnson frequently emphasized the need to avoid the mistakes committed at Munich in 1938, when the abandonment of one country had encouraged and facilitated further enemy conquests. "We know, from Munich on, that when you give, the dictators feed on raw meat," he said on February 17. "If they take South Vietnam, they take Thailand, they take Indonesia, they take Burma, they come right on back to the Philippines."[103] Johnson and the other leading officials in his administration did not develop confidence in the Munich analogy by simplistically assuming that Asia in 1965 was the same as Europe in 1938, as numerous critics were to claim.[104] Rather, their analysis was grounded in a sound understanding of local conditions in Asia. President Johnson, who was now paying closer attention to developments in individual Asian countries than before, stressed the great importance that Asia's leaders attached to Vietnam. During a meeting with Eisenhower in February, he read the former President a State Department message on Thailand as evidence of Vietnam's international significance. In the message, the U.S. ambassador to Thailand described a discussion with Thai Foreign Minister Thanat Khoman in these terms: "This morning, in my first meeting with Thanat after my return, I found him in a rosy glow over the vast improvement in morale throughout Southeast Asia as a result of American and South Vietnamese [air] strikes on North Vietnam."[105]

During the first months of 1965, the administration's leaders were reading numerous reports from embassies around the world on foreign perceptions of Vietnam. Most U.S. allies were supportive of the administration's policy, and almost every country, regardless of its alignment in the Cold War, believed that the outcome of the Vietnam conflict would have major repercussions in the global contest between China, the Soviet Union, and the United States.[106] For some of the world's non-Asian countries, the loss of Vietnam would definitely weaken, though not necessarily destroy, their confidence in the United States, while the preservation of Vietnam would have the opposite effect. H. E. Omar Sequa, the closest adviser to Saudi Arabia's King Feisal, told the Americans in February that the Flaming Dart air strikes against North Vietnam provided a welcome demonstration of American intentions, for, as a result of prior American indecisiveness, "many Arabs had been losing confidence in the United States."[107] Upon learning of Flaming Dart, Somali prime minister Ali Seamark Abdirascid told the American ambassador to his country, "It's about time.... Facts are facts, and if you do not stand up to obvious aggression in Southeast Asia, the whole world will be in danger."[108] When Dean Rusk informed the Shah of Iran in April that the United States was firmly committed to the safeguarding of South Vietnam, the Shah said that he was "delighted," for he believed that "if the United States pulled out of Vietnam, the free world would lose confidence in U.S. policy and promises."[109] President Gamal Abdul Nasser of the United Arab Republic, who was much less sympathetic towards the United States and who at this time was the most important man in the Middle East, remarked that the absence of Communist retaliation to the U.S. bombing of North Vietnam showed that the "Soviets are cowards" and that non-Western countries – presumably China was at the top of this list – "are losing ground and retreating everywhere." As a result of U.S. actions in Vietnam, said Nasser, "People in Africa and Asia will turn to the U.S. because they now see that the U.S. means what it says; other large powers talk and do nothing."[110]

Many within the Communist camp believed that the preservation of South Vietnam would abet anti-Communists across the globe, and that South Vietnam's fall would bolster Communists the world over. On April 2, Zhou Enlai told Pakistani President Ayub Khan that China's friends in Africa and Europe worried that if the United States thwarted the Vietnamese Communists, the anti-American forces in the rest of the world "will also suffer heavy losses."[111] The following month, the Chinese Army's chief of staff publicly warned that the Communists could be the victims of another Munich, contending that a failure to defeat South Vietnam could cause the Communist side to suffer further losses as had happened after the attempt to appease Hitler.[112] Conversely, Ho Chi Minh told an African diplomat that a Vietnamese Communist victory would "help the people of all nations see that they need not be afraid of the Americans," and that "once the United States is defeated in Vietnam it will never be able to win anywhere else in the world."[113]

Aside from France, which doggedly called for the neutralization of South Vietnam to gratify old grudges against the United States and assert its independence, the countries of NATO supported America's stance on Vietnam. NATO's Expert Working Group, composed of representatives from NATO countries small and large, asserted in the spring of 1965, "It remains a vital interest of the West to prevent a Communist victory in South Vietnam which would stimulate similar developments throughout Southeast Asia."[114] Many NATO nations – including the two most powerful, West Germany and Britain – said that America's willingness to defend Vietnam was a key indicator of whether America would protect its allies not only in Asia but also in Europe.[115]

During the first half of 1965, the West Germans repeatedly stressed the importance of Vietnam and urged the Americans to hold firm. They might well have contributed militarily had not the West German constitution prohibited it. During a meeting with President Johnson in the late spring, West German Chancellor Ludwig Erhard said that "Vietnam is important to most Germans because they regard it as a kind of testing ground as to how firmly the U.S. honors its commitments. In that respect there exists a parallel between Saigon and Berlin."[116] Chancellor Erhard further evidenced his sincerity by expressing the same views to the French, for whom such talk was most unwelcome. In mid-1965, the West German people as a whole approved of the defense of South Vietnam, with more than one half of West Germans believing that American intervention was justified.[117]

The British believed that their national interests were at stake in Vietnam, for they saw themselves as partners with the United States in protecting British and American interests in Southeast Asia against Communist expansionism. They were doing their part in Malaysia, and the Americans were doing their part in Vietnam. British Prime Minister Harold Wilson and other leading members of his government expressly said that the loss of Vietnam would have highly negative consequences for Southeast Asia and hence for Britain. On April 28, 1965, Wilson told the Italian President in private that "there is no alternative to the policy which the United States is pursuing" in Vietnam. If the United States withdrew from Vietnam, he asserted, "then one country after another will start to disengage from alliance with the United States and make the best terms they can with Communist China."[118] Among the general British populace, supporters of the U.S. war effort outnumbered opponents in early 1965.[119]

The fall of Vietnam in 1965, by itself, would not have immediately caused large numbers of countries outside of Asia to gravitate toward the Communist pole. America's assistance to allies in other parts of the world was only one of several factors that determined the alignment of most non-Asian countries, and for some it was a factor of only minor importance, subordinate to matters of internal politics, regional affairs, or bilateral relations with the United States. The falling of the Asian dominoes and the attendant collapse of American strength across Asia, on the other hand, could eventually have done serious harm to America's standing with its allies across the world, as it would mean a large decline in America's total power, prestige, and resolve. It was just such a falling of Asian dominoes that was a real possibility in 1965.

The argument most commonly advanced against the domino theory is that the Asian dominoes were not in danger of falling in the 1960s because they did not fall in 1975 when South Vietnam tumbled. The United States attained its objective of preventing the spread of Communism across Southeast Asia, it is conceded, but American intervention in Vietnam did not contribute to the attainment of that objective.[120] The argument is based on the unspoken premise that the countries of Asia experienced no significant changes in their capabilities or their intentions from 1965 to 1975, that the dominoes were as resistant to toppling and the Communist powers as disinclined to push them in 1965 as they were in 1975. It is a false premise, for these countries changed profoundly as the result of events during that ten-year period, including the overthrow of Sukarno in Indonesia, the Chinese Cultural Revolution, the widening of the Sino-Soviet rift, Richard Nixon's rapprochements with the two large Communist powers, and the wars in Vietnam, Cambodia, Laos, and Thailand. Nor did these events come to pass by coincidence; all of them, to varying degrees, received propulsion from the war that the United States decided to fight in Vietnam. The frustration of China's plans in 1965, the Cultural Revolution, the deterioration of Sino-Soviet relations, and the improvement of Sino-American relations during these ten years would dramatically reduce China's desire to combat U.S. influence in Southeast Asia. The struggles for power in Cambodia and Laos and the strengthening of the Soviet–North Vietnamese alliance disrupted China's friendship with North Vietnam, its principal partner in expanding Communism across Southeast Asia in the mid-1960s. In 1975, moreover, the countries of Southeast Asia were more capable of protecting themselves against Communist encroachment and more determined to do so. An assessment of the domino theory, therefore, demands a close investigation of the dominoes and the would-be topplers in 1965, not in 1975.

In early 1965, China was making considerable progress in expanding its influence abroad. Having entered the scene in Africa just a few years earlier, the Chinese were enjoying remarkable success in gaining allies on that continent by means of unconditional economic aid, covert military assistance, bribery, and propaganda. China's greatest ambitions and its greatest successes, though, were in Asia. Its Vietnamese Communist allies were scoring spectacular victories in South Vietnam, and it retained great influence in Hanoi despite its recent loss of nerve in the face of American strength. Indonesia and several other Asian countries were developing into close allies of China, and pro-Chinese insurgencies were in progress in Thailand, Malaysia, Laos, and Burma. As has been seen, Mao had definite plans for large battles in Thailand and beyond.

Of China's Asian allies in 1965, the country most directly tied to the Vietnam conflict besides North Vietnam itself was Cambodia. Cambodian Chief of State Prince Norodom Sihanouk had long distrusted the United States because of its support for his arch-enemies, Thailand and South Vietnam. As the South Vietnamese government floundered in 1964, Sihanouk became convinced that Communism would ultimately prevail in all of Southeast Asia and that therefore he had best side firmly with China and North Vietnam.[121] Over the course of 1964, Prince Sihanouk had instigated the trashing of the British and American embassies, called for an American withdrawal from South Vietnam, and allowed the Vietnamese Communists to begin shipping supplies into Sihanoukville and transporting them through Cambodian territory into South Vietnam.[122] During the spring of 1965, with a North Vietnamese victory apparently fast approaching, Sihanouk terminated diplomatic relations with the United States. Pakistan, another regional friend of China, voiced support for North Vietnam in 1965. This policy had nothing to do with what was transpiring in Vietnam, and everything to do with a desire to curry favor with the Chinese, who could help protect Pakistan against its archenemy, India.[123]

Events in Indonesia were progressing very much to China's advantage in early 1965. President Sukarno told his powerless legislature early in the year that the time had come to enter the socialist stage of the revolution, which would require that the people and the military "drastically turn the steering wheel."[124] In collaboration with the Indonesian Communists, Sukarno expropriated all American oil and rubber businesses in the country, as well as the businesses of other Western countries. He transferred the powers of his two most prominent anti-Communist ministers to pro-Communist officials, dissolved the remaining non-Communist political parties, and shut down newspapers that criticized him or the Communists. To increase his control over the military establishment, Sukarno saw to it that Communist sympathizers took over several important positions in the armed forces, among them the Air Force Chief of Staff and several regional Army commanders.[125] Most international observers warned that anti-Communist strength was declining with such rapidity that Indonesia would soon become a fully Communist country.[126] By early March, the prospect of a complete Communist takeover so worried the Americans that Dean Rusk informed the British, "Should it become necessary, I would be ready for a major war against Indonesia."[127]

Sukarno's moves at home coincided with the cementing of his alliances with North Vietnam and China. Indicative of the growing affinity between Indonesia and North Vietnam was an episode in which Indonesian "volunteers" carried weapons to the North Vietnamese embassy in Djakarta, presented them to North Vietnamese Premier Pham Van Dong, and announced that two battalions of Indonesians were ready to fight the "imperialists" in Vietnam.[128] Following a visit to Beijing by Indonesian Foreign Minister Subandrio early in the year, China and Indonesia issued a joint statement expressing "resolute support for the peoples of Vietnam, Laos and Cambodia in their just struggle to oppose U.S. imperialist aggression and intervention."[129] Zhou Enlai offered to provide 100,000 firearms for a secret Indonesian "people's army," which would give Sukarno a powerful force independent of the Indonesian army and its remaining anti-Communist officers. Urged on by Communist Party leader Aidit, Sukarno began arming such militia units at the end of February.[130] In March, almost certainly with Sukarno's knowledge, Mao told the Indonesian Communist Party to prepare an armed revolt against the anti-Communist leadership of the Indonesian armed forces, and he provided lavish sums of money – on top of the $30 million he was already giving the Indonesian Party annually – for the purpose of gaining collaborators in the military through bribery.[131]

During the first months of 1965, the Americans received very compelling indications that their actions in Vietnam would strongly influence Indonesia's military leaders as they pondered the great question of whether to resist Sukarno and the Indonesian Communist Party.[132] General Marjadi, the senior officer on Indonesian Defense Minister Nasution's staff, expressed the views of the Defense Ministry's top generals to U.S. Colonel George Benson at the end of February. Benson was the head of the U.S. military advisory group in Indonesia, and as such he was an obvious conduit for communicating with the top levels of the U.S. government. General Marjadi explained that the generals were disappointed and discouraged that the Americans had taken only "half-way measures" against North Vietnam thus far. "President Johnson should learn to use his power and should hit North Vietnam hard," Marjadi asserted. The Indonesian army would attempt to prevent a political crisis until Sukarno's death, said General Marjadi, and then would make a stand against the PKI, the Indonesian Communist Party. But such plans might not come to fruition, Marjadi warned, for "the danger of ever stronger PKI influence over Sukarno while he is alive could split the army in a time of crisis." General Marjadi made clear that what President Johnson did in Vietnam would help determine the Indonesian generals' ultimate willingness to resist the Indonesian Communists, and would indeed determine the fate of all the Asian dominoes. "The prize for victory in Vietnam is all of Asia," General Marjadi declared. "Asia respects power, and has no respect for weakness or for strong people afraid to act." General Marjadi finished his conversation with Colonel Benson by emphasizing the importance of American power in the looming confrontation between the Indonesian military and the PKI. "The United States," said Marjadi, "should be prepared to assist Indonesia quickly and fully when the showdown between the army and the PKI occurs."[133]

Seven months later, some of the Indonesian Defense Ministry's generals and Defense Minister Nasution himself were to rally anti-Communist military forces in the final conflict with Sukarno and his Communist allies. During the period of uncertainty following the failed September 30 attack on anti-Communist military leaders, the anti-Communist generals secretly asked the Americans to provide them with covert aid, saying that a failure by the United States to provide aid could reverse the rising fortunes of Indonesia's anti-Communists. Simultaneously, they urged the Americans to wield their strength in Vietnam in order to smite the Communists of Asia on multiple fronts. One emissary of the Indonesian military told the Americans: "The United States should strike while the iron is hot," and "help Indonesia crush Communism forever not only in Indonesia but in all of Southeast Asia."[134] Bolstered by quiet financial and moral support from the Americans, anti-Communist generals under the leadership of General Suharto ultimately took over the government. With a brutality that claimed hundreds of thousands of lives, the anti-Communists wiped out the huge Indonesian Communist Party. A new and long friendship between Indonesia and the United States thus took form, which was to exert perfound influence on the dynamics of power in Asia. This vital domino, tipping precariously, was transformed into a huge boulder standing squarely in the path of Chinese and North Vietnamese expansionism.

Afterward, many of the leading Indonesian anti-Communists never spoke frankly on their motives for resisting the Communists in 1965, but several did credit U.S. intervention in Vietnam with convincing key officers to make a stand. Indonesian Vice-President for Political Affairs Adam Malik, for example, told U.S. Vice-President Hubert Humphrey in 1966 that "General Suharto's success in defeating the Indonesian Communist forces was directly influenced by the U.S. determination in South Vietnam."[135] Near the end of his life, Defense Minister Nasution said that the military leadership would not have resisted the Communists during the crisis had the United States abandoned Vietnam.[136] Other Indonesian leaders made similar comments.[137]

In Southeast Asia and the surrounding areas, the elites of every nation not aligned with China greatly feared Communist expansionism and therefore they strongly supported America's efforts in South Vietnam. Among these nations were Thailand, Malaysia, Laos, Taiwan, South Korea, the Philippines, Burma, Australia, New Zealand, Japan, and India. The leading figures in these nations went well beyond the casual professions of support that one might expect from representatives of a friendly country, for their main objective was not to flatter the Americans but to protect their countries from what they viewed as aggressive and dangerous Communist powers. Asserting both publicly and privately that the preservation of South Vietnam was vital to their own security, the leaders of these nations actively urged the United States to fight for Vietnam, even though it meant that the United States would have fewer resources to distribute to them and other allies. Some made major contributions to the war effort in South Vietnam, while others contributed in smaller ways, not because of apathy, but because of a lack of capabilities, a need to combat pro-Chinese forces elsewhere in Asia, or a fear of Chinese retribution.

On the Southeast Asian mainland, the most muscular American ally besides South Vietnam was Thailand. Sandwiched between the Asian Communist powers and the Malayan peninsula, Thailand served as a critical barrier to Chinese and North Vietnamese advances. Since 1962, the Chinese and North Vietnamese had been training cadres for insertion into Thailand in order to develop a Thai insurgency similar to the insurgency in South Vietnam, with the ultimate aim of overthrowing the Thai government. The Thai resistance movement had remained relatively small prior to 1965, but at the beginning of 1965, because of heightened interest, the Chinese and the North Vietnamese attempted to jump-start it. On New Year's Day of 1965, the Chinese foreign minister announced,

"Thailand is next," and he said that there could be a guerrilla war in Thailand during the coming year. The Thai Independence Movement and the Thai Patriotic Front, both recent creations of the Thai Communist Party and its Chinese and North Vietnamese counterparts, used a covert radio station in China to exhort people of every social class and political creed to rebel. During the first part of 1965, North Vietnamese and Pathet Lao infiltrators helped their Thai compatriots recruit followers among the poor minority groups in the north and northeast of Thailand, where the Communists traditionally had been strongest. Communist assassinations of Thai officials soared in this area.[138]

The Thai government's concern over South Vietnam had begun a steep ascent in 1964, corresponding with the steep decline in the performance of the South Vietnamese government and armed forces. During 1964, Thai officials advocated sending U.S. aircraft from Thai bases to bomb targets in North Vietnam and Laos, a course of action that the United States would eventually excute. The Thais offered to deploy 10,000 "volunteers" to Laos to counter the North Vietnamese "volunteers" who were helping the Pathet Lao, but the Laotians, who had a longstanding animosity towards the Thais, torpedoed the proposal. In 1964, though, the Thais did insert over three hundred troops into Laos on a covert basis, a deployment so prized by the Americans as to discourage them from requesting that Thailand send troops to Vietnam.[139]

During the first months of 1965, the Thais were among the most vocal of all peoples in expressing both fear of the domino effect and support for American participation in South Vietnam. Like most everyone else who paid attention to Indochina, the Thais believed that Laos would fall completely into Communist hands if South Vietnam fell, leaving Hanoi and Beijing with unrestricted access to the long Lao-Thai border, and hence with the ability to provide massive support to the Thai Communists. In February, Thai Foreign Minister Thanat Khoman told a group of Americans in Bangkok that "the withdrawal of the United States from South Vietnam would provide a colossal benefit to the Chinese Communists, and Red China would have full sway over the whole of Asia." America's departure from the region would "extinguish the light of hope, leaving the free world in darkness."[140] While visiting Washington in the middle of May 1965, Thanat told the National Press Club that the 30 million people of Thailand fully supported Johnson's actions in Vietnam because they knew that if the Communists triumphed in Vietnam, they would then "move on to the next kill and come to stalk us in Thailand."[141] Many foreign observers, including the U.S. ambassador to Thailand, were saying that the fall of South Vietnam would cause the Thais to switch their allegiance from the United States to China, in accordance with their traditional policy of allying with the most powerful country in the region.[142] Because Thailand faced a growing insurgency of its own and had put troops into Laos, the Americans did not pressure the Thais to provide troops for Vietnam in 1965. During 1966, the Thai government would decide to send several thousand to South Vietnam anyway.

Malaysian Prime Minister Tunku Abdul Rahman believed that the fall of South Vietnam would make Malaysia much more vulnerable to Communist predations. "If the United States were not in South Vietnam," he told several Americans, "Malaysian security would be imperiled."[143] He firmly supported American efforts to preserve South Vietnam, as did Prime Minister Lee Kuan Yew of Singapore, whose territory at this time belonged to the Malaysian Federation.[144] The Malaysian police, heavily experienced in fighting Communist subversion, served as trainers for South Vietnamese security personnel,[145] but the Americans did not ask Malaysia to provide large-scale military assistance to South Vietnam, in the belief that the Malaysians needed all their resources to defend against the Indonesian colossus.[146] Malaysia's armed forces had just 15,000 troops, as compared with Indonesia's 400,000 – though this disparity was partially offset by British air and naval superiority and the presence of nearly 60,000 British Commonwealth troops in the region – and in early 1965 Indonesia was accelerating its troop buildup and military activities in Borneo.[147]

The Royal Laotian government endorsed America's policies in Laos and Vietnam in 1965, effusing special praise for the use of American air power in both countries. Laotian leaders believed that Rolling Thunder would convince Hanoi to sue for peace and halt its meddling in Laotian affairs, and that American strikes on North Vietnamese logistical facilities in Laos, which began in April under the code name "Steel Tiger," would in the meantime undermine Communist activities in Laos. A few weeks after Steel Tiger commenced, the U.S. ambassador to Laos reported that the Laotians "have taken great heart from our actions and have gained a new confidence in their own future."[148]

For Taiwan, robust military action against the Vietnamese Communists had always been the favorite item on the menu. In 1964, Premier Chiang Kai-shek had proposed an attack on North Vietnam using Taiwanese forces, with the United States providing support, but the Americans had nixed the idea, for they believed that the Chinese Communists would interpret any use of Taiwanese forces in Vietnam as a resumption of the Chinese Civil War, which could cause China to send its armies into Vietnam.[149] In early 1965, Taiwanese officials and journalists clamored fiercely for the deployment of Taiwanese troops to Vietnam. The Americans blocked all efforts in this direction, for the same reason as before.[150] Indicative of the importance that the Taiwanese attached to Vietnam was a speech by Taiwanese Foreign Minister Shen Chang-huan in April, in which he stated that an American withdrawal from Vietnam "would be an act of appeasement which would only further encourage the aggressors and result in a holocaust for the whole of Asia."[151]

An even greater eagerness to send soldiers to Vietnam could be found within the South Korean government of President Park Chung Hee, a man who in early 1965 held the view that "the Communist aggression in Vietnam is aggression towards Korea."[152] Since the summer of 1964, the South Koreans had repeatedly made clear an interest in sending combat forces to Vietnam, only to be told by the Americans that South Vietnam had no present need for South Korean ground units.[153] South Korea did send 200 military personnel to South Vietnam during 1964, and another 2,000 arrived in February and March 1965.[154] The Saigon government, without consulting the United States, directly asked the South Koreans in May 1965 to deploy combat troops to South Vietnam. At this very same time, because of the progressive deterioration in South Vietnam, the Americans themselves were making their own petitions to Seoul for the introduction of a full South Korean combat division into South Vietnam. President Park in turn asked the South Korean National Assembly to approve the use of a division in Vietnam, and the National Assembly overwhelmingly approved the measure.[155] The division would reach Vietnam's shores in November 1965.

In the Philippines, President Diosdado Macapagal as well as the leaders of the opposition Nacionalista Party and most of the educated population feared that the fall of South Vietnam would set the dominoes in motion toward the Philippines and gravely endanger their own national security. "The Philippines has a great stake in what is going on in Vietnam," Macapagal pronounced in April.[156] The Nacionalista chairman of the Senate Foreign Relations Committee warned that defeat in Vietnam would lead to Communist domination of Cambodia, Thailand, Malaysia, and perhaps Indonesia, and "would bring the Communist danger not only to our shores but even into the interior of our land and increase a hundredfold the dangers to our internal security." Within its borders, he noted, the Philippines had hundreds of thousands of unregistered Chinese aliens and tens of thousands of unregistered Indonesians, many of whom were likely to collude with China if the dominoes started tumbling.[157]

As the situation turned for the worse in South Vietnam, the head of the U.S. military advisory mission in the Philippines evaluated the option of sending Philippine combat troops to Vietnam. He determined that the weak Philippine armed forces were in no shape to send any combat forces abroad. The Americans, therefore, asked the Philippine government to send only military support personnel to Vietnam, and in a quantity that would not compromise the overall effectiveness of the Philippine military. Both President Macapagal and Ferdinand Marcos, a Nacionalista who would take Macapagal's place later in the year, advocated sending 2,000 military engineers to Vietnam. Political wrangling ensued, with some Philippine politicians protesting that defense spending should be devoted solely to protecting the homeland against a future Indonesian attack, but eventually the Philippine government would agree to send some of the Philippine military's non-combat personnel to South Vietnam.[158]

Burma professed neutrality with respect to the world's major powers in 1965, and its ruler, the socialist dictator General Ne Win, wanted to keep his country isolated from the rest of the world. In practice, Ne Win could not avoid interaction with foreign powers as much as he would have liked. He was generally more inclined to bow to the wishes of China than to those of the Western powers, yet he could never do enough to maintain the favor of the Chinese. Undoubtedly the Chinese had influenced the decision by the pro-Chinese Burmese Communist Party, in 1964, to renounce its policy of non-violence and commence armed warfare against the government. At first, the Communist rebels had been too few in number to constitute an immediate threat to the Burmese government, but by the spring of 1965, Ne Win believed them to pose a greater threat than the ethnic minorities who were causing major difficulties along Burma's borders. In his heart, General Ne Win hoped that the United States would hold on in South Vietnam, for it would diminish China's ability to impose its will on Burma. In April, he told a confidante, "If the whole situation gets out of hand and the U.S. has to beat China up, it would solve a long-range problem for Burma."[159] Ne Win commended America's bombing of North Vietnam, because, he said, it would allow the Americans to vanquish the Communists.[160]

Australia, another key U.S. ally in the struggle for Southeast Asia, was already embroiled in the conflict between Indonesia and Malaysia by the beginning of 1965, but it viewed the Vietnamese war as a greater threat to its safety. Indonesia was enjoying much less success than North Vietnam at this time and would likely remain frustrated in its ambitions unless South Vietnam fell, which would enable China and North Vietnam to apply direct pressure on Malaysia. The Australians were convinced that the Chinese, abetted by the North Vietnamese and Indonesians, sought hegemony over the whole of Southeast Asia and were likely to attain that objective if the Vietnamese Communists took South Vietnam. Australia was the first country besides the United States to send military advisers to South Vietnam. At the start of 1965, with the state of affairs in Saigon growing more desperate, the Australians urged the Johnson administration to attack North Vietnam without regard to the political instability in Saigon, and they offered to contribute a battalion of Australian soldiers for offensive actions aimed at saving South Vietnam. By contrast, they had repeatedly rejected British requests for major troop commitments in Malaysia. Lyndon Johnson was not yet ready for such actions at that time, and in the coming months he would consistently lag behind the Australians in belligerence.[161]

In April, after the first U.S. ground troops had stepped onto South Vietnamese soil, the Australian government decided to dispatch the 1st Battalion of the Royal Australian Regiment to Vietnam, making Australia the first country after the United States to send its infantry to South Vietnam. In explaining the deployment to the Australian Parliament, Prime Minister Robert G. Menzies declared that "the takeover of South Vietnam would be a direct military threat to Australia and all the countries of Southeast Asia. It must be seen as part of a thrust by Communist China between the Indian and Pacific oceans." Prime Minister Menzies characterized the American stand in Vietnam as "one of the greatest manifestations of justice and principle ever made," and as "the greatest act of moral courage since Britain stood alone in the Second World War."[162] The deployment of the Australian combat battalion to Vietnam enjoyed widespread support among the Australian populace.

New Zealand viewed its commitment in Malaysia as its principal contribution to the anti-Communist struggle in Southeast Asia. More dependent on Britain than was Australia, New Zealand wanted to avoid military ventures without the British at their side. By the beginning of 1965, New Zealand's armed forces had already deployed 1,100 of their 7,000 troops to Malaysia. For a country with one eightieth the population of the United States, this commitment was proportionate in size to the contemporaneous American commitment in Vietnam. The Americans were quite content to let New Zealand make its main contribution in Malaysia, rather than Vietnam. "We have full respect for the job the British, Australians, and New Zealanders face in Malaysia," Rusk told New Zealand's ambassador to the United States on March 11, 1965. "We understand the division of labor between Vietnam and Malaysia."[163] In May, New Zealand Prime Minister Keith Holyoake nonetheless sent a 120-man artillery unit to Vietnam, to join a 25-man New Zealand army engineer unit that had been sent in 1964. Reflecting the general sentiments of the government, New Zealand's defense minister argued at this time that "if South Vietnam went, it would be the beginning of the end in Southeast Asia. Cambodia would then go, followed by Laos and Thailand; Malaysia would be in jeopardy."[164]

In Japan, the ghosts of World War II precluded military participation in the Vietnam conflict and all other military conflicts of the day. The Japanese people generally paid less attention to Vietnam than most of America's other Asian friends paid, for few of them realized that the high volume of trade between Southeast Asia and Japan made the former a vital interest of the latter. Japanese intellectuals and left-wing politicians spoke disparagingly of American involvement in Vietnam, but large elements of the Japanese press preferred American involvement because they believed that in its absence calamity would befall all of Asia.[165] While Japanese Prime Minister Eisaku Sato and his Liberal Democratic Party were naturally inclined to support America's foreign policy because of Japan's economic and military dependence on the United States, they also favored defense of South Vietnam on its own merits, as they recognized the economic importance and political fragility of Southeast Asia. The Liberal Democrats fully endorsed America's Vietnam policy, both in public and in private, and sent economic aid to South Vietnam.[166] Speaking with the American ambassador to Japan in the middle of the year, Prime Minister Sato commended the United States for using force to halt North Vietnamese aggression, asserting that "it would be nonsense for the United States to withdraw troops or to stop bombing North Vietnam."[167]

If China were to become the predominant power in Southeast Asia following the defeat of South Vietnam, the Japanese would certainly feel compelled to take a more accommodating position towards the Chinese. Already, a desire for good relations with China was growing within Japanese society and some sections of the Japanese government, and Japan and China had taken preliminary steps in that direction. U.S. Ambassador to Japan Edwin Reischauer predicted in June that the defeat of the South Vietnamese government would cause a sharp rise in neutralist and leftist sentiment in Japan, resulting in a Japanese government that would break its defense agreements with the United States. The effects on America's position in the world, he said, would be "extremely adverse."[168]

India's leaders found North Vietnam's war objectionable because of their opposition to the spread of Chinese influence across Asia, particularly in Indonesia, which the Indians were already coming to view as a naval threat.[169] If China reigned supreme in Southeast Asia, India would have to kowtow to either China, the Soviet Union, or both, all of which boded ill for the United States. Once the bombing of North Vietnam began, India's leaders fervently called on all participants to negotiate an end to the fighting, out of fear that continued conflict could set off a larger war between India and China or drive the Soviet Union and China together. At the same time, nevertheless, the Indians continued to hope that the Americans would hold back the Communists in Vietnam. U.S. Ambassador to India Chester Bowles noted that the "Indians are deeply fearful of Chinese strength in Southeast Asia" and "would view our defeat there with very great alarm."[170] The Indian press, like the Indian government, favored an American defense of South Vietnam, for the purpose of preventing a dramatic power shift in Asia.[171]

No one can say with absolute certainty what would have happened had South Vietnam been defeated in 1965, considering the complex interaction of many individuals with a diverse array of personalities, cultures, and limitations, and considering the powerful role of chance in human conflict. What can be said, based on analysis of the information available then and subsequent revelations, is that staying in South Vietnam in 1965 was a much more promising option for the United States than leaving, even if it meant fighting the war in the flawed way that the United States ultimately fought it. High was the probability that the fall of Vietnam in 1965 would have knocked over many dominoes in Southeast Asia. For every Southeast Asian country that was not already in league with China, the Johnson administration possessed compelling evidence that the fall of South Vietnam would lead to either an alliance with China or defeat by Communist subversives who were supported by China and its allies. The dominoes likely to fall first after South Vietnam were Laos, Thailand, Burma, Malaysia, and two countries that were already tipping forward, Indonesia and Cambodia. Confidence in the United States would be badly shaken in the Philippines, Taiwan, South Korea, Japan, and India, and each of these countries would be very susceptible to neutralism or an alliance with China, some sooner than others. Australia and New Zealand could be counted upon to resist such pressures more effectively, but they would be left demoralized and faced with hostile neighbors that dwarfed them in population size.

Thus, in the event of South Vietnam's defeat, the United States would probably lose many of its air and naval bases, and its island defense chain would likely be broken. It could lose its access to the vital Indonesian sea lanes, which by the end of the twentieth century would host forty percent of the world's shipping.[172] It would face a serious risk of losing its trading rights with its principal Asian trading partner, Japan, and other Asian trading partners, who together conducted roughly half as much trade with the United States as did the industrialized nations of Europe in the early 1960s, and who would overtake the Europeans as America's most voluminous trading partners by the early 1980s.[173] The defection of Japan would also cost the United States the friendship of a country that, in World War II, had shown itself capable of creating and employing tremendous military power by land, sea, and air. In a relatively short period of time, the fall of the Asian dominoes could effect a major reduction in America's economic and military capabilities in Asia and a major rise in the strength of its enemies. The crumbling of American power in Asia would, in turn, decrease America's national strength and undermine confidence in the United States across the world, thereby reducing America's long-term ability to resist Communism on the remaining Cold War fronts in Europe, the Middle East, and Latin America, which might then lead to the termination of key alliances and to major alterations to the trajectory of both the Cold War and the competition between the United States and China in the twenty-first century.

The only way by which the United States might have retained some of its power in Asia after abandoning Vietnam in 1965 would have been to fight somewhere else in Asia. Strong evidence, however, indicated that relinquishing South Vietnam in 1965 would have required the United States to fight under even worse conditions in the next place, as the Munich analogy foretold. At the beginning of 1965, the South Vietnamese armed forces were tying down roughly 150,000 Vietnamese Communist regulars and irregulars in South Vietnam. If the South Vietnamese armed forces were eliminated, Hanoi could use the North Vietnamese Army, the Viet Cong's forces, and newly recruited Southerners to attack or foment insurgencies in other Southeast Asian countries. Even in South Vietnam's darkest months of 1965, no other country on the Southeast Asian mainland except North Vietnam fielded an army as strong. Acquisition of new territory, moreover, would greatly facilitate further Communist conquests by providing new sanctuaries and supply lines. It is also doubtful that Thailand and the other nations where the United States could try to hold the line would offer to help the Americans fight after watching them cut and run in South Vietnam.

Had the United States abandoned South Vietnam in 1965, it most likely would have made a stand on the Indonesian archipelago, where American air and naval superiority could inhibit the concentration of hostile land forces and the movement of materiel, rather than on the Southeast Asian mainland. Indonesia was certain to be in a close alliance with the Indonesian, Chinese, and Vietnamese Communists if South Vietnam fell, which would require, as Dean Rusk had put it, that the United States fight "a major war against Indonesia." Despite their large size, Indonesia's armed forces were not as strong as those of North Vietnam, and Indonesian forces would face considerable logistical difficulties were the U.S. Navy to establish a large presence in the vast waters surrounding the islands. America's prospects in a war against Indonesia, nevertheless, would probably not be much better than in a war against North Vietnam, particularly one in which U.S. forces entered Laos or North Vietnam. Whereas the United States had an allied government in Saigon, it would have to invade Indonesia without the help of a friendly indigenous government, and, in light of the strong anti-Western sentiments of Indonesia's military leaders, few Indonesian units would be likely to defect to the American side under such circumstances. For Lyndon Johnson, marshalling domestic and international support for an attack on a sovereign government absent the assistance of its native people would be even more difficult than marshalling support for a war in Vietnam, and international confidence in the United States would already be low as a result of the forfeiture of South Vietnam. Johnson probably would have permitted Chinese and Soviet military aid shipments to Indonesia by water as he did in the case of North Vietnam. Indonesia had a population of 100 million, roughly six times that of North Vietnam, and from 1945 to 1949 Indonesian forces had fought a guerrilla war that cost the Dutch colonialists 25,000 casualties and ended with their departure.

Under the conditions prevailing in 1965, it is highly improbable that any previous Cold War President would have attached less value to Vietnam or been less willing to fight there than Lyndon Johnson. In early 1965, Harry S. Truman expressed full support for Johnson's Vietnam policy, saying that Communist aggression had to be thwarted in South Vietnam to prevent the Communist aggressors from growing stronger and moving into other countries.[174] Eisenhower surely would have acted more strongly had he been President in the years from 1961 to 1964 and thus would not have found himself in so dire a predicament as Johnson faced in 1965; the Communists, who respected and feared Eisenhower much more than they did Kennedy or Johnson, might very well have backed off in the face of threatening behavior from Eisenhower, as they had at Korea, the Taiwan Straits, and Berlin. Eisenhower also had a different vision of how the United States should intervene, which he would soon make clear to Johnson. Once the Johnson administration had traveled into the precarious straits of 1965 and advertised its self-restrictions, nevertheless, Eisenhower repeatedly urged Johnson to hold on in Vietnam, even if it required using U.S. ground troops under adverse conditions. Said Eisenhower to Johnson during one White House meeting, "The U.S. has put its prestige onto the proposition of keeping Southeast Asia free. Indonesia is now failing. We cannot let the Indo-Chinese peninsula go."[175] John F. Kennedy, a firm anti-Communist who had viewed Southeast Asia as a critical region and had expanded the U.S. troop presence in South Vietnam twentyfold, no doubt would have wanted to fight to save South Vietnam in 1965. His like-minded brother, Senator Robert F. Kennedy, unequivocally advocated war at this time, despite his fierce contempt for Lyndon Johnson. Of America's commitment to South Vietnam, the younger Kennedy said in early 1965, "I'm in favor of keeping that commitment and taking whatever steps are necessary."[176]

CHAPTER 17

Decision

JUNE–JULY 1965

AT THE BEGINNING OF JUNE, ON THE HEELS OF THEIR SUCCESS AT BA
Gia, the Communists launched a series of major attacks in the highlands of
northern II Corps and in Quang Ngai province. The 325th North Vietnamese
Army Division and the 320th North Vietnamese Army Regiment participated
heavily in these operations, sallying from highland bases to strike government
forces and centers of power.[1] The highlands offered the Communists critical
advantages, both as bases and as operational areas. Hanoi could supply the
highlands relatively easily, via the Ho Chi Minh Trail, because of their proximity to Laos and North Vietnam. The Saigon government's trucks and armored
personnel carriers could not traverse many of the mountainous highland areas,
removing the advantages in troop mobility, logistics, and reconnaissance that
these vehicles typically conferred upon the government. In order to compound
the advantages of the highlands, the Communists had deliberately chosen to
strike during the monsoon season. From mid-May to mid-October, the southwest monsoon relentlessly dumped rain on the central highlands, turning many
of the region's dirt roads into mud and rendering them impassable to South
Vietnamese trucks. The low clouds and fog endemic to the monsoon season
often obscured the peaks of hills and mountains, which made the flying of
aircraft prohibitively dangerous. The strategically vital highland province of
Pleiku, for example, enjoyed an average of twenty-five days of good flying
weather per month during the dry season but had only six days per month
in the monsoon season. Thus, the South Vietnamese government suffered a
severe reduction in its aerial reconnaissance, air support, and air transport
capabilities.

At the beginning of the monsoon offensive, Communist forces had overrun many of the highland settlements that Diem had populated with anti-
Communist refugees as barriers to Communist intrusion, killing or driving
away large numbers of militiamen, government officials, and government sympathizers. They thus eliminated most of the government's intelligence sources
in the region,[2] which compelled the South Vietnamese forces to operate in at

least company or battalion size as protection against the sudden appearance of a large enemy force, which in turn reduced the number and geographic coverage of government operations and made those operations easier to detect and evade. Because the government had lost its intelligence assets and its ability to blanket the countryside with small patrols, it could not prevent the Communists from massing in great numbers and attacking at places and times of their choosing.

Large Communist forces assaulted dispersed government positions in sequence, in each case leaving the government with a set of options of similar unattractiveness. The South Vietnamese could send reinforcements to the point of attack by truck or on foot, which would expose the relief troops to the ambushes that the Communists set around such targets as a matter of course, unless the government units were adept at counter-ambush tactics. If weather permitted, the South Vietnamese could try to circumvent the ambush forces by flying reinforcements on helicopters, but Communist forces had learned to prepare ambushes around possible helicopter landing zones to maul the government troops as they disembarked.[3] Alternatively, the government could order the defenders to withdraw, which would remove the government's authority from that area and might also result in the ambushing of the departing defenders. Or the defenders could stand and fight, but the enemy's unrestricted ability to mass forces usually enabled the enemy to attack with overwhelming force.

The highland attacks of early June consisted largely of roadside ambushes by Communist forces in battalion strength or greater. On June 1, early in the morning, the 320th North Vietnamese Army Regiment overran the Le Thanh district capital in western Pleiku province and ambushed a Regional Force convoy that happened to be heading toward Le Thanh with the provincial chief for a routine visit. The Regional Forces in the convoy fought courageously and enjoyed the support of large air strikes, but, in a classic illustration of the supremacy of regulars in fixed battle, the North Vietnamese soldiers used their numerical superiority and their powerful Chinese weapons to overpower the militiamen. The provincial chief and some of the Regional Forces broke away and headed toward the provincial capital. On the way, they linked up with a relief unit that had been sent from Pleiku. Then another large force from the 320th NVA Regiment ambushed the combined government force from hills overlooking the road, its 57 mm recoilless rifles and rocket launchers wreaking havoc on the trucks in the South Vietnamese column. Helicopter gunships flew to the battlefield but the North Vietnamese greeted them with thick antiaircraft fire, shooting two of the gunships out of the sky. Eventually the defense broke down and the government forces scattered. Total South Vietnamese casualties for the day numbered 115, and American casualties came to four. A South Vietnamese Airborne task force subsequently arrived in the area and retook the Le Thanh district capital unopposed, but because of growing enemy strength, the South Vietnamese corps commander decided to abandon the Le Thanh district capital and create a new district headquarters in a more defensible area.[4]

Two days later, to the south and east in Phu Bon province, the 95th Regiment of the 325th North Vietnamese Army Division ambushed a battalion of the South Vietnamese Army's 40th Regiment that was strung out along Highway 7. Positioned over a distance of several kilometers in anticipation of a South Vietnamese road-clearing operation, the 95th Regiment had waited until the South Vietnamese battalion had walked deep into the trap, then attacked with overwhelming force. The South Vietnamese battalion commander, lacking the audacity and initiative that make for a good combat leader, adopted a passive defense. In the face of repeated enemy charges, the senior U.S. adviser urged the battalion commander to move the unit forward or back. Continued inertia, he warned, would spell disaster. The battalion commander did not heed this advice, and he seemed, in fact, to have lost control of the situation. In utter frustration, the senior U.S. adviser summoned a helicopter and he and two U.S. enlisted advisers flew away. The South Vietnamese battalion suffered severe casualties.[5]

Because of the strategic importance of the highlands, Communist attacks in just a few key provinces drew much of the South Vietnamese strategic reserve to the area, as North Vietnam's leaders had hoped. The strategic reserve units quickly became the primary targets of the Communist forces. As the days passed, losses among the strategic reserve units and the rest of the army climbed rapidly. In the first week of June, the Communists inflicted 1,876 casualties on the government, the highest weekly total in the history of the war, at an estimated cost of 1,305 Communist casualties.[6] By the end of that week, events on the battlefield had convinced South Vietnamese and American leaders that South Vietnam would soon lose the war unless American ground forces stepped in. Westmoreland observed in a June 7 report that the enemy, strengthened by the arrival of the 325th North Vietnamese Army division, was operating in large formations with the intention of destroying government forces and capturing provincial capitals. The Viet Cong had seven regiments that they had not yet committed to major combat, Westmoreland noted, and elements of the 304th North Vietnamese Army Division in the Laotian panhandle could move rapidly into South Vietnam to join the fighting. In the past two weeks, he emphasized, the Communists had rendered four South Vietnamese battalions combat ineffective in I and II Corps, and many other infantry battalions had very low troop levels as the result of combat losses and the especially high desertion rates and poor recruitment stemming from Quat's purges of the officer corps. I, II, and III Corps all lacked adequate reserves to contend with major enemy thrusts. General Westmoreland warned that South Vietnamese soldiers "are beginning to show signs of reluctance to assume the offensive, and in some cases their steadfastness under fire is coming into doubt." Further down in this report, Westmoreland predicted that North Vietnam "will commit whatever forces it deems necessary to tip the balance," and stated that South Vietnam "cannot stand up successfully to this kind of pressure without reinforcement."

The only viable course of action remaining, Westmoreland concluded, was a swift infusion of foreign soldiers. Specifically, Westmoreland recommended immediate deployment of two U.S. Marine battalions, 8,000 American support personnel, and the Airmobile Division – a total of 46,000 Americans on top of the 70,000 Americans who would be in Vietnam by the end of August. He also called for the deployment of a South Korean division, which would bring the number of Korean, Australian, and other third country troops to 19,000. Westmoreland envisioned the assignment of two missions to the U.S. ground forces, fundamentally different from the missions given to U.S. units heretofore: reacting to major enemy military initiatives and hunting down large enemy units. The U.S. troops would avoid operating in heavily populated areas because, in Westmoreland's view, only the South Vietnamese had sufficient local knowledge and linguistic capabilities to clear out the guerrillas, cadres, and secret agents.[7]

The Joint Chiefs backed General Westmoreland's proposal, but McNamara decided that the United States ought to bring the American troop level to 95,000, as opposed to the 116,000 Westmoreland had requested. McNamara told President Johnson that his was "a plan to cover us to the end of the year," not a plan for a long-term commitment as the men in uniform seemed to be envisioning. "I have a very definite limitation on commitment in mind," McNamara said. "I don't think the Chiefs do. In fact, I know they don't."[8]

At this same time, President Johnson received a CIA estimate on the likely enemy response to the addition of U.S. forces. The CIA predicted that Hanoi would send more North Vietnamese units to the South and intensify the fighting, but said it could not make a prediction on the most critical issue, the outcome of the fighting between Communist and American forces.[9] A separate CIA paper argued that the best way to thwart Hanoi's plans was to accelerate Rolling Thunder, hold the number of Americans at 70,000 to avoid the impression that the Americans were taking over the war, and "place major stress on a program of political, social, and economic action in South Vietnam," the same type of program that many others in Washington had been recommending for the past year and a half without comprehending that the South Vietnamese government had become too frail to implement such a program on a large scale.[10] The State Department Bureau of Intelligence and Research expressed doubt that the Communists had advanced into the final, conventional stage of Maoist warfare, lending support to the view that the United States did not need as many troops as Westmoreland had requested.[11]

The skepticism about the seriousness of the Communist threat, and the need for American troops to meet that threat, was unwarranted. By the middle of 1965, benefiting from extensive infiltration and heavy local recruitment, the Communists had 150 battalions of varying sizes in South Vietnam, and only a

few of those battalions had suffered crippling losses in battle. Of the 150 battalions, roughly one-half were main force battalions, and the total number of
main force troops exceeded 50,000, more than double what it had been in 1963.[12]
Many of the main force battalions, moreover, were filled with highly professional North Vietnamese soldiers bearing brand new conventional weapons.
Having no obligation to devote large numbers of troops to static guard duty as
the South Vietnamese and the Americans had, the Communists now had many
more mobile forces at their disposal than did their adversaries. By concentrating their conventional forces and launching numerous large attacks, the Viet
Cong and the North Vietnamese Army were chewing up the South Vietnamese
Army at an alarming rate. They might soon be able to take Saigon or other key
targets. The time for thwarting the Communists' designs with political action
or self-defense forces in the villages had long since passed – only the insertion of
mobile conventional forces could stop the onrush of large and heavily equipped
Communist main force units.

After some rumination, President Johnson adopted McNamara's recommendation to increase the American troop level to 95,000. Always striving to
keep his options open, Johnson thought that an exceedingly large deployment
would jam his escape hatch. And, as before, the fear of an uproar at home or a
provocation of the Communists still weighed on his mind.

As Washington wrestled with the issue of U.S. military participation, another
political crisis developed in Saigon, the result of a tussle between Premier Quat
and Chief of State Suu over high-level appointments. The government was stuck
in gridlock for two weeks, which the U.S. mission blamed primarily on Quat's
lack of political skills and his weak personality.[13] Quat's prestige plummeted,
to such an extent that his patron Tri Quang began to agitate for a military
government led by another of the monk's allies, General Thi.[14] On June 9, Quat
called upon the South Vietnamese generals to mediate the impasse.

At the end of the first day of mediation talks, the Saigon government ran into
a military crisis of most ominous proportions, one that would show beyond
doubt South Vietnam's need for additional conventional forces. It began shortly
before midnight at Dong Xoai, a district capital in Phuoc Long province, eighty-
five kilometers north of Saigon.[15] Dong Xoai was an excellent site for a Viet
Cong attack, as the logging and plantation roads crisscrossing the surrounding
forests permitted large troop movements that could not be seen from the air.
Defending Dong Xoai were 200 Cambodian members of a Civilian Irregular
Defense Group, 200 local Vietnamese troops with six armored cars and two
105 mm howitzers, eleven U.S. Special Forces advisers, and nine U.S. Seabees.
The U.S. Special Forces had recently taken command of the area's defenses
and had ordered the construction of new defensive fortifications around the
principal strongholds – the district headquarters, the Special Forces camp, and
armored car and artillery positions on the eastern side of the town. Many of
these fortifications were still under construction on June 9.

To conduct the assault, the Communist command assigned the 2nd Viet Cong Regiment, a battalion of the 3rd Viet Cong Regiment, a 75mm recoilless rifle company, an artillery battalion that possessed two 75mm pack howitzers and two 70mm pack howitzers, a 12.8mm anti-aircraft machine-gun company, an 82mm mortar company, and a flame-thrower company equipped with nine Chinese flame-throwers. Two additional Viet Cong regiments took up positions to the north and west of Dong Xoai to ambush relief forces and provide reserves. At 10:45 P.M. on June 9, the Communist artillery began pounding Dong Xoai while Viet Cong sappers advanced towards the outermost fences with demolition charges. The defenders gunned down some of the sappers, but enough sappers did their job that the masses of Viet Cong infantry trailing them were able to penetrate several fence lines. Soon the Viet Cong occupied much of the town. They isolated the district headquarters from the Special Forces camp, which were separated by a distance of 200 meters, but despite enjoying numerical superiority of approximately ten-to-one, failed to overrun either redoubt. The defenders deftly swept the areas beyond their perimeters with murderous machine gun, mortar, and artillery fire. One Communist history stated that these two government strongholds "provided outstanding support to one another. The fighting became ferocious." American aircraft arrived on the scene, but they accomplished little because bad weather and darkness prevented them from seeing the Viet Cong.

Incurring heavy casualties during futile assaults, the Viet Cong kept moving reserve units forward to launch new attacks on the district headquarters and the Special Forces camp. Eventually, they decided that victory would require more intensive use of heavy weaponry, so they brought their crew-served weapons forward for use in the second wave of attacks, which began at 1:00 A.M. A Communist history of the battle recounted: "Learning from the experiences of the first assault, the regiment moved its fire-support teams (75mm recoilless rifles, 75mm pack howitzers, 12.8mm machine-guns, medium machine-guns, flame-throwers) up close to the enemy wall to more effectively concentrate fire to suppress the enemy firing positions." These weapons succeeded in collapsing government bunkers, destroying government heavy weapons, and suppressing government fire as the Viet Cong infantry scrambled ahead.

At 2:00 A.M., Viet Cong flame-throwers wiped out the defenders on the western side of the Special Forces compound, and troops from the 4th Battalion of the Viet Cong 2nd Regiment streamed into the breach, entering into a frenzied, back-and-forth struggle with Cambodian irregulars and a handful of American and South Vietnamese Special Forces personnel. A twenty-year old American Special Forces sergeant who survived the battle told a reporter: "The VC would mass, come over the walls with grenades and flame throwers, then reassemble, mass and come at us again. . . . Just before each assault they'd start yelling and screaming like crazy people. Once they'd got inside there was a lot of confusion." He noted that the Cambodians "fought wonderfully. They fought to the last man." Fighting continued at the Special Forces compound until 2:30 A.M., when a VC mortar round scored a direct hit on the bunker anchoring the southwest corner of the compound. At this juncture, the Americans and a few of the Cambodians retreated to the district headquarters, where the other Americans were holding out, while other survivors split into small groups and scampered to the armored car and artillery positions.

At the district headquarters, command belonged to Second Lieutenant Charles Q. Williams of Charleston, South Carolina, the 32-year-old executive officer of the U.S. Special Forces Detachment. He had taken charge early in the battle, after the detachment's commanding officer was severely wounded. Running up and down the lines, Williams directed the American and South Vietnamese troops and put courage in them, receiving several wounds from mortar and grenade fragments for his efforts. One of the other Americans stated that Williams "was the calmest man there. He constantly exposed himself to enemy fire without any regard for his own life." At one point, when the Viet Cong began scaling the walls of the headquarters compound, some of the South Vietnamese defenders abandoned excellent fighting positions, but Williams ran to them through enemy fire and convinced them, with words and shoves, to return to the positions.

At dawn, with the skies clearing, an armada of U.S. jets and attack helicopters swarmed over Dong Xoai and struck most of the areas occupied by the Viet Cong. One Communist account of the battle noted that "savage bombing and strafing attacks" collapsed numerous bunkers and fortifications and killed "many more of our soldiers." Air power helped keep the Viet Cong from overrunning the district headquarters building during the morning. The defenders on the ground had run out of ammunition for many of their big weapons, but they still were inflicting some damage on the Viet Cong. No one showed more valor than Construction Mechanic Third Class Marvin G. Shields, a twenty-five-year-old Seabee from Port Townsend, Washington. With bullets streaking at him, Shields darted around to fire at the Viet Cong, transport ammunition, and move critically injured soldiers to safety. The Viet Cong hit Shields twice during the morning's fighting, including one shot that put a large hole in the left side of his face and tore away many of his teeth. An American witness testified that he saw Shields "jumping from position to position firing at the enemy," while another recounted that "Shields exposed himself to heavy enemy fire many times to aid the wounded and resupply others with ammunition, even after he had been shot in the face."

In the middle of the morning, the Viet Cong set up a 7.62mm machine gun in a school near the district headquarters and poured damaging fire through openings in the sides of the headquarters building. Williams considered this machine gun position so grave a threat that he decided to leave the safety of the building to attack it. Taking a 3.5-inch rocket launcher, Lieutenant Williams asked for a volunteer to join him as the loader. Shields volunteered, although he had never loaded a 3.5-inch rocket launcher before. Williams and Shields ran south to the wall near the front gate. Dashing across 100 meters of open space, they dodged hostile fire until they reached a covered position 150 meters from the enemy machine gun. Williams and Shields had brought four 3.5-inch rounds with them, and they fired all four at the school window from which the machine gun was firing. The first three missed the target, but the final round went into the window and exploded with a flash, obliterating the machine gun and its crew.

As Shields and Williams ran back to the building, another Viet Cong automatic weapon sprayed bullets at them. The VC gunner struck Shields twice in the leg and hit Williams in the lower arm. The bullets broke Shields's leg and almost tore it off. Williams's new wound was less severe, but it was sufficiently serious that he could not pick Shields up off the ground and carry him to safety, so Williams continued on to the headquarters, while Shields pulled himself into another building and attached a tourniquet to his leg, then passed out. Three other Americans subsequently made their way to Shields, and one of them carried Shields over his back to the headquarters building. Coming to his senses, Shields spent the rest of the morning laughing and joking with the other Americans. A medic gave Shields morphine, but all other medical supplies had by this time been used up or destroyed. Both Shields and Williams would be awarded the Medal of Honor for their heroism, and the Navy would eventually name one of its Knox-class frigates the USS *Marvin Shields*.

Relief forces from the ARVN 1st Battalion, 7th Regiment, meanwhile, flew from Bien Hoa to a field three kilometers from Dong Xoai, which the South Vietnamese command believed would be distant enough that the Viet Cong would not find and engage them immediately. The Viet Cong, however, had guessed that the government would land troops at this very place and were ready for them. From hidden fighting positions, soldiers of the 1st Viet Cong Regiment opened fire on the government soldiers as soon as their helicopters deposited them, and the Viet Cong commander quickly moved large reinforcements to the area. At 10:15 A.M., the Viet Cong surrounded the government troops, and at 10:30, the government unit radioed its last communication, which stated that it was being overrun.

At noon, the Viet Cong brought accurate 57mm recoilless rifle fire to bear on the district headquarters, and during the next hour they began massing for a huge attack. By one o'clock, the Viet Cong's heavy weapons had demolished two sides of the headquarters building. Williams therefore ordered the fourteen Americans in the building, along with an equal number of Vietnamese women and children, to pull back to an artillery position to the east where twenty South Vietnamese troops were holding out. Retreating safely, they continued to fight from the new position. As the Viet Cong surged through the ruins of the district headquarters and toward the last bastion, Williams radioed that he needed aircraft to hit everything around the artillery position, and that his men were running out of ammunition and could not hold off the Viet Cong much longer. Upon receiving the distress call from Williams, the commander of the 118th Aviation Company climbed aboard a helicopter and took two more helicopters with him on a rescue mission to Dong Xoai. When the helicopters came near the besieged artillery position, they learned that the Viet Cong had advanced within ninety feet of it. To clear the way for the helicopters, a swarm of fixed-wing aircraft and attack helicopters suddenly surrounded the artillery redoubt with what one witness on the ground called "a near solid wall of bullets, bombs, napalm, and rockets." The three helicopters made a quick landing, loaded up the dead and wounded while mortar rounds landed all around, and escaped safely before two o'clock. Among those loaded aboard the helicopters was Shields. The medic who had treated Shields believed that he would have survived had he been evacuated an hour earlier. By the time the helicopters arrived, Shields had suffered massive hemorrhage and gone into deep shock. Thirty minutes after he had been put on the helicopter he was dead.

Just as the Americans were abandoning the district headquarters building, the remainder of the 1st Battalion, 7th Regiment started landing at the Thuan Loi plantation, a huge forest of rubber trees that had been planted by the Michelin Corporation six kilometers north of Dong Xoai. Although twice as far from the town as the field where the battalion's first contingent had been wiped out, the plantation turned out to be an ambush site, too. Viet Cong troops immediately opened fire from the windows and rooftops of the plantation's mansions. After the first eighty South Vietnamese soldiers had landed and run into trouble, additional landings were canceled. F-100 Super Sabres and A-1E Skyraiders dropped napalm on Viet Cong forces advancing toward the landing zone from the south, but failed to stop them. Contact with the eighty soldiers was lost at 1:15 P.M., twenty minutes after they had touched the ground.

The Saigon government had no forces in Dong Xoai or its environs for a period of several hours, lasting until 4:55 P.M., when 300 men from the 52nd Ranger Battalion landed by helicopter on a road to the south of the ruined district headquarters. Advancing on foot toward the headquarters, the Rangers exploited two major Viet Cong weaknesses that had been revealed at Song Be the previous month – their inability to bring enough ammunition to fire their heavy weapons continuously for more than a few hours, and their vulnerability to massive air attack when they occupied a town. Because most of the undamaged Viet Cong artillery pieces had run out of ammunition by the late afternoon, Viet Cong artillery could cause the Rangers little harm. Viet Cong forces occupying the government's defensive positions in Dong Xoai tried to stop the Rangers with infantry weapons but were pulverized by an avalanche of bombs. A Viet Cong attack force that had started the battle with abundant artillery support and 2,000 infantrymen had been so weakened that the 300 Rangers were able to push it out of the town at a cost of a few dozen Ranger casualties. A Viet

Cong counter-attack after dark failed to dislodge the Rangers, and the rest of the night passed quietly.

In the morning, the South Vietnamese Army's 7th Airborne Battalion landed to the north of Dong Xoai against only light opposition. The battalion marched to the area where the first troops of the 1st Battalion, 7th regiment had been overrun and they collected seven survivors and fifty-five bodies. From there, they moved to the Thuan Loi rubber plantation to retrieve the remnants of the second contingent of the 1st Battalion. While searching the plantation during the afternoon, the 7th Airborne Battalion came under attack from elements of the ubiquitous 1st Viet Cong Regiment, the unit that had shredded both groups from the 1st Battalion of the 7th Regiment on the previous day and had been in the fore at Song Be and Ba Gia. The battle grew in intensity into the night, as blistering fire from both sides mangled or obliterated most of the plantation's trees. Taking advantage of their great superiority in men and organic firepower as well as poor weather that limited U.S. air strikes, the Viet Cong broke the Airborne unit into small groups and destroyed many of them. By the time the guns fell silent the next afternoon, the strength of the 7th Airborne Battalion had sunk from 470 to 159.

After the mauling of the 7th Airborne Battalion, General Westmoreland concluded that the Communists had at least five infantry battalions and one artillery battalion capable of continuing the attack in the vicinity of Dong Xoai, plus four additional battalions that could reach Dong Xoai within twenty-four hours. Although the South Vietnamese Army had flown in additional rein-forcements, it still had only four depleted battalions at Dong Xoai, and it had only one remaining strategic reserve battalion available for deployment to the area. In Westmoreland's view and that of the South Vietnamese corps com-mander, the insertion of the last strategic reserve battalion might not be enough to drive the Communists from the area and prevent them from establishing a large overt base near the Thuan Loi rubber plantation, a very logical conclu-sion in light of the 7th Airborne Battalion's defeat. As Le Duan had desired, the South Vietnamese strategic reserve had reached the point of exhaustion. Westmoreland alerted Admiral Sharp that the expulsion of the Viet Cong from the Thuan Loi plantation was "extremely important," and he proposed using U.S. forces to undertake that mission because of the lack of South Vietnamese reserve forces. "I consider that the commitment of the two battalions of the 173rd Airborne Brigade to the Dong Xoai area may be required within the next twelve hours," Westmoreland notified Sharp. "Unless directed otherwise, I intend if necessary to commit the 173rd to this action." As a preparatory step, Westmoreland sent a battalion of the 173rd Airborne Brigade by helicopter from Vung Tau to the airfield at Phuoc Vinh, thirty kilometers from Dong Xoai.[16]

In Washington, where it was two o'clock in the morning, McNamara woke President Johnson to tell him that Westmoreland was considering the inser-tion of U.S. ground forces into major combat for the first time. McNamara said that he and Rusk favored letting Westmoreland insert them if he deemed it necessary. Johnson agreed to let Westmoreland make the decision. Westmoreland, however, would be spared a final decision on committing the American battalions, for the weather at Dong Xoai improved and the U.S. brought massive air power to bear on Communist assembly areas, dealing the Viet Cong fearsome losses. Following these air strikes, the Communist leadership concluded that they themselves did not have sufficient strategic reserve forces to ensure victory at Dong Xoai, and so the Communist forces withdrew.

During five days of fierce fighting in and around Dong Xoai, the South Vietnamese incurred total losses of 416 killed, 174 wounded, and 233 missing. After the battle, search parties found several hundred VC bodies within small arms range of the Special Forces compound and the district headquarters compound, and another 126 VC bodies inside these compounds. Numerous other Viet Cong casualties had been evacuated from the town, and many hundreds, if not thousands, of Viet Cong, had been wounded or killed in the devastating fighting beyond the town's borders. During the period when they held the town, the Viet Cong had taken every civilian possession they could find – pots, mattresses, rice, livestock, and clothing – and then had used flame-throwers to destroy a large percentage of the wooden houses in the town. An American adviser commented, "The Viet Cong flame-throwers in Dong Xoai did more damage than our napalm ever has. We have hit selective targets but we have never burned down half a town that contained no enemy forces of any kind." The use of all sorts of heavy weapons by both sides had inflicted a steep toll of civilian casualties. Government troops found the bodies of 150 civilians, including many women and children, among the countless piles of corpses in the town of Dong Xoai.

On June 11, as the Battle of Dong Xoai was raging and the South Vietnamese strategic reserve was approaching exhaustion, Quat and Suu joined with fifty generals for a lengthy meeting that was to decide the fate of the Quat government. As the discussion progressed, the generals evidenced much disgust with the regime's political and military ineffectiveness. After many hours of bickering amongst the participants, the generals demanded that Quat and Suu end their disagreement immediately. Several individuals started shouting at one another, but they were interrupted by Quat, who arose and declared in a somber tone that he would resign. With Quat's concurrence, the generals commenced planning for a new government that would be controlled by the military leadership. President Johnson, observing this newest upheaval from Washington, remarked to historian Henry F. Graff, "The worst mistake we ever made was getting rid of Diem."[17]

Everything was proceeding according to Tri Quang's desires until the time came to select the top leaders of the new government. The helm was given not to Tri Quang's ally General Thi but to Air Marshal Nguyen Cao Ky, who became prime minister and executive chairman, and to General Nguyen Van

Thieu, who assumed leadership of the ruling committee of generals. To the casual observer in Saigon, this change in government might have seemed to be just another reshuffle, but the ascension of Ky and Thieu would be a watershed, akin to the ascension of Dinh Bo Linh exactly one thousand years earlier, which had ended the Period of the Twelve Warlords. The military leadership had, at last, broken Tri Quang's stranglehold on the government. Both Ky and Thieu were primarily interested in fighting the Communists, and they intended to prevent the militant Buddhists from interfering with their war-making.

Ambassador Taylor and other Americans were most pleased that the conniving General Thi had not received one of the top positions. They were not so excited by the choice of Ky as prime minister, for although Ky was a reasonably capable military officer, he had no experience in civil government and he was known to possess a greater disposition toward flamboyance and womanizing than substance and rigor. Taylor, in fact, went to the other South Vietnamese generals to object to Ky's role in the new government, but the generals ignored him. On the other hand, the U.S. leadership viewed the elevation of General Nguyen Van Thieu as a most positive development, contrary to retrospective American accounts.[18] Americans and Vietnamese who had worked with Thieu regarded him as a highly talented military leader who also possessed the political skills required in perilous Saigon. For quite some time, Thieu had been one of three generals whom the American embassy and military command viewed as excellent candidates for heading the South Vietnamese government, the others being General Pham Van Dong and General Nguyen Huu Co.[19]

Ky, Thieu, and the other generals began their rule by holding what they termed a "no breathing week." The week's scheduled activities included the imposition of censorship, the closing of many newspapers, and the curtailing of civil liberties. Ky told a gathering of Saigon journalists, "You are to suspend publication of gossip and rumors immediately. Until you are ready to act responsibly, you are allowed to publish only information provided by the government."[20] The new government resolved to consign Saigon's bickering politicians to a "village of old trees," where they would "conduct seminars and draw up plans and programs in support of government policy." On the question of opposition from religious and political groups, the leadership vowed to "ignore such opposition groups with the stipulation that troublemakers will be shot."[21] By this point in time, the factionalism and political disintegration fostered by liberalization since Diem's fall had made these sorts of measures palatable to American leaders as well as to the South Vietnamese.

The leading South Vietnamese generals infused the civil administration with energy and acted decisively to fix problems that had long needed attention. They soon had shown enough signs of promise that Tri Quang started throwing the standard grenades from his oratorical arsenal.[22] The rate of progress, however, could only be said to be modest, primarily because the government machinery had deteriorated so badly in the past twenty months.

After the great battle at Dong Xoai, the Communist military rampage continued into the middle and end of June, the heaviest blows falling in the central highlands. Viet Cong and North Vietnamese Army forces isolated the highland provinces from the coast and the highland provincial capitals from one another, then cut the roads radiating from the provincial capitals to the district capitals. The South Vietnamese government was forced to bring supplies and reinforcements to the highland capitals by emergency airlift, and it could do so only when intervals of decent weather interrupted the monsoon storms.[23] On June 25, a day chosen because the weather precluded helicopter flight, half of the 101st Regiment of the 325th North Vietnamese Army Division attacked Toumorong, an isolated district capital in the mountains of northwestern Kontum province. The other half of the regiment waited along the one substantial road into the town in order to ambush any relief forces. With two hundred territorial forces and a small contingent of regulars, Toumorong's garrison was heavily outnumbered by the attack force.

Just when one of the North Vietnamese battalions moved up to the edge of the town, South Vietnamese troops opened a gate immediately in front of the battalion and started filing out for a patrol. The North Vietnamese battalion commander ordered his soldiers to engage the South Vietnamese troops, and they fought their way in through the gate, but then were stopped by intense fire from the garrison. On another section of the town perimeter, the initial thrust went even less well for the North Vietnamese, as it quickly met fire from enemy heavy weapons. According to Nguyen Huu An, who as the 325th Division Commander was directing the entire attack, some of the North Vietnamese assault troops in this area "were confused and passive when they heard the heavy firing of the enemy guns." Every single officer in one of the North Vietnamese companies, the 9th, perished early in the battle on this part of the perimeter. The foul weather, however, prevented the defenders from calling in air support and knocking all of the wind out of the attackers.

Nguyen Huu An ordered the heavy weapons forward and insisted that the other units near the 9th company press ahead in order to draw fire away from the soldiers who had gone in through the gate. "We have to forget the issue of casualties for the moment," Nguyen Huu An told Dong Thoai, the battalion commander in that sector. Nguyen Huu An's guidance proved sound, for within a few hours the North Vietnamese troops succeeded in overwhelming the government's defenses. At 3:00 A.M., the South Vietnamese district chief fled from the town with 75 soldiers and 400 civilians, eventually making it to an area under government control. Government dead and missing during the Toumorong battle totaled 160. Because South Vietnamese II Corps Commander General Vinh Loc believed that Toumorong did not possess great strategic value and that government forces would have to fight in unfavorable weather and terrain against large enemy forces to retake it, he made no attempt to reestablish the district capital there.[24]

A few days later, the Communists targeted the capital of Thuan Man district, in the forested highlands of western Phu Bon province. Communist forces surrounded the capital, which compelled the district chief to warn higher headquarters that the enemy would soon overrun the town. This time, General Vinh Loc decided to send powerful relief forces, dispatching two Airborne battalions, the 2/40 Infantry Battalion, and an artillery battery from Cheo Reo. Traveling on the high ground on either side of the road from Cheo Reo to Thuan Man in order to avoid a classic ambush, the task force ran into a North Vietnamese Army regiment that was occupying a ridge overlooking the road. The North Vietnamese regiment charged the government forces and split them in two. South Vietnamese artillery fired into the North Vietnamese at close range, stopping them temporarily, but then North Vietnamese infantrymen supported by mortars overran the artillery positions. North Vietnamese troops now occupied the road on both sides of the government units, preventing retreat toward either Cheo Reo or Thuan Man. The weather was good, and fighters bombed and strafed the Communist forces, inflicting punishing losses and allowing the South Vietnamese forces time to consolidate their defenses. Late in the day, the South Vietnamese forces radioed that they were low on ammunition and needed medical evacuation immediately. Helicopters flew out for these purposes, but intense fire from the enemy's 12.7mm antiaircraft machine guns forced them to turn back without accomplishing their objectives. Despite the shortage of ammunition, the encircled South Vietnamese task force held out through the night.

During the night, amid reports that another North Vietnamese Army regiment lay within marching distance of the battle, the South Vietnamese command flew two Marine battalions, an Airborne task force, and the Airborne Brigade headquarters to Cheo Reo. The two Marine battalions joined the fray the next morning and battered the Communists to such a degree that they broke off the engagement. In a search of the battlefield, the Americans found 23 Communist bodies, and they estimated total enemy dead at 123, which would put total enemy casualties for the battle at several hundred. Subsequent intelligence reports indicated that the North Vietnamese Army regiment sustained severe losses in this engagement. Government forces suffered 66 dead or missing and 60 wounded, and the Americans incurred 8 casualties. Although the Communists had been driven off, the government did not succeed in keeping the Thuan Man district capital out of the enemy's clutches. Certain that Communist forces would overwhelm the district capital within the next day, the district chief and his forces evacuated the town.[25]

By the end of June, as the result of high combat losses and desertions, five South Vietnamese regiments and nine separate battalions – the equivalent of more than two full divisions – were rated combat ineffective. Among the units rated ineffective were two of the eleven general reserve battalions. Many other battalions were grossly under strength.[26] The Communists were well on their way toward achieving their objective of smashing three to four South Vietnamese divisions, and they had already attained their objective of depleting the government's general reserve to the point of exhaustion. Their only problem now was that the ultimate success of their strategy depended upon continued American abstention from the ground war. They apparently still believed that the Americans would stay out; had they believed otherwise, they could have moved most of their troops to III Corps and attempted a rapid conquest of Saigon, though it is far from certain that they could have defeated the South Vietnamese and American forces that would have been rushed to the city's defense.

In Washington, the implications of the military deterioration during June were gnawing at Lyndon Johnson. At the end of the month, the despairing President told McNamara, "I see no program from either Defense or State that gives much hope of doing anything, except just praying and gasping to hold on during monsoon and hope they'll quit. I don't believe they're ever going to quit. And I don't see ... that we have any ... plan for a victory – militarily or diplomatically."[27] Johnson asked McNamara and Under Secretary of State George Ball to draw up plans for a new U.S. strategy and submit them to him on July 1.

Subsequently portrayed by his admirers and by himself as a committed opponent of escalation, George Ball was not exactly what he seemed.[28] Ball's immediate superior, Dean Rusk, later said that Ball "did not argue vigorously inside the government for a substantially different point of view. He was named by the President as a Devil's advocate to take an opposing point of view, in order that the President would have in front of him different considerations ... and it may be that George Ball convinced himself in the process."[29] Ball made an excellent Devil's advocate, as he had long been adept at arguing whatever position needed to be argued. At times, Ball had been quite hawkish when expressing his own views, particularly in the aftermath of the February attack on Camp Holloway, and it is not clear whether at any moment in 1965 he was truly convinced that the United States ought to avoid deeper involvement in Vietnam, although by July he does seem to have convinced himself.

In the proposal he submitted to Johnson, Ball recommended holding the U.S. troop level at 72,000 and negotiating a peaceful end to the conflict. As Ball envisioned it, Hanoi would be willing to agree to such a settlement because the United States would include a provision granting South Vietnam "self-determination" at some time in the future, thereby giving the Communists hope of eventually winning control in the South.[30] All information available then and since, however, indicated that the North Vietnamese had no intention of negotiating in the middle of 1965, as they believed that they could win the war by military means in the near future.[31] According to Ball's plan, the peace agreement would be guaranteed and monitored by the United States and the Soviet Union, yet the Soviets had repeatedly and bluntly refused to facilitate such a settlement.[32] If, somehow, the North Vietnamese were willing to consider a settlement that gave them an expectation of eventual control over South Vietnam, they would not agree to anything unless the settlement required a U.S. withdrawal in the near future. The domino countries in and around Southeast Asia would recognize that such an agreement was no different from the neutralization concepts that had been floated in the past, and that it was certain to lead to a Communist takeover of South Vietnam. While Ball stated that Thailand could remain an American ally if this type of peace agreement were made, Thai leaders and many others in Asia were swearing that such a peace deal would put all of Southeast Asia under Chinese control.[33] Ball also contended that the United States could maintain Thailand's confidence by keeping the Communists out of the Mekong Valley, which, he acknowledged, would involve sending U.S. troops into western Laos. The Thais, however, were not likely to have any faith in the United States following the abandonment of South Vietnam, and even if they did, the United States would face the scenario of fighting together with a weaker ally – Thailand – against a more formidable opponent – a unified Vietnam.

McNamara, in the course of preparing his paper, turned to General Westmoreland for suggestions on how to win the war. In his reply to McNamara's inquiry, Westmoreland displayed acumen and dispassion that were quite at odds with the caricatures of the man that his detractors would later draw. "Short of decision to introduce nuclear weapons against sources and channels of enemy power, I see no likelihood of achieving a quick, favorable end to the war," the general informed the secretary of defense. "The fabric of GVN civil functions and services has been rendered so ineffective and listless by successive coups and changes, and the military arm is in such need of revitalization, that we can come to no other conclusion." Final victory was not dependent on American exertions, Westmoreland contended, but on the development of a strong South Vietnamese government. In the interim, nevertheless, U.S. troops would need to move out of their enclaves to engage the big Viet Cong and North Vietnamese Army units, so as to prevent the Communists from seizing South Vietnam's cities.

Westmoreland now advocated raising U.S. troop strength to 150,000, which he said would enable the United States to thwart Communist attacks and penetrate Communist base areas, but he added that future force requirements could not be determined because they would depend on the additional resources that the enemy subsequently introduced. In Westmoreland's estimation, chances were good that Hanoi would send many additional North Vietnamese Army troops to the South. Westmoreland noted, in addition, that American intervention might cause the Communists to disperse among the populace or hide in uninhabited areas, and under these conditions "we have no assurances that we can find, fix and destroy the VC." It would be up to the South Vietnamese to root them out of the populated areas. "U.S. troops, by virtue of their ethnic background, are not as effective as [South Vietnamese] troops in a pacification role," he explained.[34]

In his July 1 report for the President, McNamara echoed Westmoreland's recommendations to increase total U.S. strength to 150,000, supplemented by ten third-country battalions, and to use U.S. forces against the enemy's conventional forces. McNamara also recommended calling up the reserves to facilitate the additional American deployments, and advocated the mining of North Vietnam's harbors and the bombing of the twenty-eight bridges between China and Hanoi. McNamara thought it possible that Hanoi would send great numbers of North Vietnamese soldiers into the South, but unlike Westmoreland he thought the odds of such an action were low, presumably because it did not accord with McNamara's theories on the behavior of states and because McNamara believed that air strikes were holding down North Vietnamese infiltration capabilities. The Secretary of Defense was, therefore, much more optimistic than Westmoreland about the ultimate outcome of an increase to 150,000. Although "the war is one of attrition and will be a long one," McNamara stated, this program "is likely to bring about a favorable solution to the Vietnam problem."[35]

Assistant Secretary of State for Far Eastern Affairs William Bundy presented President Johnson with a third paper on a "middle way" between the Ball and McNamara plans, in which the United States would employ 85,000 troops in South Vietnam for the next two months to test whether U.S. forces could find and destroy the Communists, and whether their presence would have an adverse psychological effect on the South Vietnamese government.[36] If the test period went poorly, then, in the opinion of Bundy and other influential figures in the administration, withdrawal would be a feasible and worthy option.[37] Once other countries had seen American forces give it a go in Vietnam, the thinking went, these forces could then be withdrawn with much less damaging consequences than would come from an immediate removal of troops. John McNaughton and Daniel Ellsberg had explained this hypothesis most clearly when they had argued that the United States could portray such an abandonment of South Vietnam as the case of "a patient who died despite the extraordinary efforts of a good doctor."[38] On the question of mining North Vietnam's harbors, Bundy voiced firm opposition, on the grounds that it "would tend to throw North Vietnam into the arms of Communist China and diminish Soviet influence." He, along with the rest of the Americans, remained unaware that the North Vietnamese had already thrown themselves into the arms of the Chinese, having invited seven Chinese divisions onto North Vietnamese soil.

George Ball's ill-conceived plan did not find any friends among Lyndon Johnson's other advisers. Rusk supported all elements of McNamara's plan except for the mining of harbors and the intensification of the bombing. McGeorge Bundy backed his brother's position, emphasizing that the limited information currently available suggested that Communist forces would avoid open battle with U.S. combat units. The Joint Chiefs wanted to take the actions specified in McNamara's program and in addition they recommended striking surface-to-air missile sites in North Vietnam and the main North Vietnamese airbase. As before, however, neither Johnson nor anyone else in the President's inner circle showed much interest in the views of the Joint Chiefs, except as it related to keeping the generals' dissatisfaction from exploding in public.

Someone for whom Johnson had more respect than for the generals, and indeed more than for most of his other advisers, was also calling for bolder action within and beyond South Vietnam's frontiers. "When you go into a place merely to hold sections or enclaves," Dwight D. Eisenhower told Johnson by phone on July 2, "you are paying a price and not winning. When you once appeal to force in an international situation involving military help for a nation, you have to go all out! This is a war, and as long as [the North Vietnamese] are putting men down there, my advice is 'do what you have to do!'"[39] Eisenhower had always been more averse than Johnson or Kennedy to a "limited war" in which the United States refrained from entering the enemy's territory and sanctuaries; during Eisenhower's meeting with Kennedy on January 19, 1961, it may be remembered, Eisenhower had admonished McNamara that he did not like the term limited war and preferred to "go after the head of the snake instead of the tail."[40] Whereas Johnson, like Kennedy before him, embraced the concept of a limited war because of the low risk of provoking China, Eisenhower thought that the United States should not let fear of China compel it to stay out of Laos or North Vietnam. Earlier in 1965, Eisenhower had told Johnson that if the Chinese threatened to intervene in Southeast Asia, the President should privately threaten them with the most severe of consequences, as Eisenhower had done to his Communist adversaries during the Korean War and the Suez Crisis. If China chose to invade Southeast Asia, said Eisenhower, then the United States should "hit the head of the snake" with whatever it took, including nuclear weapons if necessary.[41]

President Johnson made no decision on the proposals he had received from Ball, McNamara, and William Bundy, nor did he act on Eisenhower's advice. He did not even say which strategy he found most attractive, though his subsequent actions would suggest that he was at least leaning toward that of McNamara. He definitely was not enamored of any of his options. "I'm pretty depressed reading all these proposals," Johnson told McNamara on July 2.[42] The President confided to his wife, "Vietnam is getting worse every day. I have the choice to go in with great casualty lists or to get out with disgrace. It's like being in an airplane and I have to choose between crashing the plane or jumping out. I do not have a parachute."[43]

During the first two weeks of July, the Communists strenuously pressed their offensive in South Vietnam, their sense of urgency heightened by reports in the Western media of possible American intervention.[44] By the middle of July, the Communists had captured six district capitals, and only in one case, Dak

To, did the Saigon government retake the capital. Communist units completely controlled the northern half of the strategically critical province of Kontum, and they held positions so close to the provincial capital that they could hit it with mortar fire. A large section of Pleiku province, another key highland province, lay in Communist hands. The provincial capitals in both Kontum and Pleiku were no longer receiving sufficient military and civilian supplies by airlift, and in both places, according to General Vinh Loc, the populace was "near panic." In the country as a whole, the Communists had isolated 12 of 45 provincial capitals and 44 of 200 district capitals.[45]

A disconsolate President Johnson had McNamara fly to Saigon on July 15 to evaluate the situation and get Westmoreland's recommendations on future force deployments. On the first day of McNamara's trip to Saigon, he met with Ky, Thieu, and the other leading South Vietnamese generals. The South Vietnamese Assistant Chief of Staff for Operations, General Nguyen Duc Thang, told McNamara that the situation in II Corps had become critical, on account of the introduction of the 325th Division, and the situation was also bleak in III Corps. General Thang recommended the deployment of two American divisions to II Corps and one American division to III Corps, which would raise the total U.S. troop commitment to 200,000. McNamara asked the South Vietnamese leaders whether their countrymen would be willing to accept 200,000 U.S. troops in their country. Prime Minister Ky replied that he did not think the deployment would cause any problems in that regard.

During McNamara's visit to Saigon, Westmoreland laid out for him a two-phase plan for the introduction and employment of American forces. As he had done several times already, Westmoreland raised the U.S. troop figures because of a worsening military situation, although his first-phase increase still was not as large as what the Vietnamese had requested. In Phase I, a total of 175,000 U.S. troops would "stem the tide," preventing further Communist military advances through the end of 1965. In phase II, which would commence in early 1966, these troops plus another 95,000 would "turn the tide" by making gains over the enemy sufficient to convince Hanoi that victory was out of reach.[46] Westmoreland was also reported to have mentioned a possible third phase, to take place one and a half years after phase II, but documentation from this period does not describe it in any detail, and the written reports of Westmoreland and McNamara show that neither man attached much significance to a third phase. Both believed that uncertainty over North Vietnam's force commitment made it impossible to forecast the duration or outcome of phase II.

Before McNamara departed, one member of his team asked Westmoreland's staff whether they were planning to cut the Laotian infiltration routes with ground forces. Major General William DePuy, Westmoreland's assistant chief of staff for operations, replied that they were making no such plans. "We are inclined to believe," DePuy said, "that it is more effective to go after VC bases than to go after infiltration parties."[47] Until now, Westmoreland's command had done its job well and made few mistakes, but in this case it made an immense error that would negate many positive achievements.

On July 20, McNamara delivered President Johnson the report from his brief trip. "A hard VC push is now on to dismember the nation and to maul the army," it read. If the United States held its troop level at 75,000, McNamara stated, it most likely would face a deeper crisis later that required an emergency infusion of U.S. forces, and such a deployment might come too late to prevent the defeat of South Vietnam. In accordance with Westmoreland's Phase I plan, McNamara recommended raising the troop level to 175,000 by October and calling up 235,000 reservists. The new troop deployments would not create resentment against the United States, McNamara maintained, citing as evidence Ky's remark to that effect and the South Vietnamese government's request for 200,000 U.S. troops. Investigations by the U.S. embassy, moreover, had found that previous deployments had occasioned neither animosity nor a slackening of Vietnamese effort. McNamara also proposed increasing the rate of air strikes against North Vietnam from 2,500 per month to at least 4,000 per month, even though he had reverted to the view that the primary purpose of the bombing was to send signals rather than to inflict material damage.[48]

Under McNamara's plan, the U.S. and third country combat units would seek out the Communist main forces "to run them to ground and destroy them." Echoing Westmoreland, McNamara noted that initial American combat successes could cause the enemy to return to the small-scale warfare that prevailed before 1965, in which case "U.S. troops and aircraft would be of limited value." But, McNamara pointed out, the enemy's return to more modest military operations would prevent the enemy from winning the war militarily and would permit the South Vietnamese to undertake pacification more easily – an important truth that was often lost on critics of U.S. conventional military operations. Looking ahead, McNamara noted that the possible arrival of additional North Vietnamese divisions might require future troop increases of undetermined magnitude, but he downplayed this eventuality, based on the false presumption that the air campaign against the Ho Chi Minh Trail was seriously impeding the enemy. "We have every reason to believe," McNamara asserted, "that the strikes on infiltration routes have at least put a ceiling on what the North Vietnamese can pour into South Vietnam, thereby putting a ceiling on the size of war that the enemy can wage there."[49] In concluding his report, McNamara predicted that his recommended course of action "stands a good chance of achieving an acceptable outcome within a reasonable time in Vietnam."[50]

On July 21 and July 22, President Johnson's top advisers gathered around the octagonal table in the White House Cabinet room for what would be the most substantive discussions on intervention preceding the President's public announcement. While it is possible that Johnson had already decided on his course of action as early as the latter part of June, the more likely conclusion is that he did not come to a decision until just after these discussions, on July 23.[51] During the meeting, their demeanors sober but firm, McNamara and the Joint Chiefs delivered their most important assessments to the President, punctuated by Johnson's questions and opinions. McNamara told the assemblage that pacifying South Vietnam would require at least two years. The Joint Chiefs, like Westmoreland, were less optimistic than McNamara. General Wheeler contended, "We might start to reverse the unfavorable trend in a year and make definite progress in three years," a forecast that events would show to be more accurate than McNamara's. Marine Corps Commandant General Wallace M. Greene, Jr., echoing the prognostication made by General Johnson in March, said that victory "will take a minimum of five years and will require at least 500,000 U.S. troops." This prophesy would prove to be the most prescient of all; it came very close to the actual size and duration of America's ultimate commitment, and when five years had passed South Vietnam would be capable of defending itself without U.S. ground forces, a victory of sorts for the United States.

President Johnson appeared to find the Joint Chiefs' predictions more convincing than those of McNamara. Waving a yellow pencil, he brought up the point that Ho Chi Minh might respond to U.S. troop deployments by dispatching an equal number of additional North Vietnamese troops to the South. Wheeler estimated that chances were fifty-fifty that Ho would send more troops to the South, but noted that Ho could send only a small portion of his forces because of the necessity of defending North Vietnam. "He would be foolhardy to put one quarter of his forces in South Vietnam," said Wheeler. "It would expose him too greatly in North Vietnam." Wheeler, however, also cautioned that he could not promise that the 100,000-man increase scheduled for 1966 would be the last troop increase needed.

Turning to China with similar concern, the President speculated that major infusions of U.S. men and money might induce the Chinese to come into the war. As had been the case in late 1964 and early 1965, Johnson was worried that forceful action would embolden the enemy, when in reality the lack of forceful action had already emboldened the enemy. General Wheeler's forecast of China's behavior differed from the President's, but it too was wrong. The Chinese, Wheeler contended, would keep their troops in China rather than send them into Vietnam because "the one thing all North Vietnamese fear is Chinese. For them to invite Chinese volunteers is to invite China's taking over North Vietnam."[52]

Like many before him, Wheeler had been misled by the myth of eternal enmity between China and Vietnam. By the time Wheeler uttered these words, tens of thousands of Chinese troops had already arrived in North Vietnam. In accordance with the Sino–North Vietnamese agreement, the seven Chinese divisions assigned to North Vietnam had begun streaming across the border one and a half months earlier. Chinese soldiers were now building railway lines, bridges, tunnels, air bases, communications systems, and coastal fortifications for their North Vietnamese hosts. The divisions' antiaircraft units occupied positions from which they defended not only Chinese forces but also key areas around Hanoi.[53] The Chinese troops served the same basic purpose that the U.S. Marines sent to Da Nang in March had originally been intended to serve – they relieved Vietnamese troops from static duties so that they could participate in mobile operations elsewhere. President Johnson's efforts to avoid another Korean War by stating and demonstrating his intention to stay out of North Vietnam ended up saddling him with the very problems that had afflicted the United States in Korea. China would use its manpower as a huge supplement to that of its small ally – even if the Chinese would not step onto the battlefield as they had in Korea because America's purely defensive strategy made it unnecessary. The substitution of Chinese for North Vietnamese troops would render false the premise, essential to General Wheeler's troop calculations, that most North Vietnamese Army units would have to remain in the North. The arrival of Chinese troops in North Vietnam also cost the United States an opportunity to fight on the ground in North Vietnam without having to worry about running into Chinese troops. Now that the Chinese forces had established a presence in North Vietnam, the Chinese leadership would be reluctant to retreat into China in the face of an American invasion, for reasons of international credibility and prestige, although in the spring and the summer of 1965 their generally oblique expressions of a willingness to fight in North Vietnam were interspersed with explicit assertions that they would fight only if the United States attacked China itself.[54]

On July 23, President Johnson received Special National Intelligence Estimate 10-9-65, which assessed the likely impact of an expansion of Rolling Thunder. According to the estimate, strikes on military targets in Hanoi and Haiphong would have little effect on Viet Cong capabilities by themselves. If, however, these strikes were combined with attacks on oil facilities in Hanoi and Haiphong and the lines of communication between North Vietnam and China, then North Vietnam's transportation and importation capabilities would suffer severe degradation. In addition, the estimate stated, such an enlargement of the target list was unlikely to cause a major war with China or the Soviet Union.[55] This estimate provided striking evidence that graduated pressure ought to be scrapped in favor of intensive strikes aimed at inflicting great tangible damage, something that the Joint Chiefs had continued to recommend to the President in June and July.[56]

In coming to his decision, Johnson remained convinced that domestic opinion did not provide compelling grounds for intervention in Vietnam. Support for intervention among the American Congress, public, and press had risen recently because Communist military advances had heightened fears of falling dominoes in Asia and because the Communists had committed several atrocities against American personnel.[57] Forty-seven percent of Americans surveyed said that they favored sending more U.S. troops to South Vietnam, nineteen percent favored keeping the current number of troops, and eleven percent favored withdrawing U.S. troops.[58] Johnson, however, said in late July that such support might evaporate once the full costs of the war became apparent.[59] Public debate would speed up the evaporation, Johnson thought. Because of his concern about such a debate, he avoided seeking a Congressional resolution supporting his decision for a larger U.S. commitment to Vietnam. Some of Johnson's aides had recommended that he ask Congress to approve this type of resolution in light of Senator Fulbright's assurances at the time of the Tonkin Gulf Resolution that the President would consult with Congress in the event of a major U.S. commitment. To prevent the Congress from thinking that he had simply ignored them, Johnson held sham "consultations" bearing some resemblance to what had been promised in August 1964. On July 27, by which time he had already made up his mind, he told the Congressional leaders that he was trying to decide between two options, and that he was inclined to take the second of the two, but gave the impression that he would consider the Congressmen's views before selecting an option. Both of these options were similar to McNamara's proposal, eliciting grumbles among those who realized that Johnson was not giving them a chance to challenge many key points. With the exception of Senator Mike Mansfield, the Congressional leaders agreed to go along with Johnson's preferred option, the one that in truth he had already chosen.[60]

Johnson decided on a troop commitment of 186,700 for Phase I, which was McNamara's 175,000 plus 11,700 more that had been added as the result of subsequent analysis. Rather than announcing an increase to 186,700 right away, Johnson decided that he would announce only an increase to 125,000 for the moment. He chose not to accelerate the bombing or mine the harbors, in spite of the claim in the recent national intelligence estimate that a comprehensive offensive against North Vietnam's supply routes would bring many rewards with low risk, because most of the senior civilians believed that external supplies were not so important and that the risk of provoking the Soviets or Chinese was high. Rejecting McNamara's proposed reserve call-up, Johnson ordered the involuntary extension of Navy and Marine Corps enlistments and increased the draft calls to compensate for the lack of reserve personnel. In addition, decided the President, the administration would not seek a large Congressional appropriation now as McNamara had advised but would instead wait until January 1966, getting by until then through the creative movement of funds.[61]

President Johnson explained to the National Security Council that he was announcing only 125,000 of the 186,700 troops, avoiding a reserve call-up, and delaying the funding request because if he did otherwise, then the North

Vietnamese would be able to persuade the Chinese and Soviets to send them more aid.[62] Johnson was indeed worried by this prospect, but other concerns also figured prominently in his thinking. McGeorge Bundy commented that in minimizing the appearance of escalation at this time, Johnson's "unspoken object was to protect his legislative program." Johnson "didn't want a big Congressional debate at a time when the whole Great Society program was in the legislative process."[63] Johnson, moreover, believed that larger actions would make it more difficult for him to pull U.S. forces out of Vietnam later should he so desire. He explained to Senator Richard Russell on July 26 that he was not prepared to call up the reserves because "it commits me where I can't get out."[64] The purpose of the new deployment, in Johnson's mind as in McNamara's, was to prevent the defeat of South Vietnam through the end of the year, not necessarily to hold off its defeat indefinitely.[65] If, by the beginning of 1966, diplomacy had failed and the war was proceeding unsatisfactorily, Johnson thought that he could withdraw the U.S. troops and abandon South Vietnam to the Communists without paying international costs as high as those involved in abandoning the South Vietnamese right away. He thus had accepted the judgment of some of his civilian advisers that fight before flight was better than immediate flight, that the rest of Asia would view the United States as the good doctor who finally had to give up on a terminally ill patient. Fight before flight seemed to offer what Johnson needed most, a means of avoiding the negative consequence of both immediate withdrawal and indefinite commitment. Johnson and other proponents of the good doctor analogy severely underestimated the diplomatic damage that would flow from the withdrawal of U.S. troops in the middle of a war and from the resultant destruction of an allied government.

Appearing on national television on July 28, Johnson announced, "I have today ordered to Vietnam the Airmobile Division and certain other forces which will raise our fighting strength from 75,000 to 125,000 men almost immediately. Additional forces will be needed later, and they will be sent as requested." Johnson emphasized the threat that China and North Vietnam posed to the rest of Asia, declaring that the insurgency in South Vietnam "is guided by North Vietnam and it is spurred by Communist China," both of which sought to "extend the Asiatic dominion of Communism." Johnson warned that "most of the non-Communist nations of Asia cannot, by themselves and alone, resist the growing might and the grasping ambition of Asian Communism. Our power, therefore, is a very vital shield."[66]

During the ensuing question-and-answer period with the Washington press corps, a smart reporter inquired, "Mr. President, does the fact that you are sending additional forces to Vietnam imply any change in the existing policy of relying mainly on the South Vietnamese to carry out offensive operations and using American forces to guard American installations and to act as an emergency backup?"

Johnson knew the correct answer to this question. Earlier in the month, he had said to McNamara, "Even though there's some record behind us, we know ourselves, in our own conscience, that when we asked for this [Tonkin Gulf] resolution, we had no intention of committing this many ground troops. We're doing so now, and we know it's going to be bad."[67] During the deliberations of July 22, McNamara had told the President, "This is a major change in U.S. policy. We have relied on South Vietnam to carry the brunt. Now we would be responsible for a satisfactory military outcome."[68] Yet in reply to the correspondent's question, Johnson said that the addition of troops "does not imply any change in policy whatever."

Another reporter asked Johnson whether he thought that the war might go on for five years or more. Johnson had no inclination to give a precise answer, both because his doubts about the likelihood of rapid success had been reinforced during the past week's discussions with the Joint Chiefs, and because he would only abet America's enemies by making public his thoughts about pulling out under unfavorable conditions in 1966. "I think the American people ought to understand that there is no quick solution to the problem that we face there," Johnson answered. "I would not want to prophesy or predict whether it would be a matter of months or years or decades."[69]

In the end, what drove Lyndon Johnson to put American ground forces into the Vietnam War was a conviction that a chain of disastrous events would unfold if he did not. North Vietnam would soon conquer South Vietnam, which would then lead to Communist control or domination of many other Asian dominoes, which in turn would severely damage America's global strategic position. Lyndon Johnson had never intended to intervene in the war with U.S. ground troops unless South Vietnam's life depended on it, for he did not think that such intervention would result in a quick or easy victory. In the middle of 1965, he concluded that South Vietnam's life did, in fact, depend on it, a correct judgment based on the evidence of Communist military capabilities and intentions available then and since. Johnson was also correct in predicting that many of the other dominoes would come crashing down if the Communists toppled South Vietnam in 1965. What would ultimately doom Johnson was neither the illness of the patient nor a faulty diagnosis but a poor choice of remedy. His refusal to order some very feasible actions in Laos and North Vietnam, the result of misplaced fears and faulty intelligence and unwarranted confidence in brainy civilians, forfeited opportunities to deny the Communists the great strategic advantages that they were to enjoy for the next ten years. The war in Vietnam that America's young men were about to fight, therefore, was not to be a foolish war fought under wise constraints, but a wise war fought under foolish constraints.

Abbreviations Used in Notes

ARVN	Army of the Republic of Vietnam
CAB	Records of the Cabinet Office
CDEC	Combined Document Exploitation Center
CIA	Central Intelligence Agency
CINCPAC	Commander in Chief, Pacific Fleet
CMH	U.S. Army Center of Military History, Washington, DC
COMUSMACV	Commander, U.S. Military Assistance Command, Vietnam
CWIHP	Cold War International History Project
DDEL	Dwight David Eisenhower Library, Abilene, Kansas
DDRS	Declassified Documents Reference System
DIA	Defense Intelligence Agency
DMUSF	Deployment of Major U.S. Forces
DRV	Democratic Republic of (North) Vietnam
FO	Foreign Office
FRUS	*Foreign Relations of the United States*
GVN	Government of (South) Vietnam
HIA	Hoover Institution Archives, Stanford, California
JCS	Joint Chiefs of Staff
JFKL	John F. Kennedy Library, Boston, Massachusetts
LBJL	Lyndon B. Johnson Library, Austin, Texas
LOC	Library of Congress, Washington, DC
MACV	Military Assistance Command, Vietnam
MCHCD	Marine Corps Historical Division, Quantico, Virginia
MHI	U.S. Army Military History Institute, Carlisle, Pennsylvania
NA II	National Archives II, College Park, Maryland
NDUL	National Defense University Library, Washington, DC
NLF	National Liberation Front
NMCC	National Military Command Center
NSA	National Security Agency
NSAM	National Security Action Memorandum
NSC	National Security Council

NSF	National Security File
POF	President's Office Files
PREM	Prime Minister's Papers
PRO	Public Record Office, London, England
RG	Record Group
RVN	Republic of (South) Vietnam
SNIE	Special National Intelligence Estimate
SWB/FE	BBC Summary of World Broadcasts, the Far East
TTU	Texas Tech University Vietnam Archive, Lubbock, Texas
USARMA	U.S. Army Attaché
USAWCL	U.S. Army War College Library, Carlisle, Pennsylvania
USVNR	*United States–Vietnam Relations, 1945–1967*
VC	Viet Cong
VCD	Viet Cong Document
VNCF	Vietnam Country File

Notes

Preface

1. For a recent overview of the orthodox-revisionist debate, see Marc Jason Gilbert, ed., *Why the North Won the Vietnam War* (New York: Palgrave Macmillan, 2002), 1–45. There are, of course, subgroups within each of these schools, some of which are discussed later in this volume. Not every historian of the war can be clearly identified with one school, but most historians generally side with one of the two groups on most of the basic issues.

2. For the Eisenhower period, recent works include Daniel Greene, "Tug of War: The Eisenhower Administration and Vietnam, 1953–1955" (Ph.D. diss., University of Texas at Austin, 1990); Philip E. Catton, *Diem's Final Failure: Prelude to America's War in Vietnam* (Lawrence, KS: University Press of Kansas, 2002); John Ernst, *Forging a Fateful Alliance: Michigan State University and the Vietnam War* (East Lansing: Michigan State University Press, 1998); Matthew Masur, "Hearts and Minds: Cultural Nation Building in South Vietnam, 1954–1963" (Ph.D. diss., Ohio State University, 2004). Recent books of note that cover the Kennedy period or the Johnson period or both are Peter Busch, *All the Way with JFK : Britain, the US, and the Vietnam War* (Oxford: Oxford University Press, 2003); Robert Buzzanco, *Masters of War: Military Dissent and Politics in the Vietnam Era* (New York: Cambridge University Press, 1996); Lawrence Freedman, *Kennedy's Wars: Berlin, Cuba, Laos, and Vietnam* (New York: Oxford University Press, 2000); Lloyd C. Gardner, *Pay Any Price: Lyndon Johnson and the Wars for Vietnam* (Chicago: Ivan R. Dee, 1995); Michael H. Hunt, *Lyndon Johnson's War: America's Cold War Crusade in Vietnam, 1945–1968* (New York: Hill and Wang, 1996); Howard Jones, *The Death of a Generation: How the Assassinations of Diem and JFK Prolonged the Vietnam War* (New York: Oxford University Press, 2003); David E. Kaiser, *American Tragedy: Kennedy, Johnson, and the Origins of the Vietnam War* (Cambridge: Harvard University Press, 2000); Fredrik Logevall, *Choosing War: The Lost Chance for Peace and the Escalation of the War in Vietnam* (Berkeley: University of California Press, 1999); Orrin Schwab, *Defending the Free World: John F. Kennedy, Lyndon Johnson, and the Vietnam War, 1961–1965* (Westport: Praeger, 1998); Frank E. Vandiver, *Shadows of Vietnam: Lyndon Johnson's Wars* (College Station: Texas A&M University Press, 1997). Gareth Porter's *Perils of Dominance: Imbalance of Power and the Road to War in Vietnam* (Berkeley: University of California Press, 2005) covers the Eisenhower, Kennedy, and Johnson periods. General histories include David L. Anderson, *The Vietnam War* (New York: Palgrave Macmillan, 2005); Robert Buzzanco, *Vietnam and the Transformation of American Life* (Malden, MA: Blackwell Publishers, 1999); William C. Gibbons, *The U.S. Government and the Vietnam War: Executive and Legislative Roles and Relationships*, vols. 1–4 (Princeton: Princeton University Press, 1986–1995); A. J. Langguth, *Our Vietnam/Nuoc Viet Ta: A History of the War 1954–1975* (New York: Simon & Schuster, 2000); Robert Mann, *A Grand Delusion: America's Descent into Vietnam* (New York: Basic Books, 2001); Jeffrey Record, *The Wrong War: Why We Lost in Vietnam* (Annapolis: Naval Institute Press, 1998); Robert D. Schulzinger, *A Time for War: The United States and Vietnam, 1941–1975* (New York: Oxford University Press, 1997). Older books on these periods that have stood up reasonably well against time include

David L. Anderson, *Trapped By Success: The Eisenhower Administration and Vietnam, 1953–1961* (New York: Columbia University Press, 1991); James R. Arnold, *The First Domino: Eisenhower, the Military, and America's Intervention in Vietnam* (New York: Morrow, 1991); David M. Barrett, *Uncertain Warriors: Lyndon Johnson and His Vietnam Advisers* (Lawrence, KS: University Press of Kansas, 1993); Larry Berman, *Planning a Tragedy: The Americanization of the War in Vietnam* (New York: W. W. Norton, 1982); Melanie Billings-Yun, *Decision Against War: Eisenhower and Dien Bien Phu, 1954* (New York: Columbia University Press, 1988); Jeffrey J. Clarke, *Advice and Support: The Final Years, 1965–1973* (Washington, DC: U.S. Government Printing Office, 1988); Mark Clodfelter, *The Limits of Air Power: The American Bombing of North Vietnam* (New York: The Free Press, 1989); William J. Duiker, *U.S. Containment Policy and the Conflict in Indochina* (Stanford: Stanford University Press, 1994); William M. Hammond, *Public Affairs: The Military and the Media, 1962–1968* (Washington, DC: U.S. Government Printing Office, 1988); Patrick L. Hatcher, *Suicide of an Elite: American Internationalists and Vietnam* (Stanford: Stanford University Press, 1990); George C. Herring, *America's Longest War: The United States and Vietnam, 1950–1975*, 4th rev. ed. (Boston: McGraw-Hill, 2002); Gary R. Hess, *Vietnam and the United States* (Boston: Twayne Publishing, 1990); George McT. Kahin, *Intervention: How America Became Involved in Vietnam* (New York: Knopf, 1986); Stanley Karnow, *Vietnam: A History*, 2nd rev. ed. (New York: Penguin Books, 1997); Yuen Foong Khong, *Analogies at War: Korea, Munich, Dien Bien Phu, and the Vietnam Decisions of 1965* (Princeton: Princeton University Press, 1992); Ernest R. May, *"Lessons" of the Past: The Use and Misuse of History in American Foreign Policy* (New York: Oxford University Press, 1973); George Donelson Moss, *Vietnam: An American Ordeal* (Englewood Cliffs, NJ: Prentice Hall, 1990); Richard E. Neustadt and Ernest R. May, *Thinking in Time: The Uses of History for Decision Makers* (New York: Free Press, 1986); William J. Rust, *Kennedy in Vietnam* (New York: Scribner, 1985); Ronald H. Spector, *Advice and Support: The Early Years of the United States Army in Vietnam, 1941–1960* (New York: The Free Press, 1985); William Turley, *The Second Indochina War: A Short Political and Military History* (Boulder: Westview Press, 1986); Brian VanDeMark, *Into the Quagmire: Lyndon Johnson and the Escalation of the Vietnam War* (New York: Oxford University Press, 1991). The historiography of the war during the period from August 1965 to April 1975 will be addressed in the sequel to this book.

3. William Prochnau, *Once Upon a Distant War: David Halberstam, Neil Sheehan, Peter Arnett – Young War Correspondents and Their Early Vietnam Battles* (New York: Times Books, 1995); Edwin Moïse, *Tonkin Gulf and the Escalation of the Vietnam War* (Chapel Hill: University of North Carolina Press, 1996); George C. Herring, *LBJ and Vietnam: A Different Kind of War* (Austin: University of Texas Press, 1994); Harold P. Ford, *CIA and the Vietnam Policymakers: Three Episodes, 1962–1968* (Langley: Center for the Study of Intelligence, 1998).

4. The best example is Catton, *Diem's Final Failure.*

5. Ilya V. Gaiduk, *Confronting Vietnam: Soviet Policy Toward the Indochina Conflict, 1954–1963* (Stanford: Stanford University Press, 2003); Ilya V. Gaiduk, *The Soviet Union and the Vietnam War* (Chicago: Ivan R. Dee, 1996); Qiang Zhai, *China and the Vietnam Wars, 1950–1975* (Chapel Hill: University of North Carolina Press, 2000); Chen Jian, *Mao's China and the Cold War* (Chapel Hill: University of North Carolina Press, 2001); Lorenz M. Lüthi, "The Sino-Soviet Split, 1956–1966" (Ph.D. diss., Yale University, 2003).

6. For the Communist side, see Robert K. Brigham, *Guerrilla Diplomacy: The NLF's Foreign Relations and the Vietnam War* (Ithaca: Cornell University Press, 1998); William J. Duiker, *Ho Chi Minh* (New York: Hyperion, 2000); William J. Duiker, *The Sacred War: Nationalism and Revolution in a Divided Vietnam* (New York: McGraw-Hill, 1994); Christopher E. Goscha, "Vietnam and the World Outside: The Case of Vietnamese Communist Advisers in Laos (1948–62)," *South East Asia Research*, vol. 12, no. 2 (July 2004); Christopher E. Goscha, "The Maritime Nature of the Wars for Vietnam," *War & Society*, vol. 23, no. 2 (October 2005); Ang Cheng Guan, *The Vietnam War from the Other Side: The Vietnamese Communists' Perspective* (London: RoutledgeCurzon, 2002); Ang Cheng Guan, *Vietnamese Communists' Relations with China and the Second Indochina Conflict, 1958–1962* (Jefferson, NC: McFarland, 1997); Kim N. B. Ninh, *A World Transformed: The Politics of Culture in Revolutionary Vietnam, 1945–1965* (Ann Arbor: University of Michigan Press, 2002); Patricia Pelley, *Postcolonial Vietnam: New Histories of the National Past* (Durham: Duke University Press, 2002); Sophie Quinn-Judge, *Ho Chi Minh: The*

Missing Years, 1919–1941 (Berkeley: University of California Press, 2002). Carlyle A. Thayer's *War By Other Means, National Liberation and Revolution in Viet-Nam, 1954–60* (Sydney: Allen & Unwin, 1989) and William J. Duiker's *The Communist Road to Power*, 2nd ed. (Boulder: Westview Press, 1996) remain very valuable studies. For the anti-Communists, see Robert K. Brigham, *ARVN: Life and Death in the South Vietnamese Army* (Lawrence, KS: University Press of Kansas, 2006); Catton, *Diem's Final Failure*; Seth Jacobs, *America's Miracle Man: Ngo Dinh Diem, Religion, Race, and U.S. Intervention in Southeast Asia, 1950–1957* (Durham: Duke University Press, 2004); Masur, "Hearts and Minds"; Edward Miller, "Grand Designs: Vision, Power and Nation Building in America's Alliance with Ngo Dinh Diem, 1954–1960" (Ph.D. diss., Harvard University, 2004); Edward Miller, "Vision, Power, and Agency: The Ascent of Ngo Dinh Diem, 1945–1954," *Journal of Southeast Asian Studies*, vol. 35, issue 3 (October 2004), 433–58. Some of the preceding works do explicitly support the orthodox position or, less often, the revisionist position in various places.

7. John M. Carland, *Combat Operations: Stemming the Tide, May 1965 to October 1966* (Washington, DC: U.S. Government Printing Office, 2000); John A. Nagl, *Counterinsurgency Lessons from Malaya and Vietnam: Learning to Eat Soup with a Knife* (Westport: Praeger, 2002); Harvey Neese and John O'Donnell, eds., *Prelude to Tragedy: Vietnam, 1960–1965* (Annapolis: Naval Institute Press, 2001); David M. Toczek, *The Battle of Ap Bac, Vietnam: They Did Everything But Learn From It* (Westport: Greenwood Press, 2001). Two others have detailed the ill-fated American and South Vietnamese attempts at covert action in North Vietnam: Conboy and Andrade, *Spies and Commandos: How America Lost the Secret War in North Vietnam* (Lawrence, KS: University Press of Kansas, 2000); Richard H. Shultz, *The Secret War Against Hanoi: Kennedy and Johnson's Use of Spies, Saboteurs, and Covert Warriors in North Vietnam* (New York: HarperCollins, 1999). On numerous naval subjects, the best source remains Edward J. Marolda and Oscar P. Fitzgerald, *The United States Navy and the Vietnam Conflict, vol. 2: From Military Assistance to Combat, 1959–1965* (Washington, DC: U.S. Government Printing Office, 1986).

8. David W. P. Elliott, *The Vietnamese War: Revolution and Social Change in the Mekong Delta, 1930–1975*, 2 vols. (Armonk: M. E. Sharpe, 2003); Eric Bergerud, *The Dynamics of Defeat: The Vietnam War in Hau Nghia Province* (Boulder: Westview Press, 1991).

9. Kai Bird, *The Color of Truth: McGeorge Bundy and William Bundy, Brothers in Arms* (New York: Simon & Schuster, 1998); Anne Blair, *Lodge in Vietnam: A Patriot Abroad* (New Haven: Yale University Press, 1995); Anne Blair, *There to the Bitter End: Ted Serong in Vietnam* (Crows Nest: Allen & Unwin, 2001); Robert Caro, *The Years of Lyndon Johnson*, 3 vols. (New York: Knopf, 1982–2002); Robert Dallek, *Lone Star Rising: Lyndon Johnson and His Times, 1908–1960* (New York: Oxford University Press, 1991); Robert Dallek, *Flawed Giant: Lyndon Johnson and His Times, 1961–1973* (New York: Oxford University Press, 1998); Robert Dallek, *An Unfinished Life: John F. Kennedy, 1917–1963* (Boston: Little, Brown and Co., 2003); Richard Reeves, *President Kennedy: Profile of Power* (New York: Simon & Schuster, 1993); Lewis Sorley, *Honorable Warrior: General Harold K. Johnson and the Ethics of Command* (Lawrence, KS: University Press of Kansas, 1998).

10. Eugenie Margareta Blang, "To Urge Common Sense on the Americans: United States' Relations with France, Great Britain, and the Federal Republic of Germany in the Context of the Vietnam War, 1961–1968" (Ph.D. diss., College of William and Mary, 2000); Busch, *All the Way with JFK?*; Ronald Bruce Frankum, *The United States and Australia in Vietnam, 1954–1968: Silent Partners* (Lewiston: Edwin Mellen Press, 2001); Lloyd C. Gardner and Ted Gittinger, eds., *International Perspectives on Vietnam* (College Station: Texas A&M University Press, 1999); Evelyn Goh, *Constructing the U.S. Rapprochement with China, 1961–1974: From "Red Menace" to "Tacit Ally"* (New York: Cambridge University Press, 2004); Christopher Goscha and Maurice Vaïsse, *La Guerre du Vietnam et L'Europe, 1963–1973* (Bruxelles: Bruylant, 2003); Matthew Jones, *Conflict and Confrontation in Southeast Asia, 1961–1965: Britain, the United States, and the Creation of Malaysia* (Cambridge: Cambridge University Press, 2001); Thomas Alan Schwartz, *LBJ and Europe: In the Shadow of Vietnam* (Cambridge: Harvard University Press, 2003); John Subritzky, *Confronting Sukarno: British, American, Australian and New Zealand Diplomacy in the Malaysian-Indonesian Confrontation, 1961–5* (New York: St. Martin's Press, 2000).

11. Logevall, *Choosing War*, xiii.

12. David L. Anderson, "One Vietnam War Should Be Enough and Other Reflections on Diplomatic History and the Making of Foreign Policy," *Society for Historians of American Foreign Relations Annual*

Meeting, College Park, Maryland, June 24, 2005. The address was reprinted in *Diplomatic History*, vol. 30, no. 1 (January 2006), 1–21. A similar claim appears in Robert Buzzanco, "Fear and (Self) Loathing in Lubbock: How I Learned to Quit Worrying and Love Vietnam and Iraq," *Counterpunch*, 16–17 (April 2005). The Society for Historians of American Foreign Relations republished Buzzanco's diatribe in the December 2005 edition of *Passport*, the organization's newsletter.

13. The book stated that "the negative repercussions of lost U.S. credibility and of Communist expansion in Asia in the event of South Vietnam's collapse could not have undermined U.S. interests critically, as American politicians of the Vietnam War era had believed they would." Mark Moyar, *Phoenix and the Birds of Prey: The CIA's Secret Campaign to Destroy the Viet Cong* (Annapolis: Naval Institute Press, 1997), 232.

14. The most significant of the early revisionist books that address this period are William Colby with James McCargar, *Lost Victory: A Firsthand Account of America's Sixteen-Year Involvement in Vietnam* (Chicago: Contemporary Books, 1989); Phillip B. Davidson, *Vietnam At War: The History, 1945–1975* (Novato: Presidio Press, 1988); Ellen J. Hammer, *A Death in November: America in Vietnam, 1963* (New York: E. P. Dutton, 1987); Norman B. Hannah, *The Key to Failure: Laos and the Vietnam War* (Lanham: Madison Books, 1987); Guenter Lewy, *America and Vietnam* (New York: Oxford University Press, 1978); Norman Podhoretz, *Why We Were in Vietnam* (New York: Simon & Schuster, 1982); Ralph B. Smith, *An International History of the Vietnam War*, 3 vols. (New York: St. Martin's Press, 1983–1991; Harry G. Summers, Jr., *On Strategy: A Critical Analysis of the Vietnam War* (Novato: Presidio Press, 1982); Robert F. Turner, *Vietnamese Communism: Its Origins and Development* (Stanford: Hoover Institution Press, 1975). Lewy's superb book was the best history of the Vietnam War when it was first published, and, despite the deluge of source materials that came afterwards, it remains one of the best.

15. Arthur J. Dommen, *The Indochinese Experience of the French and the Americans: Nationalism and Communism in Cambodia, Laos, and Vietnam* (Bloomington: Indiana University Press, 2001).

16. H. R. McMaster, *Dereliction of Duty: Lyndon Johnson, Robert McNamara, the Joint Chiefs of Staff and the Lies that Led to Vietnam* (New York: HarperCollins, 1997).

17. Michael Lind, *Vietnam, The Necessary War: A Reinterpretation of America's Most Disastrous Military Conflict* (New York: Free Press, 1999). In a somewhat similar vein is Walt Rostow, "The Case for the Vietnam War," *Parameters*, vol. 26, no. 4 (Winter 1996/1997). Rostow's scope, however, is much more limited, and he does not provide secondary source material to support his claims as Lind does. For a revisionist history that focuses on military affairs, see Mark W. Woodruff, *Unheralded Victory: The Defeat of the Viet Cong and the North Vietnamese Army, 1961–1973* (Arlington, VA: Vandamere Press, 1999).

18. C. Dale Walton, *The Myth of Inevitable U.S. Defeat in Vietnam* (London: Frank Cass, 2002).

19. Francis X. Winters, *The Year of the Hare: America in Vietnam, January 25, 1963-February 15, 1964* (Athens: University of Georgia Press, 1997); Geoffrey Shaw, "Ambassador Frederick Nolting's Role in American Diplomatic and Military Policy toward the Government of South Vietnam" (Ph.D. diss., University of Manitoba, 1999). Another noteworthy recent revisionist work concerning the Vietnamese Communists is Stephen J. Morris, "The Internationalist Outlook of Vietnamese Communism," in John Norton Moore and Robert F. Turner, eds., *The Real Lessons of the Vietnam War: Reflections Twenty-Five Years After the Fall of Saigon* (Durham, NC: Carolina Academic Press, 2002).

1. Heritage

1. Ho Chi Minh, *Selected Writings* (Hanoi: Foreign Languages Publishing House, 1977), 53–6.

2. For the argument that a unified Vietnam would have become an Asian Yugoslavia and served as a bulwark against Chinese expansionism, see Arnold, *The First Domino*; Hess, *Vietnam and the United States*; Arnold R. Isaacs, *Vietnam Shadows: The War, Its Ghosts, and Its Legacy* (Baltimore; Johns Hopkins University Press, 1997); Kahin, *Intervention*; Karnow, *Vietnam*; Gabriel Kolko, *Anatomy of a War: Vietnam, the United States, and the Modern Historical Experience* (New York: Pantheon Books, 1985); Logevall, *Choosing War*; Mann, *A Grand Delusion*; Robert McNamara with Brian VanDeMark, *In Retrospect: The Tragedy and Lessons of Vietnam* (New York: Times Books, 1995); Moss, *Vietnam*; John

Prados, *The Blood Road: The Ho Chi Minh Trail and the Vietnam War* (New York: Wiley, 1999); Record, *The Wrong War;* Schulzinger, *A Time For War;* Neil Sheehan, *A Bright Shining Lie: John Paul Vann and America in Vietnam* (New York: Random House, 1988); VanDeMark, *Into the Quagmire*.

3. The best source on the history of Vietnam before the twentieth century is Keith Weller Taylor, *The Birth of Vietnam* (Berkeley: University of California Press, 1983). Other English-language sources include Joseph Buttinger, *The Smaller Dragon* (New York: Frederick A. Praeger, 1958); Joseph Buttinger, *Vietnam: A Dragon Embattled,* 2 vols. (New York: Frederick A. Praeger, 1967); Oscar Chapuis, *A History of Vietnam: From Hong Bang to Tu Duc* (Westport: Greenwood Press, 1995); Dennis J. Duncanson, *Government and Revolution in Vietnam* (London: Oxford University Press, 1968); Neil L. Jamieson, *Understanding Vietnam* (Berkeley: University of California Press, 1993); John K. Fairbank et al., *East Asia: Tradition and Transformation,* rev. ed. (New York: Houghton Mifflin, 1989).

4. Buzzanco, *Vietnam and the Transformation of American Life;* Herring, *America's Longest War;* Frank Ninkovich, *Modernity and Power: A History of the Domino Theory in the Twentieth Century* (Chicago: University of Chicago Press, 1994); Hess, *Vietnam and the United States;* Jones, *Death of a Generation;* Karnow, *Vietnam;* Langguth, *Our Vietnam;* Archimedes L. Patti, *Why Viet Nam?: Prelude to America's Albatross* (Berkeley: University of California Press, 1980); Record, *The Wrong War;* Rust, *Kennedy in Vietnam*.

5. Hostilities would break out between China and Vietnam in 1979, but that conflict did not result from inveterate animosity between the two countries, as shall be explained in volume two of this history.

6. The most informative biographies of Ho Chi Minh are Duiker, *Ho Chi Minh* and Quinn-Judge, *Ho Chi Minh*.

7. Ho Chi Minh, *On Revolution: Selected Writings, 1920–1966* (New York: Frederick A. Praeger, 1967), 5.

8. Ho Chi Minh, *Selected Writings,* 251–2; Ho Chi Minh, *Selected Works,* vol. 4 (Hanoi: Foreign Languages Publishing House, 1962), 449–50.

9. *Theses and Statutes of the Third Communist International* (Moscow: Publishing Office of the Communist International, 1920), 66–75.

10. Ho Chi Minh, *On Revolution,* 8–10.

11. See, for example, *New York Times,* March 16, 1950; VCD 98, "World Situation and Our Party's International Mission," TTU, Viet-Nam Documents and Research Notes, box 2; Bui Tin, *Following Ho Chi Minh: The Memoirs of a North Vietnamese Colonel,* trans. by Judy Stowe and Do Van (Honolulu: University of Hawaii Press, 1995), 44; Ho Chi Minh, *Selected Works,* vol. 4, 257; Morris, "The Internationalist Outlook of Vietnamese Communism," in Moore and Turner, eds., *The Real Lessons of the Vietnam War,* 71–93.

12. An editorial in *Nhan Dan* asserted that the Hungarian people and the Soviet Army had "risen up to smash the arch enemy of the people, of the working class and socialism." SWB/FE/612/31.

13. Paul Mus, *Vietnam: Sociologie d'une Guerre* (Paris: Editions Du Seuil, 1952), 85.

14. Quinn-Judge, *Ho Chi Minh,* 51, 55.

15. Huynh Kim Khanh, *Vietnamese Communism, 1925–1945* (Ithaca: Cornell University Press, 1982), 84.

16. Ho Chi Minh, *On Revolution,* 127–9. After Chiang Kai-shek's Chinese Nationalists broke an alliance with the Chinese Communists and attacked them in 1927, the Comintern lost its enthusiasm for collaborating with non-Communists, and therefore there was no present need to produce propaganda tailored to a particular audience.

17. Hoang Van Hoan, *A Drop in the Ocean: Hoang Van Hoan's Revolutionary Reminiscences* (Beijing: Foreign Languages Press, 1988), 53. At this time, most of the Communist faithful in Siam were of Vietnamese or Chinese ethnicity, another indication of the international character of Communism in Southeast Asia. "An Internal History of the Communist Party of Thailand," translated by Chris Baker, *Journal of Contemporary Asia,* vol. 33, no. 4 (2003), 520.

18. Duiker, *Ho Chi Minh,* 197.

19. Significant biographical sources on Diem include Miller, "Grand Designs"; Edward Miller, "Vision, Power, and Agency: The Ascent of Ngo Dinh Diem, 1945–1954," *Journal of Southeast Asian Studies,* vol. 35, issue 3 (October 2004), 433–58; Catton, *Diem's Final Failure;* Ellen J. Hammer, *The*

Struggle for Indochina (Stanford: Stanford University Press, 1954); Hammer, *A Death in November*; *Time*, August 4, 1961; Robert Shaplen, *The Lost Revolution: The Story of Twenty Years of Neglected Opportunities in Vietnam and of America's Failure to Foster Democracy There* (New York: Harper & Row, 1965); Denis Warner, *The Last Confucian* (New York: Macmillan, 1963). The standard portrait of Diem is one of an obtuse reactionary unfit to lead the country. Anderson, *Trapped by Success*; Busch, *All the Way with JFK?*; Buzzanco, *Vietnam and the Transformation of American Life*; Davidson, *Vietnam at War*; Duiker, *Ho Chi Minh*; Ernst, *Forging a Fateful Alliance*; Ford, *CIA and the Vietnam Policymakers*; Freedman, *Kennedy's Wars*; Thomas X. Hammes, *The Sling and the Stone: On War in the 21st Century* (St. Paul, MN: Zenith Press, 2004); Herring, *America's Longest War*; Hess, *Vietnam and the United States*; Jones, *Death of A Generation*; Kaiser, *American Tragedy*; Karnow, *Vietnam*; Logevall, *Choosing War*; Timothy J. Lomperis, *From People's War to People's Rule: Insurgency, Intervention, and the Lessons of Vietnam* (Chapel Hill: University of North Carolina Press, 1996); Mann, *A Grand Delusion*; Moss, *Vietnam*; John M. Newman, *JFK and Vietnam: Deception, Intrigue, and the Struggle for Power* (New York: Warner Books, 1992); Prochnau, *Once Upon A Distant War*; Record, *The Wrong War*; Sheehan, *A Bright Shining Lie*; Turley, *The Second Indochina War*; Vandiver, *Shadows of Vietnam*; Marilyn B. Young, *The Vietnam Wars, 1945–1990* (New York: HarperCollins, 1991). In recent years, a growing group of scholars has viewed Diem as a more complex and more astute figure, although within the group opinions differ as to the strength of his achievements as a national leader. Catton, *Diem's Final Failure*; Masur, "Hearts and Minds"; Miller, "Grand Designs"; Shaw, "Ambassador Frederick Nolting's Role in American Diplomatic and Military Policy toward the Government of South Vietnam"; Winters, *Year of the Hare*. Earlier works that take a similar view of Diem are Colby, *Lost Victory*; Hammer, *A Death in November*; Marguerite Higgins, *Our Vietnam Nightmare* (New York: Harper & Row, 1965).

20. PBS, *Vietnam: A Television History: America's Mandarin (1954–1963)* (Boston: WGBH, 1983).

21. Duiker, *Ho Chi Minh*, 143–5, 225; Quinn-Judge, *Ho Chi Minh*, 108, 182–3, 202–3.

22. Hammer, *A Death in November*, 47.

23. Bui Tin, *Following Ho Chi Minh*, 60. See also *Time*, April 4, 1955; Hoang Hai Van and Tan Tu, *Pham Xuan An: A General of the Secret Service* (Hanoi: The Gioi Publishers, 2003), 203; Saigon to State, 7 September 1962, NA II, RG 59, C0092, reel 8.

24. Bui Tin, "The View from Hanoi," paper presented at Texas Tech University conference on Ngo Dinh Diem, 24 October 2003.

25. *Time*, August 4, 1961.

26. For the depiction of the Viet Minh as a broad and diverse nationalist movement, see Anderson, *Trapped By Success*, 4–7; Loren Baritz, *Backfire: A History of How American Culture Led Us Into Vietnam and Made Us Fight the Way We Did* (New York: William Morrow, 1985), 58–9; Buzzanco, *Vietnam and the Transformation of American Life*, 14; Kahin, *Intervention*, 10; Langguth, *Our Vietnam*, 58–9; Mark A. Lawrence, *Assuming the Burden: Europe and the American Commitment to War in Vietnam* (Berkeley: University of California Press, 2005), 18; Schulzinger, *A Time for War*, 12; Young, *The Vietnam Wars*, 8.

27. The best sources on this subject are Dommen, *The Indochinese Experience of the French and the Americans*; Duiker, *Ho Chi Minh*.

28. His birth name was Nguyen Sinh Cung. He had taken on the name Nguyen Ai Quoc, meaning Nguyen the Patriot, during World War I.

29. Paris to State, 13 March 1945, *FRUS*, 1945, vol. 6, 300.

30. For Roosevelt's Indochina policy, see Walter LaFeber, "Roosevelt, Churchill, and Indochina: 1942–45," *American Historical Review*, vol. 80, no. 5 (December 1975), 1277–1295; George C. Herring, "The Truman Administration and the Restoration of French Sovereignty in Indochina," *Diplomatic History*, vol. 1, no. 2 (Spring 1977), 97–117; Duiker, *U.S. Containment Policy and the Conflict in Indochina*, 25.

31. Hoang Van Chi, *From Colonialism to Communism* (New York: Frederick A. Praeger, 1964), 33–5.

32. David Chanoff and Doan Van Toai, *Portrait of the Enemy* (New York: Random House, 1986), 37. See also Truong Nhu Tang with David Chanoff and Doan Van Toai, *A Vietcong Memoir* (San Diego: Harcourt Brace Jovanovich, 1985), 11–12.

33. Patti, *Why Viet Nam?*; Duiker, *U.S. Containment Policy and the Conflict in Indochina*, 37.

34. Patti, tel. 36, 29 August 1945, NA II, RG 226, Field Station Files, Box 199.

35. For the killing of specific individuals during this period, see Duiker, *Ho Chi Minh;* Buttinger, *Vietnam: A Dragon Embattled,* vol. 1; David G. Marr, *Vietnam 1945: The Quest for Power* (Berkeley: University of California Press, 1995); Bernard Fall, *The Two Viet-Nams: A Political and Military Analysis* (New York: Frederick A. Praeger, 1963).

36. Ho Chi Minh, *Selected Writings,* 42.

37. Edward Miller, "Vision, Power, and Agency: The Ascent of Ngo Dinh Diem, 1945–1954," *Journal of Southeast Asian Studies,* vol. 35, issue 3 (October 2004), 433–58.

38. *Time,* August 4, 1961.

39. Hammer, *The Struggle for Indochina,* 150; Gullion, memcon, 7 May 1953, *FRUS,* 1952–1954, vol. 13, 553–4; Duncanson, *Government and Revolution in Vietnam,* 212.

40. Marr, *Vietnam 1945,* 519.

41. Vo Nguyen Giap, *People's War, People's Army: The Viet Cong Insurrection Manual for Underdeveloped Countries* (New York: Frederick A. Praeger, 1962), 18. See also Hanoi to State, 1 July 1946, NA II, RG 59, LM070, reel 2.

42. Intra-Vietnamese killings, which the Communists perpetrated in greater numbers than everyone else combined, came to a total of as high as 50,000 in this period, according to recent estimates. Shawn Frederick McHale, *Print and Power: Confucianism, Communism, and Buddhism in the Making of Modern Vietnam* (Honolulu: University of Hawaii Press, 2003), 193.

43. Leon Blum, the Socialist Premier, proclaimed before the French Assembly, "We have been obliged to deal with violence. I declare that the men who are fighting out there, the French of Indochina, the friendly populations, may count unreservedly on the vigilance and resolution of the government. It was our common task to try everything to spare the blood of our children – and also the blood that is not ours, but which is blood all the same, that of a people whose right to political liberty we recognized ten months ago, and who should keep place in the union of peoples federated around France." Hammer, *The Struggle for Indochina,* 191.

44. In February 1947, the French located the Viet Minh leadership in a canyon near Ha Dong. The French could have captured Ho and his colleagues by sending a parachute unit to the location, but Marius Moutet, Minister for Overseas Territories, forbade such an operation on the grounds that it would be dishonorable. Philippe Devillers and Jean Lacouture, *End of a War: Indochina, 1954,* trans. by Alexander Lieven and Adam Roberts (New York: Frederick A. Praeger, 1969), 13.

45. Mark Bradley, *Imagining Vietnam and America: The Making of Postcolonial Vietnam, 1919–1950* (Chapel Hill: University of North Carolina Press, 2000), 176. See also Nguyen Vu Tang, "Coping with the United States," in Peter Lowe, ed., *The Vietnam War* (New York: St. Martin's Press, 1998), 33.

46. Ho Chi Minh, *Selected Works,* vol. 3, 184. On another occasion, Ho declared, "We are deeply impressed and most grateful for the Chinese people's lofty spirit of internationalism and their friendship with the Vietnamese people." Hoang Van Hoan, *A Drop in the Ocean,* 293.

47. Duiker, *Ho Chi Minh,* 415–6.

48. Ibid., 422; Jian, *Mao's China,* 121–2.

49. Zhai, *China and the Vietnam Wars,* 18–21; Jian, *Mao's China,* 124–37; Military History Institute of Vietnam, *Lich Su Quan Doi Nhan Dan Viet Nam,* Tap 1, (Hanoi: People's Army Publishing House, 1994), 291.

50. Ho Chi Minh, *On Revolution,* 208.

51. Bui Tin, *Following Ho Chi Minh,* 15–6, 29. Bui Tin also said that while the unsophisticated peasant masses readily accepted the Communist propaganda line that Ho Chi Minh was leading a nationalist struggle, the Vietnamese elites both inside and outside the Communist movement understood that the Communists waged the struggle under the guidance of China and the Soviet Union "to protect the whole socialist camp" from "U.S.-led 'imperialist aggression'." Bui Tin, *From Enemy to Friend: A North Vietnamese Perspective on the War,* trans. by Nguyen Ngoc Bich (Annapolis: Naval Institute Press, 2002), 4–9.

52. Bui Tin, *Following Ho Chi Minh,* 29.

53. This policy received its most famous articulation in the document NSC-68. "Any substantial further extension of the area under the domination of the Kremlin would raise the possibility that no coalition adequate to confront the Kremlin with greater strength could be assembled," NSC-68 stated.

"A defeat of free institutions anywhere is a defeat everywhere." NSC-68, 14 April 1950, *FRUS*, 1950, vol. 1, 235–92. Truman was at first reluctant to embrace NSC-68, but events – especially the Korean War – led him to accept its main tenets by the middle of 1950. The extent to which NSC-68 influenced Truman in the period from March to May 1950, when he made the decisions that led to the funding of the war in Indochina, is unclear. On Truman's decisions during those months, see Lawrence, *Assuming the Burden*, 267–75; Duiker, *U.S. Containment Policy and the Conflict in Indochina*, 87–98. To implement the expanded containment strategy spelled out in NSC-68, Truman was to authorize huge increases in U.S. military spending and military aid. On the subject of foreign policy under the Truman administration, see Michael J. Hogan, *A Cross of Iron: Harry S. Truman and the Origins of the National Security State, 1945–1954* (New York: Cambridge University Press, 1998); David G. McCullough, *Truman* (New York: Simon & Schuster, 1992); John Lewis Gaddis, *The Long Peace: Inquiries into the History of the Cold War* (New York: Oxford University Press, 1987); John Lewis Gaddis, *We Now Know: Rethinking Cold War History* (New York: Oxford University Press, 1997); Allan R. Millett, *The War for Korea, 1945–1950: A House Burning* (Lawrence, KS: University Press of Kansas, 2005).

54. Although the term "domino" would not become associated with this concept until Eisenhower used the term in public during his Presidency, the "domino theory" espoused by the Eisenhower administration and subsequent administrations originated with the Truman administration. A National Security Council document of February 27, 1950, stated, "The neighboring countries of Thailand and Burma could be expected to fall under Communist domination if Indochina were controlled by a Communist-dominated government. The balance of Southeast Asia would then be in grave hazard." NSC 64, 27 February 1950, *FRUS*, 1950, vol. 6, 745–7.

55. The most recent and detailed example of such caricaturing is Porter, *Perils of Dominance*.

56. The following histories contend that the Truman administration viewed the Communist world as an unbreakable monolith: Kahin, *Intervention*, 29; Karnow, *Vietnam*, 14, 190; Mann, *A Grand Delusion*, 69; Moss, *Vietnam*, 44; James S. Olson and Randy Roberts, *Where the Domino Fell: America in Vietnam, 1945–1990* (New York: St. Martin's Press, 1991), 28; Patti, *Why Viet Nam?*, 385; Record, *The Wrong War*, 15–16; Sheehan, *A Bright Shining Lie*, 169; VanDeMark, *Into the Quagmire*, 5; Young, *Vietnam Wars*, 267.

57. Gaddis, *The Long Peace*; Gaddis, *We Now Know*.

58. King C. Chen, *Vietnam and China, 1938–1954* (Princeton: Princeton University Press, 1969), 231.

59. On Sino-Soviet relations during this period, see Jian, *Mao's China*; Lüthi, "The Sino-Soviet Split, 1956–1966."

60. Of the 150,000 foreign troops, 70,000 were French nationals. Bernard Magnillat, "Notre guerre d'Indochine: 2/Le duel (1951–1955)," *Historia*, hors série 25 (1972), 42–3.

61. Jian, *Mao's China*, 130.

62. The circumstances at this fateful moment have been widely misunderstood. At the time and since, many Westerners believed that by early 1954 the Viet Minh had grown into a colossus that was about to take the inevitable last step to victory. The Communists did their best to reinforce this impression through propaganda. For histories that have attributed overwhelming strength to the Viet Minh in 1954, see Buzzanco, *Vietnam and the Transformation of American Life*, 45–47; Herring, *America's Longest War*, 33; Jacobs, *America's Miracle Man in Vietnam*, 47; Kahin, *Intervention*, 44–45; Khong, *Analogies At War*, 74; Lomperis, *From People's War to People's Rule*, 95; Mann, *A Grand Delusion*, 130.

63. Janos Radvanyi, *Delusion and Reality: Gambits, Hoaxes, & Diplomatic One-Upmanship in Vietnam* (South Bend: Gateway, 1978), 8. See also Nikita S. Khrushchev, *Khrushchev Remembers*, trans. by Strobe Talbott (Boston: Little, Brown and Co., 1970), 482; Shaplen, *Lost Revolution*, 113. At the time of the release of Khrushchev's memoirs, rumors flew that they were not authentic. In 1990, however, Khrushchev's son Sergei confirmed, in great detail, that the memoirs were truly those of his father. Sergei Khrushchev, *Khrushchev on Khrushchev* (Boston: Little Brown and Company, 1990).

64. Bui Tin, *Following Ho Chi Minh*, 21; Le Duan, *Letters to the South* (Hanoi: Foreign Languages Publishing House, 1986), 38; Gaiduk, *Confronting Vietnam*, 33.

65. Chen, *Vietnam and China*, 276; Nguyen Van Phap et al., *Lich Su Quan Chung Phong Khong*, Tap I (Hanoi: People's Army Publishing House, 1991), 30–34.

66. *Tap Chi Lich Su Quan Su*, July–August 1997, 58. Chinese advisers would play a prominent role throughout the battle; Ho Chi Minh informed Giap that military activities at Dien Bien Phu did not require the approval of the top Vietnamese Communist leader but did require the approval of the

Chinese advisers. Vo Nguyen Giap with Huu Mai, *Dien Bien Phu: Diem Hen Lich Su* (Hanoi: People's Army Publishing House, 2001), 63.

67. Gaiduk, *Confronting Vietnam*, 23; Khrushchev, *Khrushchev Remembers*, 482.

68. For Eisenhower's national security policies, see Robert R. Bowie and Richard H. Immerman, *Waging Peace: How Eisenhower Shaped an Enduring Cold War Strategy* (New York: Oxford University Press, 1998); Stephen Ambrose, *Eisenhower: Soldier and President* (New York: Simon & Schuster, 1990); Gaddis, *We Now Know*.

69. NSC meeting notes, 8 January 1954, *FRUS*, 1952–1954, vol. 13, 947–54. At a press conference on February 10, the President told reporters, "No one could be more bitterly opposed to ever getting the United States involved in a hot war in that region than I am; consequently, every move that I authorize is calculated, so far as humans can do it, to make certain that that does not happen." *Public Papers of the Presidents of the United States: Dwight D. Eisenhower, 1954*, 250.

70. Memorandum for the File of the Secretary of State, 5 April 1954, *FRUS*, 1952–1954, vol. 13, 1224–5. See also memcon, Dulles with Eisenhower, 3 April 1954, DDEL, Dulles Papers, Telephone Calls Series, box 10.

71. Numerous histories have likewise contended that China and the Soviet Union compelled the Vietnamese Communists to settle for less than they had wanted or deserved at Geneva. Anderson, *Trapped By Success*, 44–5; Arnold, *The First Domino*, 214; Bradley, *Imagining Vietnam and America*, 183; Buzzanco, *Vietnam and the Transformation of American Life*, 53–5; Duiker, *The Sacred War*, 90–1; Hammes, *The Sling and the Stone*, 61; Herring, *America's Longest War*, 48–9; Hess, *Vietnam and the United States*, 47–9; Hunt, *Lyndon Johnson's War*, 32–3; Anthony James Joes, *The War for South Viet Nam, 1954–1975*, rev. ed. (Westport: Praeger, 2001), 31–2; Karnow, *Vietnam*, 217–18; Khong, *Analogies At War*, 78–9; Lind, *Vietnam, The Necessary War*, 10; Moss, *Vietnam*, 59; Olson and Roberts, *Where the Domino Fell*, 47–8; Record, *The Wrong War*, 13–14; Turley, *The Second Indochina War*, 5; Young, *The Vietnam Wars*, 38–41.

72. Gaiduk, *Confronting Vietnam*, 33–8; Zhai, *China and the Vietnam Wars*, 43–53; Cutler, "Outline of General Smith's Remarks," 23 June 1954, DDEL, OSANSA, NSC, Briefing Notes, Box 11; Nguyen Quy, ed., *Van Kien Dang*, Tap 20, 1959 (Hanoi: Nha Xuat Ban Chinh Tri Quoc Gia, 2002), 59; Hoang Van Hoan, *A Drop in the Ocean*, 285; *Beijing Review*, December 7, 1979; Khrushchev, *Khrushchev Remembers*, 482–3; Saigon to State, 27 October 1954, *FRUS*, 1952–1954, vol. 13, 2190–1; Hammer, *The Struggle for Indochina*, 333–5.

73. Wesley Fishel, ed., *Vietnam: Anatomy of a Conflict* (Ithaca: F. E. Peacock, 1968), 124.

74. NSC meeting notes, 15 July 1954, *FRUS*, 1952–1954, vol. 13, 1835.

75. U.S. Delegation to State, 21 July 1954, *FRUS*, 1952–1954, vol. 16, 1500–1501.

76. *Public Papers of the Presidents of the United States: Dwight D. Eisenhower, 1954*, 642.

2. Two Vietnams: July 1954–December 1955

1. Dulles to Eisenhower, 21 May 1954, DDEL, Whitman File, Dulles-Herter Series, box 2; Cutler, "Outline of General Smith's Remarks," 23 June 1954, DDEL, OSANSA, NSC, Briefing Notes, Box 11.

2. *United States Treaties and Other International Agreements*, vol. 6, part 1 (Washington, DC: U.S. Government Printing Office, 1956), 81–92. The signatories agreed that if any protected country came under attack, each signatory would "act to meet the common danger in accordance with its constitutional processes." This language, which watered down the treaty considerably, was the work of Dulles and Eisenhower. They knew that the U.S. Senate would not ratify a treaty mandating war with China under a particular set of conditions, as it would want to reserve its right to declare war.

3. Andrew H. Berding, *Dulles on Diplomacy* (Princeton: Princeton University Press, 1965), 63.

4. Bao Dai, *Le Dragon D'Annam* (Paris: Plon, 1980), 328–9. On Diem's accession to power, see also Edward Miller, "Vision, Power, and Agency: The Ascent of Ngo Dinh Diem, 1945–1954," *Journal of Southeast Asian Studies*, vol. 35, issue 3 (October 2004), 433–58.

5. USARMA Saigon to Deptar, 23 October 1954, NA II, RG 59, C0014, reel 25; Purnell to Young, 7 October 1954, NA II, RG 59, Lot Files, Entry U052.

6. *USVNR*, book 11, 37.

7. Higgins, *Our Vietnam Nightmare*, 195.

8. Cao The Dung and Luong Minh Khai, *Lam The Nao De Giet Mot Tong Thong* (San Jose, CA: Dong Phuong Cultural Foundation, 1988), 196. After her husband's death, Madame Nhu herself said that Nhu had viewed her as a "babe in the woods," and that when he spoke to her he simply said, "You just keep quiet – don't say anything." PBS, *Vietnam: A Television History: America's Mandarin (1954–1963)* (Boston: WGBH, 1983).

9. Vietnamese of many political stripes viewed Confucianism as a critical part of Vietnamese tradition, but Confucianism was considerably less influential in pre-colonial Vietnam than was widely believed. See K. W. Taylor, "Vietnamese Confucian Narratives," and Shawn McHale "Mapping a Vietnamese Confucian Past and Its Transition to Modernity," in Benjamin A. Elman et al., eds., *Rethinking Confucianism: Past and Present in China, Japan, Korea, and Vietnam* (Los Angeles: UCLA Asian Pacific Monograph Series, 2002), 337–69, 397–430.

10. Catton, *Diem's Final Failure*, 37.

11. Diem explained, "All the underdeveloped countries are under authoritarian or dictatorial regimes, which is a historical and general phenomenon having nothing to do with individuals or government and which corresponds to a historical need for centralization of power to wipe out the age-old poverty and humiliation of the people.... The governments which have tried to establish Western-style democracy from the top down in an underdeveloped country have all been liquidated by military coups d'état." *U.S. News and World Report*, February 18, 1963.

12. For histories containing this criticism, see Bergerud, *The Dynamics of Defeat*; Brigham, *ARVN*; Catton, *Diem's Final Failure*; Karnow, *Vietnam*; Kolko, *Anatomy of a War*; Rust, *Kennedy in Vietnam*; Spector, *Advice and Support*.

13. The contention that the United States was doomed by a lack of Vietnam experts appeared, most famously, in McNamara, *In Retrospect*, 32–3, 322. From the mid-1950s through 1963, Americans in Vietnam who demonstrated a strong understanding of Vietnamese culture and politics included General Samuel T. Williams, Kenneth T. Young, Sterling Cottrell, William Colby, Theodore Heavner, Fredrick E. Nolting, General Paul Harkins, and John H. Richardson.

14. Edward Lansdale Oral History Interview I, LBJL.

15. Cecil B. Currey, *Edward Lansdale: The Unquiet American* (Boston: Houghton Mifflin, 1988), 45.

16. Useful sources on the roles of Lansdale and Magsaysay in fighting the Huk rebellion include Currey, *Edward Lansdale*; Lawrence Greenberg, *The Hukbalahap Insurrection: A Case Study of a Successful Anti-Insurgency Operation in the Philippines 1946–1955* (Washington, DC: United States Army Center of Military History, 1995); Benedict J. Kerkvliet, *The Huk Rebellion: A Study of Peasant Revolt in the Philippines* (Lanham: Rowman & Littlefield Publishers, 2002). The precise extent of Lansdale's influence remains controversial, but the evidence clearly shows that Magsaysay followed Lansdale's advice on many occasions.

17. *The Pentagon Papers: The Defense Department History of United States Decisionmaking on Vietnam*, Senator Gravel edition, vol. 1 (Boston: Beacon Press, 1971–1972), 578–9; Fall, *The Two Viet-Nams*, 153–4.

18. Gibbons, *The U.S. Government and the Vietnam War*, vol. 1, 265.

19. On Communist obstruction and the anti-Communist sentiments that caused great numbers of individuals to flee, see Saigon to State, 5 August 1954, *FRUS*, 1952–1954, vol. 13, 1921–2; Hammer, *The Struggle for Indochina*, 345; Richard W. Lindholm, ed., *Viet-Nam: The First Five Years* (East Lansing: Michigan State University Press, 1959), 58; Douglas A. Ross, *In the Interests of Peace: Canada and Vietnam, 1954–1973* (Toronto: University of Toronto Press, 1984); Shaplen, *The Lost Revolution*, 114–5.

20. Lindholm, ed., *Viet-Nam*, 54.

21. Greene would later deny that Lansdale had served as the model for Pyle, but the similarities between Lansdale and Pyle make Greene's explanation difficult to believe.

22. On one occasion, after receiving information that Frenchmen were blowing up American-owned cars, Lansdale approached a French colonel whom he believed to be the head perpetrator. "Don't forget that you are ten thousand miles from metropolitan France," Lansdale warned the colonel. "Whatever happens to you from now on is on your own heads." That night, grenades exploded outside the quarters of Frenchmen suspected of complicity in the car bombings. The French colonel stomped into

the American embassy the next morning to demand Lansdale's removal, one of several instances where the French asked to have him ousted. The Americans refused. Zalin Grant, *Facing the Phoenix* (New York: W.W. Norton, 1991), 125–6. Rufus Phillips, who was working for Lansdale at that time, confirmed most aspects of this account. Phillips, interview with author.

23. Nguyen Van Chau, *Ngo Dinh Diem va No Luc Hoa Binh Dang Do* (Los Alamitos, CA: Xuan Thu Publishers, 1989), 96. See also Ton That Dinh, *20 Nam Binh Nghiep* (San Jose: Chanh Dao, 1998), 154; Hoang Lac and Ha Mai Viet, *Why America Lost the Vietnam War* (Sugarland, TX: Hoang Lac and Ha Mai Viet, 1996), 135, 152; Saigon to State, 19 December 1961, NA II, RG 59, C0092, reel 5.

24. The American Army attaché in Saigon reported that "Hinh and Vietnamese National Army, primarily preoccupied with politicking, have done little or nothing to retrain, reorganize, and reforge defeated and demoralized men into effective military force." USARMA Saigon to Deptar, 23 October 1954, NA II, RG 59, C0014, reel 25.

25. Dulles to State, 8 September 1954, *FRUS*, 1952–1954, vol. 13, 2012–3.

26. Saigon to State, 26 August 1954, *FRUS*, 1952–1954, vol. 13, 1984–5. The Cao Dai Pope himself was in attendance, as were General Soai and the political counselor of the Binh Xuyen.

27. Saigon to State, 27 August 1954, *FRUS*, 1952–1954, vol. 13, 1990–1.

28. Saigon to State, 16 September 1954, *FRUS*, 1952–1954, vol. 13, 2030–1.

29. USARMA Saigon to Deptar, 23 October 1954, NA II, RG 59, Lot Files, Southeast Asia, Entry 1200, box 7.

30. Saigon to State, 25 September 1954, *FRUS*, 1952–1954, vol. 13, 2059–61.

31. NSC meeting notes; 22 October 1954, *FRUS*, 1952–1954, vol. 13, 2153–8.

32. Joseph Lawton Collins, *Lightning Joe: An Autobiography* (Baton Rouge: Louisiana State University Press, 1979), 379.

33. Saigon to State, 15 November 1954, *FRUS*, 1952–1954, vol. 13, 2250–6.

34. Collins to Dulles, 20 January 1955, DDRS, 1978, 295A.

35. Miller, "Grand Designs," 166–7.

36. Kidder to State, 4 March 1955, *FRUS*, 1955–1957, vol. 1, 53; Saigon to State, 8 March 1955, NA II, RG 59, C0008, reel 2.

37. Dulles to Eisenhower, 1 March 1955, DDRS, Document number CK3100182677.

38. Collins to State, 22 March 1955, *FRUS*, 1955–1957, vol. 1, 69.

39. At one point in the conversation, when Diem said that the Binh Xuyen would have surrendered quickly, Collins snapped, "No one I have consulted agrees with your analysis." Collins to State, 30 March 1955, *FRUS*, 1955–1957, vol. 1, 80.

40. Collins to State, 30 March 1955, *FRUS*, 1955–1957, vol. 1, 82; Collins to State, 31 March 1955, *FRUS*, 1955–1957, vol. 1, 85; Collins to Dulles, 19 April 1955, *FRUS*, 1955–1957, vol. 1, 127.

41. Collins to State, 31 March 1955, *FRUS*, 1955–1957, vol. 1, 84; Wisner to Robinson, "Reply by General Collins to Your Cable of 1 April," n. d., *FRUS*, 1955–1957, vol. 1, 99.

42. Dulles to Collins, 20 April 1955, DDRS, Document Number CK3100195454; Telcon, 4 April 1955, *FRUS*, 1955–1957, vol. 1, 96n.

43. Kidder to State, 30 April 1955, *FRUS*, 1955–1957, vol. 1, 159.

44. For Collins' discussions in Washington, see Sebald to Dulles, 23 April 1955, *FRUS*, 1955–1957, vol. 1, 132; Davis to Hensel, 25 April 1955, *FRUS*, 1955–1957, vol. 1, 133; Young to Robertson, 30 April 1955, *FRUS*, 1955–1957, vol. 1, 161. The telegrams are State to Paris, 27 April 1955, *FRUS*, 1955–1957, vol. 1, 140; State to Paris, 27 April 1955, *FRUS*, 1955–1957, vol. 1, 141.

45. Saigon to State, 29 April 1955, NA II, RG 59, C0008, reel 3; *Newsweek*, May 9, 1955.

46. *New York Times*, April 30, 1955.

47. Kidder to State, 30 April 1955, *FRUS*, 1955–1957, vol. 1, 159.

48. Upon hearing Kidder's answer, Ely demanded, "How do you know that?" Kidder replied, "General, I know American foreign policy." Kidder, unpublished article, *FRUS*, 1955–1957, vol. 1, 157n.

49. *Time*, May 16, 1955.

50. Dulles to State, 8 May 1955, *FRUS*, 1955–1957, vol. 1, 177; Paris to State, 11 May 1955, *FRUS*, 1955–1957, vol. 1, 184; Dulles to State, 12 May 1955, *FRUS*, 1955–1957, vol. 1, 186.

51. Saigon to State, 29 November 1955, *FRUS*, 1955–1957, vol. 1, 278.

52. Duiker, *Ho Chi Minh*, 462–3.

53. *New York Times*, October 21, 1954, December 31, 1954, and January 5, 1955; Hammer, *The Struggle for Indochina*, 337–41; Turner, *Vietnamese Communism*, 109–46.

54. Gerard Tongas, a French historian and former Communist, ran Hanoi's French high school under the Viet Minh for a time. He observed that "in North Vietnam, a man of reasonable culture, education and learning is one who has been continuously subjected to indoctrination in Marxist-Leninist ideology (or what passes for it), one who no longer thinks for himself but accepts in their entirety as Gospel truth all the concepts systematically inculcated by carefully graded propaganda." Gerard Tongas, "Indoctrination Replaces Education," in P. J. Honey, ed., *North Vietnam Today: Profile of a Communist Satellite* (New York: Frederick A. Praeger, 1962), 93.

55. Gaiduk, *Confronting Vietnam*, 109. To ring in the New Year of 1955, the Communists organized a mass demonstration in a square that they had renamed Red Square in which, surrounded by portraits of Ho, Malenkov, and Mao, the masses denounced Diem and "American imperialism" and praised Ho and his Soviet and Chinese allies on cue from Party cadres. Saigon to State, 4 January 1955, NA II, RG 59, C0008, reel 1.

56. Sebald, "Status of Information on Viet Minh Truce Violations," 1 March 1955, *FRUS*, 1955–1957, vol. 1, 47.

57. Thayer, *War By Other Means*, 45.

58. From 1955 to 1960, the Chinese would provide a total of 1.4 billion yuan in economic aid to North Vietnam, and the Soviets would contribute approximately half that amount. Gaiduk, *Confronting Vietnam*, 90.

59. Le Kinh Lich, ed., *The 30-Year War: 1945–1975*, vol. 2 (Hanoi: The Gioi Publishers, 2001), 13. By interviewing sailors who had participated in the evacuation, two historians from the Polish Navy recently verified that roughly 100,000 people went north by ship. Adrzej Makowski and Krzysztof Kubiak, presentation at Texas Tech University, April 11, 2002.

60. For extensive discussion of Communist concepts of political *dau tranh* (struggle), as well as military *dau tranh*, see Davidson, *Vietnam At War*.

61. *Time*, April 4, 1955.

62. *Time*, January 17 and February 7, 1955. See also Dommen, *The Indochinese Experience of the French and the Americans*, 294; Miller, "Grand Designs," 158–9.

63. Military History Institute of Vietnam, *Victory in Vietnam: The Official History of the People's Army of Vietnam, 1954–1975*, trans. by Merle L. Pribbenow (Lawrence, KS: University Press of Kansas, 2002), 15–16.

64. Just three days after the signing of the Geneva agreement, Dulles had said, "In view of the population distribution – 13 million in North Vietnam, 9 million in the South – we will have to take the position in 1956 that conditions are not favorable for the free expression of the will of the population." Meeting notes, 24 July 1954, *FRUS*, 1952–1954, vol. 12, part 1, 665–71. Less than one week later, Ambassador Heath commented, "Truly free elections in North Vietnam would require not only neutral international supervision of actual voting but absolute freedom of non-Communist parties to campaign for months preceding elections without restraint or surveillance by Communist authorities. Last will never happen." Saigon to State, 30 July 1954, *FRUS*, 1952–1954, vol. 13, 1892–3.

65. Ha Dang, ed., *Van Kien Dang*, Tap 29, 1968 (Hanoi: Nha Xuat Ban Chinh Tri Quoc Gia, 2004), 3. Immediately after the completion of the Geneva agreement, Pham Van Dong was asked who he thought would win the elections. "You know as well as I do that there won't be any elections," he responded. P. J. Honey, *Communism in North Vietnam: Its Role in the Sino-Soviet Dispute* (Cambridge: M.I.T. Press, 1963), 6. See also Radvanyi, *Delusion and Reality*, 24; Race, *War Comes to Long An: Revolutionary Conflict in a Vietnamese Province* (Berkeley: University of California Press, 1972), 34. The Communists' lack of serious interest in free elections was evident at the time in public pronouncements, starting at the beginning of 1955, that the existing Communist government was the one and only true government of Vietnam and that Diem was a "lackey of American imperialism." On January 18, 1955, the Party newspaper *Nhan Dan* published on its front page the following declaration above the signature Ho Chi Minh: "The DRV now declares to all governments of the world that it is the only official and legal Government of the Vietnamese people and that now the DRV is ready to establish diplomatic relations with any government which respects the DRV as an equal, sovereign power and

respects its territorial integrity, and wishes to live in peace and build a democratic world." Below this statement was a list of nations, including China and the Soviet Union, that had recognized North Vietnam. Gaiduk, *Confronting Vietnam*, 67; Dommen, *The Indochinese Experience of the French and the Americans*, 261.

66. Allan Cole et al., eds., *Conflict in Indo-China and International Repercussions: A Documentary History, 1945–1955* (Ithaca: Cornell University Press, 1956), 226–7; *Major Policy Speeches by President Ngo Dinh Diem* (Saigon: Presidency of the Republic of Vietnam Press Office, 1957), 13.

3. Peaceful Coexistence: 1956–1959

1. "In the countries where capitalism is still strong and has a huge military and police apparatus at its disposal," Khrushchev said, "the reactionary forces will, of course, inevitably offer serious resistance. There the transition to socialism will be attended by a sharp class, revolutionary struggle." Geoffrey F. Hudson et al., *The Sino-Soviet Dispute* (New York: Frederick A. Praeger, 1961), 42–6.

2. Ho Chi Minh, *Selected Works*, vol. 4, 153–6; *USVNR*, book 2, IV.A.5, tab 3, 46–7.

3. The North Vietnamese informed the Soviets of some of the proceedings of the ninth plenum, but did not divulge Ho's aforementioned words. Gaiduk, *Confronting Vietnam*, 92–4. Hanoi continued to hide its reunification plans from the Soviets from 1957 to 1959. Zhai, *China and the Vietnam Wars*, 80.

4. Jian, *Mao's China*, 65; Gaiduk, *Confronting Vietnam*, 100, 106; Lüthi, "The Sino-Soviet Split, 1956–1966," 82ff.

5. Guan, *Vietnamese Communists' Relations with China*, 19–20.

6. SWB/FE/610/40. On August 18, 1956, Ho wrote a letter to peasants and cadres stating, "A number of our cadres have not thoroughly grasped the land-reform policy or correctly followed the mass line.... The status of those who have been wrongly classified as landlords or as rich peasants should be reviewed. Party membership, rights, and honor should be restituted to Party members, cadres, and others who have been wrongly convicted." Ho Chi Minh, *On Revolution*, 304–6.

7. Saigon to State, 21 November 1973, NA II, RG 59, Central Files, 1970–1973, box 2801. Bernard Fall, who was conducting research in Vietnam during this period, put the total number killed at 50,000. Fall, *The Two Viet-Nams*, 155–6. In a more recent study, Edwin Moïse concluded that the death toll lay between 3,000 and 15,000 and was probably close to 5,000. Moïse contended that some of Fall's evidence was unreliable, but his alternative approach of extrapolating from incomplete data provided by the Communists rested on the dubious assumption that the Communists would show accurate figures to outsiders. Edwin Moïse, *Land Reform in China and North Vietnam: Consolidating the Revolution at the Village Level* (Chapel Hill: University of North Carolina Press, 1983), 217–22.

8. Thayer, *War By Other Means*, 96.

9. Bernard Fall, "Power and Pressure Groups in North Vietnam," in Honey, ed., *North Vietnam Today*, 68. See also Fall, *The Two Viet-Nams*, 188–90; Ninh, *A World Transformed*.

10. SWB/FE/616/25.

11. SWB/FE/615/25.

12. According to a North Vietnamese news broadcast, "the reactionary elements rushed on the soldiers to beat them, and the soldiers were forced to fight back. As a result, a number of persons were killed or wounded." SWB/FE/616/24.

13. An official Communist history recounted that in October 1956, "Vietnamese reactionary organizations that had worked before in Laos again reared their ugly heads and began operations." A man named Gia Le organized a group of "bandits" in Laos, and "our border areas from Thanh Hoa to Quang Binh were under continuous attack by this group." Vo Van Minh, *Quan Khu 4: Lich Su Khang Chien Chong My Cuu Nuoc (1954–1975)* (Hanoi: People's Army Publishing House, 1994), 14.

14. Nguyen Hung Linh and Hoang Mac, *Luc Luong Chong Phan Dong: Lich Su Bien Nien (1954–1975)* (Hanoi: Public Security Publishing House, 1997), 105–13.

15. Fall, *The Two Viet-Nams*, 139.

16. Turner, *Vietnamese Communism*, 188.

17. William Kaye, "A Bowl of Rice Divided: The Economy of North Vietnam," in Honey, ed., *North Vietnam Today*, 105–13; Bui Tin, *Following Ho Chi Minh*, 38.

18. One Communist historian observed that in late 1955, "Many of our cadre and Party members were ordered to join the ranks of the dissident Hoa Hao Army factions opposing Diem." Forty-seven Communist Party members infiltrated the ranks of a new rebel force created by General Soai. Nguyen Viet Ta et al., *Mien Dong Nam Bo Khang Chien (1945–1975)*, Tap II (Hanoi: Nha Xuat Ban Quan Doi Nhan Dan, 1993), 36, 47.

19. An official Communist history boasted, "We succeeded in exploiting the enemy's legal organizations, such as worker and schoolboy unions, women's associations, etc. Through these organizations we successfully guided the people to struggle." Thayer, *War By Other Means*, 70.

20. *The Pentagon Papers*, vol. 1, 255.

21. *Hearings Before the Subcommittee on the Far East and the Pacific of the House Committee on Foreign Affairs*, 86th Cong., 1st sess., July 27, August 3, 11, 14, 1959, 4.

22. *Hearings Before the Subcommittee on the Far East and the Pacific of the House Committee on Foreign Affairs*, 86th Cong., 1st sess., July 27, August 3, 11, 14, 1959, 23–4; Thayer, *War By Other Means*, 115; *Life*, May 13, 1957; Hue to State, 16 June 1960, NA II, RG 59, C0092, reel 1.

23. The Communist complaint is in Thayer, *War By Other Means*, 117. The Canadian component of the International Control Commission observed that the violence was substantially worse in the North than in the South. Ross, *In the Interests of Peace*, 121–2.

24. Numerous historians have echoed this charge. Anderson, *Trapped By Success*, 166; Arnold, *The First Domino*, 330; Bergerud, *The Dynamics of Defeat*, 14; Hess, *Vietnam and the United States*, 61; Kahin, *Intervention*, 96–98; Kaiser, *American Tragedy*, 61; Karnow, *Vietnam*, 242–3; Khong, *Analogies At War*, 239; Kolko, *Anatomy of a War*, 88–90; Langguth, *Our Vietnam*, 99–100; Moss, *Vietnam*, 88; Porter, *Perils of Dominance*, 90.

25. Vien Nghien Cuu Chu Nghia Mac Lenin Va Tu Tuong Ho Chi Minh, *Lich Su Dang Cong San Viet Nam, Tap II (1954–1975)* (Hanoi: Nha Xuat Ban Chinh Tri Quoc Gia, 1995), 89.

26. Government mistreatment of the population did ultimately assist the Communists in obtaining support from the peasants, as shall be seen in chapter four. Most of the government actions in question, however, were not the result of the Denounce the Communists campaigns but of simple disrespect for the welfare of the people. Witnesses seldom attributed abusive actions specifically to the Denounce the Communists campaigns or generally to the hunt for Communists.

27. At the end of 1956, the *Economist* noted that the apathy one had found on Vietnamese faces in the Bao Dai era was gone: "The ministers and civil servants of the new Vietnam do not merely work hard – fourteen to sixteen hours a day is common – but also with will, enthusiasm and brimming confidence." *Economist*, December 22, 1956.

28. William Henderson, "South Viet Nam Finds Itself," *Foreign Affairs*, January 1957, 283–94.

29. Saigon to State, 22 February 1957, NA II, RG 59, C0008, reel 14; Saigon to State, 6 March 1957, NA II, RG 59, C0008, reel 14; *Lich Su Bo Doi Dac Cong*, Tap I (Hanoi: People's Army Publishing House, 1987), 85; Ho Chi Minh National Political Studies Institute, *Lich Su Bien Nien Xu Uy Nam Bo Va Trung Uong Cuc Mien Nam (1954–1975)* (Hanoi: Nha Xuat Ban Chinh Tri Quoc Gia, 2002), 134.

30. The State Department told the International Control Commission that the new personnel were coming solely to salvage equipment abandoned by the French, and that they would leave within one year. The new contingent of Americans was responsible for salvage activities, but from the beginning a large fraction of its 350 members was involved in training the South Vietnamese in logistics, an area in which help was badly needed. At first the commission went along, as they similarly had allowed Chinese personnel into North Vietnam on a temporary basis, but eventually the Poles and the Indians started complaining. In the end, the Indians consented to the increase, which, together with Canada's support, overcame the Polish opposition. The new ceiling became 692. See Evans to O'Donnell, 16 June 1959, *FRUS*, 1958–1960, vol. 1, 80.

31. Harold J. Meyer, *Hanging Sam: A Military Biography of General Samuel T. Williams from Pancho Villa to Vietnam* (Denton, TX: University of North Texas Press, 1990).

32. "The Vietnamese do not like to be threatened, talked down to, nor pushed around," Williams once observed. "Furthermore it is not necessary. They can be influenced to do as we wish by showing sympathetic understanding of their particular problems, close friendly liaison and suggestions or

recommendations made, sometimes many times over, in a straightforward, man-to-man way." Williams to Stump, 16 November 1957, *FRUS, 1955–1957*, vol. 1, 405. Durbrow required Williams to give him a written report of all his conversations with Diem, and also compelled Williams to clear with him all messages sent to CINCPAC, the officer above Williams in the military chain of command. Williams viewed the former as "idiotic" and the latter as "an unwarranted interference between me and my immediate military superior." Williams to Lansdale, 10 December 1961, HIA, Edward G. Lansdale Papers, box 42.

33. Anderson, *Trapped by Success*, 185–6.

34. Spector, *Advice and Support*, 280.

35. For example, Robert B. Asprey, *War in the Shadows: The Guerrilla in History*, rev. ed. (New York: William Morrow, 1994), 611–12; Buzzanco, *Masters of War*, 55–79; Andrew F. Krepinevich, Jr., *The Army and Vietnam* (Baltimore: Johns Hopkins University Press, 1986), 22–26; Kaiser, *American Tragedy*, 62–64; Mann, *A Grand Delusion*, 196–7.

36. Memcon, 28 December 1955, *FRUS, 1955–1957*, vol. 1, 284; Williams to Diem, 28 December 1955, *FRUS, 1955–1957*, vol. 1, 285.

37. Conventional organization did not prevent South Vietnamese forces from operating in small units and conducting counter-guerrilla operations. On many occasions during the war, U.S. and South Vietnamese regulars performed well in such a capacity. The North Vietnamese Army was organized along the lines of a conventional force, and it did not suffer from an inability to operate in small units or in guerrilla fashion.

38. Williams to Diem, 28 December 1955, *FRUS, 1955–1957*, vol. 1, 285; memcon, 5 March 1958, HIA, Samuel T. Williams Papers, box 13.

39. Diem once explained to a group of Americans that during the Franco-Viet Minh war, "a system of auto-defense units in Vietnam had been supported by the French administration. Since they were made up of local personnel who knew the community in which they lived, they had been, in fact, a more effective anti-Communist instrument than the army itself." Saigon to State, 17 November 1955, *FRUS, 1955–1957*, vol. 1, 276.

40. On the Michigan State University Group and the Civil Guard controversy, see Ernst, *Forging a Fateful Alliance*; Spector, *Advice and Support*.

41. The most detailed and influential critique of South Vietnamese and American employment of conventional military forces is Krepinevich, *The Army and Vietnam*. Others include Asprey, *War in the Shadows*; Baritz, *Backfire*; Douglas Blaufarb, *The Counterinsurgency Era: U.S. Doctrine and Performance, 1950 to the Present* (New York: Free Press, 1977); Buzzanco, *Masters of War*; Larry E. Cable, *Conflict of Myths: The Development of American Counterinsurgency Doctrine and the Vietnam War* (New York: New York University Press, 1986); Cincinnatus, *Self-Destruction: The Disintegration and Decay of the United States Army During the Vietnam Era* (New York: W. W. Norton, 1981); William R. Corson, *The Betrayal* (New York: W. W. Norton, 1968); James William Gibson, *The Perfect War: Technowar in Vietnam* (Boston: Atlantic Monthly Press, 1986); Hammes, *The Sling and the Stone*; Herring, *LBJ and Vietnam*; Kaiser, *American Tragedy*; Robert Komer, *Bureaucracy At War: U.S. Performance in the Vietnam Conflict* (Boulder: Westview Press, 1986); Lind, *Vietnam, The Necessary War*; Moss, *Vietnam*; Nagl, *Counterinsurgency Lessons from Malaya and Vietnam*; Olson and Roberts, *Where the Domino Fell*; Record, *The Wrong War*; D. Michael Shafer, *Deadly Paradigms: The Failure of U.S. Counterinsurgency Policy* (Princeton: Princeton University Press, 1988); Vandiver, *Shadows of Vietnam*. Among the best expositions of traditional counterinsurgency theory are David Galula, *Counterinsurgency Warfare: Theory and Practice* (New York: Frederick A. Praeger, 1964); John McCuen, *The Art of Counter-Revolutionary War: The Strategy of Counter-Insurgency* (Harrisburg: Stackpole Books, 1966); Blaufarb, *The Counter-Insurgency Era*; Nathan Leites and Charles Wolf, Jr., *Rebellion and Authority: An Analytic Essay on Insurgent Conflicts* (Chicago: Markham Publishing, 1970).

42. For the early development of the party by Nhu, see Edward Miller, "Vision, Power, and Agency: The Ascent of Ngo Dinh Diem, 1945–1954," *Journal of Southeast Asian Studies*, vol. 35, issue 3 (October 2004), 433–58.

43. Memcon, 1 August 1957, *FRUS, 1955–1957*, vol. 1, 392; memcon, 13 December 1957, HIA, Samuel T. Williams Papers, box 13.

44. In early 1956, Lansdale and Rufus Phillips sought funding to train new civic action cadres and administrators, but Ambassador Reinhardt and the U.S. director of development programs, Leland Barrows, turned down the request. Reinhardt and Barrows preferred to rely on the existing civil administrators, and they wanted to spend money on industrial and infrastructure projects. Neese and O'Donnell, eds., *Prelude to Tragedy*, 22–3.

45. Thayer, *War By Other Means*, 119; Robert G. Scigliano, *South Vietnam: Nation Under Stress* (Boston: Houghton Mifflin, 1963), 121; Wolf I. Ladejinsky, "Agrarian Reform in the Republic of Vietnam," in Wesley Fishel, ed., *Problems of Freedom: South Vietnam Since Independence* (New York: Free Press of Glencoe, 1961), 155. When Diem took office, the Vietnamese peasants faced some of the highest rental rates in Asia, paying between one-third and one-half of their crop to their landlord. The rates went down in 1955, however, when Diem passed a law limiting the rent to one-quarter of the crop.

46. Philip E. Catton, "Parallel Agendas: The Ngo Dinh Diem Regime, the United States and the Strategic Hamlet Program, 1961–1963," (Ph.D. diss., Ohio University, 1998), 76.

47. William Colby Oral History Interview I, LBJL.

48. VCD 257, September 1962, TTU, Pike Collection, Unit 1, box 1.

49. Roy L. Prosterman, "Land Reform in Vietnam," *Current History*, vol. 57, no. 340 (December 1969), 327–32.

50. Memcon, 30 January 1958, *FRUS*, 1958–1960, vol. 1, 3. For discussion of the investment environment, see Lloyd D. Musolf, "Public Enterprise and Development Perspectives in South Vietnam," *Asian Survey*, 3:8 (August 1963), 357–71; John Dorsey, "South Vietnam in Perspective," *Far Eastern Survey*, December 1958.

51. The U.S. National Security Council pronounced on one occasion that Diem's government "is the least corrupt of all governments in Southeast Asia." Burke, NSC meeting notes, 28 April 1961, *FRUS*, 1961-1963, vol. 1, 36. One ARVN general recalled that there was much less corruption during Diem's rule than afterwards because "President Diem was a moral person, who carefully picked individuals for important positions and promotions. President Diem and his staff paid a lot of attention to the honorable conduct and morality of the officer corps." Triet Minh Nguyen, "Army of the Republic of Vietnam, 1954-1963: At War and In Politics" (master's thesis, University of Calgary, 2005), 106. See also Wesley R. Fishel, "Problems of Democratic Growth in Free Vietnam," in Fishel, ed., *Problems of Freedom*, 24-5; Kent, "President Diem," 26 January 1962, *FRUS*, 1961-1963, vol. 2, 35.

52. Scigliano, *South Vietnam*, 107; Fall, *The Two Viet-Nams*, 296.

53. Pike, *Viet Cong: The Organization and Techniques of the National Liberation Front of South Vietnam* (Cambridge: M.I.T. Press, 1966), 59.

54. *Congressional Record*, vol. 103, 6700.

55. The assembly's membership included a substantial number of purportedly independent persons, but most of these individuals were really Diem supporters. Saigon to State, 17 March 1956, NA II, RG 59, C0008, reel 7.

56. Saigon to State, 7 December 1959, *FRUS*, 1958–1960, vol. 1, 97.

57. *New York Times*, May 9, 1957.

58. *Congressional Record*, vol. 103, 6764.

59. Ibid., 6759.

60. *New York Times*, May 10, 1957.

61. *Life*, May 13, 1957. John Osborne, who wrote the article, noted that although Diem was running a "police state," his government "must be viewed in the context of postwar Asia. The simple truth is that all of the new governments produced by liberated Asian nationalism since World War II are more or less authoritarian in nature."

62. Memcon, 9 May 1957, *FRUS*, 1955–1957, vol. 1, 375.

63. Memcon, 20 May 1957, *FRUS*, 1955–1957, vol. 1, 386.

64. Guan, *Vietnamese Communists' Relations with China*, 86-7; Le Kinh Lich, ed., *The 30-Year War*, vol. 2, 42.

65. Race, *War Comes to Long An*, 83.

66. Philippe Devillers, "The Struggle for the Unification of Vietnam," in Honey, ed., *North Vietnam Today*, 35–8.

67. Crimp document, undated, TTU, Pike Collection, Unit 1, box 3.

68. "A Party Account of the Situation in the Nam Bo Region of South Vietnam From 1954–1960" (William Duiker kindly provided a copy of this document); "Study of Military Situation in South Vietnam, 1955–1960," April 1974, TTU, Pike Collection, Unit 2, box 1.

69. Tran Van Quang, et al., *Tong Ket Cuoc Khang Chien Chong My Cuu Nuoc: Thang Loi va Bai Hoc* (Hanoi: Nha Xuat Ban Chinh Tri Quoc Gia, 1995), 310. For a description of this period in the central highlands, see Nguyen Van Minh et al., *Luc Luong Vu Trang Nhan Dan Tay Nguyen Trong Khang Chien Chong My Cuu Nuoc* (Hanoi: Nha Xuat Ban Quan Doi Nhan Dan, 1980), 18–19.

70. *New York Times*, July 7, 1959.

71. Williams later said that the Civil Guard's firearms and the Civil Guard units themselves were "in a deplorable condition" in this period. *U.S. News and World Report*, November 9, 1964.

72. Ernst, *Forging A Fateful Alliance*, 80.

73. Spector, *Advice and Support*, 320–1.

74. Diem gave this explanation as to why the people from Annam, the central third of Vietnam, outperformed those in the southern third in defending themselves: "There is security in Central Vietnam because the people there have confidence and the offensive spirit.... The people of the Center lead a hard life. They are tough." Memcon, 3 December 1957, HIA, Samuel T. Williams Papers, box 13.

75. Neese and O'Donnell, eds., *Prelude to Tragedy*, 188–9.

76. Hue to State, 16 June 1960, NA II, RG 59, C0092, reel 1.

77. Nguyen Quy, ed., *Van Kien Dang*, Tap 20, 1959, 57–92; Ho Chi Minh National Political Studies Institute, *Lich Su Bien Nien Xu Uy Nam Bo Va Trung Uong Cuc Mien Nam (1954–1975)*, 168–71; Le Kinh Lich, ed., *The 30-Year War*, vol. 2, 45–6; High-Level Military Institute, *Vietnam: The Anti-U.S. Resistance War for National Salvation, 1954–1975, Military Events* (Arlington, VA: Foreign Broadcast Information Service, 1982), 30.

78. Hoang Van Hoan, *A Drop in the Ocean*, 324; Duiker, *Ho Chi Minh*, 520–1; Guan, *The Vietnam War from the Other Side*, 39–40.

79. Military History Institute of Vietnam, *Victory in Vietnam*, 52.

80. Le Kinh Lich, ed., *Tran Danh Ba Muoi Nam*, vol. 2 (Hanoi: People's Army Publishing House, 1995), 82–7; Military History Institute of Vietnam, *Victory in Vietnam*, 52–3; Tran Van Quang, et al., *Tong Ket Cuoc Khang Chien Chong My Cuu Nuoc*, 224.

81. *The Pentagon Papers*, vol. 1, 336.

82. Thayer, *War By Other Means*, 152, 154.

83. "A Party Account of the Situation in the Nam Bo Region of South Vietnam From 1954–1960."

4. Insurgency: 1960

1. Nguyen Thi Dinh, *No Other Road to Take: Memoirs of Mrs. Nguyen Thi Dinh*, trans. by Mai Van Elliott (Ithaca: Southeast Asia Program, Cornell University, 1976), 62–74; An Bao Minh, "Uprising in Ben Tre," TTU, Pike Collection, Unit 2, box 1; Military History Institute of Vietnam, *Victory in Vietnam*, 60–64; Saigon to State, 10 May 1960, NA II, RG 59, C0092, reel 11; Saigon to State, 12 July 1960, NA II, RG 59, C0092, reel 11.

2. High-Level Military Institute, *Vietnam: The Anti-U.S. Resistance War for National Salvation*, 39; Nguyen Viet Ta et al., *Mien Dong Nam Bo Khang Chien*, Tap II, 74–5.

3. *U.S. News and World Report*, 2 May 1960; Spector, *Advice and Support*, 338; Williams to Myers, 20 March 1960, *FRUS*, 1958–1960, vol. 1, 121. With characteristic exaggeration, a Communist history stated that the Viet Cong had killed or wounded 400 government troops in the engagement and captured more than 1,000, in addition to seizing more than 5,000 weapons. High-Level Military Institute, *Vietnam: The Anti-U.S. Resistance War for National Salvation*, 39.

4. Spector, *Advice and Support*, 338.

5. Gareth Porter, ed., *Vietnam: The Definitive Documentation of Human Decisions* (Stanfordville, NY: E. M. Coleman, 1979), vol. 2, 59–68. See also Nam Bo Regional Committee to All Members of Cells, 28 March 1960, TTU, Pike Collection, Unit 5, box 30. A top-level missive from Hanoi explained, "With their money, their power, and especially with the reactionary attitude among a number of the upper

levels of society and among the crooks and thugs, the enemy still possesses a political base, he still has a firm grip on the state apparatus, on the army, on the police, and on his intelligence organizations that he can use to suppress the revolution. . . . We must recognize that the enemy has military superiority." While the Communist forces could win guerrilla actions, they would find it very difficult to defend fixed positions in the villages because of "the large number of powerful regular military units and the destructive instruments of war that the enemy currently possesses (such as heavy artillery, bombs, etc)." Trinh Nhu, ed., *Van Kien Dang*, Tap 21, 1960 (Hanoi: Nha Xuat Ban Chinh Tri Quoc Gia, 2002), 291–2.

6. Le Duan asserted, "In the present conjuncture, when the possibility exists to maintain a lasting peace in the world and create favorable conditions for the world movement of socialist revolution and national independence to go forward, we can and must guide and restrict within the South the solving of the contradiction between imperialism and the colonies in our country." Le Duan, *On the Socialist Revolution*, vol. 1 (Hanoi: Foreign Languages Publishing House, 1965), 48. See also Gaiduk, *Confronting Vietnam*, 112.

7. Trinh Nhu, ed., *Van Kien Dang*, Tap 21, 1960, 289–90.

8. The Viet Cong had risen to approximately 10,000 armed men by the end of 1960, while the GVN had lost only 3,000 small arms. Even if the Communists had acquired every one of the 3,000 weapons and lost no weapons of their own – neither of which possibly could have happened – the captured weapons would account for only thirty percent of the total. Saigon to State, 6 April 1961, NA II, RG 59, C0092, reel 3; Saigon to State, 24 December 1960, *FRUS*, 1958–1960, vol. 1, 271; SNIE 53–2-61, "Bloc Support of the Communist Effort Against the Government of Vietnam," 5 October 1961, JFKL, NSF, box 194. The caches established in 1954 provided few weapons. During the Denounce the Communists campaigns, the Diem government had seized a large number of the weapons, using information obtained from prisoners and defectors. Other weapons were found to be unusable when they were dug up. A Communist history covering the northern provinces of South Vietnam recounted, "Most of these weapons were cached for so long that they were either lost or became damaged." Hoi Dong Bien Soan Lich Su Nam Trung Bo Khang Chien, *Nam Trung Bo Khang Chien, 1945–1975* (Hanoi: National Political Publishing House, 1995), 230. The Communist history of Military Region 6 explained that the weapons had to be hidden quickly, and therefore "the weapons were not properly packed and concealed, and later most of the weapons were either lost or damaged and inoperable." Tran Duong et al., *Lich Su Khu 6 (Cuc Nam Trung Bo-Nam Tay Nguyen) Khang Chien Chong My, 1954–1975* (Hanoi: People's Army Publishing House, 1995), 29.

9. *The Pentagon Papers*, vol. 1, 336.

10. *Rand Vietnam Interviews*, ser. PIE, no. 73.

11. On the importance of longstanding family ties to the Communists, see especially Phillips, "A Report on Counter-insurgency in Vietnam," 31 August 1962, HIA, Edward G. Lansdale Papers, box 49.

12. CIA, "National Intelligence Survey, South Vietnam," April 1960, TTU, Pike Collection, Unit 1, box 1.

13. *Rand Vietnam Interviews*, ser. V, no. 105.

14. VCD 866, "National Liberation Front Central Committee Resolutions Numbers Four and Five," 1961, TTU, Pike Collection, Unit 5, box 19.

15. Race, *War Comes to Long An*, 98.

16. "The Political Struggle Movement in Nam Bo," October 1961, TTU, Pike Collection, Unit 6, box 1. An April 1960 cable from the Communist Party headquarters in Cochinchina to the Communist Party Central Committee in Hanoi explained: "If we follow the right policy, causing the power and prestige of the enemy to decline and that of the revolution to increase, the masses will immediately rise up against the enemy." Trinh Nhu, ed., *Van Kien Dang*, Tap 21, 1960, 292.

17. *Rand Vietnam Interviews*, ser. AG, no. 154.

18. During World War II, eighty-five percent of Americans harmed during combat survived. The primary reasons for the disparity were the greater Vietnamese tendency to kill wounded enemies and the inferiority of medical care for wounded Vietnamese soldiers. *Executive Sessions of the Senate Foreign Relations Committee*, 1963, 692–3.

19. Pike, *Viet Cong*, 122–3.

20. *Rand Vietnam Interviews*, ser. Z-ZH, no. 41. In this case and all other cases where a Rand interviewee is mentioned by name, that name is a pseudonym, because the interview transcripts do not contain actual names.

21. *Rand Vietnam Interviews*, ser. AG, no. 362.

22. *Rand Vietnam Interviews*, ser. PIE, no. 42.

23. Simulmatics Corporation, "Studies of the Chieu Hoi Program: Interviews with the Hoi Chanh," interview CH-32.

24. *Hop Tac*, 35th Party Anniversary Issue, February 1965.

25. Conley, *The Communist Insurgent Infrastructure in South Vietnam: A Study of Organization and Strategy* (Washington, DC: U.S. Government Printing Office, 1967), 331.

26. Trullinger, *Village At War: An Account of Conflict in Vietnam* (Stanford: Stanford University Press, 1994), 71.

27. *Rand Vietnam Interviews*, ser. PIE, no. 21. As has happened with many other revolutionaries, the Vietnamese Communists were not very effective in sustaining this same dedication after the war ended, for they had greater access to money and their survival no longer depended on winning over the people.

28. A Viet Cong military proselyting cadre from Kien Phong described one such area: "It was very difficult for the villagers to decide their behavior toward both sides. . . . They listened to the VC and also to the GVN. Both sounded right to them. They didn't know who their master was. . . . They had to be good to both sides in order to protect themselves." *Rand Vietnam Interviews*, ser. AG, no. 543.

29. Conley, *Communist Insurgent Infrastructure*, 348–60.

30. *Rand Vietnam Interviews*, ser. DT, no. 143.

31. Williams, "Remarks, MAAG Chiefs Conference," 18 April 1960, HIA, Samuel T. Williams Papers, box 16.

32. Williams to Tran Trung Dung, 29 February 1960, *FRUS*, 1958–1960, vol. 1, 109; Williams to Lansdale, 10 March 1960, *FRUS*, 1958–1960, vol. 1, 113; Saigon to State, 29 March 1960, *FRUS*, 1958–1960, vol. 1, 125; Williams to Durbrow, 1 June 1960, *FRUS*, 1958–1960, vol. 1, 167.

33. Saigon to State, 16 February 1960, NA II, RG 59, C0092, reel 11.

34. Saigon to State, 6 April 1961, NA II, RG 59, C0092, reel 3.

35. Trinh Nhu, ed., *Van Kien Dang*, Tap 21, 1960, 296–99. On the lowlands, see Hue to State, 16 June 1960, NA II, RG 59, C0092, reel 1.

36. Nguyen Van Minh et al., *Luc Luong Vu Trang Nhan Dan Tay Nguyen Trong Khang Chien Chong My Cuu Nuoc*, Saigon to State, 14 January 1961, NA II, RG 59, C0092, reel 3; Saigon to State, 24 January 1961, NA II, RG 59, C0092, reel 3.

37. High-Level Military Institute, *Vietnam: The Anti-U.S. Resistance War for National Salvation*, 44–5. See also Guan, *Vietnamese Communists' Relations with China*, 148.

38. Gaiduk, *Confronting Vietnam*, 114.

39. Zhai, *China and the Vietnam Wars*, 84–5; Guan, *Vietnamese Communists' Relations with China*, 149.

40. Lüthi, "The Sino-Soviet Split, 1956–1966," 272–3.

41. Zhai, *China and the Vietnam Wars*, 86–8; Hoang Van Hoan, *A Drop in the Ocean*, 314; Gaiduk, *Confronting Vietnam*, 117.

42. Khrushchev, *Khrushchev Remembers*, 483–4; Gaiduk, *Confronting Vietnam*, 121. Immediately after the conference, apparently in an effort to rally the big Communist powers as well as to discredit Titoism, Le Duan declared that "each socialist country must constantly pay due attention to correctly handling the relationship between national interests and those of the world revolutionary movement." The world's Communist parties "have the obligation to ceaselessly educate their peoples in a spirit of socialist internationalism and socialist patriotism, and to resolutely struggle against all manifestations of nationalism and chauvinism." Le Duan, *On Some Present International Problems*, 2nd ed. (Hanoi: Foreign Languages Publishing House, 1964), 49–50.

43. Le Kinh Lich, ed., *Tran Danh Ba Muoi Nam*, vol. 2, 87–8, 156–7; Nguyen Viet Phuong, *Lich Su Bo Doi Truong Son Duong Ho Chi Minh* (Hanoi: People's Army Publishing House, 1994), 37–9.

44. Vietnam Workers' Party, *Third National Congress of the Viet Nam Workers' Party* (Hanoi: Foreign Languages Publishing House, 1960), vol. 1, 62, and vol. 2, 31–3, 62; SWB/FE/435/C/5.

45. Many historians have asserted that the creation of the National Liberation Front marked the beginning of the armed insurgency, when in fact the armed insurgency had begun a year earlier. Among those accounts making this claim is a well-known history of the National Liberation Front itself. Brigham, *Guerrilla Diplomacy*, 1.

46. "Program of the South Viet Nam National Front for Liberation," 20 December 1960, TTU, Pike Collection, Unit V, box 1.

47. Trinh Muu, ed., *Van Kien Dang*, Tap 22, 1961 (Hanoi: Nha Xuat Ban Chinh Tri Quoc Gia, 2002), 653–4. The directive explained, "Although the overt name will be different than that used in North Vietnam, secretly, internally and from the organizational standpoint, the Party Chapter for South Vietnam will still be a part of the Vietnamese Labor Party and will be under the leadership of the Party Central Committee, headed by Chairman Ho Chi Minh." Ibid. At the third Congress, the central committee had explained the rationale behind the front organization as follows: "The weakness of our movement in South Vietnam over the past several years has been that we have not been able to attract widespread support of the anti-Diem elements of the upper classes, that we have not been able to form a united Front with elements opposed to the U.S. and Diem, and that we have not had a name to use in public to appeal to the population and to use in our strategy to sow division and isolate Diem." Trinh Nhu, ed., *Van Kien Dang*, Tap 21, 1960, 1021. See also Duiker, *The Communist Road to Power in Vietnam*, 211–2.

48. Race, *War Comes to Long An*, 107.

49. *The Pentagon Papers*, vol. 1, 316–21.

50. Durbrow Oral History Interview, LBJL.

51. Williams to Lansdale, 17 May 1960, *FRUS*, 1958–1960, vol. 1, 164; Saigon to State, 11 June 1960, *FRUS*, 1958–1960, vol. 1, 173.

52. Saigon to State, 3 May 1960, *FRUS*, 1958–1960, vol. 1, 150; Wood, memcon, 5 May 1960, NA II, RG 59, C0092, reel 1.

53. "Notes on State msg. Saigon 3095," 4 May 1960, *FRUS*, 1958–1960, vol. 1, 153. The memorandum was not signed, but the tone, content, and circumstances of its publication leave no doubt as to its author.

54. For recent examples of Diem's visits to the countryside, see Williams to Durbrow, "Conference (trip) with President," 26 January 1960, HIA, Samuel T. Williams Papers, box 14; memcon, 15 March 1960, HIA, Samuel T. Williams Papers, box 14; Dolan, summary of discussion, 13 April 1960, HIA, Samuel T. Williams Papers, box 14.

55. NSC meeting notes, 9 May 1960, *FRUS*, 1958–1960, vol. 1, 156.

56. Saigon to State, 30 August 1960, *FRUS*, 1958–1960, vol. 1, 187; Saigon to State, 16 September 1960, *FRUS*, 1958–1960, vol. 1, 197.

57. Colby, *Lost Victory*, 70–75.

58. Lansdale to O'Donnell, 20 September 1960, *FRUS*, 1958–1960, vol. 1, 198.

59. Saigon to State, 15 October 1960, *FRUS*, 1958–1960, vol. 1, 203; Saigon to State, 15 October 1960, *FRUS*, 1958–1960, vol. 1, 205.

60. Rust, *Kennedy in Vietnam*, 1; Saigon to State, 12 November 1960, *FRUS*, 1958–1960, vol. 1, 232.

61. Rust, *Kennedy in Vietnam*, 2.

62. Durbrow's actions both before and during the coup attempt suggest that he would not have minded a change in government, and the plotters' demands were virtually identical to the changes that Durbrow had been pushing on Diem in recent months. On the other hand, Durbrow did not back the coup as fully as one would expect had he been intent on ousting Diem. A more likely American catalyst than Durbrow was George Carver, a thirty-year-old CIA officer who was on good terms with some of the key plotters, including Hoang Co Thuy. Carver later said that he agreed with the plotters' objections to Diem and their desire to replace him, though he denied any involvement in inciting the coup. "I was absolutely convinced that to achieve American objectives in Vietnam, Diem had to be ousted," Carver recalled. Rust, *Kennedy in Vietnam*, 9. Several hours into the coup, Carver would telephone Hoang Co Thuy, and Thuy invited Carver to his house, where the Civilian Revolutionary Committee was meeting. Carver went, but it is not clear whether he did more than serve as a means of communication with the rebels. One other possible American instigator was Russ Miller, who, several months earlier, allegedly

had dropped a hint to General Don about replacing Diem. Tran Van Don, *Viet Nam Nhan Chung: Hoi Ky Chanh Tri* (Xuan Thu Publishing, 1989), 157.

63. Saigon to State, 11 November 1960, *FRUS*, 1958–1960, vol. 1, 219.

64. *FRUS*, 1958–1960, vol. 1, 235. Durbrow also said, "I had no confidence in any rebels doing any good for Vietnam or for us or for anybody else." Ibid.

65. Langguth, *Our Vietnam*, 108–9.

66. Rust, *Kennedy in Vietnam*, 14; Nguyen Khanh, interview with author.

67. Saigon to State, 12 November 1960, *FRUS*, 1958–1960, vol. 1, 228.

68. Saigon to State, 12 November 1960, *FRUS*, 1958–1960, vol. 1, 232.

69. Knowing that Carver had followed orders to urge compromise on the plotters during the coup attempt, Colby had told Nhu that Carver had not provided encouragement, and he urged Nhu not to expel Carver. To avoid blowing Carver's cover, Colby also said that Carver was not a CIA man, but he could tell that Nhu was unconvinced. William Colby with Peter Forbath, *Honorable Men: My Life in the CIA* (New York: Simon & Schuster, 1978), 164; Colby, *Lost Victory*, 79.

70. Rust, *Kennedy in Vietnam*, 19.

71. French to Erskine, 6 December 1960, *FRUS*, 1958–1960, vol. 1, 259; Saigon to State, 1 December 1960, NA II, RG 59, C0097, reel 24.

72. McGarr to Lansdale, 13 November 1960, *FRUS*, 1958–1960, vol. 1, 234.

73. Lansdale concluded that Durbrow had done so much damage that only McGurr could repair America's relations with Diem. Lansdale to Gates, 12 November 1960, *FRUS*, 1958–1960, vol. 1, 230.

74. Memcon, 18 November 1960, *FRUS*, 1958–1960, vol. 1, 245.

75. When the State Department proposed that Eisenhower congratulate Diem for overcoming the rebellion, Durbrow objected, contending that such a message would deter Diem from "grasping and heeding lessons of coup." Saigon to State, 18 November 1960, *FRUS*, 1958–1960, vol. 1, 246.

76. Saigon to State, 4 December 1960, *FRUS*, 1958–1960, vol. 1, 257.

77. Saigon to State, 31 December 1960, NA II, RG 59, C0092, reel 2.

78. Le Kinh Lich, ed., *Tran Danh Ba Muoi Nam*, vol. 2, 157.

79. For events in Laos, see Dommen, *The Indochinese Experience of the French and the Americans;* Guan, *Vietnamese Communists' Relations with China;* George C. Eliades, "United States Decision-making in Laos, 1942–1962" (Ph.D. diss., Harvard University, 1999); Charles A. Stevenson, *The End of Nowhere: American Policy Toward Laos Since 1954* (Boston: Beacon Press, 1972).

80. Vo Van Minh, *Quan Khu 4*, 50–53.

81. Gaiduk, *Confronting Vietnam*, 166–170. The North Vietnamese regularly derided their Laotian allies for their fear of artillery and hand-to-hand combat and their preference for flight over fight. When the Soviets and Czechs sent modern firearms to North Vietnam for transportation to the Laotian fighters, the North Vietnamese kept the new weapons for their own tough soldiers and sent the old weapons from the French war to the Pathet Lao. See also Marek Thee, *Notes of a Witness: Laos and the Second Indochinese War* (New York: Random House, 1973), 129.

82. Vo Van Minh, *Quan Khu 4*, 52.

83. Merchant, memcon, 31 December 1960, *FRUS*, 1958–1960, vol. 16, 498; Eisenhower, *Waging Peace, 1956–1961: The White House Years* (Garden City: Doubleday, 1965), 610.

5. Commitment: 1961

1. John F. Kennedy, "America's Stake in Vietnam," in Fishel, ed., *Vietnam: Anatomy of a Conflict*, 142–7.

2. For insightful biographies of Kennedy, see Dallek, *An Unfinished Life;* Reeves, *President Kennedy;* Thomas C. Reeves, *A Question of Character: A Life of John F. Kennedy* (New York: Free Press, 1991).

3. Reeves, *President Kennedy*, 25; McNamara, *In Retrospect*, 14–15.

4. *Public Papers of the Presidents, John F. Kennedy*, 1961, 1–3.

5. Country Team Staff Committee, "Basic Counterinsurgency Plan for Vietnam," 4 January 1961, *FRUS*, 1961–1963, vol. 1, 1.

6. After Durbrow's foiled attempt to deny aid to Diem in May 1960, high Defense officials had attempted to send Lansdale on a visit to Vietnam, telling the State Department that Diem would listen to Lansdale and respond more favorably to a friendly face. They did not mention what was undoubtedly another motive, the desire for new appraisals of Durbrow and Diem. Ambassador Durbrow subsequently notified Washington that he objected to a Lansdale visit because he believed that Diem "hopes use an 'old sympathetic friend' to reverse pressure Department and Embassy putting on Diem to take what we consider needed steps his and our interests." Saigon to State, 17 May 1960, FRUS, 1958–1960, vol. 1, 163. The State Department concurred with Durbrow, and came up with additional reasons for opposing a Lansdale mission. One State official asserted, "Knowing something of Lansdale's views and methods, it is very unlikely that he would strongly support our views and policies – particularly on Vietnam's attitude toward Cambodia – during private talks with Diem." Anderson to Parsons, 18 May 1960, FRUS, 1958–1960, vol. 1, 165n. In the face of State's strenuous objections, the Defense Department had backed away from its recommendation to send Lansdale.

7. Lansdale to Gates, 17 January 1961, HIA, Edward G. Lansdale Papers, box 49.

8. Rust, Kennedy in Vietnam, 21; Reeves, President Kennedy, 46–7.

9. Meeting notes, 28 January 1961, FRUS, 1961–1963, vol. 1, 3; Rostow to Bundy, 30 January 1961, FRUS, 1961–1963, vol. 1, 4.

10. Kennedy, in fact, sensed that the Counterinsurgency Plan did not go far enough. On a piece of paper summarizing the proposed force augmentations, Kennedy scribbled in the margin, "Why so little?" Rust, Kennedy in Vietnam, 26. Kennedy did decide that the forty-one million dollars needed for this effort would not be released until the South Vietnamese agreed to enact a variety of reforms. On this point, Kennedy took the advice of the Country Staff Team over that of Lansdale, who opposed using aid to coerce Diem.

11. The man responsible for covert action in North Vietnam, CIA Saigon station chief William Colby, complied with Kennedy's demands for covert action in the North, but he did not devote great resources to the task. Colby preferred to use most of the CIA's resources in South Vietnam rather than North Vietnam, believing that they would be largely wasted in the North. Diem, whose support for such operations was vital, held similar views. Colby and Diem made limited attempts to send individuals and small teams of ex-Northerners into North Vietnam to conduct sabotage and harassment operations. Saboteurs were able to blow up a number of tanks and trucks and to set fire to factories and warehouses. Almost all of the agents, however, were apprehended in little time by the North Vietnamese internal security apparatus, which controlled territory and people as effectively as its counterparts in China and the Soviet Union. See Conboy and Andrade, Spies & Commandos; Shultz, The Secret War Against Hanoi.

12. Maxwell D. Taylor, Swords and Plowshares (New York: W. W. Norton, 1972), 221. See also Hue to State, 31 August 1961, NA II, RG 59, C0092, reel 4.

13. Le Duan, Thu Vao Nam (Hanoi: Su That Publishing House, 1985), 41.

14. Military History Institute of Vietnam, Victory in Vietnam, 88; Guan, Vietnamese Communists' Relations with China, 175–6.

15. Persons, meeting notes, 19 January 1961, FRUS, 1961–1963, vol. 24, 8; Herter, meeting notes, 19 January 1961, FRUS, 1961–1963, vol. 24, 9; Clifford, meeting notes, 24 January 1961, FRUS, 1961–1963, vol. 24, 9n; Reeves, President Kennedy, 31–2.

16. Judith Banister, China's Changing Population (Stanford, CA: Stanford University Press, 1987), 85, 230.

17. Kennedy told Arthur Schlesinger that it was "hard to fight for a country whose people evidently could not care less about fighting for themselves." Arthur M. Schlesinger, A Thousand Days: John F. Kennedy in the White House (Boston: Houghton Mifflin, 1965), 331–2.

18. New York Times, March 24, 1961.

19. McGarr to Felt, 6 May 1961, FRUS, 1961–1963, vol. 1, 41.

20. USVNR, book 11, 62–66; Bowles to Kennedy, 26 April 1961, FRUS, 1961–1963, vol. 24, 61.

21. See Aleksandr Fursenko and Timothy Naftali, "One Hell of a Gamble": Khrushchev, Castro, and Kennedy, 1958–1964 (New York: W. W. Norton, 1997). William Bundy recalled, "Never thereafter would civilian leaders and advisers accept military and professional judgments without exploring them so fully as to make them, in effect, their own." Rust, Kennedy in Vietnam, 32.

22. Edwin O. Guthman and Jeffrey Shulman, eds., *Robert Kennedy in His Own Words: The Unpublished Recollections of the Kennedy Years* (Toronto: Bantam, 1988), 247–8. Walt Rostow, who in general had more respect for the military leadership than did other civilian officials, later wrote, "I must observe that I never saw the American military less clear in mind, less helpful to a President, than in the first four months of Kennedy's administration.... The fact should be noted because it had a distinctly unsettling effect on Kennedy in his first year." Walt W. Rostow, *Diffusion of Power: An Essay in Recent History* (New York: Macmillan, 1972), 664–5.

23. Brown, memcon, 3 February 1961, *FRUS*, 1961–1963, vol. 24, 13. In later years, Souvanna would come to appreciate the true objectives and methods of the Communists, but by then crucial sections of his country had been lost to the North Vietnamese and the Pathet Lao.

24. Clifton, "Notes from the Meeting of Congressional Leaders with the President on April 27, 1961," 2 May 1961, JFKL, NSF, Chester V. Clifton Series, box 345.

25. In reference to the offensive in Laos during the spring of 1961, a Vietnamese Communist history recounted: "Its principal value was that it opened up the strategic route down the western side of the Annamite Mountains to link up with the Central Highlands and Cochinchina." Le Kinh Lich, ed., *Tran Danh Ba Muoi Nam*, vol. 2, 155–6.

26. Vo Van Minh, *Quan Khu 4*, 63.

27. Le Kinh Lich, ed., *Tran Danh Ba Muoi Nam*, vol. 2, 155–8; Nguyen Viet Phuong, *Lich Su Bo Doi Truong Son Duong Ho Chi Minh*, 58, 63. At this time, Communist planes were flying crates of ammunition and food into the Tha Khong airfield at Tchepone, thirty miles west of the South Vietnamese border, which were then picked up by Group 559 and transported into South Vietnam.

28. In the course of this conversation, Kennedy also dismissed de Gaulle's suggestion that the United States try to cultivate Titoism in North Vietnam, arguing that the Communists were likely to remain united in hatred against the West as long as the West was present. Glenn, memcon, 31 May 1961, *FRUS*, 1961–1963, vol. 24, 103. In July 1961, Kennedy himself said of Berlin, "We cannot and will not permit the Communists to drive us out of Berlin, either gradually or by force. For the fulfillment of our pledge to that city is essential to the morale and security of Western Germany, to the unity of Western Europe, and to the faith of the entire Free World.... If we do not meet our commitments to Berlin, where will we later stand? If we are not true to our word there, all that we have achieved in collective security, which relies on these words, will mean nothing. And if there is one path above all others to war, it is the path of weakness and disunity." Kennedy, "Radio and Television Report to the American People on the Berlin Crisis," 25 July 1961, <http://www.jfklibrary.org/jfk_berlin_crisis_speech.html>.

29. Peter Collier and David Horowitz, *The Kennedys: An American Drama* (New York: Summit Books, 1984), 274. See also Rostow, *Diffusion of Power*, 268; *The Pentagon Papers*, vol. 2, 76; Gibbons, *The U.S. Government and the Vietnam War*, vol. 2, 41–4; Jones, *Death of a Generation*, 39.

30. National Security Action Memorandum 52, 11 May 1961, *FRUS*, 1961–1963, vol. 1, 30, 52. For the Joint Chiefs' position, see *The Pentagon Papers*, vol. 2, 49.

31. Vietnam Task Force, "A Program of Action to Prevent Communist Domination of South Vietnam," 6 May 1961, DDRS, 1998, 28.

32. *USVNR*, book 11, 38.

33. Rostow to Kennedy, 15 April 1961, *FRUS*, 1961–1963, vol. 1, 30.

34. Saigon to State, 14 July 1961, *FRUS*, 1961–1963, vol. 1, 92.

35. Kennedy to Diem, 8 May 1961, JFKL, NSF, box 193.

36. "We now know that as a small nation we cannot hope to meet all of our defense needs alone and from our own resources," was Diem's reply. "We are prepared to make the sacrifices in blood and manpower to save our country and I know that we can count on the material support from your great country which will be so essential for achieving final victory." Diem to Kennedy, 15 May 1961, JFKL, NSF, box 193.

37. *USVNR*, book 11, 159–66.

38. Vladislav Zubok and Constantine Pleshakov, *Inside the Kremlin's Cold War* (Cambridge: Harvard University Press, 1996), 243.

39. Reeves, *President Kennedy*, 166.

40. Akalovsky, memcon, 3 June 1961, *FRUS*, 1961–1963, vol. 24, 107; Akalovsky, memcon, 4 June 1961, *FRUS*, 1961–1963, vol. 24, 108.

41. Akalovsky, memcon, 4 June 1961, *FRUS*, 1961–1963, vol. 14, 32; Akalovsky, memcon, 4 June 1961, *FRUS*, 1961–1963, vol. 14, 33.

42. Reeves, *President Kennedy*, 166.

43. Alistair Horne, *Macmillan*, vol. 2 (London: Macmillan, 1989), 303–4.

44. Reeves, *President Kennedy*, 172–3.

45. Diem to Kennedy, 9 June 1961, JFKL, NSF, box 193.

46. At this time, Kennedy also authorized full funding for the 20,000-man increase in the South Vietnamese Army approved in late January, which had been held up by State Department efforts to pry concessions from Diem.

47. *USVNR*, book 11, 241–4.

48. CIA, "Infiltration of Communist Bloc Trained Sabotage Personnel into South Vietnam," 12 July 1961, JFKL, NSF, box 193; CIA, SNIE 53-2-61, "Bloc Support of the Communist Effort Against the Government of Vietnam," 5 October 1961, JFKL, NSF, box 194; Saigon to State, 10 October 1961, JFKL, NSF, box 194; Hilsman to Rusk, 16 July 1962, *FRUS*, 1961–1963, vol. 2, 243; Military History Institute of Vietnam, *Victory in Vietnam*, 456.

49. Saigon to State, 27 November 1961, NA II, RG 59, C0092, reel 11.

50. Saigon to State, 18 September 1961, *FRUS*, 1961–1963, vol. 1, 133; Saigon to State, 6 October 1961, *FRUS*, 1961–1963, vol. 1, 147.

51. Hannah, *The Key to Failure*, 39.

52. State to Saigon, 12 October 1961, *FRUS*, 1961–1963, vol. 1, 161; Lemnitzer to Felt, 13 October 1961, *FRUS*, 1961–1963, vol. 1, 163.

53. For background information on Taylor, see Clay Blair, *Ridgway's Paratroopers: The American Airborne in World War II* (Garden City, NY: The Dial Press, 1985).

54. Saigon to State, 13 October 1961, NA II, RG 218, CJCS File 091, box 138; Saigon to State, 28 November 1961, NA II, RG 59, C0092, reel 5.

55. Saigon to State, 18 October 1961, *FRUS*, 1961–1963, vol. 1, 174; Taylor to Johnson, 25 October 1961, *FRUS*, 1961–1963, vol. 1, 190; Saigon to State, 25 October 1961, *FRUS*, 1961–1963, vol. 1, 192; Taylor, *Swords and Plowshares*, 232–3.

56. Rostow, *Diffusion of Power*, 272–4.

57. Taylor to Kennedy, 3 November 1961, *FRUS*, 1961–1963, vol. 1, 210.

58. *USVNR*, book 11, 337–42.

59. For example, *Newsweek*, 13 November 1961.

60. Galbraith to Kennedy, 21 November 1961, TTU, Pike Collection, Unit 1, box 2; *USVNR*, book 11, 406–9.

61. Harris Wofford, *Of Kennedy and Kings: Making Sense of the Sixties* (New York: Farrar, Straus, and Giroux, 1980), 379.

62. Talbot, memcon, 21 November 1961, *FRUS*, 1961–1963, vol. 19, 63. Rusk and McNamara favored holding South Vietnam because if it fell, "We would have to face the near certainty that the remainder of Southeast Asia and Indonesia would move to a complete accommodation with Communism, if not formal incorporation within the Communist bloc." *The Pentagon Papers*, vol. 2, 110–16.

63. Rostow, *Diffusion of Power*, 270.

64. Ho Chi Minh, *Selected Writings*, 264.

65. Gaiduk, "Containing the Warriors," in Gardner and Gittinger, eds., *International Perspectives on Vietnam*, 72–3.

66. Chin Peng, *My Side of History* (Singapore: Media Masters, 2003), 428–30; Zhai, *China and the Vietnam Wars*, 117–19.

67. For Stalin's views on this subject, see Gaiduk, *Confronting Vietnam*, 8.

68. Young to Taylor, 27 October 1961, *FRUS*, 1961–1963, vol. 23, 13.

69. Chin Peng, *My Side of History*, 433.

70. Saigon to State, 9 November 1961, NA II, RG 59, C0092, reel 4.

71. Battle to Bundy, 13 July 1961, *FRUS*, 1961–1963, vol. 23, 354.

72. Taipei to Hong Kong, 15 May 1961, *FRUS*, 1961–1963, vol. 22, 26.

73. Young to Rusk, 22 May 1961, JFKL, NSF, box 193.

74. Reeves, *President Kennedy*, 111.

75. On Japan's relations with Indonesia during this period, see Masahi Nishihara, *The Japanese and Sukarno's Indonesia: Tokyo-Jakarta Relations, 1951–1966* (Honolulu: University Press of Hawaii, 1976).

76. Meeting notes, 11 November 1961, *FRUS*, 1961–1963, vol. 1, 236.

77. State to Saigon, 15 November 1961, JFKL, NSF, box 195.

78. Taylor to Kennedy, 3 November 1961, *FRUS*, 1961–1963, vol. 1, 210.

79. Saigon to State, 18 November 1961, NA II, RG 59, C0092, reel 5; Saigon to State, 26 November 1961, NA II, RG 59, C0092, reel 11.

80. CIA, "Views of President Ngo Dinh Diem," 29 November 1961, *FRUS*, 1961–1963, vol. 1, 295.

81. Saigon to State, 22 November 1961, *FRUS*, 1961–1963, vol. 1, 270.

82. Saigon to State, 4 December 1961, NA II, RG 59, C0092, reel 5.

83. After Chinese Communist armies had vanquished their Chinese Nationalist foes, Kennedy stood up on the floor of the House of Representatives and declared, "Mr. Speaker, over this weekend we have learned the extent of the disaster that has befallen China and the United States. The responsibility for the failure of our foreign policy in the Far East rests squarely with the White House and the Department of State. The continued insistence that aid would not be forthcoming unless a coalition government with the Communists were formed was a crippling blow to the National Government. So concerned were our diplomats and their advisers, the Lattimores and the Fairbanks, with the imperfection of the democratic system in China after twenty years of war and the tales of corruption in high places that they lost sight of our tremendous stake in a non-Communist China." John F. Kennedy, *A Compendium of Speeches, Statements, and Remarks Delivered During His Service in the Congress of the United States* (Washington, DC: U.S. Government Printing Office, 1964), 41–2.

84. Parker to Lemnitzer, 18 December 1961, *FRUS*, 1961–1963, vol. 1, 325.

85. On February 13, 1962, the Republican National Committee charged that Kennedy had been "less than candid" about American involvement in South Vietnam and demanded that the President come clean on the question of whether the United States had 4,000 men in South Vietnam, not just the 685 that the Kennedy administration continued to claim in public. *New York Times*, February 14, 1962.

86. Reeves, *President Kennedy*, 37, 58.

87. Mary S. McAuliffe, ed., *CIA Documents on the Cuban Missile Crisis, 1962* (Washington, DC: Central Intelligence Agency, 1992), 123–5.

88. John Mecklin, *Mission in Torment: An Intimate Account of the U.S. Role in Vietnam* (Garden City: Doubleday, 1965), 110.

89. Hilsman to Rusk, 16 July 1962, *FRUS*, 1961–1963, vol. 2, 243.

90. COSVN draft resolution, October 1961, CDEC Doc Log No. 01–0529–70, TTU, Pike Collection, Unit 6, box 7; Porter, *Vietnam: The Definitive Documentation of Human Decisions*, vol. 2, 119–23; Nguyen Viet Ta et al., *Mien Dong Nam Bo Khang Chien*, Tap II, 107.

91. Bui Tin, *Following Ho Chi Minh*, 45–6; Zhai, *China and The Vietnam Wars*, 113; Porter, *Perils of Dominance*, 46.

6. Rejuvenation: January–June 1962

1. Gilpatric, "President's Meeting with JCS," 3 January 1962, *FRUS*, 1961–1963, vol. 2, 2.

2. Gilpatric to Lemnitzer, 4 January 1962, *FRUS*, 1961–1963, vol. 2, 3.

3. *New York Times*, February 19, 1962.

4. State to Saigon, 21 February 1962, *FRUS*, 1961–1963, vol. 2, 75; Carl T. Rowan, *Breaking the Barriers: A Memoir* (Boston: Little, Brown, 1991), 211–14; Pierre Salinger, *With Kennedy* (Garden City: Doubleday, 1966), 322–4. On March 9, Assistant Secretary of Defense for Public Affairs Arthur Sylvester notified Admiral Felt, "Radio and newspaper stories in last 24 hours have caused concern here at highest level, also Joint Chiefs. Suggest you urge General Harkins to begin moving away from present policy which results in stories indicating combat participation.... The problem is that too much emphasis is being put on U.S. participation implying all-out U.S. combat involvement plus operational details and weaknesses. Please discourage direct quotes of American officers involved and impression that

Americans are leading the combat missions against the Viet Cong." Sylvester to Felt, 9 March 1962, JFKL, Newman Papers.

5. Ambassador Nolting once remarked that the young reporters "have yet to learn that the mark of a great nation is tolerance and understanding of such tortured people as the Vietnamese and their petty, often rather pathetic, maneuvers to save face. And they forget that the face of the government has vital bearing on support of its people in conduct of war." Saigon to State, 5 February 1963, *FRUS, 1961–1963*, vol. 3, 30. See also Frederick Nolting, *From Trust to Tragedy: The Political Memoirs of Frederick Nolting, Kennedy's Ambassador to Diem's Vietnam* (New York: Praeger, 1988), 43.

6. In Lodge's case, it must be noted, the success was partially the result of a shift in the U.S. policy toward Diem that pleased the press, as is covered in chapter 8.

7. Nolting, *From Trust to Tragedy*, 87, 92.

8. Mecklin, *Mission in Torment*, 126.

9. Ibid., 143.

10. Ibid., xi.

11. Hilsman, "A Strategic Concept for South Vietnam," 2 February 1962, *FRUS, 1961–1963*, vol. 2, 42. Joseph Mendenhall, the most senior opponent of Diem in the American Embassy at the time, observed that South Vietnam's educated class "exerts a strong, probably predominant influence on international opinion because of the tendency of the foreign press to accept this class's judgment of the GVN rather than the official views which we and the GVN put forth." Saigon to State, 23 March 1962, *FRUS, 1961– 1963*, vol. 2, 127. See also Robert Hopkins Miller, *Vietnam and Beyond: A Diplomat's Cold War Education* (Lubbock: Texas Tech University Press, 2002), 60.

12. On March 1, for instance, the *New York Times* editorial page stated that the attack "does reflect serious discontent." *New York Times*, March 1, 1962. Historical accounts that draw the same conclusion include Busch, *All the Way with JFK?*, 135; Kaiser, *American Tragedy*, 177; Rust, *Kennedy in Vietnam*, 78; Schulzinger, *A Time for War*, 113.

13. Wheeler to JCS, "JCS Team Report on South Vietnam," January 1963, *FRUS, 1961–1963*, vol. 3, 26.

14. Saigon to State, 20 March 1962, *FRUS, 1961–1963*, vol. 2, 118.

15. Prochnau, *Once Upon a Distant War*, 51.

16. *U.S. News and World Report*, February 18, 1963.

17. "Status Report of Developments Since March 21," 28 March 1962, JFKL, NSF, box 203.

18. *New York Times*, April 1, 1962.

19. Hilsman, "A Strategic Concept for South Vietnam," 2 February 1962, *FRUS, 1961–1963*, vol. 2, 42; Gilpatric to Taylor, 6 February 1962, *FRUS, 1961–1963*, vol. 2, 49; Roger Hilsman, *To Move a Nation: The Politics of Foreign Policy in the Administration of John F. Kennedy* (Garden City: Doubleday, 1967), 436–8. While Diem did not acknowledge the army's shortcomings in public, he displayed great dissatisfaction in private. McGarr to Nolting, 12 January 1962, *FRUS, 1961–1963*, vol. 2, 13; Gardiner, "Points of special interest in President Diem's meeting with AID administrator Fowler Hamilton," 16 January 1962, *FRUS, 1961–1963*, vol. 2, 23.

20. Felt to JCS, 22 February 1962, *FRUS, 1961–1963*, vol. 2, 81; Saigon to State, 27 November 1961, NA II, RG 59, C0092, reel 11.

21. Burris to Johnson, 16 March 1962, *FRUS, 1961–1963*, vol. 2, 112.

22. *New York Times*, April 8, 1962.

23. *New York Times*, April 7, 1962.

24. *Newsweek*, April 30, 1962. Roger Hilsman contended in June that the enemy "is now meeting more effective resistance and having to cope with increased aggressiveness by the Vietnamese military and security forces." Hilsman to Harriman, "Progress Report on South Vietnam," 18 June 1962, JFKL, Hilsman Papers, Countries, Vietnam, box 3.

25. Cao Minh et al., *Quan Khu 8: Ba Muoi Nam Khang Chien (1945–1975)* (Hanoi: People's Army Publishing House, 1998), 429. See also Truong Minh Hoach and Nguyen Minh Phung, *Quan Khu 9: 30 Nam Khang Chien, 1945–1975* (Hanoi: People's Army Publishing House, 1996), 328–9.

26. Phillips, "A Report on Counter-insurgency in Vietnam," 31 August 1962, HIA, Edward G. Lansdale Papers, box 49. As Taylor's report of November 1961 indicated, the results had already begun to show by

the end of 1961. In the document of August 31, Phillips noted that the central government's functionaries in Saigon were still lacking in skill and motivation, but the Ngo brothers could bypass them by working directly with the provincial chiefs, which is what they did.

27. For a detailed discussion of the origins of the strategic hamlet program, see Catton, *Diem's Final Failure*.

28. Living with their families in these forts, militiamen tended to stay inside at night to protect wives and children, rather than patrol the countryside. Even then, their presence often was not enough to prevent massed Viet Cong forces from wiping out the outposts and seizing the defenders' arms, ammunition, and food. A South Vietnamese government document on the strategic hamlet program emphasized the need to steer clear of "small military posts which cut off and immobilize three or five Civil Guards uselessly in each place." Republic of Vietnam, "From the Strategic Hamlet to the Self-Defence Village," ca. May 1962, PRO, FO 371/166748.

29. Peasants who lived far from the hamlet center sometimes had to move closer to the center, but they still could work the same lands and reach them on foot in a few minutes. Only in a small number of Viet Cong-dominated areas did the government move entire hamlets, typically to places closer to government strongholds or major roads. Nolting to Cottrell, 15 October 1962, *FRUS*, 1961–1963, vol. 2, 302; Rufus Phillips, interview with author; Albert Fraleigh, interview with author; John O'Donnell, interview with author.

30. Heavner to Nolting, 27 April 1962, *FRUS*, 1961–1963, vol. 2, 173. For the impact of this strong leadership on the performance of the militiamen, see Robert Thompson, *Defeating Communist Insurgency: The Lessons of Malaya and Vietnam* (New York: Frederick A. Praeger, 1966), 143.

31. Theodore Heavner was among those who recognized the irrelevance of Western democracy to the strategic hamlet program. Heavner found, at the end of 1962, that little had changed since the 1959 National Assembly elections, which he had witnessed closely. Then and now, the peasants were not wondering "whom should I chose to represent me?" but rather "what do they want of me?" Heavner expressed agreement with a missionary who had told him, "Of course the elections are decided in advance. The people would be very uncomfortable if they were not." The missionary explained that "the kind of direct confrontation involved in western-style elections is repugnant to the Vietnamese; they would rather make such decisions informally to prevent loss of face." Heavner concluded, "I am not convinced that there is any present need to impose our political ideas on the Vietnamese peasants. Free elections and town meetings can come later. If we can get effective local administration – albeit paternalistic – plugged into the national administration, if we can open up a few lines of communication up as well as down, and if we can involve the peasant in the defense of a felt stake in a developing hamlet economy tied into the national economy, we will have done quite enough to freeze out the VC." Heavner, "Visit to Vietnam," 11 December 1962, *FRUS*, 1961–1963, vol. 2, 328. See also Saigon to State, 11 March 1963, NA II, RG 59, Central Files, 1963, box 4048.

32. Rufus Phillips, the American who was to become the head U.S. adviser to the strategic hamlet program, reported in August that the program's recent successes were attributable to "a continuous stream of instructions being sent out from Saigon," much of which was the result of Nhu's trips to the countryside, and to "the quality of local leadership and their understanding of the program." Phillips, "A Report on Counter-insurgency in Vietnam," 31 August 1962, HIA, Edward G. Lansdale Papers, box 49. For the Ngo brothers' leadership of the strategic hamlet program, see also Neese and O'Donnell, eds., *Prelude to Tragedy*, 30, 34–8; Hilsman, memo for the record, 2 January 1963, *FRUS*, 1961–1963, vol. 3, 3; notes of the meetings of the Interministerial Committee on Strategic Hamlets, NA II, RG 59, C0092.

33. Roger Hilsman remarked in April, "I thought it likely before that Diem would beat the Viet Cong, but now, with the new program, I think it will be easy." *Newsweek*, April 30, 1962.

34. Carl W. Schaad, "The Strategic Hamlet Program in Vietnam: The Role of the People in Counterinsurgency Warfare," (student thesis, U.S. Army War College, 1964), 64–7.

35. There is no truth to the oft-heard allegation that the Communist agent Pham Ngoc Thao was Nhu's top lieutenant for the strategic hamlet program and used his influence to overextend the hamlets. For the allegation, see Bergerud, *The Dynamics of Defeat*, 35; Duiker, *The Sacred War*, 154; Karnow, *Vietnam*, 274; Khong, *Analogies At War*, 94; Olson and Roberts, *Where the Domino Fell*, 98; Prochnau, *Once Upon A Distant War*, 76; Truong Nhu Tang, *A Vietcong Memoir*, 46–7. Col. Hoang Lac headed the

program, while Thao spent most of the program's duration serving as a provincial chief. Both Hoang Lac and Rufus Phillips said that Thao did not exert any influence over the program at the national level. Hoang Lac, interview with author; Rufus Phillips, interview with author. In addition, most South Vietnamese leaders suspected that Thao was working secretly for the Communists because of his past Communist affiliation. See Harkins to Taylor, 31 August 1963, *FRUS*, 1961–193, vol. 4, 33; Saigon to State, 29 October 1963, *FRUS*, 1961–193, vol. 4, 225.

36. Nhu had intended to influence the fighting in this way. He explained in March 1962, "With the strategic hamlets, we disrupt the Viet-Cong liaison channels, food supplies, information sources; they cannot infiltrate any longer. They then have to come out in the open and attack the hamlets in mass. We force them into the type of warfare in which we are superior to them." Ngo Dinh Nhu, speech, 19 March 1962, PRO, FO 371/166702.

37. Hilsman argued, "Some easing of the United States pressure on Diem for major reforms and reorganization of his government at the top seems called for. Although desirable, none of these are fundamental to the problem of cutting the Viet Cong's access to the villages and the people." Hilsman, "A Strategic Concept for South Vietnam," 2 February 1962, *FRUS*, 1961–1963, vol. 2, 42.

38. Cottrell to Harriman, 17 February 1962, *FRUS*, 1961–1963, vol. 2, 68.

39. Heavner to Wood, 3 August 1962, *FRUS*, 1961–1963, vol. 2, 257.

40. *Time*, June 22, 1962.

41. Ho Chi Minh National Political Studies Institute, *Lich Su Bien Nien Xu Uy Nam Bo Va Trung Uong Cuc Mien Nam*, 322–3; Gareth Porter, *A Peace Denied: The United States, Vietnam, and the Paris Agreement* (Bloomington: Indiana University Press, 1975), 17; Porter, *Perils of Dominance*, 120.

42. Le Duan, *Thu Vao Nam*, 50–67. In December, the North Vietnamese reiterated that the strengthening of the South Vietnamese government had placed military victory out of reach. Busch, *All the Way with JFK?*, 127. That same month, the North Vietnamese Politburo expressed hope that "many limited victories" would compel the enemy to yield control of South Vietnam. The Politburo acknowledged, though, that the South Vietnamese government might in the future still be able to "continue the war by making new efforts and using new plots and tricks," and therefore the Politburo called for expansion of the armed forces in the South over a period of "several years" to fight larger battles. Vien Nghien Cuu Chu Nghia Mac Lenin Va Tu Tuong Ho Chi Minh, *Lich Su Dang Cong San Viet Nam*, Tap II, 239–41. For the next year, nevertheless, Hanoi would act as if it did not foresee decisive military actions any time soon, continuing to rely primarily on small attacks aimed at wearing down Diem's forces.

43. Bernard Fall, *Viet-Nam Witness, 1953–1966* (New York: Frederick A. Praeger, 1966), 105–14.

44. Guan, *Vietnamese Communists' Relations with China*, 226.

45. Chen Xiaolu, "Chen Yi and China's Diplomacy," in Michael H. Hunt and Niu Jun, eds., *Toward a History of Chinese Communist Foreign Relations, 1920s–1960s: Personalities and Interpretive Approaches* (Washington, DC: Woodrow Wilson Center, 1992), 104; Zhai, *China and the Vietnam Wars*, 115–6; Jian, *Mao's China*, 207; *Beijing Review*, 30 November 1979.

46. Christopher E. Goscha, "Vietnam and the World Outside," 182; Xiaoming Zhang, "China's Involvement in Laos During the Vietnam War, 1963–1975," *Journal of Military History*, vol. 66, issue 4 (October 2002), 1158.

47. Department of Defense, "Visit to Southeast Asia by the Secretary of Defense, 8–11 May 1962," *FRUS*, 1961–1963, vol. 2, 187.

48. Forrestal, memcon, 11 May 1962, *FRUS*, 1961–1963, vol. 24, 355n; McCone, memcon, 13 May 1962, *FRUS*, 1961–1963, vol. 24, 363.

49. *Richmond News Leader*, June 9, 1962.

50. State to Saigon, 9 July 1962, *FRUS*, 1961–1963, vol. 2, 238.

7. Attack: July–December 1962

1. Neil Sheehan, Introduction to Jules Roy, *The Battle of Dienbienphu* (New York: Harper & Row, 1965), xvii.

2. Mecklin, *Mission in Torment*, 18.

3. General Harkins's executive assistant, Brig. Gen. Michael Greene, provided a telling description. Sorley, *Honorable Warrior*, 156. Harkins also was subjected to spurious accusations that he was dimwitted. Harkins's words and deeds in Vietnam and elsewhere revealed strong mental faculties, and those who knew him well considered him to be an intelligent man. Roger Hilsman, for example, a senior State Department official with a Ph.D. from Yale, commented that "Harkins is a much more sophisticated man than General McGarr." Hilsman, "Visit with General Paul Harkins and Ambassador Nolting," 19 March 1962, JFKL, Hilsman Papers, Countries, Vietnam, box 3. On October 29, 1963, as a terrible crisis neared its climax, President Kennedy said, "I think we all have confidence in [Harkins]." Recording of meeting, 29 October 1963, Tape No. 118/A54, JFKL, POF, Presidential Recordings.

4. Memo for the record, 31 July 1962, *FRUS*, 1961–1963, vol. 2, 244.

5. Saigon to State, 19 December 1962, *FRUS*, 1961–1963, vol. 2, 331. See also Wood to Johnson, 11 October 1962, *FRUS*, 1961–1963, vol. 2, 298. During July, when asked how long it would take the South Vietnamese government to weaken the Viet Cong to the point that a large American advisory presence would no longer be necessary, Harkins had told McNamara that it would take one year from the time that all South Vietnamese units were fully operational and taking the war to the Viet Cong. McNamara and others interpreted this comment to mean one year from the present time, which was a misinterpretation since South Vietnam had not yet fulfilled Harkins's conditions. McNamara told Harkins that it was better to take a conservative view and estimate that the large American advisory apparatus would no longer be needed in three years. Meeting notes, 23 July 1962, *FRUS*, 1961–1963, vol. 2, 248; *The Pentagon Papers*, vol. 2, 175. McNamara himself did not believe that all Americans would be out by the end of this three year period. Lyndon Johnson's military aide Col. Howard L. Burris, commenting on McNamara's three-year time frame one month later, reported, "This is not to say that the effort will be terminated or phased out in this period, but rather it is a realistic expression of a reasonable period during which success must be achieved or at least be in sight." Burris to Johnson, 17 August 1962, *FRUS*, 1961–1963, vol. 2, 269.

6. Meeting notes, 10 September 1962, *FRUS*, 1961–1963, vol. 2, 277.

7. Nguyen Anh Tuan, *Du Thao Lich Su Dang Bo Tinh Tien Giang*, Tap 2 (1954–1975) (My Tho City: Tien Giang Province Party History Research Section, 1986), 35.

8. For general appraisals, in addition to sources cited in subsequent sections on the South Vietnamese armed forces, see meeting notes, 10 September 1962, *FRUS*, 1961–1963, vol. 2, 277; Saigon to State, 11 September 1962, NA II, RG 59, C0092, reel 8; Saigon to State, 16 November 1962, NA II, RG 59, C0092, reel 9; Heavner, "Visit to Vietnam," 11 December 1962, *FRUS*, 1961–1963, vol. 2, 328; *Pentagon Papers*, vol. 2, 690–716.

9. Vo Tran Nha, ed., *Lich Su Dong Thap Muoi: Gui Nguoi Dang Song* (Ho Chi Minh City: Ho Chi Minh City Publishing House, 1993), 251.

10. Truehart also noted that intelligence activities had been "greatly improved." Meeting notes, 19 September 1962, *FRUS*, 1961–1963, vol. 2, 286; Saigon to State, 18 September 1962, NA II, RG 59, C0092, reel 8. See also Saigon to State, 29 October 1962, RG 59, C0092, reel 8; Forrestal to Kennedy, 18 September 1962, *FRUS*, 1961–1963, vol. 2, 283.

11. *Newsweek*, August 20, 1962.

12. Hammond, *Public Affairs: The Military and the Media, 1962–1968*, 26–7; Mecklin, *Mission in Torment*, 132–5.

13. *Newsweek*, 24 September 1962.

14. *New York Times*, November 28, 1962; Associated Press, "U.S. Press Assailed in Vietnam," November 29, 1962, TTU, Pike Collection, Unit 2, box 2; Mecklin, *Mission in Torment*, 136.

15. Mecklin, *Mission in Torment*, 135.

16. Ibid., 138.

17. Prochnau, *Once Upon a Distant War*, 248–9. Keyes Beech commented, "I never could understand why some of my colleagues got so upset in Vietnam when the military occasionally lied to them. What the hell did they expect? It was part of the game." Strategic Studies Institute, "Press Coverage of the Vietnam War: The Third View," 25 May 1979, A-4.

18. Sheehan, *A Bright Shining Lie*, 319.

19. Mecklin, *Mission in Torment*, 139–40.

20. Prochnau, *Once Upon a Distant War*, 52.

21. In an article covering the battle, Halberstam stated that the Viet Cong "climbed up the main ridges to attack. One American military observer surveying the scene said he believed this was their big mistake. He said they should have come up the little corridors running between the ridges. It was easier for government troops to defend against the main ridges and concentrate their fire than against the corridors." *New York Times*, November 27, 1962.

22. Prochnau, *Once Upon a Distant War*, 90.

23. David Halberstam, *The Best and the Brightest* (New York: Random House, 1972), 814.

24. David Halberstam, *The Making of a Quagmire* (New York: Random House, 1965), 315–19. Halberstam's pro-war words were deleted from later editions of *The Making of a Quagmire*.

25. Sheehan, *A Bright Shining Lie*, 317.

26. For Vann's life prior to his deployment to Vietnam, see Sheehan, *A Bright Shining Lie*.

27. Sheehan, *A Bright Shining Lie*, 494.

28. Cao was not given a high post simply because of his loyalty to Diem, as the U.S. press claimed. Many Americans and South Vietnamese considered him a strong leader. An evaluation of Cao produced by his American adviser two years earlier described him as "an alert, competent, intelligent officer of great potential" who "is constantly on the go visiting and inspecting his units at all hours of the day and night." In addition, it stated, Cao "is one of the few Vietnamese officers who appears to take an interest in his enlisted personnel." Burns to Williams, "Evaluation of Officer," 22 June 1960, HIA, Samuel T. Williams Papers, box 15.

29. In December, Heavner of the State Department reported that U.S. advisers in different areas had told him that fear of incurring Diem's wrath by suffering high casualties was inhibiting Vietnamese commanders. Heavner, "Visit to Vietnam," 11 December 1962, *FRUS*, 1961–1963, vol. 2, 328.

30. Halberstam, *The Making of a Quagmire*, 141.

31. "The Seventh Division struck me as being as good a litmus paper of the war as any." Halberstam, *The Making of a Quagmire*, 80. Many historians have similarly argued that the South Vietnamese armed forces performed poorly during the last three months of 1962. Asprey, *War in the Shadows*; Freedman, *Kennedy's Wars*; Hammond, *Public Affairs: The Military and the Media, 1962–1968*; Herring, *America's Longest War*; Kahin, *Intervention*; Krepinevich, *The Army and Vietnam*; Mann, *A Grand Delusion*; Prochnau, *Once Upon a Distant War*; Rust, *Kennedy in Vietnam*; Sheehan, *A Bright Shining Lie*.

32. The Seventh Division figures for losses and strength include the division's regulars as well as the Rangers who operated in the division's area of operations. Sheehan, *A Bright Shining Lie*, 55.

33. "Diem's cold propaganda line," explained one American, "is that there must never be a defeat, even a small one, but only one long series of victories." Hilsman, memcon, 2 January 1963, *FRUS*, 1961–1963, vol. 3, 4.

34. *New York Times*, October 6, 1962. Halberstam wrote that the Rangers' losses in the battle amounted to "one of the highest tolls in a Government-initiated operation." *New York Times*, October 9, 1962.

35. Hammond, *Public Affairs: The Military and the Media, 1962–1968*, 29–30; *New York Times*, November 22, 1962; State to Saigon, 12 November 1962, NA II, RG 59, C0092, reel 9; Saigon to State, 15 December 1962, NA II, RG 59, C0092, reel 9.

36. Brooks D. Simpson and Jean V. Berlin, eds., *Sherman's Civil War: Selected Correspondence of William T. Sherman, 1860–1865* (Chapel Hill: University of North Carolina Press, 1999), 396.

37. Charles Roland, *An American Iliad: The Story of the Civil War* (New York: McGraw-Hill, 1991), 92.

38. Saigon to State, 15 December 1962, NA II, RG 59, C0092, reel 9; Headquarters United States Army, Pacific, "USARPAC Intelligence Bulletin," December 1962, JFKL, Newman Papers; "CINCPAC's Booklet for SECDEF Meeting," 6 May 1963, JFKL, Newman Papers. While the South Vietnamese were known to misrepresent their casualty statistics on purpose, there is little chance that they suddenly decided to report their casualties more accurately in late 1962, when the topic was so controversial.

39. CIA Office of Current Intelligence, "Current Status of the War in South Vietnam," 11 January 1963, *FRUS*, 1961–1963, vol. 3, 11.

40. Richard Tregaskis, *Vietnam Diary* (New York: Holt, Rinehart, and Winston, 1963), 312–5.

41. Ibid., 214–5.

42. Ibid., 180–88, 217.

43. Ibid., 287–94.

44. *Newsweek*, December 10, 1962.

45. *Saturday Evening Post*, November 24, 1962.

46. *Time*, November 2, 1962.

47. *Plain Dealer*, October 22, 1962.

48. *New York Times*, November 4, 1962; Harkins to JCS, 3 November 1962, JFKL, Newman Papers.

49. Halberstam also noted that "in many areas, for the first time in years, the Vietcong must be careful because of the Government's new striking power." *New York Times*, October 21, 1963.

50. *New York Times*, November 15, 1962.

51. Winterbottom, "Captured Viet Cong Documents," 1 December 1962, JFKL, Newman Papers; *New York Times*, November 27, 1962; *Stars and Stripes*, November 28, 1962.

52. *New York Times*, December 8, 1962.

53. Headquarters United States Army, Pacific, "USARPAC Intelligence Bulletin," December 1962, JFKL, Newman Papers.

54. Ziegler, journal, 1962–1963, LOC, Sheehan Papers, box 83.

55. Sheehan, cable, 19 October 1962, LOC, Sheehan Papers, box 225.

56. *New York Times*, November 9, 1962; Saigon to State, 10 November 1962, NA II, RG 59, C0092, reel 9.

57. Sheehan, cable, 26 November 1962, LOC, Sheehan Papers, box 225.

58. Sheehan, cable, 28 November 1962, LOC, Sheehan Papers, box 225.

59. Robert F. Futrell, *The Advisory Years to 1965* (Washington, DC: U.S. Government Printing Office, 1981), 156–7.

60. Heavner, "Visit to Vietnam," 11 December 1962, *FRUS*, 1961–1963, vol. 2, 328.

61. Vien Nghien Cuu Chu Nghia Mac Lenin Va Tu Tuong Ho Chi Minh, *Lich Su Dang Cong San Viet Nam*, Tap II, 239.

62. High-Level Military Institute, *Vietnam: The Anti-U.S. Resistance War for National Salvation*, 49, 53. See also VCD 257, September 1962, TTU, Pike Collection, Unit 1, box 1.

63. MACV, "Translation of VC Document on Ap Bac Battle 2 Jan 63," 20 April 1963, USAWCL. In late 1962, according to a different Communist history of this same area, "the enemy continued to cause us many problems and considerable losses." Cao Minh et al., *Quan Khu 8*, 433.

64. In October 1962, according to this history, the South Vietnamese government began launching thirteen waves of operations into Viet Cong base areas and transportation corridors, each wave employing two to three South Vietnamese battalions plus some tribal commandos. Government forces and the Viet Cong battled fiercely for the next two months. As a consequence of these operations, the history stated, "a number of cadre became discouraged, wavered, and wanted to retreat." Tran Duong et al., *Lich Su Khu 6*, 98–100.

65. The performance of the South Vietnamese Army remains a much misunderstood subject. In a new, but poorly researched and argued, history of the South Vietnamese Army (ARVN), Robert K. Brigham argues that because of poor leadership and training, "the ARVN never coalesced into an effective fighting force." Brigham, *ARVN*, 27. Brigham specifically contends that the South Vietnamese Army fared poorly in 1962 and 1963. Ibid., 9–10.

66. Numerous histories have described the strategic hamlet program as an abject failure. Asprey, *War in the Shadows*; Bergerud, *The Dynamics of Defeat*; Brigham, *Guerrilla Diplomacy*; Buzzanco, *Masters of War*; Cable, *Conflict of Myths*; Freedman, *Kennedy's Wars*; Gibson, *The Perfect War*; Hess, *Vietnam and the United States*; Herring, *America's Longest War*; Hunt, *Lyndon Johnson's War*; Kahin, *Intervention*; Karnow, *Vietnam*; Krepinevich, *The Army and Vietnam*; Logevall, *Choosing War*; Lomperis, *From People's War to People's Rule*; Nagl, *Counterinsurgency Lessons from Malaya and Vietnam*; Newman, *JFK and Vietnam*; Olson and Roberts, *Where the Domino Fell*; Prochnau, *Once Upon a Distant War*; Rust, *Kennedy in Vietnam*; Schulzinger, *A Time for War*; Schwab, *Defending the Free World*; Sheehan, *A Bright Shining Lie*. The other histories that mention the program credit it with causing some initial problems for the Viet Cong but contend that the program deteriorated over the course of 1963.

67. VCD 35, October/November 1962, TTU, Pike Collection, Unit 5, box 18.

68. Taylor to McNamara, 17 November 1962, *FRUS*, 1961–1963, vol. 2, 319. See also Harkins to AIG, 8 September 1962, JFKL, NSF, box 196; Saigon to State, 11 September 1962, NA II, RG 59, C0092, reel 8; Heavner and Wood, "Developments in Viet-Nam Between General Taylor's Visits – October 1961– October 1962," n.d., *FRUS*, 1961–1963, vol. 2, 297; Saigon to State, 16 November 1962, NA II, RG 59, C0092, reel 9.

69. For Communist rapacity in the highlands and the South Vietnamese and CIA efforts to gain the support of the Uplanders, see Saigon to State, 23 May 1962, *FRUS*, 1961–1963, vol. 2, 203; Southeast Asia Task Force, "Status Report on Southeast Asia," 27 June 1962, *FRUS*, 1961–1963, vol. 2, 230; JCS to McNamara, 28 July 1962, *FRUS*, 1961–1963, vol. 2, 251; Saigon to State, 11 September 1962, NA II, RG 59, C0092, reel 8; Saigon to State, 15 September 1962, NA II, RG 59, C0092, reel 8; Heavner and Wood, "Developments in Viet-Nam Between General Taylor's Visits – October 1961–October 1962," n.d., *FRUS*, 1961–1963, vol. 2, 297; *Saturday Evening Post*, November 24, 1962; Johnson, trip notes, 10 December 1962, *FRUS*, 1961–1963, vol. 2, 327; Heavner, "Visit to Vietnam," 11 December 1962, *FRUS*, 1961–1963, vol. 2, 328; Mansfield, "Southeast Asia – Vietnam," 18 December 1962, *FRUS*, 1961–1963, vol. 2, 330; UPI, "Viet Cong Burn Montagnard Villages in New Terror Wave," December 20, 1962; Tregaskis, *Vietnam Diary*, 318.

70. Military History Institute of Vietnam, *Victory in Vietnam*, 110.

71. Cao Minh et al., *Quan Khu 8*, 424–8.

72. Truong Minh Hoach and Nguyen Minh Phung, *Quan Khu 9*, 328–9.

73. The Geneva agreement permitted the United States to send military supplies to Souvanna's government and to the rightists, and the United States did so in the hope of influencing their future conduct. The lack of warlike qualities among these groups, though, ensured that they would not disrupt the infiltration traffic. Two CIA officers remained in the mountains with the fierce Hmong tribesmen, who had agreed to the ceasefire at the urging of the Americans. The North Vietnamese and the Pathet Lao, however, continued to attack the Hmong and push them out of their settlements, a development that the CIA officers detailed in reports back to headquarters. Colby repeatedly pleaded with Harriman to assist the tribesmen, but Harriman refused. Finally, after months of escalating Communist military action, Harriman permitted secret shipments of ammunition to the Hmong armies, with the unrealistic stipulation that the ammunition be used only for defensive purposes. Colby, *Honorable Men*, 192–4.

74. Stevenson, *End of Nowhere*, 178–9. At the end of 1962, according to Hanoi's own figures, the North Vietnamese forces assigned to the Ho Chi Minh Trail alone numbered nearly 5,000. Nguyen Viet Phuong, *Van Tai Quan Su Chien Luoc Tren Duong Ho Chi Minh Trong Khang Chien Chong My*, 2nd ed. (Hanoi: General Department of Rear Services, 1988), 424.

75. Nguyen Viet Phuong, *Lich Su Bo Doi Truong Son Duong Ho Chi Minh*, 63, 68; Gaiduk, *Confronting Vietnam*, 179–80. Many of the infiltrators arrived in battalions that had been organized and outfitted in North Vietnam, giving them superior competence and cohesion.

76. Nguyen Viet Phuong, *Lich Su Bo Doi Truong Son Duong Ho Chi Minh*, 63. The first shipment of military supplies from North Vietnam to the Mekong Delta by sea also took place in 1962. Tran Van Quang et al., *Tong Ket Cuoc Khang Chien Chong My Cuu Nuoc*, 223; Nguyen Tu Duong, *Duong Mon Tren Bien* (Hanoi: People's Army Publishing House, 1986), 50–51; Pham Hong Thuy et al., *Lich su Hai Quan Nhan Dan Viet Nam* (Hanoi: People's Army Publishing House, 1985), 155.

77. Histories contending that South Vietnam was not viable for this reason include Anderson, *Trapped by Success;* Buzzanco, *Vietnam and the Transformation of American Life;* Gardner, *Pay Any Price;* Kaiser, *American Tragedy;* Khong, *Analogies At War;* Moss, *Vietnam;* Record, *The Wrong War.*

78. Wilfred Burchett, *Vietnam: Inside Story of the Guerrilla War* (New York: International Publishers, 1965), 193–4.

8. The Battle of Ap Bac: January 1963

1. The account of the Battle of Ap Bac in Sheehan's *A Bright Shining Lie* has been accepted unquestioningly by almost all subsequent historians. One recent history that examined the battle in depth using primary sources is Toczek, *The Battle of Ap Bac*. Toczek's account diverges in some respects from

Sheehan's account, but his overall conclusions are closer to Sheehan's than they are to those in this account.

2. Elliott, *The Vietnamese War*, 399–403; *New York Times*, Western Edition, January 4, 1963.

3. Nguyen Tu Duong, *Duong Mon Tren Bien*, 73.

4. Sheehan, *A Bright Shining Lie*, 209.

5. MACV, "Translation of VC Document on Ap Bac Battle 2 Jan 63," 20 April 1963, USAWCL.

6. Captain Kenneth Good of Ewa Beach, Hawaii, the battalion's senior advisor, sustained grievous wounds during the fighting and was taken by helicopter to Tan Hiep, where he died. Neil Sheehan was to report that Good had been killed while vainly urging the South Vietnamese troops to fight, but this report turned out to be false. Halberstam, *The Making of a Quagmire*, 157.

7. John Paul Vann, after action report, 9 January 1963, LOC, Sheehan Papers, box 38; John Paul Vann, interview with Charles von Luttichau, 22 July 1963, LOC, Sheehan Papers, box 39.

8. *Time*, January 11, 1963. Lieutenant Lewis Stone of Alexandria, Virginia, a crewman on one of the helicopters that failed to leave the landing zone, recalled that the Viet Cong "really pinned us down. Several of the ARVN troops were with us in the paddy. They would raise up and get hurt. There were a lot of wounded when they got us out of there." Tregaskis, *Vietnam Diary*, 379.

9. Carlton Nysewander, interview with author. See also *Wall Street Journal*, August 12, 1998.

10. James Scanlon, interview by Neil Sheehan, LOC, Sheehan Papers, box 76.

11. *Time*, January 11, 1963.

12. Le Quoc San, *Cuoc Do Suc Than Ky*, (Hanoi: People's Army Publishing House, 1991), 108.

13. Scanlon recalled, "Everybody started to become casualties because all of a sudden we were really getting raked." James Scanlon, interview by Neil Sheehan, LOC, Sheehan Papers, box 76.

14. Said Scanlon, "We were going through the same routine we had always gone through.... No one had any idea that the VC had prepared these positions ahead of time and had decided they were going to fight from them and had been in position and on alert since dawn. No one realized it because the VC had never done that before." James Scanlon, interview by Neil Sheehan, LOC, Sheehan Papers, box 76.

15. Dave R. Palmer, *Summons of the Trumpet: U.S. – Vietnam in Perspective* (Novato: Presidio Press, 1978), 37.

16. Sheehan, *A Bright Shining Lie*, 261.

17. Fletcher Ware, interview with author; Cao Van Vien, *Leadership* (Washington, DC: U.S. Army Center of Military History, 1980), 54. Ware jumped with the 8th Airborne Battalion on January 2, 1963. The only other American who parachuted in with the unit, Russell Kopti, is deceased. At the time of the Battle of Ap Bac, Cao Van Vien was the commanding officer of the South Vietnamese Airborne Brigade.

18. Sun Tzu, *The Art of War*, trans. by Samuel B. Griffith (Oxford: Oxford University Press, 1963), 109.

19. Cao reportedly said that he wanted to avoid cornering the Viet Cong force. Later in the war, General William Westmoreland was to conclude that South Vietnamese forces were giving great weight to Sun Tzu's dictum. William C. Westmoreland, *A Soldier Reports* (Garden City: Doubleday, 1976), 102. When attacking, the Viet Cong themselves liked to use the technique of leaving one exit route open and waiting until the enemy fled before swooping down onto the exit route to crush the departing troops. Two years later, at the much larger battle of Binh Gia, the Viet Cong would annihilate a South Vietnamese Ranger company by using this technique.

20. Diem undoubtedly had Vann in mind when he told Nolting, in April, that "the men at the top of your mission understand the psychological and political problems, but many junior officers among such a large and increasing American contingent do not, and are prone to insist upon their own ideas when they do not have sufficient experience of the country, its people, its traditions, and its way of doing things. The resulting frustration on the part of some Americans is the root cause of a great deal of unfavorable publicity, and of much uncoordinated reporting to Washington." Saigon to State, 5 April 1963, *FRUS*, 1961–1963, vol. 3, 81.

21. Fletcher Ware, interview with author.

22. John Paul Vann, after action report, 9 January 1963, LOC, Sheehan Papers, box 38.

23. If a force of three to four hundred men were to lose more than one hundred dead, it most likely would suffer an even greater number of wounded and thus would have a casualty rate well above fifty percent. Under such circumstances, it would face great difficulty in evacuating its casualties, even with sampans nearby, unless large numbers of civilians helped them carry the dead and wounded. The number of civilians who assisted them is unknown.

24. Le Quoc San, *Cuoc Do Suc Than Ky*, 116, 118. Le Quoc San also asserted that only twelve civilians were killed in the battle, which undercuts the argument that the Americans included large numbers of civilians in their total estimate of one hundred dead.

25. Halberstam, *The Making of a Quagmire*, 154; Sheehan, *A Bright Shining Lie*, 277.

26. *Washington Post*, January 4, 7, 1963. In the January 4 edition of the *New York Times*, Halberstam wrote that "in the eyes of one American observer" – the journalists rarely mentioned Vann by name – the government's troops "lost the initiative from the first moment and never showed much aggressive instinct and consequently suffered heavier casualties than they might have had they tried an all-out assault of the Vietcong positions." *New York Times*, Western Edition, January 4, 1963. See also *New York Times*, Western Edition, January 7, 1963.

27. *New York Times*, January 11, 1963.

28. *New York Times*, Western Edition, January 7, 1963.

29. Vann told Tregaskis that his bosses had been grilling him about his decisions at Ap Bac. One of the questions the brass had asked, Vann divulged, involved the distance between the tree line and the landing zone where the helicopters had been shot down. "Why did you land them so close to the enemy?" they had asked him. Vann had answered, "I'm delighted when I get a chance to get at the enemy." Tregaskis, *Vietnam Diary*, 389.

30. Daniel Boone Porter Oral History Interview, LBJL.

31. Hilsman and Forrestal to Kennedy, 25 January 1963, *FRUS*, 1961–1963, vol. 3, 19. According to a report by the British, who were in regular contact with the American advisory group, U.S. military advisers took a more positive view of the battle once it became clear that the Viet Cong defenders had "taken a bad mauling." Saigon to FO, 8 January 1963, PRO, FO 371/170131.

32. Tregaskis, *Vietnam Diary*, 380–1.

33. Andrew P. O'Meara, interview with author.

34. *New York Times*, October 27, 1963.

35. Sheehan, *A Bright Shining Lie*, 582. Sheehan approvingly quoted a military engineer who said that regardless of how many helicopters an army had, "you don't have much mobility in a full rice paddy."

36. Highly capable officers who occupied critical military positions in 1963 included Cao Van Vien, Do Cao Tri, Huynh Van Cao, Le Nguyen Khang, Le Quang Tung, Le Van Kim, Ly Tong Ba, Nguyen Huu Co, Nguyen Khanh, Nguyen Ngoc Khoi, Nguyen Van Thieu, Ton That Dinh, and Tran Thien Khiem. The quality of the provincial officials during 1963 is covered in later chapters.

37. Bruce Catton, *A Stillness at Appomattox* (Garden City: Doubleday, 1953), 210. For more on the political and military significance of the "political generals," see Thomas J. Goss, *The War Within the Union High Command: Politics and Generalship During the Civil War* (Lawrence, KS: University Press of Kansas, 2003).

38. James Robertson, *Stonewall Jackson: The Man, The Soldier, The Legend* (New York: Macmillan, 1997), 371.

39. Williams to Wurfel, 31 January 1963, HIA, Edward G. Lansdale Papers, box 49.

40. Robert Leckie, *George Washington's War: The Saga of the American Revolution* (New York: Harper Collins, 1992), 357; Burke Davis, *George Washington and the American Revolution* (New York: Random House, 1975), 223.

41. Davis, *George Washington and the American Revolution*, 373–4.

42. *Time*, January 11, 1963.

43. Porter to Harkins, "Final Report," 13 February 1963, NA II, RG 472, MACJ03, Military Historians Branch, Historians Background Files, Policy & Precedent Files, box 2.

44. John Paul Vann, "Senior Advisor's Final Report," 1 April 1963, LOC, Sheehan Papers, box 38.

45. Halberstam, for example, called the delta "the crucial area" of the war. *New York Times*, March 1, 1963. Sheehan later wrote that the "northern half of the delta" was "where the course of the war was going to be decided." Sheehan, *A Bright Shining Lie*, 41.

46. John Michael Dunn Oral History Interview I, LBJL, 3–4.

47. Tregaskis, *Vietnam Diary*, 6.

48. Le Duan, *Letters to the South*, 116.

49. Crimp document, undated, TTU, Pike Collection, Unit 1, box 3. During 1963, the central committee of the Vietnamese Communist Party issued a resolution stating that the mountainous highlands were "the area where we can build up a large armed force and annihilate many enemy troops in large-scale attacks. We can also use the mountainous area as a stepping stone to expand our activities to the lowlands and, when the situation allows, to attack the key positions of the enemy." Resolution of the Ninth Conference, December 1963, TTU, Viet-Nam Documents and Research Notes, box 2. See also Nguyen Van Minh et al., *Luc Luong Vu Trang Nhan Dan Tay Nguyen Trong Khang Chien Chong My Cuu Nuoc* (Hanoi: People's Army Publishing House, 1980); Trinh Nhu, ed., *Van Kien Dang*, Tap 21, 1960, 296; *Newsweek*, December 10, 1962.

50. *Mot So Van Kien Cua Dang Ve Chong My, Cuu Nuoc*, Tap I (1954–1965) (Hanoi: Su That, 1985), 146. Hanoi would, in fact, deliberately and successfully isolate the highlands in 1965 by gaining a strong position in Military Region 5. At its 11th Plenum in March 1965, the Vietnamese Communist Party leadership resolved, "Particular note should be made of the fact that the destruction of the strategic hamlets and the expansion of the liberated zones in the lowlands of Region 5 are increasingly cutting off and isolating the enemy's military forces stationed in the Central Highlands." Ibid., 212.

51. See, for example, *Executive Sessions of the Foreign Relations Committee*, 1963, 698–9.

52. Sheehan wrote afterwards that Harkins "really believed that the battle had not been a defeat for the Saigon troops." With Harkins, "anything which contradicted the official optimism was simply ignored or derided as false or inconsequential." Until Ap Bac, Sheehan asserted, the journalists and Vann "had been profoundly underestimating Harkins's capacity for self-delusion." Sheehan, *A Bright Shining Lie*, 283; Sheehan, Introduction to Roy, *The Battle of Dienbienphu*, xvii. Such would be Halberstam's indignation with Harkins over his handling of Ap Bac and other aspects of the war that he would tell some of his fellow journalists later in the year that "Paul D. Harkins should be court-martialed and shot!" Sheehan, *A Bright Shining Lie*, 350–1. Another such outburst occurred after the press learned in February of a confidential memorandum by John Mecklin that contained some positive remarks about the correspondents but also stated, "The American commitment to Vietnam has been badly hampered by irresponsible, astigmatic, and sensationalized reporting." The newsmen temporarily turned against Mecklin and threatened to boycott him for life. *Time* correspondent Mert Perry, knowing that Mecklin was soon to undergo surgery, told his colleagues, "I hope the son of a bitch dies!" David Halberstam Oral History Interview I, LBJL.

53. Saigon to FO, 10 February 1963, PRO, FO 371/170132; Prochnau, *Once Upon a Distant War*, 243.

54. Harkins to Dodge, 4 January 1963, JFKL, NSF, box 197.

55. Futrell, *Advisory Years to 1965*, 159; Saigon to State, 9 January 1963, NA II, RG 59, C0092, reel 13. Although Diem himself said little on record about the battle, he must have been thoroughly aware of what had transpired, given his intimate familiarity with other battles. Just days after Ap Bac, in conversation with Roger Hilsman and Michael Forrestal, he discussed in great depth an attack on the American Special Forces camp at Plei Mrong, which the Viet Cong had overrun a few days earlier. Hilsman and Forrestal had just visited the site. "Diem drew us a remarkably detailed sketch of the defenses of the camp," Hilsman reported, "and accompanied it with a devastatingly correct and completely fair critique of the mistakes in siting weapons, in cutting fields of fire, and so on made by the West Point commander of the camp. It made me squirm, particularly when Diem recalled that I, too, was a West Pointer." Hilsman recounted that Diem displayed a "very profound knowledge of his own country. There is no facet of it that he does not know everything about." Hilsman, *To Move a Nation*, 461; Hilsman, memcon, January 1963, *FRUS*, 1961–1963, vol. 3, 6.

56. A U.S. military delegation that visited Vietnam in January reported that Harkins was continuing to urge changes on Diem. Wheeler to JCS, "JCS Team Report on South Vietnam," January 1963, *FRUS*, 1961–1963, vol. 3, 26; Harriman, memcon, 9 February 1963, *FRUS*, 1961–1963, vol. 3, 36. In a February letter to Diem, Harkins remarked that the enemy "is being driven from the base of his support, the people" with the help of the strategic hamlet program, which "is the real core of our effort," but warned that "to relent now, in optimism over the favorable results and achievements of the past few months, could be ruinous or fatal to the RVN counterinsurgency." CINCPAC to RUEPDA/DIA, 13 March 1963, JFKL, NSF,

box 197. On March 11, Harkins urged the South Vietnamese to eliminate many of the small outposts in the countryside. Harkins to Thuan, 11 March 1963, JFKL, Newman Papers. Harkins told Diem in another letter that his commanders needed to reduce the number of large operations and pursue fleeing enemy forces with greater determination. Harkins to Diem, 15 May 1963, *FRUS*, 1961–1963, vol. 3, 123.

57. Felt to Rusk, 11 January 1963, JFKL, NSF, box 197.

58. Nolting to Harriman, 19 November 1962, *FRUS*, 1961–1963, vol. 2, 320. See also Michael Forrestal Oral History, JFKL.

59. Ambrose, *Eisenhower: Soldier and President*, 82, 88. Sheehan actually had cited Eisenhower as an example of all the negative qualities that Harkins, in Sheehan's view, possessed. Sheehan, *A Bright Shining Lie*, 284–7.

60. Thomas J. Lewis, *Year of the Hare: Bureaucratic Distortion in the U.S. Military View of the Vietnam War in 1963* (Master's thesis, George Washington University, 1972), 57; Daniel Boone Porter Oral History Interview, LBJL.

61. Sorley, *Honorable Warrior*, 156.

62. Halberstam, *The Making of a Quagmire*, 147.

9. Diem on Trial: February–July 1963

1. While some histories have taken note of certain successes of the South Vietnamese armed forces and the strategic hamlets in 1962, none have appreciated the successes of 1963. The war from January to October 1963 either receives little attention or is portrayed as a period of decline for the government. This characterization applies even to those histories that have tried to give serious consideration to Diem's achievements – Hammer, *A Death in November;* Catton, *Diem's Final Failure;* Winters, *The Year of the Hare;* Dommen, *The Indochinese Experience of the French and the Americans*.

2. NIE 53–63, "Prospects in South Vietnam," 17 April 1963, JFKL, Newman Papers.

3. Col. Bryce F. Denno, "Report of Duty Tour in a Country Confronted with Insurgency," 19 July 1963, JFKL, Newman Papers.

4. Wilbur Wilson, "Estimate of the Situation III Corps – 30 June 1963," 8 July 1963, MHI, Wilbur Wilson Papers.

5. Krulak, "Visit to Vietnam, 25 June-1 July 1963," NDUL. For the situation in Quang Ngai, see also JCS J-3, "South Vietnam Operations – Intelligence Summary," 27 April 1963, NA II, RG 218, JCS Central File, 1963, box 9; Saigon to State, 29 April 1963, NA II, RG 59, Central Files, 1963, box 3763. Long considered one of the military's most innovative thinkers, Krulak was also a man who told it as he saw it. A few years later, he would bluntly tell the nation's top brass that they were fighting the war in Vietnam the wrong way. But the war was much different then from what it was in the summer of 1963, and in the summer of 1963 Krulak believed that the war was moving along a favorable path.

6. Krulak to Bundy, "Long An Province," 11 September 1963, JFKL, Newman Papers.

7. Saigon to State, 6 July 1963, *FRUS*, 1961–1963, vol. 3, 209. In this document, Truehart noted that "progress here is afoot. There remains no doubt that military defeat of the Viet Cong is attainable, barring catastrophic political or social developments in the Republic of Vietnam."

8. Saigon to State, 17 May 1963, NA II, RG 59, Central Files, 1963, box 4050; Denney, "Strategic Hamlets," 1 July 1963, *FRUS*, 1961–1963, vol. 3, 197; Saigon to State, 18 July 1963, NA II, RG 59, Central Files, 1963, box 4049; Saigon to State, 27 July 1963, NA II, RG 59, C0096, reel 5. Thompson told President Kennedy in April that "Diem has much support in the country where it counted," while he had "written off the Saigon intelligentsia." Wood, memcon, 4 April 1963, *FRUS*, 1961–1963, vol. 3, 77.

9. Serong noted that the strategic hamlets in the central Vietnamese lowlands were "beautifully done, almost copy book versions of the strategic hamlet concept." Memcon, 22 May 1963, NA II, RG 59, Central Files, 1963, box 4137; Dingeman, meeting notes, 23 May 1963, *FRUS*, 1961–1963, vol. 3, 132. In a March 1963 report, Serong had stated that the Diem government, despite some problems in a variety of areas, was winning the war and that the Viet Cong had not found a way to counter the strategic hamlet program. Serong, "Strategic Review," 14 March 1963, MHI, Westmoreland Papers, box 28. In a recent book, historian David Kaiser laid great stress on the problems identified in Serong's March 14 report but left out its positive overall conclusion, and he made no mention of Serong's remarks in May. Kaiser, *American Tragedy*, 190–2.

10. Robert Thompson, "The Situation in South Vietnam, March 1963," 11 March 1963, PRO, FO 371/170100.

11. Gibbons, *The U.S. Government and the Vietnam War*, vol. 2, 140; Dingeman, meeting notes, 4 April 1963, *FRUS, 1961–1963*, vol. 3, 78; Busch, *All the Way with JFK?*, 129. Chester Cooper, whom CIA Director John McCone dispatched to Vietnam during the spring for an independent appraisal, decided that "the GVN can probably defeat the Viet Cong militarily," and, with the exception of parts of the delta, victory would "probably take place within about three years." Ford, *CIA and the Vietnam Policymakers*, 16.

12. Rufus Phillips, interview with author; William Truehart Oral History Interview, LBJL; Saigon to State, 11 March 1963, NA II, RG 59, Central Files, 1963, box 4048; Saigon to State, 15 April 1963, NA II, RG 59, C0096, reel 5; Saigon to State, 27 July 1963, NA II, RG 59, C0096, reel 5; Saigon to State, 19 August 1963, NA II, RG 59, Central Files, 1963, box 3763; Saigon to State, 30 September 1963, NA II, RG 59, C0092, reel 5; O'Donnell, "The Strategic Hamlet Program in Kien Hoa Province, South Vietnam: A Case Study of Counter-Insurgency," 11 May 1965, TTU, John Donnell Collection, box 6. In an earlier report, Phillips had observed that "the provincial representatives of USOM, and the sector advisors of MAAG, get around as much as they can, and visit as many hamlets as possible." He added that many hamlets had not been visited by U.S. personnel simply because of time constraints, but this report and others make clear that Americans visited enough hamlets on an impromptu basis to estimate accurately the ratio of hamlets actually completed to hamlets reportedly completed. Phillips to York, 24 January 1963, HIA, Charles T. R. Bohannon Papers, box 34.

13. Phillips to Brent, 1 May 1963, *FRUS, 1961–1963*, vol. 3, 102. One day before the issuance of the report, Phillips had noted that "we are winning the war in Vietnam," and that "it is our belief that the GVN and the majority of its leaders have made an admirable effort to overcome almost insuperable obstacles." Phillips, "Financing, and the Future of the Counter-Insurgency Effort in Vietnam," 30 April 1963, HIA, Edward G. Lansdale Papers, box 40

14. In a June 1963 report, Harkins's command reported, "Throughout Vietnam there are great differences in the quality and conditions of strategic hamlets that are reported as completed." The American military advisers were aware of the discrepancy from visiting the strategic hamlets: "Based on observations during field visits, it is estimated that about 40 to 50% of those reported as 'completed hamlets' are in fact fully and properly developed." Krulak, "Visit to Vietnam, 25 June-1 July 1963," NDUL. Nhu stated in March 1963 that of the five thousand officially completed strategic hamlets, only one third satisfied all of the criteria for completion. Catton, *Diem's Final Failure*, 131. See also memcon, 1 May 1963, HIA, Edward G. Lansdale Papers, box 40.

15. Ray A. Bows, *Vietnam Military Lore* (Hanover, MA: Bows & Sons, 1997), 362.

16. *New York Times*, July 22, 1963.

17. *Washington Post*, July 21, 1963. See also Saigon to State, 23 July 1963, JFKL, Newman Papers; Saigon to State, 27 July 1963, NA II, RG 59, C0096, reel 5; Thang and Stilwell to Ty and Harkins, 29 July 1963, NA II, RG 472, MACJ3–12, JGS Joint Operations Center Weekly Resume, box 1; Elliott, *The Vietnamese War*, 420–1.

18. Nguyen Phu Cuong, "U.S. 'Special War' (1961–1965)," *Vietnamese Studies*, no. 18/19, 1968, 173–4.

19. "COSVN Standing Committee Directive Discussing the Tasks for the Last Six Months of 1963," September 1963, TTU, Pike Collection, Unit 6, box 1.

20. Dang Uy va Tu Lenh Quan Khu 5, *Quan Khu 5: Thang Loi va Nhung Bai Hoc Trong Khang Chien Chong My*, vol. 1 (Hanoi: Nha Xuat Ban Quan Doi Nhan Dan, 1981), 46–9.

21. Military History Institute of Vietnam, *Victory in Vietnam*, 110.

22. Ibid., 113.

23. Le Quoc San, *Cuoc Do Suc Than Ky*, 144.

24. Vietnam News Agency, "The South Vietnam Revolution Must Be Long-Drawn, Arduous, and Complicated But Certainly Victorious," 19 March 1963, TTU, Pike Collection, Unit 1, box 2.

25. For a particularly emphatic example, see *Washington Post*, May 14, 1995. Histories that have echoed this claim are Bird, *The Color of Truth*; Ford, *CIA and the Vietnam Policymakers*; Freedman, *Kennedy's Wars*; Hammond, *Public Affairs: The Military and the Media, 1962–1968*; Hunt, *Lyndon Johnson's War*; Kahin, *Intervention*; Krepinevich, *The Army and Vietnam*; Langguth, *Our Vietnam*; Logevall, *Choosing War*; Moss, *Vietnam*; Prochnau, *Once Upon a Distant War*; Schwab, *Defending the Free World*.

26. Albert Fraleigh, interview with author.

27. Edward Rowny, *Lieutenant General Edward L. Rowny, Former Ambassador* (Alexandria, VA: U.S. Army Corps of Engineers, 1995).

28. *New York Times*, July 28, 1963. See also *New York Times*, April 13, 1963 and May 5, 1963.

29. The Joint Chiefs of Staff team that visited Vietnam in January observed that Diem could not defeat the Viet Cong any time soon if the Communists retained the use of Laotian and Cambodian territory, remarking, "to cauterize the 900 miles of border and 1500 miles of coastline presents a problem which even the most dynamic of efforts on the part of the Vietnamese will not greatly diminish." The problem, they said, "must be solved by methods more practicable than surveillance of the country's borders." Wheeler to JCS, "JCS Team Report on South Vietnam," January 1963, *FRUS*, 1961–1963, vol. 3, 26. Concerned that direct U.S. action against North Vietnam would lead to a larger conflict, Wheeler and the others advocated an increase in South Vietnam's covert sabotage and subversion activities in North Vietnam. Earle Wheeler Oral History, JFKL.

30. During the first half of 1963, the CIA transferred control of its Uplander forces to the U.S. military assistance command, which chose to assign the Uplanders to numerous mobile operations against Communist base areas and infiltration routes. Critics assailed the military for using the Uplanders in such conventional operations, contending that this departure from the original village-defense mission was counterproductive. They attributed the change to the military's lack of imagination and flexibility. Blaufarb, *The Counterinsurgency Era*, 106–7, 259–60; Krepinevich, *The Army and Vietnam*, 69–75; Nagl, *Counterinsurgency Lessons from Malaya and Vietnam*, 128–9. But, given that conventional warfare posed the greatest threat to South Vietnam and that the highlands provided critical supply routes and base areas to the Communist forces, the mobile operations were more important strategically than the village-defense operations. When the Uplander forces were well led, moreover, the mobile operations did not prevent the Uplanders from resisting Communist intrusion into their villages.

31. Wheeler to JCS, "JCS Team Report on South Vietnam," January 1963, *FRUS*, 1961–1963, vol. 3, 26; Rostow to Rusk, 4 July 1963, *FRUS*, 1961–1963, vol. 3, 206.

32. Military History Institute of Vietnam, *Victory in Vietnam*, 115; High-Level Military Institute, *Vietnam: The Anti-U.S. Resistance War for National Salvation*, 32; Tran Van Quang et al., *Tong Ket Cuoc Khang Chien Chong My Cuu Nuoc*, 311; Gaiduk, *Confronting Vietnam*, 197. The infiltration rate for 1963 was calculated by deducting the infiltration figures for 1959–1962 provided in chapters 3–7 from the total of 40,000 for 1959–1963 cited in several of the Communist histories.

33. At the end of June, Krulak reported that 11,700 people had already left the Viet Cong via Diem's Chieu Hoi amnesty program, which had been created in April 1962. Krulak, "Visit to Vietnam, 25 June-1 July 1963," NDUL.

34. Crimp document, undated, TTU, Pike Collection, Unit 1, box 3.

35. Memcon, 26 April 1963, *FRUS*, 1961–1963, vol. 24, 466.

36. Diem's order to his province chiefs and city mayors stated: "Direct that all places of worship of all religions that the only flag that may be flown above places of worship (churches, pagodas, etc.) is our national flag." Le Cung, *Phong Trao Phat Giao Mien Nam Viet Nam, Nam 1963* (Hanoi: Nha Xuat Ban Dai Hoc Quoc Gia Ha Noi, 1999), 298.

37. Hue to State, 10 May 1963, *FRUS*, 1961–1963, vol. 3, 116.

38. For an earlier case of a quite similar nature, see Saigon to State, 29 October 1962, NA II, RG 59, C0092, reel 8.

39. Hue to State, 10 May 1963, *FRUS*, 1961–1963, vol. 3, 117.

40. The U.S. correspondents would soon be telling anyone who would listen that they were hoping for the overthrow of the government. See, for example, Saigon to State, 10 July 1963, *FRUS*, 1961–1963, vol. 2, 210n. When American officials offered a toast to Diem at an official reception in July, Halberstam held his glass to his chest and yelled, "I'd never drink to that son of a bitch!" Prochnau, *Once Upon a Distant War*, 324. Numerous historians have advanced the journalists' argument that the Buddhist crisis demonstrated the bankruptcy of the Diem government. Anderson, *The Vietnam War*; Buzzanco, *Vietnam and the Transformation of American Life*; Dallek, *An Unfinished Life*; Davidson, *Vietnam At War*; Duiker, *U.S. Containment Policy and the Conflict in Indochina*; Ford, *CIA and the Vietnam Policymakers*; Freedman, *Kennedy's Wars*; Hammond, *Public Affairs: The Military and the Media, 1962–1968*; Herring,

America's Longest War; Jacobs, *America's Miracle Man in Vietnam;* Jones, *Death of a Generation;* Kahin, *Intervention;* Kaiser, *American Tragedy;* Karnow, *Vietnam;* Logevall, *Choosing War;* Lomperis, *From People's War to People's Rule;* Nagl, *Counterinsurgency Lessons from Malaya and Vietnam;* Prochnau, *Once Upon a Distant War;* Record, *The Wrong War;* Schwab, *Defending the Free World;* Sheehan, *A Bright Shining Lie;* Robert J. Topmiller, *The Lotus Unleashed: The Buddhist Peace Movement in South Vietnam, 1964–1966* (Lexington: University Press of Kentucky, 1992); Turley, *The Second Indochina War;* Young, *Vietnam Wars;* Zhai, *China and the Vietnam Wars.*

41. David Halberstam, *The Powers That Be* (New York: Knopf, 1979), 452. Halberstam put part of the blame on U.S. embassy officials, stating that the press's political reporting "was limited by the absence of serious skilled Asia experts in the American Embassy. The McCarthy era had taken care of that." As explained in chapter 2, the United States did not lack Asia experts. It did have some officials who were ignorant of Vietnamese culture and politics, and the press paid much heed to such individuals, primarily because these people tended to be the fiercest critics of Diem.

42. Halberstam, *The Making of a Quagmire,* 279.

43. Hoang Hai Van and Tan Tu, *Pham Xuan An,* 196.

44. Karnow, *Vietnam,* 39.

45. Halberstam, *The Making of a Quagmire,* 229. Pham Xuan An later denied that he had fed false information to his press corps colleagues, and some of those colleagues have accepted that claim. Morley Safer, *Flashbacks: On Returning to Vietnam* (New York: Random House, 1990), 178–81; Thomas A. Bass, "The Spy Who Loved Us," *The New Yorker,* May 23, 2005; Karnow, *Vietnam,* 40. This claim is implausible, in light of the fact that Pham Xuan An was recruited in order to influence the foreign press, and the fact that the journalists who were to cite him as their best source on the officer corps routinely wrote inaccurate stories on the officer corps in 1963, to the detriment of the South Vietnamese government.

46. Hammer, *A Death in November,* 139; Richard Critchfield, *The Long Charade: Political Subversion in the Vietnam War* (New York: Harcourt, Brace, and World, 1968), 70; Piero Gheddo, *The Cross and the Bo-Tree: Catholics and Buddhists in Vietnam* (New York: Sheed and Ward, 1970), 187; Higgins, *Our Vietnam Nightmare,* 47; CIA, Office of Current Intelligence, "The Buddhists in South Vietnam," 28 June 1963, JFKL, NSF, Box 197; CIA, "Tri Quang and the Buddhist-Catholic Discord in South Vietnam," 19 September 1964, LBJL, NSF, VNCF, box 9.

47. "The Buddhist Movement in Vietnam and its Difficulties with the Present Government," April 1961, TTU, John Donnell Collection, box 6.

48. Gheddo, *The Cross and the Bo-Tree,* 176. John Mecklin, who became one of the Diem regime's most ardent detractors, later said that the allegations of "religious persecution" leveled by Buddhist leaders and their proponents were "absurd." Mecklin, *Mission in Torment,* 159.

49. Halberstam, for example, wrote that the Buddhists "form the bulk of South Vietnam's population," but "President Ngo Dinh Diem and most of his officials are Roman Catholic." *New York Times,* July 20, 1963.

50. Winters, *Year of the Hare,* 178. Diem, moreover, had strenuously resisted efforts by Catholic clergymen to exert influence over the government. Gheddo, *The Cross and the Bo-Tree,* 143–5.

51. The press's interpretation has been echoed in Hammond, *Public Affairs: The Military and the Media, 1962–1968;* Jones, *Death of a Generation;* Kahin, *Intervention;* Karnow, *Vietnam;* Lomperis, *From People's War to People's Rule;* Mann, *A Grand Delusion;* Prochnau, *Once Upon a Distant War;* Sheehan, *A Bright Shining Lie;* Young, *Vietnam Wars.*

52. Two good examples were the Vietnamese labor leader Tran Quoc Buu and his number-two man, Dam Sy Hien, both of them respected and independent-minded individuals. Displaying full approval of Diem's policies towards the Buddhists, they dismissed the Buddhist monks as "uninformed and unsophisticated." Saigon to State, 18 July 1963, MHI, Gard Papers, box 1.

53. Most historians have similarly concluded that the Buddhist protesters were upstanding citizens motivated only by dissatisfaction with the government's alleged religious intolerance. Duiker, *The Communist Road to Power in Vietnam;* Jacobs, *America's Miracle Man in Vietnam;* Kahin, *Intervention;* Kaiser, *American Tragedy;* Karnow, *Vietnam;* Langguth, *Our Vietnam;* Rust, *Kennedy in Vietnam;* Schulzinger, *A Time for War;* Schwab, *Defending the Free World;* Sheehan, *A Bright Shining Lie;* Topmiller, *The Lotus Unleashed;* Young, *Vietnam Wars.*

54. A high-level Communist resolution prepared a few years earlier had described the general approach: "We should strive to plant our agents in religious organizations.... Once our agents are planted, they then lead these organizations to work for the cause of the people." COSVN draft resolution, October 1961, CDEC Doc Log No. 01-0529-70, TTU, Pike Collection, Unit 6, box 7.

55. MACV J2 Translation Section, "Translation of Document per Request of IV Corps," HIA, Charles T. R. Bohannon Papers, box 5. From the early stages of the tumult, the National Liberation Front added to the suspicions about the Buddhists' relations with the Communists by issuing declarations supporting the Buddhists' claims. Nguyen Phuc Khanh et al., ed., *Chung Mot Bong Co (ve Mat Tran Dan Toc Giai Phong Mien Nam Viet Nam)* (Ho Chi Minh City: Nha Xuat Ban Chinh Tri Quoc Gia, 1993), 214.

56. Hoi Dong Bien Soan Lich Su Nam Trung Bo Khang Chien, *Nam Trung Bo Khang Chien*, 300, 302. See also Le Cung, *Phong Trao Phat Giao Mien Nam Viet Nam*, 292–3.

57. Nguyen Phuc Khanh et al., ed., *Chung Mot Bong Co*, 217–18. See also Vien Nghien Cuu Chu Nghia Mac Lenin Va Tu Tuong Ho Chi Minh, *Lich Su Dang Cong San Viet Nam*, Tap II, 250.

58. One official history explained that the Saigon-Gia Dinh Region Party Committee "urged all classes of the population of the city to join the demonstrations alongside the monks and Buddhist followers, and it decided to send in cadre to fight alongside the movement to awaken the revolutionary awareness of the masses and to establish and expand the leadership role of the Party in the urban struggle movement. Implementing the Region Party Committee's decision, large numbers of workers, students, and small businessmen, acting under the banner of 'Buddhism,' joined the Buddhist movement and made even more aggressive demands." Nguyen Viet Ta et al., *Mien Dong Nam Bo Khang Chien*, Tap II, 142.

59. Saigon to State, 21 November 1963, NA II, RG 59, Central Files, 1963, box 4047; CIA, "An Analysis of Thich Tri Quang's Possible Communist Affiliations, Personality and Goals," 28 August 1964, DDRS, 1976, 22E; Critchfield, *The Long Charade*, 62–81; Higgins, *Our Vietnam Nightmare*, 29; Jean Lacouture, *Vietnam: Between Two Truces*, trans. by Konrad Kellen and Joel Carmichael (New York: Random House, 1966), 222.

60. CIA, "Situation Appraisal of the Political Situation," 8 July 1963, *FRUS, 1961–1963*, vol. 3, 212.

61. At the beginning of June, as the Buddhist protesters continued to denounce the government, Truehart was to inform Washington, "Chief bonze Tri Quang, among staunchest of militants, has reportedly stated earlier this week that situation in his view beyond compromise and, in direct confrontation with GVN, Buddhists should seek help from any source, including VC." Saigon to State, 1 June 1963, *FRUS, 1961–1963*, vol. 3, 142.

62. CIA, "An Analysis of Thich Tri Quang's Possible Communist Affiliations, Personality and Goals," 28 August 1964, DDRS, 1976, 22E; Topmiller, *The Lotus Unleashed*, 156; *New York Herald Tribune*, April 11, 1966.

63. *New York Times*, July 14, 1979. In April 1975, as the end of South Vietnam approached, Tri Quang turned down an American offer to take him out of the country. Langguth, *Our Vietnam*, 660. What happened to Tri Quang after the war remains something of a mystery. According to one Western press account, the Communists gave Tri Quang a job in Hue and the activist monk did not object to their regime, in sharp contrast to many other politically inclined monks whom the Communist rulers imprisoned. *Washington Post*, November 2, 1983. Another account, however, stated that the Communists imprisoned Tri Quang for one and a half years after the fall of Saigon. *New York Times*, July 14, 1979.

64. Colby, *Lost Victory*, 124.

65. Moore to Wilson, 1 February 1963, *FRUS, 1961–1963*, vol. 3, 28.

66. Saigon to State, 31 May 1963, *FRUS, 1961–1963*, vol. 3, 140.

67. Saigon to State, 4 June 1963, *FRUS, 1961–1963*, vol. 3, 149.

68. Saigon to State, 8 June 1963, JFKL, NSF, box 197.

69. Beneath the caption, the ad condemned "our country's military aid to those who denied him religious freedom" and "the loss of American lives and billions of dollars to bolster a regime universally regarded as unjust, undemocratic, and unstable." *New York Times*, June 27, 1963.

70. Memo for the record, 14 June 1963, *FRUS, 1961–1963*, vol. 3, 169n.

71. State to Saigon, 14 June 1963, JFKL, NSF, box 197.

72. Saigon to State, 16 June 1963, *FRUS, 1961–1963*, vol. 3, 179; Saigon to State, 19 June 1963, *FRUS, 1961–1963*, vol. 3, 180.

73. Saigon to State, 16 June 1963, *FRUS*, 1961–1963, vol. 3, 177.

74. Halberstam, *The Making of a Quagmire*, 212–3; Prochnau, *Once Upon a Distant War*, 319. See also DIA to Clifton, "Special Intelligence Summary," 26 June 1963, DDRS, document number CK3100171742.

75. Saigon to State, 22 June 1963, *FRUS*, 1961–1963, vol. 3, 185.

76. Saigon to State, 29 June 1963, *FRUS*, 1961–1963, vol. 3, 193.

77. CIA, "Situation Appraisal of the Political Situation," 8 July 1963, *FRUS*, 1961–1963, vol. 3, 212.

78. Schlesinger, *A Thousand Days*, 989. At the time of Lodge's appointment, a senior administration official reportedly sneered, "If we have to lose Vietnam, we might as well let a Republican take the blame." Mecklin, *Mission in Torment*, 221.

79. Saigon to State, *FRUS*, 1961–1963, vol. 3, 186; Saigon to State, 27 June 1963, *FRUS*, 1961–1963, vol. 3, 189.

80. Saigon to State, 29 June 1963, *FRUS*, 1961–1963, vol. 3, 194; Saigon to State, 6 July 1963, NA II, RG 59, Central Files, 1963, box 4047; Saigon to State, 12 July 1963, NA II, RG 59, Central Files, 1963, box 4047; Saigon to State, 27 July 1963, NA II, RG 59, C0096, reel 5.

81. Saigon to State, 7 July 1963, *FRUS*, 1961–1963, vol. 3, 210.

82. Salinger, *With Kennedy*, 327.

83. Kattenburg, memcon, 26 July 1963, *FRUS*, 1961–1963, vol. 3, 238; Manning, "Report on the Saigon Press Situation," n.d., *FRUS*, 1961–1963, vol. 3, 239.

84. *New York Times*, July 3, 1963. Later in the month, the *Washington Post*, which to the Vietnamese seemed another meter of official U.S. opinion, openly recommended that the United States engineer Diem's overthrow because of his "continuing persecution of Buddhists." *Washington Post*, July 19, 1963.

85. Saigon to State, 11 December 1963, NA II, RG 59, Central Files, 1963, box 4049.

86. Grant, *Facing the Phoenix*, 198–9; Karnow, *Vietnam*, 298–301.

87. CIA, "Comments on reports of Ngo Dinh Nhu's coup plotting," 13 July 1963, *FRUS*, 1961–1963, vol. 3, 220.

88. Nolting, *From Trust to Tragedy*, 111–14; Nolting, "William C. Truehart, Deputy Chief of Mission," 17 August 1963, University of Virginia Library, Nolting Papers, box 13.

89. Saigon to State, 28 July 1963, *FRUS*, 1961–1963, vol. 3, 241; Hilsman, "Buddhist Problem in Viet-Nam," 6 August 1963, *FRUS*, 1961–1963, vol. 3, 246.

90. State to Saigon, 23 July 1963, *FRUS*, 1961–1963, vol. 3, 234.

10. Betrayal: August 1963

1. Higgins, *Our Vietnam Nightmare*, 165–176. Diem gave a similarly insightful interview earlier in the year. *U.S. News and World Report*, February 18, 1963.

2. Saigon to State, 6 August 1963, MHI, Gard Papers, box 1.

3. Ho Son Dai and Tran Phan Chan, *Lich Su Saigon-Cho Lon-Gia Dinh Khang Chien (1945–1975)* (Ho Chi Minh City: Ho Chi Minh City Publishing House, 1994), 364.

4. Warner, *The Last Confucian*, 230.

5. Saigon to State, 21 August 1963, DDRS, 1985, 22; Saigon to State, 21 August 1963, JFKL, NSF, box 198; Carroll to McNamara, 21 August 1963, *FRUS*, 1961–1963, vol. 3, 264; CIA Saigon to CIA, 24 August 1963, *FRUS*, 1961–1963, vol. 3, 275; CIA Saigon to CIA, 10 September 1963, *FRUS*, 1961–1963, vol. 4, 80; Higgins, *Our Vietnam Nightmare*, 192.

6. Saigon to State, 21 August 1963, DDRS, 1985, 22; Saigon to State, 21 August 1963, *FRUS*, 1961–1963, vol. 3, 261; CIA Saigon to CIA, 24 August 1963, *FRUS*, 1961–1963, vol. 3, 275; CIA Saigon to CIA, 10 September 1963, *FRUS*, 1961–1963, vol. 4, 80; Higgins, *Our Vietnam Nightmare*, 190–2; *New York Times*, August 23, 1963. Many of South Vietnam's senior generals also signed a document stating, "All the responsible commanders of the Army had unanimously and respectfully proposed to the President of the Republic and obtained from him the establishment of the state of martial law, as well as the measures related to it, and the Army has directly taken all the necessary steps to carry out that mission." *New York Herald Tribune*, August 29, 1963. See also General Dinh's remarks in *New York Times*, August 30, 1963.

7. At a press conference on August 29, as reported by Halberstam, Dinh announced that he had commanded the pagoda clearing operations. *New York Times*, August 30, 1963. In 1999, a Vietnamese Communist historian published General Dinh's report to Diem on the events of 20–21 August, in which Dinh described in detail how he, as the military governor of Saigon and III Corps commander, carried out the evacuation of the pagodas using military and other security forces. Le Cung, *Phong Trao Phat Giao Mien Nam Viet Nam*, 305–9.

8. On the organization and execution of the pagoda raids, see Saigon to State, 21 August 1963, MHI, Gard Papers, box 2; USAIRA Saigon to State, 21 August 1963, NA II, RG 59, Central Files, 1963, box 4048; USARMA Saigon to State, 22 August 1963, NA II, RG 59, Central Files, 1963, box 4137; Harkins to Taylor, 22 August 1963, NA II, RG 59, Central Files, 1963, box 4138; Le Cung, *Phong Trao Phat Giao Mien Nam Viet Nam*, 305–9; Blair, *There to the Bitter End*, 59–60; Blair, *Lodge in Vietnam*, 32–33. Tri Quang escaped arrest and disappeared mysteriously for ten days before seeking and obtaining asylum at the U.S. embassy. Saigon to State, 1 September 1963, JFKL, NSF, box 199. Embassy officials who listened to him denounce the Diem government found that he changed his position on an issue as soon as he discovered that it had not convinced the Americans of Diem's undesirability. Saigon to State, 21 November 1963, NA II, RG 59, Central Files, 1963, box 4047.

9. Kattenburg, memcon, 14 October 1963, NA II, RG 59, Central Files, 1963, box 4046. See also Harkins to Taylor, 22 August 1963, DDRS, 1995, 208; Saigon to State, 26 August 1963, MHI, Gard Papers, box 2; Canberra to State, 3 October 1963, NA II, RG 59, Central Files, 1963, box 4047.

10. Saigon to FO, 5 September 1963, PRO, FO 371/170146.

11. *New York Times*, August 22, 24, 1963.

12. *New York Times*, August 23, 1963. Halberstam's report on a "semi-coup" led by the Nhus appeared on the front page of the *New York Times* right next to a detailed story on Vietnam by Tad Szulc that correctly identified the military leadership's central role in conceiving and carrying out the eviction of the Buddhists from the pagodas.

13. *New York Times*, August 24, 1963.

14. Halberstam, *The Making of a Quagmire*, 231.

15. United Nations General Assembly, Eighteenth Session, Document A/5630, "Report of the United Nations Fact-Finding Mission to South Viet-Nam," 7 December 1963, 75–6.

16. *New York Times*, August 25, 1963.

17. *New York Times*, August 27, 29, and 31, 1963.

18. Saigon to State, 24 August 1963, *FRUS*, 1961–1963, vol. 3, 274.

19. Saigon to State, 24 August 1963, JFKL, NSF, box 198.

20. Hoang Lac and Ha Mai Viet, *Why America Lost the Vietnam War*, 154.

21. Saigon to State, 24 August 1963, *FRUS*, 1961–1963, vol. 3, 273.

22. Two weeks later, Phillips reported on another conversation with Thuan as follows: "Thuan opened the conversation by saying that he felt completely useless now. Nhu says he has been bought by the Americans, and would certainly kill him if he tried to resign. . . . Thuan said that Nhu was definitely trying to destroy him. He is telling Diem that Thuan is an American agent, and Thuan senses that Diem's attitude toward him has changed." Saigon to State, 9 September 1963, *FRUS*, 1961–1963, vol. 4, 76.

23. CIA Saigon to CIA, 24 August 1963, *FRUS*, 1961–1963, vol. 3, 275. Don also lauded the effective execution of the raids and indicated that Dinh was involved in carrying them out, but he claimed that he personally did not know that the raids had occurred until after the fact. Ibid. A reliable Vietnamese officer, however, informed an American colonel that Don had been briefed about the operation in advance. CIA Saigon to CIA, 10 September 1963, *FRUS*, 1961–1963, vol. 4, 80.

24. Historians have been equally inaccurate in analyzing the pagoda raids. See Anderson, *The Vietnam War*; Catton, *Diem's Final Failure*; Dallek, *An Unfinished Life*; Freedman, *Kennedy's Wars*; Gardner, *Pay Any Price*; Hess, *Vietnam and the United States*; Gibbons, *The U.S. Government and the Vietnam War*, vol. 2; Hammond, *Public Affairs: The Military and the Media, 1962–1968*; Herring, *America's Longest War*; Jones, *Death of a Generation*; Kahin, *Intervention*; Karnow, *Vietnam*; Langguth, *Our Vietnam*; Lomperis, *From People's War to People's Rule*; Mann, *A Grand Delusion*; Moss, *Vietnam*; Newman, *JFK and Vietnam*; Olson and Roberts, *Where the Domino Fell*; Prochnau, *Once Upon A Distant War*; Reeves, *President Kennedy*; Rust, *Kennedy in Vietnam*; Schulzinger, *A Time for War*; Sheehan, *A Bright Shining Lie*; Topmiller, *The Lotus Unleashed*; VanDeMark, *Into the Quagmire*.

25. State to Saigon, 24 August 1963, *FRUS*, 1961–1963, vol. 3, 281.

26. Gerald S. Strober and Deborah H. Strober, *"Let Us Begin Anew": An Oral History of the Kennedy Presidency* (New York: HarperCollins, 1993), 410.

27. Grant, *Facing the Phoenix*, 205. Regarding Dunn's working relationship with Lodge, see also Mecklin, *Mission in Torment*, 222–3. The other embassy staffer who enjoyed Lodge's confidence, Frederick Flott, remembered that when the journalists and General Harkins gave Lodge conflicting accounts of developments in South Vietnam, Lodge usually believed the journalists on the grounds that "they probably had more of a hands-on grasp of the story." Flott, interview with author.

28. *New York Herald Tribune*, 26–28 August 1963.

29. Prochnau, *Once Upon a Distant War*, 397–8.

30. Saigon to State, 24 August 1963, *FRUS*, 1961–1963, 276. See also Blair, *Lodge in Vietnam*, 14–15.

31. CIA Saigon to CIA, 25 August 1963, *FRUS*, 1961–1963, vol. 3, 285n; Acting Secretary of State to Lodge, 25 August 1963, *FRUS*, 1961–1963, vol. 3, 286; telcon, 25 August 1963, LBJL, Ball Papers, box 7.

32. Voice of America Broadcast, 26 August 1963, *FRUS*, 1961–1963, vol. 3, 287.

33. Saigon to State, 21 August 1963, DDRS, 1985, 22.

34. Higgins, *Our Vietnam Nightmare*, 208. See also Stephen Pan and Daniel Lyons, *Vietnam Crisis* (New York: East Asian Research Institute, 1966), 133.

35. Higgins, *Our Vietnam Nightmare*, 200. For McCone's reaction, see John H. Richardson, *My Father the Spy: An Investigative Memoir* (New York: HarperCollins, 2005), 176.

36. Kaiser, *American Tragedy*, 234.

37. Dictation, 4 November 1963, Tape M, JFKL, POF, Presidential Recordings.

38. Herbert S. Parmet, *JFK: The Presidency of John F. Kennedy* (New York: Dial Press, 1983), 139.

39. Rust, *Kennedy in Vietnam*, 119.

40. Krulak, memo for the record, 26 August 1963, *FRUS*, 1961–1963, vol. 3, 289; Hilsman, memcon, 26 August 1963, JFKL, Hilsman Papers, box 4; *The Joint Chiefs of Staff and the War in Vietnam, 1960–1968* (Christiansburg, VA: Dalley Book Service, 2001), chp. 6, 25.

41. Saigon to State, 28 August 1963, *FRUS*, 1961–1963, vol. 3, 306.

42. Harkins to Taylor, 29 August 1963, *FRUS*, 1961–1963, vol. 4, 4.

43. Reeves, *President Kennedy*, 570.

44. Krulak, meeting notes, 28 August 1963, NDUL, Taylor Papers, box 50; Smith, memcon, 28 August 1963, *FRUS*, 1961–1963, vol. 4, 1; *FRUS*, 1961–1963, vol. 4, 2.

45. Saigon to State, 29 August 1963, *FRUS*, 1961–1963, vol. 4, 10.

46. Saigon to State, 29 August 1963, DDRS, Document number CK3100447109.

47. CIA Saigon to CIA, 31 August 1963, *FRUS*, 1961–1963, vol. 4, 32.

48. Michael Charlton and Anthony Moncrieff, *Many Reasons Why: The American Involvement in Vietnam* (New York: Hill and Wang, 1978), 89.

11. Self-Destruction: September–November 2, 1963

1. State to Saigon, 28 September 1963, *FRUS*, 1961–1963, vol. 4, 157. Some American officials who thought ill of Diem suspected that he would negotiate a deal with Hanoi involving an American withdrawal from South Vietnam, to the detriment of U.S. interests in Asia, but this issue never became a central complaint of the American officials who favored a coup. In their view, the government's central weakness was always that its heavy-handed methods were alienating the South Vietnamese people to such an extent that the war effort would soon deteriorate. Many Americans, of differing opinions on Diem, believed that rumors of a deal between Nhu and the North Vietnamese were merely a ploy by the Diem government to induce the Americans to ease their pressure on the regime, which they most probably were – Diem had always been a staunch anti-Communist and had always understood that his country could not survive without U.S. aid. Hints by the South Vietnamese and North Vietnamese governments concerning a rapprochement were scant and did not lead anywhere. For a recent analysis of this diplomatic episode employing newly available Polish documents, see Margaret K. Gnoinska, "Poland Vietnam, 1963: New Evidence on Secret Communist Diplomacy and the 'Maneli Affair,'" Cold

War International History Project Working Paper #45 (Washington, DC: Woodrow Wilson International Center for Scholars, 2005).

2. *Executive Sessions of the Senate Foreign Relations Committee,* 8 October 1963, 737.

3. Thompson to Peck, 9 October 1963, PRO, FO 371/170102.

4. Thompson to Peck, 30 October 1963, PRO, FO 371/170102.

5. Guthman and Shulman, eds., *Robert Kennedy in His Own Words,* 403. See also telcon, 4 October 1963, LBJL, Ball Papers, box 7.

6. Louis Harris, *Anguish of Change* (New York: W. W. Norton, 1973), 54.

7. *American Foreign Policy: Current Documents, 1963,* 870–1.

8. Krulak, "Visit to Vietnam," 10 September 1963, *FRUS, 1961–1963,* vol. 4, 82.

9. *Chicago Daily News,* September 13, 1963.

10. Bows, *Vietnam Military Lore,* 467–73.

11. Saigon to State, 16 September 1963, NA II, RG 59, Central Files, 1963, box 3763.

12. The Viet Cong left twenty-eight dead behind. Saigon to State, 23 September 1963, NA II, RG 59, C0096, reel 5.

13. *Washington Post,* September 10, 1963; Associated Press, "Viet Armor Raid Kills 80 Reds," September 10, 1963; Harkins to JCS, "USMACV Weekly Headway Report," 13 September 1963, JFKL, Newman Papers; Saigon to State, 16 September 1963, NA II, RG 59, Central Files, 1963, box 3763; Le Quoc San, *Cuoc Do Suc Than Ky,* 136; Thang and Stilwell to Ty, Harkins, and Don, 16 September 1963, NA II, MACJ3-12, JGS Joint Operations Center, Weekly Resume, box 1.

14. USMACV Weekly Headway Reports, June–October 1963, JFKL, Newman Papers. As mentioned in the following note, total attacks actually declined in July and August, before rising slightly in September and then falling back to the rate of the early summer.

15. Thomas L. Hughes, the director of the State Department's Bureau of Intelligence and Research, presented the weapon loss figures in a report that was plagued by the misperceptions characteristic of State Department analysis at this time. The report was reprinted in *The Pentagon Papers,* vol. 2, 770–780, and Hughes reiterated its conclusions in Hughes, "Experiencing McNamara," *Foreign Policy,* 100 (Fall 1995), 154–171. Concerning the real reasons for the higher weapon losses, see CINCPAC to JCS, 17 August 1963, DDRS, 1975, 267B; *Executive Sessions of the Senate Foreign Relations Committee, 1963,* 693. Hughes also stated that nationwide attacks increased sharply starting in July, but his argument was misleading, for he was only comparing the average rate from January to June 1963 with the average rate from July to September 1963. The average rate in the first six months of 1963 was lower because of low numbers of Viet Cong attacks in January and February. Viet Cong attacks actually declined after June, going from 410 in June to 407 in July and 368 in August, before rising to 503 in September and then subsiding to 369 in October. Harkins to JCS, "USMACV Weekly Headway Report," 27 September 1963, JFKL, Newman Papers; Saigon to State, "Saigon's Weekly Progress Report," 30 September 1963, NA II, RG 59, C0092, reel 5; Honolulu Meeting Briefing Book, 20 November 1963, JFKL, NSF, box 204; CIA, "The Situation in South Vietnam," 4 June 1965, DDRS, 1978, 35A. Failing to analyze the critical regional differences, Hughes portrayed the aggregate statistics as evidence of numerous Viet Cong attacks across the country, when in fact they were evidence only of numerous attacks in four provinces. Historians have used Hughes's faulty claims to support the contention that the war effort was deteriorating near the end of the Diem regime. Freedman, *Kennedy's Wars,* 401; Kaiser, *American Tragedy,* 268; Krepinevich, *The Army and Vietnam,* 89; Logevall, *Choosing War,* 438; Newman, *JFK and Vietnam,* 419–22; Prochnau, *Once Upon a Distant War,* 361; Schwab, *Defending the Free World,* 83–4; Sheehan, *A Bright Shining Lie,* 366; Zhai, *China and the Vietnam Wars,* 120.

16. Robert Thompson, "Report on Visits to Delta Provinces, June-August, 1963," n.d., NA II, RG 200, Records of Robert S. McNamara, box 63.

17. In Vinh Binh, "hamlet militia response to attacks has generally been encouraging." The new provincial chief had chosen as his top priority the consolidation of existing hamlets, rather than further expansion. In Kien Hoa, "security has steadily improved, and optimism and pro-government commitment are growing among hamlet residents." Viet Cong attacks in Kien Phong "have been successfully met by hamlet militia." An Giang reportedly had the largest percentage of its people in strategic hamlets of any delta province, and "anti-communist spirit in An Giang is strong." In Kien Giang, "there has been appreciable progress, although the situation is still far from satisfactory." USOM Rural Affairs,

"Second Informal Appreciation of the Status of the Strategic Hamlet Program," 1 September 1963, JFKL, NSF, box 204. The American adviser to the strategic hamlet program in Phu Bon, a highland province of considerable military importance, announced a few days later that "the Viet Cong have lost their war in Phu Bon province." Young to Phillips, "Mid-Year Progress Report," 6 September 1963, HIA, Edward G. Lansdale Papers, box 49.

18. Nguyen Viet Ta et al., *Mien Dong Nam Bo Khang Chien*, Tap II, 144. See also Ho Son Dai and Tran Phan Chan, *Lich Su Saigon-Cho Lon-Gia Dinh Khang Chien*, 369; "A COSVN Standing Committee Account of the Situation in South Vietnam from the End of 1961 to the Beginning of 1964," 20 April 1964, TTU, Pike Collection, Unit 6, box 1; "Binh Duong Monthly Report," August 1963, TTU, Pike Collection, Unit 5, box 19.

19. Saigon to State, 9 September 1963, *FRUS*, 1961–1963, vol. 4, 78.

20. Neese and O'Donnell, eds., *Prelude to Tragedy*, 50.

21. Smith, memcon, 10 September 1963, JFKL, NSF, Meetings & Memoranda, box 316; memcon, 10 September 1963, *FRUS*, 1961–1963, vol. 4, 83.

22. Saigon to State, 2 September 1963, *FRUS*, 1961–1963, vol. 4, 44.

23. Neese and O'Donnell, eds., *Prelude to Tragedy*, 197–8. Diem had reacted in this way with respect to another individual whose removal the Americans had recommended. Scigliano, *South Vietnam*, 210.

24. Saigon to State, 9 September 1963, *FRUS*, 1961–1963, vol. 4, 77.

25. Saigon to State, 11 September 1963, *FRUS*, 1961–1963, vol. 4, 86.

26. McCone, "Summary of Cable from Sheldon," 13 September 1963, *FRUS*, 1961–1963, vol. 4, 105.

27. State to Saigon, 15 September 1963, DDRS, Document number CK3100164618.

28. Saigon to State, 11 September 1963, *FRUS*, 1961–1963, vol. 4, 86.

29. *Washington Post*, September 15, 1963.

30. *Saturday Evening Post*, September 28, 1963. While he was in Vietnam, Karnow received a message from one coup plotter which he then delivered to another conspirator in Hong Kong. Hong Kong to State, 19 October 1963, NA II, RG 59, Central Files, 1963, box 4050.

31. Harkins to Rusk, 11 September 1963, DDRS, 1998, 73; Harkins to Felt, 20 September 1963, NA II, RG 59, Central Files, 1963, box 4049.

32. CIA Saigon to CIA, 10 September 1963, *FRUS*, 1961–1963, vol. 4, 80.

33. Lodge to Rusk, 13 September 1963, *FRUS*, 1961–1963, vol. 4, 104.

34. Since early July, Phillips had been recommending the dispatch of Lansdale to Vietnam as a means of saving Diem, whom Phillips viewed as essential to the survival of South Vietnam. Demonstrating a considerable degree of prescience, Phillips predicted that "unless President Diem remains as head of the State, chaos is probable. The prospects are that an initial reach for power would be followed by ruthless suppression of potential rivals, followed, in turn, by repeated coup attempts which could result in real civil war with an eventual splitting of the country into independent domains. In such an eventuality a Communist takeover by default seems likely unless the U.S. massively intervenes." Phillips to Truehart, 5 July 1963, HIA, Edward G. Lansdale Papers, box 49.

35. Lodge to Rusk, 24 September 1963, *FRUS*, 1961–1963, vol. 4, 104n.

36. *New York Times*, 15 September 1963.

37. Ford, *CIA and the Vietnam Policymakers*, 35n; John Michael Dunn Oral History Interview I, LBJL. Similar divisions could be found among the State Department officials in the Saigon embassy. Miller, *Vietnam and Beyond*, 71.

38. *Washington Daily News*, October 2, 1963.

39. Ford, *CIA and the Vietnam Policymakers*, 35.

40. *New York Times*, October 4, 1963.

41. *Washington Post*, September 16, 1963.

42. *Washington Post*, September 23, 1963. This article did contain some sharp criticisms of the Diem government, which Alsop was later to regret. He was to write that after Diem's overthrow, "I came to revise my assessment of Diem and, indeed, felt some measure of guilt for having turned against him. . . . The alternatives to Diem favored by his official enemies Cabot Lodge, Averell Harriman, and Roger Hilsman as well as by most of the American press turned out to be flat busts in a matter of months. The assassination of Diem left South Vietnam without any sort of government for a considerable period and can now be judged as a grim and perhaps decisive turning point for the worse in the Vietnam War."

Joseph Alsop with Adam Platt, *"I've Seen the Best of It": Memoirs* (New York: W. W. Norton, 1992), 462–3.

43. Bundy, memo for the record, 23 September 1963, *FRUS*, 1961–1963, vol. 4, 143.

44. CIA, "David Halberstam's Reporting on South Vietnam," 26 September 1963, JFKL, NSF, box 204.

45. Robert Kennedy later recalled that Rusk was "not really helping at all." The Secretary of State "was for a coup and then he was against it. He was all over the lot." Guthman and Shulman, eds., *Robert Kennedy in His Own Words*, 403.

46. Taylor, "Farewell Call on Major General Duong Van Minh," 1 October 1963, *FRUS*, 1961–1963, vol. 4, 162.

47. Memcon, 29 September 1963, *FRUS*, 1961–1963, vol. 4, 158.

48. They stated that most of the remaining advisers could be withdrawn by 1965, for the war would be won in I, II, and III Corps by the end of 1964, and in the delta by 1965. McNamara and Taylor did not really think that the United States would be able to withdraw by 1965, given the extensive North Vietnamese activities in Cambodia and Laos. They set the 1965 deadline to spur on the South Vietnamese and influence American public opinion. Said Taylor, "We've got to make these people put their noses to the wheel – or the grindstone or whatever. If we don't give them some indication that we're going to get out sometime, they're just going to be leaning on us forever." William Sullivan Oral History, JFKL. McNamara told the President on October 2 that a specified withdrawal date would "meet the view of Senator Fulbright and others that we are bogged down forever in Vietnam." NSC meeting notes, 2 October 1963, *FRUS*, 1961–1963, vol. 4, 169.

49. McNamara and Taylor, "Report of McNamara-Taylor Mission to South Vietnam," 2 October 1963, *FRUS*, 1961–1963, vol. 4, 167.

50. Bundy to Lodge, 5 October 1963, *FRUS*, 1961–1963, vol. 4, 182.

51. "The aid cuts," General Minh recalled, "erased all our doubts." Higgins, *Our Vietnam Nightmare*, 208. Minh, however, was exaggerating the impact of the cuts, for the generals still had many doubts and they had additional means for gauging American attitudes towards a coup.

52. CIA, "Events and Developments in South Vietnam, 5–18 October" 19 October 1963, JFKL, NSF, box 201.

53. Saigon to State, 5 October 1963, JFKL, NSF, box 204; Saigon to State, 7 October 1963, *FRUS*, 1961–1963, vol. 4, 186; Saigon to State, 17 October 1963, NA II, RG 59, Central Files, 1963, box 4047.

54. Saigon to State, 18 October 1963, NA II, RG 59, Central Files, 1963, box 4046; Saigon to State, 19 October 1963, *FRUS*, 1961–1963, vol. 3, 202.

55. CIA Saigon to CIA, 5 October 1963, *FRUS*, 1961–1963, vol. 4, 177.

56. CIA to Lodge, 9 October 1963, *FRUS*, 1961–1963, vol. 4, 192.

57. Neither the authors of the classified Pentagon Papers study nor anyone else has found any U.S. government reports on this conversation. *The Pentagon Papers*, vol. 2, 257–8. This meeting was not mentioned in an October 1963 CIA document listing all contacts with the generals. CIA, "Contacts with Vietnamese Generals, 23 August through 23 October 1963," 23 October 1963, DDRS, 1978, 142A. Subsequent developments show that Kennedy had not been informed of the meeting. The content of the meeting was revealed by Robert Shaplen, a respected journalist to whom Conein divulged much of the conspiracy. Shaplen, *Lost Revolution*, 203–4. General Don, in the English version of his memoirs, mentioned this meeting between Conein and Minh but did not elaborate. Tran Van Don, *Our Endless War: Inside Vietnam* (Novato: Presidio Press, 1978), 97. Conein's official history of the coup reveals that Lodge, on October 10, authorized Conein to deliver the message if the generals made contact with him, though it does not mention the meeting itself. Conein's history contains Lodge's quoted message. Conein and Richardson, "History of the Vietnamese Generals' Coup," NA II, RG 46, Church Committee Records, box 47. Owing to the secrecy surrounding these contacts, almost all historians have missed the critical events in the middle of October that set the plotters on a path towards a coup, largely out of the sight of President Kennedy. See, for instance, Bird, *The Color of Truth*; Dallek, *An Unfinished Life*; Dommen, *The Indochinese Experience of the French and the Americans*; Duiker, *U.S. Containment Policy and the Conflict in Indochina*; Freedman, *Kennedy's Wars*; Gardner, *Pay Any Price*; Gibbons, *The U.S. Government and the Vietnam War*, vol. 2; Hammond, *Public Affairs: The Military*

and the Media, 1962–1968; Jones, *Death of a Generation;* Kaiser, *American Tragedy;* Langguth, *Our Vietnam;* Logevall, *Choosing War;* Mann, *A Grand Delusion;* Newman, *JFK and Vietnam;* Prochnau, *Once Upon a Distant War;* Reeves, *President Kennedy;* Schulzinger, *A Time for War;* Sheehan, *A Bright Shining Lie.*

58. Stromberg, memo for the record, 8 March 1964, *FRUS, 1964–1968,* vol. 1, 75. Recounting his dealings with the Americans as the coup approached, Don remarked, "We wanted to be certain that if we succeeded with the coup we would have American support afterward, that the Americans agreed with us, because we needed their aid to continue the war." PBS, *Vietnam: A Television History: America's Mandarin (1954–1963)* (Boston: WGBH, 1983).

59. Halberstam, *The Making of a Quagmire;* Halberstam, *The Best and the Brightest.*

60. Harkins to JCS, "USMACV Weekly Headway Report," 25 October 1963, JFKL, Newman Papers; Saigon to State, 28 October 1963, NA II, RG 59, C0096, reel 5; *New York Times,* 21 and 27 October 1963; Thang and Stilwell to Ty, Harkins and Don, 28 October 1963, NA II, MACJ3–12, JGS Joint Operations Center, Weekly Resume, box 2.

61. *Newsweek,* November 4, 1963. On October 19, the CIA reported that the South Vietnamese war effort had not slackened at all. CIA, "Events and Developments in South Vietnam, 5–18 October," 19 October 1963, JFKL, NSF, box 201.

62. Saigon to State, 21 October 1963, NA II, RG 59, Central Files, 1963, box 3763; Thang and Stilwell to Ty, Harkins and Don, 21 October 1963, NA II, MACJ3–12, JGS Joint Operations Center, Weekly Resume, box 2.

63. Thang and Stilwell to Harkins and Don, 11 November 1963, NA II, MACJ3–12, JGS Joint Operations Center, Weekly Resume, box 2.

64. Halberstam, *The Making of a Quagmire,* 172, 187–9.

65. *New York Times,* October 23, 1963.

66. Hickerson to Committee on Province Rehabilitation, "Report of the Delta Sub-Committee," 14 October 1963, NA II, RG 59, Bureau of Far Eastern Affairs, Vietnam Working Group, Subject Files, 1963–1966, box 3.

67. Weede to CINCPAC, 18 November 1963, NA II, RG 59, Lot Files, Entry 5305, box 3.

68. Saigon to State, 28 October 1963, NA II, RG 59, C00096, reel 5.

69. *FRUS, 1961–1963,* vol. 4, 209.

70. CIA, "Contacts with Vietnamese Generals, 23 August through 23 October 1963," 23 October 1963, DDRS, 1978, 142A. Suspicion about Lodge's dealings with oppositionists had been building for some time. On October 10, the day of the fateful meeting between Minh and Conein, McCone complained to Harriman about Lodge's lack of reporting on potential acts of rebellion. Harriman promised to look into the matter, although it is doubtful that he actually did since he had no desire to interfere with anti-Diem activity. Telcon, 10 October 1963, *FRUS, 1961–1963,* vol. 4, 193n. On October 14, Kennedy sent a message to Lodge expressing concern that he had not heard Lodge's views since the beginning of the month, and he asked Lodge to start sending him an evaluation of the situation at least once per week. State to Saigon, 14 October 1963, *FRUS, 1961–1963,* vol. 4, 195.

71. CIA, Telegram 1925, 23 October 1963, JFKL, NSF, box 201; Harkins to Taylor, 24 October 1963, *FRUS, 1961–1963,* vol. 4, 214.

72. Recording of meeting, 25 October 1963, Tape No. 117/A53, JFKL, POF, Presidential Recordings.

73. Bundy to Lodge and Harkins, 24 October 1963, *FRUS, 1961–1963,* vol. 4, 211.

74. Lodge to Bundy, 25 October 1963, *FRUS, 1961–1963,* vol. 4, 216.

75. Saigon to State, 28 October, 1963, *FRUS, 1961–1963,* vol. 4, 221.

76. Lodge to State, 29 October 1963, *FRUS, 1961–1963,* vol. 4, 225.

77. Lodge to State, 29 October 1963, *FRUS, 1961–1963,* vol. 4, 226.

78. Krulak, "Visit to Representative Zablocki," 28 October 1963, *FRUS, 1961–1963,* vol. 4, 222. For the full text of the Congressional report, see "Report of the Special Study Mission to Southeast Asia (October 3–19, 1963)," House Report No. 893, November 7, 1963.

79. *New York Times,* October 30, 1963.

80. On the following day, Kennedy himself pinpointed what Lodge had done: "The Ambassador feels that 74228 does change 63560 and that a change in government is desired." Recording of meeting, 30

October 1963, Tape No. 118/A54, JFKL, POF, Presidential Recordings. Message 63560 is Bundy to Lodge, 5 October 1963, *FRUS*, 1961–1963, vol. 4, 182; message 74228 is CIA to Lodge, 9 October 1963, *FRUS*, 1961–1963, vol. 4, 192.

81. Recording of meeting, 29 October 1963, Tape No. 118/A54, JFKL, POF, Presidential Recordings; Smith, memcon, 29 October 1963, *FRUS*, 1961–1963, vol. 4, 234; Smith, memcon, 29 October 1963, *FRUS*, 1961–1963, vol. 4, 235; Mendenhall, memcon, 29 October 1963, JFKL, Hilsman Papers, Box 4.

82. Bundy to Lodge, 29 October 1963, *FRUS*, 1961–1963, vol. 4, 236.

83. Lodge to State, 30 October 1963, *FRUS*, 1961–1963, vol. 4, 242.

84. Just a week later, Lodge himself conceded, "In a country like this, exhortations, argument, rhetoric, and facial expressions mean very little. Actions apparently are an international language." Saigon to State, 6 November 1963, *FRUS*, 1961–1963, vol. 4, 302.

85. Harkins to Taylor, 30 October 1963, *FRUS*, 1961–1963, vol. 4, 240; Harkins to Taylor, 30 October 1963, *FRUS*, 1961–1963, vol. 4, 246; Harkins to Taylor, 30 October 1963, *FRUS*, 1961–1963, vol. 4, 247.

86. Recording of meeting, 30 October 1963, Tape No. 118/A54, JFKL, POF, Presidential Recordings. David Kaiser has asserted that Kennedy spoke positively of a coup at this meeting. According to Kaiser, Kennedy said that Lodge favored a coup "for very good reasons." Kaiser, *American Tragedy*, 272. Kennedy actually did not endorse Lodge's view. He said of Lodge: "He's for a coup for what he thinks are very good reasons." Recording of meeting, 30 October 1963, Tape No. 118/A54, JFKL, POF, Presidential Recordings. For the claim that Kennedy favored the coup in the end, see also Jones, *Death of a Generation*.

87. Bundy to Lodge, 30 October 1963, *FRUS*, 1961–1963, vol. 4, 249.

88. Tran Van Don, *Viet Nam Nhan Chung: Hoi Ky Chanh Tri* (Xuan Thu Publishing, 1989), 185.

89. Ibid., 186.

90. *U.S. News and World Report*, October 10, 1983.

91. Saigon to State, 1 November 1963, *FRUS*, 1961–1963, vol. 4, 262.

92. Tran Van Don, *Viet Nam Nhan Chung*, 215. Additional evidence of the conspirators' doubts about Khiem's loyalties surfaced later, upon the discovery of rebel documents showing that Khiem had received the equivalent of seven thousand U.S. dollars for his participation in the coup, making him the only general besides Dinh to receive so large a sum. Dommen, *The Indochinese Experience of the French and the Americans*, 545.

93. CIA Saigon to State, 1 November 1963, NA II, RG 59, Central Files, 1963, box 4048; Conein and Richardson, "History of the Vietnamese Generals' Coup," NA II, RG 46, Church Committee Records, box 47.

94. Do Tho, *Nhat Ky Do Tho: Tuy Vien Mot Tong Thong Bi Giet* (Glendale, CA: Co So Xuat Ban Dai Nam, 1970), 232; Hien Anh, "The Coup D'État of November 1, 1963," 17 November 1971, TTU, Echols Collection, EK 29, Fiche 1–5, 67.

95. Saigon to State, 23 October 1963, JFKL, NSF, box 201.

96. Tran Van Don, *Viet Nam Nhan Chung*, 223; *New York Times*, May 14, 1972.

97. *Alleged Assassination Plots Involving Foreign Leaders: An Interim Report of the Select Committee to Study Governmental Operations with Respect to Intelligence Activities* (New York: W. W. Norton, 1976), 222–3; CIA Saigon to State, 1 November 1963, NA II, RG 59, Central Files, 1963, box 4048.

98. Hoang Lac and Ha Mai Viet, *Why America Lost the Vietnam War*, 165–6.

99. Do Tho, *Nhat Ky Do Tho*, 181, 231.

100. Saigon to State, 1 November 1963, *FRUS*, 1961–1963, vol. 4, 259.

101. Frederick W. Flott, interview with author; Frederick W. Flott Oral History Interview I, LBJL.

102. Blair, *Lodge in Vietnam*, 69.

103. Nguyen Cao Ky, *Buddha's Child: My Fight to Save South Vietnam* (New York: St. Martin's Press, 2002), 96.

104. Hien Anh, "The Coup D'État of November 1, 1963," 17 November 1971, TTU, Echols Collection, EK 29, Fiche 1–5, 70–71, 78.

105. Hammer, *A Death in November*, 293.

106. Helms to Hilsman, 16 August 1963, *FRUS*, 1961–1963, vol. 3, 256; Taylor, "Probable Loyalties of Vietnamese Units and Commanders," 30 August 1963, *FRUS*, 1961–1963, vol. 4, 24.

107. Hien Anh, "The Coup D'État of November 1, 1963," 17 November 1971, TTU, Echols Collection, EK 29, Fiche 1–5, 78–81.

108. Associated Press, "Thieu Tells Role in Diem Overthrow," July 21, 1971.

109. Tran Van Don, *Viet Nam Nhan Chung*, 228.

110. Do Tho, *Nhat Ky Do Tho*, 236.

111. Grant, *Facing the Phoenix*, 211. The other source that mentioned a second conversation between Lodge and Diem was journalist Joseph Fried, who provided an on-the-spot report. *New York Daily News*, 5 November 1963.

112. *Hearing before the Senate Select Committee to Study Governmental Operations with Respect to Intelligence Activities*, 20 June 1975, NA II, RG 46, Church Committee Records on the JFK Assassination, box 47.

113. Sheehan, *A Bright Shining Lie*, 371.

114. Higgins, *Our Vietnam Nightmare*, 215.

115. Ibid.

12. The Return of the Twelve Warlords: November 3–December 1963

1. *New York Times*, November 2 and 3, 1963.

2. *Washington Post*, November 2, 1963.

3. Under orders from the chief conspirators, Col. Do Mau had released imprisoned student and Buddhist protesters during the coup and transported them in dozens of GMC trucks to Saigon to lead the demonstrations. Hien Anh, "The Coup D'État of November 1, 1963," 17 November 1971, TTU, Echols Collection, EK 29, Fiche 1–5, 73–4; Conein and Richardson, "History of the Vietnamese Generals' Coup," NA II, RG 46, Church Committee Records, box 47. For U.S. suspicions that the demonstrations had been choreographed, see Smith, meeting notes, 4 November 1963, *FRUS, 1961–1963*, vol. 4, 288.

4. Saigon to State, 12 November 1963, NA II, RG 59, Central Files, 1963, box 4048: Hien Anh, "The Coup D'État of November 1, 1963," 17 November 1971, TTU, Echols Collection, EK 29, Fiche 1–5, 121.

5. Saigon to State, 4 November 1963, *FRUS, 1961–1963*, vol. 4, 291.

6. Galbraith to Harriman, LOC, W. Averell Harriman Papers, box 463. In his memoirs, Galbraith recounted no such euphoria, and indeed he tried to exonerate himself by explaining away the 1961 letters to Kennedy in which he had argued that Diem's removal would improve the war effort tremendously and that "nothing succeeds like successors." In one of the most fantastic attempts by a coup supporter to dissociate himself from the catastrophe, Galbraith wrote incongruously of those letters, "In saying that the Diem regime was hopeless, which I believed, and in saying that it could not be propped up by our troops, which I believed and wanted to believe, I came close to saying, 'Let the insurgents take over.' But that no one could say. Such an admission was all that those arguing for intervention needed to put me in my place." John Kenneth Galbraith, *A Life in Our Times: Memoirs* (Boston: Houghton Mifflin, 1981), 473–4. See also Winters, *Year of the Hare*, 42–3.

7. Taylor, *Swords and Plowshares*, 301.

8. ABC News, "The Death of Diem," 22 December 1971, TTU, Echols Collection, EK 29, Fiche 1–5. Diem's death also shocked the previous U.S. President and the two Presidents who would follow Kennedy. Richard Nixon wrote to Eisenhower on November 4, 1963 that "our complicity in Diem's murder was a national disgrace." Eisenhower replied, "I cannot believe that any American would have approved the cold-blooded killing of a man who had, after all, shown great courage when he undertook the task some years ago of defeating communist's (sic) attempts to take over his country." Mann, *A Grand Delusion*, 297. Lyndon Johnson's reaction is described later in this chapter.

9. Collier and Horowitz, *The Kennedys*, 309.

10. Saigon to State, 5 November 1963, JFKL, NSF, box 201.

11. Guthman and Shulman, eds., *Robert Kennedy in His Own Words*, 394–5.

12. *American Foreign Policy: Current Documents, 1963*, 870–1.

13. Smith, memcon, 3 September 1963, *FRUS, 1961–1963*, vol. 4, 54.

14. See chapter five of this volume.

15. Recent histories alleging that Kennedy was planning to withdraw from Vietnam include Jones, *Death of a Generation;* Kaiser, *American Tragedy;* Newman, *JFK and Vietnam;* Porter, *Perils of Dominance.* The authors have emphasized Kennedy's alleged statements expressing an interest in withdrawal. They have also cited Kennedy's authorization of plans for incremental U.S. troop reductions, but in reality Kennedy authorized those plans in the expectation that he could afford to withdraw the troops in the future because of South Vietnamese progress in prosecuting the war, a realistic expectation given the positive state of military affairs prior to Diem's assassination. President Kennedy showed no inclination towards removing U.S. troops if it might mean defeat for South Vietnam. Another major piece of supporting evidence offered by proponents of the withdrawal thesis was a supposed major shift in policy in NSAM 273 of November 26, 1963, yet NSAM 273 did not actually represent a significant change, nor did Johnson's other early Vietnam policies veer substantially from Kennedy's. For the document, see NSAM 273, 26 November 1963, *FRUS*, 1961–1963, vol. 4, 331. Adherents of the withdrawal thesis, moreover, have not explained persuasively why the contrary evidence is not compelling. The withdrawal thesis has been effectively refuted in Larry Berman, "NSAM 263 and NSAM 273: Manipulating History," in Lloyd C. Gardner and Ted Gittinger, eds., *Vietnam: The Early Decisions* (Austin: University of Texas Press, 1997), 177–203; Noam Chomsky, *Rethinking Camelot: JFK, The Vietnam War, and U.S. Political Culture* (Boston: South End Press, 1993); Logevall, *Choosing War;* Lind, *Vietnam, The Necessary War;* Kahin, *Intervention;* Reeves, *A Question of Character.*

16. McCone, memcon, 24 November 1963, *FRUS*, 1961–1963, vol. 4, 330.

17. Johnson was also disgusted by Halberstam's actions in the months preceding the coup. Several years later, he told *Time-Life* journalist Robert Sherrod, "David Halberstam killed Diem. He made us assassinate him. That man is a traitor – so they give him a Pulitzer Prize. They give Pulitzer Prizes to traitors nowadays." Dallek, *Flawed Giant,* 379.

18. Averell Harriman Oral History, JFKL.

19. Lodge to State, 4 November 1963, *FRUS*, 1961–1963, vol. 4, 289.

20. Conein and Richardson, "History of the Vietnamese Generals' Coup," NA II, RG 46, Church Committee Records, box 47.

21. CIA, "Situation Appraisal as of 30 November 1963," 2 December 1963, *FRUS*, 1961–1963, vol. 4, 335.

22. *Newsweek,* December 23, 1963.

23. *Time,* December 13, 1963.

24. *Newsweek,* December 23, 1963.

25. Memcon, 20 December 1963, *FRUS*, 1961–1963, vol. 4, 370.

26. *Time,* December 13, 1963.

27. Neese and O'Donnell, eds., *Prelude to Tragedy,* 114. A countrywide assessment of the strategic hamlet program noted that after the coup, "no workable policy instructions were forthcoming from the national level of the GVN, and provincial officials working with strategic hamlets were generally inactive in anticipation of such direction.... Many excellent programs in the areas of public works, education, health, safety, administration, agriculture, communication media, and industrial development were slowed or stopped by lack of GVN guidance and positive and thorough cross agency coordination." Saigon to State, 3 February 1964, LBJL, NSF, VNCF, box 2. See also Saigon to State, 15 November 1963, NA II, RG 59, Central Files, 1963, box 4048.

28. Rufus Phillips's report contained detailed comments on individual chiefs. For example, in Kontum province: "Substantial progress continues in Kontum under the leadership of an extremely capable provincial chief." In Phu Bon: "Forceful and intelligent action on the part of the provincial chief combined with close coordination between the U.S. military and economic assistance programs have resulted in a degree of security and economic activity previously unknown in this area." In Quang Ngai: "The provincial chief and his strategic hamlet assistant continue to be energetic, farsighted, considerate of the population, and, in general, astute counter-insurgents." The summary for III Corps stated: "All present provincial chiefs in this Region appear competent, effective, and dedicated. Most are keenly concerned with their civil as well as military responsibilities, an attitude usually reflected by the people." There were still some ineffective provincial chiefs, mainly in the strategically unimportant delta, but, in general, Diem and Nhu were employing strong men and inspiring them to energetic action.

USOM Rural Affairs, "Second Informal Appreciation of the Status of the Strategic Hamlet Program," 1 September 1963, JFKL, NSF, box 204.

29. Jorden to Harriman, 31 December 1963, *FRUS, 1961–1963,* vol. 4, 383. Even John Mecklin, a fervent supporter of Diem's overthrow, would come to lament that the purges had wrecked the South Vietnamese government. Mecklin, *Mission in Torment,* 283. See also Blair, *There to the Bitter End,* 65.

30. Lodge to Rusk, 11 December 1963, DDRS, 1986, 27.

31. The removal of numerous provincial chiefs, one American report noted, "has produced a certain indecisiveness in [provincial] administration, the effect of which has been transmitted downwards through the district chiefs and into the villages." Forrestal to Johnson, 11 December 1963, TTU, Pike Collection, Unit 1, box 3. See also Saigon to State, 3 February 1964, LBJL, NSF, VNCF, box 2.

32. Wilson to Chief USMAAG, "Status G-5 Programs," 13 January 1964, MHI, Wilbur Wilson Papers, box 4; Saigon to State, 3 February 1964, LBJL, NSF, VNCF, box 2; Helms to Rusk, 18 February 1964, *FRUS, 1964–1968,* vol. 1, 50.

33. Honolulu Meeting Briefing Book, 20 November 1963, JFKL, NSF, box 204.

34. Lodge to Rusk, 11 December 1963, DDRS, 1986, 27.

35. State to Saigon, 6 December 1963, *FRUS, 1961–1963,* vol. 4, 351.

36. Krulak, "Report on the Visit of the Secretary of Defense to South Vietnam," 19–20 December 1963, *FRUS, 1961–1963,* vol. 4, 372.

37. CIA, "Situation Appraisal as of 14 December 1963," 16 December 1963, *FRUS, 1961–1963,* vol. 4, 368.

38. McNamara to Johnson, 21 December 1963, *FRUS, 1961–1963,* vol. 4, 374. See also Sullivan, "Report of McNamara Visit to Saigon, December 19–20, 1963," 21 December 1963, *FRUS, 1961–1963,* vol. 4, 373.

39. McCone, "Highlights of Discussions in Saigon," 21 December 1963, *FRUS, 1961–1963,* vol. 4, 375.

40. For the misuse of the McNamara and McCone reports, see Davidson, *Vietnam At War,* 303; Ford, *CIA and the Vietnam Policymakers,* 21; Hammond, *Public Affairs: The Military and the Media, 1962–1968,* 64; Herring, *America's Longest War,* 133; Jones, *Death of a Generation,* 448; Karnow, *Vietnam,* 341; Langguth, *Our Vietnam,* 270; Logevall, *Choosing War,* 90; Prochnau, *Once Upon a Distant War,* 483; Reeves, *President Kennedy,* 610; Rust, *Kennedy in Vietnam,* 180; Schulzinger, *A Time for War,* 131; Sheehan, *A Bright Shining Lie,* 376.

41. The downward statistical trends that began in July, stated McCone, "were gradual until 1 November, the date of the coup, and then moved very sharply against the GVN." McCone, "Highlights of Discussions in Saigon," 21 December 1963, *FRUS, 1961–1963,* vol. 4, 375. In January 1964, the CIA noted, "The Diem government's key pacification effort – the strategic hamlet program – progressed steadily during 1963 except in the delta area, where it suffered serious reverses in several provinces." CIA, "Trends of Communist Insurgency in Vietnam," 17 January 1964, DDRS, 1976, 232A. In December 1963, McNamara also noted the alleged inadequacy of reporting under Diem and said that the situation had deteriorated to a greater extent than he had thought. He did not, however, specify whether most of the deterioration had occurred before or after the coup. His negative remarks about the new government suggested that he too thought that the worst had come after the coup. McNamara to Johnson, 21 December 1963, *FRUS, 1961–1963,* vol. 4, 374. McNamara clarified his views somewhat in a report on January 31, 1964, stating, "After the coup in November, South Vietnamese military operations were neglected. A period of uncertainty ensued and the Viet Cong took advantage of the confusion in government and the weakness in administration of both political and military affairs. Serious setbacks to the counterinsurgency program resulted, particularly in the Delta." Rusk and McNamara to Lodge and Harkins, 31 January 1964, *FRUS, 1964–1968,* vol. 1, 25.

42. Helms to Rusk, 18 February 1964, FRUS, 1964–1968, vol. 1, 50.

43. "NLF Study of War History 1961 thru 1964," 20 April 1964, CDEC Doc Log No. 01-0519-70, TTU Pike Collection, Unit 1, box 5.

44. *Mot So Van Kien Cua Dang Ve Chong My, Cuu Nuoc,* Tap I, 212, 216.

45. Dang Uy va Tu Lenh Quan Khu 5, *Quan Khu 5,* vol. 1, 50–65. This account is corroborated by Le Duan's February 1965 letter to Nguyen Chi Thanh. Le Duan, *Thu Vao Nam,* 68–93. See also Hoi Dong Bien Soan Lich Su Nam Trung Bo Khang Chien, *Nam Trung Bo Khang Chien,* 304.

46. Tran Duong et al., *Lich Su Khu* 6, 115, 118, 136–7, 150.

47. Nguyen Van Minh et al., *Luc Luong Vu Trang Nhan Dan Tay Nguyen Trong Khang Chien Chong My Cuu Nuoc*, 34–42.

48. "NLF Study of War History 1961 thru 1964," 20 April 1964, CDEC Doc Log No. 01-0519-70, TTU Pike Collection, Unit 1, box 5. In November 1964, the Communist leadership reported that the Viet Cong had by that time taken control of only half of the delta areas. Nguyen Chi Thanh, "The Political Bureau's Assessment of the Situation," 20 November 1964, TTU, Pike Collection, Unit 6, box 1.

49. Nguyen Huu Nguyen, *Long An: Lich Su Khang Chien Chong My Cuu Nuoc (1954–1975)* (Hanoi: People's Army Publishing House, Hanoi, 1994), 109–15.

50. Ibid., 109, 118–9, 128. See also Nguyen Viet Ta et al., *Mien Dong Nam Bo Khang Chien,* Tap II, 147–8. A post-coup American assessment of Long An recounted: "The VC virtually seized control of much of Long An in November. . . . More than two-thirds of the hamlet militia turned in their weapons and quit when faced with lack of support by GVN military and paramilitary forces. Dissipation of the Republican Youth organization also helped undermine their discipline and local leadership. . . . Hamlet and village officials throughout much of the province surrendered their authority to the VC or adopted a passive and ineffective attitude towards their duties." Saigon to State, 3 February 1964, LBJL, NSF, VNCF, box 2.

51. Elliott, *The Vietnamese War,* 427–30; Nguyen Anh Tuan, *Du Thao Lich Su Dang Bo Tinh Tien Giang,* Tap II, 43–4. Communist sources do not make clear how many of the 184 strategic hamlets were believed to have been destroyed before November 1963.

52. Saigon to State, 3 February 1964, LBJL, NSF, VNCF, box 2. Concerning deliberate attempts by Diem's successors to misrepresent his record, see also Neese and O'Donnell, eds., *Prelude to Tragedy,* 82–3; *New York Times,* 23 December 1963; Washington to FO, 27 December 1963, PRO, FO 371/170096.

53. For the Vietnamese, such a slandering of a deposed leader conformed to a long and storied tradition. Whenever a dynasty was destroyed – and for many Vietnamese the November 1963 coup was tantamount to the destruction of a dynasty – its successors went to extraordinary lengths to discredit its last king to justify the rebellion. Oftentimes, the allegations bore little or no resemblance to the truth. The last king of the early Le dynasty, Le Long Dinh, offers a good example of how the next dynasty tended to behave. According to the court histories produced after his death in 1009, Le Long Dinh entertained himself by wrapping people in oil-coated straw and setting them on fire. Other victims were put at the tops of trees that the king then chopped down, or placed in cages that he immersed in the sea. His favorite pastime, allegedly, was the use of a monk's head as a cutting board. Independent evidence did not support the allegations of Le Long Dinh's successors, just as independent evidence did not support the claims of Diem's successors.

54. Higgins, *Our Vietnam Nightmare,* 302.

55. Political Bureau Resolution, November 1963, TTU, Pike Collection, Unit 6, box 1.

56. *Washington Post,* November 14, 1964. See also Burchett, *Vietnam,* 216–9; Truong Nhu Tang, *Vietcong Memoir,* 90; Military History Institute of Vietnam, *Victory in Vietnam,* 121–2; "NLF Study of War History 1961 thru 1964," 20 April 1964, CDEC Doc Log No. 01-0519-70, TTU Pike Collection, Unit 1, box 5.

57. The official history of the Vietnamese Communist Party explained, "As far back as January 1961 the Politburo had predicted the possibility that army mutinies and coups would occur and had directed that we make ideological preparations and that we prepare organizations, forces, and plans so that we could gain larger victories when a coup took place. This was a very favorable opportunity for our troops to step up their attacks and annihilate enemy soldiers. However, our main force units were all new, having been formed just in the period 1961–1963, and in actuality they had only begun to fight at the battalion level after our victory at Ap Bac. In comparison with the situation in the past, great progress had been made in the organization, equipment, and combat abilities of our troops, but this progress had not kept pace with the rapid development of the situation. For that reason, we were unable to fully exploit the advantages that the Saigon puppet government's state of critical, perpetual crisis presented." Vien Nghien Cuu Chu Nghia Mac Lenin Va Tu Tuong Ho Chi Minh, *Lich Su Dang Cong San Viet Nam,* Tap II, 253.

58. Vo Cong Luan and Tran Hanh, eds., *May Van De ve Tong Ket Chien Tranh va Viet Su Quan Su* (Hanoi: Military History Institute of Vietnam and Ministry of Defense, 1987), 285; Resolution of the Ninth Conference of the Central Committee of the Viet-Nam Workers' Party, December 1963, TTU, Pike Collection, Unit 1, box 3. As in 1959, Ho and the preponderance of the Party leadership ended up siding with Le Duan, the advocate of Maoist militancy, rather than those who favored a less intense struggle out of concern for American and Soviet reactions, of whom the most notable were Giap, Truong Chinh, and Pham Van Dong.

13. Self-Imposed Restrictions: January–July 1964

1. The most informative biographies of Lyndon Johnson are Robert Caro, *The Years of Lyndon Johnson*, 3 vols., and Robert Dallek's much more positive *Lone Star Rising* and *Flawed Giant*. Thomas Schwartz, in a study of Johnson's European diplomacy, has argued persuasively that scholars have failed to appreciate Johnson's diplomatic skills and positive diplomatic achievements. Schwartz, *Lyndon Johnson and Europe*. As shall be shown, Johnson's judgments on diplomatic issues related to Vietnam were more astute than is widely believed. In setting policy and strategy for Vietnam, Johnson generally committed his biggest errors and misdeeds in the military and political realms, not the diplomatic realm.

2. Memo for the File of the Secretary of State, 5 April 1954, *FRUS, 1952–1954*, vol. 13, 1224–5. Some Johnson supporters and historians have contended that Johnson was opposed to U.S. participation in united action. Baritz, *Backfire,* 86; Barrett, *Uncertain Warriors*, 35; Lind, *Vietnam, The Necessary War,* 200; VanDeMark, *Into the Quagmire,* 9. The notes from the April 5 meeting, however, point toward the conclusion that Johnson gave it his conditional approval.

3. Lyndon Johnson, address, 6 May 1954, LBJL, Statements of LBJ, box 15.

4. Alexander Haig, *Inner Circles: How America Changed the World* (New York: Warner Books, 1992), 146.

5. Doris Kearns, *Lyndon Johnson and the American Dream* (New York: Harper & Row, 1976), 177. Johnson once told his wife, "If I got word that Bob had died or quit, I don't believe I could go on with this job." Johnson, tape-recorder diary, 14 February 1965, Michael Beschloss, ed., *Reaching for Glory: Lyndon Johnson's Secret White House Tapes, 1964–1965* (New York: Simon & Schuster, 2001), 178.

6. Early in the Johnson administration, Marine Commandant General M. Wallace Greene, Jr. complained that McNamara "appeared to think that he knew more about all the military aspects of the problems in Vietnam and the cures therefor than any of the military persons present." Greene, summary of discussions, 17 March 1964, MCHD, Greene Papers. After recording the contents of one meeting with McNamara, Greene drew an arrow toward McNamara's name with the notation, "an arrogant individual who eventually will have his comeuppance!" Greene, "Escalation of effort in South Vietnam," 10 July 1965, MCHD, Greene Papers.

7. Barrett, *Uncertain Warriors;* Berman, *Planning a Tragedy;* Buzzanco, *Masters of War;* Kahin, *Intervention;* Kolko, *Anatomy of a War;* Logevall, *Choosing War;* Schulzinger, *A Time for War;* VanDeMark, *Into the Quagmire;* Vandiver, *Shadows of Vietnam;* Young, *Vietnam Wars.*

8. *The Pentagon Papers,* vol. 3, 694–702.

9. Robert McNamara, interview with author.

10. Ted Gittinger, ed., *The Johnson Years: A Vietnam Roundtable* (Austin: Lyndon B. Johnson Library, 1993), 96.

11. See, for example, McNamara to Johnson, "South Vietnam," 16 March 1964, *FRUS, 1964–1968,* vol. 1, 84; William Bundy, unpublished manuscript, LBJL, William Bundy Papers, box 1, chap. 12, 22–3; State to Saigon, 27 May 1964, LBJL, NSF, VNCF, box 53; Telcon, 1 June 1964, LBJL, Recordings of Telephone Conversations, tape WH6406.01; Bundy and Forrestal, "Position Paper on Expanding U.S. Action in South Vietnam to the North," 31 July 1964, LBJL, NSF, VNCF, box 6; McNamara to Johnson, "Comment on Memoranda by Senator Mansfield," 7 January 1964, *FRUS, 1964–1968,* vol. 1, 8; Bundy to Johnson, draft memorandum, 18 May 1964, DDRS, 1988, 39.

12. McNamara explained on one occasion, "Southeast Asia has great significance in the forward defense of the United States. Its location across east-west air and sea lanes flanks the Indian subcontinent

on one side and Australia, New Zealand, and the Philippines on the other and dominates the gateway between the Pacific and Indian Oceans. In Communist hands this area would pose a most serious threat to the security of the United States and to the family of free-world nations to which we belong. To defend Southeast Asia, we must meet the challenge in South Vietnam." *Department of State Bulletin,* 13 April 1964, 563. Some observers have maintained that the Johnson administration believed that it was facing a monolithic threat in Vietnam. Gibson, *The Perfect War;* Herring, *America's Longest War;* Hunt, *Lyndon Johnson's War;* Mann, *A Grand Delusion;* McNamara, *In Retrospect;* Olson and Roberts, *Where the Domino Fell;* Record, *The Wrong War;* VanDeMark, *Into the Quagmire;* Young, *Vietnam Wars.* The administration's leadership, however, was well aware of the Sino-Soviet split, and it knew that China was supporting Communist expansionism in Southeast Asia while the Soviet Union was not. See, for example, telcon, 21 March 1964, Michael Beschloss, ed., *Taking Charge: The Johnson White House Tapes, 1963–1964* (New York: Simon & Schuster, 1997), 293–4.

13. Smith, NSC meeting notes, 7 January 1964, *FRUS,* 1964–1968, vol. 26, 8. On March 26, McNamara referred to Indonesia as "what the Chinese Communists may consider the greatest prize of all." *Department of State Bulletin,* 13 April 1964, 563. Robert Komer, an influential member of McGeorge Bundy's National Security Council staff who would later succeed Bundy as National Security Adviser, asserted that Indonesia's "strategic location and 100 million people make it a far greater prize than Vietnam." Komer to Johnson, 19 August 1964, *FRUS,* 1964–1968, vol. 26, 61.

14. The mounting troubles in Malaysia and Vietnam also caused the Australians to increase defense expenditures from 2.6 percent of GNP to 4.6 percent of GNP and to expand the regular army from 22,750 men to 33,000. As part of enlarging the army, the Australian government instituted a draft, for which there was widespread public support. The top priority of the new army was the development of expeditionary forces for use in Southeast Asia. Subritzky, *Confronting Sukarno,* 134; Gregory Pemberton, *All the Way: Australia's Road to Vietnam* (Sydney: Allen & Unwin, 1987), 213; Glen Barclay, *A Very Small Insurance Policy: The Politics of Australian Involvement in Vietnam, 1954–1967* (St. Lucia: University of Queensland Press, 1988), 66; P. G. Edwards, *Crises and Commitments: The Politics and Diplomacy of Australia's Involvement in Southeast Asian Conflicts, 1948–1965* (North Sydney: Allen & Unwin, 1992), 328–9.

15. Manila to State, 21 August 1964, LBJL, NSF, Country File, Malaysia, box 275.

16. Yang Kuisong, "Changes in Mao Zedong's Attitude toward the Indochina War, 1949–1973," CWIHP, 26; NIE 55–64, 22 July 1964, *FRUS,* 1964–1968, vol. 26, 56; CIA, "Sukarno and the Communists," 23 October 1964, LBJL, NSF, Country File, Indonesia, box 246; Odd Arne Westad, *The Global Cold War: Third World Interventions and the Making of Our Times* (Cambridge: Cambridge University Press, 2005), 187.

17. A. C. A. Dake, *In the Spirit of the Red Banteng: Indonesian Communists Between Moscow and Peking, 1959–1965* (The Hague: Mouton, 1973), 253; Howard Palfrey Jones, *Indonesia: The Possible Dream* (New York: Harcourt Brace Jovanovich, 1971), 321; Djakarta to State, 9 May 1964, *FRUS,* 1964–1968, vol. 26, 47. The United States had already cut most of its aid to Indonesia before Kennedy's assassination. On the development of Indonesia's "Confrontation" with Malaysia and the early American responses, see Subritzky, *Confronting Sukarno;* J. A. C. Mackie, *Konfrontasi: The Indonesia-Malaysia Dispute, 1963–1966* (Kuala Lumpur: Oxford University Press, 1974); Pemberton, *All the Way.*

18. Kuala Lumpur to State, 23 July 1964, LBJL, NSF, Country File, Malaysia, box 276; Jones, *Indonesia,* 342; *New York Times,* 23 July 1964.

19. During this same appearance, Sukarno also said, in line with Communist theory, that the current "bourgeois" and "democratic" revolution in Indonesia would be followed by a socialist revolution, and he spoke approvingly of Communist land seizures. OCI, "Sukarno's Independence Day Speech," 20 August 1964, *FRUS,* 1964–1968, vol. 26, 62; *New York Times,* August 17 and 18, 1964. Ho Chi Minh reciprocated with expressions of support for Indonesia's war against Malaysia. In 1966, after he had been removed from power, Sukarno would say publicly that he was a Marxist. *New York Times,* September 7, 1966.

20. Most significantly, Logevall, *Choosing War;* Robert McNamara et al., *Argument Without End: In Search of Answers to the Vietnam Tragedy* (New York: Public Affairs, 1999).

21. Memcon, 12 April 1964, *FRUS*, 1964–1968, vol. 27, 129; memcon, 20 July 1964, *FRUS*, 1964–1968, vol. 1, 237.

22. See, for example, Le Duan, *Thu Vao Nam*, 87, 90.

23. Bui Tin, *From Enemy to Friend*, 90–1.

24. Berman, *Planning a Tragedy;* Buzzanco, *Masters of War;* Dallek, *Flawed Giant;* Gardner, *Pay Any Price;* Herring, *America's Longest War;* Kahin, *Intervention;* Karnow, *Vietnam;* Mann, *A Grand Delusion;* McMaster, *Dereliction of Duty;* VanDeMark, *Into the Quagmire*. Others have argued that a leading factor or the principal factor in Johnson's decision was his determination to protect his personal reputation and his ego against charges of failure. Dallek, *Flawed Giant;* Logevall, *Choosing War;* Mann, *A Grand Delusion*.

25. Telcon, 27 May 1964, *FRUS*, 1964–1968, vol. 27, 52; telcon, 27 May 1964, Beschloss, ed., *Taking Charge*, 365.

26. In January 1964, just 2 percent of Americans surveyed said that Vietnam was an important issue. Harris, *Anguish of Change*, 55. When asked two months later whether they favored air strikes against North Vietnam, 26 percent of respondents supported air strikes while 45 percent opposed them. *Washington Post*, March 30, 1964. Few Congressmen were interested in Vietnam at this time, and fewer still had strong views on the subject. Dutton, "Loose Congressional Breakdown on Southeast Asia Situation," 2 June 1964, LBJL, NSF, VNCF, box 53. When Republican leaders, in the middle of 1964, tried to turn Americans against Johnson by accusing him of fighting the war half-heartedly, the public largely ignored them.

27. In 1964, to Johnson's chagrin, the press generally considered Vietnam less strategically important than Johnson did. Although some elements of the mainstream press – including Halberstam, who was no longer in Vietnam – contended that the United States had to maintain South Vietnam if it wanted to avert catastrophe elsewhere, others were less convinced and they were critical of Johnson's handling of the situation. Repeatedly meeting with press critics, Johnson and his lieutenants tried to sell them on the administration's Vietnam policies, but seldom with any success. Johnson also tried to stop the flow of gloomy press stories out of Saigon, as Kennedy had tried, because he believed that such stories were providing encouragement to the enemy, which in fact they were. Johnson issued orders to fire individuals who gave negative accounts to the press and attempted to cut off the press's access to sources within the government. These efforts, however, accomplished little, aside from increasing the press's distrust of the government. Hammond, *Public Affairs: The Military and the Media, 1962–1968*, 72, 81–2, 93. On Halberstam's views, see *New York Times*, March 6, 1964.

28. Telcon, 27 May 1964, *FRUS*, 1964–1968, vol. 27, 52; Telcon, 27 May 1964, Beschloss, ed., *Taking Charge*, 363–70.

29. Telcon, 1 June 1964, LBJL, Recordings of Telephone Conversations, tape WH6406.01.

30. See, for example, Forrestal to McGeorge Bundy, 4 February 1964, DDRS, 1975, 175B.

31. Telcon, 27 May 1964, *FRUS*, 1964–1968, vol. 27, 52.

32. Telcon, 2 March 1964, Beschloss, ed., *Taking Charge*, 261–2.

33. Johnson told Gen. Earle Wheeler that he "didn't want any problems to arise with respect to Vietnam that would have any effect on the election." Barksdale Hamlett, Oral History, Barksdale Hamlett Papers, Box 1, MHI. Michael Forrestal recalled, "He did everything to convey to his associates that their principal job in foreign affairs was to keep things on the back burner." Forrestal Oral History, LBJL. Additional instances are cited in subsequent footnotes.

34. Johnson to Lodge, 28 April 1964, *FRUS*, 1964–1968, vol. 1, 129.

35. Shaplen, *Lost Revolution*, 224–6.

36. Blair, *There to the Bitter End*, 82.

37. Sibley, memo for the record, 14 August 1964, *FRUS*, 1964–1968, vol. 1, 309.

38. Harkins Interview, Senior Officers Debriefing Program, MHI; Harkins Oral History, LBJL; Nguyen Khanh, interview with author; Harkins to Taylor, 30 January 1964, DDRS, 1975, 156C; Dunn Oral History, LBJL.

39. CIA to White House, 30 January 1964, LBJL, NSF, VNCF, box 2.

40. *Time*, February 14, 1964.

41. Assailed by constant criticism from intellectuals and political factions, Khanh also condemned the "intellectuals who sit around in teahouses and talk and don't support us," and the political schemers who were engaged in "a mere scramble for individual interests" and "represent only themselves." Shaplen, *Lost Revolution*, 240, 252, 256; Saigon to FO, 17 April 1964, PRO, 175469; CIA, "Comments of Prime Minister Nguyen Khanh," 31 May 1964, LBJL, NSF, VNCF, box 5.

42. Saigon to State, 4 May 1964, LBJL, NSF, VNCF, box 4.

43. Greene, memo for the record, 3 June 1964, MCHD, Greene Papers.

44. Some commentators have attached relatively little weight to the inferior quality of South Vietnam's leadership in the period between Diem's overthrow and the entrance of U.S. ground forces into the war, emphasizing instead supposed inadequacies in the methods selected for countering the insurgency. Had South Vietnam's government and its American advisers chosen methods more consistent with traditional counterinsurgency theory, they contend, the government would have performed much better. Asprey, *War in the Shadows;* Cable, *Conflict of Myths;* Cincinnatus, *Self-Destruction;* Krepinevich, *The Army and Vietnam;* Nagl, *Counterinsurgency Lessons from Malaya and Vietnam.* The foregoing conclusion is repeatedly contradicted by developments in Vietnam. The majority of historians have recognized, correctly, that the weakness of the South Vietnamese leadership powerfully affected the government's performance. Few, however, have studied the causes of the leadership problems. In most instances, the only cause cited is the poor quality of the ruling elite. Buzzanco, *Masters of War;* Kahin, *Intervention;* Kolko, *Anatomy of a War;* Logevall, *Choosing War;* Moss, *Vietnam;* Record, *The Wrong War;* Schwab, *Defending the Free World;* VanDeMark, *Into the Quagmire;* Vandiver, *Shadows of Vietnam.* The political activities of the militant Buddhists during 1964 and 1965 have received surprisingly little attention. In *Intervention,* George McT. Kahin analyzed the Buddhists in some depth, but he did not include a great amount of information that reflected poorly on the Buddhists. Orthodox historians usually have portrayed the Buddhists during this period in the same way they portrayed them in 1963, as non-Communists who were merely seeking freedom from religious intolerance and repression. The only previous scholarly account that has attributed South Vietnam's political problems in this period to duplicitous and destructive Buddhist scheming, albeit less comprehensively than this account, is Dommen, *The Indochinese Experience of the French and the Americans.*

45. Saigon to State, 27 February 1964, LBJL, NSF, VNCF, box 2.

46. Lodge remarked, "Tri Quang, the Buddhist leader, is a potential trouble maker. Having overthrown one government, he may feel like trying again against Khanh. He has indicated to me that he does not regard Khanh as a 'good Buddhist' – meaning, presumably, that he is a Buddhist who does not follow Tri Quang's direction." On another occasion, Lodge said that Tri Quang "is ambitious, anti-Christian, full of hatreds, and agitating against Khanh," and that "some communist infiltration of Buddhists exists." Memcon, 11 May 1964, *FRUS,* 1964–1968, vol. 1, 147; Memcon, 12 May 1964, *FRUS,* 1964–1968, vol. 1, 151.

47. Bui Tin, *Following Ho Chi Minh,* 66.

48. King Chen, "North Vietnam in the Sino-Soviet Dispute, 1962–1964," *Asian Survey,* vol. 4, issue 9 (September 1964), 1029–34; Thomas Kennedy Latimer, "Hanoi's Leaders and Their South Vietnam Policies, 1954–1968" (Ph.D. diss., Georgetown University, 1972), 167; Zhai, *China and the Vietnam Wars,* 126; Bui Tin, *Mat That: Hoi Ky Chinh Tri cua Bui Tin* (Turpin Press, 1994), 189–90.

49. Military History Institute of Vietnam, *Dai Tuong Nguyen Chi Thanh: Nha Chinh Tri Quan Su Loi Lac* (Hanoi: People's Army Publishing House, 1997), 148; Latimer, "Hanoi's Leaders and Their South Vietnam Policies," 174–7.

50. Le Kinh Lich, ed. *The 30-Year War,* vol. 2, 113; Military History Institute of Vietnam, *Victory in Vietnam,* 102–4; MACV, "Infiltration Study," 31 October 1964, *FRUS,* 1964–1968, vol. 1, 392.

51. Douglas Pike, *Vietnam and the Soviet Union: Anatomy of an Alliance* (Boulder: Westview Press, 1987), 74; Gaiduk, *The Soviet Union and the Vietnam War,* 7–11.

52. Yang Kuisong, "Changes in Mao Zedong's Attitude toward the Indochina War, 1949–1973," 28.

53. Record of talk, 19 July 1964, PRO, FO 371/180988.

54. Yang Kuisong, "Changes in Mao Zedong's Attitude toward the Indochina War, 1949–1973," 28–9; Zhai, *China and the Vietnam Wars,* 131–2.

55. Military History Institute of Vietnam, *Victory in Vietnam,* 126–7; Nguyen Viet Phuong, *Van Tai Quan Su Chien Luoc Tren Duong Ho Chi Minh Trong Khang Chien Chong My,* 55; CIA, "Viet Cong

Infiltration into Northern South Vietnam," 23 October 1964, LBJL, NSF, VNCF, box 9. Hanoi's ambitious plans called for an even more dramatic increase in shipments, but the goals were not met owing to the incapacitation of roadways by heavy rains and enemy attacks.

56. Vientiane to State, 9 February 1964, DDRS, 1981, 206C; Vientiane to State, 1 March 1964, *FRUS, 1964–1968*, vol. 28, 11; Vientiane to State, 10 April 1964, DDRS, 1981, 210A.

57. The strikes had a larger impact on the foreign press, which criticized the administration for evading questions on air operations over Laos and attributed the administration's reticence to the coming Presidential election. The true reason for the evasiveness was Souvanna's insistence that the Americans keep quiet, a policy intended to prevent the Communists from gaining material for their propaganda mill, in imitation of North Vietnam's own silence about its assistance to the Pathet Lao.

58. Pham Hong Thuy et al., *Lich su Hai Quan Nhan Dan Viet Nam,* 158–61; Nguyen Tu Duong, *Duong Mon Tren Bien,* 10, 65–67, 74.

59. Political Department of the Navy, *35 Nam Duong Ho Chi Minh Tren Bien va Thanh Lap Lu Doan 125 Hai Quan* (Hanoi: People's Army Publishing House, 1996), 23–5; Nguyen Tu Duong, *Duong Mon Tren Bien,* 109–10.

60. Ho Chi Minh National Political Studies Institute, *Lich Su Bien Nien Xu Uy Nam Bo Va Trung Uong Cuc Mien Nam,* 438. The Politburo resolved in June, "We must quickly increase our shipment of supplies and equipment to give our troops sufficient strength to attack continuously in order to annihilate the enemy." Ibid.

61. Marolda and Fitzgerald, *The United States Navy and the Vietnam Conflict,* vol. 2, 299, 309–333.

62. From 1962 to 1964, the North Vietnamese transported 4,920 tons of equipment and supplies to the South via the maritime infiltration routes, of which 1,318 were transported in 1962 and 1963. Tran Van Quang et al., *Tong Ket Cuoc Khang Chien Chong My Cuu Nuoc,* 223, 318; Pham Hong Thuy et al., *Lich su Hai Quan Nhan Dan Viet Nam,* 158–65.

63. Ibid.; Nguyen Viet Phuong, *Van Tai Quan Su Chien Luoc Tren Duong Ho Chi Minh Trong Khang Chien Chong My,* 382.

64. Tran Phan Tran and Dinh Thu Xuan, *Lich Su Quan Gioi Nam Bo va Cuc Nam Trung Bo (1954–1975)* (Hanoi: People's Army Publishing House, 1998), 175.

65. From 1960 to early 1965, the South Vietnamese government lost 39,000 weapons and captured 25,000, giving the Viet Cong a net gain of 14,000 weapons. The total strength of the Viet Cong armed forces in early 1965 was approximately 150,000. *Department of State Bulletin,* 17 May 1965, 749–50; CIA-DIA-State, "Strength of Viet Cong Military Forces in South Vietnam," 17 March 1965, LBJL, NSF, VNCF, box 15; CIA, "Status of the War in South Vietnam," 12 May 1965, DDRS, 1977, 28D.

66. Le Quoc San, *Cuoc Do Suc Than Ky,* 550.

67. Resolution of the Ninth Conference of the Central Committee of the Viet-Nam Workers' Party, December 1963, TTU, Pike Collection, Unit 1, box 3.

68. Nguyen Tu Duong, *Duong Mon Tren Bien,* 74.

69. This account is drawn from Roger Donlon Congressional Medal of Honor Recommendation, 15 August 1964, NA II, RG 472, Medal of Honor Award Case Files, box 6; Roger Donlon, *Outpost of Freedom* (New York: McGraw-Hill, 1965); Roger Donlon, *Beyond Nam Dong* (Leavenworth, KS: R and N Publishers, 1998); Blair, *There to the Bitter End,* 90–3; Roger Donlon, interview with author.

70. Sheehan, *A Bright Shining Lie,* 3.

71. The State Department, in which this view was especially popular, recommended projects such as irrigation works in the Phan Rang Valley, a village cistern and well program, and new agricultural financing policies. State to Saigon, 25 July 1964, *FRUS, 1964–1968,* vol. 1, 246. President Johnson himself expressed considerable interest in providing additional political and economic benefits to the peasants to win them over, remarking, "We've got to see that the South Vietnamese government wins the battle, not so much of arms, but of crops and hearts and caring, so their people can have hope and belief in the word and deed of their government." Jack Valenti, *A Very Human President* (New York: W. W. Norton, 1975), 133–4. See also Johnson to Lodge, 28 April 1964, *FRUS, 1964–1968,* vol. 1, 129; Merle Miller, *Lyndon: An Oral Biography* (New York: Putnam, 1980), 466.

72. William Colby explained in May that the basic South Vietnamese pacification concept was sound, but "the middle levels of the GVN machinery, civilian and military, have failed to translate the concept

into new forms of action." Colby to Forrestal, 11 May 1964, NSF, VNCF, box 4. See also Nes to Lodge, 17 February 1964, *FRUS, 1964–1968*, vol. 1, 52; Read, summary record of meeting, 30 May 1964, *FRUS, 1964–1968*, vol. 1, 184; Washington to FO, 30 May 1964, PRO, PREM 11/4759; Sullivan, "Memorandum on Situation in Vietnam," 13 June 1964, *FRUS, 1964–1968*, vol. 1, 214.

73. Summary Record of National Security Council Meeting, 3 April 1964, DDRS, 1999, 34.

74. *The Pentagon Papers*, vol. 3, 69; summary record of meeting, 1 June 1964, *FRUS, 1964–1968*, vol. 1, 187.

75. "Operations must be aimed at retention and extension of control," Westmoreland argued. "This means more clear and hold operations and fewer 'safaris' with large formations which start from a secure area, sweep through a contested area, then return to a secure area – and with no lasting contribution to pacification." Summary record of meeting, 1 June 1964, *FRUS, 1964–1968*, vol. 1, 187.

76. *The Joint Chiefs of Staff and the War in Vietnam*, chap. 8, 17.

77. Shultz, *The Secret War Against Hanoi*, 37–38, 45, 94–6, 324.

78. Ibid., 101, 276–7.

79. Vien Nghien Cuu Khoa Hoc Cong An, Bo Noi Vu, *Cong An Nhan Dan Viet Nam, Tap II (1954–1965)* (Ho Chi Minh City, 1978), 160.

80. Conboy and Andrade, *Spies & Commandos*; Shultz, *The Secret War Against Hanoi*; *The Joint Chiefs of Staff and the War in Vietnam*, chap. 8, 23.

81. Conboy and Andrade, *Spies & Commandos*; Shultz, *The Secret War Against Hanoi*.

82. McNamara to Johnson, 16 March 1964, *FRUS, 1964–1968*, vol. 1, 84.

83. *The Pentagon Papers*, vol. 3, 496–9.

84. Bruce Palmer, *The 25 - Year War: America's Military Role in Vietnam* (Lexington: University Press of Kentucky, 1984), 28.

85. Taylor to McNamara, 2 March 1964, *FRUS, 1964–1968*, vol. 1, 65; Taylor to McNamara, 2 March 1964, *FRUS, 1964–1968*, vol. 1, 66; Greene, meeting notes, 4 March 1964, MCHD, Greene Papers; Taylor, memcon, 4 March 1964, *FRUS, 1964–1968*, vol. 1, 70; Taylor to McNamara, 14 March 1964, *FRUS, 1964–1968*, vol. 1, 82; Davis to McNamara, 2 June 1964, *FRUS, 1964–1968*, vol. 1, 191; Taylor to McNamara, 5 June 1964, *FRUS, 1964–1968*, vol. 1, 199; *The Pentagon Papers*, vol. 3, 165–6, 496–9; *The Joint Chiefs of Staff and the War in Vietnam*, chap. 9, 18–19.

86. *The Joint Chiefs of Staff and the War in Vietnam*, chap. 9, 20; McCone, "Memorandum on Vietnam," 3 March 1964, *FRUS, 1964–1968*, vol. 1, 68.

87. Clifton, Memo for the Record, 4 March 1964, DDRS, 1999, 91; Greene, meeting notes, 4 March 1964, MCHD, Greene Papers; memcon, 4 March 1964, *FRUS, 1964–1968*, vol. 1, 70. These comments rapidly generated grumbling in the Pentagon's hallways that the President was choosing strategy in the interest of his Presidential campaign rather than in the interest of the country.

88. Rusk to McNamara, 5 February 1964, *FRUS, 1964–1968*, vol. 1, 36; Sullivan to Rusk, 25 February 1964, *FRUS, 1964–1968*, vol. 1, 61; memcon, 10 June 1964, *FRUS, 1964–1968*, vol. 28, 88; Bundy and Forrestal, "Position Paper on Expanding U.S. Action in South Vietnam to the North," 31 July 1964, LBJL, NSF, VNCF, box 6. A sizeable group of historians has also espoused this view. Asprey, *War in the Shadows*; Ford, *CIA and the Vietnam Policymakers*; Hess, *Vietnam and the United States*; Kahin, *Intervention*; Kolko, *Anatomy of a War*; Krepinevich, *The Army and Vietnam*; McNamara et al., *Argument Without End*; Record, *The Wrong War*; VanDeMark, *Into the Quagmire*.

89. America's Asian allies – even the normally militant Chiang Kai-shek – opposed the use of nuclear weapons in Asia. Greene, meeting notes, 4 March 1964, MCHD, Greene Papers; Rusk to State, 1 June 1964, *FRUS, 1964–1968*, vol. 1, 186; Imhof, memcon, 20 July 1964, *FRUS, 1964–1968*, vol. 1, 237.

90. President Johnson told McGeorge Bundy on May 27, "I just stayed awake last night thinking of this thing, and the more that I think of it I don't know what in the hell, it looks like to me that we're getting into another Korea. It just worries the hell out of me. I don't see what we can ever hope to get out of there with once we're committed. I believe the Chinese Communists are coming into it. I don't think that we can fight them 10,000 miles away from home and ever get anywhere in that area." Telcon, 27 May 1964, *FRUS, 1964–1968*, vol. 27, 53.

91. For the influence of these theorists, see McNamara, *Argument Without End*, 159–60.

92. Davidson, *Vietnam At War*, 338.

93. Thomas C. Schelling, *Strategy of Conflict* (Cambridge: Harvard University Press, 1960).

94. See Zubok and Pleshakov, *Inside the Kremlin's Cold War*; Naftali and Fursenko, *"One Hell of a Gamble."*

95. *New York Times,* 27 May 1964.

96. Khanh told Lodge that because the South Vietnamese government lacked the necessary trained personnel, "we Vietnamese want the Americans to be responsible with us and not merely be advisers." Lodge to Johnson, 30 April 1964, *FRUS,* 1964–1968, vol. 1, 132.

97. McCone, memo for the record, 24 May 1964, *FRUS,* 1964–1968, vol. 28, 62; Goodpaster, "Four Meetings on Extension of Operations Against North Viet-Nam," 25 May 1964, NA II, RG 218, 091 Vietnam, May 1964, box 13; "Discussions with Mr. Bundy," 28 May 1964, PRO, PREM 11/4761; "Record of Discussions with Mr. Bundy," 29 May 1964, PRO, PREM 11/4761; Bundy, unpublished manuscript, chap. 14, 10.

98. CANDEL Saigon, "Initial Visit to Hanoi," 20 June 1964, LBJL, NSF, VNCF, box 54; George C. Herring, *The Secret Diplomacy of the Vietnam War: The Negotiating Volumes of the Pentagon Papers* (Austin: University of Texas Press, 1983), 7–8, 31–3; Luu van Loi and Nguyen Anh Vu, *Tiep Xuc Bi Mat Viet Nam-Hoa Ky Truoc Hoi Nghi Pa-Ri* (Hanoi: International Relations Institute, 1990), 16–24.

99. Saigon to FO, 23 June 1964, PRO, PREM 11/4759; Saigon to State, 28 July 1964, LBJL, NSF, VNCF, box 6; CIA, "South Vietnamese Government Contacts with the Viet Cong and National Liberation Front," 26 November 1965, DDRS, 1977, 279G.

100. Joseph C. Goulden, *Truth is the First Casualty: The Gulf of Tonkin Affair–Illusion and Reality* (Chicago: Rand McNally, 1969), 32; Moïse, *Tonkin Gulf,* 39; *New York Times,* July 20 and 24, 1964.

101. Telcon, 15 June 1964, Beschloss, ed., *Taking Charge,* 407–409; telcon, 16 June 1964, Beschloss, ed., *Taking Charge,* 410–411; telcon, 18 June 1964, Beschloss, ed., *Taking Charge,* 415–16.

102. *The Joint Chiefs of Staff and the War in Vietnam,* chap. 11, 13–15.

103. The details of Westmoreland's life are drawn primarily from Samuel Zaffiri, *Westmoreland: A Biography of William C. Westmoreland* (New York: Morrow, 1994); Westmoreland, *A Soldier Reports;* and *New York Times Magazine,* November 15, 1964.

104. Sorley, *Honorable Warrior,* 192.

14. Signals: August–October 1964

1. Pham Hong Thuy et al., *Lich su Hai Quan Nhan Dan Viet Nam,* 92–4.

2. Bui Tin, *Mat That,* 191–2.

3. Ibid.; Moïse, *Tonkin Gulf,* 73, 90.

4. The official history of the North Vietnamese Navy described the arriving aircraft: "Enemy sky pirates insanely poured a stream of rockets and 20mm cannon shells down on our torpedo-boat formation.... Taking advantage of the fact that our anti-aircraft armament was weak and dispersed between several vessels, the American sky pirates concentrated their attacks on one boat at a time." Pham Hong Thuy et al., *Lich su Hai Quan Nhan Dan Viet Nam,* 96–7.

5. Moïse, *Tonkin Gulf,* 72–82; Vo Van Tri, et. al., *Mot So Tran Danh cua Hai Quan 1964–1978,* Tap 1 (Hanoi: Navy Headquarters, 1993), 7–36.

6. *New York Times,* August 4, 1964; CIA, "The Situation in South Vietnam," 5 August 1964, LBJL, NSF, VNCF, box 7.

7. Saigon to State, 3 August 1964, *FRUS,* 1964–1968, vol. 1, 262.

8. Top U.S. officials evidently thought that the belated North Vietnamese cancellation order, which the NSA had decrypted rapidly, was an order from the central command overruling the local command, rather than what it really was – an order from the central command canceling its own previous command.

9. The radar operators on the *Turner Joy* were firmly convinced that their ship had engaged and destroyed enemy sea craft. The contacts had not behaved like phantom contacts would, they observed, a conclusion supported by a subsequent investigation. Moïse, *Tonkin Gulf,* 125, 135, 137, 203–4; Andy Kerr, *A Journey Amongst the Good and the Great* (Annapolis: Naval Institute Press, 1987), 178; William Cogar,

ed., *New Interpretations in Naval History: Selected Papers from the Eighth Naval History Symposium* (Annapolis: Naval Institute Press, 1989), 323–8.

10. Marolda and Fitzgerald, *The United States Navy and the Vietnam Conflict*, vol. 2, 432–3; Moïse, *Tonkin Gulf*, 126, 203–4; CTG 72.1 to CINCPACFLT, 4 August 1964, NA II, RG 59, Central Files, 1964–1966, box 2944; Telcon, 4 August 1964, LBJL, NSF, VNCF, box 228; *The Pentagon Papers*, vol. 3, 184–6; *FRUS, 1964–1968*, vol. 1, 276.

11. Robert J. Hanyok, "Skunks, Bogies, Silent Hounds, and the Flying Fish: The Gulf of Tonkin Mystery, 2–4 August 1964," *Cryptologic Quarterly*, Winter 2000/Spring 2001 (vol. 19, no. 4/vol. 20, No. 1), 1–55; *U.S. News and World Report*, July 23, 1984; Haig, *Inner Circles*, 122–3; Ray Cline OH II, LBJL.

12. The most compelling arguments against the existence of a second attack are made in Moïse, *Tonkin Gulf*, and Hanyok, "Skunks, Bogies, Silent Hounds, and the Flying Fish." Moïse contends that most of the reported North Vietnamese activity on August 4 definitely did not take place, but acknowledges that it is possible, though unlikely, that a single North Vietnamese vessel did make an attack during the first minutes of the incident. Moïse, *Tonkin Gulf*, 203–7.

13. Smith, NSC meeting notes, 4 August 1964, *FRUS, 1964–1968*, vol. 1, 278; Jenkins, meeting notes, 4 August 1964, *FRUS, 1964–1968*, vol. 1, 280.

14. Telcon, 4 August 1964, LBJL, NSF, VNCF, box 228.

15. Jenkins, meeting notes, 4 August 1964, *FRUS, 1964–1968*, vol. 1, 280.

16. *Department of State Bulletin*, 24 August 1964, 259.

17. CIA, "The Situation in South Vietnam," 5 August 1964, LBJL, NSF, VNCF, box 7; Westmoreland to Sharp, 8 August 1964, *FRUS, 1964–1968*, vol. 1, 303; *Time*, August 14, 1964; Furness, memcon, 21 August 1964, *FRUS, 1964–1968*, vol. 1, 320.

18. *New Republic*, 10 July 1965.

19. Philippine Vice President Emmanuel Pelaez pronounced that the American action represented "the kind of firmness that can rally the people of Southeast Asia against Red aggression." *New York Times*, August 7, 1964.

20. *Department of State Bulletin*, 24 August 1964, 268.

21. Telcon, 3 August 1964, Beschloss, ed., *Taking Charge*, 493–4; telcon, 3 August 1964, Beschloss, ed., *Taking Charge*, 494–5; *American Foreign Policy: Current Documents, 1964*, 985–9; *Executive Sessions of the Senate Foreign Relations Committee*, 6 August 1964, 291–6.

22. Robert David Johnson, *Ernest Gruening and the American Dissenting Tradition* (Cambridge: Harvard University Press, 1998), 253–4.

23. *Congressional Record*, vol. 110, 18398–18471.

24. *Washington Post*, August 10, 1964. Most elements of the press also supported Johnson's reaction.

25. *Congressional Record*, vol. 110, 18398–18471.

26. Ibid., 18539.

27. Sharp warned that a drop off in American action "could easily be interpreted as a period of second thoughts about Pierce Arrow and the events leading thereto as well as a sign of weakness and lack of resolve." Marolda and Fitzgerald, *The United States Navy and the Vietnam Conflict*, vol. 2, 453.

28. Bundy, "Next Courses of Action in Southeast Asia," 13 August 1964, *FRUS, 1964–1968*, vol. 1, 313.

29. The new measures were needed, Khanh explained, because "the Communist authorities in North Vietnam, on orders from their Chinese Communist masters, have continually ignored the national sentiments and have ruthlessly brought the calamities of war into free and peaceful South Vietnam." Saigon to State, 7 August 1964, LBJL, NSF, VNCF, box 7; *Time*, 14 August 1964; Shaplen, *Lost Revolution*, 270.

30. Saigon to State, 23 August 1964, LBJL, NSF, VNCF, box 7; Saigon to State, 26 August 1964, NA II, RG 59, Central Files, 1964–1966, box 2933; CIA, "The Situation in South Vietnam," 27 August 1964, LBJL, NSF, VNCF, box 7; *New Yorker*, September 19, 1964; *New York Times*, September 10, 1964; Lacouture, *Vietnam*, 211.

31. Saigon to State, 23 August 1964, LBJL, NSF, VNCF, box 7.

32. *Time*, September 4, 1964.

33. Saigon to FO, 25 August 1964, PRO, FO 371/175472; Lacouture, *Vietnam*, 207–8; *New York Times*, August 24, 27, 1964.

34. *Time*, September 4, 1964; *New York Times*, August 31, 1964.

35. Saigon to FO, 24 August 1964, PRO, FO 371/175472.

36. Of those individuals whom the police did choose to arrest during the disturbances, a substantial number were not carrying a national identity card, something possessed by most everyone in the cities except the Viet Cong. For suspicions and evidence of Communist influence in the Buddhist and student movements, see Saigon to FO, 24 August 1964, PRO, FO 371/175472; CIA, "Situation in Vietnam," 27 August 1964, LBJL, NSF, VNCF, box 7; CIA, "Situation in South Vietnam," 1 September 1964, DDRS, 1979, 20C; SNIE 53-64, 8 September 1964, *FRUS*, 1964–1968, vol. 1, 341; Saigon to State, 24 September 1964, *FRUS*, 1964–1968, vol. 1, 360; SNIE 53-2-64, 1 October 1964, *FRUS*, 1964–1968, vol. 1, 368; *New Yorker*, September 19, 1964; *New York Times*, August 29, 1964.

37. Nguyen Phuc Khanh et al., eds., *Chung Mot Bong Co*, 156–7.

38. Among those installed right after the coup by the Minh junta was Colonel Tran Ba Thanh, who upon becoming the deputy director of the National Police released important Viet Cong prisoners, destroyed police files on the Viet Cong, and assigned a Viet Cong agent to a high post in the police. Thanh was removed when Khanh took over, but in the subsequent months, according to a U.S. intelligence report prepared in September, "the Saigon police and security services have not recovered their anti-Communist capabilities." SNIE 53-2-64, 1 October 1964, *FRUS*, 1964–1968, vol. 1, 368; "A COSVN Standing Committee Account of the Situation in South Vietnam from the End of 1961 to the Beginning of 1964," 20 April 1964, TTU, Pike Collection, Unit 6, box 1.

39. Higgins, *Our Vietnam Nightmare*, 285–6; CIA, "Tri Quang and the Buddhist-Catholic Discord in South Vietnam," 19 September 1964, LBJL, NSF, VNCF, box 9; *New Yorker*, September 19, 1964; Shaplen, *Lost Revolution*, 279.

40. Saigon to State, 25 August 1964, *FRUS*, 1964–1968, vol. 1, 324.

41. In order to secure a signed letter from Tri Quang and Tam Chau expressing support for the government, Khanh had to give them $300,000 in cash. *New Yorker*, September 19, 1964. This letter, moreover, put yet more demands on Khanh, conditioning continued support on the government's stifling of the Can Lao and the creation a new national assembly in one year. Saigon to State, 26 August 1964, LBJL, NSF, VNCF, box 7.

42. CIA, "Details of the 26 and 27 August 1964 Meetings of the Military Revolutionary Council," 1 September 1964, DDRS, 1977, 278A; Saigon to State, 28 August 1964, LBJL, NSF, VNCF, box 7.

43. Westmoreland to Taylor, 6 September 1964, *FRUS*, 1964–1968, vol. 1, 340.

44. *New York Times*, September 3 and 10, 1964.

45. Thomas M. Coffey, *Iron Eagle: The Turbulent Life of General Curtis LeMay* (New York: Crown Publishers, 1986), 436; Curtis LeMay with MacKinlay Kantor, *Mission With LeMay* (Garden City: Doubleday, 1965), 565; *The Joint Chiefs of Staff and the War in Vietnam*, chap. 12, 16.

46. Gibbons, *The U.S. Government and the Vietnam War*, vol. 3, 13.

47. *The Pentagon Papers*, vol. 3, 556–9; Gibbons, *The U.S. Government and the Vietnam War*, vol. 2, 348.

48. *The Joint Chiefs of Staff and the War in Vietnam*, chap. 12, 15; Vincent Demma, "Suggestions for the Use of Ground Forces, June 1964–March 1965," unpublished manuscript, CMH, 11–12.

49. The creators of the first SIGMA game, which was held in April, had admitted that the game was "scarcely a conclusive medium for evaluating such things as North Vietnamese ability to withstand military pressures." According to the SIGMA-I-64 report, the members of the team that played the North Vietnamese could not decide how much punishment they would tolerate before backing off, because "it was impossible for any of them to think exactly like a North Vietnamese leader as to just how much they could take." In addition, the study was based on the faulty premise that Hanoi's contribution to the Viet Cong was "mainly psychological and disciplinary, not material." Joint War Games Agency, "Sigma-I-64 Final Report," n.d., DDRS, 1987, 91. The second game, conducted in September, had been specifically designed to examine what would happen if the bombing of North Vietnam did not stop the enemy. Joint War Games Agency, "Sigma-II-64 Final Report," 5 October 1964, DDRS, 1986, 205. Historians have committed the same errors in interpretation as contemporary observers. Bird, *The Color of Truth*, 276–7; Buzzanco, *Masters of War*, 162, 174–5; Ford, *CIA and the Vietnam Policymakers*, 57–58, 67; Gibbons, *The U.S. Government and the Vietnam War*, vol. 2, 353; Karnow, *Vietnam*, 415; Krepinevich, *The Army and*

Vietnam, 133; Logevall, *Choosing War,* 123, 242; McMaster, *Dereliction of Duty,* 89–91, 156–63; Schwab, *Defending the Free World,* 123.

50. SNIE 50-2-64, 25 May 1964, *FRUS,* 1964–1968, vol. 1, 174.

51. *New York Times,* September 5, 1964.

52. The destroyer commanders reported afterwards that they believed the contacts to be genuine surface vessels. An intercepted enemy message suggested that North Vietnamese vessels were under attack at this very time, but subsequent analysis cast doubt on the validity of this message, and a search conducted after the incident found no debris. The only visual evidence consisted of a pilot's aerial sighting of two wakes trailing the destroyers and reports from two sailors that they had seen unidentified silhouettes. CTG to RUATUL, 18 September 1964, LBJL, NSF, VNCF, box 227; CINCPAC to AIG, 18 September 1964, LBJL, NSF, VNCF, box 227; COMSEVENTHFLT to CINCPACFLT, 19 September 1964, LBJL, NSF, VNCF, box 227; CTU 77.6.6 to RUECW, 19 September 1964, LBJL, NSF, VNCF, box 227; Bundy, "The Gulf of Tonkin Incident," 20 September 1964, *FRUS,* 1964–1968, vol. 1, 356; Marolda and Fitzgerald, *The United States Navy and the Vietnam Conflict,* vol. 2, 454–8; telcon, 18 September 1964, Beschloss, ed., *Reaching for Glory,* 38–9.

53. Bundy, "Meeting on South Vietnam," 14 September 1964, LBJL, NSF, Memos to the President, box 2.

54. In addition to sources cited previously, see CIA, "Peiping's Views on 'Revolutionary War,'" 14 December 1964, DDRS, 1997, 248; Rangoon to State, 31 July 1964, LBJL, NSF, Country File, Burma, box 235; Xiaoming Zhang, "China's Involvement in Laos During the Vietnam War, 1963–1975," 1163; Melvin Gurtov and Byong-Moo Hwang, *China Under Threat: The Politics and Strategy of Diplomacy* (Baltimore: Johns Hopkins University Press, 1980), 160.

55. CIA, "The Sino-Vietnamese Effort to Limit American Actions in the Vietnam War," 9 June 1965, DDRS, 1979, 244B.

56. Zhai, *China and the Vietnam Wars,* 149–50.

57. Xiaoming Zhang, "The Vietnam War, 1964–1969: A Chinese Perspective," *Journal of Military History,* vol. 60, issue 4 (October 1996), 739–42; Jian, *Mao's China and the Cold War,* 215; Barry Naughton, "The Third Front: Defence Industrialization in the Chinese Interior," *China Quarterly,* no. 115 (September 1988), 351–86. China built new airfields near North Vietnam, but not for offensive purposes. They were designed to accommodate North Vietnamese jets in case the Americans compelled them to leave. Gurtov and Hwang, *China Under Threat,* 160–1.

58. Bui Tin, *From Enemy to Friend,* 40; Bin Yu, "What China Learned From Its 'Forgotten War' in Korea," in Ziaobing Li et al., eds., *Mao's Generals Remember Korea* (Lawrence, KS: University Press of Kansas, 2001), 9–29.

59. Congressional briefing, 23 February 1965, LBJL, Congressional Briefings on Vietnam, box 1; Congressional reception, 2 March 1965, LBJL, Congressional Briefings on Vietnam, box 1; JIC, "The Chinese Threat in the Far East Up to 1969," 10 May 1965, PRO, CAB 158/54.

60. Mao told Pham Van Dong that "you," not "we," would fight the Americans if they entered North Vietnam. In the event of such an invasion, Mao said, "you can win it." Mao explained to Pham Van Dong, "If the Americans are determined to invade the inner land, you may allow them to do so.... You must not engage your main forces in a head-to-head confrontation with them, and must well maintain your main forces. My opinion is that so long as the green mountain is there, how can you ever lack firewood?" Memcon, Mao Zedong and Pham Van Dong, Hoang Van Hoan, 5 October 1964, CWIHP. Historians have generally accepted the Johnson administration's argument that an American invasion of North Vietnam would cause China to intervene. See, for example, Duiker, *Sacred War;* Kahin, *Intervention;* Krepinevich, *The Army and Vietnam;* Zhai, *China and the Vietnam Wars.*

61. Given that the Saigon government was near its political nadir in 1964, an American expedition to North Vietnam might well have been accompanied by the creation of a separate anti-Communist government in the North, drawn from the one million Northern refugees in South Vietnam. These refugees had shown fierce anti-Communism and strong organizational skill in the South, and could be expected to do the same in the North. The South Vietnamese government, relieved of massive infiltration from the North, likely would have been able to handle the South without major foreign help, as it had done until Hanoi's rapid acceleration of the infiltration in late 1964 and early 1965. In the

longer-term, prospects for a combined anti-Communist effort across all of Vietnam were good, for the Saigon government was destined to improve dramatically several years hence.

62. Bui Tin, *From Enemy to Friend*, 82.

63. While the Joint Chiefs and others repeatedly recommended cutting the Ho Chi Minh Trail with U.S. troops during the war, advocacy of this approach has most often been associated with Col. Harry Summers Jr., who made it a central theme of his book *On Strategy*. Summers, though, did not have access to most of the pertinent U.S. archival material and North Vietnamese sources that are now available.

64. Several historians have argued that interdiction of the trail was infeasible because the United States would have needed thousands of engineers and as many as nine months of logistical preparation. The argument has its origins in Krepinevich, *The Army and Vietnam*, 263. But the fact remains that MACV, the only organization that studied this proposed undertaking in depth, concluded that while the time and resource requirements were large, it was nonetheless a feasible course of action. Westmoreland, "Commander's Estimate of the Situation in South Vietnam, 26 March 1965, LBJL, Westmoreland Papers, History Backup, box 5. If necessary, U.S. forces could have been used to hold the enemy in check in South Vietnam during an initial logistical preparation period.

65. The argument that the North Vietnamese would have responded by shifting the infiltration routes into Thailand can be found in Krepinevich, *The Army and Vietnam*, 145, 263; Prados, *The Blood Road*, 376; Duiker, *U.S. Containment Policy and the Conflict in Indochina*, 375. Prados also contends that U.S. intervention in Laos might have caused China to intervene. Considering China's strong aversion to fighting the Americans in North Vietnam and the absence of evidence that China was even contemplating intervention in southern Laos, a Chinese troop deployment into Laos at the 17th parallel – far from China's border with Laos – was very unlikely.

66. The size of the Thai armed forces was provided in Special State-Defense Study Group, "Communist China (Short Range Report)," 30 April 1965, DDRS, 1998, 114.

67. Bui Tin, *From Enemy to Friend*, 74–6. See also Lacouture, *Vietnam*, 183–4.

68. In November, the North Vietnamese Political Bureau noted that American weakness began to manifest itself with the Americans' limited and unrepeated retaliatory attack following the Tonkin Gulf incidents. Nguyen Chi Thanh, "The Political Bureau's Assessment of the Situation," 20 November 1964, TTU, Pike Collection, Unit 6, box 1.

69. Memcon, Mao Zedong and Pham Van Dong, Hoang Van Hoan, 5 October 1964, CWIHP.

70. Luu van Loi and Nguyen Anh Vu, *Tiep Xuc Bi Mat Viet Nam-Hoa Ky Truoc Hoi Nghi Pa-Ri*, 26–8.

71. Military History Institute of Vietnam, *Victory in Vietnam*, 137. See also memcon, Mao Zedong and Pham Van Dong, Hoang Van Hoan, 5 October 1964, CWIHP.

72. That North Vietnamese actions were heavily dependent on American actions and that Hanoi would restrain itself if it feared the United States both disprove the prevailing view that the North Vietnamese were so intent on victory that no American strategy could have saved South Vietnam in the long run. The orthodox view is espoused in Buzzanco, *Masters of War*; Duiker, *Sacred War*; Herring, *America's Longest War*; Kahin, *Intervention*; Karnow, *Vietnam*; Record, *The Wrong War*; Schulzinger, *A Time for War*; Schwab, *Defending the Free World*.

73. Eric F. Goldman, *The Tragedy of Lyndon Johnson* (New York: Knopf, 1969), 235–6.

74. Bundy to Johnson, 1 October 1964, LBJL, NSF, Memos to the President, box 2. Walt Rostow admonished that if the President continued to promise peace unequivocally and then employed force soon after the election, it "could reopen charges of alleged Democratic campaigning deceit, against the background of 1916 and 1940." Rostow to Bundy, 9 September 1964, LBJL, Office Files of Bill Moyers, box 53.

75. *Public Papers of the Presidents, Lyndon B. Johnson, 1963–1964*, vol. 2, 1387–93.

76. Cao Minh et al., *Quan Khu 8*, 515–6; Vien Nghien Cuu Chu Nghia Mac Lenin Va Tu Tuong Ho Chi Minh, *Lich Su Dang Cong San Viet Nam*, Tap II, 267; Duiker, *Communist Road to Power*, 250; Ho Chi Minh National Political Studies Institute, *Lich Su Bien Nien Xu Uy Nam Bo Va Trung Uong Cuc Mien Nam*, 453; *Quan Doi Nhan Dan*, 16 June 2004. The Communists' southern headquarters observed that "a favorable opportunity for the South Vietnamese revolution is approaching and the puppet army and the puppet government are collapsing." Nguyen Viet Ta et al., *Mien Dong Nam Bo Khang Chien*, Tap II, 167.

77. The Politburo noted, "Our main force army in South Vietnam is still weak and is not yet ready to mount massed combat operations to destroy the puppet regular army." Military History Institute of Vietnam, *Victory in Vietnam*, 137. Under the new plans, North Vietnamese main force units would enter the South and, together with the Viet Cong main forces, "conduct battles of annihilation to shatter a significant portion of the enemy's regular army." Cao Minh et al., *Quan Khu 8*, 516. See also Gareth Porter, "Coercive Diplomacy in Vietnam," in Jayne S. Werner and David Hunt, eds., *The American War in Vietnam* (Ithaca: Southeast Asia Program, Cornell University, 1993), 19–20; SVNLA Military Affairs Party Committee Resolution, January 1965, CDEC Doc Log No. 01-0520-70, TTU, Pike Collection, Unit 6, box 12.

78. Yang Kuisong, "Changes in Mao Zedong's Attitude Toward the Indochina War, 1949–1973," 29–30.

79. Vien Nghien Cuu Chu Nghia Mac Lenin Va Tu Tuong Ho Chi Minh, *Lich Su Dang Cong San Viet Nam,* Tap II, 267.

80. Ho Son Dai and Tran Phan Chan, *Lich Su Saigon-Cho Lon-Gia Dinh Khang Chien*, 391–4.

81. Special National Intelligence Estimate 10–3-64, produced on October 9, explained that the North Vietnamese "probably will avoid actions that would in their view unduly increase the chances of a major U.S. response against North Vietnam or Communist China. We are almost certain that both Hanoi and Peiping are anxious not to become involved in the kind of war in which the great weight of U.S. weaponry could be brought against them." CIA, SNIE 10–3-64, 9 October 1964, NA II, RG 59, Lot Files, Entry 5175, box 35.

82. William H. Sullivan, *Obbligato, 1939–1979: Notes on a Foreign Service Career* (New York: W. W. Norton, 1984), 200–2; Saigon to State, 13 September 1964, LBJL, NSF, VNCF, box 8.

83. Saigon to State, 4 November 1964, DDRS, 1985, 122.

84. The Vietnamese Confederation of Labor had long been suspected of harboring Viet Cong spies, and the strike heightened these suspicions, coming as it did right after a National Liberation Front appeal for the urban masses to rise up. Lacouture, *Vietnam*, 197–9.

85. Saigon to State, 24 September 1964, *FRUS, 1964–1968*, vol. 1, 359.

86. Saigon to State, 28 September 1964, LBJL, NSF, VNCF, box 8; CIA, "Deterioration in South Vietnam," 28 September 1964, LBJL, NSF, VNCF, box 9; SNIE 53–2-64, 1 October 1964, *FRUS, 1964–1968*, vol. 1, 368.

87. Westmoreland to Taylor, 6 September 1964, *FRUS, 1964–1968*, vol. 1, 340; Bundy, meeting notes, 9 September 1964, *FRUS, 1964–1968*, vol. 1, 343.

88. Saigon to State, 17 October 1964, DDRS, 1983, 119; CIA, "Viet Cong Infiltration into Northern South Vietnam," 23 October 1964, LBJL, NSF, VNCF, box 9.

89. Taylor to Johnson, 30 September 1964, *FRUS, 1964–1968*, vol. 1, 366.

90. The air attack did not signify a change toward a more belligerent U.S. policy, for Johnson had already been making plans to strike the North after the election. A Congressional resolution had been part of that plan, and in the absence of the August 1964 events he most likely could have used another Communist provocation in late 1964 or early 1965 to obtain Congressional approval of the same document.

15. Invasion: November–December 1964

1. McNamara, *In Retrospect*, 159; Wheeler to McNamara, 4 November 1964, NA II, RG 218, CJCS Wheeler, box 182; Darmstandler, "Chronology of Significant Requests and Decisions Affecting the Air War Against North Vietnam," 15 December 1967, DDRS, 1988, 217; Chairman of the Joint Chiefs of Staff Private Diary, 1964, NA II, RG 218, CJCS Wheeler, box 201.

2. Harris, *Anguish of Change*, 23; Gibbons, *The U.S. Government and the Vietnam War*, vol. 2, 364.

3. Rusk to Taylor, 1 November 1964, *FRUS, 1964–1968*, vol. 1, 397. The accusations that Johnson was using retaliation as a political device, the message stated, would "weaken intended signal" to Hanoi, but, given Moyers's phone call to Harris and Johnson's obsession with winning the election up until this time, this consideration could not have been as important as the potential impact on the election results. The message further stated that retaliation would commit the United States to a sustained program of

retaliation and that such a decision ought not be taken quickly. Such concerns, however, had not swayed Johnson during the Tonkin Gulf incidents, and Johnson had been planning post-election strikes since May.

4. Greene, memo for the record, 2 November 1964, MCHD, Greene Papers.

5. Telcon, 5 November 1964, Beschloss, ed., *Reaching for Glory,* 133. Johnson later told U Thant that he retired LeMay in early 1965 because of his "outdated attitudes," particularly his disposition toward bombing China. U Thant, *View from the UN* (Garden City: Doubleday, 1978), 68.

6. This argument received its most thorough and compelling articulation in McMaster, *Dereliction of Duty.*

7. For thoughtful examinations of this issue, see Sorley, *Honorable Warrior;* Herring, *LBJ and Vietnam.*

8. *New York Times,* November 1, 3, and 8, 1964. U.S. relations with France had been increasingly strained in the previous year by de Gaulle's public advocacy of a neutralized Vietnam and his denigration of the South Vietnamese government.

9. Gaiduk, *The Soviet Union and the Vietnam War,* 20; Oleg Sarin and Lev Dvoretsky, *Alien Wars: The Soviet Union's Aggression Against the World, 1919 to 1989* (Novato: Presidio Press, 1996), 90–1; Duiker, *Ho Chi Minh,* 542; Latimer, "Hanoi's Leaders and Their South Vietnam Policies," 183. The North Vietnamese reciprocated by promising to keep the war inside South Vietnam and replacing their denunciations of revisionism with cautious praise of the new Soviet leadership.

10. Nguyen Chi Thanh, "The Political Bureau's Assessment of the Situation," 20 November 1964, TTU, Pike Collection, Unit 6, box 1.

11. Tran The Long et al., *Su Doan Chien Thang, Ky Su,* vol. 2 (Hanoi: People's Army Publishing House, 1980), 28; Phan Chi Nhan et al., *Su Doan 308 Quan Tien Phong* (Hanoi: People's Army Publishing House, 1999), 179; Dang Uy va Tu Lenh Quan Khu 5, *Quan Khu 5,* vol. 1, 50.

12. Military History Institute of Vietnam, *Victory in Vietnam,* 126–42; Pham Gia Duc, *Su Doan 325,* vol. 2 (Hanoi: People's Army Publishing House, 1986), 44–6.

13. The promise of nuclear assistance carried new significance because the Chinese had just detonated their first nuclear device a few weeks earlier, although the Chinese probably had no more intention of giving Indonesia nuclear weapons than they did North Vietnam. Dake, *In the Spirit of the Red Banteng,* 326–8; Robert Shaplen, *Time Out of Hand: Revolution and Reaction in Southeast Asia* (New York: Harper & Row, 1969), 79–80. On November 27, Chinese Foreign Minister Chen Yi flew to Indonesia, where he presented Sukarno with an economic aid package worth fifty million U.S. dollars. The Indonesians and Chinese subsequently issued a joint declaration stating that during Chen Yi's visit they had discussed "ways of raising the level of struggle." Jay Taylor, *China and Southeast Asia: Peking's Relations with Revolutionary Movements* (New York: Praeger, 1974), 98.

14. Shaplen, *Time Out of Hand,* 80.

15. *New York Times,* November 1, 1964.

16. Higgins, *Our Vietnam Nightmare,* 261.

17. *Time,* December 11, 1964.

18. *Time,* December 4, 1964.

19. Lacouture, *Vietnam,* 212–13.

20. *Time,* December 4, 1964.

21. Taylor to Johnson, 24 November 1964, *FRUS,* 1964–1968, vol. 1, 421.

22. *Time,* December 4, 1964.

23. The total strength of the armed forces rose to 482,000, and most units were on track to reach their authorized strengths within a few months. Westmoreland to Taylor, "Assessment of the Military Situation," 24 November 1964, DDRS, 1977, 288E. Although recruiting outpaced desertions, the desertion rate remained high, with total desertions for the year totaling 73,010, more than twice as many as in 1963. Clarke, *Advice and Support,* 43.

24. *Congressional Record,* vol. 114, 12618–20; Saigon to State, 14 October 1964, DDRS, 1985, 121; Tran Van Quang et al., *Tong Ket Cuoc Khang Chien Chong My Cuu Nuoc,* 311.

25. The North Vietnamese Navy opened new maritime routes to the northern coastal provinces, according to a Communist history, because the "armed forces were expanding rapidly, but the area

faced a serious shortage of weapons." The first ship to navigate these routes arrived on South Vietnam's northern coast on November 11, and several more followed before the year was out, enabling Hanoi to give the new battalions all of the arms befitting conventional battalions. Nguyen Tu Duong, *Duong Mon Tren Bien*, 110–36.

26. Taylor, "The Current Situation in South Viet-Nam – November 1964," n.d., *FRUS*, 1964–1968, vol. 1, 426.

27. Saigon to State, 27 February 1965, LBJL, NSF, VNCF, box 14.

28. U. S. G. Sharp and William C. Westmoreland, *Report on the War in Vietnam, as of June 30, 1968* (Washington, DC: U.S. Government Printing Office, 1969), 88; Westmoreland, *A Soldier Reports*, 99–100; Le Kinh Lich, ed., *Tran Danh Ba Muoi Nam*, vol. 2, 230; Nguyen Tri Huan et al., *Su Doan Sao Vang* (Hanoi: People's Army Publishing House, 1984), 16.

29. See the works cited in chapter 3, note 41 of this volume.

30. Military History Institute of Vietnam, *Mot So Tran Danh Trong Khang Chien Chong Phap, Khang Chien Chong My, 1945–1975* (Hanoi: Ministry of Defense, 1991), Tap I, 204–29; Le Kinh Lich, ed., *Tran Danh Ba Muoi Nam*, vol. 2, 227–9; Political Department of the Navy, *35 Nam Duong Ho Chi Minh Tren Bien va Thanh Lap Lu Doan 125 Hai Quan*, 24–5; Pham Hong Thuy et al., *Lich su Hai Quan Nhan Dan Viet Nam*, 158–9; Nguyen Viet Ta et al., *Mien Dong Nam Bo Khang Chien*, Tap II, 170–81; Le Hao and Nguyen Viet Ta, *Chien Dich Tien Cong Binh Gia, Dong Xuan 1964–1965 (Luu Hanh Noi Bo)* (Hanoi: Ministry of Defense, 1988), 11; Nguyen Khac Tinh et al., *Phao Binh Nhan Dan Viet Nam: Nhung Chang Duong Chien Dau*, Tap II (Hanoi: Artillery Command, 1986), 80–83; Le Duan, *Letters to the South*, 69; MACV Daily Staff Journal, 28 December 1964 to 4 January 1965, NA II, RG 472, MACV, MACJ3-08, Daily Journal, box 3; Wheeler to Bundy, "Binh Gia Engagements," 5 January 1965, LBJL, NSF, VNCF, box 12; CIA, "The Situation in South Vietnam," 6 January 1965, DDRS, 1979, 133A; Tran Ngoc Toan, "The Binh Gia Front," *Song Than*, 2002, 287–94; Tran Ve, "I Still Recall Binh Gia," in Tran Xuan Dung, ed., *History of the Vietnamese Marine Corps* (Vietnamese Marine Division Headquarters, 1997), 72–88; Robert H. Whitlow, *U.S. Marines in Vietnam: The Advisory & Combat Assistance Era 1954–1964* (Washington, DC: Government Printing Office, 1977), 136–8; *New York Times*, January 3, 1965.

31. A Communist history of the Binh Gia battle explained that the people of the hamlet "had been brainwashed by the enemy and were ferociously anti-communist, so we had virtually no revolutionary organizations or assets inside the hamlet." Military History Institute of Vietnam, *Mot So Tran Danh Trong Khang Chien Chong Phap, Khang Chien Chong My, 1945–1975*, Tap I, 208.

32. Vo Cong Luan and Tran Hanh, eds., *May Van De ve Tong Ket Chien Tranh va Viet Su Quan Su*, 267. The Southern Party headquarters analyzed the situation facing the Communists at the end of 1964: "We have gained many great successes, but we are not yet strong enough to defeat [the enemy] completely.... The concentrated [Communist] troops increased quickly, but their quality was still poor. Their annihilating attacks were still not so good. Their technical and tactical experiences were insufficient and as a result, no strong and continuous blows were carried out." COSVN Resolution 3, January 1965, TTU, Pike Collection, Unit 6, box 12. See also SVNLA Military Affairs Party Committee Resolution, January 1965, CDEC Doc Log No. 01-0520-70, TTU, Pike Collection, Unit 6, box 12.

33. Several variants of these two options were discussed over the course of November, and there was some confusion over the differences between them, but the two basic ideas did not change. The group also considered a third option, in which the United States would continue its present Vietnam policy, but everyone in the administration quickly ruled this option out and Johnson himself showed no inclination to cancel his earlier plans to take action against the North after the election.

34. NSC working group, "Courses of Action in Southeast Asia," 21 November 1964, *FRUS*, 1964–1968, vol. 1, 418.

35. Bundy to Rusk, 24 November 1964, *FRUS*, 1964–1968, vol. 1, 423.

36. Thompson to FO, 18 November 1964, PRO, FO 371/175503.

37. JCS to McNamara, "Courses of Action in Southeast Asia," 23 November 1964, DDRS, 1999, 9.

38. Johnson to Taylor, 3 December 1964, *FRUS*, 1964–1968, vol. 1, 435.

39. Meeting Notes, 1 December 1964, DDRS, 1984, 197. MacArthur made this prediction at Wake Island on October 15, 1950. See William Stueck, *The Korean War: An International History* (Princeton: Princeton University Press, 1995), 106–7.

40. Bundy, unpublished manuscript, chap. 18, 31–2.

41. Meeting Notes, 1 December 1964, DDRS, 1984, 197.

42. Executive Committee, "Position Paper on Southeast Asia," 2 December 1964, FRUS, 1964–1968, vol. 1, 433; State to London, 4 December 1964, FRUS, 1964–1968, vol. 1, 437; The Joint Chiefs of Staff and the War in Vietnam, chap. 14, 34.

43. Most notably Logevall, Choosing War, and Kaiser, American Tragedy.

44. Ambassador Sullivan explained to Souvanna that the United States would need to make public some information about the aerial bombardment; otherwise, the American people might learn that their government was not being forthright and would stop supporting military action in Southeast Asia. Souvanna, however, stipulated that there be no public disclosure. Laos and the United States should deny everything, he insisted, just as North Vietnam had endlessly denied the presence of North Vietnamese soldiers in Laos. Souvanna remarked that the strikes violated the 1962 agreement, and if they were publicized, Laos would come under "intolerable international and domestic pressures." Vientiane to State, 10 December 1964, FRUS, 1964–1968, vol. 28, 150. Ultimately it would be Souvanna, not the Americans, who won out on this point, as the United States agreed in the end to strike the Ho Chi Minh Trail while refraining from any public comment on the matter.

45. Jackson, "Operations in Laos," 11 December 1964, DDRS, 1991, 132; The Pentagon Papers, vol. 3, 253–4.

46. CIA, "Communist Reaction to Barrel Roll Missions," 29 December 1964, DDRS, 1976, 233B.

47. Far Eastern Economic Review, March 12, 1965.

48. Nguyen Cao Ky, Twenty Years and Twenty Days (New York: Stein and Day, 1976), 55.

49. Airgram A-493, 24 December 1964, DDRS, 1978, 433D; Nguyen Cao Ky, Twenty Years and Twenty Days, 53.

50. Saigon to State, 20 December 1964, FRUS, 1964–1968, vol. 1, 451; Saigon to State, 20 December 1964, FRUS, 1964–1968, vol. 1, 452.

51. Newsweek, January 18, 1965.

52. Memcon, 21 December 1964, FRUS, 1964–1968, vol. 1, 454; Saigon to State, 21 December 1964, DDRS, 1979, 206D.

53. Saigon to State, 22 December 1964, DDRS, 1979, 206E; Tran Van Don, Our Endless War, 139.

54. Saigon to State, 22 December 1964, NA II, RG 59, Central Files, 1964–1966, box 2949.

55. New York Herald Tribune, December 23, 1964.

56. One of the Young Turks commented, "Far less emphasis should be given to finding a completely legal and democratic solution to the Vietnam problem. What is acceptable procedure in the United States, where there is a long tradition of respect for law, cannot be applied without minor or perhaps major modifications in Vietnam." CIA Watch Office to State, 25 December 1964, DDRS, 1979, 132C. See also CIA, cable 240442Z, 24 December 1964, DDRS, 1979, 132A.

57. CIA, cable 240442Z, 24 December 1964, DDRS, 1979, 132A.

58. Saigon to State, 26 December 1964, DDRS, 1978, 433E.

59. Porter, ed., Vietnam: The Definitive Documentation of Human Decisions, vol. 2, 345–6.

60. Nguyen Phuc Khanh et al., eds., Chung Mot Bong Co, 581–4.

61. Karnow, Vietnam, 423–5; New York Times, December 25, 1964; Westmoreland, A Soldier Reports, 90. At his Christmas day performance, Hope opened by saying, "I've gone from many airports to my hotel, but this is the first time I've found the hotel on its way out to meet me." Peer De Silva, Sub Rosa: The CIA and the Uses of Intelligence (New York: Times Books, 1978), 254.

62. The Joint Chiefs of Staff and the War in Vietnam, chap. 15, 20–1.

63. Johnson to Taylor, 30 December 1964, FRUS, 1964–1968, vol. 1, 477.

64. Wheeler to Westmoreland, 31 December 1964, FRUS, 1964–1968, vol. 1, 479. William Bundy offered one more explanation in 1992, saying that Johnson did not want to undertake such a momentous initiative while he was celebrating Christmas at his ranch. Duiker, U.S. Containment Policy and the Conflict in Indochina, 429.

65. At the 3rd conference of the Communist headquarters in the South, a few weeks after the Brink Hotel attack, the conferees expressed strong confidence that the Americans lacked the will to strike North Vietnam or shield South Vietnam from the mortal blow. "Resolution Issued by 3rd Conference

of COSVN," 15 January 1965, CDEC Doc Log No. 01–0526–70, TTU, Pike Collection, Unit 6, box 12.

66. *Public Papers of the Presidents,* 1965, 449.

16. The Prize for Victory: January–May 1965

1. CIA, "Thich Tri Quang's Campaign to Bring Down the Tran Van Huong Government," 21 January 1965, DDRS, 1976, 24E.

2. Rosenthal, memcon, 17 January 1965, LBJL, NSF, VNCF, box 12.

3. Saigon to State, 20 January 1965, *FRUS,* 1964–1968, vol. 2, 29.

4. Saigon to State, 25 January 1965, LBJL, NSF, VNCF, box 12.

5. Saigon to State, 20 January 1965, LBJL, NSF, VNCF, box 12; Saigon to State, 31 January 1965, DDRS, 2000, 9; *Newsweek,* February 8, 1965.

6. Rosenthal, memcon, 17 January 1965, LBJL, NSF, VNCF, box 12; Saigon to State, 20 January 1965, LBJL, NSF, VNCF, box 12.

7. In early 1965, thanks to the government's inability to thwart subversion, the Communists were building up their presence in the cities by infiltrating ostensibly non-Communist political and religious organizations. Nguyen Phuc Khanh et al., eds., *Chung Mot Bong Co,* 353, 905; *Mot So Van Kien Cua Dang Ve Chong My, Cuu Nuoc,* Tap I, 216; Truong Nhu Tang, *A Vietcong Memoir,* 95–8. For the widespread disillusionment with the militant movement among South Vietnam's Buddhists, see *New York Times,* January 23, 1965; *Newsweek,* February 8, 1965.

8. Saigon to State, 25 January 1965, LBJL, NSF, VNCF, box 12; Saigon to State, 31 January 1965, DDRS, 2000, 9; *New York Times,* 24 January 1965.

9. Saigon to State, 30 January 1965, LBJL, NSF, VNCF, box 12.

10. CIA, "Situation in South Vietnam," 26 January 1965, *FRUS,* 1964–1968, vol. 2, 39; CIA, "Decisions and Discussions at the 31 January Armed Forces Council meeting," 2 February 1965, LBJL, NSF, VNCF, box 13.

11. Saigon to State, 30 January 1965, LBJL, NSF, VNCF, box 12.

12. Saigon to State, 6 January 1965, *FRUS,* 1964–1968, vol. 2, 9. See also Bundy, unpublished manuscript, chap. 20, 19.

13. McGeorge Bundy, meeting notes, 27 January 1965, LBJL, Papers of McGeorge Bundy, box 1.

14. 52d Aviation Battalion, "Camp Holloway Attack Narrative," 12 February 1965, MHI, Harold K. Johnson Papers, box 35; Nguyen Van Minh et al., *Luc Luong Vu Trang Nhan Dan Tay Nguyen Trong Khang Chien Chong My Cuu Nuoc,* 37. The Americans concluded that Hanoi had struck at this moment because of the presence of two people in Vietnam: McGeorge Bundy in Saigon and Alexei Kosygin in Hanoi. According to this interpretation, Hanoi believed that the attacks would put the Americans on the horns of a dilemma: if they did not retaliate, they would lose face, and if they did retaliate, then the Soviets would feel insulted and provide more assistance to North Vietnam. But, in fact, the Communists' decision to strike had not involved such cunning. The attack had been conceived and ordered by the local commander of the Viet Cong forces in Pleiku province, who knew nothing about the visits of Bundy and Kosygin and was simply trying to hurt his adversaries. Dang Vu Hiep, *Ky Uc Tay Nguyen,* 13.

15. Smith, NSC meeting notes, 6 February 1965, *FRUS,* 1964–1968, vol. 2, 76; Colby, "White House Meeting on Vietnam," 6 February 1965, *FRUS,* 1964–1968, vol. 2, 77.

16. Bundy to Johnson, 7 February 1965, *FRUS,* 1964–1968, vol. 2, 84.

17. On one occasion, as recounted by a journalist who was on hand, Johnson explained that "the slow escalation of the air war in the North and the increasing pressure on Ho Chi Minh was seduction, not rape. If China should suddenly react to slow escalation, as a woman might react to attempted seduction, by threatening to retaliate (a slap in the face, to continue the metaphor), the United States would have plenty of time to ease off the bombing. On the other hand, if the United States were to unleash an all-out, total assault on the North – rape rather than seduction – there could be no turning back, and Chinese reaction might be instant and total." *USVNR,* book 4, IV-C-3, 94.

18. At the beginning of March, by which time most of the 325th Division had arrived in the northern II Corps area, American analysts contended that there were probably new Communist main force units in northern II Corps, but they misidentified these units as Viet Cong units; Hanoi's efforts to disguise the North Vietnamese Army units as Viet Cong had worked. Saigon to State, 2 March 1965, *FRUS*, 1964–1968, vol. 2, 177.

19. Taylor asserted, "If there were any great likelihood of DRV forces crossing the demilitarized zone in conventional attack, there would be no question of need for strong U.S. ground force to assist ARVN in defense of coastal plain. However, this situation would not arise suddenly and we should have ample time to make our deployments before situation got out of hand." Taylor to JCS, 22 February 1965, *FRUS*, 1964–1968, vol. 2, 153.

20. Westmoreland to Sharp, 16 February 1965, LBJL, NSF, NSC History, DMUSF, box 40; Taylor to JCS, 22 February 1965, *FRUS*, 1964–1968, vol. 2, 153; Sharp to JCS, 24 February 1965, LBJL, NSF, NSC Histories, DMUSF, box 40; Bundy, "Notes Concerning the President's Major Decisions on Vietnam of February and July, 1965," NA II, RG 59, Lot Files, Entry 5408, box 9.

21. Telcon, 26 February 1965, Beschloss, ed., *Reaching for Glory*, 193–5.

22. Telcon, 6 March 1965, Beschloss, ed., *Reaching for Glory*, 213–6.

23. *Congressional Record*, vol. 111, 784–6. Another such liberal Democrat, New York Rep. Jonathon Bingham, said on February 24 that the experiences of Munich and the Sudetenland had proven to the world that "appeasement is not the way to measure the peace.... As the polls show, majority sentiment in this country is not for a pullout from Vietnam. There is wide recognition of what such a decision would do to the morale of our friends around the world who are resisting communism – in Thailand, in the Philippines, in West Berlin, in Venezuela – and to their confidence in us. I found last summer, even in countries such as Burma and India, people hoping that the United States would not withdraw and leave Southeast Asia completely unprotected against the Chinese Communists." Ibid., 3411–12. Another, Fred R. Harris of Oklahoma, said, "We must again apply the principle that unless we are willing, now, to take the risks involved ... in drawing the line in South Vietnam, we shall have to draw it somewhere. I, for one, would like to see it drawn in South Vietnam, rather than in Thailand, in Malaysia, in the Philippines, in Hawaii, or in San Francisco and Seattle." Ibid., 3783.

24. Telcon, 6 March 1965, Beschloss, ed., *Reaching for Glory*, 213–6.

25. *The Joint Chiefs of Staff and the War in Vietnam*, chap. 19, 5; *The Pentagon Papers*, vol. 3, 417; Marolda and Fitzgerald, *The United States Navy and the Vietnam Conflict*, vol. 2, 526.

26. *Department of State Bulletin*, 29 March 1965, 442.

27. Nguyen Huu An with Nguyen Tu Duong, *Chien Truong Moi* (Hanoi: People's Army Publishing House, 2002), 9–12.

28. Pham Gia Duc, *Su Doan 325*, vol. 2, 49; Dang Vu Hiep, *Ky Uc Tay Nguyen*, 26; Military History Institute of Vietnam, *Victory in Vietnam*, 138.

29. Bundy to Johnson, 7 February 1965, *FRUS*, 1964–1968, vol. 2, 84.

30. CIA, "Situation in Vietnam," 6 April 1965, DDRS, 1977, 279F.

31. Political Department of the Navy, *35 Nam Duong Ho Chi Minh Tren Bien va Thanh Lap Lu Doan 125 Hai Quan*, 26, 30; Military History Institute of Vietnam, *Victory in Vietnam*, 144; Pham Hong Thuy et al., *Lich su Hai Quan Nhan Dan Viet Nam*, 162–5.

32. Political Department of the Navy, *35 Nam Duong Ho Chi Minh Tren Bien va Thanh Lap Lu Doan 125 Hai Quan*, 30.

33. CIA-DIA-State, "Strength of Viet Cong Military Forces in South Vietnam," 17 March 1965, LBJL, NSF, VNCF, box 15; CIA-DIA, "An Assessment of Present Viet Cong Military Capabilities," 21 April 1965, DDRS, 1976, 233F.

34. Nguyen Ngoc, *Co Mot Con Duong Tren Bien Dong: Ky Su cua Doan Lam Phim* (Hanoi: Hanoi Publishing House, 1994), 110–25; Nguyen Tu Duong, *Duong Mon Tren Bien*, 137–8; *Department of State Bulletin*, 22 March 1965, 417–18; Marolda and Fitzgerald, *The United States Navy and the Vietnam Conflict*, vol. 2, 513–19.

35. Tran Van Quang et al., *Tong Ket Cuoc Khang Chien Chong My Cuu Nuoc*, 223; Nguyen Ngoc, *Co Mot Con Duong Tren Bien Dong*, 137–232; Nguyen Tu Duong, *Duong Mon Tren Bien*, 142; Xiaoming

Zhang, "The Vietnam War, 1964–1969: A Chinese Perspective," 748–9. The arrival of the seventh Fleet also shut down the shipment of materials from China to islands off the central Vietnamese coast whence North Vietnamese boats had taken them to South Vietnam.

36. McNamara to Johnson, 1 July 1965, *FRUS, 1964–1968*, vol. 3, 38.

37. McGeorge Bundy summed up the administration's opposition to a naval quarantine as follows: "nearly everyone agrees the real question is not in Hanoi, but in South Vietnam." The threat of a naval quarantine was more valuable than an actual naval quarantine, Bundy also noted, for the threat could serve as a means of "communication to Hanoi." Bundy to McNamara, 30 June 1965, *FRUS, 1964–1968*, vol. 3, 35.

38. Le Duan, *Thu Vao Nam*, 68–93.

39. "The faster we score a decisive victory in South Vietnam," the committee resolved, "the better chance we have of preventing the enemy from switching from a 'special war' in South Vietnam into a 'limited war' and of preventing the enemy from expanding his 'limited war' into North Vietnam." *Mot So Van Kien Cua Dang Ve Chong My, Cuu Nuoc*, Tap I, 222. See also Cao Minh et al., *Quan Khu 8*, 520; Nguyen Viet Phuong, *Van Tai Quan Su Chien Luoc Tren Duong Ho Chi Minh Trong Khang Chien Chong My*, 60; Thai Van Tinh, *Chien Dich Tien Cong Ba Gia, He 1965* (Hanoi: Military History Institute of Vietnam, 1987), 14–16; Ho Son Dai and Tran Phan Chan, *Lich Su Saigon-Cho Lon-Gia Dinh Khang Chien*, 402–3.

40. Ho Chi Minh, *On Revolution*, 361–2.

41. Zhai, *China and the Vietnam Wars*, 150; CIA, "Asian Communist and Soviet Views on the War in Vietnam," 25 May 1965, LBJL, NSF, VNCF, box 50; CIA, "Special DCI Briefing for Senator Stennis," 9 April 1965, DDRS, 1978, 32A; Ramesh Chandra Thakur and Carlyle A. Thayer, *Soviet Relations with India and Vietnam* (New York: St. Martin's Press, 1992), 117–18.

42. Moscow to FO, 23 March 1965, PRO, PREM 13/693.

43. Gaiduk, *The Soviet Union and the Vietnam War*, 38.

44. Anatoly Dobrynin, *In Confidence: Moscow's Ambassador to America's Six Cold War Presidents* (New York: Times Books, 1995), 140.

45. London to State, 22 June 1965, LBJL, NSF, Country File, United Kingdom, box 207.

46. Snow, "An Interview with Mao Tse-Tung," n.d., DDRS, 1977, 318B. Even after the Chinese troop deployment to North Vietnam later in the year, the Chinese asserted on several occasions that they would not fight the Americans unless they attacked the Chinese homeland, as is noted in the next chapter.

47. On February 9, for instance, the Chinese government declared that in the face of American aggression against North Vietnam, the Chinese people "will definitely not stand idly by." "Statement of the Government of the People's Republic of China," 9 February 1965, PRO, FO 371/180594. See also Gurtov and Hwang, *China Under Threat*, 164–5. The Chinese had stated that they would not "stand idly by" prior to intervening in the Korean War. Stueck, *The Korean War*, 106. By 1965, however, the phrase had lost much of its effect, as it had been used after the Tonkin Gulf incidents without any accompanying military action. See China's announcement of August 6, 1964 in *American Foreign Policy: Current Documents, 1964*, 990–1. After Flaming Dart, moreover, the Chinese displayed their fear of the United States by actively attempting to discourage the Americans from attacking China, telling the Americans soon thereafter through a third party that they were not building up their ground troop strength on China's southern border. CIA, "The Sino-Vietnamese Effort to Limit American Actions in the Vietnam War," 9 June 1965, DDRS, 1979, 244B. CIA analysts emphasized that China's inaction following Flaming Dart led other countries to conclude that China was too fearful or weak to defend North Vietnam. CIA, "The Sino-Vietnamese Effort to Limit American Actions in the Vietnam War," 9 June 1965, DDRS, 1979, 244B. On February 11, Kosygin chided Mao for failing to retaliate against the Americans with Chinese aircraft, stating, "Presently the Americans bomb North Vietnam, but not the South. Unfortunately, we have no air force there, which could come forward with counter strikes against American bases. Only you could do this, but you don't do it, and you do not give an appropriate rebuke to the American imperialists, although you could do it." Mao replied that the "South Vietnamese people" would "drive the Americans away by themselves." Lüthi, "The Sino-Soviet Split, 1956–1966," 545.

48. Luu Van Loi and Nguyen Anh Vu, *Cac Cuoc Thuong Luong Le Duc Tho-Kissinger tai Paris* (Hanoi: People's Public Security Publishing House, 2002), 47; Bui Tin, *From Enemy to Friend*, 40–1.

49. Memcon, Mao Zedong and Pham Van Dong, Hoang Van Hoan, 5 October 1964, CWIHP, footnote 4.

50. Walsh to Smith, "Recent History of U.S. Negotiating Efforts in Southeast Asia," n.d., LBJL, NSF, VNCF, box 18.

51. Chen Xiaolu, "Chen Yi and China's Diplomacy," 104; Yang Kuisong, "Changes in Mao Zedong's Attitude toward the Indochina War, 1949–1973," 32.

52. For Hanoi's position on negotiations in the spring, see Moscow to FO, 7 April 1965, PRO, FO 371/180524; CIA, "North Vietnamese References to Negotiations on Vietnam," 23 April 1965, DDRS, 1983, 92; Herring, ed., *The Secret Diplomacy of the Vietnam War*, 9, 41.

53. See, for example, Warsaw to State, 1 March 1965, DDRS, 1990, 218. Johnson authorized these pronouncements in disregard of new advice from Eisenhower to send stern threats to the Communists. For the Chinese reaction, see memcon, Zhou Enlai and Ayub Khan, 2 April 1965, CWIHP.

54. After Khrushchev's ouster, the new Soviet leaders and the Chinese had made several attempts to mend relations, but they had failed badly. By February 1965, Mao was telling Kosygin that China would continue its struggle against the Soviet "revisionists" for 9,000 years. Chen Jian, "Deng Xiaoping, Mao's 'Continuous Revolution,' and the Path toward the Sino-Soviet Split: A Rejoinder," CWIHP.

55. The most influential proponent of the dovish view was Mike Mansfield. See, for instance, Colby, "White House Meeting on Vietnam," 6 February 1965, *FRUS, 1964–1968*, vol. 2, 77.

56. Eventually, arrangements were made to transport Soviet armaments through China by rail, but disputes over the issue of air and rail transport would continue in the coming years. Lüthi, "The Sino-Soviet Split, 1956–1966," 554–6. On April 13, Zhou and Chernovenko entered into a shouting match over dinner, in which the Chinese accused the Soviets of communicating with the Americans "behind the backs of China and Vietnam." Ibid., 566–67. In May, Le Duan complained to the Soviets that the Chinese, through their refusal to cooperate with the Soviets, were showing a lack of concern about the greater good of the socialist camp. Ibid., 565.

57. Memcon, Zhou Enlai and Ho Chi Minh, 1 March 1965, CWIHP; Chen Xiaolu, "Chen Yi and China's Diplomacy," 104–5.

58. Warsaw to State, 26 April 1965, DDRS, 1990, 218. CIA, "The Sino-Vietnamese Effort to Limit American Actions in the Vietnam War," 9 June 1965, DDRS, 1979, 244B. On the same day, Chinese officials told a Japanese correspondent that it was not yet time for Chinese Army forces to go to North Vietnam or South Vietnam, but if the Americans appeared likely to take all of North Vietnam, then Chinese forces would intervene. CIA, "The Sino-Vietnamese Effort to Limit American Actions in the Vietnam War," 9 June 1965, DDRS, 1979, 244B. On March 28, Chinese Foreign Minister Chen Yi wrote to his North Vietnamese counterpart, "the Chinese people will exert every effort to send the heroic South Vietnamese people the necessary material aid, including arms and all other war material, and stand ready to fight shoulder to shoulder with the South Vietnamese people whenever the latter so require." CIA, "The Situation in Vietnam," 2 April 1965, DDRS, 1979, 236A.

59. Memcon, Liu Shaoqi and Le Duan, CWIHP, 8 April 1965.

60. Yang Kuisong, "Changes in Mao Zedong's Attitude toward the Indochina War, 1949–1973," CWIHP, 33. On July 16, China backed out of sending Chinese pilots to North Vietnam. Zhai, *China and the Vietnam Wars*, 134–5.

61. Memcon, Mao Zedong and Ho Chi Minh, 16 May 1965, CWIHP; Jian, *Mao's China and the Cold War*, 219.

62. Jian, *Mao's China and the Cold War*, 228.

63. MACV to NMCC, 19 February 1965, LBJL, NSF, VNCF, box 13.

64. CIA, "Individuals and Cliques in South Vietnam," 25 February 1965, LBJL, NSF, VNCF, box 14; CIA, "The Situation in Vietnam," 26 February 1965, DDRS, 1983, 91; Harold K. Johnson, "Report on the Survey of the Military Situation in Vietnam," 14 March 1965, LBJL, NSF, VNCF, box 191; Westmoreland, "Commander's Estimate of the Situation in South Vietnam, 26 March 1965, LBJL, Westmoreland Papers,

History Backup, box 5; CIA, "The Situation in South Vietnam," 14 April 1965, DDRS, 1979, 239A; CIA, "The Situation in South Vietnam," 26 May 1965, DDRS, 1979, 244A.

65. High-Level Military Institute, *Vietnam: The Anti-U.S. Resistance War for National Salvation*, 64–65; Military History Institute of Vietnam, *Victory in Vietnam*, 142.

66. Tran Duong et al., *Lich Su Khu 6*, 137–41; 152, 442.

67. Stuart A. Herrington, *Silence Was a Weapon: The Vietnam War in the Villages* (Novato: Presidio Press, 1982), 29.

68. Sharp and Westmoreland, *Report on the War in Vietnam*, 83–4. For a very similar Communist appraisal, see *Mot So Van Kien Cua Dang Ve Chong My, Cuu Nuoc*, Tap I, 211–16.

69. Hong Kong to State, 20 February 1965, LBJL, NSF, Country File, Asia and the Pacific, China, box 238.

70. Rosenthal, memcon, 27 February 1965, LBJL, NSF, VNCF, box 14.

71. Saigon to State, 15 May 1965, NA II, RG 59, Central Files, 1964–1966, box 2959.

72. Shaplen, *Lost Revolution*, 319–21; CIA, "The Situation in Vietnam," 28 February 1965, DDRS, 1978, 31 C; *New York Times*, March 7, 1965.

73. Saigon to State, 8 March 1965, DDRS, 1981, 235 C.

74. Darmstandler, "Chronology of Significant Requests and Decisions Affecting the Air War Against North Vietnam," 15 December 1967, DDRS, 1988, 217; Clodfelter, *The Limits of Air Power*, 85–8; Gittinger, ed., *The Johnson Years*, 56.

75. McCone to Johnson, n.d., *FRUS*, 1964–1968, vol. 2, 234.

76. Lady Bird Johnson, tape-recorded diary, 7 March 1965, Beschloss, ed., *Reaching for Glory*, 216.

77. Greene, "Conference with the President," 8 April 1965, MCHD, Greene Papers.

78. Telcon, 26 February 1965, Beschloss, ed., *Reaching for Glory*, 194.

79. McDonald and von Luttichau, "Interview of General Harold Keith Johnson," 20 November 1970, CMH.

80. Harold K. Johnson, "Report on the Survey of the Military Situation in Vietnam," 14 March 1965, LBJL, NSF, VNCF, box 191; Gibbons, *The U.S. Government and the Vietnam War*, vol. 3, 166.

81. Saigon to State, 18 March 1965, *FRUS*, 1964–1968, vol. 2, 204.

82. Saigon to State, 26 March 1965, LBJL, NSF, VNCF, box 15.

83. Westmoreland, "Commander's Estimate of the Situation in South Vietnam," 26 March 1965, LBJL, Westmoreland Papers, History Backup, box 5.

84. The first U.S. contact with enemy forces would take place on April 22, when a small U.S. Marine patrol exchanged fire with the Viet Cong near Da Nang. The 173rd Airborne Brigade started airlifting troops further from its base to search for the enemy on May 15. It would not make contact with the enemy until May 26, on which day three of its companies engaged in minor skirmishes with Communist forces, resulting in eight American wounded.

85. NSAM 328, 6 April 1965, *FRUS*, 1964–1968, vol. 2, 242. See also Westmoreland, *A Soldier Reports*, 135.

86. CIA, "The Situation in South Vietnam," 14 April 1965, DDRS, 1979, 239A; CIA, "North Vietnamese References to Negotiations on Vietnam," 23 April 1965, DDRS, 1983, 92; Le Duan, *Letters to the South*, 42.

87. Herring, ed., *The Secret Diplomacy of the Vietnam War*, 71. The Chinese called the bombing pause a "peace swindle" and "a despicable trick." Walsh to Smith, "Recent History of U.S. Negotiating Efforts in Southeast Asia," n.d. LBJL, NSF, VNCF, box 18. The bombing pause lasted from May 12 to May 18.

88. CIA, "The Situation in South Vietnam," 7 April 1965, DDRS, 1979, 238A.

89. CIA, "Study on Possible Viet Cong Intention to Launch Major Campaigns in Both Central and Southern South Vietnam in the Near Future," 15 April 1965, DDRS, 1979, 239B; CIA, "Current Trends in Vietnam," 30 April 1965, DDRS, 1979, 241 B; Saigon to State, 4 May 1965, DDRS, 1981, 116A.

90. Saigon to State, 17 April 1965, *FRUS*, 1964–1968, vol. 2, 258; Saigon to State, 17 April 1965, *FRUS*, 1964–1968, vol. 2, 260.

91. Telcon, 20 April 1965, Beschloss, ed., *Reaching for Glory*, 282–3; Taylor, diary entry, 20 April 1965, *FRUS*, 1964–1968, vol. 2, 264.

92. McNamara to Johnson, 21 April 1965, *FRUS*, 1964–1968, vol. 2, 265; Taylor, diary entry, 20 April 1965, *FRUS*, 1964–1968, vol. 2, 264. By the time of the conference, McNamara had lost faith in the idea that Hanoi could be convinced to stop the war solely with "signals" sent via air strikes. The change in opinion among his civilian advisers confused Johnson, who himself seems to have changed his views on the purpose of the bombing without fully realizing it. Upon McNamara's return, the President asked him, "Are we pulling away from our theory that bombing will turn 'em off?" McNamara replied, "That wasn't our theory. We wanted to lift morale; we wanted to push them toward negotiation." Bundy, NSC meeting notes, 21 April 1965, *FRUS*, 1964–1968, vol. 2, 266n. Yet during the development of Rolling Thunder, McNamara himself had said that its purpose was "to destroy the will of the DRV." Goodpaster, memcon, 17 February 1965, *FRUS*, 1964–1968, vol. 2, 133.

93. Le Duan, *Letters to the South*, 19–45; CDEC Doc Log No. 01–0515–70, "Meeting of Current Affairs Committee, COSVN," 30 May 1965, TTU, Pike Collection, Unit 6, box 12. The Communist history of Military Region 7 stated, "The COSVN Military Party Committee and the COSVN Military Headquarters decided to exploit the victories we had already won by launching a follow-up wave of operations in the rainy season, including an offensive campaign designed to drive the puppet army to its knees before U.S. troops could begin massively pouring into South Vietnam." Nguyen Viet Ta et al., *Mien Dong Nam Bo Khang Chien,* Tap II, 190.

94. Asprey, *War in the Shadows;* Baritz, *Backfire;* Clodfelter, *The Limits of Air Power;* Corson, *The Betrayal;* Krepinevich, *The Army and Vietnam;* Record, *The Wrong War.* Robert Buzzanco asserted that "the instability of 1964–5 continued to work in the Revolution's favor. The VC actually slowed down its military activity to let the RVN self-destruct even more, and by the early months of 1965, NLF victory was imminent." Buzzanco, *Vietnam and the Transformation of American Life,* 77.

95. After one of the Communists' big attacks, an American military adviser remarked, "It is all very well to win the heart and the mind of the peasant, but when there are three hundred on your side, and three thousand VC surrounding you on all sides, and when the VC has mortars, recoilless rifles, and heavy machine guns, the sympathies of the peasant are irrelevant to what happens. If the peasant is smart he'll go hide while he can." Higgins, *Our Vietnam Nightmare,* 250.

96. Witness statements, n.d., NA II, RG 472, 5th Special Forces Group, Det B-34, box 22; "Weapons used by the Viet Cong in the Attack at Song Be," n.d., NA II, RG 472, 5th Special Forces Group, Det B-34, box 22; CIA, "The Situation in South Vietnam," 19 May 1965, TTU, Central Intelligence Agency Collection, box 2; *Washington Post,* May 13, 1965; Tran Duong et al., *Lich Su Khu 6,* 137–41; Nguyen Viet Ta et al., *Mien Dong Nam Bo Khang Chien,* Tap II, 191–2; *Quan Doi Nhan Dan,* 16 June 2004.

97. CIA, "Status of the War in South Vietnam," 12 May 1965, DDRS, 1977, 28D; CIA, "The Situation in South Vietnam," 4 June 1965, DDRS, 1978, 35A; Saigon to State, 5 June 1965, *FRUS*, 1964–1968, vol. 2, 332; CIA, "Developments in South Vietnam During the Past Year," 29 June 1965, DDRS, 1976, 231D.

98. Westmoreland to Sharp, 7 June 1965, NA II, RG 550, MACV and USARV Command Reporting Files, USMACV Military Reports, box 1; USMACV, "1965 Command History," 20 April 1966, NA II; MACV, Daily Staff Journal, 8 June 1965, NA II, RG 472, MACV J3-08, Daily Journal, box 5; Thai Van Tinh, *Chien Dich Tien Cong Ba Gia,* 18–49; Tran The Long et al., *Su Doan Chien Thang,* vol. 2, 28; *Stars and Stripes,* June 2, 1965; Saigon to State, 1 June 1965, *FRUS*, 1964–1968, vol. 2, 322; CIA, "The Situation in South Vietnam," 9 June 1965, LBJL, NSF, VNCF, box 18; Blair, *There to the Bitter End,* 114–116; Carland, *Combat Operations,* 45.

99. Valenti, meeting notes, 21 July 1965, *FRUS*, 1964–1968, vol. 3, 71. See also McCone, Memorandum for the Record, 3 July 1965, DDRS, 1999, 263; NSC meeting notes, 8 February 1965, *FRUS*, 1964–1968, vol. 2, 87; Tyler, memcon, 19 February 1965, *FRUS*, 1964–1968, vol. 12, 43; Bundy to Mission Chiefs, 24 March 1965, LBJL, NSF, VNCF, box 54; Hubert H. Humphrey, *The Education of a Public Man: My Life and Politics* (Garden City: Doubleday, 1976), 320; *The Pentagon Papers,* vol. 3, 686; Bundy, unpublished manuscript, chap. 20, 22–3; Henry L. Trewhitt, *McNamara* (New York: Harper & Row, 1971), 217. Even George Ball, the senior official most skeptical about the importance of Vietnam, conceded that if the United States left Vietnam, "We will have to take the risk of Southeast Asia becoming Communist." Cooper, meeting notes, 21 July 1965, *FRUS*, 1964–1968, vol. 3, 72. Ball is also on the record as having said, "If the Communists fail in Vietnam, there is a good chance that they will also do so in Indonesia.

Conversely, if Vietnam goes Communist it will not be long before Indonesia does so as well." Record of discussion, 2 May 1965, PRO, PREM 13/694.

100. Bundy, unpublished manuscript, chap. 26, 22–23.

101. *Department of State Bulletin*, 26 April 1965, 607; *Public Papers of the Presidents*, 1965, 522.

102. NIE 13-9-65, 5 May 1965, DDRS, 1998, 262.

103. Telcon, 17 February 1965, Beschloss, ed., *Reaching for Glory*, 181–2.

104. Histories that have advanced this claim include Gibson, *The Perfect War;* Kaiser, *American Tragedy;* Karnow, *Vietnam;* Khong, *Analogies at War;* Logevall, *Choosing War;* Schwab, *Defending the Free World;* VanDeMark, *Into the Quagmire.*

105. Goodpaster, memcon, 17 February 1965, *FRUS*, 1964–1968, vol. 2, 133. The telegram itself is Bangkok to State, 17 February 1965, DDRS, 1976, 298B. For Johnson's attentiveness to developments in Indonesia, see William Bundy Oral History Interview, LBJL.

106. Fredrik Logevall, who has produced the only recent broad assessment of international views on Vietnam, contends that America's Vietnam policy enjoyed very little support in Southeast Asia and the rest of the world. "At the start of 1965," Logevall asserts, "the United States had the unequivocal support for its Vietnam policy of exactly one" country. Logevall, *Choosing War,* 378. The analysis in the rest of this chapter draws upon a large amount of evidence that Logevall did not use.

107. Jidda to State, 8 February 1965, NA II, RG 59, Central File, 1964–1966, box 2950. See also Komer, memo for the record, 5 March 1964, *FRUS*, 1964–1968, vol. 18, 26.

108. Mogadiscio to State, 8 February 1965, NA II, RG 59, Central Files, 1964–1966, box 2950. Maurice Yameogo, the President of the Republic of Upper Volta, told President Johnson in March that America's Vietnam policy enjoyed unanimous approval in the Organisation Commune Africaine et Malgache, an organization of a dozen French-speaking countries in Africa and Mauritius. "Africans know that if the United States were to give up the struggle," Yameogo said, "this would mean the end of freedom not only in Vietnam, but also in Africa." Glenn, memcon, 29 March 1965, NA II, RG 59, Lot Files, Entry 5159, box 1.

109. Rusk to State, 8 April 1965, *FRUS*, 1964–1968, vol. 22, 72. See also Tehran to State, 18 June 1965, *FRUS*, 1964–1968, vol. 22, 90; Tehran to State, 4 July 1965, *FRUS*, 1964–1968, vol. 22, 93.

110. CIA, "Nasir's Account of his Talks with Chou en-Lai, Sukarno, Ayub Khan, and Shastri," 3 July 1965, DDRS, 1977, 167E.

111. Memcon, Zhou Enlai and Ayub Khan, 2 April 1965, CWIHP.

112. Harold C. Hinton, ed., *The People's Republic of China, 1949–1979*, vol. 2 (Wilmington: Scholarly Resources, 1980), 1205–13. See also *Peking Review,* 14 May 1965.

113. Luu van Loi and Nguyen Anh Vu, *Tiep Xuc Bi Mat Viet Nam-Hoa Ky Truoc Hoi Nghi Pa-Ri*, 86. See also *Mot So Van Kien Cua Dang Ve Chong My, Cuu Nuoc*, Tap I, 224; Vien Nghien Cuu Chu Nghia Mac-Lenin va Tu Tuong Ho Chi Minh, *Ho Chi Minh: Bien Nien Tieu Su*, Tap IX (1964–1966) (Hanoi: Nha Xuat Ban Chinh Tri Quoc Gia, 1996), 216.

114. London to State, 1 September 1964, LBJL, NSF, VNCF, box 8; Ball to Johnson, 13 February 1965, *FRUS*, 1964–1968, vol. 2, 113; McKillop, memcon, 20 April 1965, NA II, RG 59, Lot Files, Entry 5159, box 1; Record of Meeting, 28 April 1965, PRO, PREM 13/694; Lawrence S. Kaplan, "The Vietnam War and Europe: The View From NATO," in Goscha and Vaïsse, eds., *La Guerre du Vietnam et L'Europe 1963–1973,* 89–102; Rimko Van Der Maar, "Dutch Minister for Foreign Affairs Joseph Luns and the Vietnam War (1963–1971)," in Goscha and Vaïsse, eds., *La Guerre du Vietnam et L'Europe 1963–1973*, 103–115.

115. Kaplan, "The Vietnam War and Europe," 95. On October 4, 1965, NATO Secretary-General Manlio Brosio told the NATO Parliamentarians' Conference that "a setback of the United States in Asia, for example, in Vietnam, would also be a grave setback for the whole of the West. An American retreat or a humiliating compromise in Vietnam, far from ending U.S. commitments in Asia, would extend them on an even greater scale to all sorts of other areas, from Thailand to the Philippines." Ibid., 96.

116. Obst, memcon, 4 June 1965, *FRUS*, 1964–1968, vol. 2, 331. For a German account of the meeting, see Horst Osterheld, *Aussenpolitik unter Bundeskanzler Ludwig Erhard 1963–1966: Ein dokumentarischer Bericht aus dem Kanzleramt* (Düsseldorf: Droste Verlag, 1992), 195. See also Erhard to Johnson, n.d., *FRUS*, 1964–1968, vol. 15, 36; Porter, *Paul Hasluck: A Political Biography* (Nedlands: University of West

Australia Press, 1993), 244. On May 11, 1965, West German Foreign Minister Gerhard Schroeder declared that "withdrawal or defeat of the United States in Vietnam would have an effect on the situation in Europe, especially in Berlin, comparable to that of the test of strength over Cuba in 1962 on the situation in Berlin." Kaplan, "The Vietnam War and Europe," 99.

117. Schwartz, *Lyndon Johnson and Europe,* 86–7; Blang, "To Urge Common Sense on the Americans," 176.

118. Record of Conversation, 28 April 1965, PRO, PREM 13/694. From time to time, each side asked the other for help with its side of the conflict, but both responded negatively to the other's entreaties, saying that they already had heavy commitments in their principal area of operations. See also Saigon to FO, 14 January 1965, PRO, FO 371/180558; Cabinet Conclusions, 30 March 1965, PRO, CAB 128/39; Record of meeting, 2 April 1965, PRO, PREM 13/693; State to London, 29 April 1965, *FRUS,* 1964–1968, vol. 27, 64; Record of discussion, 2 May 1965, PRO, PREM 13/694. In early 1965, British Prime Minister Harold Wilson repeatedly urged Johnson to seek a negotiated end to the war, much to Johnson's annoyance, so as to placate members of the British Labor Party who deemed Johnson too inflexible toward negotiations. Some observers would take Wilson's appeals as evidence of British opposition to the war, but they were not. While Wilson contended that the United States should use the olive branch, he also said privately that "the Americans would have to continue to use the club." Record of Conversation, 24 March 1965, PRO, PREM 13/693.

119. John W. Young, "British Governments and the Vietnam War," in Goscha and Vaïsse, eds., *La Guerre du Vietnam et L'Europe 1963–1973*, 127.

120. See, for example, Arnold, *The First Domino*, 389; Baritz, *Backfire*, 229; Isaacs, *Vietnam Shadows*, 176; Moss, *Vietnam*, 371–2; Ninkovich, *Modernity and Power*, 315.

121. *New York Times*, September 20, 1987.

122. As compensation, the North Vietnamese gave Sihanouk 10 percent of the shipped materiel and refrained from promoting armed revolution in Cambodia. Milton E. Osborne, *Sihanouk: Prince of Light, Prince of Darkness* (Honolulu: University of Hawaii Press, 1994), 172; Dommen, *The Indochinese Experience of the French and the Americans*, 612–3.

123. JIC, "The Chinese Threat in the Far East Up to 1969," 10 May 1965, PRO, CAB 158/54.

124. Andrew H. Wedeman, *The East Wind Subsides: Chinese Foreign Policy and the Origins of the Cultural Revolution* (Washington, DC: Washington Institute Press, 1987), 197.

125. *New York Times*, April 1, 1965; Djakarta to State, 5 June 1965, NA II, RG 59, Central Files, 1964–1966, box 2313; CIA, "Prospects for Indonesia and Malaysia," 1 July 1965, DDRS, 1993, 153.

126. Djakarta to State, 14 January 1965, LBJL, NSF, Country File, Indonesia, box 246; JIC, "Possible Political Developments in Indonesia Within the Next Few Months," 23 March 1965, PRO, CAB 158/58; Djakarta to State, 5 June 1965, NA II, RG 59, Central Files, 1964–1966, box 2313.

127. Memcon, 6 March 1965, PRO, PREM 13/693. See also Washington to FO, 29 July 1965, PRO, FO 371/180543.

128. Djakarta to State, 21 April 1965, LBJL, NSF, Indonesia Country File, box 247.

129. "Text of China-Indonesia Joint Statement," 28 January 1965, PRO, FO 371/181468.

130. Djakarta to State, 22 October 1965, DDRS, 1993, 118; Dake, *In the Spirit of the Red Banteng*, 331–2, 358–60.

131. Nishihara, *The Japanese and Sukarno's Indonesia*, 170–1.

132. Even the most recent studies of Indonesia have not drawn a connection between the Vietnam conflict and the political behavior of the Indonesian armed forces. See R. E. Elson, *Suharto: A Political Biography* (Cambridge: Cambridge University Press, 2001); Theodore Friend, *Indonesian Destinies* (Cambridge: Harvard University Press, 2003); Jones, *Conflict and Confrontation in Southeast Asia;* Bradley Simpson, "Modernizing Indonesia: United States–Indonesia Relations, 1961–1967" (Ph.D. diss., Northwestern University, 2003); Subritzky, *Confronting Sukarno.*

133. Djakarta to State, 26 February 1965, LBJL, NSF, Country File, Indonesia, box 246. See also Arnold C. Brackman, *The Communist Collapse in Indonesia* (New York: W. W. Norton, 1969), 196.

134. Djakarta to State, 11 December 1965, DDRS, document number CK3100357672; Djakarta to State, 15 December 1965, DDRS, 1976, 83 E; Djakarta to State, 17 December 1965, DDRS, 1976, 83 H.

135. Humphrey to Johnson, 25 September 1966, DDRS, 1995, 101.

136. Novarin Gunawan, interview with author. Novarin Gunawan is the Indonesian Marine officer to whom Nasution made the remarks.

137. An Indonesian general later told Brig. Gen. Theodore Mataxis that the Indonesian military would not have tried to throw out the Communists had the United States not intervened in Vietnam. Theodore C. Mataxis, interview with author. For additional evidence, see Dean Rusk, *As I Saw It* (New York: W. W. Norton, 1990), 496. The silence of many individuals on this subject is probably a function of their reluctance to admit their reliance on foreigners. The overthrow of Sukarno will be treated in greater detail in volume two of this history.

138. Donald E. Weatherbee, *The United Front in Thailand: A Documentary Analysis* (Columbia, SC: Institute of International Studies, 1970), 37–43; Meeting notes, 29 January 1965, *FRUS, 1964–1968,* vol. 27, 286; JIC, "The Chinese Threat in the Far East Up to 1969," 10 May 1965, PRO, CAB 158/54; Peking to FO, 12 January 1965, LBJL, NSF, VNCF, box 12; "An Internal History of the Communist Party of Thailand," translated by Chris Baker, *Journal of Contemporary Asia,* vol. 33, no. 4 (2003), 528.

139. Bangkok to State, 4 May 1964, *FRUS, 1964–1968,* vol. 27, 268; Smith, NSC meeting notes, 15 May 1964, *FRUS, 1964–1968,* vol. 1, 156; Burchinal to LeMay, 22 June 1964, *FRUS, 1964–1968,* vol. 27, 278; Forrestal to Johnson, "Third Country Assistance to Vietnam," 11 December 1964, LBJL, NSF, VNCF, box 11.

140. Bangkok to FO, 8 February 1965, PRO, FO 371/180414. See also Tokyo to FO, 19 May 1965, PRO, FO 371/180414; *New York Times,* February 9, 1965.

141. *Washington Post,* May 12, 1965.

142. For the ambassador's position, see Bangkok to State, 30 June 1965, NA II, RG 59, Lot Files, Entry 5408, box 8.

143. Kuala Lumpur to State, 21 May 1965, NA II, RG 59, Central Files, 1964–1966, box 2959.

144. Kuala Lumpur to State, 6 April 1965, LBJL, NSF, Country File, Malaysia, box 276; Record of conversation, 28 April 1965, PRO, FO 371/180209; Walker, report, 7 May 1965, PRO, PREM 13/304.

145. Hughes, "Third Country Assistance to South Vietnam," 28 August 1964, LBJL, NSF, VNCF, box 7.

146. Kuala Lumpur to State, 22 December 1964, LBJL, NSF, Country File, Malaysia, box 276.

147. Subritzky, *Confronting Sukarno,* 137–40; Edwards, *Crises and Commitments,* 343–4; State to UN, 15 January 1965, *FRUS, 1964–1968,* vol. 26, 98.

148. Vientiane to State, 21 April 1965, *FRUS, 1964–1968,* vol. 28, 178. See also Walker, report, 7 May 1965, PRO, PREM 13/304; Paris to State, 8 July 1965, *FRUS, 1964–1968,* vol. 28, 189; *The Joint Chiefs of Staff and the War in Vietnam,* chap. 24, 16.

149. Taipei to State, 24 February 1964, LBJL, NSF, Country File, Asia and the Pacific, China, box 237; Komer to Bundy, 7 April 1964, DDRS, 1977, 195 B; Taipei to State, 7 November 1964, LBJL, NSF, Country File, Asia and the Pacific, China, box 238; Forrestal to Johnson, "Third Country Assistance to Vietnam," 11 December 1964, LBJL, NSF, VNCF, box 11.

150. Tamsui to FO, 21 February 1965, PRO, FO 371/181058.

151. Tamsui to FO, 6 April 1965, PRO, FO 371/181052.

152. Donohue, memcon, 15 January 1965, NA II, RG 59, Central Files, 1964–1966, box 2402.

153. Seoul to State, 30 June 1964, *FRUS, 1964–1968,* vol. 29, part 1, 5; State to Seoul, 3 July 1964, DDRS, 1993, 120; Forrestal to Johnson, "Third Country Assistance to Vietnam," 11 December 1964, LBJL, NSF, VNCF, box 11.

154. Pemberton, *All the Way,* 202; *FRUS, 1964–1968,* vol. 29, part 1, 32; *The Joint Chiefs of Staff and the War in Vietnam,* chap. 22, 26.

155. The opposition members of the National Assembly walked out before the vote, but many of them supported the combat force deployment. Of those who remained, 101 voted for the measure, 1 voted against it, and 2 abstained. Rusk to Johnson, 17 May 1965, *FRUS, 1964–1968,* vol. 29, part 1, 46; *FRUS, 1964–1968,* vol. 29, part 1, 58.

156. McArthur, "DM Favors Keeping American Bases Here," PRO, FO 371/180386. See also Manila to FO, 9 February 1965, PRO, FO 371/180386.

157. Manila to State, 9 October 1964, NA II, RG 59, Central Files, 1964–1966, box 2947. In February 1965, the U.S. embassy in Manila cabled to Washington that the "majority of Filipinos support U.S. policy in South Vietnam and consider that success of South Vietnamese, U.S. and other free-world effort in South Vietnam is vital to future security of Philippines." Manila to State, 25 February 1965, LBJL, NSF, Country File, Philippines, box 278. See also Manila to State, 10 June 1965, LBJL, NSF, Country File, Philippines, box 278; Manila to FO, 20 July 1965, PRO, FO 371/180390.

158. *The Joint Chiefs of Staff and the War in Vietnam*, chap. 16, 45, and chap. 22, 27; Manila to State, 10 June 1965, LBJL, NSF, Country File, Philippines, box 278. The first Philippine troops arrived in 1966.

159. Rangoon to State, 19 April 1965, LBJL, NSF, Country File, Burma, box 235. See also CIA, "The Situation in Burma," 27 July 1964, LBJL, NSF, Country File, Burma, box 235; Rangoon to State, 30 July 1964, LBJL, NSF, Country File, Burma, box 235; Taylor, *China and Southeast Asia*, 202; Rangoon to State, 25 April 1965, LBJL, NSF, Country File, Burma, box 235; Rumbold to Stewart, 5 April 1965, PRO, FO 371/180207; JIC, "The Chinese Threat in the Far East Up to 1969," 10 May 1965, PRO, CAB 158/54; Rangoon to State, 10 June 1965, NA II, RG 59, Central Files, 1964–1966, box 2961.

160. Fearey, memcon, 12 July 1965, LBJL, NSF, Country File, Japan, box 250.

161. Pemberton, *All the Way*, 260–3; Frankum, *The United States and Australia in Vietnam*, 233; Barclay, *A Very Small Insurance Policy*, 79–86, 97–8, 110; Edwards, *Crises and Commitments*, 341–4; Porter, *Paul Hasluck*, 242–3.

162. Subritzky, *Confronting Sukarno*, 153; Edwards, *Crises and Commitments*, 360–75; Pemberton, *All the Way*, 308, 321. Upon arriving in South Vietnam in June, the Australian battalion was attached to the U.S. 173rd Airborne Brigade and it began operating in Phuoc Tuy province.

163. Conlon, memcon, 11 March 1965, NA II, RG 59, Central Files, 1964–1966, box 2954. See also Subritzky, *Confronting Sukarno*, 139–40; Bundy, memcon, 28 June 1965, LBJL, NSF, Country File, New Zealand, box 277.

164. Record of discussion, 2 May 1965, PRO, PREM 13/694. See also Roberto Rabel, "The Most Dovish of the Hawks," in Jeffrey Grey and Jeff Doyle, eds., *Vietnam: War, Myth, and Memory* (St. Leonards, Australia: Allen & Unwin, 1992), 20; Subritzky, *Confronting Sukarno*, 154.

165. *New York Times*, February 22, 1965.

166. Tokyo to State, 30 June 1964, NA II, RG 59, Central Files, 1964–1966, box 2944; record of conversation, 28 April 1965, PRO, FO 371/180209; Thomas Havens, *Fire Across the Sea: The Vietnam War and Japan, 1965–1975* (Princeton: Princeton University Press, 1987), 42–3; Tokyo to FO, 21 May 1965, PRO, FO 371/181073; Tokyo to State, 15 June 1965, LBJL, NSF, Country File, Japan, box 250. That the government's support of America's Vietnam policy did not arouse public indignation can be seen from the results of the upper house elections of July 4, in which the Liberal Democratic Party won 71 of 127 seats. Havens, *Fire Across the Sea*, 48.

167. Tokyo to State, 27 July 1965, DDRS, 1998, 284.

168. Reischauer to Bundy, 24 June 1965, NA II, RG 59, Lot Files, Entry 5408, box 8. Reischauer thought that a negotiated American exit from Vietnam could have less damaging consequences in Japan than a forced exit, but at this time it was most doubtful that such a negotiation could be arranged. It was also very doubtful that the Japanese people would have viewed it as something less than defeat; in all of the other countries of east and southeast Asia, neutralization was viewed at this time as a thinly disguised means of American capitulation. See also Brackman, *The Communist Collapse in Indonesia*, 15.

169. On January 26, the British ambassador to India commented, "Any evidence of Western withdrawal before the Chinese would be likely to cause the Indians to retreat further into their shells. But they would be likely to attempt a more positive line, if it appeared that the Chinese were being held. Moreover, apart from their major pre-occupation with the Chinese threat from the North, the Indians are becoming increasingly concerned at Indonesian behaviour and at evidence of an emerging Djakarta-Peking-Karachi axis. They realise that if the Indonesians are successful over Malaysia, they would be likely to turn their attentions further afield to the detriment of Indian interests. Already the Indians are looking to the defence of the Andaman and Nicobar islands, and the Indian Navy considers the Indonesian Navy its most likely opponent." New Delhi to FO, 26 January 1965, PRO, FO 371/180205.

170. New Delhi to State, 4 May 1965, LBJL, NSF, Country File, India, box 129. See also Peck, "Impressions of a Visit to Southeast Asia," 19 February 1965, PRO, FO 371/180206; Manila to State, 7 March 1965, LBJL, NSF, Country File, Philippines, box 278; *Congressional Record,* vol. 111, 3411–12.

171. *New York Times,* February 22, 1965.

172. James J. Przystup and John T. Dori, *Indonesia After Suharto: How the U.S. Can Foster Political and Economic Reform* (Washington, DC: The Heritage Foundation, 1998). Sukarno had already shown an intention to deny the Western powers access to Indonesia's sea lanes. In August 1964, he threatened to attack British ships if they passed through the Sunda Strait, which he claimed as territorial water. Medan to State, 11 September 1964, LBJL, NSF, Country File, Malaysia, box 275. The British prime minister, Sir Alec Douglas-Home, chose not to back down, on the grounds that the strait was international water and a British retreat "might be followed by an attempt on Sukarno's part progressively to deny the use by Royal Navy Ships of other waters in the Far East." DO(64) 35th meeting, 7 September 1964, PRO, CAB 148/1; "Conclusions of a Cabinet Meeting," 10 September 1964, PRO, CAB 128/38. In the face of British determination, Sukarno backed down.

173. The trade statistics are given in Paul M. Kennedy, *The Rise and Fall of Great Powers: Economic Change and Military Conflict from 1500 to 2000* (New York: Random House, 1987), 441.

174. Gardner, *Pay Any Price,* 207.

175. Goodpaster, meeting notes, 17 February 1965, *FRUS,* 1964–1968, vol. 2, 133. See also Goodpaster, "Meeting with General Eisenhower," 16 June 1965, DDRS, 1982, 6.

176. *New York Times,* February 24, 1965.

17. Decision: June–July 1965

1. The Communists also had the 709th Artillery Battalion and an antiaircraft battalion in northwestern II Corps. Thai Van Tinh, *Chien Dich Tien Cong Ba Gia,* 14–16; Nguyen Huu An with Nguyen Tu Duong, *Chien Truong Moi,* 13.

2. Vinh Loc, "Road-Clearing Operation," *Military Review,* April 1966; Theodore C. Mataxis, "Monsoon Offensive in the Highlands," TTU, Mataxis Collection.

3. Theodore C. Mataxis, "Monsoon Offensive in the Highlands," TTU, Mataxis Collection; Theodore C. Mataxis, interview with author; CIA, "The Situation in South Vietnam," 9 June 1965, LBJL, NSF, VNCF, box 18; Pham Gia Duc, *Su Doan 325,* vol. 2, 52–58.

4. MACV, Daily Staff Journal, 1–2 June 1965, NA II, RG 472, MACV J3–08, Daily Journal, box 5; MACV, Monthly Evaluation Report, June 1965, NA II, RG 472, MACJ3–05, Evaluation Reports, box 1; Theodore C. Mataxis, "Monsoon Offensive in the Highlands," TTU, Mataxis Collection; Nguyen Van Minh et al., *Luc Luong Vu Trang Nhan Dan Tay Nguyen Trong Khang Chien Chong My Cuu Nuoc,* 39–40.

5. Pham Gia Duc, *Su Doan 325,* vol. 2, 58; Theodore C. Mataxis, "Monsoon Offensive in the Highlands," TTU, Mataxis Collection; MACV, Daily Staff Journal, 3–4 June 1965, NA II, RG 472, MACV J3–08, Daily Journal, box 5.

6. Westmoreland to Sharp, 7 June 1965, NA II, RG 550, MACV and USARV Command Reporting Files, USMACV Military Reports, box 1; CIA, "The Situation in South Vietnam," 9 June 1965, LBJL, NSF, VNCF, box 18.

7. Westmoreland to JCS, 7 June 1965, *FRUS,* 1964–1968, vol. 2, 337; Westmoreland to Sharp, 13 June 1965, *FRUS,* 1964–1968, vol. 3, 1.

8. Bundy, notes, 10 June 1965, *FRUS,* 1964–1968, vol. 2, 343; Telcon, 10 June 1965, Beschloss, ed., *Reaching for Glory,* 349–52.

9. CIA, "Reactions to a Further U.S. Buildup in South Vietnam," 10 June 1965, LBJL, NSF, VNCF, box 18.

10. CIA, "US Options and Objectives in Vietnam," 10 June 1965, *FRUS,* 1964–1968, vol. 2, 344.

11. State to Saigon, 11 June 1965, LBJL, NSF, NSC History, DMUSF, box 42; Hughes to Rusk, "Giap's Third Phase in Prospect in South Vietnam?" 23 July 1965, LBJL, NSF, VNCF, box 20.

12. Saigon to State, 11 July 1965, LBJL, NSF, NSC History, DMUSF, box 43; "Intensification of the Military Operations in Vietnam," 14 July 1965, DDRS, 1986, 203.

13. Saigon to State, 5 June 1965, *FRUS, 1964–1968,* vol. 2, 332.

14. Saigon to State, 12 June 1965, LBJL, NSF, VNCF, box 18.

15. Jay to Johnson, 10 June 1965, TTU, Larry Berman Collection, box 2; Westmoreland to Sharp, 13 June 1965, NA II, RG 319, Westmoreland Personal Papers, box 11; Sharp to Westmoreland, 13 June 1965, LBJL, Westmoreland Papers, History Backup, box 6; Westmoreland to Sharp, 13 June 1965, MHI, Westmoreland Papers, box 46; NMCC to White House, 13 June 1965, LBJL, NSF, VNCF, box 18; MACV, Weekly Talking Paper, June 1965, NA II, RG 472, Military History Branch, MACV Weekly Talking Papers, box 1; Holt to Spears, "Dong Xoai After Action Report," 7 July 1965, NA II, RG 472, 5th Special Forces Group, Headquarters Assistant Chief of Staff for Operations, After Action Reports, box 1; Military History Institute of Vietnam, *Mot So Tran Danh Trong Khang Chien Chong Phap, Khang Chien Chong My, 1945–1975*, Tap II, 125–143; Nguyen Viet Ta et al., *Mien Dong Nam Bo Khang Chien (1945–1975)*, Tap II, 192–5; *Quan Doi Nhan Dan*, 16 June 2004; Chanoff and Toai, *Portrait of the Enemy*, 158–61; 145th Combat Aviation Battalion History, "Battle of Dong Xoai, 10–20 June 1965," <www.145cab.com>; Charles Q. Williams Medal of Honor Award Recommendation, 9 August 1965, NA II, RG 472, Medal of Honor Awards Case File, box 24; Critchfield, *The Long Charade*, 144–5; Higgins, *Our Vietnam Nightmare*, 250, 310; *Washington Post*, June 11, 14, and 15, 1965; *New York Times*, June 14, 1965; telcon, 13 June 1965, Beschloss, ed., *Reaching for Glory*, 354; Hammond, *Public Affairs: The Military and the Media, 1962–1968*, 170; Carland, *Combat Operations*, 27, 46–7.

16. U.S. press correspondents were present at the airfield, and they filed reports on the arrival of the 173rd Airborne Brigade at Phuoc Vinh in which they stated that the American paratroopers were preparing to go into action against the Viet Cong. Major U.S. newspapers such as the *Washington Post* and the *Los Angeles Times* printed these reports, to the great consternation of Westmoreland.

17. Henry F. Graff, *The Tuesday Cabinet: Deliberation and Decision on War and Peace Under Lyndon B. Johnson* (Englewood Cliffs: Prentice Hall, 1970), 53.

18. The following works state or imply that the American leadership held a negative view of Thieu as well as Ky: Anderson, *The Vietnam War*, 46; Bird, *The Color of Truth*, 329; Karnow, *Vietnam*, 401; McNamara, *In Retrospect*, 186; Herring, *America's Longest War*, 162; VanDeMark, *Into the Quagmire*, 150.

19. CIA, "Nguyen Van Thieu," 29 January 1965, LBJL, International Meetings and Travel, box 29; Manfull, memcon, 4 February 1965, *FRUS, 1964–1968*, vol. 2, 63; CIA Vietnam Working Group, "Implications of the Saigon Coup Events," 20 February 1965, LBJL, NSF, VNCF, box 14; CIA Office of Central Reference, "Nguyen Van Thieu," 24 June 1965, DDRS, 1987, 87. In 1960, an American evaluation of Thieu had stated that he was "the outstanding colonel in the Vietnamese Army." Stromberg to Williams, 21 June 1960, HIA, Samuel T. Williams Papers, box 15.

20. Nguyen Cao Ky, *Buddha's Child*, 142.

21. CIA, "Military Plans for a Revolutionary Government to Replace the Present Government of Vietnam," 11 June 1965, DDRS, 1978, 35 B.

22. Tri Quang denounced Thieu as a "Can Lao remnant" and accused him of having "fascistic tendencies." The monk alleged that the "ex-Can Lao around General Ky were sabotaging his program." As was to be expected, Tri Quang's generalizations far exceeded his specific charges. When pressed to provide an example of the sabotaging of Ky's program, Tri Quang could offer only this bizarre answer: "Ky's decision to shoot all speculators, since such a move could obviously never be implemented." Memcon, 9 July 1965, LBJL, NSF, VNCF, box 20; Saigon to State, 11 July 1965, LBJL, NSF, NSC History, DMUSF, box 43; memcon, 14 July 1965, LBJL, NSF, VNCF, box 20; Saigon to State, 27 July 1965, LBJL, NSF, VNCF, box 19.

23. Theodore C. Mataxis, "Monsoon Offensive in the Highlands," TTU, Mataxis Collection; Vinh Loc, "Road-Clearing Operation," 22–8; Saigon to State, 30 June 1965, *FRUS, 1964–1968*, vol. 3, 32. Elsewhere, in I Corps and III Corps, the Communists attempted to sever major governmental transportation arteries by means of ambushes and acts of sabotage, but with less success than in the highlands.

24. Pham Gia Duc, *Su Doan 325*, vol. 2, 58; CIA, "The Viet Cong Campaign in South Vietnam's Highlands," 9 July 1965, LBJL, NSF, VNCF, box 50; MACV, Daily Staff Journal, 26–28 June 1965, NA II, RG 472, MACV J3–08, Daily Journal, box 5; Westmoreland to JCS, 28 June 1965, NA II, RG 550, MACV and USARV Command Reporting Files, USMACV Military Reports, box 1; Theodore C. Mataxis, "Monsoon

Offensive in the Highlands," TTU, Mataxis Collection; Nguyen Van Minh et al., *Luc Luong Vu Trang Nhan Dan Tay Nguyen Trong Khang Chien Chong My Cuu Nuoc*, 40; Nguyen Huu An with Nguyen Tu Duong, *Chien Truong Moi*, 15–20.

25. MACV, Daily Staff Journal, 30 June-3 July 1965, NA II, RG 472, MACV J3–08, Daily Journal, box 5; MACV, Monthly Evaluation Report, June 1965, NA II, RG 472, MACJ3–05, Evaluation Reports, box 1; MACV, Monthly Evaluation Report, July 1965, NA II, RG 472, MACJ3–05, Evaluation Reports, box 1; Nesbit to Westmoreland, Combat Operations After Action Report, 3 August 1965, NA II, RG 472, MACJ3–05, After Action Reports, box 1; Theodore C. Mataxis, "Monsoon Offensive in the Highlands," TTU, Mataxis Collection.

26. CIA, "Developments in South Vietnam During the Past Year," 29 June 1965, DDRS, 1976, 231 D; Westmoreland, "GVN Civil Defense Decree," 6 July 1965, MHI, Westmoreland Papers, box 29. Government recruiting continued to lag behind losses, because of both administrative weakness and the success of the Communist main forces in eroding the remnants of government authority in the countryside. The government lost control of nearly 3 percent of the country's population during June alone. *The Joint Chiefs of Staff and the War in Vietnam*, chap. 27, 14–15.

27. Telcon, 21 June 1965, Beschloss, ed., *Reaching for Glory*, 364–6.

28. In Ball's memoirs, which are unusually self-serving even by the standards of political memoirs, Ball repeatedly misrepresented or distorted his conduct during this period. George W. Ball, *The Past Has Another Pattern: Memoirs* (New York: W. W. Norton, 1982). Historical depictions of Ball as a staunch opponent of greater U.S. involvement can be found in Barrett, *Uncertain Warriors*; Bird, *The Color of Truth*; Hunt, *Lyndon Johnson's War*; Kaiser, *American Tragedy*; Khong, *Analogies At War*; Langguth, *Our Vietnam*; Mann, *A Grand Delusion*; Schwab, *Defending the Free World*; Schulzinger, *A Time for War*; VanDeMark, *Into the Quagmire*; Vandiver, *Shadows of Vietnam*.

29. Rusk Oral History II, LBJL. See also Graff, *The Tuesday Cabinet*, 50.

30. Ball, "A Compromise Solution for South Viet-Nam," n.d., *FRUS*, 1964–1968, vol. 3, 40.

31. Pham Van Dong told a *Mussawar* reporter on July 6 that Hanoi would negotiate for nothing less than an American withdrawal that was tantamount to an American capitulation. "We will fight to the end, and will help them withdraw by pushing them in the sea so long as they insist on not withdrawing," Pham Van Dong bellowed. Cairo to State, 6 July 1965, NA II, RG 59, Central Files, 1964–1966, box 2962. Later in the month, Ho Chi Minh told a Ghanaian delegation that he had no need for negotiations because Communist forces might win the war before the end of the monsoon season. W. Scott Thompson, *Ghana's Foreign Policy, 1957–1966: Diplomacy, Ideology and the New State* (Princeton: Princeton University Press, 1969), 411. See also CIA, "The Situation in South Vietnam," 9 June 1965, LBJL, NSF, VNCF, box 18; Accra to Commonwealth Relations Office, 16 August 1965, PRO, PREM 13/697; Gaiduk, *The Soviet Union and the Vietnam War*, 43–4.

32. For recent examples, see Cabinet Conclusions, 18 March 1965, PRO, CAB 128/39; CIA, "Soviet References to Negotiations on Vietnam," 23 April 1965, DDRS, 1983, 92; Moscow to State, 13 May 1965, *FRUS*, 1964–1968, vol. 2, 298; Rusk to Ball, 15 May 1965, *FRUS*, 1964–1968, vol. 2, 303; Cabinet Conclusions, 20 May 1965, PRO, CAB 128/39.

33. "Asians want peace, stability, independence, freedom, not surrender by installment or submission by stages to Communist expansionists," Thanat Khoman had recently declared in Tokyo. "South Viet Nam's struggle against the Viet Cong is a determined resistance against a new form of colonialism.... Neutralization of South Vietnam or the whole of Southeast Asia means surrender and wholesale delivery of the entire region to the neo-colonialists." Tokyo to FO, 19 May 1965, PRO, FO 371/180414.

34. Westmoreland to Wheeler, 24 June 1965, *FRUS*, 1964–1968, vol. 3, 17; Westmoreland to Wheeler, 26 June 1965, MHI, Westmoreland Papers, box 46; Westmoreland to Wheeler, 30 June 1965, *FRUS*, 1964–1968, vol. 3, 30; Gibbons, *The U.S. Government and the Vietnam War*, vol. 3, 373–4.

35. McNamara to Johnson, 1 July 1965, *FRUS*, 1964–1968, vol. 3, 38.

36. Bundy, "A 'Middle Way' Course of Action in South Vietnam," 1 July 1965, *FRUS*, 1964–1968, vol. 3, 41.

37. Two days earlier, William Bundy had told his boss Dean Rusk, "85,000 may be a good figure with which to fight out the summer, but any commitment beyond that needs careful assessment of the

possible negative factors." Bundy to Rusk, "Ground Force Deployments to South Vietnam," 29 June 1965, LBJL, Gibbons Papers, box 1.

38. *The Pentagon Papers,* vol. 3, 556–9, 683–4; Gibbons, *The U.S. Government and the Vietnam War,* vol. 2, 348.

39. Brown, Memorandum of Telephone Conversation, 2 July 1965, DDEL, Eisenhower Post-Presidential Papers, Augusta Series, box 10.

40. See chapter 5, note 15.

41. Goodpaster, meeting notes, 17 February 1965, *FRUS, 1964–1968,* vol. 2, 133.

42. Telcon, 2 July 1965, Beschloss, ed., *Reaching for Glory,* 381–3.

43. Johnson, tape-recorded diary, 8 July 1965, Beschloss, ed., *Reaching for Glory,* 390. The Johnson tapes provide conclusive evidence that Johnson was not optimistic about the prospects for U.S. intervention. Johnson's advisers were not blindly optimistic about intervention, either, though McNamara did make some optimistic predictions in the latter part of the month, as discussed below. Accusations of blind optimism on the part of Johnson and his advisers have been made in, among others, Buzzanco, *Masters of War;* Herring, *LBJ and Vietnam;* Kaiser, *American Tragedy;* Karnow, *Vietnam;* Krepinevich, *The Army and Vietnam;* Mann, *A Grand Delusion;* Moss, *Vietnam;* Record, *The Wrong War;* Sheehan, *A Bright Shining Lie;* VanDeMark, *Into the Quagmire.*

44. Le Duan told a conference of cadres early in the month of July, "The best way to cope, and not let the U.S. broaden the direct warfare in the South or in the North, is to fight even more strongly and more accurately in the South, and make the puppet military units – the primary mainstay of the United States – rapidly fall apart, push military and political struggle forward, and quickly create the opportune moment to advance to complete the defeat of U.S. imperialism and its lackeys in the South." Porter, ed., *Vietnam: The Definitive Documentation of Human Decisions,* vol. 2, 383–5.

45. CIA, "The Viet Cong Campaign in South Vietnam's Highlands," 9 July 1965, LBJL, NSF, VNCF, box 50; Saigon to State, 11 July 1965, LBJL, NSF, NSC History, DMUSF, box 43; Vinh Loc, "Road-Clearing Operation," 22–8; Valenti, NSC meeting notes, 27 July 1965, LBJL, Meeting Notes File, box 1.

46. *The Joint Chiefs of Staff and the War in Vietnam,* chap. 22, 6.

47. Gibbons, *The U.S. Government and the Vietnam War,* vol. 3, 378.

48. A few days later, McNamara explained that Rolling Thunder "should be structured to capitalize on fear of future attacks. At any time, 'pressure' on the DRV depends not upon the current level of bombing but rather upon the credible threat of future destruction which can be avoided by agreeing to negotiate or agreeing to some settlement in negotiations." McNamara to Johnson, 30 July 1965, *FRUS, 1964–1968,* vol. 3, 100.

49. McNamara made this comment ten days after the initial report, in an evaluation of Rolling Thunder. McNamara to Johnson, 28 July 1965, DDRS, 1979, 366C.

50. McNamara to Johnson, 20 July 1965, *FRUS, 1964–1968,* vol. 3, 67.

51. The testimonials of most of Johnson's advisers put the President's decision sometime between late June and his July 28 speech. Bundy, unpublished manuscript, chap. 27, 1, 13, 23–4; Barrett, *Uncertain Soldiers,* 215; Gibbons, *The U.S. Government and the Vietnam War,* vol. 3, 343; Gittinger, ed., *The Johnson Years,* 48, 61; Kahin, *Intervention,* 366. The evidence is clear that until at least the second half of June, Johnson hoped to avoid enmeshing American combat forces in the ground war, as he envisioned much calamity stemming from it. In late June, he had come to the realization that the United States would probably have to enter the ground war soon to prevent a total defeat, and in early July he appears to have decided to expand the U.S. commitment in some fashion. One recently declassified document points toward the conclusion that by July 8, 1965, before McNamara left for his mid-July trip, Johnson had decided to raise the troop strength to 175,000. On July 10, according to the notes of General Wallace Greene, McNamara told the Joint Chiefs to prepare to raise the U.S. troop strength to 115,000 in September and 175,000 by mid-November. Greene recorded that Johnson seemed to have authorized such an increase on July 8. At the same time, however, McNamara said that there remained some uncertainty with respect to Johnson's plans. "The President intends to move forward in South Vietnam," McNamara told the Joint Chiefs, but "the President has not yet decided on a specific program." Greene, "Escalation of effort in South Vietnam," 10 July 1965, MCHD, Greene Papers. One day after McNamara's team left for Saigon, according to a message written by Deputy Secretary of Defense

Cyrus Vance, Johnson said it was his "current intention" to raise the troop level to 175,000. Vance to McNamara, 17 July 1965, *FRUS, 1964–1968*, vol. 3, 61. This document led early historians of the war to conclude that Johnson had firmly decided on a course of action. In 1988, however, Vance disputed this interpretation. The President's "current intention," Vance said, was not necessarily his "final decision," and "there was continuing uncertainty about his final decision." John P. Burke and Fred I. Greenstein, *How Presidents Test Reality: Decisions on Vietnam, 1954 and 1965* (New York: Russell Sage Foundation, 1989), 215. The documentary record from July 21 to July 23 supports Vance's contention. Johnson at this time was telling his advisers – with whom he tended to be substantially more candid than with Congress – that he still was considering alternatives to McNamara's plan, and he encouraged Ball, in front of the others, to present his arguments in favor of withdrawing from Vietnam. Alone with his wife he showed the agony of a man still struggling to decide what to do. Valenti, meeting notes, 21 July 1965, *FRUS, 1964–1968*, vol. 3, 71; Cooper, "Meetings on Vietnam," 21 July 1965, *FRUS, 1964–1968*, vol. 3, 72; Valenti, *A Very Human President*, 319–40; Bundy, unpublished manuscript, chap. 27, 30–33; Johnson, tape-recorded diary, 22 July 1965, Beschloss, ed., *Reaching for Glory*, 403. Considering that Johnson and McNamara had deceived their military subordinates about their intentions in the past, it is possible that Johnson misrepresented his thinking even in private during June and July. It may also be that much of his uncertainty and agonizing concerned the size of the U.S. troop deployment, as opposed to whether he would pull out right away or not. All that can be said with complete certainty is that Johnson came to his decision at some point between late June and July 23. That he had definitely reached a decision by July 23 can be seen in the notes from a meeting that day in which Secretary of the Navy Nitze said that McNamara had just decided to meet Westmoreland's newest troop request. Greene, "Developing Situation in South Vietnam," 24 July 1965, MCHD, Greene Papers. By the afternoon of July 27, Johnson had firmly decided on the exact program. Smith, NSC meeting notes, 27 July 1965, *FRUS, 1964–1968*, vol. 3, 93.

52. Valenti, meeting notes, 21 July 1965, *FRUS, 1964–1968*, vol. 3, 71; Cooper, "Meetings on Vietnam," 21 July 1965, *FRUS, 1964–1968*, vol. 3, 72; Valenti, *A Very Human President*, 319–52; Bundy, unpublished manuscript, chap. 27, 30–33; Valenti, meeting notes, 22 July 1965, *FRUS, 1964–1968*, vol. 3, 76; Greene, record of conference, 22 July 1965, MCHD, Greene Papers.

53. Zhai, *China and the Vietnam Wars*, 135; Jian, *Mao's China and the Cold War*, 222–5, 229; Xiaoming Zhang, "The Vietnam War, 1964–1969: A Chinese Perspective," 749–53; Nguyen Van Minh et al, *Lich Su Khang Chien Chong My Cuu Nuoc, 1954–1975*, Tap V (Hanoi: National Political Publishing House, Hanoi, 2001), 270–1.

54. On a few occasions in April, the Chinese expressed a willingness to fight the Americans on Vietnamese territory. Memcon, Zhou Enlai and Ayub Khan, 2 April 1965, CWIHP; Jian, *Mao's China and the Cold War*, 216. It was nonetheless possible, even in late March and April, that the Chinese merely would have withdrawn their units quietly when an American invasion started, especially if the Americans had attacked only North Vietnamese military and logistical facilities rather than the entire country, because of fear in Beijing of another war like the Korean War. In 1954 and 1964, the Chinese had shown a willingness to make the Vietnamese Communists promises of military intervention that they did not intend to keep. The Chinese boldness of late March and April began to recede in May. In the middle of May, the Chinese said that they would not fight the Americans unless they attacked China. *New York Times*, May 11, 1965; *Peking Review*, May 14, 1965. It is most doubtful that they would have made such claims insincerely, for China had little to gain and much to lose by encouraging the United States to invade North Vietnam and then attacking the Americans there. For logistical reasons, China would face much higher costs if it fought in Vietnam than in China, and the Americans could move supplies and smash Chinese conventional forces more easily in the confines of Vietnam than in the vast expanses of China. Later in May, on the other hand, Zhou privately assured two North Vietnamese envoys, "We will go to Vietnam if Vietnam is in need, as we did in Korea." Memcon, Zhou Enlai, Nguyen Van Hieu, and Nguyen Thi Binh, 16 May 1965, CWIHP. Because Ayub Khan's visit to the United States was postponed, the Chinese attempted to use a different intermediary at the end of May, and now they softened their stance again, making clear to British chargé Donald Charles Hopson that they would not fight the United States unless the United States attacked China. Peking to FO, 31 May 1965, PRO, FO 371/180990. Chen Yi conveyed the same message to the Soviet ambassador on the same day. James Hershberg and

Chen Jian, "Reading and Warning the Likely Enemy: China's Signals to the United States about Vietnam in 1965," *International History Review,* vol. 27, issue 1 (March 2005), 78. According to Chinese sources, Liu Ruiqing told Van Tien Dung in June that Chinese forces, including ground forces, would assist the North Vietnamese if the Americans invaded North Vietnam, but the form of assistance was left vague, as the Chinese said the use of their ground troops would depend on the circumstances and they would probably operate primarily as "strategic reserves" – which could mean that they would be based in China. Vietnamese accounts have disputed this rendition of events, asserting in particular that the Chinese said they could not provide air cover over North Vietnam. Jian, *Mao's China and the Cold War,* 219–20; Zhai, *China and the Vietnam Wars,* 134; Xiaoming Zhang, "The Vietnam War, 1964–1969: A Chinese Perspective," 750. According to Chen Jian, who has studied Chinese sources on this period in great detail, the Chinese government has yet to release critical documents on China's policy towards North Vietnam, especially in May and June 1965. Chen Jian, email to author, 6 November 2005. In July 1965, the Chinese sent the Americans messages through third parties stating that China did not want war with the United States and would not attack American forces unless the Americans attacked mainland China. Fearey, memcon, 12 July 1965, LBJL, NSF, Country File, Japan, box 251; Hershberg and Jian, "Reading and Warning the Likely Enemy: China's Signals to the United States about Vietnam in 1965," 76–7. Had the United States found itself at war with China following an invasion of North Vietnam, it would have fought from a favorable strategic position. As was noted earlier, America's armed forces were far stronger than China's, and China did not have nuclear capabilities. The Soviets might have provided aid or sanctuary to the Chinese in the name of Communist internationalism, but given the dreadful state of Sino-Soviet relations, the introduction of Soviet forces into China was highly unlikely. Occupying and controlling such an enormous and populous country, though, would have posed major challenges for the United States and its allies.

55. SNIE 10-9-65, 23 July 1965, *FRUS,* 1964–1968, vol. 3, 81.

56. Darmstandler, "Chronology of Significant Requests and Decisions Affecting the Air War Against North Vietnam," 15 December 1967, DDRS, 1988, 217; *The Joint Chiefs of Staff and the War in Vietnam,* chap. 25, 14. By the middle of 1965, Rolling Thunder had destroyed only 5% of North Vietnam's total barracks capacity, 5% of supply depot capacity, 27% of ammo depot capacity, 18% of oil storage capacity, and 9% of power plant capacity. Of North Vietnam's 475 bridges, only 27 had been hit, and some of those had been only partially damaged. Ports and railroad yards remained almost entirely intact, for with few exceptions they had been left off of the Rolling Thunder target list. McNamara to Johnson, 30 July 1965, *FRUS,* 1964–1968, vol. 3, 100.

57. The most notable atrocity was the execution of U.S. Army Sergeant Harold G. Bennett, who had been taken captive during the Battle of Binh Gia. The Viet Cong accompanied this killing with this public announcement: "Harold G. Bennett, who has just paid for his crimes, was but a leaf falling in a revolutionary storm. Again, this storm will sweep away all the aggressive castles built by the U.S. puppets in their nightmare. Bennett has paid for his crimes. Tomorrow will be the turn of all the bloodthirsty devils of whom Maxwell Taylor, Alexis Johnson, Westmoreland, and Thieu and Ky . . . will come first in the death list." *Washington Post,* June 27, 1965.

58. Redmon to Johnson, 17 June 1965, LBJL, Confidential File, box 71; *Washington Post,* June 28, 1965.

59. When, on July 22, someone told the President that a Gallup poll showed strong support for the war, Johnson snapped, "But if you make a commitment to jump off a building, and you find out how high it is, you may withdraw the commitment." Valenti, meeting notes, 22 July 1965, *FRUS,* 1964–1968, vol. 3, 76.

60. Bundy, meeting notes, 27 July 1965, *FRUS,* 1964–1968, vol. 3, 94; meeting notes, 27 July 1965, LBJL, Meeting Notes File, box 1.

61. McNamara had initially favored raising taxes to pay for the additional troop deployments, but Johnson stifled the recommendation. "Obviously you don't know anything about politics," Johnson told him. "I'll tell you what's going to happen. We'll put it forward; they are going to turn it down. But in the course of the debate they'll say: 'You see, we've been telling you so. You can't have guns and butter, and we're going to have guns.'" Gibbons, *The U.S. Government and the Vietnam War,* vol. 3, 389. Johnson planned to avoid raising taxes and to seek no more than $400 million from Congress for the time being, because, as Deputy Secretary of Defense Cyrus Vance explained to McNamara, "If a

larger request is made to the Congress, he believes this will kill domestic legislative program." Vance to McNamara, 17 July 1965, *FRUS, 1964–1968,* vol. 3, 61.

62. Valenti, NSC meeting notes, 27 July 1965, LBJL, Meeting Notes File, box 1.

63. Bundy, meeting notes, 27 July 1965, *FRUS, 1964–1968,* vol. 3, 93n; Mark A. Lorell et al., *Casualties, Public Opinion, and Presidential Policy During the Vietnam War* (Santa Monica, CA: Rand, 1985), 45. See also Greene, "Developing Situation in South Vietnam," 24 July 1965, MCHD, Greene Papers; Read, "Actions Agreed on at Special Meeting of the Assistant Secretaries," 23 July 1965, DDRS, 1988, 21.

64. Telcon, 26 July 1965, Beschloss, ed., *Reaching for Glory,* 410.

65. Johnson told the National Security Council, "This course of action will keep us there during the critical monsoon season." The forces would "hold until January" so that American diplomats could work toward a diplomatic resolution. Smith, NSC meeting notes, 27 July 1965, *FRUS, 1964–1968,* vol. 3, 93; Valenti, NSC meeting notes, 27 July 1965, LBJL, Meeting Notes File, box 1. Johnson's lack of appreciation of the problems arising from a U.S. ground force withdrawal offers compelling evidence that he was not drawn into Vietnam by the commitment of U.S. ground forces to South Vietnam that began in March.

66. *Public Papers of the Presidents,* 1965, 794–803.

67. Telcon, 2 July 1965, Beschloss, ed., *Reaching for Glory,* 381–3.

68. Valenti, meeting notes, 22 July 1965, *FRUS, 1964–1968,* vol. 3, 76.

69. *Public Papers of the Presidents,* 1965, 794–803.

Index

CPSIA information can be obtained
at www.ICGtesting.com
Printed in the USA
LVHW081620110822
725746LV00004B/59